FOURTH EDITION

Introduction
to
Clinical Psychology

MICHAEL T. NIETZEL

University of Kentucky

DOUGLAS A. BERNSTEIN

University of Illinois

RICHARD MILICH

University of Kentucky

PRENTICE HALL, Englewood Cliffs, New Jersey 07632

Library of Congress Cataloging-in Publication Data

NIETZEL, MICHAEL, T.
  Introduction to clinical psychology / Michael T. Nietzel, Douglas
A. Bernstein, Richard Milich. — 4th ed.
    p.   cm.
  Includes bibliographical references and index.
  ISBN 0-13-098518-X
  1. Clinical psychology. I. Bernstein, Douglas A. II. Milich.
Richard. III. Title.
  [DNLM: 1. Psychology, Clinical. WM 105 N677i 1994]
RC467.N54 1994
616.89—dc20
DNLM/DLC
for Library of Congress   93–33601
                                                               CIP

Acquisitions editor: Peter Janzow

Managing editor: Heidi Freund

Editorial production/supervision
  and interior design: F. Hubert

Manufacturing buyer: Tricia Kenny

Cover design: Tommy Boy

© 1994, 1991, 1987 by Prentice-Hall, Inc.
A Paramount Communications Company
Englewood Cliffs, New Jersey 07632

Printed in the United States of America

10 9 8 7 6 5 4 3 2 1

ISBN 0-13-098518-X

PRENTICE-HALL INTERNATIONAL (UK) LIMITED, *London*
PRENTICE-HALL OF AUSTRALIA PTY. LIMITED, *Sydney*
PRENTICE-HALL CANADA INC., *Toronto*
PRENTICE-HALL HISPANOAMERICANA, S.A., *Mexico*
PRENTICE-HALL OF INDIA PRIVATE LIMITED, *New Delhi*
PRENTICE-HALL OF JAPAN, INC., *Tokyo*
SIMON & SCHUSTER, PTE. LTD., *Singapore*
EDITORA PRENTICE-HALL DO BRASIL, LTDA., *Rio de Janeiro*

To our students,
who will join in the advance
of the science of clinical psychology

Contents

APPENDIX

Preface

In the earlier editions of this book, we tried to accomplish three goals. First, we wanted a book that, while appropriate for graduate students, was written especially with sophisticated undergraduates in mind. Many undergraduate psychology majors express an interest in clinical psychology without having a clear understanding of what the field involves and requires. An even larger number of nonmajors also wish to know more about clinical psychology. We felt that both groups of undergraduates would benefit from a thorough survey of the field which does not go into all the details typically found in "graduate study only" texts.

Second, we wanted to present a scholarly portrayal of the history of clinical psychology, its scope, functions, and future that reviewed different theoretical perspectives. For this reason, we did not limit ourselves to our own preferences for cognitive-behavioral theory but instead described three theoretical systems—psychoanalytic, behavioral, and phenomenological—in as neutral a manner as possible. We do champion the empirical research tradition of clinical psychology throughout the book because we believe it is a necessary and useful perspective for all clinicians to follow, regardless of their theoretical orientation.

Third, we wanted to write a book that would be interesting and enjoyable to read. Because we like being clinical psychologists and because we enjoy teaching students about the field, we tried to create a book that would pass that enthusiasm on to others.

Our goals for this fourth edition remain the same. However, in addition to the comprehensive updating of all chapters, we have introduced significant new material in this edition. We cover the latest developments in clinical diagnosis and assessment (e.g., *DSM-IV* and new versions of standard psychological tests). We have strengthened our attention to the empirical foundations that must support good clinical practice. We discuss a host of professional issues that have emerged in the last few years—a new ethics code for psychologists, proposed plans for funding mental health care, and new forms of legal regulation over clinical psychology. In prior editions, we included a chapter on biological factors that surveyed clinical research and techniques in health psychology, psychopathology, and neuropsychology. Because of the tremendous expansion of knowledge and practice in these areas, our former single-chapter review of these areas is no longer adequate. In this edition, we discuss health psychology and psychopathology in one chapter, and neuropsychology is covered in a new, separate chapter.

ACKNOWLEDGMENTS

We want to thank several people for their valuable contributions to this book. Our colleagues, Doug Snyder, David Berry, Art Nonnerman, Ruth Baer, Charles Carlson, Greg Smith, Sandy D'Angelo, Monica Harris, and Tom Widiger carefully read parts of the manuscript and offered many valuable suggestions for its improvement. We want to express special appreciation to Dr. Wendy Heller of the University of Illinois for her preparation of the new chapter on neuropsychology.

Countless undergraduate and graduate students asked the questions, raised the controversies, and argued opposing positions that have found their way into the text; they are really the people who stimulated this book. Now, we hope they read it.

We want to pay special tribute to Frank Hubert for his dedicated and skilled coordination of the production of the manuscript. His judgments about the manuscript were superb.

Finally, and once again, we owe our deepest appreciation to Shirley Jacobs for her overall coordination of the manuscript's preparation, the reference list's compilation, and a multitude of other arrangements that made completion of the project possible. She pulled us through one more time.

MICHAEL T. NIETZEL
DOUGLAS A. BERNSTEIN
RICHARD MILICH

CHAPTER 1

Clinical Psychology: Definitions and History

Psychology has been one of the most popular undergraduate majors in the United States for many years. Among the arts and sciences, psychology ranks first in the number of majors (National Center for Education Statistics, 1991). By the end of the 1980s, more than 45,000 bachelor's degrees were being awarded to psychology majors annually, a figure that had been increasing by about 5% per year since 1985. In 1988, more bachelor's degrees were awarded to psychology majors than to majors in chemistry, physics, all foreign languages, geology, sociology, and zoology combined.

At many American universities, more PhDs are awarded in psychology than in any other discipline. Throughout the 1980s, 3,000 or more doctoral degrees in psychology were granted each year (Howard et al., 1986), with the largest group of them (about 40%) earned by students studying clinical psychology (Stapp, Fulcher, & Wicherski, 1984).

This continuing popularity is associated with dramatic changes in the demographic characteristics of clinical psychologists. Women received 37% of the bachelor's degrees and 15% of the doctoral degrees in psychology in 1950; but by the end of the 1980s, women were earning 70% of the undergraduate degrees and 57% of the PhDs in psychology (Kohout & Wicherski, 1991; National Center for Education Statistics, 1991).

The appeal of clinical psychology is also reflected in the membership of the American Psychological Association (APA), the largest organization of psychologists in the United States. APA has more than 113,000 members, associates, and affiliates. Almost half of the members of APA list clinical psychology as their major field (Howard et al., 1986). Of the 49 recognized divisions within APA, the Division of Clinical Psychology is the largest.

The immense popularity of clinical psychology is remarkable considering that it is only about 100 years old and did not begin to grow rapidly until after World War II. What is it that a clinical psychologist does that makes so many people want to become one? To put it more generally, what is clinical psychology?

1

The answer to this question is not simple, but in this book we attempt to describe the field in a way that will allow you to draw your own conclusions. In the process, we examine the history, current status, and future of the field; its uniqueness and its overlap with other fields; the training and activities of its members; the factors that unite it; and the issues that threaten to divide it.

SOME ATTEMPTS AT DEFINITION

We would like to provide a simple and easily remembered definition of clinical psychology from which the rest of the material in this book would logically flow. However, no such definition exists. For many years the field has been expanding in so many different directions that any attempt to capture it in a sentence or two is bound to be too vague, too narrow, or soon outdated. This lack of definition has caused confusion in the public's mind over what clinical psychology is all about. The same problem exists to a certain extent among clinical psychologists themselves, who find that the ever-expanding boundaries of the field threaten to make traditional notions of clinical psychology obsolete. In spite of continual changes within the field, there is a set of factors underlying most definitions of clinical psychology which provides a workable definition of the discipline.

First, clinical psychology is a field within the larger discipline of psychology. Clinical psychologists, like all psychologists, study *behavior and mental processes.* Unlike some psychologists, however, clinicians are concerned almost entirely with *humans;* they study animals mainly when the use of human subjects is impractical or unsafe and when the behavior of animals can illuminate general behavioral principles and relationships that are relevant at the human level.

Second, clinical psychologists do *research* on human behavior and mental processes. Clinical psychology also applies the knowl-

edge and principles gained from research in a practical way, but this alone does not make the field unique; other specialties, such as industrial and educational psychology, are also noted for their applied orientation.

A third aspect of clinical psychology is *assessment or measurement* of the abilities and characteristics of individual human beings. The clinician collects information that will be analyzed and used to support conclusions about the person observed. While such information might be collected from large groups as part of a clinical research project, it is more frequently employed by the clinician to understand the particular individual at hand. However, many nonclinicians (e.g., personality researchers and industrial psychologists) administer and score tests of various kinds. Assessment activities alone cannot fully define clinical psychology or account for its distinctiveness.

A fourth characteristic of clinical psychology is that clinicians *help* people who are psychologically distressed. Therapeutic work is the most recently evolved aspect of the field, but it rivals assessment activities in the general public's image of the clinical psychologist. Nevertheless, providing therapy is not unique to clinical psychology: Psychiatrists, family physicians, social workers, counselors, nurses, educators, and the clergy also intervene to alleviate psychological problems.

In summary, clinical psychology is a subarea of psychology that, like other subareas, applies psychological knowledge; and its members generate research about human behavior, engage in individual assessment, and provide various forms of psychological assistance. However, the defining characteristic that distinguishes clinical psychology from the other branches of psychology is what has been called the *clinical attitude* or the *clinical approach* (Korchin, 1976). This term means that clinical psychologists combine knowledge generated by clinical and other research with their own efforts at individual assessment in order to understand and help a particular person.

The clinical attitude sets clinicians apart

from other psychologists whose interests, though often related to clinical psychology, tend to be more abstract because they involve a search for principles and relationships that apply to human behavior problems on a general, or *nomothetic,* level. Clinical psychologists are interested in research of this kind because they must know how general principles shape lives, problems, and treatments on an individual, or *idiographic,* level.

The clinical attitude is distinctive with respect to the helping professions outside psychology. Psychiatrists, social workers, and others assist people in psychological distress, but their fields are not traditionally noted for research into or systematic assessment of the problems they seek to alleviate. Their involvement with a given case is more likely to focus on treatment.

The clinical attitude and the ways it contrasts with related approaches are most obvious with respect to a given case. For example, in reading a description of the problems of a person just admitted to a mental institution, the psychopathologist would search for psychological or biological relationships that might explain the "disorder," while the psychiatrist (a physician who specializes in psychological problems) might weigh the potential benefits of psychological, medical, or combined treatment. The clinical psychologist, however, would plan a strategy for further assessment of the problem and, depending upon the outcome of the assessment process, develop an intervention for reducing the person's distress. The research evidence that guides the clinical psychologist in these pursuits (and also aids other helping professions) often comes from the work of fellow clinical psychologists.

So it is not the research, the individual assessment, the treatment, or any of the other activities that makes clinical psychology unique. Rather, it is the clinical attitude, the idea of not only learning about behavior (particularly problematic behavior) but also doing something about it that is indigenous to clinical psychology (Wyatt, 1968, p. 235).

This emphasis on combining several functions *within a single field* is consistent with the "official" definition of clinical psychology that was adopted in 1991 by the Division of Clinical Psychology of APA: "The field of Clinical Psychology involves research, teaching, and services relevant to the applications of principles, methods, and procedures for understanding, predicting, and alleviating intellectual, emotional, biological, psychological, social and behavioral maladjustment, disability and discomfort, applied to a wide range of client populations" (Resnick, 1991). No single skill defines clinical psychology. Its uniqueness stems from the use of science and theory to guide specific interventions for persons experiencing adjustment problems or mental disorders.

CLINICAL PSYCHOLOGISTS AT WORK

Now that we have outlined the nature of clinical psychology, we will survey the range of things that clinical psychologists do, the variety of places in which they are employed, and the array of clients and problems with which they work. Our examples of clinical activities, work settings, clients, and problems are only a small sample; it is possible to describe others. On the other hand, our coverage is so broad that it is unlikely any given clinical psychologist will be associated with all the functions, locations, clients, and problems listed.

We look first at some isolated examples of clinical activities, settings, clients, and problems. Later we shall see how these dimensions are combined for individual clinicians.

The Activities of Clinical Psychologists

The popular stereotypes of the clinician as mind reader, hypnotist, psychotherapist, or mental tester are, like most stereotypes, only partly accurate at best. Empirical research by clinical psychologists is a vital though underpublicized aspect of the field. In addition, clinicians often engage in teaching, consultation, and administration. It is probably fair to say that 95% of all clinical psychologists spend their working lives engaged in some combination of six activities: *assessment, treatment, research, teaching, consultation,* and *administration.*

Assessment

Assessment involves the collection of information about people: their behavior, problems, unique characteristics, abilities, and intellectual functioning. This information may be used to diagnose problematic behavior, to guide a client toward an optimal vocational choice, to facilitate selection of job candidates, to describe a client's personality characteristics, to select treatment techniques, to aid legal decisions regarding the commitment of individuals to institutions, to provide a more complete picture of a client's problems, to screen potential participants in a psychological research project, to establish pretreatment baseline levels of behavior against which to measure posttreatment improvement, and for literally hundreds of other purposes. Most clinical assessment devices fall into one of three categories: *tests, interviews,* and *observations.*

Tests, interviews, and observations are not always distinct means of assessment. For example, a clinician may observe the nonverbal behavior of a client during a testing session or an interview to estimate the client's level of discomfort in social situations. Further, a test may be embedded in an interview, as when the client is asked to provide specific information whose accuracy provides clues to reality contact.

Various modes of assessment are combined in assessment *batteries* and *multiple assessment* strategies. Here, information necessary for the clinician's work is collected through a series of procedures sometimes including a variety of tests; often, a more elaborate combination of tests, interviews, and observations is used to focus not only on the client, but also on significant others who can provide additional information.

Treatment

This function of the clinical psychologist involves helping people better understand and solve distressing psychological problems. The intervention may be called psychotherapy, behavior modification, psychological counseling, or other names, depending upon the orientation of the clinician, and may involve many combinations of clients and therapists. Though psychotherapy is the single most frequent activity of clinicians (Norcross, Prochaska, & Gallagher, 1989a), it is also common for one psychologist to deal with groups of clients (e.g., family members, co-workers, hospital residents). Sometimes two or more clinicians work as a team to deal with the problems of an individual, couple, or group. The emphasis of treatment may be on alleviating the distress and/or problematic behavior of one or more troubled individuals, or may include prevention of psychological problems by altering the institutions, social or environmental situation, or behavioral skills of persons "at risk" (e.g., teenage parents) or of an entire community. Herink (1980) lists more than 250 different "brand names" of therapy ranging literally from A (Aikido) to Z (Zaraleya psychoenergetic technique).

Treatment by a clinical psychologist may be on an outpatient basis (the client lives in the community) or may be part of the services for residents (inpatients) of an institution. It may be as brief as one session or extend over several years. Treatment sessions may consist of anything from client or therapist monologues to painstaking construction of new behavioral skills to episodes of intense emotional drama, and may range from highly structured to totally spontaneous interactions. The goals of clinician and client may be limited (as when a solution to a specific problem is sought), ambitious (as when a complete analysis and reconstruction of the client's personality is planned), or may fall somewhere between these extremes. Therapy may be conducted free of charge, on a sliding scale based on client income, or in return for large fees. In given cases, treatment can result in anything from worsening of client problems to no change to vast improvement.

Research

By training and by tradition, clinical psychologists are research oriented. This research activity makes them notable among other helping professions; we believe that it is in this area that clinicians make their greatest contribution (see Box 1–1). In the realm of psychotherapy, for example, theory and practice were once based mainly upon case study evidence, subjective impressions of treatment efficacy, and rather poorly designed research. This "prescientific" era (Paul, 1969a) in the history of psychotherapy research has now evolved into an "experimental" era in which the quality of research has improved greatly and the conclusions we can draw about the effects of therapy are much stronger (Smith, Glass, & Miller, 1980). This development is due in large measure to the research of clinical psychologists.

Recent years have seen a shift away from the research emphasis in the training of clinicians. This change is due in part to an erosion of the number of academic-research jobs available and in part to students' greater interests in careers that emphasize clinical service. We discuss this issue more extensively in Chapter 14, but for now we want to point out that clinical psychology will risk its special identity and value as a mental health profession if it neglects research training in favor of purely professional objectives.

The areas investigated by clinicians include neuropsychology, behavioral medicine, stress and social support, social problems, childhood problems, community development, psychopharmacology, developmental problems, geriatrics, test construction and validation, personality diagnosis and adjustment, psychoanalytic theory, therapeutic processes, brain damage and mental retardation, behavior disorders, marriage and family problems, outcomes of various forms of psychological treatment, the design and analysis of experiments, and the value and training of nonprofessionals as therapeutic agents. A journal called *Psychological Abstracts* contains brief summaries of clinical and other psychological research; a glance at a few issues will document the diversity and intensity of the clinician's involvement in research. Another journal, *Clinical Psychology Review,* first published in 1981, includes longer reviews of topics germane to clinical psychology. The *Journal of Consulting and Clinical Psychology, Psychological Assessment,* and the *Journal of Abnormal Psychology* publish many of the most influential research studies conducted by clinical psychologists (Feingold, 1989).

Clinical investigations vary greatly with respect to their setting and scope. Some are conducted in the controlled confines of a laboratory, while others are run in the more natural but often uncontrollable circumstances of the real world. Some projects are carried out by clinicians who are aided by paid research assistants and clerical personnel and supported by funds from governmental or private sources, but a great deal of research is performed by clinicians whose budgets are limited and who depend on volunteer help and their own ability to scrounge for space, equipment, and subjects.

Teaching

A considerable portion of many clinical psychologists' time is spent in educational activities. Clinicians who hold full- or part-time academic positions conduct graduate and undergraduate courses in such areas as personality, abnormal psychology, introductory clinical psychology, psychotherapy, behavior modification, interviewing, psychological testing, research design, and clinical assessment.

One issue that may confuse students who are considering clinical psychology as a career is why so much emphasis is placed on research methods and skills. Graduate school admission committees may give more weight to students' performance in a statistics course than to how they have done in abnormal psychology, and show more interest in their research activities than in their clinical experiences (Purdy, Reinehr, & Swartz, 1989). Most students who are fortunate enough to be invited to interview at graduate programs in clinical psychology know that it is important that they present a balance of research and clinical interests, even if they ultimately plan to go into private practice.

This emphasis on research methodology differentiates clinical psychology programs from other mental health professions. For example, medical students are not required to undertake their own research projects, and they may obtain only brief exposure to issues in experimental methods.

The research emphasis in clinical psychology does not reflect a desire to steer all graduates toward an academically oriented career. As noted earlier, only about 20% of clinical psychologists wind up in academic positions, and the market could not support increased numbers even if the desire were there. It is also not assumed that most graduates of clinical programs will combine research and clinical work in their professional lives. In fact, surveys of clinical psychologists consistently indicate that approximately 25% never publish any research (Barrom, Shadish, & Montgomery, 1988). This is in contrast to PhDs in biology, where less than 5% have no publications (Schuckman, 1987).

Given that the majority of graduates of clinical psychology programs pursue clinically oriented careers, why do training programs place strong emphasis on research training? We can list at least three reasons. First, an attempt is made to produce clinicians who can critically evaluate the published research to determine what assessment procedures and therapeutic interventions are most effective for clients. A therapist who relies only upon summaries of published studies is likely either to apply effective therapies to the wrong clients, or to rely upon interventions that are ineffective.

A second purpose is to give clinicians the means to evaluate the effectiveness of their own clinical work. This goal is accomplished by intensively exposing students to factors that influence therapeutic outcomes, as well as offering training in objective means of evaluating effectiveness.

Finally, many psychologists who work in medical or community mental health centers find that they are the ones to whom other professionals turn when research is needed, whether to write a grant proposal or undertake assessments of program effectiveness. In fact, a survey by Barrom et al. (1988) found that over half of the clinical psychologists reported currently being engaged in some form of research activity. Thus, whether they intend to pursue research activities, the majority of clinical psychologists can assume that their research skills will be called upon sometime in their professional careers.

BOX 1–1
The Clinician and Research

Clinicians often conduct specialized graduate seminars on advanced topics; frequently they supervise the work of graduate students who are learning assessment and therapy skills in practicum courses. Supervision of a practicum is a special kind of teaching that combines the use of research evidence and other didactic material with the clinician's own experience to guide students' assessment and treatment of actual clients. Practicum teaching usually involves a model in which the student sees a client on a regular basis and, between these sessions, also meets with the supervisor (the client is aware of the student's status and of the participation of the supervisor). Supervision may occur on an individual basis or may be part of a meeting with a small group of practicum students, all of whom maintain the confidentiality of any material discussed.

The clinician's teaching task is particularly delicate in practica since a balance must be struck between directing the student and allowing sufficient independence. The therapist-in-training may feel stifled if supervision is too heavy-handed. At the same time, the supervisor is ultimately responsible for the case and cannot allow the student to make serious errors that would be detrimental to client welfare.

A good deal of teaching by clinical psychologists involves supervising undergraduate and graduate students' research efforts. This kind of teaching begins when a student comes to the supervisor with a research topic and asks for advice and a list of relevant readings. In addition to providing the reading list, most research supervisors help the student frame appropriate research questions, apply basic principles of research design in answering those questions, and introduce the student to research skills relevant to the problem at hand. These tasks require considerable skill if the supervisor is to avoid giving the student so much guidance and direction that the student simply becomes an assistant who, instead of wrestling with and learning from research problems, merely carries out orders.

Much teaching by clinical psychologists involves in-service (i.e., on-the-job) training of psychological, medical, or other interns, as well as social workers, nurses, institutional aides, ministers, police officers, suicide prevention and other hotline personnel, prison guards, teachers, administrators, business executives, day-care workers, lawyers, probation officers, dentists, and many other groups whose vocational skills might be enhanced by increased psychological sophistication. Some clinical psychologists also teach in the context of therapy (particularly those who adopt a behavioral approach to treatment; see Chapter 9) since part of therapy involves helping people learn more adaptive ways of behaving.

One last point about clinical psychologists as teachers: They are often not formally trained for the job. The same might be said, of course, about other psychologists (and many other PhDs, for that matter), but the lack of attention to teaching in clinical training programs is unfortunate because educational activities are such an integral part of clinicians' work. This significant omission is due in part to the fact that clinical training time is so precious that most of it is taken up with research, assessment, and treatment functions.

Consultation

Clinical psychologists often provide advice to organizations about a variety of problems. This activity is called consultation; it combines research, assessment, treatment, and teaching. Perhaps this is why some clinicians find consultation satisfying and lucrative enough that they engage in it full time. Organizations that benefit from consultants' expertise range in size and scope from one-person medical or law practices to huge government agencies and multinational corporations. The consultant may also work with neighborhood associations, walk-in treatment centers, and many other community-based organizations.

Rather than cataloging all the consulting activities in which a clinical psychologist might engage, we will review basic dimensions of the consulting function. The first of these is the *orientation* or *goal* of the consultation. When consulting is *case* oriented, the clinician focuses attention on a case and either deals with it directly or offers advice as to how it might be handled. An example would be providing treatment for a problem case in a mental health agency or medical facility. When consultation is *program* or *administration* oriented, it focuses not on case-level problems but on those aspects of organizational function or structure that are causing trouble. For example, the consultant may develop new procedures for screening candidates for various jobs within an organization, set up criteria for identifying promotable personnel, or reduce staff turnover rates by increasing administrators' awareness of the psychological impact of their decisions on employees.

A second dimension of consultation is *locus of responsibility*. In some cases, responsibility for the solution to an organization's problem is transferred to the consultant, as when a mental health clinic contracts for the assessment of suspected cases of brain damage among new clients. In such instances, responsibility for the cases rests with the clinician; giving advice and then going home is not appropriate. More commonly, however, the responsibility for problem resolution remains with the organization served. A clinician may participate in decisions about which treatment would be of greatest benefit to a client, but if the client gets worse instead of better, the consultant is not held culpable. The ultimate responsibility remains with the clinic.

A third major consulting dimension involves *functions*. A partial account of what a consultant could do for an organization might include education (e.g., familiarizing staff with relevant reading materials), advice (e.g., about cases or programs), direct service (e.g., assessment, treatment, and evaluation), and reduction of intraorganizational conflict (e.g., eliminating sources of trouble by altering personnel assignments).

Successful consultation is not easy. The clinician must be aware of his or her role as an outsider and of the implications of that role. The consultant's presence might be resented and resisted by rank-and-file personnel if they see it as a threat to their jobs. Interpersonal rivalries may color the information the consultant receives about a problem. Consultants make great scapegoats. Administrators often blame them for ideas and strategies that later prove unpopular.

Administration and Management

This function, involving the management or day-to-day running of an organization, might be named by most clinical psychologists as their least-preferred activity. The reasons given would include aversion to paperwork, lack of interest and expertise in routine details of business and budget, impatience with conflicts among employees, reluctance to deal with the time-consuming and often acrimonious process of hiring and firing, and the frustration that sometimes attends dealing with other administrators. Nevertheless, clinical psychologists sometimes find themselves in administrative roles by choice. They may be asked to take on administrative jobs because of the sensitivity, interpersonal skill, research expertise, and organizational abilities associated with their field. On the other hand, some of the clinician's skills can be liabilities in administration because they may lead to overanalysis of problems and to conflicts between helping and managerial roles. Whatever the circumstances, many clinicians find it satisfying to guide an organization toward reaching its goals and improving its services.

Examples of the administrative posts held by clinical psychologists include: head of a university psychology department, director of a graduate training program in clinical psychology, director of a student counseling center, head of a consulting firm or testing center, superintendent of a school system, chief psychologist at a hospital or clinic, director of a mental hospital, director of a community mental health center, manager of a governmental agency, and director of the psychology service at a Veterans Administration (VA) hospital.

Administration and management have become increasingly popular professional activities for psychologists. Kilburg (1984) contends that management is the third most important job market for psychologists behind direct clinical services and academic jobs. In one survey (Norcross et al., 1989a), clinicians reported spending an average of 16% of their time on administrative work.

Distribution of Clinical Functions

Not all clinical psychologists perform each of the six functions we have discussed. Some spend all their time at one task, while others spread themselves around. To many clinicians, the potential for distributing their time among several functions is one of the most attractive aspects of their field, and the data from several surveys conducted over the last 30 years provide some idea of the work pattern that results.

Although these surveys asked about clinical functions in different ways, making direct comparisons between them difficult, some patterns are still obvious. For example, considering all types of psychologists (the majority of whom are clinicians), more than 50% report holding more than two jobs and about 19% report holding at least three (Stapp, Tucker, & VandenBos, 1985). In addition, the majority of those clinicians who have only one employment position participate in several functions within it.

Clinicians spend more time in various service activities than they do in research, and the majority of clinicians identify themselves primarily as practitioners rather than as researchers or academicians. Data like these have caused concern in the field over what is feared to be the erosion of the traditionally strong research contributions of clinical psychologists.

There have also been trends in recent years toward more involvement in treatment and less in traditional psychological testing (Norcross et al., 1989a).

The surveys summarized in Box 1–2 highlight other striking changes across the almost 30 years represented. The percentage of clinicians engaged in full-time private practice has doubled; if we add to this figure the 30% of clinicians who are employed in some kind of direct service agency, we see that by 1990 two thirds of clinicians were working primarily in a health service provider role.

Work Settings for Clinical Psychology

There was a time when most clinical psychologists worked in a single type of facility: child clinics or guidance centers; however, the settings in which clinicians now function are expanding in all directions.

Clinical psychologists are now found in college and university psychology departments; law schools; public and private medical and psychiatric hospitals; city, county, and private mental health clinics; community mental health centers; student health and counseling centers; medical schools; the military; university psychological clinics; child treatment centers; public and private schools; institutions for the mentally retarded; police departments; prisons; juvenile offender facilities; business and industrial firms; probation departments; rehabilitation centers for the handicapped; nursing homes and other geriatric facilities; orphanages; alcoholism treatment centers; health maintenance organizations; and many other places. Further, a large number of clinicians function independently in full- or part-time private practice.

Why has the number of clinicians in private practice grown so dramatically? In one study, private practitioners reported greater satisfaction with their careers than did clinicians working in institutional settings (Norcross & Prochaska, 1983). In other studies, clinicians in

Type	Kelly (1961) (N = 1,024)	Goldschmid et al. (1969) (N = 241)	Garfield & Kurtz (1976) (N = 855)	Stapp & Fulcher (1983) (N = 2,436)	Norcross, Prochaska, & Gallagher (1989b) (N = 579)
Academic	20%	17%	29%	17.9%	21%
Direct service[a]	50%	28%	35%	39.8%	30%
Research	c	c	c	c	c
Community agency	c	16%	b	d	c
Schools	3%	c	b	1.3%	c
Private practice	17%	28%	23.3%	31.1%	35%
Industry	3%	c	b	8.6%	c
Military	1.5%	c	b	c	c
Other	5.5%	11%	12.7%	c	10%

[a] Includes hospitals, clinics, medical schools, mental health centers, etc.

[b] Included under "other."

[c] Not included.

[d] Included under "direct service."

BOX 1–2

Percentage of Clinicians Employed in Various Work Settings

private practice reported substantially less job-related stress than did psychologists in academia (Boice & Myers, 1987) or psychologists in mental health agencies (Raquepaw & Miller, 1989).

If you suspected that the greater satisfaction of private practitioners might be linked to larger financial rewards, you'd be right. According to an APA survey of 25 metropolitan areas in the United States, the median 1991 salary of psychologists in independent practice was $63,750 compared to $44,750 for psychology faculty in the same 25 cities (*APA Monitor*, August 1992, p. 55). Even if we adjust the faculty salaries from the 9- to 10-month academic work schedule to the 11- to 12-month period worked by most practitioners, the academicians' annual salaries are still about $9,000 less than their practitioner colleagues.

Clients and Problems

Within the limits imposed by their areas of expertise, clinical psychologists work on almost any kind of human behavior problem. Clinical contracts may be voluntarily arranged by the client (or the client's family), prescribed by a court or other legal agency, or take place in the client's hospital ward, school, or community.

Having already considered the problems the clinician deals with as teacher, researcher, consultant, and administrator, one should also be aware of the problems she or he faces in the assessment and treatment areas. Client complaints are often complex and frequently stem from a combination of biological, psychological, and social factors, with the result that the clinical psychologist does not always work independently. A given case is sometimes referred to a psychiatrist or social worker or dealt with through an assessment and treatment team composed of experts from several related helping professions.

The average practicing clinician sees between 5 to 10 clients per day and encounters a wide range of client problems. According to one survey of more than 6,500 psychologists (VandenBos & Stapp, 1983), the most commonly treated problems are, in order of frequency: (a) anxiety and depression, (b) difficulties in interpersonal relations, (c) marital problems, (d) school difficulties, (e) psychosomatic and physical symptoms, (f) job-related difficulties, (g) alcohol and/or drug abuse, (h) psychoses, and (i) mental retardation.

Work Schedules and Specific Illustrations

We can now pull together what we have said about clinical functions, settings, clients, and problems by considering some examples of how and where various clinicians actually spend their time.

A Professor's Day

Shemberg and Leventhal (1978) surveyed 244 full-time faculty members in 120 doctoral clinical programs to determine how clinicians in academia spent their time. The results, summarized in Box 1–3, confirm the fact that clinical faculty members spend less time than other clinicians in direct clinical work and devote most of their time to graduate and undergraduate teaching, research, and supervision of research.

The Work of Other Clinicians

As scientific discoveries advance, particularly in the areas of childhood psychopathology and treatment (Chapter 11), behavioral medicine (Chapter 12), and neuropsychology (Chapter 13), clinicians have continued to expand their assessment and intervention techniques and have entered more diverse practice

BOX 1–3

Percentage of Academic Clinicians
Devoting Various Amounts of Time to Professional Activities

	% TIME SPENT IN ACTIVITY		
Activity	*< 10%*	*10%–29%*	*> 30%*
Graduate courses	7	77	16
Undergraduate courses	29	58	13
Own research	21	63	15
Supervising research	26	67	5
Own clinical work	53	39	8
Clinical supervision	38	55	7
Administration	35	55	10

Note: All percentages are rounded to the nearest whole number. Based on Shemberg and Leventhal (1978, Table 2).

and academic settings (DeSantis & Walker, 1991). The 1990s promise to be a decade in which clinical psychologists devote more of their expertise to specialized services for substance abusers, forensic agencies, and medical settings and to traditionally underserved groups (older persons, the poor, and minority populations). Clinicians also find themselves increasingly called upon to guide policy decisions in the areas of health care, child care, education, and social services.

Does greater specialization mean that clinicians will or should replace their traditional work activities with new roles? To a certain extent, specialization will require new activities, but recent surveys of clinicians indicate that the six functions already described (assessment, treatment, research, teaching, consultation, and administration) remain the core skills in which modern clinicians are most engaged (Watkins, Tipton, Manus, & Hunton-Shoup, 1991).

A comparison of two surveys illustrates that different types of clinicians continue to concentrate on the "bread and butter" activities that have long characterized the field. Norcross, Nash, and Prochaska (1985) surveyed a randomly selected group of clinicians in APA Division 42 (Psychologists in Independent Practice), and Norcross et al. (1989a) surveyed a random group of respondents from Division 12 (Division of Clinical Psychology). Division 42 is comprised of psychologists who identify themselves as being in private practice at least part time, while members of Division 12 are more likely to work in a mix of independent, public agency, and academic settings. Box 1–4 summarizes some of the findings of these two surveys. Regardless of division, clinicians are most involved in psychotherapy and assessment, and more than half of the clinicians in each group are active in teaching (which includes clinical supervision), administration, and consultation. The clearest difference is in the area of research, where Division 12 psychologists report a considerably greater investment than do Division 42 members.

The combination of clients, settings, and clinical functions we have discussed stems partly from each clinical psychologist's interests and expertise and partly from the influence of larger social factors. For example, a clinician could not work in a VA hospital unless legislation had been passed creating such settings. Similarly, much clinical research depends on grants from federal agencies like The National Institute of Mental Health, whose existence depends on continued congressional appropriations. Many clinical functions are legitimized by the perceptions of other professions and the general public. If no one saw the clinician as capable of doing effective therapy, that function would soon disappear from the field. Thus, the current state and future development of clinical psychology depend on the society in which it is embedded. The history of clinical psychology illustrates this point well.

THE ROOTS OF CLINICAL PSYCHOLOGY

Anyone born in the United States after World War II might assume that the field of clinical psychology has always existed. However, clinical psychology is a child of the postwar era. Now, about 50 years after World War II, clinical psychology is experiencing its own version of a "midlife crisis" centered on several of the same issues that occupied its adolescence: How should clinical psychologists be trained? What is the role of science in the field? What are the best ways to ensure that clinicians offer high-quality services to the public?

The roots of clinical psychology extend back to periods before the field was ever named and to prewar years when it appeared only in embryonic form. Just as full understanding of clients' problems is easier when their social, cultural, educational, and vocational backgrounds are known, it is easier to understand the current dimensions, new developments, and critical issues in clinical psy-

Activity	DIVISION 12 CLINICIANS[a] (N = 579)		DIVISION 42 CLINICIANS[b] (n = 157)	
	% Involved	Mean % Time	% Involved	Mean % Time
Psychotherapy	87	35	99	40
Diagnosis and assessment	75	16	75	12
Teaching	55	14	51	9
Clinical supervision	67	11	70	9
Research	54	15	35	4
Consultation	63	11	68	7
Administration	55	16	56	14

[a]Based on Norcross, Prochaska, and Gallagher (1989a).
[b]Based on Norcross et al. (1985).

BOX 1–4
Professional Activities of Clinicians

chology when its historical background is reviewed. In the rest of this chapter we provide that review. We look first at the factors that were most influential in the formal birth of clinical psychology in 1896, and then follow the growth of the new field to the present. Many of the details mentioned here are drawn from Reisman (1976) and Watson (1953), to which the interested reader should turn for more intensive historical coverage. Box 1–5 provides a general chronology of important events in the development of clinical psychology.

To understand modern clinical psychology, one must be aware of three sets of social and historical factors that initially shaped the field and that continue to influence it. They include (a) the use of scientific research methods by psychology in general, (b) the study of human individual differences, and (c) the ways in which behavior disorders have been viewed and treated over the years.

1. The Research Tradition in Psychology. From its 19th-century beginnings in the psychophysics of Fechner and Weber, the experimental physiology of Helmholtz, and the work of the first "real" psychologist, Wilhelm Wundt, psychology sought to establish itself as a science that employed the methods of natural sciences like biology and physics. Though the roots of psychology were partly in philosophy, and though many early psychologists were preoccupied with philosophical questions, the discipline was determined to study human behavior by conducting *research* that employed two powerful tools of science, observation and experimentation. Thus, the early history of psychology, which began "officially" in Wundt's psychological laboratory at the University at Leipzig in 1879, is primarily the history of *experimental* psychology (Boring, 1950; Leahey, 1987).

By the time clinical psychology began to emerge, 17 years after the founding of

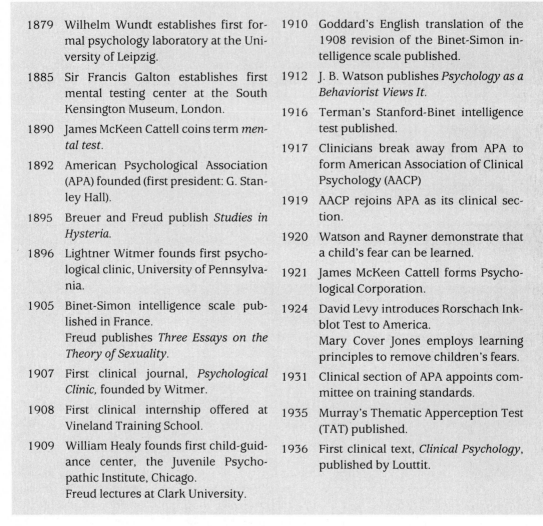

1879	Wilhelm Wundt establishes first formal psychology laboratory at the University of Leipzig.
1885	Sir Francis Galton establishes first mental testing center at the South Kensington Museum, London.
1890	James McKeen Cattell coins term *mental test*.
1892	American Psychological Association (APA) founded (first president: G. Stanley Hall).
1895	Breuer and Freud publish *Studies in Hysteria*.
1896	Lightner Witmer founds first psychological clinic, University of Pennsylvania.
1905	Binet-Simon intelligence scale published in France. Freud publishes *Three Essays on the Theory of Sexuality*.
1907	First clinical journal, *Psychological Clinic*, founded by Witmer.
1908	First clinical internship offered at Vineland Training School.
1909	William Healy founds first child-guidance center, the Juvenile Psychopathic Institute, Chicago. Freud lectures at Clark University.
1910	Goddard's English translation of the 1908 revision of the Binet-Simon intelligence scale published.
1912	J. B. Watson publishes *Psychology as a Behaviorist Views It*.
1916	Terman's Stanford-Binet intelligence test published.
1917	Clinicians break away from APA to form American Association of Clinical Psychology (AACP)
1919	AACP rejoins APA as its clinical section.
1920	Watson and Rayner demonstrate that a child's fear can be learned.
1921	James McKeen Cattell forms Psychological Corporation.
1924	David Levy introduces Rorschach Inkblot Test to America. Mary Cover Jones employs learning principles to remove children's fears.
1931	Clinical section of APA appoints committee on training standards.
1935	Murray's Thematic Apperception Test (TAT) published.
1936	First clinical text, *Clinical Psychology*, published by Louttit.

BOX 1–5
Some Significant Dates and Events in the History of Clinical Psychology

Wundt's laboratory, the experimental research tradition in psychology was well established. Psychology laboratories had been set up at major universities in Europe and the United States, and early psychologists were experimenting on human behavior. The first clinicians, already trained to think in scientific terms and use laboratory methods, also applied research methods to clinical problems. The research tradition they brought to their work took root and grew in the new field until clinical psychologists attained special recognition among the helping professions as experts in research.

The scientific orientation and the skill that forms the basis of clinicians' continuing reputation for research expertise also form the strongest link between clinical psychology and psychology itself. The question of whether this link should be maintained, intensified, or deemphasized in the training and

1937   Clinical section of APA breaks away to form American Association for Applied Psychology (AAAP).

1938   First Buros *Mental Measurement Yearbook* published.

1939   Wechsler-Bellevue Intelligence Test published.

1942   Carl Rogers publishes *Counseling and Psychotherapy.*

1943   Minnesota Multiphasic Personality Inventory (MMPI) published.

1945   AAAP rejoins APA.

1946   Veterans Administration and National Institute of Mental Health begin support for training of clinical psychologists.

1947   American Board of Examiners in Professional Psychology organized.

1949   Boulder, Colorado, conference on training in clinical psychology convenes.

1952   American Psychiatric Association's *Diagnostic and Statistical Manual (DSM-I)* published.

1953   APA *Ethical Standards for Psychologists* published.

1956   Stanford Training Conference.

1958   Miami Training Conference.

1965   Chicago Training Conference.

1968   PsyD training program begun at the University of Illinois.
Second edition of *Diagnostic and Statistical Manual (DSM-II)* published.

1969   California School of Professional Psychology founded.

1973   Vail, Colorado, Training Conference.

1980   Third edition of *Diagnostic and Statistical Manual (DSM-III)* published.
Smith, Glass, and Miller publish *The Benefits of Psychotherapy.*

1981   APA publishes its revised *Ethical Principles of Psychologists.*

1987   *DSM-III-R* published.
Conference on graduate education in psychology, Salt Lake City, Utah.

1988   American Psychological Society formed.

1994   *DSM-IV* published.

BOX 1–5
Continued

daily activities of clinical psychologists continues to be one of the liveliest issues in the field. We consider this point in more detail later.

The research tradition of experimental psychology has directed clinical psychology. It has provided a methodology for approaching clinical subject matter, engendered empirical evaluation of clinical functions, and acted as a point of contention that keeps clinicians engaged in healthy self-examination.

2. Attention to Individual Differences. Because clinical psychology deals with the individual, it could not appear as a discipline until differences among human beings began to be recognized and measured. There would be little impetus for learning about individuals in a world where everyone is thought to be about the same.

Differences among people have always been noticed and assessed. In his *Republic,*

Plato pointed out that people should do work for which they are best suited; he suggested specifically that prospective soldiers be tested for military ability prior to their acceptance in the army. DuBois (1970) and McReynolds (1975) refer to Pythagoras (sixth century B.C.) selecting members of his brotherhood on the basis of facial characteristics, intelligence, and emotionality, and to the 4,000-year-old Chinese system of ability testing for prospective government employees. However, it was not until the early 1800s that the idea of paying systematic attention to subtle psychological differences really caught on. Until then, people were thought of as falling into a few categories such as male–female, good–evil, sane–insane, wise–foolish.

The earliest developments in the scientific measurement of individual differences came from astronomy and anatomy. The astronomical story began in 1796, when Nevil Maskelyne was Astronomer Royal at the Greenwich (England) Observatory. He had an assistant named Kinnebrook, whose recordings of the moment at which various stars and planets crossed a certain point in the sky consistently differed from those of his boss by five- to eight-tenths of a second. Maskelyne assumed that his readings were correct and that Kinnebrook was in error. Result: Kinnebrook lost his job.

This incident drew the attetion of F. W. Bessel, an astronomer at the University of Konigsberg (Germany) observatory. Bessel wondered whether Kinnebrook's "error" might reflect something about the characteristics of various observers, and, during the next several years, he compared his own observations with those of other experienced astronomers. Bessel found that discrepancies appeared regularly and that the size of the differences depended upon the person with whom he compared notes. The differences associated with each observer became known as the "personal equation," since they allowed for correction of calculations based upon personal characteristics. Bessel's work led to later research by

psychologists on the speed of, and individual differences in, reaction time.

The second source of interest in variations among individuals began with the study of phrenology by the anatomist Franz Gall and his pupil, Johann Spurzheim, at the beginning of the 19th century. As a child in Germany, Gall thought he saw a relationship between the shape of his schoolmates' heads and their mental characteristics. This idea later became the basis for phrenology, which assumed (a) that each area of the brain was associated with a different faculty or function (like self-esteem, language, or reverence); (b) that the better developed each of these areas was, the more strongly that faculty or function would manifest itself in behavior; and (c) that the pattern of over- or underdevelopment of each faculty would be reflected in corresponding bumps or depressions in the skull.

Although the brain plays a major role in determining behavior, and although its functions are localized to a certain extent, Gall's theory was mostly fallacious. The conclusions he drew and the procedures he used to test them were scorned by the scientists of his day. Nevertheless, Gall went around Europe measuring the bumps on people's heads. He began with prisoners and mental patients whose behavioral characteristics seemed well established (he thought the "acquisitiveness" bump was especially strong among pickpockets). Later, under Spurzheim's influence, phrenology was applied to more respectable segments of society, and an elaborate map of the brain was developed which showed the 37 "powers" or "organs" of the mind.

The importance for clinical psychology of the now discredited field of phrenology lies in its orientation toward assessment of individual characteristics. The phrenologists specialized in feeling heads and providing the owners with a profile of mental makeup. This process may have been the origin of the expression "having your head examined"; it certainly anticipated one of the purposes (though not the procedures) of assessment in clinical psychology.

Measuring individual mental or behavioral characteristics through physical dimensions survived in the 1876 work of Cesare Lombroso, an Italian psychiatrist who correlated facial features with criminal behavior, and in the 20th-century bodytype systems of Ernst Kretschmer and William Sheldon. Today these approaches are not taken seriously by scientists, but they remain a part of our folklore.

Later in the 19th century procedures began to appear that were to form the foundation of clinical psychology's assessment function. These procedures differed from those we have discussed so far. Rather than measuring physical dimensions or observing differences in performance among a few selected individuals, these methods involved systematically collecting *samples of behavior* from large groups of individuals responding to standard sets of stimuli. Such behavior samples were first used to make general statements about individual mental characteristics. Later, as statistical sophistication increased, they were used to establish group norms against which a person could be evaluated quantitatively. By 1890 these procedures had been named *mental tests*. The story of their origin began some 30 years earlier.

In 1859 Charles Darwin published his momentous work, *The Origin of Species,* in which he proposed two important ideas: (a) Variation of individual characteristics occurred within and between species (including humans), and (b) natural selection took place based in part upon those characteristics. Darwin's cousin, Sir Francis Galton, was fascinated by these ideas, and quickly applied Darwin's notions to the inheritance of individual differences.

Galton's tests were aimed at measuring the relatively fixed capacities, structures, and functions he thought comprised the mind. Many of these tests focused on sensorimotor capacity. For example, Galton (1883) tried to discriminate high from low intelligence on the basis of individuals' ability to make fine discriminations among objects of differing weight and among varying intensities of heat, cold,

and pain. He sought to measure individual differences in vividness of mental imagery; for this purpose, he invented the questionnaire. Galton's interests also extended to associative processes, so he developed the word association test to explore this phenomenon. Galton set up a laboratory in London where, for a small fee, anyone could take a battery of tests and receive a copy of the results. This operation comprised the world's first *mental* testing center; and it appeared as part of the health exhibition in the 1884 International Exhibition (an early world's fair).

By the late 1880s psychologists began to show interest in the measurement of individual differences in mental functioning. The person usually credited with merging individual mental measurement with the new science of psychology is James McKeen Cattell, an American who in 1886 took his doctorate in psychology under Wundt in Leipzig. Cattell's interest in the application of psychological methods to the study of individual differences, already evident in his doctoral dissertation on individual variation in reaction time, was intensified by his contact with Galton while lecturing at Cambridge University in 1887. In 1888 Cattell founded the third psychological laboratory in the United States. (The first lab was set up by William James at Harvard in 1879; the second was established by G. Stanley Hall at Johns Hopkins in 1883.) Cattell was one of the first psychologists to appreciate the practical uses of tests for selection and diagnosis of people. This recognition of the applied potential of mental tests foreshadowed the emergence of clinical psychology.

His experience in Wundt's laboratory taught Cattell that "psychology cannot attain the certainty and exactness of the physical sciences unless it rests on a foundation of experiment and measurement" (Dennis, 1948, p. 347), so one of his first tasks was to construct a standard battery of mental tests for use by researchers interested in individual differences. He chose 10 tests that reflected his orientation toward using sensorimotor functioning

FIGURE 1-1 James McKeen Cattell (1860–1944). (From *Scientific Monthly,* 1929, *28,* 25. Reprinted by permission of the American Association for the Advancement of Science.)

as an index of mental capacity. Cattell was interested in measuring how well a person could perform under different conditions. He also collected less systematic information from subjects about personal qualities such as dreams, diseases, preferences, recreational activities, and future plans (Shaffer & Lazarus, 1952).

In spite of their popularity at other universities like Wisconsin, Clark, and Yale, sensorimotor mental tests were criticized because of their low correlations with most criteria (e.g., Sharp, 1899, cited in Reisman, 1976). By this time, however, an alternative approach to testing had evolved from several quarters. In 1891 Hugo Munsterberg, a psychologist at the University of Freiburg (Germany) who later came to Harvard, constructed a set of 14 tests to assess children's mental ability. These tests went beyond Galton-Cattell tasks to include more complex functions like reading, classification of objects, and mathematical operations. The German psychiatrist Emil Kraepelin (originator of an early classification system for behavior disorders) also designed tests of more complex mental functions such as memory, fatigue, and attention.

Finally, and most important, in 1895, Alfred Binet, a French lawyer and scientist who founded the first French psychology lab with Henri Beaunis, began to develop measures of complex mental ability in normal and defective children. Binet's involvement in this testing grew out of the recognition that retarded children (who had been distinguished from psychotics only as late as 1838) might be helped if they could be identified and given special educational attention. By 1896 Binet and his colleague Victor Henri had described a battery of tests that measured not just "simple part processes" such as space judgment, motor skill, muscular effort, and memory, but also comprehension, attention, suggestibility, aesthetic appreciation, and moral values.

Thus, by 1896 psychology was involved in the measurement of individual differences in mental functioning. It also hosted two overlapping approaches to the task: (a) the Cattell-Galton sensorimotor tests, aimed at assessing inherited, relatively fixed mental *structures;* and (b) the instruments of Binet and others, which emphasized complex mental *functions* and which could be taught to some degree. Each of these approaches was important to the development of clinical psychology, the former because it fostered the appearance of the first psychological clinic and the latter because it provided a mental test which was to give the new field its first clear identity. Although early American psychologists came to rely on Binet's test, they embraced Galton's belief that intelligence was largely inherited.

The rest of this story must wait, however, until we examine a third major influence on clinical psychology: changing views of behavior disorder and its treatment.

3. Conceptions of Behavior Disorder.

From the beginning of recorded history, human beings have been faced with the problem of how to explain behavior that is bizarre or apparently irrational. The explanations that have appeared over the centuries make stimulating reading (e.g., Brems, Thevenin, & Routh, 1991; Ullmann & Krasner, 1975; Zilboorg & Henry, 1941), but rather than covering that material in detail here, we shall merely outline the historical progression of ideas about behavior disorder to show how they have influenced various professions, including clinical psychology.

The earliest explanations of disordered behavior involved magical forces and supernatural agents. Persons who acted "crazy" were thought to be possessed by demons or spirits, and treatment involved various forms of exorcism (including *trephining,* or boring small holes in the skull to provide evil spirits with an exit).[1] In Greece before Hippocrates, these

---

[1]This idea continues today in some primitive cultures and parts of Western society. The popularity of *The Exorcist,* the tenets of certain religions, and scattered reports of modern-day demon possession and antidevil procedures all point to the tenacity of demonological notions.

ideas continued in revised form: Disordered behavior was attributed to the influence of one or more of the gods. In early cultures that practiced monotheism, God was seen as a possible source of behavior problems. In the Old Testament, for example, we are told that "the Lord shall smite thee with madness, and blindness, and astonishment of heart" (Deuteronomy 28:28).

As long as supernatural approaches to behavior disorders were prevalent, philosophy and religion were dominant in explaining and dealing with them. Sometimes the practitioners in these fields came from the ranks of the "disturbed." In some primitive groups the shamans, or healers, had themselves been possessed or influenced by supernatural beings.

Supernatural explanations of behavior disorders were still strong when, in about the fourth century B.C., the Greek physician Hippocrates suggested that these aberrations were due to natural causes. Hippocrates argued that behavior disorders, like other behaviors, are a function of the bodily distribution of four fluids, or humors: blood, black bile, yellow bile, and phlegm. This theory, generally acknowledged as the first medical model of behavioral problems, paved the way for the concept of mental illness and legitimized the involvement of the medical profession in its treatment. From Hippocrates until the fall of Rome in A.D. 476, physicians provided the dominant approach to behavior disorders.

In the Middle Ages, naturalistic explanations were swept away and replaced by a return to demonological explanations of behavior problems. The church became the primary social and legal institution in Europe, and religious personnel again took over responsibility for understanding and dealing with unusual behavior. Physicians were expected to confine their ministrations to physical illnesses only. Many medical men solved this problem by becoming priests.

The church began treating the "insane" by exorcising spirits. For example, Zilboorg and Henry (1941, pp. 131–132) quote from a 10th-century invocation designed to alleviate hysteria, then believed to be a female disorder caused by a wandering uterus under demonic control.

O womb, womb, womb, cylindrical womb, red womb, white womb, fleshy womb, bleeding womb, large womb, neufredic womb, bloated womb, O demoniacal one! . . . I conjure thee, O womb, in the name of the Holy Trinity to come back to the place from which thou shouldst neither move nor turn away . . . and to return, without anger, to the place where the Lord has put thee originally. . . . I conjure thee not to harm that maid of God, N., not to occupy her head, throat, neck, chest, ears, teeth, eyes, nostrils, shoulderblades, arms, hands, heart, stomach, spleen, kidneys, back, sides, joints, navel, intestines, bladder, thighs, shins, heels, nails, but to lie down quietly in the place which God chose for thee, so that this maid of God N. be restored to health.

People suspected of deviant behavior were treated as heretics under the control of the devil. Physician-priests "diagnosed" such cases by looking for signs of the devil (*stigmata diaboli*) on the skin (Spanos, 1978). Demon possession was also diagnosed by "dead spots" or local anesthesias which were disclosed by pricking the body with sharp instruments. Once a "diagnosis" of possession was made (and it usually was), "treatment" began. This consisted of torture to produce confessions of heresy, or burning at the stake. These practices continued in varying forms in Europe and in America until the 18th century.

However, long before these atrocities finally ended, the demonological model of disorder was questioned by physicians and scholars, and treatment of deviant individuals gradually began to take the form of confinement in newly established hospitals and asylums such as London's St. Mary of Bethlehem (organized in 1547 and referred to by locals in contracted form as "bedlam"). The hospital movement saved many lives, but it did not necessarily make them worth living. Even though many 18th-century scholars agreed that the insane were suffering from mental illness (not possession), the medical profession, which was now back in charge of the problem, had little to offer in the way of treatment. Because of fear and misunderstanding by the general public, the insane became little more than prisoners who lived under abominable conditions and received grossly inadequate care. The doctors who treated them thought mental illness resulted from brain damage or from an overabundance of blood in the brain. At St. Mary of Bethlehem

> A physician would visit once a year to prescribe treatment: bleeding of all patients in April, purges and "vomits" of surviving patients in May, and once again bleeding all patients in October. At smaller private institutions . . . a physician might visit once in ten years to prescribe a regime of treatment for the next decade. As a continuing feature of institutionalization, patients were chained to posts in dungeons, whipped, beaten, ridiculed, and fed only the coarsest of slops. (Reisman, 1976, p. 10)

Thanks to the efforts of European and American reformers of the 18th and early 19th centuries (Philippe Pinel, William Tuke, Benjamin Rush, and Eli Todd), improved living conditions and more humane treatment aimed at improving patient behavior were instituted. Pinel ushered in this Moral Era of treatment with the following comment: "It is my conviction that these mentally ill are intractable only because they are deprived of fresh air and liberty" (quoted in Ullmann & Krasner, 1975, p. 135). Thus began a new awareness of the possibility that patients could be helped, rather than simply hidden.

During this period physicians retained the responsibility for treatment. Late in the 19th century, syphilis was identified as the organic cause of general paresis, a deteriorative brain syndrome that had once been treated as a form of insanity. This event bolstered the view that all behavior disorder was organically based and that other disease entities awaited

discovery by doctors. The notion that there could be "no twisted thought without a twisted molecule" (Gerard, 1956, quoted in Abood, 1960), along with the crusading of Dorothea Dix to enlarge and improve the mental hospitals in the United States, hastened the decline of the short-lived (but effective) "moral treatment" era. These factors further established medical doctors as the only legitimate agents for the treatment of mental illness.

The search by doctors for organic causes and physical treatment of mental illness resulted in what Zilboorg and Henry (1941) called a "psychiatric revolution." It started when a few French physicians of the mid-19th century began to explore what Franz Anton Mesmer had called "animal magnetism" and which James Braid, an English surgeon, later termed "hypnotism." Research and demonstrations of the relationship between hypnosis and behavior disorders (particularly hysteria) by Jean-Martin Charcot, Hippolyte Bernheim, and Pierre Janet sparked interest in the possibility that mental illness might be partially psychological in nature and thus might respond to psychological, as opposed to organic, treatment.

The issue attracted the attention of a young Viennese neurologist named Sigmund Freud, who by 1896 had proposed the first stage of a theory that saw behavior disorders not as a result of organic conditions, but as a consequence of the dynamic struggle of the human mind to satisfy instinctual (mainly sexual) desires, while at the same time coping with the rules and restrictions of the outside world. Freud's theory brought a less-than-enthusiastic reaction from his medical colleagues. One doctor called Freud's idea "a scientific fairy tale" (Krafft-Ebing, quoted in Reisman, 1976, p. 41). Nevertheless, the idea grew to become a comprehensive theory of the dynamic nature of behavior and behavior disorder, and it ultimately redirected the entire course of the mental health professions, including clinical psychology.

FIGURE 1–2 Tony Robert-Fleury's 1876 painting of Pinel freeing the insane from chains in the Bicetre is one of the most famous artistic interpretations of the Moral Era's reformist and humanitarian spirit. Artists depicting life in the early asylums present a terrifying portrait to our enlightened eyes. However, we must acknowledge that abuses in institutions for the mentally ill have continued well into the second half of the 20th century. Examples of such abuse can be seen in films such as *Titicut Follies,* a documentary by Frederick Wiseman about life in a Massachusetts institution. In fact, this film was so damning in its indictment of the treatment of the inmates that the state sued to prevent its distribution. Cinematic accounts of the abuses of psychiatric hospitals include *Frances,* based on the autobiography of Frances Farmer, and *One Flew Over the Cuckoo's Nest,* an adaptation of Ken Kesey's novel about an institution's attempt to crush the spirit of its inmates. (Photo reprinted by permission of Sander L. Gilman, John Wiley & Sons, Inc.)

Freud's influence on clinical psychology was slight at first because his theory was so controversial and because it dealt with the problem of mental illness, therefore remaining within the province of the medical profession. Psychologists laid no claim to a treatment function at this time, but we shall see that dynamic approaches to behavior pioneered by Freud and his followers shaped the activities of clinical psychologists in other areas and ultimately provided the foundation for their involvement in therapy.

THE BIRTH OF CLINICAL PSYCHOLOGY: 1896–1917

We have now examined the three main roots of clinical psychology, and it should be clear that by the end of the 19th century, the ground had been prepared for its appearance. Psychology had been identified as a science; psychologists had begun to apply scientific methods to the study of individual differences; and Freud's dynamic approach to behavior disorder was about to open up vast new areas of subject matter for psychologists interested in understanding deviance.

It was in this historical context that the first recognized clinical psychologist appeared, an American named Lightner Witmer. Following graduation from the University of Pennsylvania in 1888, Witmer studied for his PhD in psychology with Wundt at the University in Leipzig. Upon completion of his doctorate in 1892, Witmer was appointed director of the University of Pennsylvania psychology laboratory.

In March of 1896 a schoolteacher named Margaret Maguire asked Witmer to help one of her students who was a "chronic bad speller." When Witmer took the case, he became the first clinical psychologist and began an enterprise that became the world's first psychological clinic. The willingness of a psychologist to work with a child's scholastic problem may not now seem significant enough to mark the founding of a profession, but remember that until this point, psychology had dealt with people only to study their behavior in general, not to become concerned about them as individuals. Witmer's decision was as unusual then as would be an attempt by a modern astronomer to determine the "best" orbit for the moon in order to alter its path.

Witmer's approach was to assess the child's problem and then arrange for appropriate remedial procedures. For example, he discov-

ered that Ms. Maguire's bad speller also had reading and memory problems that Witmer termed "visual verbal amnesia." Witmer recommended intensive tutoring aimed at helping the boy recognize words without having to spell them first. This procedure was successful in bringing the boy to a point where he could read ordinary material (McReynolds, 1987).

Not everything Witmer did was to be equally influential later, but several aspects of his new clinic came to characterize subsequent clinical work for some time.

1. The clients were children, a natural development since Witmer had been offering a course on child psychology and had attracted the attention of teachers concerned about their students.

2. Recommendations for helping clients were preceded by diagnostic assessment.

FIGURE 1-3 Lightner Witmer (1867–1956). A man of some idiosyncracies and with a demanding nature, Witmer is reported to have insisted that the temperature in his lecture room always be held exactly at 68 degrees (McReynolds, 1987). (Courtesy of George Eastman House. Reproduced by permission.)

3. Witmer did not work alone. He used a team approach whereby members of various professions would consult and collaborate on a given case.

4. There was a clear interest in preventing future problems through early diagnosis and remediation.

5. Clinical psychology would be built on the foundations of basic, scientific psychology.

At the 1896 meeting of the 4-year-old American Psychological Association, Witmer described his new brand of psychology to his colleagues. His friend Joseph Collins recounted the scene as follows:

[Witmer said] that clinical psychology is derived from the results of an examination of many human beings, one at a time, and that the analytic method of discriminating mental abilities and defects develops an ordered classification of observed behavior, by means of postanalytic generalizations. He put forth the claim that the psychological clinic is an institution for social and public service, for original research, and for the instruction of students in psychological orthogenics which includes vocational, educational, correctional, hygienic, industrial, and social guidance. The only reaction he got from his audience was a slight elevation of the eyebrows on the part of a few of the older members. (Quoted in Brotemarkle, 1947, p. 65).

The lead-balloon reception accorded Witmer's talk was based on four factors:

For *one,* the majority of psychologists considered themselves scientists and probably did not regard the role described by Witmer as appropriate for them. *Two,* even if they had considered his suggestions admirable, few psychologists were prepared by training or experience to perform the functions he proposed. *Three,* they were not about to jeopardize their identification as scientists, which

was tenuous enough in those early years, by plunging their profession into what they felt were premature applications. *Four,* aside from any prevalent skeptical and conservative attitude, Witmer had an unfortunate talent for antagonizing his colleagues. (Reisman, 1976, p. 46)

These objections provided the first clue that conflicts would arise between psychology as a science and psychology as an applied profession. As noted earlier, this issue is as active today as it was in 1896.

In spite of objections, Witmer continued his work and expanded his clinic in order to deal with the increasing caseload, which at first consisted mainly of "slow" or retarded children. Later, the clinic accepted other kinds of cases: speech disorders, sensory problems, and learning disabilities. Consistent with his orthogenic (preventive guidance) orientation, Witmer also worked with "normal" and intellectually superior children, providing guidance and advice to parents and teachers.

In 1897 the new clinic began offering a 4-week summer course in child psychology. It consisted of case presentations, instruction in diagnostic testing, and demonstrations of remedial techniques. By 1900 three children were being seen per day and the clinic staff had grown to 11 members. By 1909 over 450 cases had been seen in Witmer's facilities. Under Witmer's influence, the University of Pennsylvania began offering formal courses in clinical psychology during the 1904–1905 academic year. In 1907 Witmer set up a residential school for training retarded children and founded and edited the first clinical journal, *The Psychological Clinic.* Clinical psychology was on its way.

However, the influence of Witmer's clinic, school, journal, and training courses was limited. Witmer got clinical psychology rolling but had little to do with steering it, mainly because Witmer ignored most of the developments that would later become prominent in clinical psychology.

Specifically, Witmer ignored the introduction in the United States of Alfred Binet's new intelligence test, the Binet-Simon scale. Like Binet's earlier tests, this instrument dealt with complex mental processes rather than the fixed mental structures with which Witmer was concerned. Binet and Simon had developed their test to identify school children whose mental abilities were too low to include them in regular classes. In spite of Binet's warning that it did not provide a wholly objective measure of intelligence, the Binet-Simon gained wide attention. Henry H. Goddard of the Vineland (New Jersey) Training School heard about the Binet-Simon scale while in Europe in 1908 and brought it to the United States for assessing the intelligence of "feeble-minded" children in the clinic he had set up 2 years earlier.

The popularity of Goddard's translation of the Binet-Simon scale and Lewis Terman's 1916 American revision of it (known as the Stanford-Binet) grew so rapidly in the United States that they overshadowed other tests of intelligence, including those used by Witmer. The Binet scales provided a focus for clinical assessment that, until 1910, had been disorganized. All over the country, new university psychological clinics (more than twenty of them by 1914) and institutions for the retarded were adopting the Binet approach while de-emphasizing Witmer's "old-fashioned" methods.

Witmer also ignored the clinical assessment of adults, which was initially designed to aid psychiatrists diagnose and plan treatment for brain damage and other problems. After 1907, psychological examination of mental patients in some hospitals became routine. Similar assessments began in prisons to assist staff in identifying disturbed convicts or planning rehabilitation programs.

Finally, Witmer did not join other clinicians in adopting the Freudian approach to behavior disorder. Freud's approach became known to clinical psychology through association with psychiatry in mental hospitals and also through child-guidance clinics which, though often run by psychiatrists, routinely employed psychologists.

The child-guidance movement in America was stimulated by the National Committee for Mental Hygiene, a group founded by a former mental patient, Clifford Beers, and supported by William James, a Harvard psychologist, and Adolf Meyer, the country's most prominent psychiatrist. With funds from philanthropist Henry Phipps, the committee (which ultimately became the National Association for Mental Health) worked to improve treatment of the mentally ill and to prevent psychological disorders. Guidance clinics for children were very much in line with Witmer's ideal of prevention. The first of them was founded in Chicago in 1909 by an English-born psychiatrist named William Healy.

Like Witmer, Healy worked with children, employed a team approach, and emphasized prevention, but otherwise his orientation was different. Instead of dealing mainly with learning disabilities or other educational difficulties, Healy focused on cases of child misbehavior that required the attention of school authorities, the police, or the courts. Healy's clinic operated on the assumption that juvenile offenders were suffering from mental illness that should be prevented before it caused more serious problems later. Finally, Freud's ideas influenced the tone of Healy's Chicago clinic (first called the Juvenile Psychopathic Institute and later the Institute for Juvenile Research).

This dynamic approach differed from Witmer's and it received a huge boost in popularity when, in the same year Healy opened his clinic, G. Stanley Hall, a psychologist, arranged for Sigmund Freud and two of his followers, Carl Jung and Sandor Ferenczi, to speak at the 20th anniversary celebration of Clark University in Worcester, Massachusetts. This event and the lectures associated with it "sold" psychoanalysis to American psychologists. Freud's theory was compatible with their interest in the way the mind deals with its environment (the functionalism of William James and G. Stanley Hall) as opposed to what it is made of (the structuralism of Wundt). It also appealed to the emphasis on pragmatism in the United States.

One result of this excitement over Freud was that psychological and child-guidance clinics followed Healy's model, not Witmer's. This fact, coupled with the spreading use of Binet intelligence tests, left Witmer in the background. He stayed involved with activities and clients that have since become more strongly associated with school psychologists, vocational counselors, speech therapists, and remedial teachers than with clinical psychologists.

After clinical psychology adopted the Binet-Simon scales it became identified primarily with the testing of problematic children in clinics and guidance centers. This image led critics to argue that clinicians spent too much time diagnosing hopeless cases and that they were not sufficiently psychoanalytic in orientation. At the same time, schools and other institutions that dealt with children were desperately searching for clinical psychologists to do the testing which was fast becoming fashionable.

The need for clinicians' services outweighed the effects of their critics, and the field continued its slow advance during the 1910–1917 period. Its practitioners gave established tests, constructed new ones, and conducted research on the reliability and validity of them all. Most of the new instruments were aimed at measuring intelligence, but a few began to focus on the assessment of personality through word associations or questionnaire items.

Training for clinical psychology was a problem during this period. A few internships were available at places like the Vineland Training School, and courses in intelligence testing and related subjects were taught here and there, but training was not formalized. Virtually anyone could use the title of clinical psychologist. APA was little help in this regard because it was largely preoccupied with the scientific as-

pects of psychology. It took no official notice of the problems of the new field except to pass a 1915 resolution discouraging the use of mental tests by unqualified persons.

A group of disgruntled clinicians agreed that they could best advance the interests of their new profession by forming a separate organization; so in December 1917, the American Association of Clinical Psychologists (AACP) was established. This step was not successful, and, after the APA promised to give more consideration to professional issues and problems, the AACP rejoined the APA as its clinical section in 1919.

BETWEEN THE WARS: 1918–1941

When America became involved in World War I, large numbers of men had to be classified in terms of their intellectual prowess and psychological stability. No techniques existed to do this, so the Army asked Robert Yerkes (then APA president) to head a committee of assessment-oriented experimental psychologists who were to develop appropriate measures.[2] This group produced the Army Alpha and Army Beta intelligence tests, which could be administered to groups of literate or nonliterate adults. To help detect behavior disorders among the recruits, Yerkes's committee recommended Robert Woodworth's Psychoneurotic Inventory (when given to soldiers, it was more politely titled "personal data sheet"; see Yerkes, 1921, in Dennis, 1948). By 1918 psychologists had evaluated nearly two million men for the army.

After the war, clinical psychologists still assessed children, but they began to find increased employment as testers in adult-oriented facilities as well. Clinicians were also

---

[2]The group included Henry Goddard of the Vineland School; Guy Whipple, publisher of a 1910 *Manual of Mental and Physical Tests;* and Lewis Terman, developer of the Stanford-Binet scales.

using a wide variety of intelligence tests for children and adults and adding new measures of personality, interests, specific abilities, emotions, and traits. They developed many of these tests themselves, while adopting others from the psychoanalytically oriented psychiatrists of Europe. Some of the more familiar instruments of this period include the Seashore Musical Ability Test (1919), Jung's Word Association Test (1919), the Rorschach Inkblot Test (1921), the Miller Analogies Test (1926), the Goodenough Draw-A-Man Test (1926), the Strong Vocational Interest Test (1927), the Thematic Apperception Test (1935), the Bender-Gestalt Test (1938), and the Wechsler-Bellevue Intelligence Scale (1939).

So many psychological tests appeared (over 500 by 1940) that a *Mental Measurements Yearbook* was needed to catalog them (Buros, 1938). The development, administration, and evaluation of these instruments continued to stimulate clinicians' assessment and research functions. In 1921 Cattell formed the Psychological Corporation to sell tests and provide consultation and research to business and industry. Clinical psychologists of this period also researched and theorized on such topics as the nature of personality, the source of human intelligence (i.e., heredity or environment), the causes of behavior disorders, the uses of hypnosis, and the relationship between learning principles and deviance.

By the mid-1930s there were 50 psychological clinics and at least a dozen child-guidance clinics in the United States. Clinical psychologists in these settings "perceived themselves as dealing with educational, not psychiatric problems. But this distinction was growing increasingly difficult to maintain" (Reisman, 1976, pp. 176–177). Slowly, clinicians began to add a treatment function to their assessment, training, and research roles. By the late 1930s a few had even gone into private practice.

Therapy focused initially on children and was a natural outgrowth of clinicians' involvement in diagnostic and remedial work with children. It also stemmed from the prestige of

clinicians' use of personality tests, such as the Rorschach and the Thematic Apperception Test (TAT). These techniques provided a common language for diagnostician (psychologist) and therapist (psychiatrist) to discuss patients, thus increasing the clinician's association with treatment. Engaging in treatment also allowed clinical psychologists to obtain better-paying, more responsible jobs, to be less dependent on testing for their professional identities, and to become involved with the "whole patient."

Even though its settings, clients, and functions were expanding, clinical psychology was not a recognized profession in the 1930s. At the beginning of World War II there were still no official training programs for clinicians. Few of them held PhDs, some had MAs, and many had BAs or less. To get a job as a clinical psychologist, all one needed was a few courses in testing, abnormal psychology, and child development, along with an "interest in people."

While clinicians did not like their second-class reputation as mental testers, they received little help from their university colleagues or the APA in upgrading that image through standardized training programs or official certification. Discomfort on the part of academic psychologists over the appropriateness of "applied" psychology, combined with the cost of clinical training, led to a slow response by university psychology departments to develop graduate programs in clinical psychology.

Although the APA had appointed committees on clinical training at various times during the 1920s and 1930s (and had even set up a short-lived certification program), its involvement was halfhearted. For example, in 1935 the APA Committee on Standards of Training in Clinical Psychology suggested that a PhD plus 1 year of supervised experience was necessary to become a clinical psychologist, but after issuing its report the committee disbanded; little came of its efforts.

The discontent of clinical and other nonacademic psychologists erupted in 1937, and they again broke away from APA to form a separate organization, this time called the American Association of Applied Psychology (AAAP). It contained divisions of consulting, clinical, educational, and industrial psychology and remained independent for 8 years before rejoining APA.

By the end of the 1930s all the ingredients for the modern field of clinical psychology had been assembled: Its six functions (assessment, treatment, research, teaching, consultation, and administration) had appeared. Clinical psychology had expanded beyond its original clinics into hospitals, prisons, and other settings. It worked with adults as well as children, and was motivated to stand on its own; only the support of its parent discipline and the society it served was still needed. This support came as a result of World War II.

THE POSTWAR EXPLOSION

America's entry into World War II again necessitated mass testing of military personnel on intelligence, ability, and personality dimensions, and again a committee of psychologists was formed to help with the task. Because psychometric and clinical sophistication had increased greatly since the time of the Yerkes committee, this new group of psychologists produced a correspondingly wider range of military-oriented tests, including the Army General Classification Test (a group intelligence instrument), a psychiatric screening questionnaire called the Personal Inventory, brief measures of intelligence, short forms of the Rorschach and the TAT, and several ability tests for selection of officers, pilots, and the like.[3]

The involvement of psychology in World War II was far greater than in World War I. For example, about 1,500 psychologists (nearly 25% of those available) served in World War II. Reisman (1976) reports that in 1944 alone, over 60 million psychological tests were given to 20 million soldiers and civilians. In addition to giving tests, psychologists conducted interviews, wrote psychological reports, and, because of the overwhelming caseload of psychological casualties, performed psychoanalytically oriented therapy. For those who had been clinicians before the war, military life meant an opportunity to consolidate and expand their clinical functions, but such individuals were a minority. Most wartime psychologists came from academic settings. For them, the army's desperate need for applied psychological services meant taking on clinical responsibilities for the first time.

These converted clinicians found they were able to handle their new jobs remarkably well, and many of them began to like the work. Authorities in the military and civilian establishment were impressed with the clinical skills of psychologists. Psychologists became commissioned military officers, just like physicians. By the end of the war, many clinicians were hooked on therapy with adults, and former experimentalists became enamored of clinical functions. Their wartime testing and therapeutic activities brought psychologists increasing public attention and prestige.

This awakening of interest in clinical work might have come to nothing if there had not been so much of it to do. The war left over 40,000 people in VA neuropsychiatric hospitals, and there were not enough clinical psychologists and psychiatrists to serve these patients adequately. Where the APA and university psychology departments had vacillated over the education and roles of clinicians, the needs of the VA prompted immediate action. A 1946 VA circular defined clinical psychology as a profession that engaged in diagnosis, treatment, and research relating to adult disorders; it described clinicians as holders of the

---

[3]Some of the latter techniques included behavioral measures that required candidates to perform various tasks under frustrating or stressful conditions. Such "real-life" observation is now a popular clinical assessment strategy (see Chapter 6).

PhD. More important, the VA said it needed 4,700 of these individuals to fill lucrative, high-prestige jobs and that it would help pay for clinical training. Hathaway (1958, p. 107) said, "This document, more than any other single thing, has served to guide the development of clinical psychology."

Here was the support clinical psychology had been waiting for. Early in 1946 the chief medical director of the VA met with representatives of major universities to ask them to start formal clinical training programs; by that fall, 200 graduate students became VA clinical trainees at 22 institutions (Peck & Ash, 1964). By 1951 the VA had become the largest single employer of psychologists in the United States.

Not all psychology departments that began clinical training programs after the war were enthusiastic about doing so. Faculty members sympathetic to clinical work saw governmental support as a boon, while others who were devoted to psychology as a pure science objected to the intrusion of professional training which, to their way of thinking, was begun merely because the government (first through the VA and then through the United States Public Health Service, USPHS) was willing to pay for it. Shakow (1965) characterized this as a conflict between the "virgins" and the "prostitutes." Whatever one calls it, it was a continuation of the same "science versus profession" issue that has been brewing ever since 1896.

Nevertheless, the VA and USPHS went ahead with their funding plans and turned to the APA for guidance about which university clinical programs merited federal support. Accordingly, an initial evaluation of existing programs was provided by a Committee on Graduate and Professional Training in 1947 (Kelly, 1961). Later that year, a more extensive report came from David Shakow's Committee on Training in Clinical Psychology, which had been appointed by the APA to (a) recommend the content of clinical programs, (b) set up training standards to be followed by universities and internship facilities, and (c) report on current programs (Shakow, 1978, presents details of the history and composition of this committee).

This Shakow report was meant only to provide training guidelines, but since it was so intimately tied to the dispensation of federal money to individual students and whole departments, the "guidelines" were adopted as policy "and soon became the 'bible' of all departments of psychology desirous of having their programs evaluated and reported on favorably by the APA" (Kelly, 1961, p. 110). Shakow felt that this reaction prematurely forced the nature of clinical training, and that, if things had gone more slowly, the resulting programs might have been better.

The Shakow report laid the groundwork for later controversy over how clinicians should be trained, an issue that related directly to the science–profession problem. The recommendations of greatest contemporary importance include the following (APA, 1947):

1. Clinical psychologists should be trained first as psychologists (i.e., as scientists) and second as practicing professionals.
2. Clinical training should be as rigorous as that given to nonclinicians and thus should consist of a 4-year doctorate, including a year of supervised clinical internship experience.
3. Clinical training should focus on the "holy trinity" (assessment, research, and treatment) by offering courses in general psychology, psychodynamics, assessment techniques, research methods, and therapy (see Shakow, 1978, for a summary of the full report).

Thus began "what later came to be recognized as something of an educational experiment: the training of persons both as scientists and as practitioners, not in a separate professional school [as is the case in medicine or law], but in the graduate schools of our universities" (Kelly, 1961, p. 112). This experiment continued with the support of the APA, the federal government, internship facilities, and universities. Two years after the Shakow report appeared, a national conference on clinical training at Boulder, Colorado, formally adopted its recommendations. In addition, APA created an Education and Training Board to evaluate and publish lists of accredited doctoral-level clinical programs and internship settings.

The scientist–professional training package described in the Shakow report and adopted at Boulder in 1949 came to be known as the "Boulder model"; it set the pattern for clinical training for the next 25 years. Nevertheless, not everyone in the field was enthusiastic about it, and though its official APA status was reaffirmed at subsequent training conferences in 1955, 1958, 1962, 1965, and 1973, discontent remained. In Chapter 14 we consider the details of these conferences and the modifications of the Boulder model that have ensued. Suffice it to say here that psychologists committed to professional practice felt that the model emphasized research training at the expense of preparation for applied work, while more research-oriented psychologists failed to see the need for so much emphasis on application.

In spite of such problems, government support of university-based Boulder model training contributed to the explosive growth of clinical psychology. By 1948 there were 22 APA-approved clinical training programs, 60 by 1962, 83 by 1973, and more than 150 by 1993. Personality and intelligence assessment mushroomed following the introduction of tests like the Minnesota Multiphasic Personality Inventory (MMPI), new scoring procedures for projectives like the Rorshach, and new adult intelligence scales. Clinical psychologists' treatment roles, now recognized by the government and by the public, blossomed as well. Three times as many clinical psychologists engaged in therapy after the war as before it, and the emphasis swung toward work with adults as well as with children. The clinician in private practice became more common as practitioners sought to pattern themselves after physicians.

Legal recognition of clinical psychology as a profession was growing as well. In the postwar years, states passed laws providing for licensure or certification of qualified clinicians, and the APA set up an independent certification group to identify individuals who had attained particularly high levels of clinical experience and expertise. The APA also developed a code of ethics governing the behavior of all its members, but focusing on those engaged in applied activities. These and other aspects of clinical psychology as a profession are discussed more fully in Chapter 14.

Clinical research also expanded after World War II and produced some disturbingly negative conclusions on the usefulness of some personality tests (e.g., Magaret, 1952), the value of clinicians' diagnostic judgments when compared to statistically based decisions (Meehl, 1954), and the effectiveness of traditional (e.g., mainly Freudian) psychotherapy (Eysenck, 1952). Such research influenced a shift away from standard clinical assessment and the development of new treatment approaches, including those of Carl Rogers and many behavior therapists.

By the 1980s, almost everything that could have been said about clinical psychology before World War II had changed. The clinical psychologist before the war was primarily a diagnostician whose clients were children. Since 1945 the functions, settings, and clients of clinical psychology have expanded dramatically. Today's clinician enjoys a wider range of theoretical approaches and practical tools for assessing and altering human behavior.

Although the field has advanced in spectacular fashion during the last 50 years, neither its development nor its self-examination has been completed. Clinicians are an introspective and self-critical group. The issues clinical psychologists continue to debate include society's needs for psychological service, the value of clinical assessment and psychotherapy, the problems and prospects of private practice, the prevention of psychological problems, the relationship of psychology to physical health, and ways of providing services to segments of the population (such as the poor) who do not usually receive them.

Clinicians also still focus on the scientist–professional issue: How can the clinician be a scientifically minded psychologist who waits for carefully validated evidence before diagnosing a condition or proceeding with treatment and, at the same time, function as a "front-line" practitioner who tries to help distressed people with complex problems about which little knowledge may be available? Some observers feel that the scientific and professional roles are basically incompatible, and that a psychologist must choose one or the other. Accordingly, some clinical students become intuitive practitioners to whom *data* is a nasty word, while others work as full-time researchers in hopes of generating empirical findings that will someday make all clinical practice scientific.

This either–or polarization has unfortunate consequences. It isolates the practitioner from research that may be useful in applied work, and it may place the researcher in a laboratory that is so artificial that results apply only to other laboratory settings or situations where the most interesting and important clinical problems may not appear. The cumulative result of this polarization could be a reduction in the mutual stimulation between clinic and laboratory that most careful thinkers in the field consider to be vital to the future of clinical psychology (Cohen, Sargent, & Sechrest, 1986; Strupp, 1989).

Another indication of the conflict between academic psychologists and practitioners centers around the type of professional organization that best represents their respective views. In 1988, the American Psychological Society (APS) was formed by a group of psychologists who desired a more scientifically oriented organization than APA. Although some research-oriented clinicians belong to both APA and APS, most full-time practitioners appear to prefer APA over APS for their professional "home."

If the past is any indication of the future, clinical psychologists will continue to debate the scientist–professional issue. Those who see clinical psychology as an art learned from practice and who have little use for scientific verification will line up on one side of the question, while those who mistrust the value of subjective impressions and other non-scientific aspects of clinical work will be found on the other side. Less predictable are psychologists who view clinical psychology as a field with artistic characteristics, a scientific base, and a capability to exploit both (Hoshmand & Polkinghorne, 1992; Mahoney, 1991).

While clinical psychologists passionately argue these issues, we have come to believe that, as a profession and a scholarly field, clinical psychology will advance and prosper only to the degree that it remains firmly grounded in the foundations of science. We recognize that science can be defined in several ways (Gergen, 1985), but for our purposes in this book the essential feature of a scientific clinical psychology is that clinicians evaluate the validity of their theories, the effectiveness of their techniques, and the impact of their practice with public, replicable, and well-controlled empirical research methods. The clearest call for building a scientific clinical psychology has been sounded in Richard McFall's (1991) "Manifesto for a Science of Clinical Psychology." McFall's Manifesto has been echoed by other clinical psychologists (Sechrest, 1992) and consists of the following three principles:

1. Scientific clinical psychology is the only legitimate and acceptable form of clinical psychology.

2. Psychological services should not be delivered to the public (except under strict experimental control) until they meet four criteria: The service is described clearly, its claimed benefits are stated explicitly, its effects are validated scientifically, and its positive effects are shown to outweigh its possible negative effects.

3. The primary and overriding objective of doc-

toral training programs in clinical psychology must be to produce the most competent clinical scientists possible.

As the size and stature of clinical psychology have grown, the field has become more tolerant of divergent ideas about clinical training, professional roles, and basic issues like the development of human problems and the means through which they can best be alleviated. Throughout this book we review the most important of these contrasting ideas and illustrate their importance for clinical psychologists. We describe the different models and methods of clinical psychology fairly, but we also intend the book to reflect our conviction that these models and methods are best judged against the scientific standards suggested by McFall's Manifesto.

CHAPTER 2

Models
of
Clinical Psychology

To appreciate fully the dimensions of an object, one must examine it from several angles; this is why sculpture is often displayed where the viewer can walk around it. Events are also subject to multiple interpretations, depending on one's point of view. This phenomenon is so reliable that instructors often stage sudden and unusual classroom events (such as the attempted "murder" of the professor by a "disgruntled former student") and then ask students to describe what they saw, to demonstrate the inevitable variability in observer recollection.

Listening to differing accounts of the same occurrence from varying points of view can be confusing. But it may also be illuminating in the sense that, as with a statue, one is allowed to examine all the angles. And though the "absolute truth" about an event, relationship, or a person may not necessarily be revealed, there is at least the assurance that potentially important material has not been totally overlooked.

Clinical psychologists follow a similar strategy when they gather assessment information about a client from multiple sources. In this regard, clinicians are like competent investigative reporters who try to understand a subject fully by talking to several sources. The same open and comprehensive orientation can be of value to the beginning student of clinical psychology. There are many ways to look at the field. Each view reveals some aspects and obscures others. The whole picture cannot emerge unless one is familiar with the variety of viewpoints that are available.

This chapter examines four of the most prominent of these points of view: the psychodynamic, behavioral, phenomenological, and interpersonal models of clinical psychology. They are referred to as *models* because they describe on a miniature scale the ways various thinkers have approached human behavior in general and clinical psychology in particular. Each model tries to explain how behavior develops and becomes problematic, and each influences the assessment, treatment, and research styles of its adherents.

For example, if one's model of clinical psychology were based on the assumption that behavior is determined by the foods people eat, that assumption would lead to predictions about how diet affects behavioral development through the life span (e.g., "Mushy foods produce mushy thinking and uncoordinated behavior, while solid food and mature eating habits result in clear thought processes"). Further, a dietary model might suggest hypotheses about disordered behavior in which excess carbohydrates are associated with anxiety, consumption of large quantities of soft drinks are thought to result in hallucinations, or too little protein is implicated in obsessive rituals. Specialized measurement procedures might be developed to assess clients' eating patterns and to monitor the nutritional components of each meal. The model would also emphasize certain treatments. Carefully programmed alterations in diet would be prescribed, while simply talking about one's problems would be regarded as a waste of time. Finally, the targets of research would be shaped by the model. Experiments designed to evaluate diet-assessment or diet-modification procedures would appear in large numbers.

THE VALUE OF MODELS

The positive features of a model of clinical psychology are that it helps clinicians (a) organize their thinking about behavior, (b) guide their clinical decisions and interventions, and (c) communicate in a common, systematic language with their colleagues. It imposes order on vast amounts of material that might seem otherwise unrelated.

A model encourages an ordered understanding of a complicated subject. Human behavior is extremely complex and can be examined on several levels, from the activity of cells to the processes of social interaction. There also is an endless number of ways in which behavior can be interpreted, assessed, researched, and altered. One must decide which aspects of behavior deserve special attention,

which kinds of assessment data are of greatest interest, which treatment techniques merit more exploration, and which research targets are the most fruitful. A model guides these decisions, thereby helping the clinician bring order to what may have been conceptual chaos.

The appeal of a model as a compass or guide attracts followers whose commitment to it ranges from healthy skepticism to fanatic zeal. However, the usefulness of the major models of clinical psychology must be evaluated on dimensions other than superficial attractiveness or number of adherents. In scientific terms, the best clinical models are those whose implications and hypotheses can be rigorously investigated in a wide range of contexts. A good model for a clinical psychologist should include a complete and testable account of the development, maintenance, and alteration of both problematic and non-problematic human behavior. Models that meet these requirements are open to experimental evaluation. They will stand or fall as the data accumulate. Those that hold themselves aloof from scientific evaluations must base their claims to legitimacy on clinical intuition, subjective appeal, or logical coherence alone.

SOME CAUTIONS ABOUT MODELS

The strengths of clinical models can also be construed as their weaknesses. For example, a given model may organize one's thinking about behavior so completely that it becomes rigid and closed to new and valuable ideas. This closure promotes a fossilized rather than organized approach to clinical psychology.

Blind adherence to a particular model can reduce a clinician's functioning to a level where objective evaluation and subsequent modification of professional practices become unlikely. As a result, clinicians who become dependent on a model may perform their professional activities in strict accordance with the dictates of the model because they have always performed them that way, regardless of empirical evidence that might indicate the need for change. A model's consistent perspective is turned from an asset to a liability when it produces such a narrow focus that other points of view are overlooked.

Finally, a model is like a region of the country that tends to develop its own "language." It eases communication among those conversant in it, but it can obstruct discussions between "natives" and "foreigners." Often, the exchange of ideas between persons espousing different models of clinical psychology is hampered by this kind of language barrier. Both parties think they are speaking clearly and comprehensibly when, in fact, they are not understanding each other because their model-based terms and specialized meanings are in the way. We have heard heated theoretical arguments of this type that ended when the participants finally realized that they agreed with one another. Fortunately, most problems associated with the adoption of a clinical model can be reduced by avoiding the overzealous commitment to it that fosters conceptual rigidity, behavioral inflexibility, and semantic narrowness. This is not to say that systematic reference to a particular model is detrimental; quite the opposite. However, understanding and appreciating other points of view can act as insurance against a narrowmindedness that could be detrimental to clinicians and clients alike. We intend the material in this chapter to assist in this regard. For those acquainted with psychodynamic, behavioral, interpersonal, and phenomenological personality theories, much of what follows may be familiar, but we will attempt to go beyond abstract theory and outline the clinical conceptualization, assessment, and treatment that flow from each model and can be applied to individual cases. In subsequent chapters, we will consider the specific tactics that translate these strategies into action.

One final point: None of the models discussed in this chapter is a single, unitary entity. Each is made up of variations on a basic theme; thus, to characterize adequately each model, we must describe several of these variations.

THE PSYCHODYNAMIC MODEL

The psychodynamic model is rooted in the 19th- and 20th-century writings of Sigmund Freud, but it has broadened to include the ideas of those who revised and challenged many of Freud's concepts. The model is based upon the following assumptions:

1. Human behavior is determined by impulses, desires, motives, and conflicts that are *intrapsychic* (within the mind) and often unconscious (out of awareness).

2. Intrapsychic factors cause both normal and abnormal behaviors. Thus, just as disabling anxiety or delusions of persecution in a patient would be attributed to unresolved conflicts or unmet needs, the outgoing and friendly behavior of an acquaintance might be seen as stemming from contrasting inner feelings of fear or worthlessness or from a hidden desire to be more popular than a sibling.

3. The foundations for behavior are set down in childhood through satisfaction or frustration of basic needs and impulses. Because of their central role in these needs, early relationships with parents, siblings, grandparents, peers, and authority figures are given special attention. There is a historical flavor to the psychodynamic model because of its focus on early childhood events.

4. Clinical assessment, treatment, and research should emphasize the subtle aspects of intrapsychic activity which, though often hidden from direct observation, must be uncovered if behavior is to be understood and behavior problems are to be alleviated.

Freudian Psychoanalysis

Some scholars (Ullmann & Krasner, 1975) have described the Freudian approach, or *psychoanalysis,* as a *medical model* because the theory focused on abnormality and was introduced at a time when there was interest in discovering organic causes for "mental illness."

This atmosphere, along with Freud's own training as a physician, emphasized the parallels between his psychological thinking and the disease orientation to behavior dominant at the time. Unconscious conflicts and other psychological factors were seen as analogous to *disease processes,* and problematic behaviors became the *symptoms* of those processes. Troubled people who came to medical doctors or were confined in hospitals because of what might, according to Freud, be psychologically based problems, were still called *patients,* and the standard medical concepts of *diagnosis, prognosis, treatment,* and *cure* were applied to them.

Freud's psychodynamic model was founded on a few basic principles. One of these is *psychic determinism,* the notion that behavior is related to causes often hidden from outside observers and the behaving individual as well. From this perspective, almost all behaviors (even "accidents") are seen as meaningful because they provide clues to hidden conflicts and motivations (Freud, 1901). Thus, reading the word *breast* when the text says *beast,* forgetting a relative's name, or losing a borrowed book may all be interpreted as expressing feelings or impulses that may not appear in awareness. Freud called *unconscious* the part of mental functioning that was out of awareness and not readily accessible to it.

Another of Freud's basic postulates was that human behavior is derived from a continual struggle between the individual's desire to satisfy inborn sexual and aggressive instincts and the need to respect the rules and realities of the outside world. He saw each individual facing a lifelong search for ways of expressing instinctual urges without incurring punishment or other negative consequences. The case of the 7-year-old boy who, after being told by his mother that he cannot go to the mall, eats 16 oatmeal raisin cookies and then throws up all over her desk, provides a perfect example of the expression of aggressive impulse in light of the facts of reality. Freud saw the human mind as an arena where what the person *wants* to do (instinct) must be reconciled with

the controlling requirements of what *can* or *should* be done (reason and morality).

Mental Structure

In Freud's system, unconscious instincts make up the *id,* which is present at birth and contains all the psychic energy or *libido* available to motivate behavior. Id seeks to gratify its desires without delay, and therefore it is said to operate on the *pleasure principle* (i.e., "If it feels good, do it!"). As the newborn grows and the outside world imposes more limitations on direct id gratification, the *ego* begins to organize as an outgrowth of id around the age of 1 year and begins to find safe outlets for expression of instincts. It was our 7-year-old's ego, for example, that engineered the revenge wreaked upon his mother. Since ego adjusts to external demands, it operates on the *reality principle* (i.e., "If you are going to do it, at least do it quietly"). A third mental agency, *superego,* is another result of the socializing influence of reality. It contains all the teachings of family and culture regarding ethics, morals, and values, and according to Freud, these teachings are internalized to become the "ego ideal," or how one would like to be. Superego also contains the conscience, which seeks to promote perfect, conforming, and socially acceptable behavior usually opposed by id.

Mechanisms of Defense

Freud's three-part mental structure is constantly embroiled in internal conflicts (see Box 2–1) resulting in anxiety. Ego attempts to keep these conflicts and their discomfort from reaching consciousness by employing a variety of *defense mechanisms,* usually at an unconscious level. One of the most common—and for Freud, the most prototypic of these mechanisms—is *repression,* where ego simply holds an unacceptable thought, feeling, or impulse out of consciousness. Repression has also been called *motivated forgetting.* An individual whose hatred is not consciously experi-

Conflict	Example
Id vs. ego	Choosing between a small immediate reward and a larger reward that requires some period of waiting (delay of gratification).
Id vs. superego	Deciding whether to return the difference when you are overpaid or undercharged.
Ego vs. superego	Choosing between acting in a realistic way (telling a white lie) and adhering to a potentially costly or unrealistic standard (always telling the truth).
Id and ego vs. superego	Deciding whether to retaliate against the attack of a weak opponent or to turn the other cheek.
Id and superego vs. ego	Deciding whether to act in a realistic way that conflicts both with your desires and your moral convictions (the decision faced by devout Roman Catholics as to the use of contraceptive devices).
Ego and superego vs. id	Choosing whether to act on the impulse to steal something you want and cannot afford. The ego would presumably be increasingly involved in such a conflict as the probability of being apprehended increases.

Source: Robert M. Liebert and Michael D. Spiegler, *Personality: Strategies and Issues,* 6th ed. Homewood, IL: The Dorsey Press, 1990, p. 100; © by the Dorsey Press.

BOX 2–1
Some Examples of Intrapsychic Conflict

enced may be repressing that hatred (when a person is aware of an impulse and *consciously* denies its existence, the process is called *suppression*). However, repression takes great, constant effort (somewhat like trying to hold an inflated balloon under water), and the undesirable urge may threaten to surface at times.

To guard against this, ego employs additional unconscious defenses. One of these is *reaction formation,* in which the person thinks and acts in a fashion diametrically opposed to the unconscious impulse. A son who hates his father may enthusiastically express unbounded love and doting concern for his father. If the defense mechanism called *projection* is used, the son may attribute negative feelings to others and accuse them of mistreat-

ing their fathers. A mechanism of *displacement* allows some expression of id impulses, but it aims their expression at safer targets, such as co-workers or others who may be father figures. The son's harsh criticism of an older colleague, for example, might be viewed this way. Displacement also works in dreams. If the son expresses id impulses by criticizing his father, he may *rationalize* or explain away the behavior by pointing out that it is "for his father's own good." The defense mechanism Freud saw as most socially adaptive is *sublimation*. Here, the expression of taboo impulses is directed into productive and creative channels such as writing, painting, acting, dance, or other activities.

While sublimation may provide a relatively

permanent defense against anxiety, the other mechanisms are less desirable because they waste psychic energy. Further, they may fail under stress, forcing the troubled person to fall back, or *regress,* to levels of behavior characteristic of earlier, less mature stages of development. Partial regression may produce behaviors inappropriate to one's age and social status; more profound regression is associated with more severely disturbed behavior. The depth of regression in a given case is partly a function of the individual's history of *psychosexual development.*

Developmental Stages

Freud postulated that as children develop, they pass through several psychosexual stages, each named for the part of the body most associated with pleasure at the time. The first year or so is called the *oral* stage, because eating, sucking, biting, and other oral activities are the predominant sources of pleasure. The oral child is busy *incorporating* or taking in the external world. If, because of premature or delayed weaning from the bottle or breast, oral needs are frustrated or overindulged, the child may fail to pass through the oral stage without clinging to, or becoming *fixated* on, behavior patterns associated with it. Adults who depend inordinately upon oral behavior patterns such as smoking, overeating, excessive talking, or biting sarcasm may be seen as orally fixated. As adults, oral characters also may appear to be gullible, passive, and optimistic. Freud felt that the stronger an individual's fixation at a given psychosexual stage, the more behaviors typical of that stage would be shown at a later point and the more likely it would be that regression to that level would occur under stress. Cases in which a person becomes very dependent upon others or very depressed when dependency needs are not met are sometimes viewed by Freudians as regression to the oral stage.

The second year or so is called the *anal* stage, because Freud saw the anus and the stimuli associated with eliminating and with-holding feces as the important sources of pleasure at that point. The significant feature of this period is toilet training, in which there is a clash of wills between parents and child. The passivity of the oral stage gives way to the defiance of the anal period, a change suggested by the popular description of this period as the "terrible 2s." Anal fixation was thought to result from overly prohibitive or particularly indulgent practices in this area. Adult behaviors associated with anal fixation include tight, controlled behavior or loose, disorderly habits. Persons who are stingy, obstinate, highly organized, concerned with cleanliness or detail, and those who are sloppy, disorganized, and markedly generous with money might be seen as displaying anal characteristics.

The child enters Freud's *phallic* stage at about age three or four, as the genitals become the primary source of pleasure. As the name of this period implies, Freud paid more attention to psychosexual development in the male than in the female. He theorized that during the phallic stage the young boy begins to have sexual desire for his mother and wants to do away with his father's competition. This situation was labeled *Oedipal* because it recapitulates the plot of the Greek tragedy *Oedipus Rex.* Because the boy fears castration as punishment for his incestuous and murderous desires, the Oedipus complex and its attendant anxiety are normally resolved by repressing sexual desires toward the mother, *identifying* with the father, and ultimately finding an appropriate female sex partner.

Freud discussed a female Oedipus complex (he rejected the term *Electra complex,* used by some of his students) in which a little girl suffers *penis envy* and a sense of inferiority because she believes she has already been castrated. She ultimately sublimates these feelings by substituting a desire to have a baby for a desire to have a penis, in this way coming to identify with her mother. Freud thought that a woman's superego was less developed than a man's because it was not forged from a strong fear like castration anxiety. (These views have not made Freud a popular figure among feminists.)

Freud believed that successful resolution of conflicts in the phallic stage was crucial to healthy psychological development. For example, he saw superego as the result of the Oedipus complex; "Conform or be castrated" provides the boy's first motive for moral behavior. Fixation at the phallic stage was seen as common and responsible for many adult interpersonal problems, including rebellion, aggression, and socially discouraged sexual practices like homosexuality, exhibitionism, and fetishism.

Freud believed a dormant or *latency* period follows the phallic stage. During latency, the reality principle becomes a stronger force in the child's life. A quieting of the Oedipal conflict allows the child to develop social and educational skills and extends until adolescence, when the individual's physical maturity ushers in the *genital* period. In this final stage (which lasts through the adult years), pleasure is again focused in the genital area, but if all has gone well in earlier stages, sexual interest is directed not just toward the kind of self-satisfaction characteristic of the phallic period, but toward establishment of a stable, long-term heterosexual relationship in which the needs of another are valued and considered.

Related Psychodynamic Approaches

Freud's original ideas have undergone many changes.[1] His constant alterations of psychoanalysis make it possible to speak of many editions of Freud's theory, but he remained committed to a few cardinal principles, notably the sexual and aggressive basis of human behavior. This often unpopular dogma promoted others to create variations on the psychodynamic model. Some of these variants involved minimal shifts of emphasis, while others represented a substantial break with Freud's notions. Several trends mark the evolution of alternative psychoanalytic theories (Liebert & Spiegler, 1990): (a) dissatisfaction with the central role of unconscious instincts in motivation, (b) increased recognition of the influence of social and cultural variables on human behavior, (c) greater emphasis on conscious aspects of personality, and (d) belief that personality development is not completed in childhood but continues through the adult years.

In the less radical variations, ego is characterized as a positive, creative, coping mechanism in addition to being an arbiter of intrapsychic conflict. In these versions of psychoanalysis (e.g., Hartmann, 1939), ego is not seen as developing entirely out of id and its conflicts with the environment, but rather as having some of its own independent energy and growth potential not tied up in unconscious defensive functions. This neo-Freudian thinking is attractive to many psychoanalytically oriented clinicians because it presents a more positive, less instinct-ridden portrait of human behavior.

Another important revision of psychoanalysis was presented by Erik H. Erikson, an American psychologist who emphasized social factors in human development. Erikson (1959, 1963) outlined a sequence of *psychosocial* stages that was more elaborate than Freud's psychosexual scheme and also more oriented toward individuals' interactions with other people. At each of Erikson's eight stages (see Box 2–2), a social crisis is faced and either successfully handled or left partly unresolved. Positive outcomes at each stage facilitate the individual's ability to deal with the next crisis, while unsettled problems interfere with later development. The parallel with Freud is obvious here, as is the attention paid to the social nature of human development.

Several early acquaintances of Freud re-

---

[1]For example, Freud first believed that neurotics had been sexually seduced or abused as children because so many of his patients reported early childhood sexual experiences with an adult. Later, unwilling to accept such widespread sexual misconduct, Freud decided that such recollections were not factual but fantasies from the phallic period. This revision laid the cornerstone for Freud's theory of infantile sexuality (see Masson, 1983, for a controversial account of this aspect of Freud's work). Ironically, current revelations of frequent child sexual abuse suggest that Freud may have been right the first time.

Stage	Age	Successful Resolution Leads to:	Unsuccessful Resolution Leads to:
I. Trust vs. Mistrust (Oral)*	Birth–1 yr.	Hope	Fear
II. Autonomy vs. Shame and Doubt (Anal)*	1–3 yr.	Willpower	Self-doubt
III. Initiative vs. Guilt (Phallic)*	4–5 yr.	Purpose	Unworthiness
IV. Industry vs. Inferiority (Latency)*	6–11 yr.	Competency	Incompetency
V. Ego Identity vs. Role Confusion	12–20 yr.	Fidelity	Uncertainty
VI. Intimacy vs. Isolation	20–24 yr.	Love	Promiscuity
VII. Generativity vs. Stagnation	25–65 yr.	Care	Selfishness
VIII. Ego Integrity vs. Despair	65 yr.–death	Wisdom	Meaninglessness and despair

*Roughly corresponding Freudian stage.

Source: E. J. Phares, *Introduction to Personality,* 2nd ed. Glenview, IL: Scott, Foresman and Company, 1988, p. 123.

BOX 2–2
Erikson's Eight Stages or Crises and Associated Emerging Traits

jected rather than revised certain aspects of psychoanalysis. For example, Alfred Adler, one of the original members of the psychoanalytic school of thought, disavowed the instinct theory of behavior, broke away from Freud, and developed his own approach. In Adler's *Individual Analysis,* the most important psychological factor in human behavior and development is considered to be inferiority, not instinct. Adler also emphasized the importance of sociocultural, goal-oriented dynamics. He was interested in the family as a whole rather than just the Oedipal situation and proposed an extensive theory on the effects of *birth order* in a family.

Noting that each person begins life in a helpless and inferior position, Adler suggested that subsequent behavior represents a compensatory "striving for superiority" (first within the family, then in the larger social world). The particular ways each individual seeks superiority comprise a *style of life.* Adaptive lifestyles are characterized by cooperation, social interest, courage, and common sense. Maladaptive styles are reflected in extreme competitiveness or dependency, lack of concern for others, and distortion of reality. Adler believed that maladaptive lifestyles and behavior problems are due to misconceptions the individual has about the world and other people.

Consider the little boy who discovers early that he can have a measure of control over others (and thus attain feelings of superiority) by requiring their assistance in everything from dressing to eating. Over time, such a child might develop the misconception that he is a "special case" and that he cannot deal with the world and its requirements on his own. He learns that his dependency can become a means of reigning supremely over others. The person whose lifestyle evolves from such a mistaken idea might appear frightened, sick, or handicapped in ways that demand special attention and consideration from others. (See Mosak & Dreikurs, 1973, for more details of Adlerian theory.)

Otto Rank was another of Freud's original disciples who broke from the master. Like Adler, Rank rejected Freud's emphasis on sex and aggression as the bases of human behavior, and focused instead on the developing child's basic dependency and inborn potential for positive growth. Rank saw the *trauma of birth* as significant because it involves an abrupt change from the passive, dependent world of the fetus to a chaotic outside world that requires ever-increasing independence. Birth provides the prototype for a basic human conflict between the desire to be dependent (return to the womb) and the innate tendency within each person to grow physically and psychologically toward full independence. Failure to resolve this fundamental conflict was, for Rank, the root of human behavior problems.

Several other revisions and reformulations of Freud's ideas contribute to the psychodynamic model of clinical psychology. Carl Jung, Karen Horney, Erich Fromm, Melanie Klein, and Harry Stack Sullivan have influenced clinical psychology over several decades. Summaries of different psychodynamic theories can be found in such reference works as Munroe's *Schools of Psychoanalytic Thought* (1955), or more recent books by Roazen (1975) or Brenner (1974).

Some theorists made such dramatic breaks with Freud's theory that they are often included under a different label. For example, *object relations theorists* like W. R. D. Fairbairn (1952) and Heinz Kohut (1977) have replaced most of Freud's ideas with very different explanations of how our relationships with other people develop. We discuss the object relations theorists further in Chapter 8. Harry Stack Sullivan is another theorist whose ideas depart sufficiently from Freud's that he is sometimes identified with the interpersonal viewpoint. We consider Sullivan and his ideas, after evaluating the other major clinical models.

Evaluation of Freud's Psychodynamic Model

Sigmund Freud's influences on psychiatry and clinical psychology are hard to overestimate. He presented the most comprehensive and revolutionary theory of behavior ever articulated. In the process, he introduced concepts that captured the imagination of psychiatry, psychology, and other helping professions, not to mention literature, religion, sociology, and anthropology. The intensive study of a single individual, the one-to-one assessment or treatment session, the view that overt behavior is systematically related to identifiable psychological causes, the possibility that individuals' behavior may be influenced by factors of which they are unaware, the continuity of childhood and adult behavior, the symbolic significance of overt behavior, the importance of conflict and anxiety, and other features characteristic of all types of clinicians are directly traceable to Freud. Freud's concepts have become a part of everyday language and guide the way nonpsychologists think about behavior. It is not uncommon to hear people refer to Freudian slips, the Oedipus complex, unconscious motivation, defense mechanisms, or ego in the context of ordinary conversation.

In spite of its broad acceptance, Freud's approach has been the target of several criticisms. You have probably anticipated some objections as you read about Freud's ideas. What are the most frequent criticisms of the psychodynamic perspective? The following six problems are most often cited as deficiencies of the psychodynamic model.

1. Psychodynamic concepts such as id, ego, superego, projection, unconscious motivation, and repression consist of vague abstractions that are difficult to measure and test scientifically. The techniques that have been designed to measure various Freudian personality concepts have often shown themselves to be unreliable and invalid (see Chapter 5), and the effects of clinical treatment based on those concepts have been questioned (see Chapter 8). Recent attempts to investigate psychoanalytic constructs empirically (e.g., Silverman & Weinberger, 1985) have not satisfied critics (Balay & Shevrin, 1988) who complain about the methodological problems of this research. However, empirical research on selected aspects of psychodynamic theory has become more sophisticated and has supported some aspects of psychodynamic treatment (Crits-Christoph, Cooper, & Luborsky, 1988) while it has challenged others (Wallerstein, 1989).

2. Freud's approach was built on his clinical experiences with a small number of upper-class patients living in Vienna around the turn of the century. This raises questions about the generalizability of his ideas to people from other socioeconomic groups and other cultural backgrounds. Some anthropologists have suggested, for example, that psychoanalytic concepts of behavior are not universal (e.g., Lindesmith & Strauss, 1950; Mead, 1928, 1939). Also, Freud's biases against women have caused many male and female feminists to reject his account of human development (Chesler, 1972).

3. Psychoanalytic thinking places too much emphasis on the negative side of human character (i.e., sexual and aggressive instincts) and not enough on inherent growth potential and the influence of society and culture on behavior.

4. The psychoanalytic view represents a closed system that is not easily influenced by contradictory data; any results can be interpreted as confirming Freudian principles. For example, if an analyst concludes that a person harbors unconscious feelings of hostility, subsequent hostile behavior would be taken as evidence for the emergence of unconscious impulses. But the appearance of calm and friendly behavior could also provide evidence for underlying hostility because it could be seen as a reaction formation.

5. The psychodynamic model overinterprets behavior as indicative of unconscious motivation and related pathology. A man who is a successful go-getter might be distressed to learn that he may merely be compensating for unconscious feelings of inadequacy.

6. The psychodynamic model's emphasis on childhood causes of adult behavior neglects the role of more contemporary, situational influences on behavior. This weakness of classic psychoanalysis led many neo-Freudians to stress the importance of factors that stretch across the life span, an emphasis that the other models of clinical psychology share.

THE BEHAVIORAL MODEL

Instead of emphasizing intrapsychic conflicts, basic instincts, or unconscious motivation in the development and alteration of human behavior, the behavioral model focuses directly on that behavior and its relationship to the environmental and personal conditions that affect it. The basic assumption of this model is that behavior is primarily influenced by *learning*,[2] which takes place in a *social context*. As a result, this

---

[2]Familiarity with learning principles such as reinforcement, punishment, extinction, partial reinforcement, generalization, discrimination, and stimulus control is assumed in the discussion which follows. Those not acquainted with these terms should consult a standard introductory psychology text or a more specialized text like Leahey and Harris (1989).

perspective is sometimes called a *learning theory model*.

In this model individual differences in behavior are attributed to a person's unique learning history in relation to specific people and situations, not to traits, personality characteristics, or "mental illness." For example, under the stressful conditions of an academic examination, a student who has benefited in the past from cheating may cheat again to earn a high grade, while an individual who has been rewarded in the past for diligent study may be less likely to behave dishonestly. Each individual's cultural background also is seen as a part of his or her unique learning history, which plays a significant role in the appearance of both "normal" and problematic behavior. Upon receiving a failing grade on a vital exam, some students' cultural values may prompt so much shame as to engender a suicide attempt; for others, the failure may evoke a culturally traditional desire for revenge and an ensuing attack on the professor.

Similarities among people are accounted for within the behavioral model by noting commonalities in rules, values, and learning history shared by most people in the same culture. Thus, students' attentiveness during a lecture would not be seen as a collective manifestation of some intrapsychic process, but rather as a group fulfillment of the socially learned *student role,* which appears in certain academic situations for specified periods of time. By the same token, an instructor's behavior reflects prior learning of appropriate *professor role* responses and may be just as situation specific and time limited as that of the students.

The same principles of learning that account for behavioral differences and similarities *among* individuals are also employed to explain consistencies and discrepancies *within* individuals. Behaviorists view behavioral consistency (which other models might refer to as "personality") as stemming from generalized learning, stable cognitive abili-

ties, and/or from the stimulus similarities that exist among related situations. For example, a person may appear calm under most circumstances if calmness has been rewarded over a period of years in a wide range of social situations.

The behavioral model explains *inconsistencies* in behavior and other unpredictable human phenomena in terms of *behavioral specificity.* Mischel (1971, p. 86) summarizes this point well:

> Consider a woman who seems hostile and fiercely independent some of the time but passive, dependent, and feminine on other occasions. . . . Which one of these two patterns reflects the woman that she really is? Is one pattern in the service of the other, or might both be in the service of a third motive? Might she be a really castrating lady with a facade of passivity—or is she a warm, passive-dependent woman with a surface defense of aggressiveness? Social behavior theory suggests that it is possible for the lady to be *all* of these—a hostile, fiercely independent, passive, dependent, feminine, aggressive, warm, castrating person all in one. . . . Of course which of these she is at any particular moment would not be random and capricious; it would depend on discriminative stimuli—who she is with, when, how, and much, much more. But each of these aspects of her self may be a quite genuine and real aspect of her total being.

There are three main versions of the behavioral model—operant learning, respondent learning, and social learning (also known as cognitive-behavioral). Though differing substantially among themselves on certain specifics, these three views share a common core of characteristics:

1. Measurable behavior is emphasized as the subject matter of clinical psychology. *Measurable* does not always mean "overt." The behaviorally oriented clinician may be interested in be-

haviors ranging from the objective and countable (number of cigarettes smoked, time spent talking) to the subtle and covert (clarity of visualization, content of thoughts). Almost any behavior can be the target of a behavioral approach; the only requirement is that a way of measuring it be available.

2. The importance of environmental influences on behavior is stressed. Genetic and biological factors are not ignored, but they are seen as a general foundation upon which the environment shapes the specifics of behavior. Genetic endowment may set limits on a person's behavioral or intellectual potential, but it is assumed that within those limits, learning factors predominate in determining behavior.

3. The methods of empirical research are employed as the primary means of learning about the assessment, development, and modification of behavior. Within clinical psychology, the behavioral model has led the way in operationalizing and experimentally investigating clinical subject matter. The emphasis is on systematic manipulation of independent variables (e.g., treatment techniques) and observation of the effects of such manipulations on specifically defined and quantified dependent variables (eg., alcohol consumption, social assertiveness, depressed behavior, or sexual arousal).

4. Clinical assessment and treatment are tied to the results of empirical research. Many clinical methods of the behavioral variety are derived from laboratory-based principles of learning and social behavior, and they are subjected to continuing research conducted in laboratory and clinical settings. Further, this model encourages its practitioners to scrutinize the empirical evidence regarding an assessment or treatment procedure before deciding to adopt it and to proceed with caution in areas where there is little empirical guidance.

5. Clinical assessment and treatment are integrated. The behavioral model assumes that the same principles of learning determine both problematic and nonproblematic behaviors; therefore, clinical assessment should be designed to determine how a client's current difficulties were learned and how they are being maintained so that more adaptive, individually tailored learning can be arranged. A kindergarten child's fear of school, for example, might be based on a specific conditioned response to a particular setting, a generalized anxiety response to new situations, the intimidating presence of a classmate, or other environmental factors. The behaviorally oriented clinician's treatment would not be based on standard procedures for dealing with children diagnosed as phobic. The specific techniques chosen would depend on what the assessment data have to say about etiological and maintenance factors.

The three versions[3] of the behavioral model differ primarily in the learning processes they emphasize. *Operant learning* stresses the relationship between a behavior and its environmental consequences; *respondent learning* concentrates on the temporal association between stimuli and responses; and *social learning (cognitive-behavioral)* emphasizes the relationship between overt behavior and the cognitions (thoughts) or expectations that a person has about that behavior. A brief review

---

[3]From a historical perspective, one could speak of a fourth behavioral model that involved an attempt to translate Freud's concepts into learning theory language. This task was undertaken in the 1940s by John Dollard, a sociologist, and Neal Miller, a psychologist, and culminated in their book *Personality and Psychotherapy* (1950). Dollard and Miller sought to recast Freudian concepts into testable, environmentally determined phenomena rather than unconscious patterns. Their attempt represented an important effort to bridge the gap between psychoanalysis and mainstream experimental psychology. However, as learning theorists developed their own independent model of human behavior, they became less dependent on attempts to graft their views onto the roots of other theories. As a consequence, the Dollard and Miller model has little current influence on clinical psychology.

of the three variations of the behavioral model is presented next.

Operant Learning: B. F. Skinner and the Functional Analysis of Behavior

The operant version of the behavioral model reflects the ideas of B. F. Skinner, who maintained that behavior is learned and that nonobservable constructs such as need and drive are unnecessary to understand it. Skinner asserted that observation of learned relationships between environmental stimuli and overt behavior will allow for a complete picture of the development, maintenance, and alteration of human behavior. Instead of relying on internal factors (such as id), Skinner advocated observation and description of the ways behavior is controlled by its antecedents and consequences. This approach is called *functional analysis* because it focuses on functional relationships among stimuli, responses, and consequences.

Consider the notion of need. Rather than assuming that human behavior reflects various needs (e.g., "aggressive behavior indicates needs for dominance"), the Skinnerian would look at the relationship between aggressive behavior and its consequences. If a client's aggressive behavior has been and continues to be rewarded, at least part of the time, no further explanation in terms of internal need is necessary. The client has simply learned to behave aggressively.

The same analysis can account for more severe behavior disorders. A mental hospital resident who spends the day staring into space, loses control over bladder and bowels, and must be fed from a spoon need not be considered "mentally ill." Instead, these behaviors (not symptoms) would be thought of as learned responses prompted by environmental factors and maintained by the reinforcement of "crazy" behavior provided by society and especially by the hospital (see Ullmann & Krasner, 1975). Details of the Skin-

nerian approach to human behavior in general and to the analysis of problematic behavior in particular can be found in Skinner (1953, 1971) and other sources (Masters, Burish, Hollon, & Rimm, 1987).

Classical Conditioning

Skinner's views highlight the importance of *operant* or *instrumental* learning for clinical psychology. Another version of the behavioral model is exemplified by the writings of Joseph Wolpe (1958, 1982) and Hans Eysenck (1982). They focus on the applications of *classical* or *respondent* conditioning principles (Hull, 1943; Pavlov, 1927) to the understanding and elimination of human distress, particularly anxiety. Classical conditioning broadens the concepts available to the behavioral model by emphasizing the role of anxiety-based clinical problems that include clients' subjectively experienced distress.

The importance of operant reinforcement and punishment in shaping behavior is not denied, but there is an accent on learning that takes place through the association of conditioned and unconditioned stimuli. For example, a man who fearfully avoids social events may do so because of past negative experiences (i.e., operant conditioning: He enters a room and everyone laughs at his clothes), but also because the discomfort from those experiences has become associated with parties (i.e., classical conditioning: He gets a stomachache upon receiving a party invitation). Thus, both operant and classical conditioning may be involved in the appearance of specific behavior patterns (Mowrer, 1939). Wolpe and Eysenck provided a complement to Skinner's operant position by directing attention to classical conditioning.

Social Learning (Cognitive-Behavioral) Theory

The views of Skinner, Wolpe, Eysenck, and other behavioral theorists who focus on overt behaviors as the targets of clinical assessment and treatment have attracted many ardent followers, prompted the birth of specialized professional journals, and stimulated the growth of the behavioral model. They have not been universally accepted, however. Some *social-learning* theorists believe that too little attention has been paid to the role of cognitive or symbolic (i.e., thought) processes in the development, maintenance, and modification of behavior.

Social-learning theory developed from the early work of Edward Tolman (1932), who emphasized that behavior was purposive. Two of the most prominent representatives of this point of view are Albert Bandura and Walter Mischel, who have generated a great deal of research and writing (Bandura, 1969, 1986; Mischel, 1968, 1984, 1986) about the ways cognitive activity contributes to learning.

A major feature of Bandura's theory is its attention to *observational learning* or *vicarious cognitive processes*. In his view, behavior develops not only through what the individual learns directly by operant and classical conditioning, but also through what is learned *indirectly* (vicariously) through observation and symbolic representation of other people and events.

Bandura has shown that humans can acquire new behaviors without obvious reinforcement and even without the opportunity to practice. All that may be required is for the person to observe another individual, or *model,* engage in the behavior. Later, especially if the model was visibly rewarded for his or her performance, the observer may also display the new response if given the opportunity. In an illustrative experiment, Bandura, Ross, and Ross (1963) arranged for preschoolers to observe models either vigorously attacking or sitting quietly near an inflatable "Bobo" doll. In subsequent tests, the children who had observed aggression tended to match the models' behavior, while those who had seen a passive model tended to be nonaggressive. According to Bandura, the effects of vicarious processes can be as substantial as the effects of direct learning. They can bring about acquisition of new responses, inhibition or disinhibition of already learned responses (as when a person violates a Don't Walk sign after watching someone else do so), and facilitation or prompting of behavior (as when everyone in an airline waiting lounge forms a line at an unattended check-in counter after a single prankster stands in front of it).

In the case of the socially fearful man discussed in the last section, Bandura would point out that there are at least two sources of discomfort. One is *external* and includes the anxiety-signaling aspects of social situations themselves (e.g., other people, invitations, laughter), while the other is *internal,* or cognitive. This second source consists of thoughts by the fearful individual about socializing (e.g., "I will make a fool of myself" or "I'm no good at making friends") that serve to support continued avoidance.

The role of cognitive variables was stressed in the social-learning theory of Julian Rotter (1954), who emphasized the importance of *expectancies* in human activity. In Rotter's system, the probability that a given behavior will occur depends on (a) what the person expects to happen after the response, and (b) the value the person places on that outcome. Thus, a woman will pay for a ticket because she expects that this will result in admission to a movie theater (outcome) showing a desirable film (value). Rotter assumes that the expectancies that influence behavior are acquired through learning. To have an expectancy about an outcome or make a judgment regarding its value, the person must have had direct or vicarious experience with similar situations in the past.

Bandura has stressed the influence of another type of expectancy he calls *self-efficacy* (Bandura, 1977, 1982, 1986). In contrast to Rotter's emphasis on the expectancy of outcomes, efficacy expectations refer to the belief that one *can* successfully perform a given behavior regardless of the outcome that follows the behavior. Bandura believes that overt behavior is controlled by the perceived self-effi-

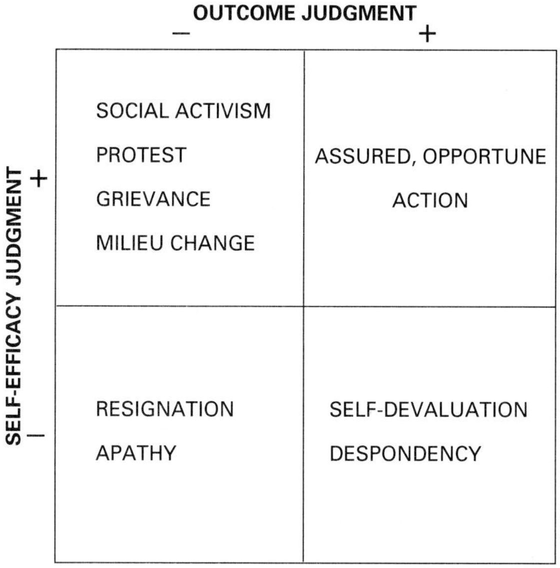

OUTCOME JUDGMENT

FIGURE 2–1 Interactive effects of self-percepts of efficacy and response outcome expectations on behavior and affective reactions. (From A. Bandura, 1982, Self-efficacy mechanism in human agency. *American Psychologist, 37,* 122–147.)

cacy a person holds; the higher the level of self-efficacy, the higher one's performance accomplishments will be. For example, perceived self-efficacy can reduce stress reactions, empower bold behavior in previously feared situations, and lead to self-control of addictive behaviors (Bandura, 1986). (See Figure 2–1 and Box 2–3.)

Mischel (1986) has described five types of cognitive variables that social-learning theo-

BOX 2–3
Self-Efficacy and Emotions

Bandura (1982) proposes that many emotions, such as depression, result from the interaction between two expectancies held by the individual—self-efficacy beliefs and outcome judgments. According to Bandura, the interplay of these two beliefs accounts for an individual's psychological well-being. Thus, for example, when individuals have little self-efficacy and they perceive that nothing anyone does matters, apathy results. However, self-inefficacy beliefs combined with a belief that others are able to enjoy the benefits of their efforts produces self-disparagement and depression. In contrast, high self-efficacy combined with a perceived unresponsive environment can produce resentment and social activism, whereas self-efficacy and a responsive environment produce a self-assured, active individual. Interventions designed to alter efficacy-based futility would differ from those targeted at outcome-based futility.

Bandura further argues that by considering the perceived nature of the outcomes one attempts to control, he can predict when low self-efficacy will produce anxiety versus depression. Both emotional states result from perceived inefficacy. Anxiety results from individuals perceiving a lack of control over harmful consequences, whereas depression results from an inability to control desired outcomes.

rists use in understanding the interaction between individuals and their environments. (See Box 2–4.) These cognitive factors are a bit unusual in the behavioral model because they represent *individual difference* variables, a notion that this model has typically downplayed. Box 2–4 summarizes the five cognitive social learning variables; Bandura's self-efficacy and Rotter's outcome expectancies are both included under expectancies in this table.

While early attempts to integrate cognitive processes with learning theory focused on expectancies about future events, recent work has been directed toward appraisals of (Beck, 1976) and attributions for (Abramson, Seligman, & Teasdale, 1978) current behaviors, as well as long-standing beliefs (Ellis, 1962). These views have proven fruitful in developing theories of and interventions for clinical depression and anxiety disorders.

Appraisals are the way we evaluate our own behavior, as well as actions directed toward us. According to Beck (1976), appraisals are the intervening thoughts that precede and influence our emotional reactions to events. For example, individuals who continually evaluate their performance as inadequate are

likely to interpret compliments as evidence that others are merely being polite. Thus, they gain no pleasure from positive reinforcement. Individuals who see the world in such a negative light see themselves as worthless and inadequate and are predisposed to depressive thoughts and symptoms. According to Beck, these thoughts become automatic through maturation and experience, and they influence our emotional reactions without our consciously thinking about them. The goal of Beck's cognitive-behavioral therapy (see Chapter 10) is to make these automatic thoughts conscious, so the individual can logically appraise their merit.

Attributions are the causes we perceive for behavior, how we explain why events have occurred. Attributions for behavior occur along three dimensions: *internality*—whether we see the cause of an event as due to something about ourselves or something about the environment; *stability*—whether we see the cause as persisting in time or being transitory; and *globality*—whether we see the cause as specific to a given task or general to all situations. For example, the explanation that you failed an important test because it was too

---

BOX 2–4
Summary of Cognitive Social Learning Person Variables

1. *Competencies:* Ability to construct (generate) particular cognitions and behaviors. Related to measures of IQ, social and cognitive (mental) maturity and competence, ego development, social-intellectual achievements and skills. Refers to what the person knows and can do.

2. *Encoding Strategies and Personal Constructs:* Units for categorizing events, people, and the self.

3. *Expectancies:* Behavior-outcome and stimulus-outcome relations in particular situations; self-efficacy or confidence that one can perform the necessary behavior.

4. *Subjective Values:* Motivating and arousing stimuli, incentives, and aversions.

5. *Self-Regulatory Systems and Plans:* Rules and self-reactions for performance and for the organization of complex behavior sequences

Source: Mischel (1986)

hard would be seen as an external, specific, and unstable attribution, whereas the statement "I am stupid" is internal, global, and stable. Research has shown that individuals who make internal, stable, and global attributions for failure experiences are less likely to persist on subsequent tasks (Diener & Dweck, 1978); more likely to experience depressive symptoms (Seligman, Abramson, Semmel, & von Baeyer, 1979); and have a greater likelihood of subsequent depressive episodes (Seligman et al., 1984).

Whereas expectancies, appraisals, and attributions refer to relatively short-term cognitive processes, Ellis has been concerned with the long-term, entrenched *beliefs* that individuals hold, and how *irrational* beliefs can produce psychological distress. These irrational beliefs are often associated with "should" statements ("Everyone should like me") and such unrealistically high standards that the individual is doomed to failure or disappointment. Ellis's rational-emotive therapy (see Chapter 10) consists of attacking these irrational beliefs until the client realizes they are counterproductive and lets go of them.

To theorists like Bandura, Rotter, Beck, Seligman, and Mischel, attention to cognitive components of behavior is an important aspect of a comprehensive behavioral model of clinical psychology and represents a wing of the model that emphasizes covert as well as overt behavior in clinical assessment, treatment, and research. This end of the behavioral spectrum, at which there is strong interest in what people say to themselves, helps illustrate the breadth and diversity of the model (see Chapter 10). It also separates modern behavior theory, in which all aspects of behavior are targets of scientific attention, from the earlier radical behaviorism of J. B. Watson (1913, 1924), which placed cognitive activity off limits to scientific psychologists.

In conjunction with basic research in cognition and social cognition, social learning theorists have stimulated the growth of cognitive behavior therapy to the point that it represents the most popular version of behavior therapy among clinicians (Zook & Walton, 1989). This popularity may rest, in part, on the fact that cognitive behavior therapy shares a great deal with certain psychodynamic viewpoints (remember Adler's emphasis on misconceptions) and with some versions of the phenomenological model, which we discuss after providing a brief evaluation of the behavioral model.

Evaluation of the Behavioral Model

Since its beginnings in the late 1950s, the behavioral approach has enjoyed enthusiastic support from an increasing number of adherents. The model's attractiveness lies in its objective and experimentally oriented approach to human behavior. It defines its concepts operationally, relies on empirical data for its basic principles, ties its applied work to the results of research, and evaluates its procedures through a series of critical investigations. In short, the behavioral model is seen as the best approach to the advancement of psychology *as a science of behavior* in the clinical field.

What are the shortcomings of the behavioral model? At times it seems that behaviorists have misplaced the person in their approach to the study of personality; they may have also overlooked some complexity in human behavior in an attempt to study it objectively. We discuss some limitations of the behavioral model next.

1. The behavioral approach reduces human beings to a set of acquired responses derived from a mechanistic relationship with the environment. This view tends to exclude genetic, physiological, and other non-learning-based influences and, most important, fails to recognize the importance of subjective experience. In other words, behaviorists deal with an individual's behavior, but ignore the individual.

2. The behavioral model cannot conceptualize adequately human problems of a complex, in-

ternal nature. Learning principles are fine for explaining phobias and other relatively simple stimulus-response relationships, "but how about grief at the loss of a loved one, shame at failures, guilt whether real or fancied over moral transgressions, a pervasive sense of impotence, and other negative affects? Likening human to animal behavior, and focusing on visible behavior rather than inner states, minimizes precisely those values, feelings, fantasies, and motives which most distinguish and trouble human life" (Korchin, 1976, p. 349).

3. The principles of learning on which the behavioral model is based are neither well established nor agreed on by learning theorists themselves. The role of reinforcement in the learning process is still a matter of debate, for example. Even if all learning principles were established, there is the question of whether their animal-laboratory origins allow them to be applied meaningfully to human beings. A cat faced with an insoluble task may display "experimental neurosis," but the human behavior called "neurotic" may not be equivalent and may result from entirely different processes.

4. Behavioral approaches to clinical psychology are not as uniquely scientific or clearly validated as their practitioners would have us believe. Many assessment and treatment procedures representing the model are based more on clinical experience than experimental research, and, where research evidence is available, it is often not unequivocally supportive of learning-based techniques.

THE PHENOMENOLOGICAL MODEL

So far we have considered models of clinical psychology in which human behavior is viewed as primarily influenced by (a) instincts and intrapsychic conflicts or (b) the environment and cognitive factors. A third approach, known generally as the phenomenological model, rejects many assumptions of the other

two and asserts that the behavior of each human being at any given moment is determined primarily by that particular person's *perception of the world*. Phenomenological theories assume that each person's view of reality is different from anyone else's, and that each person's behavior reflects that view as it is constructed from moment to moment.

Consider two students who listen to the same lecture on the first day of a new term. One may be enthralled, while the other stomps out and drops the course. Phenomenologists would attribute these divergent reactions to each listener's perceptions of the speaker during the lecture. Most versions of the phenomenological model share the following features:

1. Human beings are seen as active, thinking people who are individually responsible for what they do and fully capable of making choices about their behavior. In fairness, it should be pointed out that neither the psychodynamic nor the behavioral model fails to recognize these human attributes. Psychoanalysts who emphasize the autonomous role of ego and learning-oriented psychologists who focus upon individuals' capabilities for self-control provide illustrations of this point. However, both models tend to look at the processes producing such uniquely human characteristics as creativity, self-discipline, and decision making, rather than to focus on those characteristics themselves.

2. Phenomenologists believe that no one can understand another person's behavior unless she or he can perceive the world through that person's eyes. In line with this notion, the phenomenological model assumes that all human activity is comprehensible *when viewed from the point of view of the person being observed*. Thus, a woman who is violent toward others would be seen neither as acting out id impulses nor as displaying the results of reinforcement; she is behaving in line with her perception of those around her at the time.

Phenomenological views have evolved from several sources. In part, they represent a reaction against Freud that began when Adler rejected instincts as the basis of behavior and emphasized individual perceptions and positive growth potential. Attention to the individual's perception of reality was also prompted by the philosophies of Husserl, Heidegger, Kierkegaard, and Sartre, who assert that the meaning and value of life are not intrinsic, but are provided by the perceiver. Thus, a person is not actually attractive or ugly; these qualities are assigned when someone else reacts to the person in question, and they reflect a different reality in the eye of each beholder.

The focus on individual views of reality was sharpened by a group of German psychologists known as the gestalt school (Koffka, 1935; Kohler, 1925; Wertheimer, 1923). In contrast to the structuralism of Wundt, they asserted that the mind was more than the sum of its parts and that with respect to perception, the individual was an active participant, not just a passive receptor. To support their view, gestaltists pointed out that there are many cases in which a person's subjective perception goes beyond the stimuli that are "objectively" there and where the "same" object may be interpreted in different ways (see Figure 2–2).

As a result of these different traditions, there are two versions of phenomenological clinical psychology. On the one hand, we have a primarily North American version linked with clinicians such as Carl Rogers and with devotees of the human potential movement; it is the phenomenology best known to American students because it is the version usually described in our psychology textbooks. These phenomenologists emphasize humanistic values and stress the primacy of conscious experience for each individual. They assume each person possesses a potential for growth that gives impetus to most behavior. These theorists see people as basically good, striving naturally toward creativity, love, and other positive goals. Their practice of clinical psychology does not seek to gather as-sessment data about the past or to help a person solve particular behavior problems. Their emphasis is on the here and now. Their clinical interventions are designed to facilitate personal growth and choice.

The other version of the phenomenological model has been called "philosophically grounded phenomenology" (Fischer, 1989). It is based on a philosophical foundation established by such European philosophers as Edmund Husserl (1969), Martin Heidegger (1968), and Maurice Merleau-Ponty (1962). This tradition is devoted to the rigorous analysis of how human beings participate in what appears to us, how we take part in the world we attempt to know. It involves the qualitative study of human knowledge and human consciousness. While philosophically grounded phenomenologists may adopt a humanistic or existential perspective as practicing therapists, their theoretical approach to psychology differs from the humanistic wing of phenomenology in several ways. Unlike the humanistic tradition, the philosophically grounded phenomenologist does not concentrate only on conscious experience, does not deny the importance of exploring the past to enrich understanding of the present, and does not assume that all behavior is rational or that all human beings are basically good in nature.

Let us now examine specific phenomenological views that have grown from these different roots.

Kelly's Personal Construct Theory

George Kelly developed a theory of behavior which, though not as well known as others in the phenomenological model, provides a good place to start because it illustrates how that model relates to social-learning theory. Kelly's (1955) theory is based on the fundamental assumption that human behavior is determined by *personal constructs,* or ways of anticipating the world.

Kelly believed individuals act in accord with their unique set of expectations about the

FIGURE 2–2   Some perceptual phenomena which illustrate the perceiver's role in organizing "objective" stimuli: (A) Closure results in the appearance of a circle and a person on horseback even though many parts are omitted; (B) reversible figure-ground relationship allows viewer to see a vase or a pair of silhouettes; (C) interpretive shifts allow shaded area of a Necker Cube to appear as the front or back surface, and allows the drawing to be seen as a young woman or an old hag. (Part B and the Necker Cube are from Ernest R. Hilgard, Richard C. Atkinson, and Rita L. Atkinson, *Introduction to Psychology,* 5th ed., copyright © 1971 by Harcourt Brace Jovanovich, Inc., reproduced by permission of the publisher; Part A and the young woman/old hag are from *Psychology* by Lyle Bourne and Bruce Ekstrand, copyright © 1973 by The Dryden Press, a division of Holt, Rinehart and Winston, Inc., reprinted by permission of the publisher.)

consequences of behavior (note the similarity to Rotter) and that people's constructs about life comprise their reality and guide their behavior. For example, a person may consider sharp knives to be capable of inflicting severe harm. This construct would lead to cautious behavior in relation to sharp knives; since such behavior reflects an accurate anticipation of the consequences of carelessness and does avoid accidents, the construct "sharp knives are dangerous" is *validated*.

Validation of personal constructs is, in Kelly's view, the major goal of every human being. He believed that human behavior does not reflect instinctual desires or the effects of reinforcement, but rather individuals' attempts to make sense of the world as they see it. Like the scientist who revels in discovering why a phenomenon occurs and how that phenomenon can be controlled, each person seeks to understand and to predict the phenomena in his or her life.

In Kelly's system, problematic behavior results when a person develops inaccurate, oversimplified, or otherwise faulty constructs about social experience. If someone has only a few constructs with which to anticipate and comprehend the vast number of events that occur every day, behavior based on those constructs is almost sure to be inappropriate or inadequate at least part of the time, such as a "bad" scientist whose incorrect predictions are based on inadequate constructs. Similarly, a man who construes everything in life as either good or bad is going to have problems, because not all events and people can be classified accordingly without distortion. He may totally reject or unreservedly welcome the friendship of others according to this overall perception of their value and thus completely miss the positive qualities of enemies and the negative qualities of allies. He may stereotype college students, political activists, and anyone with a foreign accent as bad, and children, grandmothers, and the clergy as good. Such a person would probably be seen by others as selfish, strongly prejudiced, and a poor judge of character. His interpersonal relations would be stormy.

Kelly's views are compatible with the social-learning theorists. Both views are interested in how cognitive activity influences overt behavior. Kelly also saw people as capable of *learning to change* their personal constructs and, in turn, the patterns of response flowing from them. This latter notion blended phenomenological concepts with social-learning principles and resulted in the development of new, mixed-model approaches to clinical treatment, first by Kelly himself and later by others (e.g., Ellis, 1962). We shall discuss the specifics of these approaches in Chapters 9 and 10.

Rogers's Self-Actualization Theory

In contrast to Kelly's social-learning-flavored views, the prolific writings of Carl Rogers (1942, 1951, 1961, 1970) have clearly differentiated the phenomenological model from all others and, in the process, made his name practically synonymous with the humanistic version of it. Among Rogers's basic assumptions, we find the following (1951, pp. 483–486): (a) "Every individual exists in a continually changing world of experience of which he is the center"; (b) "The organism reacts to the field as it is experienced and perceived. This perceptual field is, for the individual, reality"; and (c) "The organism reacts as an organized whole to this phenomenal field."

Rogers assumed that people have an innate motive toward growth, which he called *self-actualization*. This motive is thought to account for all human behavior, from basic food seeking to sublime artistic creativity. Self-actualization is defined as "the directional trend which is evident in all organic and human life—the urge to expand, extend, develop, mature—the tendency to express and activate all the capacities of the organism" (Rogers, 1961, p. 351). Rogers saw human behavior, whether problematic or not, as reflecting the individual's efforts at self-actualization in a uniquely perceived world. These efforts begin at birth and continue throughout life; they are sometimes unimpeded and successful, but they may also be thwarted, with problematic results.

As Rogers described the process, a person's growth is accompanied by a differentiation between self and the rest of the world. This produces an awareness of a part of experience recognized as "I" or "me." According to Rogers, all of a person's experiences, including "self" experiences, are subject to evaluation as positive or negative, depending on whether they are consistent or inconsistent with the self-actualizing tendency. These evaluations are made partly on the basis of direct or *organismic* feelings (as when a child evaluates the taste of candy as positive), and partly on the basis of other people's judgments. For example, a young boy may end up negatively evaluating the experience of fondling his genitals (even though the direct feelings are positive) because his parents tell him that he is a bad boy to do so. Thus, the self or self-concept emerges as a set of *evaluated experiences* whose positive or negative valence is influenced by the opinions of others.

These socializing influences help integrate the developing individual into society, especially when the judgments of others coincide with organismic feelings. For example, if a child practices reading skills and experiences both positive direct feelings upon gaining competence and positive regard from a parent for doing so, the result will be a positively evaluated self-experience ("I like to read"). Here, the self-experience is congruent with the organismic experience and the child is able to reconcile accurately his or her own behavior ("I read a lot") and the evaluation of it ("I enjoy reading").

According to Rogers, people value the positive regard of others so highly that they will seek it even if it means thinking and acting in ways that are *incongruent* with organismic experience and the self-actualizing motive. This tendency is encouraged by what Rogers called *conditions of worth*. These are circumstances in which one receives positive regard from others (and, ultimately, from the self) only if certain approved behaviors, attitudes, and beliefs are displayed. These conditions are set up first by parents, family, and other societal agents, but they are later maintained internally by the individual (note the similarity to Freud's concept of superego).

Persons facing conditions of worth are likely to be uncomfortable. If they behave to please others, it may be at the expense of personal growth, as in the case of a woman who fulfills traditional housewife roles in spite of genuine desires to do other things. On the other hand, displaying authentic feelings and behaviors that are discrepant with conditions of worth risks loss of the positive regard of others and the self.

Rogers believed that to reduce discomfort stemming from such incongruity, the individual may distort reality in ways that may be seen as problematic by others. A man whose parents set up conditions of worth in which displays of emotional behavior (like crying) were discouraged and unemotional "masculinity" was praised may deny that emotional expression feels good. As an adult, his often-repeated, judgmental statements that "anyone who cries is weak" represent a distortion of his real feelings. According to Rogers, the greater the discrepancy between real feelings and self-concept, the more severe will be the resulting problematic behavior. Consider a mild case: A young man with a strong interest in women claims that he is too busy to go out with them when, in fact, it would be too discrepant with his self-concept to admit that his invitations are routinely rejected. He even goes so far as to profess disdain for members of the opposite sex. (Note the relationship to some of Freud's ego defense mechanisms.)

In a more extreme instance, a man whose self-concept characterizes him as self-sufficient and career oriented may feel quite the opposite. Thus, failure to receive a promotion and less-than-adequate performance on the job (all based on lack of real interest in his field) are misinterpreted. Instead of recognizing that he may not be very interested in his work, he asserts that others are out to get him. Ideas of persecution may grow to such proportions that he trusts no one and sees conspiracies on every side. Ultimately, his behavior may become so troublesome as to require hospitalization.

Rogers believed that these problems can be avoided. "If an individual should experience only unconditional positive regard, then no conditions of worth would develop, self-regard would never be at variance with organismic evaluation, and the individual would continue to be psychologically adjusted, and would be fully functioning" (Rogers, 1959, p. 224). Even if these optimal conditions have not existed in the past, they may help in the present. Accordingly, Rogers developed a therapeutic approach that employs unconditional positive regard and other factors to help troubled people reduce incongruity without having to distort reality (see Chapter 10).

Maslow and Humanistic Psychology

Abraham Maslow (1954, 1962, 1971) provides another humanistic version of the phenomenological model. Maslow emphasized subjective experience and each person's unique perception of reality. In founding the movement known as humanistic psychology, Maslow emphasized that which is positive and creative about human beings. Like Rogers, Maslow saw people as capable of (and needing) self-actualization, but he suggests that failure to realize one's full potential is caused not by incongruity between self-experience and organismic experience, but by the presence of unmet needs.

Maslow believed that those needs form a hierarchy starting with basic physiological requirements (like food and water) and moving to higher-level requisites like safety, security, love, belongingness, self-esteem, and, finally, self-actualization. Satisfaction of each need

level must be preceded by meeting all lower-level needs. Thus, one will not be concerned with fulfilling the need for love and belongingness when there is uncertainty over where one's next meal is coming from. Although each person contains the potential for full actualization, that potential cannot be achieved if lower-level needs remain unfulfilled.

Maslow points out that most people seek to meet needs below the self-actualization level, and are thus oriented toward that which they do not have. Such individuals are *deficiency motivated.* For most people in our culture, incompletely satisfied needs involve security, love, belongingness, and self-esteem, and according to Maslow, often produce adult need-seeking behaviors that are neurotic or problematic. In rare cases all lower-order needs are satisfied, thus freeing the person to seek fulfillment of the highest need, self-actualization. Such people are in a position to focus on what they can *be*, not on what they do not *have*. Maslow called this process *growth motivation.*

These fortunate few can experience the full potential of humanness. Because they are unfettered by concern over lower-level needs, they can expand their potential and search for abstractions like truth, beauty, and goodness. Momentary experiential high points, or *peak experiences,* at which full self-actualization is reached, are common in these individuals and represent the best that is within all of us. Maslow underscores the importance of helping people overcome the obstacles that block natural growth, happiness, and fulfillment.

Fritz Perls and Gestalt Psychology

Freidrich S. (Fritz) Perls was a European psychiatrist whose dissatisfaction with traditional Freudian theory first evidenced itself in his 1947 book, *Ego, Hunger and Aggression: A Revision of Freud's Theory and Method.* Perls felt that Freud put too much emphasis on sexual instincts and not enough on what he called *hunger:* an instinct or tendency toward self-preservation and self-actualization. Like Freud,

Perls emphasized the function of ego in facilitating growth and self-preservation by mediating between the person's internal needs and the demands of the environment. However, he thought of ego not as a psychic structure, but as a *process* whose goal is the reduction of tension between the person and the environment.

As this balancing act continues over time, the individual grows psychologically. She or he finds new ways to meet internal needs while becoming better able to deal with the requirements of the outside world. For this growth to occur, the person must remain aware of internal needs and the environment. However, since each person is an active participant in attending to and organizing his or her perceptions, and since the tendency to avoid conflict and keep tension as low as possible may make certain perceptions more comfortable than others, each person's awareness can become incomplete or distorted. When this happens, growth stops and problems start.

For example, a person with strong sexual desires who grows up in a moralistic, antisexual family may find certain distortions temporarily comfortable but ultimately problematic. Repression of sexual feelings or perceptions of the world as a place filled with unrelenting pressure for sexual promiscuity may occur. None of this accurately reflects either the external circumstances or the internal needs. (Note the similarity to Rogers's concept of incongruence.)

According to Perls, when conflict avoidance prompts disturbances in awareness, symptoms of psychological disorders appear. Intense anxiety about being away from home may result when a person projects hostile feelings (usually kept out of awareness) onto others, thus making everyone else seem hostile. Or the same person may selectively attend to the ordinary risks that surround us all and, "because the world is so dangerous," refuse to go out. When disturbances in awareness become severe, psychotic symptoms may occur.

Perls developed a treatment approach called *gestalt therapy,* aimed at restarting growth by reestablishing aware processes. We shall describe the methods involved in Chapter 10.

There are several other phenomenological approaches to behavior, but this brief outline conveys the flavor of the model. Those interested in more detailed coverage of this and the other models discussed should consult the original sources already cited as well as comparative presentations provided by Hall, Lindzey, Loehlin, and Manosevitz (1985); Liebert and Spiegler (1990); Phares (1988); and Rychlak (1970).

Evaluation of the Phenomenological Model

The phenomenological orientation has a strong intrinsic appeal. It gives a central role to each person's experience, a perspective that is appreciated by anyone who attends to such experience. Further, it emphasizes the uniqueness of each individual, providing reassurance that the person is not just an extension of lower animals and is not just like everyone else. Finally, humanistic phenomenologists stress an optimistic approach that focuses on the potential of human life and places faith in the individual's capability to grow toward fulfillment of ultimate capacities.

In spite of these encouraging views, the phenomenological model has received its share of criticism. For the most part, the following criticisms are directed at the humanistic version of the phenomenological model, and not the more philosophically sophisticated version that we traced to Husserl and others.

1. Humanistic phenomenology is too concerned with immediate conscious experience and does not pay sufficient attention to unconscious motivation, reinforcement contingencies, situational influences, and biological factors.

2. The model does not deal adequately with the *development* of human behavior. Postulation of an innate tendency toward actualization can account for development, but does not explain its processes. Saying that a child develops because of an actualizing tendency is like saying that one eats because of hunger; this may be true, but it says little about what hunger is or how it influences behavior.

3. A related criticism has been that phenomenological theories provide excellent descriptions of human behavior but are not focused on the scientific exploration of its causes. To suggest that people act as they do because of their unique perceptions of reality may be personally satisfying, but this is not very informative in terms of understanding the variables that develop, maintain, and alter human behavior.

4. Phenomenological concepts are vague and difficult to comprehend, let alone investigate. When human beings are described as "a momentary precipitation at the vortex of a transient eddy of energy in the enormous and incomprehensible sea of energy we call the universe" (Kempler, 1973, p. 225), it becomes difficult to generate testable hypotheses about their behavior. Although phenomenologists have been chided for being unscientific, it may be more accurate to describe them as pursuing a different approach to science than we are accustomed to. Their methods are more qualitative than quantitative, and they approach psychology as a human science rather than as a natural science.

5. The phenomenological model's clinical applicability is limited to those segments of the population whose intellectual and cultural background is compatible with the introspective nature of this approach. Further, the range of problems addressed by the model is limited: To the person struggling with a crisis of identity or values, phenomenological notions may be of great subjective value, but these notions (like the tenets of most other models) may not be very useful in situations where unmet needs near the bottom of Maslow's hierarchy (food, decent housing, and a job) are the bases of human distress.

THE INTERPERSONAL PERSPECTIVE

Related to the psychodynamic model of clinical psychology—and to a lesser extent the behavioral and the phenomenological models—is a collection of theories grouped under the label of interpersonal perspectives. Whether these interpersonal theories are unified enough in their emphases and whether they provide sufficiently comprehensive views on psychological assessment, disorders, and treatment to be called a model is questionable. Most textbooks on personality theory, abnormal psychology, and psychopathology pay scant attention to interpersonal viewpoints, except to offer a passing wave to Harry Stack Sullivan, generally agreed to be the intellectual father of the interpersonal perspective in psychology and psychiatry. There are several reasons for this unfortunate neglect. First, the prevailing theoretical models in clinical psychology, especially the behavioral and psychoanalytic, have absorbed many interpersonal principles into their systems so that the distinctiveness of interpersonal theories is obscured. As Carson (1983) observed, "the interpersonal viewpoint is increasingly coming to occupy a central position within the domain of the many competing evaluations of human behavior and its findings" (p. 146).

A second reason why interpersonal perspectives have been slighted is that most of their main proponents were not popularizers who sought to convert a group of followers or build a movement. Sullivan, a controversial and eccentric character within psychiatry, wrote little about his system. Timothy Leary, whose interpersonal circumplex (described later) is one of the cornerstone concepts of modern interpersonal theory, abandoned his study of this area in the 1960s, when his interests turned to other matters. The theories of current-day interpersonalists like Jerry Wiggins, Lorna Smith Benjamin, and Donald Kiesler are often perceived by practicing clinicians as too statistically complicated for them to understand or appreciate. Besides Eric Berne's (1964) faddish transactional analysis, the author who most succeeded in stimulating interest in interpersonal ideas among clinicians is Robert Carson, whose *Interaction Concepts of Personality* (1969) integrated and interpreted the ideas of Sullivan, Leary, and subsequent interpersonal researchers.

A final impediment to widespread appreciation of interpersonal perspectives is that, historically, they have not been associated with particular forms of psychopathology to which they seemed ideally suited as explanations and interventions. Psychoanalysis had the hysterical neuroses, behavioral theories had childhood problems and discrete adult disorders, and the phenomenological-humanists had existential neuroses—in each case the model had clinical phenomena for which it could claim special expertise and then extend its ideas to other pathology. Interpersonal theories have not had a disorder they could call their own, although that is changing with the new emphasis on personality disorders, to which interpersonal theories seem well matched (Kiesler, 1986a).

While these characteristics prevent us from calling the interpersonal perspective a model equivalent to the three major models of clinical psychology, it is clear that this viewpoint is distinctive enough to merit attention and that its future importance may outstrip some of the classic theories that commonly receive attention in most textbooks. With this in mind, we summarize a few major principles of interpersonal theory. Readers interested in more detailed coverage of this material should consult Anchin and Kiesler (1982), Carson (1969), Kiesler (1983), and Wiggins (1982).

Sullivan

Harry Stack Sullivan was an American psychiatrist who received his medical degree in 1917 from the Chicago College of Medicine and Surgery. Although he is often described as a neo-Freudian, he actually developed a personality theory and corresponding form of treatment that was much different from prior versions of psychoanalysis. Sullivan's system derived from his own analysis with Dr. Clara Thompson, his association with William Alanson White and Adolph Meyer and their interdisciplinary view of psychiatry, and his exposure to several of the leading theorists of what was known as the Chicago School of Social Science. Sullivan worked briefly at St. Elizabeth's Hospital in Washington, DC, followed by a longer tenure at the Sheppard and Enoch Pratt Hospital in Towson, Maryland, where he was given unusual autonomy in establishing special methods for treating schizophrenics. Around 1930, Sullivan left Maryland to begin private practice of psychiatry in New York City. Prior to his death in 1949 he became involved in applying psychiatric concepts to international issues and was one of the founders of the World Federation for Mental Health.

Sullivan (1953) believed that personality consisted of "the relatively enduring pattern of recurrent interpersonal situations which characterize a human life" (pp. 110–111). Sullivan sought to understand personality as it was revealed in the pattern of what a person did with others, said to others, and believed about others. By the same token, psychological disorders involved disturbed interpersonal relationships that had become so taxing, cumbersome, or frustrating that constructive interactions with others were not possible. Sullivan believed that one overcame these problems by becoming aware of one's interpersonal relations and understanding them in a way that was consistent with the views of others.

From this perspective, the development of personality begins with the infant's biological and acquired needs. These needs require the infant to interact repeatedly with parents, especially the mother. Out of these interactions the infant comes to experience the moods of the mother by what Sullivan called "empathy."

The infant becomes anxious through empathy with an anxious mother. Likewise, the child experiences pleasant moods ("euphoria" was Sullivan's term) in conjunction with the mother's actions. Through a primitive form of understanding Sullivan called the "prototaxic" mode of experience, the infant comes to associate approval and disapproval from mother into two "personifications" of the mothering person (a personification is the mental image, or organized understanding, we construct of a person and it guides our subsequent behavior toward that person in a powerful manner, even if it is not accurate). The "good mother" personification grows from satisfying, pleasurable experiences the infant has in mother's presence; the "bad mother" image develops from experiencing anxiety in her presence. Gradually, the infant comes to develop a personification of "me," which is the beginning of the self. This personification is based on what Sullivan called "reflected appraisals"; the infant gains an early sense of self based on the way significant others in the environment behave toward the infant. It is as if others' reactions to us provide a kind of mirror in which we can see ourselves. As we develop, the personifications we construct of real or imaginary people come to exert a powerful influence on how we interact with others throughout our lives.

The major aspects of the self, established in these early years, are based on what the child comes to believe about himself or herself. It consists of a "good me," the result of reflected appraisals conveying tenderness and acceptance of positive feelings; a "bad me," the outcome of anxiety and reflected disapproval from others; and the "not me," the result of such intense anxiety or panic that the person feels that the associated experience is not really happening. The self develops in a child to preserve feelings of security in an interpersonal world in which feelings of anxiety are the major threat. The self functions like a benevolent authority figure who guides the development of personality, tries to maintain se-

curity with other people, seeks prestige, and protects against anxiety and jeopardized self-esteem. This is accomplished by selective inattention (ignoring upsetting information about oneself), dissociation (a more extreme form of denial in which information is cut off completely from one's awareness), sublimation (substituting an acceptable activity for one less socially approved), and obsessionalism (a preoccupation with details that distract oneself and others from sources of anxiety). When anxiety becomes too severe, these maneuvers becomes so extreme or so rigid that disturbed interpersonal relationships result.

Like Freud, Sullivan thought that personality developed according to a series of eras in which important skills and tasks appeared. Unlike Freud's emphasis on the psychosexual qualities of these developmental periods, Sullivan concentrated on the major interpersonal issues typical of each stage.

Infancy, already discussed briefly, extends from birth to the development of meaningful speech around the age of 15 to 18 months. Throughout this period, the child shifts more from prototaxic understanding to "parataxic" thought in which she or he associates events because of their close proximity in time to each other. Parataxic thought is impulsive, highly idiosyncratic, and based on hunches; while more sophisticated than the prototaxic mode, it is not much more advanced than thinking in stereotypes.

In *Childhood,* an era extending to about the age of four, language becomes more developed and the child engages in greater amounts of "syntaxic" thinking, which requires the use of consensually understood language and other symbols. This type of experience is essential to the ability to communicate effectively and accurately with one another. Children also begin to experience punishment more frequently in this era as their parents attempt to train them to behave in a socialized manner. The child, on the other hand, begins to learn ways to manipulate parents. Language is important in this regard; what parent hasn't been dissuaded from following through on a threatened punishment by their child's plea of "I'm sorry," followed by the plaintive promise, "I won't do it again." Language also makes possible dramatizations by children in which they act as if they were a grown-up and imitate desirable behaviors.

The *Juvenile* era, lasting from about 4 to 10 years of age, finds the child learning to cooperate and compete with peers. Rejection is a painful experience of the juvenile era, and juveniles will go to great lengths to avoid exclusion. Strong identification with a close-knit group of schoolmates is commonly observed.

The *Preadolescent* era is an important phase because its main interpersonal task is learning how to be psychologically intimate with another person. Such relationships usually involve a same-sex friend, who Sullivan termed a "chum." A chum is central to a later capacity for closeness because the chum serves as the first peer to whom we divulge our secrets and disclose our fears. The chum helps us realize we are not so different from anyone else because the chum reveals to us the same fantasies, doubts, and preoccupations that we were sure revealed our unique bizarreness. For the first time, friendship leads to feelings of intimacy among equals; conversely, when we are separated from our chum we feel the first ache of loneliness and a potential emptiness of self.

In *Early Adolescence,* ushered in by the onset of puberty, the person becomes more driven by lustful urges. The ideal resolution of this period is that the person is able to integrate lustful needs with a desire for psychological intimacy with a partner. *Late Adolescence* requires more and more syntaxic understanding so that the person can be free to enter into a range of satisfying interpersonal relationships. To the extent that the person's behavioral options are restricted because of inaccurate personifications, widespread anxiety, or continuing parataxic distortions, she or he will not be able to participate fully in satisfying interpersonal relationships.

Sullivan (1953) believed adult interpersonal relationships were governed by a rule of reciprocity: "Integration in an interpersonal (relationship) is a reciprocal process in which (1) complementary needs are resolved, or aggravated; (2) reciprocal patterns of activity are developed, or disintegrated; and (3) foresight of satisfaction, or rebuff, of similar needs is facilitated" (p. 198). When two persons engage each other interpersonally, the goal is to achieve satisfaction under conditions of maintained security for both individuals. In relationships that work well, the parties usually negotiate these complementary needs so smoothly that they remain largely unaware of why they interact easily. Smooth transactions might occur, for example, when both parties share a friendly attitude toward each other or when a dominant person interacts with someone who is typically submissive. However, if one person in an interpersonal situation approaches it with anxiety and inordinately strong needs for security developed over the long stretch of an interpersonally troubled infancy, childhood, and adolescence, that person will almost inevitably frustrate the relationship to the point that it is terminated or that it is continued with feelings of desperation and unhappiness by both parties.

Leary and Other Contemporary Interpersonal Theorists

While Sullivan described how interpersonal styles developed and why they constituted the essence of personality as he understood it, he left it to others to chart the specific form of these styles and their relationship to one another. A major system for organizing interpersonal behavior was developed by Timothy Leary and his associates at the Kaiser Foundation in Oakland, California. Described in Leary's (1957) *Interpersonal Diagnosis of Personality,* this system organizes different styles of interpersonal behavior around a circle, called a circumplex.

The original interpersonal behavioral circle

is depicted in Figure 2–3. There are two primary dimensions that define different portions of the circle. The vertical axis runs along a dimension of dominance to submission; the horizontal axis travels between the polar opposites of love and hate. Each of the eight sections, or octants, described along the perimeter of the circle represents a blend of power (dominance–submission) and affiliation (love–hate) in interpersonal behavior. The first word in each octant label describes a mild form of the interpersonal behavior represented in that slice of the circle; the second word refers to an extreme form of the behavior. In addition, as one moves from the center of the circle to the perimeter, the intensity of the behavior depicted increases. For example, "guide, advise, teach" in its extreme form becomes "seeks respect compulsively, pedantic, dogmatic actions."

This circular arrangement of interpersonal behavior has several other implications. First, sectors adjacent to each other are assumed to be maximally positively correlated (cooperative–overconventional behavior should correlate more highly with docile–dependent behavior

FIGURE 2–3 The Interpersonal Behavior Circle. (Source: Timothy Leary, *Interpersonal Diagnosis of Personality—A Functional Theory and Methodology for Personality Evaluation,* copyright © 1957 The Ronald Press Company, New York.)

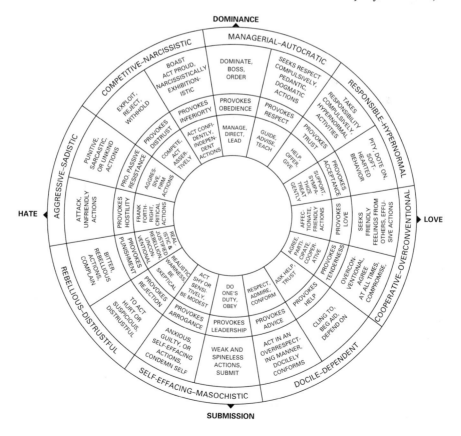

than it would with self-effacing–masochistic behavior). Second, sectors lying directly opposite each other on the circle (aggressive–sadistic and cooperative–overconventional) should be strongly negatively correlated. A large amount of empirical research has been conducted on Leary's system as well as other two- and even three-dimensional models that bear remarkable resemblance to Leary's ideas (see Wiggins, 1982, or Wiggins & Broughton, 1985, for a review). In general, the research has supported the circular ordering of interpersonal styles, although certain octants are not as well understood or described as others.

A prominent feature of Leary's model and other circular models is that a person can pull for certain behaviors from others by deploying a typical interpersonal style. As Carson (1969) observed, this pull is Leary's way of describing Sullivan's original notion that people often sought to protect security and prevent anxiety in their interactions:

> The purpose of interpersonal behavior . . . is to induce from the other person behavior that is complementary to the behavior proffered. It is assumed that this induced, complementary behavior has current utility for the person inducing it, in the sense that it maximizes his momentary security. Leary suggests that we learn how to "train" others to respond to us in security-maintaining ways . . . and that each of the eight categories of interpersonal behavior may be viewed as a distinct set of learned operations for prompting desired behavior from others. (p. 112)

Are certain pulls or combinations of interpersonal actions and reactions more common than others? In general, the rule of *complementarity* predicts the following interpersonal matches: Along the dominance–submission axis, dominant behavior is reciprocated by submissiveness and vice versa; along the love–hate dimension, the relationship is one of correspondence with love inviting love and hate evoking hate.

Currently, interpersonal theories are concentrating on two major implications of their ideas for clinical psychology. First, is it possible to understand psychological disorders in primarily interpersonal terms? Second, can interpersonal theory be extended to psychotherapy and therefore suggest to therapists specific kinds of interventions to employ with specific clients? We examine each of these areas briefly next.

Clinical Implications of Interpersonal Theory

Since Sullivan, a number of clinicians have argued that mental illness should be understood in terms of rigid and extreme patterns of interpersonal behaviors. Kiesler (1986a) illustrates this idea:

> Abnormal behavior . . . consists of a rigid, constricted, and extreme pattern of interpersonal behaviors by which the abnormal person, without any clear awareness, engages others who are important in his or her life. The abnormal person, rather than possessing the flexibility to use the broad range of interpersonal behaviors warranted by different social situations, is locked into a rigid and extreme use of limited classes of interpersonal actions. (p. 572)

One group of disorders to which interpersonal theory seems very well suited is the personality disorders. Personality disorders refer to different collections of behaviors or traits that are so extreme and inflexible that they cause substantial difficulties in a person's social or occupational life or lead to repeated unhappiness and distress. A few examples include the antisocial personality disorder defined by a long pattern of irresponsible and unlawful behavior about which the person seems to have little remorse; the dependent personality disorder characterized by a pervasive pattern of submissive behavior where the person is unable to make even simple decisions without a lot of advice and reassurance from others; and the schizoid personality disorder typified by a person who is indifferent to social relationships and shows a constricted range of emotional feelings and expression. You have probably noticed from these brief descriptions what several researchers and clinicians have observed—many of the troubling qualities of personality disorders consist of disturbances in interpersonal behavior. In fact, it is possible to understand some personality disorders as extreme and rigid instances of different octants around the interpersonal circle (see Kiesler, 1986a; Widiger & Frances, 1985; and Wiggins & Pincus, 1989, for illustrations). As examples, the antisocial personality illustrates extreme versions of the hateful and dominant behaviors one finds in the upper left section of the interpersonal circle. The dependent personality would seem to live in the docile–dependent octant where extremes of clingy submissiveness are encountered. Finally, the schizoid personality is an extension of the introverted aloofness that one finds at the extremes of the lower left portion of the circle (Soldz, Budman, Demby, & Merry, 1993).

Interpersonal descriptions have also been extended to other disorders such as depression. Depressed persons commonly feel inferior and powerless so they look to others for help and support. Many people react to these requests by providing suggestions and advice intended to help the depressed person snap out of it. However, such advice often simply confirms depressed persons' feelings of inadequacy, and they reject the advice or become even more demandingly dependent on others. Irritated and frustrated with depressed persons' failure to heed their well-intentioned advice, other people begin to avoid them or show their anger which, of course, further increases the patients' distress (see Coyne, 1976; Horowitz & Vitkus, 1986). Some authors, convinced of interpersonal theory's relevance to abnormal behavior, have recommended that we abandon traditional types of psychological di-

agnosis (described in Chapter 3) in favor of a system in which abnormal behavior would be described almost exclusively in interpersonal terms (Benjamin, 1980; McLemore & Benjamin, 1979).

Interpersonal theory also leads to suggestions for how therapists should respond to clients' standard interpersonal maneuvers. Because a client tends to perpetuate maladaptive behavior by evoking complementary behaviors from others that reinforce the problem behavior, one goal for a therapist would be to adapt a noncomplementary stance toward the client's usual gambits. The therapist would try to respond antidotally to the client to induce new behaviors. For example, the hostile dominance of an antisocial client typically pulls for hostile submissiveness from others. The therapist, however, could try to act in a friendly, dominant manner toward this client in an attempt to swing him or her around the circle toward increased friendly submissiveness. As you will discover in Chapters 8, 9, and 10, psychodynamic, behavioral, and phenomenological therapists have all incorporated various interpersonal strategies into their own treatment approaches.

SOME IMPLICATIONS OF CLINICAL MODELS

We can now go beyond abstract conceptualizations of the models of clinical psychology and examine their implications for assessment, treatment, and research. Perhaps the best way to do this is to consider the clinical strategy that would be used for a hypothetical case by adherents of each model. Descriptions of these strategies provide only a general representation of their parent models and, because there are several versions of each model, these descriptions will not be comprehensive. Nevertheless, we hope that by applying the general principles and assumptions of each model to the problems of a troubled person, the role of model as guide will become clear.

Discussing the same person from different points of view can also highlight an important point about clinical models: Human behavior does not have to appear in any particular form in order to be dealt with by a model. For example, clinicians sometimes say things like "I feel comfortable working with clients who have poor self-concepts, but I am really not prepared to deal with conditioned anxiety responses," or "The behavioral approach is a good one for learned problems, but it can't handle unconscious conflicts very well." In both cases, the speaker has taken clinical models so seriously that he or she assumes that human behavior conforms to the concepts described by theoreticians instead of the other way around, and has failed to see that any sample of behavior can be approached by any model. It is instructive, therefore, to consider the behavior of a single fictitious person and to see that no model has a monopoly on describing and explaining that behavior.

The following examples reveal other features of models. Models attempt to provide an organized, systematic explanation of some phenomena. The various models of clinical psychology give different theoretical justifications for how behavior is caused, how it can be assessed, and how it can be changed. But models often suggest a theorist's general vision of the world, and they point to the values that the theorist may hold about human behavior. Models may even bear some relationship to the personality of their creators. Do different theorists have personal styles that are reflected in their models' most prominent ideas? Andrews (1989) has compared the different models of clinical psychology and concluded there is some resemblance between a model's overall perspective and the characteristic style of that model's originator. For example, Carl Rogers's model reveals a romantic vision in which unconditional affiliation with the client is thought to allow good to triumph over evil and optimism to replace pessimism. Psychodynamic theorists, on the other hand, have a more ironic vision by which they are always looking beneath the surface of appearances, constantly skeptical of conscious motives and experiences.

To illustrate the special emphases of the different clinical models, the authors asked one representative of the psychoanalytic, behavioral, phenomenological, and interpersonal schools to read a fictitious case report on Mr. A. and provide (I) an initial reaction, (II) an assessment strategy, (III) some hypotheses about the etiology (cause) of the client's problems, (IV) some ideas about additional assessment data needed, and (V) an outline of treatment. Here is the case study, followed by each clinician's responses.

A Case Example

Mr. A. is a 42-year-old Caucasian who lives in a comfortable home in the middle-class suburb of a large city on the west coast of the United States. He has been married for 20 years, has two daughters (aged 16 and 18), and is employed as an electrical engineer at a large aircraft corporation. He was raised a Protestant, but his attendance at church has been sporadic and is now completely terminated. There are no remarkable aspects to his medical history; his general health is good. Though Mr. and Mrs. A. were on a tight budget at the beginning of their marriage, several promotions and pay raises over the years have made them financially secure.

Mr. A. is an only child. He was born in a small midwestern city that is the home of a prestigious university. His father, now retired, was for many years head of that university's chemical engineering department and then dean of the college of engineering. His mother is also retired, but taught high school English before being elevated to the post of vice principal. Mr. A. had a happy and uneventful childhood. He did well in school and was a serious youngster who usually followed his parents' teachings about the importance of hard work and superior performance. His parents were loving but somewhat unemotional. He had never seen them display overt signs of affection for each other, and his father had become really angry only once (when Mr. A. talked about dropping out of high school).

In elementary and high school, Mr. A. was part of a small group of male and female friends. Its members were a lot like him: quiet, serious, and studious. His social activities included meetings of special interest groups (the German and stamp clubs) as well as movies and concerts, which he attended in a group rather than on a date. When he enrolled as an engineering student at the local university, Mr. A. continued to live with his parents and retained his well-established study and social patterns. By the middle of his junior year, he had become especially friendly with an intelligent and compatible young woman who had been in several courses with him. He had first invited her to join him and other friends for concerts, football games, and plays; later they began to socialize as a couple. Mr. A. was delighted with her company but was never physically or verbally demonstrative of his feelings. When she brought up the subject of marriage, he was surprised but thought it would be a fine idea. Mr. A.'s parents were pleased, and the wedding took place right after graduation. The births of the couple's daughters were welcome, and life settled into a pleasant cycle of work, play, and child rearing.

Problems first appeared when Mr. and Mrs. A.'s attractive girls reached adolescence. Arguments over boyfriends, politics, the effects of drug use, the existence of God, and curfews became frequent, and the family atmosphere was often turbulent. These relatively commonplace, though stressful, difficulties were later overshadowed by a set of more serious and totally unanticipated problems.

For a little over a year, Mr. A. has had attacks of dizziness, accelerated heartbeat, and fainting. Though he has received extensive medical attention, no organic basis for the problem

has been detected. The severity of the attacks has increased in recent months to the point that Mr. A. was forced to ask for an indefinite leave of absence from his job. Though insurance benefits and Mrs. A.'s income as a substitute teacher have prevented a financial crisis, he has become increasingly depressed over his problem. After exhausting hope that the attacks would cease spontaneously, Mr. A. reluctantly accepted his physicians' conclusion that psychological factors may be involved and has contacted a clinical psychologist.

He reports that he never has an attack at home unless his older daughter is there, but that he is almost sure to become dizzy and faint shortly after leaving home for any purpose. For this reason, he cannot drive a car. For a while he stayed active by having his wife or a friend act as chauffeur, but he is now completely housebound. Mr. A.'s days are spent reading, watching television, or gazing out the living room window. His appetite is poor and he is losing weight. He does not sleep well and has frequent arguments with his wife and children, during which he accuses them of being the cause of his problems. He has become so morose about the current situation and so pessimistic about the future that he contemplates suicide.

A Psychoanalytic Approach to Mr. A.: Dr. Thomas A. Widiger*

I. Initial Reaction. My initial impression is that Mr. A. is suffering from agoraphobia and an adjustment disorder with depressed mood, complicated by a compulsive personality disorder. Mr. A. meets the criteria for a major affective disorder, depressive episode, but the diagnosis should emphasize that the depression is reactive to the loss of his career. Mr. A. might not meet the criteria for a com-

*Professor, Department of Psychology, University of Kentucky.

pulsive personality disorder, but he has inflexible and maladaptive compulsive personality traits that could contribute to the development of the anxiety and depressive disorders.

Mr. A.'s character traits of isolation and constriction of affect, restricted ability to express warmth and tender emotions, and excessive devotion to work appear to represent a defensive identification with a demanding and withholding father. They help repress the anger and depression he experienced but could not express during childhood. In addition, Mr. A. denies any psychological conflicts in order to maintain the ego ideals of self-control and productivity. However, he was unable to maintain this myth when his daughter not only directly challenged his personality but also symbolically re-created his own conflict with his father. His anxiety symptoms were a signal that his denial and repression were being threatened. Mr. A., however, maintained his denial, and his anxiety escalated to the point of a crack in his character armor. He then became depressed not only because of the loss of his ego ideals of productivity and self-control, but also because of an emerging recognition of the emptiness of his past and current relationships.

II. Assessment Strategy. The preceding tentative formulation would need to be verified in the course of treatment. I would be careful not to impose this formulation, but would test it with an evenly hovering consideration of the material presented by the patient.

I would first obtain a structured anamnesis (i.e., a life history with particular attention to the course of his symptomatology and relationships). I would like to hear the patient describe his life in his own words. I would assess his motivation for treatment and his capacity for insight. Mr. A. has been reluctant to acknowledge psychological conflicts and I would want to assess whether an insight-oriented treatment would be appropriate. His interpretation of psychosocial events and recent dreams would be particularly helpful. I am as-

suming that the degree of Mr. A.'s anxiety and depression would not prohibit an insight-oriented psychotherapy.

Following the anamnesis, I would begin a trial analysis. Freud suggested an initial, time-limited analysis to assess the suitability of analytic therapy. We would meet for 6 weeks to allow Mr. A. to gain an understanding of what therapy would be like, and to give me further opportunity to assess his motivation and capacity for insight.

III. Etiological Hypotheses. Mr. A.'s symptoms appear to be the result of unconscious conflicts that resulted from pathologic object-relations during childhood. The repression of childhood conflicts is evident in the unrealistic, blanket denial of any traumas or problems during childhood. Mr. A. is described as having a "happy and uneventful childhood." This is difficult to imagine in any family. The facade is illustrated further in the next sentence. Mr. A. was a "rather serious youngster who usually behaved in accordance with his parents' teachings about the importance of hard work and superior performance." This describes an affectively constricted child who conformed to a parental ideal of perfectionism and productivity. Achievement and productivity probably were his symbolic means of obtaining a sense of worth and love from his parents. His mother and father were "loving but somewhat unemotional." This is another contradiction. Can loving be unemotional? Only inadequate loving. It is likely he found his relationship with his parents to be unsatisfying, but was unable to express his dissatisfaction since affective expression was suppressed. Denied overt expressions of affection and love, he obtained parental approval through a realization of their ideals of achievement, self-control, and perfectionism. However, symbolic satisfaction is not as satisfying as the real thing, especially if it entails a lifestyle that denies normal human expression and desires. He almost attempted a rebellion by dropping hints of quitting high school. Dropping out of high school would have been a clear and direct rejection of his parents' repressive and constrictive ideals. It was a "good" way of letting them know he was dissatisfied. It forced his father to deviate from his own constrictive character style and express some emotion, although an unpleasant and negative anger. Mr. A. desired an expression of love and affection, but his own constriction of affect prevented him from expressing this directly and effectively responding to his father's anger. Therefore, he resumed the identity imposed by his parents. A lack of emotion was easier to live with than anger and hostility.

The aforementioned compulsive character defenses were maintained throughout college and marriage. They were not, however, without cost. Mr. A. was able to repress his anger and depression, but at the price of a constriction of his own feelings of affection. It was necessary for his girlfriend to suggest marriage, an idea that took him by surprise and was accepted with little feeling. He simply "thought it would be a fine idea," comparable to the purchase of a new book. "Life settled into a pleasant and serene cycle of work, play, and child rearing," continuing the myth of a successful denial and repression of tension, depression, and anger.

Mr. A.'s daughter, however, was unable or unwilling to perpetuate the family myth. She rebelled, and her rebellion challenged his character armor. Their continual arguments over boyfriends, drug usage, God, and curfews exacerbated his unconscious conflicts. The fact that her rebellion occurred at the same stage of life as his own failed rebellion contributed to its symbolic significance. Mr. A. was able to deny his ambivalence regarding his values, impulses, and desires when his family corroborated them, but not if a family member openly challenged them. Repression and denial were not so easily maintained in the company of his daughter. Her sexual attractiveness, rebellious behavior, and verbal assaults were too strong for his defensive armor.

As his defenses became ineffective, Mr. A. began to experience symptoms of anxiety, especially in the presence of the rebellious daughter. To his own detriment, he continued to deny psychological conflicts, searching for a physician to discover an organic basis.

The denial was now not only ineffective but very costly. Severity of anxiety attacks increased to the point that he had to abandon his career. Mr. A., however, may have obtained some unconscious satisfaction in the loss of his career. He was finally able to reject his parents' ideals without an overt, hostile rebellion.

However, the anxiety attacks not only fulfilled an unconscious desire to rebel, they also resulted in the loss of Mr. A.'s symbolic source of parental affection (i.e., self-worth). His identity revolved around hard work, self-control, and productivity. Loss of career through anxiety attacks shattered these ideals and he became severely depressed. Knowing that company benefits and his wife's income prevented a financial crisis only reaffirmed his crippled state.

His depression may also have been overdetermined by the emergence of repressed depressive affect. Mr. A. had dealt with his withholding parents by denying throughout his adolescent and adult life the need for close and loving relationships. With a breakdown of his character armor he perhaps began to recognize the emptiness of his past and current relationships. Denial was now impossible. Anxiety and depression had broken down the controlled but productive facade. "Mr. A. reluctantly accepted his physicians' conclusions that psychological factors may be involved."

IV. Potential Influence of Further Assessment Data. The etiological hypotheses focused on the patient's relationships with his father and with his daughter. It is likely that during assessment the importance of other relationships would be revealed. Mr. A.'s relationships with his mother and his wife would be crucial to consider. It would also be of interest to explore his relationship with his parents prior to adolescence. Conflicts regarding emotional expression and intimacy, and the compulsive character defenses, were developed prior to adolescence, and it would be important to explore their genesis in the context of the parent–child relationships.

V. General Approach to Relief of Distress. Treatment would consist of insight-oriented psychotherapy. I would prefer to meet at least twice a week, for the intensity and effectiveness of insight are diminished by long intervals between sessions. Mr. A., however, would probably find twice-weekly sessions too threatening.

I would be nondirective within the sessions, allowing Mr. A. to govern the focus and pace of the sessions. This does not imply a passive tolerance of resistance, but a respect for the patient's readiness and receptivity. I would encourage Mr. A. to discuss and reflect on his problems, attempting to discover why they developed, how they were being maintained, and what to do about them. He would be instructed to say whatever came to mind, freely associating to his thoughts and fantasies.

Mr. A. probably would proceed slowly, demonstrating considerable denial, intellectualization, and rationalization. My initial efforts would consist of reflecting and clarifying Mr. A.'s comments and associations to highlight what I believe are the important issues. I would not interpret his comments in terms of his underlying conflicts until enough material had emerged and sufficient rapport was established that he would be ready to receive them. The interpretations would focus on the relationship of Mr. A.'s associations, dreams, symptoms, and underlying conflicts. Interpretations would be offered in a nonthreatening and suggestive manner, always encouraging the patient to offer his own insights and interpretations. Each interpretation would be followed by a considerable amount of working through, or elicitation of further material, to clarify and expand on the initial insight.

Treatment would eventually focus on the therapeutic relationship itself, for I would expect him to transfer to me the conflicts he has experienced with his father (and mother). In this case the transference analysis is likely to be problematic and, for the same reasons, therapeutic, for Mr. A.'s relationship with his father appears to be central to his unconscious conflicts. It is anticipated that initially he would be deferential and detached, preferring to engage in intellectual discussions. Beneath this superficial obedience would be a hostile rebellion and a yearning for an intimate and affectionate relationship. The hostile rebellion would likely appear first, perhaps expressed through arguments and rejections. Treatment will have progressed successfully if Mr. A. could acknowledge his unsatisfied needs for affection and intimacy.

A Behavioral Approach to Mr. A.: Dr. Barry Edelstein*

I. Initial Reaction. My initial impression is that Mr. A. is experiencing several problems, one of the most important of which is his consideration of suicide. No matter how one would proceed with this case, the possibility of suicidal behavior should be assessed in depth. Space limitations preclude an adequate description of how one would assess suicide potential, so I will proceed with the understanding that it was assessed and judged not to be an imminent problem.

Assigning diagnoses is a common practice among most clinicians; however, it can distract one from an analysis of the presenting problem and may not translate into meaningful decisions regarding treatment. Thus, some behavioral clinicians would not formulate a diagnosis until required to do so. For the sake of this exercise, I will offer an initial diagnostic impression to allow comparison with other ap-

---

*Professor, Department of Psychology, West Virginia University.

proaches. Mr. A. appears to be experiencing agoraphobia with panic attacks accompanied by symptoms of major depressive disorder. The depressive symptoms are probably secondary to the panic attacks, loss of job, inability to deal with the stressful difficulties with his children, and general loss of reinforcement. The more specific problems that might be articulated by a behavioral clinician rather than a diagnosis would include: reports of fear, avoidance behavior, physiological arousal, marital dysfunction, child behavior management, interpersonal problem solving, employment, anger control, sleep, appetite, finances, and the reduced number and intensity of many daily behaviors.

II. Assessment Strategy. The initial reaction is based upon very limited information and may not be accurate. Further assessment would occur throughout all future meetings with the client, a practice common among behavioral clinicians.

An initial interview would be conducted at Mr. A.'s home since he is housebound. The interview would begin with a survey of general problem areas and their history. Mr. A. would be encouraged to provide concrete examples of each problem and, if possible, specify related thoughts and observable environmental events. Mr. A. would be asked about the frequency, duration, and intensity of each behavior problem across settings, individuals, times, and occasions. The effects of these problem behaviors on Mr. A. and others would also be assessed. A functional analysis of Mr. A.'s dysfunction would be performed to describe the relationship between environmental events that set the occasion for and maintain (reinforce) the problem behaviors that constitute the dysfunction. Thus, I would look for the events in the observable environment as well as in Mr. A.'s thoughts that are functionally related to each problem.

I would also assess the probable consequences (motivation) for Mr. A. attending sessions with me and completing any homework assignments. His motivation for change will partially determine the method of treatment.

The client is only one member of a family system, the members of which influence each other on a daily basis. I would therefore attempt to meet with members of Mr. A.'s family to gain their perspective on the problem, determine how the problem affects the family, determine how the family affects the problem, and determine the extent to which other family members could assist with or hamper treatment. It is possible that Mr. A. is also gaining something positive from his problem behaviors. I would attempt to determine whether some of his problem behaviors were being maintained by their positive consequences (secondary gain).

During the initial visit I would also obtain two additional types of assessment information: self-report ratings on standardized questionnaires and an actual sample of the avoidance behavior and the associated verbal reports of Mr. A.'s reaction to feared situations. I would have Mr. A. complete the Mobility Inventory, the Body Sensations Questionnaire, and the Beck Depression Inventory. The Mobility Inventory lists several places and situations and asks the client to rate the amount of avoidance of these situations when alone or when accompanied. The Body Sensations Questionnaire asks the client questions about bodily sensations that are common among individuals experiencing anxiety in various situations (e.g., "I am going to pass out"). The Beck Depression Inventory is a measure of level of depression which can be completed quickly and can be readministered over time/sessions to evaluate change in level of depression. For a behavior sample, I would have Mr. A. attempt to walk away from his home and monitor the number of steps he is able to take and his ratings of anxiety at several points along the way.

I would also teach Mr. A. to gather relevant information and collaborate in the development of the treatment program that arises from this information. I would teach Mr. A. how to evaluate the severity of his problem by rating the intensity of anxiety and describing his avoidance behavior in various situations. Intensity of anxiety can be rated on a 100-point scale where 1 = as relaxed as I have ever been and 100 = as anxious as I have ever been. Avoidance can be measured by noting what is avoided when he is alone or accompanied by someone.

Mr. A. would be asked to begin keeping a log of his anxiety and avoidance behavior throughout each day so that I could gain a detailed picture of the situations that occasion avoidance and elicit anxiety. He would also be asked to record any panic attacks, those situations in which he may feel dizzy, experience an accelerated heartbeat, and sometimes faint. In summary, Mr. A. would record where he goes, when he goes there, who accompanies him, and what he experiences every day.

If Mr. A. is able to record everything as I requested and his family is cooperative, I could have enough information to begin treatment in about 2 weeks.

My understanding of the problem would be checked repeatedly against the new evaluative information obtained from the client. Should new information reveal errors in my assessment, the treatment strategies would be adjusted accordingly. Similarly, if a treatment does not produce significant improvement in level of functioning in a relatively short period of time, the treatment strategy would be reconsidered and altered to bring about the desired change.

III. Etiological Hypotheses. Mr. A. appears to have had a long history of conservative behavior with little risk taking. His study habits, method of socializing, and living at home until marriage reduced the chances of having to face new challenges and their associated anxiety. Just as he controlled sources of anxiety, he also controlled his emotional expression (as had his parents). Consequently,

he rarely had the opportunity to learn to cope with problems and their associated anxiety. The confrontations associated with his children reaching adolescence challenged his skills for coping with major interpersonal problems as well as the accompanying anxiety. The anxiety experienced when confronting the problems with his daughters may well have been of a greater magnitude than any previously experienced. Those initial intense feelings of anxiety would have been paired with previously neutral stimuli that were present. In light of the panic attacks in the presence of his older daughter, I would guess that she was present during the initial experiences of intense anxiety. Once anxiety became associated with thoughts about his daughters and related problems, he might experience anxiety anywhere he was thinking about these issues. Thus, anxiety responses would generalize across a variety of situations, including Mr. A.'s work environment. The internal cues of anxiety would come to signal a possible recurrence of the original panic attack. The more anxious he became, the more he feared becoming anxious. Panic attacks resulted from increased anxiety and strengthened his fear of becoming anxious. Thus, his failure to meet the demands of the problem situations resulted in increased anxiety which developed into a fear of fear itself. Depression probably resulted from his inability to control his problems and the significant reduction in reinforcement that was normally associated with his job and family.

IV. Potential Influence of Further Assessment Data. Additional assessment data would be gathered on the relationship of Mr. A.'s problems to other family members as well as the situation at work prior to development of the presenting problems. It is possible that the problems were brought on and maintained by family members; or that problems at work developed into a phobia of work rather than agoraphobia. The extent to which Mr. A. is considering suicide could alter the analysis as well as the nature of treatment. Depression could become the major priority for treatment. Family therapy would be considered, particularly if the family is contributing significantly to the problem's maintenance. Child behavior management or parent–child communication skills could be so poor that teaching both parents appropriate parenting skills could have a significant impact on Mr. A.'s presenting problems.

V. General Approach to Relief of Distress. If agoraphobia seems to be the major problem, I would address it first with the expectation that symptoms of depression would abate once the avoidance behavior was reduced. The psychological treatment most strongly supported by research is an exposure procedure. Two drugs, imipramine and phenelzine, have also been used successfully in combination with exposure procedures to reduce the frequency and intensity of panic attacks. If I were working with a psychiatrist I might consult with him or her regarding the advisability of employing one of these drugs in addition to using an exposure procedure. Regardless of whether one of these drugs was employed, I would begin with an exposure procedure. Exposure procedures can be either *in vivo* or imaginal, where clients are exposed to the anxiety-arousing stimuli via direct contact with the stimuli or by having them imagine the stimuli. The object of stimulus exposure is to elicit anxiety to a moderate extent and have the client experience the anxiety without escaping from the situation or thoughts. The exposure procedures would first be performed by me and then by cooperative family members in concert with Mr. A. Progress would be monitored continually using the same assessment methods previously noted. Treatment would be terminated when Mr. A. was able to return to work on a regular basis and when suicidal ideation and the other related problems were alleviated to an extent agreed upon by Mr. A. and me.

A Phenomenological Approach to Mr. A.: Dr. Constance T. Fischer *

I. Initial Impressions. In terms of the prevailing diagnostic classification system *(DSM-III-R)*, Mr. A. meets criteria for major depressive disorder, for agoraphobia with panic attacks, and for some long-standing features of compulsive personality disorder. That framework helps me to think broadly about research and theory on how these patterns evolve and on how best to engage the client and his family in assessing and altering his present state.

My point of departure into classifications and my point of return from that framework is Mr. A.'s life. I ask myself how the "disorders" point back to a disordering of his life—a disruption of a personal world that used to make sense and support his goals, values, and actions. Now he finds himself immobilized, anxious, depressed. What has changed for him? Who was he trying to be? What were his assumptions about life? Where was he going? What obstacles did he encounter that he now apparently perceives his basic goals as unreachable? How is he contributing to these obstacles and to his perceptions of them? What purposes does his comportment now serve?

My initial impression is that Mr. A. had lived his life in an orderly, disciplined manner. He seems to have avoided spontaneity, strong feelings, and introspection in an implicit belief that a controlled and logical life rendered him worthy, accepted, and safely on course. His successful life at work and at home validated his values and strengthened his assumption that his children would honor him as he had his parents. However, as his daughters entered adolescence, Mr. A. found that they chose not to live in a controlled manner, that in effect they had disrupted his course. His tried-and-true problem-solving approach, logic, and dis-

───────

*Professor, Department of Psychology, Duquesne University.

cipline failed him. He not only found himself to be unaccustomedly confused, but he also found himself experiencing unusually strong feelings, such as anger and perhaps jealousy of his daughters' freedom. I suspect that he also was not prepared for his daughters' emerging sexuality. In short, his fundamental personal rules are no longer viable; Mr. A. does not know how to continue his life. The world and his own reactions have become unpredictable. He cannot imagine how to continue being himself. When he confronts this disorderly world (and self), he becomes anxious; when he retreats, he again finds himself helpless and demoralized.

II. Assessment Strategy. Before meeting with Mr. A., I would review my initial impressions and conjectures so that I could revise them as I came to know Mr. A. more directly. I would not be looking for proof of my impressions nor for causes of his condition, but rather for a deepened understanding of what that condition is, especially in terms of how he is living and perpetuating it. In my meeting with Mr. A., I would try to assess how viable his prior life course might still be, and how I and others might help him revise his assumptions, his goals, his participation in bringing about his circumstances, and his ways of being the person he has strived to be.

Our starting point would be Mr. A.'s own story, which would be our common ground for collaborative exploration. We would try to make sense of his life in its own terms, using his language and his themes. That life would be my point of departure into reflections about my initial impressions, recollections of similar clients, my more personal reactions, and my knowledge of research findings and theory. Mr. A.'s everyday life would also be my point of return, where we could refine our understandings in light of our respective reflections. The purpose of assessment would be to understand his circumstance, and to identify viable interventions and points at which he might opt for alternate routes. I would hope that during the assessment process he would redis-

cover that he does participate in directing his life. In this sense, recovery is initiated prior to formal psychotherapy.

I would use psychological tests, largely as a means of engaging Mr. A. in ways that are familiar to him—looking at visual evidence, taking a problem-solving approach. I might start with subtests from the Wechsler intelligence test. After witnessing his performance with the block designs, I might remark that his engineering background is certainly evident. I could affirm his logical, systematic approach. We might discuss its advantages, and how he has accomplished various objectives through it. I might then ask when this approach hasn't worked so well. We would continue this inquiry through other subtests. For example, we might note on Picture Arrangement that he was less facile at ordering scenes in that he was disinclined to put himself in others' shoes. We might continue this exploration by looking together at a self-report personality inventory. By the end of our assessment session(s) I would have a sense of which forms of psychotherapy would best suit Mr. A., and I would propose this to him, along with a summary of the goals we had agreed on. I also would acknowledge disagreements between our respective understandings. Although I would have strived to express my impressions in ways that would be sensible to Mr. A., inevitably our different backgrounds and motives and our ways of attuning to nonrational realms would leave several issues unsettled between us. Nevertheless, Mr. A. would have experienced a positive working relationship and could anticipate that psychotherapy could proceed safely and productively in a similar manner.

III. Etiological Hypotheses. Mr. A. seems to have grown up in a setting that one-sidedly rewarded academic, intellectual pursuit. He did not become familiar with open affection, nor with give-and-take interpersonal argument. Nor did his parents model spontaneity or openness to new lifestyles. His one effort to leave school and home was summarily disallowed. Moreover, Mr. A. had no siblings with whom to learn that being aggressive, angry, and jealous can occur within a good family. He seems to have restricted himself so closely to schoolwork and to his parents' home that he probably was not familiar with how other youngsters were growing up, with their struggles and perspectives. He was slow to discover the other gender and sexuality.

As he moved into marriage and an engineering career, the consequences of his life seemed to be totally positive. He continued to honor his parents through perpetuating their approach to life. He was a good provider, a respected person at home, work, and in the community. His daughters were growing up in a reserved, respectable home. Surely this course would continue. His daughters would affirm his rightness and the appropriateness of his careful life by respecting his values, worth, and power, just as he has respected his parents'.

But by the time his daughters entered adolescence, they were living in a different time and different social world than the one in which Mr. A. grew up. They were more independent and less restrained. They challenged Mr. A., perhaps showed more affection toward boyfriends than toward their father, argued emotionally, and possibly talked outright about their father's uptightness about their interest in young men. I wonder what Mrs. A.'s participation in this evolution has been. Might she be supporting the daughters' growth, for both selfless and vicarious reasons? Does Mr. A. perceive this as disloyal?

At any rate, Mr. A.'s lifelong, and up until now valid, philosophy no longer works for him. He is helpless in that all he knows to do is to assert authority and logic, which now appear to others to be rigid, narrow, inappropriate. The proverbial rug has been pulled out from under him. In a sense, he doesn't know who he is or how to be. The more he takes refuge in isolation from work and family, the more alienated he feels, and the more frightened he is at the prospect of reasserting himself. He is agoraphobic and depressed. I wonder, though, whether his daughters' freedom has not also put him in touch with his own previously disallowed yearnings, leaving him implicitly angry at his parents and at himself. I wonder whether his present state is also one of feeling sorry for himself; of mourning what might have been; of avoiding current choice; of punishing parents, wife, and daughters; and of still retaining power, recognition, and order by disrupting the family's pursuits. I wonder too whether being depressed serves to keep Mr. A. from more fully experiencing the aforementioned.

IV. Potential Influence of Further Assessment Data. Formal psychotherapy would continue the assessment, as I would listen and revise it in light of what Mr. A. and his family present and in light of response to therapeutic efforts. The preceding formulations would allow me to revise continually and systematically. Even if the initial formulations prove incorrect, they move us closer to understanding Mr. A.'s circumstance.

There are five additional areas I would want to assess: (a) the likelihood, method, and lethality of Mr. A.'s attempting to kill himself; (b) Mrs. A.'s and the daughters' participation in what is happening; (c) what intolerable possibilities are evoked by the older daughter's presence; (d) what was happening in Mr. A.'s work setting: were younger people, new ideas, and a changing world threatening his way of life there too?; and (e) whether medication might interrupt Mr. A.'s panic attacks, thereby assisting his reentry into his community and job.

V. Therapeutic Efforts. If I were to continue as Mr. A.'s therapist, I would use multiple and flexible methods geared to help him develop revised ways of continuing his orderly, reasonable, worthy, respected, but now broadened life. Choice of methods would depend on how Mr. A. related to me and how reflective he was. First, I would use our relationship, letting him know that we *can* make sense of what has happened, and that I respect him and his goals even though I know that they've gone awry. We would look at his early developmental years to the extent that he found such exploration useful. I would help him to see that although there were good reasons for his earlier style, he no longer has to continue it in exactly the same way.

I would intervene in his environment so that it became more manageable for him. In addition to the possibility of medication to lessen his being lethargic and panic prone, I would encourage family meetings, at which his wife and daughters could affirm those aspects of Mr. A.'s life they still see as worthy. I might also instruct all members of the family in specific ways to stop reinforcing Mr. A.'s withdrawal. I would encourage a return to healthy diet, taking up household tasks, excursions out of the house, and a partial return to work.

In an openly paradoxical manner, I might congratulate Mr. A. on having demonstrated to his daughters that our actions have consequences. Similarly, I might caution him not to return to his old self until he was sure he was ready. Both messages affirm that in certain ways Mr. A. has known and knows what he is doing, and that he can continue his life in a more fulsome manner.

These and other efforts would be based on continual reappraisal of "what is possible from here?," particularly in terms of how Mr. A. takes up what his body, environment, other people, his history, and opportunity present to him.

An Interpersonal Approach to Mr. A.: Dr. Donald J. Kiesler*

I. Initial Reaction. Interpersonal treatment of Mr. A. would concentrate on the long-standing personality aspects of his problems.

*Professor, Department of Psychology, Virginia Commonwealth University. Thanks are due Dr. Todd F. Van Denburg for his helpful comments and feedback regarding an earlier version of this treatment plan.

The apparent diagnoses of panic disorder with agoraphobia and adjustment disorder with depressed mood would not be targeted initially for treatment. Instead, their significance within the patient's central interpersonal maladaptive pattern would be assessed throughout the therapy. I expect that treatment of his basic interpersonal problem will begin to alleviate Mr. A.'s emotional symptoms. If necessary, amelioration of the latter symptomatology would become the focus of intervention after Mr. A.'s maladaptive pattern becomes less extreme and rigid. However, an immediate and continuing priority would be the close monitoring of Mr. A.'s recent depressive "vegetative" symptoms and suicidal ideation; if this pattern worsens, antidepressant medication may temporarily be necessary to reverse the process.

The data suggest diagnosis of compulsive personality disorder which, in turn, suggests a preliminary profile translation onto the 1982 Interpersonal Circle at the *Detached* and *Inhibited* categories (see Figure 2–4). This hypothesized interpersonal profile, however, needs to be more thoroughly validated through further interpersonal assessment.

FIGURE 2–4 Kiesler's 1982 version of the Interpersonal Circle (Kiesler, 1983) has a similar configuration to Leary's original circular arrangement, depicted in Figure 2–3. However, because Kiesler names the segments differently from Leary, we include this figure so that Kiesler's clinical conception of Mr. A. can be more easily visualized.

II. Assessment Strategy. A basic assumption of interpersonal therapy is that the patient's central problems reside in maladaptive transaction cycles (MTC) with significant others, including the therapist. The therapist must identify the specific components of this repetitious, self-defeating maladaptive pattern: the patient's covert experience (Mr. A.: "My family brought this on"); the patient's overt actions with significant others (Mr. A.'s angry outbursts and social withdrawal); the covert experience of others in reaction to the patient (Mr. A.'s family: "He won't listen to anything we say"); and the overt reactions of significant others (his family's criticism of Mr. A.) which, in turn, confirm the patient's covert experience of himself. The patient's specific MTC needs to be the central target of psychotherapy; the therapist attempts to disrupt the patient's maladaptive vicious cycle at any or all of the four MTC components (Kiesler, 1986a, 1988).

The Interpersonal Circle helps the therapist to identify the specific content present in the four causally linked components of the patient's MTC. The circle both guides interpersonal diagnosis and permits formulation of interpersonal interventions with a particular patient. A repertoire of interpersonal measures is available to locate and describe a given patient's interpersonal behavior at specific segments of the circle.

With our present case, I would concentrate on determining Mr. A.'s predominant interpersonal action pattern with significant others in his life. I would use Kiesler's Check List of Interpersonal Transactions (CLOIT-R; Kiesler, 1987a) and Impact Message Inventory (IMI; Kiesler, 1987b; Kiesler et al., 1985), Horowitz and colleagues' Inventory of Interpersonal Problems (IIP), and Larus and colleagues' Significant Other Inventory (SOI). I would use three sources of assessment: (a) Mr. A.'s wife and two daughters, especially the older (who would rate Mr. A.'s interpersonal behavior on the CLOIT-R); (b) Mr. A. himself (who would describe his own interpersonal behavior on the CLOIT-R, characterize his interpersonal problems on the IIP, and characterize significant others throughout his life on the SOI); and (c) myself as therapist (rating Mr. A.'s actions with me on the CLOIT-R, and reporting the impacts I experience with him on the IMI). The result would be circle profiles of Mr. A.'s interpersonal behavior with his spouse, his daughters, and his therapist—as well as Mr. A.'s perceptions of his own interpersonal behavior patterns, of his interpersonal problems, and of his historical and present significant others (Kiesler, 1991).

It's likely that the various perspectives on Mr. A.'s interpersonal behavior would show a high degree of consistency/generality, with the possible exception that his older daughter might show some important differences in her perceptions of her father's behavior. Since patients are often unaware of the negative impacts their interpersonal styles have on others, it's expected also that there would be important discrepancies between Mr. A.'s characterizations of himself and those from his interactants. Let's assume that generality prevails among interactants with the result that Mr. A.'s peak segments on the circle, as determined by our assessment, are at *Hostile* (often ignores family members' feelings; quick to dispute their statements; eager to provoke them; etc.), *Detached* (disregards family members' presence; slow to speak or respond to them; keeps things to self; etc.) and *Inhibited* (deliberates carefully before speaking; tries to be undemonstrative of feelings; procrastinates; etc.). These three segments fall in the hostile–submissive quadrant of the circle.

III. Etiological Hypotheses. Mr. A.'s most prototypic self-definition (Sullivan's "self-personification") seems to be that he is serious, hardworking, intelligent/rational, and has demonstrated superior performance in his career as an electrical engineer. This style developed in order to gain acceptance and security in his relationships with his parents and peers, who appeared to value this stance. Any other enactments (such as to drop out of high school, or to be affectionate, emotional, or gregarious) likely resulted in disapproval or anger from these significant others; in turn, this seriously threatened his self-esteem. In similar manner, his personification (schema) of significant others seems to have been modeled by his parents and further confirmed by his adolescent friends. From Mr. A.'s perspective, significant others are expected to be *Mistrusting* (watching Mr. A. for harmful intent, claiming they are judged unfairly by Mr. A., etc.); *Cold* (critical of Mr. A., expecting exact compliance by Mr. A. to the rules, etc.); and *Hostile* (becoming angry with Mr. A. when they are crossed or antagonized, etc.).

His older adolescent daughter's current age- and role-appropriate behaviors, and his family's apparent alignment against him, seem to be challenging the validity of Mr. A.'s lifelong self-definition. The results of his recent behavior are producing major dissonance to his self-conception and lowering his self-esteem. Depressed and agoraphobic, he has lost the success of his job performance; instead of remaining rational and undemonstrative, he is arguing constantly with his family; instead of being competent, he cannot find a solution to his recent dilemmas and symptoms. Mr. A., however, is blind to the automatic process in which his own rigid and extreme actions with his family *actually evoke and reinforce* these complementary behaviors (that is, these reactions that are so consistent with his personification of others). Unsuccessful in changing their reactions, he escalates his maladaptive pattern ("transactional escalation") and develops symptoms of depression and agoraphobia.

IV. Potential Influence of Further Assessment Data. In assisting Mr. A. to tell and explore his story of his life and problems, I would be especially attentive to those interpersonal situations I hypothesize to be problematic. First, I would explore the area of sexual and emotional intimacy with his wife, as well as the manner in which they negotiate disagreement and anger. Mr. A.'s wife seems to have aligned with the daughters against

him; it's likely that their relationship will have to be realigned before the daughters' adolescent rebellions can be constructively addressed. Second, it would be important to pursue any differences in the way Mr. A. relates to men, in contrast to women. It seems he is pursuing traditional male strategies in pursuit of intimacy with the women in his life. Clarification of this pattern would also require close examination of his earlier relationships with his mother and father.

V. General Approach to Relief of Distress. Although Mr. A.'s agoraphobia seems to confine him to home, a contract for individual therapy at my office would be negotiated, with either his wife or daughters transporting him. Because of his several problems, I would contract initially for two sessions per week.

My earlier circle assessment permits me to make predictions about the goals of treatment and the interpersonal processes that will be encountered in attempting to achieve these objectives. The goal of therapy for Mr. A. would be an increased frequency and intensity of interpersonal actions with significant others (wife, children, therapist) from segments polar opposite on the circle to the Hostile, Detached, and Inhibited segments that define Mr. A.'s pattern of rigid and extreme maladaptive interpersonal behavior. The opposite segments are *Friendly* (thoughtful of others, smoothes over disagreements, quick to offer help, etc.), *Sociable* (chats easily, seeks others' company, inquires into others' activities, etc.), and *Exhibitionistic* (takes clear stands on issues, his statements often pop out, jumps into action, etc.).

In early therapy sessions especially, Mr. A.'s interpersonal behavior will evoke or pull covert and overt responses from me. This is expected, because the patient's interpersonal behavior is more rigid and extreme than the therapist's and therefore has more controlling power in the relationship. As therapist, then, I would show a pattern of overt behavior in early sessions in which I would be "hooked" into the complementary interpersonal stance (a therapist cannot *not* be hooked in early sessions). This is the "objective" countertransference—I would be experiencing negative impacts similar to those others experience when interacting with Mr. A. This hooked stance would consist of my enactment of Hostile, Cold, and Mistrusting behaviors (as described earlier). By automatically enacting these behaviors with Mr. A. in our early sessions, I would be inadvertently reinforcing and confirming his maladaptive interpersonal approach to living.

My therapeutic priority would be to disengage myself from the complementary covert and overt responses being pulled from me by Mr. A. To accomplish this, I must first detect and label the complementary engagements (thoughts, feelings, action tendencies, images, etc.) being evoked during our sessions. This disengagement would permit me to discontinue the complementary responses and to begin applying asocial interventions (longer silences, reflection of feelings). The goal would be to assist Mr. A. to experience cognitive/emotional ambiguity and uncertainty from this new situation in which his preferred maladaptive style does not produce the expected consequences.

I would emphasize interpersonal feedback in the form of "therapeutic metacommunication" (Kiesler, 1988) throughout the middle and late stages of therapy. With these interventions I would disclose to Mr. A. my perceptions of and reactions to his interpersonal actions during our relationship. Disclosure would target any of the four components of the maladaptive transaction cycle: my covert experiences (impacts); my overt reactions and any discrepancies or incongruities I notice; Mr. A.'s covert experience as inferred by me; and Mr. A.'s overt maladaptive pattern as it occurs in and outside our sessions. For example, I might say to Mr. A., "I'm trying to figure out why I feel so emotionally distant from you—feel that you have to do all this by yourself without any help from me," or "Often I find

myself being cautious and careful about what I'm going to say to you—as if, if I'm not careful, you will disapprove of what I say and lose respect for me." In collaboration, we would continue to validate these components until their cyclical regularity with me and with his family are overwhelmingly apparent. As the crucial first step in discovering more adaptive interpersonal alternatives, Mr. A. and I would seek to "etch in marble" the vicious MTC cycle that represents his central problem in living with his significant others.

In the pretermination stage of therapy, we would focus on enactment of the needed alternative interpersonal behaviors (Friendly, Sociable, Exhibitionistic) in his transactions with me and with his family members. We also would explore ways for Mr. A. to give interpersonal feedback to his family members as a powerful alternative to his previously unsuccessful strategies for intimacy (Kiesler, 1988). Finally, we would assess amelioration of his symptoms of depression and agoraphobia and design further interventions for any residues of these symptomatic problems.

There are similarities among the conceptualizations of Mr. A.'s case offered by the four clinicians. They all note Mr. A.'s interpersonal difficulties, his rigid personality style, and his depressive mood. However, it is also evident from these four presentations that the type of therapeutic experience Mr. A. would have would depend on whose office door he enters. These therapists reveal dramatic differences in the ways they conceptualize Mr. A.'s difficulties, the types of assessment data they would gather, the issues they would focus on in therapy, and the way they would conduct the interventions. For example, the behavioral model focuses on the present-day nature of Mr. A.'s depression and interpersonal problems, whereas the psychodynamic approach downplays these symptoms and attempts to uncover unresolved conflicts from childhood. Similarly, the four therapeutic approaches differ in how directive (behavioral), confrontive (interpersonal), or nondirective (phenom-enological) the therapist would be with Mr. A. The diversity of the four presentations demonstrates that a clinician's theoretical orientation influences all aspects of the therapeutic process.

BIOLOGICAL CHALLENGES TO PSYCHOLOGICAL MODELS

In the past 2 decades, the role of biological factors in the regulation of normal behavior and mental processes and in the causation of various behavioral disorders has been highlighted by growing research evidence from psychiatry, neuroscience, and experimental psychopathology. Three areas of biological discoveries are particularly important to clinical psychologists: (a) *biopsychology,* the study of specific relationships between brain processes and behavior; (b) *behavioral genetics,* the study of causes of individual differences in behavior within a species; and (c) *sociobiology,* the study of the biological bases of social behavior, particularly in terms of the evolutionary value of these behaviors. No matter which model they prefer, all clinical psychologists must take these new findings into account as they conduct their research, assessment, and treatment activities. In fact, the growing recognition of biology–behavior relationships suggests that the biological perspective may one day also attain the status of a model in clinical psychology. Some psychologists see this development as a threat in which reductionistic thinking endangers psychology of "losing its status as an independent body of knowledge" (Peele, 1981). On the contrary, we believe the growing impact of biological progress in understanding behavior and mental processes has not diminished the importance of clinical psychologists but has expanded their professional roles and research interests.

The *diathesis-stress* model provides an increasingly popular way of integrating biologi-cal concepts into psychological models. This perspective, which we discuss more fully in Chapter 12, views many mental disorders as the result of an interaction between a biological *predisposition* or risk for a disorder and an environmental trauma or life stress. In some disorders, like schizophrenia or major depression, the diathesis appears to be genetically influenced, although we do not yet know the exact nature of its manner of genetic transmission.

Chapters 12 and 13 survey three areas of activity—neuropsychology, psychopathology, and health psychology—that reveal how essential it is for psychologists to study the interactions between biological and psychological variables and how exciting areas of professional work grow from this understanding. For now, we want to emphasize that as psychoanalytic, behavioral, interpersonal, and humanistic psychologists advance and revise their particular models of behavior, they need to do so with a thorough appreciation for the new biology–behavior relationships that are constantly being discovered.

THE POPULARITY OF CLINICAL MODELS

The main models of clinical psychology present a kind of approach-avoidance conflict for the person trying to decide which one to adopt. They all present positive and negative features and, even after a tentative choice is made, one still faces diversity of emphasis within each model. There are no universally agreed-upon criteria available to guide one's choice; even the advice offered at the beginning of this chapter regarding a preference for scientifically testable models is based on the authors' personal bias, which, though shared by many, is a bias nonetheless.

What determines one's choice of a model? Freudians might suggest that unconscious motivation compels our choice, while behaviorists would point to the role of learning principles. Some would seek the answer in congruity between a model's principles and the self-concepts of its adherents. Or the choice may be made on the basis of "cognitive style" (Kaplan, 1964), emotional and personality characteristics (L'Abate, 1969), world view (Andrews, 1989), or just plain "personal preference" (Zubin, 1969). The truth is, we really do not know exactly why clinicians choose a particular model, but we can examine what models they choose.

Here the answers are fairly clear. Most clinicians do not make a single choice; instead, they adopt those aspects of two or more models that are personally satisfying to them (Zook & Walton, 1989). To those who value open-mindedness, flexibility, and moderation above systematic consistency, this solution to the choice-of-model problem is called *eclecticism*. To those who emphasize the value of an integrated and unitary point of view, eclectics are merely confused individuals destined to spin their intellectual wheels for lack of theoretical traction. In any case, the ranks of the eclectic or the confused have remained heavily populated among clinical psychologists. Over the past 25 years, anywhere from 30% to 55% of clinicians have described themselves as primarily eclectic.

The diathesis-stress approach is a form of eclecticism. Many versions of this approach integrate biological predispositions with psychological stressors as the main ingredients, but in some cases the diathesis can be primarily psychological in nature. For example, cognitive theorists emphasize chronic negative beliefs about oneself as a predisposing vulnerability that interacts with stressful life events to produce depression in some individuals. Likewise, certain early childhood personality characteristics described by psychoanalysts appear to increase the negative impact that later behavioral events exert on the development or recurrence of depression (Nietzel & Harris, 1990).

Evidence presented by Smith (1982) and Conway (1988) suggests that Freudian and neo-Freudian models have lost popularity among clinicians lately, while phenomenological and behavioral views have gained. Behavioral and cognitive-behavioral models appear to be especially attractive to scientist-practitioners and to younger psychologists (Zook & Walton, 1989). While these data are probably accurate reflections of trends within clinical psychology, they may not be entirely representative. For example, many noneclectic clinicians are not members of the Clinical Division of the APA, joining instead model-oriented clinical groups such as the Association for the Advancement of Behavior Therapy or the Association of Humanistic Psychology. Although there are claims that some models do not "mix well" (Messer & Winokur, 1980), the spirit of current times favors a search for commonalities among various therapeutic schools, even by the skeptics (Messer & Winokur, 1986). Goldfried (1980) has suggested that such commonalities are most likely at a level of abstraction somewhere between general theory and specific techniques, a level he calls the *strategic* because of its focus on principles of change. We will discuss these common strategies in detail in Chapter 7.

CHAPTER 3

Assessment
in
Clinical Psychology

Dictionaries define *assessment* as an estimate of value or worth. A county assessor, for example, looks at a house and estimates its value. On the basis of that estimate, the homeowner's property tax is established. Assessment does not take place in isolation; it is a process leading to a goal. While some assessments involve determination of value or worth, a more useful definition of assessment for our purposes would be *the process of collecting information to be used as the basis for informed decisions by the assessor or by those to whom results are communicated*. In Chapter 1 we saw that assessment was the earliest function of clinical psychology and is still a mainstay of the field. However, it is important to understand that assessment is not performed only by clinicians; almost everyone engages in some type of assessment at one time or another.

Decisions in everyday life are guided by an (often unrecognized) assessment process paralleling that associated with clinical psychology. We meet other people and get to know

them firsthand. The data we collect about their background, attitudes, behaviors, and characteristics are then processed and interpreted in light of our own experience and frame of reference. We form impressions that guide our social decisions; when given a choice, we seek out certain individuals and avoid others.

When accurate social assessment data are processed efficiently, beneficial decisions result. For example, we correctly see through a person's tough talk to appreciate other, rarely revealed aspects of his or her behavior. Individuals who do this regularly are described as good judges of character and become valued sources of opinion and advice.

However, social-decision errors often occur because of problems in data collection, processing, or both. It is easy to jump to false conclusions about another person on the basis of inadequate information ("As soon as he said he hated ballet, I knew I wasn't going to like him"), unrepresentative behavior (someone in a foul mood seldom leaves a good impression), stereotypes ("Her accent really turned me off"), and personal biases ("I love people who wear sweaters like that!"). These and other sources of error make the collecting of information that guide decisions about other people a hazardous process.

Similar problems plague assessment in clinical psychology. Even though the clinician may have access to more systematic assessment information than is normally available to nonprofessionals, the task of forming an accurate understanding of other people is a difficult challenge. That challenge is complicated by the fact that the consequences of errors in clinical assessment can be more dramatic and enduring than buying the wrong car or spending an evening with a clod. Because of the complexity of clinical assessment and the seriousness of the decisions tied to it, the study of clinical decision making is a growing and important area of research (see Garb, 1989; Kleinmuntz, 1984; Rock, Bransford, Maisto, & Morey, 1987 for reviews).

This chapter provides an overview of how the clinical psychologist, as a human being who is not possessed of special powers of perception and judgment and who is susceptible to the same data collection and processing errors that plague other human beings, attempts to meet the challenge of assessment.

COMPONENTS OF THE CLINICAL ASSESSMENT PROCESS

Psychologists have proposed several different outlines for the activities involved in assessment (Tallent, 1992). In general, these approaches recognize that assessment is a process of gathering information to solve a problem and that a systematic, logically related sequence of steps is the most effective organization for good problem solving. Four interrelated components of clinical assessment are illustrated in Figure 3–1. Each component involves issues we have to confront in order to comprehend the process as a whole. With respect to planning and data collection, for example, one might ask how much information about a person is enough, which kinds of data are most valuable, how inaccurate information can be detected and eliminated, and where information should be sought. The data-processing phase raises questions such as: How does the clinician go about integrating available data? Is the assessor able to remain unbiased? Could a computer combine assessment data more competently than a human being? Consideration of the fourth assessment segment leads to other inquiries: Who uses the results and for what purposes? What is the impact of assessment on the lives of those assessed? Are people protected from misuse or abuse of assessment information?

We will examine these and many other issues of clinical assessment in subsequent sections.

Planning for Assessment

McReynolds (1975) points out that two related questions must be answered before clinical assessment can begin: (a) What do we want to know? (b) How should we go about learning it? A reply to the first question is dictated by what one believes are important human vari-

FIGURE 3–1 A schematic view of the clinical assessment process.

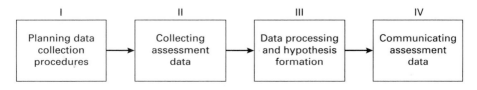

ables; it also shapes the answer to the second question.

The world view that has guided most clinical assessment in American psychology emphasizes variables that operate *within* or *immediately around* the individual being assessed. As we saw in Chapter 2, this orientation toward the individual takes many forms, which we described as *models*. Personality dynamics and traits, learning history and current environmental factors, interpersonal interactions, biological variables, as well as perceptions of self and reality are each accorded varying emphasis from one clinician to the next. However, regardless of specifics, modern clinical assessment seeks to learn things about people *by focusing on them directly, mainly through the use of interviews, tests, observations, and life records.*[1]

The notion that clinical assessment focuses on individuals through certain data sources provides the clinician with only the most general guidelines. The particulars of what to look for and what tools to use can still vary enormously and make the planning, organization, and implementation of an efficient and useful assessment strategy a challenging process.

To illustrate the problem, consider the sheer *number* of things that can be asked about a single person. The list might begin with age, sex, height, and weight, and go on endlessly to include bank balance, favorite food, and hat size. Assessment questions can also tap several interrelated *levels,* ranging from physiological functioning to relations with family and other social systems. The most common levels are listed in Box 3–1, along with a few examples of data associated with each.

The diversity of assessment data means that we can never learn all there is to know about

another person. Even if total knowledge were possible, it would not be a practical goal for the clinician. Exploring every level of assessment for a given client would turn up a lot of important information, but the process would be extremely expensive and time consuming. It would also reveal much that is trivial, redundant, or outdated.

Making Assessment Choices

The clinician must decide (a) how much attention should be devoted to each assessment level, (b) what questions to ask at each level, and (c) what assessment techniques to employ.

The theoretical model adopted by each clinician plays a major role in such choices. As noted in Chapter 2, the dynamically oriented methods favored by an orthodox Freudian will differ substantially from the functional-analytic techniques emphasized by a strict Skinnerian. Models lead clinicians to favor different types of data, look for information in different time periods, emphasize some kinds of tests over others, and resolve discrepancies between the data in alternative ways. A clinician's preferred theoretical model and his or her favorite assessment techniques are usually tightly linked. The clinician's familiarity with relevant research also shapes the assessment strategy. Studies of the relative value of interviews, tests, observations, and life records can be helpful guides which, along with research on the *reliability* and *validity* of these procedures, can make the clinician's planning task more empirically oriented.

These concepts are important enough to merit explanation. In fact, they are the primary criteria by which any assessment instrument should be judged. An *unreliable* or *invalid* assessment method is a poor foundation on which to base any clinical decision. *Reliability* refers to *consistency* in or *agreement* among assessment data. It can be evaluated in several ways. If the results of repeated measurements of the same client are very similar, the assess-

---

[1]Life records include various kinds of personal documents (e.g., diaries and letters), archival and "trace" data (e.g., college transcripts), and other environmental and achievement measures (e.g., honors or awards).

Assessment Level	Type of Data
1. Somatic	Blood type, RH factor, autonomic stress response pattern, kidney and liver function, genetic characteristics, basal metabolism, visual acuity, diseases
2. Physical	Height, weight, sex, eye color, hair color, body type
3. Demographic	Name, age, address, telephone number, occupation, education, income, marital status, number of children
4. Overt behavioral	Reading speed, eye–hand coordination, frequency of arguments with other people, conversational skill, interpersonal assertiveness, occupational competence, smoking habits
5. Cognitive/intellectual	Response to intelligence test items, reports on thoughts, performance on tests of information processing or cognitive complexity, response to tests of reality perception and structuring
6. Emotional/affective	Reports of feelings, responses to tests measuring mood states, physiological responsiveness
7. Environmental	Location and characteristics of housing; number and description of cohabitants; job requirements and characteristics; physical and behavioral characteristics of family, friends, and co-workers; nature of specific cultural or subcultural standards and traditions; general economic conditions; geographical location

BOX 3–1
Levels of Assessment and Some Representative Data From Each

ment procedures are said to have high *test–retest reliability*. Another way to evaluate reliability is to examine internal consistency. If one part of an assessment method provides evidence similar to that coming from other parts, the method is *internally consistent*. This dimension is sometimes called *split-half reliability*. Finally, if different clinicians come to the same conclusions after using a particular assessment system to diagnose, rate, or observe a particular client, that system is described as having high *interrater reliability*.

The *validity* of assessment methods reflects the degree to which they measure what they are supposed to measure. Like reliability, validity can be evaluated in several ways. For example, if an assessment device measures all aspects of its target, it is said to have high *content validity*. An intelligence test which measures only memory would be low on this dimension. If a test is capable of forecasting accurately something about a client (e.g., suicide attempts or college grades), that test has high *predictive validity*. When two assessment devices agree about the measurement of the same quality, they are said to have *concurrent validity*. Predictive and concurrent validity are subtypes of *criterion validity*, which is a measure of how strongly an assessment result correlates with external criteria of interest.

Finally, there is *construct validity* (Cronbach & Meehl, 1955). To oversimplify somewhat, an assessment has construct validity when its results are shown to be systematically related to the thing or construct it is supposed to be measuring. Construct validity is studied when a psychologist is interested in determining whether some measure yields results that a theory about an underlying trait indicates it should yield. For example, scores on a measure of anxiety should increase under circumstances thought to increase anxiety (e.g., facing major surgery). If no change occurs, the measure's construct validity would be suspect. A single observation of this type is too limited to establish construct validity; a more elaborate set of operations in a series of experiments is required (Campbell & Fiske, 1959).

To summarize the differences between reliability and validity, consider a situation in which 50 people use their eyes to assess the sex of a female impersonator. All 50 observers might agree that the person in question is a female, but they would all be wrong. Their observations would thus be *reliable* but *invalid* because they were not accurately measuring gender.

The concepts of reliability and validity have been integrated under a broader concept called *generalizability* (Cronbach, Gleser, Nanda, & Rajaratnam, 1972). Within this framework, an assessment instrument is evaluated in terms of how well its results generalize over certain conditions. Thus, instead of saying that a device has high test-retest reliability, one says that its data generalize over time. Generalizability theory and its use of analysis of variance procedures have played an increasingly important role in the evaluation of clinical assessment methods.

To return to the topic of planning, clinicians are influenced not only by the reliability and validity of available tools, but also by personal preferences and training experiences. A clinical psychologist may never administer a particular test simply because its use was not included in his or her graduate training program. Similarly, some clinicians rely on a specific assessment technique because their professors at graduate school were enthusiastic about it. Those who find certain measurement tactics tedious or unrewarding will seek answers to assessment questions through other procedures with which they are more comfortable.

As a result of these practices, some assessment methods continue to be used by clinicians despite their having inadequate reliability and validity.

The clinician's assessment strategy is further guided by what in electronic information theory has been called the "bandwidth-fidelity" problem (Shannon & Weaver, 1949). Just as greater bandwidth is associated with lower fidelity, the more extensively one explores a client's behavior, the less intensive each aspect of that exploration becomes. In an interview, for example, the clinician could spend 3 hours trying to cover an extensive outline, but the result would probably be superficial information about a wide range of topics. It works the other way, too. The interviewer could use the same 3 hours to explore the client's relationship with parents. At the end of the interview, a lot of detailed information would be available about one part of the client's life, but there might be few data about other parts. Cronbach and Gleser (1965) have referred to the *breadth* of an assessment device as its *bandwidth* and the *intensity* or exhaustiveness of the measure as its *fidelity*. Increasing the bandwidth of an assessment strategy will be accompanied by a decrease in fidelity, while increasing fidelity narrows the bandwidth.

A significant problem in assessment planning is to choose a package of measures that will allow both bandwidth and fidelity to be as high as possible. This choice is guided by the time and resources available and also by the goal of the assessment. Goals have an enormous impact on assessment planning. The questions, levels of inquiry, and techniques relevant for the problem of selecting business executives differ substantially from those regarding detection of brain damage in a 4-year-old child. Accordingly, the major assessment goals deserve some attention.

The Goals of Clinical Assessment

The specific aims of assessment can be placed in one of three general categories:

classification, description, and *prediction.* Each of these goals may be sought in assessment focused on one individual or as part of projects in which large groups of subjects are assessed.

1. Classification. After clinical psychologists began working with adults, they came under the influence of medical personnel, particularly psychiatrists. As a result, clinical psychologists' assessment skills were often used for diagnostic classification of psychiatric patients.[2] Accurate psychodiagnosis is important for several reasons. Proper treatment decisions may depend on the correct differentiation of one disorder from another. Research about the causes of psychological disorders requires accurate and reliable identification of these disorders. Finally, classification allows an efficient way for clinicians to talk about disorders, almost like a form of professional shorthand.

Clinicians' preoccupation with assessment for the purpose of diagnostic classification during the late 1930s and early 1940s was evident in their day-to-day work with clients and in the kind of research they conducted. During this period, numerous studies were designed to relate responses on instruments like the Rorschach inkblot test to certain diagnoses. Many clinical psychologists were not comfortable with this search for specific indicators (called *pathognomonic signs*) of clinical conditions, because they felt that it oversimplified assessment in ways that could result in errors (e.g., Klopfer & Kelley, 1942). Nevertheless, the goal of diagnostic classification was prominent in clinical research and practice during the 1940s and continues to be a reason why clinicians do assessment today, especially if they work in psychiatric or other medically oriented settings.

Although various systems for classifying mental disorders had been in use since the early 1900s, classification of mental disorders became more formalized when, in 1952, the American Psychiatric Association published its first official classification system, called the *Diagnostic and Statistical Manual of Mental Disorders.* The system, abbreviated *DSM,* provided a uniform nomenclature for mental health professionals to use in describing and diagnosing abnormal behavior.

Research conducted in the 1950s on the reliability and validity of psychiatric diagnoses raised serious concerns about the accuracy and meaning of *DSM* diagnostic labels as they were being applied. These studies suggested that labels had little effect on how different clients were treated and did not predict the course of disorders the way a valid classification should (Dailey, 1953; Little & Shneidman, 1959; Schmidt & Fonda, 1956; Ullmann & Hunrichs, 1958). This research showed the need for changes in the classification system.

Since its initial appearance in 1952, the *DSM* has been revised several times, but for the past 5 decades, some version of the *DSM* has been the standard format for classifying the realm of abnormal behavior. *DSM-II* was introduced in 1968 to make the *DSM* system more like the World Health Organization's International Classification of Diseases.

DSM-II stayed in use until 1980, when *DSM-III* was published. In 1987, a revised form (*DSM-III-R*) was released to eliminate some inconsistencies and weaknesses in *DSM-III's* criteria that had become apparent through research and clinical experience with the system.

Some of the problems *DSM-III* and *DSM-III-R* were designed to correct included the lack of a uniform, organizing principle for assigning diagnoses; vague definitions of many disorders, which lowered the reliability and validity of their use; and a general failure to consider such background factors as medical problems and psychosocial stress that could affect mental disorders. Three of the most important

---

[2]This is also called *psychodiagnosis, differential diagnosis,* or *diagnostic labeling.*

changes in the *DSM,* each a response to these problems, are summarized next.

1. *DSM-III-R* diagnoses were made by referring to specific, clearly defined criteria, some combination of which must be present for the disorder to be classified. This use of *operational criteria* was intended to improve the reliability and validity of diagnoses, and there is evidence that this aim was accomplished to some extent (American Psychiatric Association, 1980; Grove, 1987). The operational criteria make use of what is called a *polythetic* approach. With a polythetic system, a person can be diagnosed as having a disorder if she or he meets a preestablished number of criteria out of a larger set of criterion items (e.g., symptoms). In other words, not every criterion, or even the same list of criterion items, is necessary for a specific diagnosis to be made. Polythetic diagnoses often result in the same diagnosis being given to patients with similar, but not identical, sets of criterion symptoms. Use of a polythetic system will produce the same diagnosis for patients that resemble each other (somewhat like the physical similarity of relatives within a family), but who are not identical in their manifestation of the disorder.

2. *DSM-III-R* was formulated in a *descriptive* as opposed to a theoretical or etiological manner. By avoiding theoretical assumptions about disorders, *DSM-III-R* was designed to eliminate many of the disagreements that arise between clinicians holding different views of the causes of pathology.

3. Another advantage of *DSM-III-R* was its *multiaxial classification.* This scheme allows the client to be described along five dimensions, or *axes,* which are intended to provide a more complete picture of the client's life, inform clinicians about factors that could affect the disorder, suggest what kind of treatment might be most successful, and serve as a basis for additional research about the nature of mental disorders.

Axis 1 contained the major mental disorders, organized into 16 groupings. Included on this axis were schizophrenia, mood disorders (including depression and bipolar disorder in which depressed and manic episodes both occur), anxiety disorders, organic mental disorders, and psychological problems typical of infancy, childhood, and adolescence.

On Axis II, two other categories of disorder, developmental problems and personality disorders, were listed. These difficulties develop early in life and continue relatively unchanged into adulthood. They were placed on a separate axis to ensure that they are not overlooked when an Axis 1 disorder is also present.

Axis III classified any physical disorder or condition that might be relevant to understanding a person's mental disorder. Axis IV provided a scale (from 1 to 6) on which the clinician can rate the severity of psychosocial stressors the person suffered in the past year that may have contributed to an Axis I or II disorder in some way. Axis V was a scale, ranging from 1 to 90, on which the clinician rated the person's psychological, social, and occupational functioning.

Despite improvement over earlier versions, *DSM-III* and *DSM-III-R* were criticized on several grounds, including the fact that diagnostic criteria were still vaguely defined, that Axes II, IV, and V had measurement deficiencies, that too little emphasis was placed on the construct validity of diagnoses, and that biases were still present in the criteria (for extensive criticisms of *DSM-III* and *DSM-III-R,* see Bellack & Hersen, 1988; Kaplan, 1983; Last & Hersen, 1987; McReynolds, 1989; Millon & Klerman, 1986; Nathan, 1987; Vaillant, 1984).

Partly in response to these criticisms, 1 year after the publication of *DSM-III-R,* the American Psychiatric Association established a task force to begin to develop *DSM-IV.* Several factors spurred the rush to begin work on the new classification system. First, the World Health Organization (WHO) was set to publish the 10th edition of its *International Classification of Diseases (ICD-10)* in 1993. Because the United States is under treaty obligation to maintain classification systems consistent with those of the WHO, it was desirable to proceed promptly with development of *DSM-IV* (Frances, Widiger, & Pincus, 1989). Though the drafting of *DSM-IV* was coordinated with work on *ICD-10,* several differences in the two systems persist, both in terms of specific diagnostic criteria and overall orientation.

The second impetus for *DSM-IV* was the intention to increase the empirical foundation of diagnostic practices. Although both *DSM-III* and *DSM-III-R* were designed to reflect available research, this goal was not well achieved, partly because, prior to *DSM-III,* few adequate diagnostic studies had been conducted. Further, no specific guidelines were given on how to translate research findings into specific diagnostic criteria. This deficiency produced final decisions that often reflected experts' best clinical judgments rather than available empirical findings (Widiger, Frances, Pincus, Davis, & First, 1991). Finally, neither *DSM-III* nor *DSM-III-R* documented the rationale or the empirical support for the diagnostic criteria they established. Thus, it was difficult to evaluate critically the decisions reflected in those classification systems.

DSM-IV was designed to rectify these problems. Thirteen different work groups followed a three-step plan to study various disorders and how best to diagnose them (Widiger et al., 1991). First, each group was to review all the clinical and empirical literature relevant to a given disorder in order to guide initial suggestions for changes in the diagnosis of that disorder. Second, the groups were to obtain and analyze relevant but unpublished data sets that might shed light on the effects of using different diagnostic criteria. Finally, focused *field trials* were to be conducted to resolve specific diagnostic controversies. (In general, a field trial is a research project conducted in the natural environment that examines questions about a disorder as clinicians encounter it; in

this case, the questions concern the reliability and utility of diagnoses made by different clinicians.) To increase the likelihood of reaching final decisions that were unbiased by the preconceptions of any one expert, the decisions of each work group were reviewed by as many as 100 outside advisers. These reviews were made possible by the publication of *source materials* that documented the decision making by each work group. They contained abbreviated versions of the specific procedures used by each group so that individuals outside of the formal *DSM-IV* process could critically review the groups' final decisions (Frances et al., 1989).

Box 3–2 summarizes the basic categories of disorder in *DSM-IV* and illustrates how a diagnosis of a client would look.

Like its predecessors, *DSM-IV* has been criticized. As soon as work began on *DSM-IV,* some charged that it was premature to be revising a classification system that had been in use for only 1 year. When *DSM-III-R* was published in 1987, research studies aimed at validating the diagnostic categories had been started. Revising the criteria so soon thereafter would render these ongoing studies obsolete.

Other criticisms of *DSM-IV* concern the process by which it was derived, as well as the basic philosophy behind it. For example, despite the intention to rely strictly on research findings when making decisions, expert consensus on some matters will still be necessary because empirical justification is simply not available for many decisions (Spitzer, 1991). Some psychologists object to the disease model of psychopathology that underlies *DSM-IV* and its implication that disorders are either present or absent (Carson, 1991; Millon, 1991).

Psychological disorders are heterogeneous in nature, and they are present in varying degrees. In contrast, the *DSM* systems involve all-or-none decisions: If individuals meet a certain number of criteria, they have the disorder; while if they do not reach the cutoff they do not have the disorder. *DSM-IV* developers an-

DSM-IV retains the basic multiaxial system of classification and diagnosis first introduced in *DSM-III*, with some modifications in the earlier terminology and rating schemes used on the various axes.

Axis I contains the major mental disorders, organized under 16 major categories. The following categories are listed:

A. Disorders Usually First Diagnosed in Infancy, Childhood, or Adolescence

B. Delirium, Dementia, Amnestic and Other Cognitive Disorders

C. Mental Disorders Due to a General Medical Condition

D. Substance-Related Disorders

E. Schizophrenia and Other Psychotic Disorders

F. Mood Disorders

G. Anxiety Disorders

H. Somatoform Disorders

I. Factitious Disorders

J. Dissociative Disorders

K. Eating Disorders

L. Sexual Disorders

M. Sleep Disorders

N. Impulse Control Disorders Not Elsewhere Classified

O. Adjustment Disorders

P. Other Clinically Significant Conditions.

DSM-IV also retains the polythetic approach of its predecessors; a person is diagnosed with an Axis I mental disorder by meeting a preset number of criteria out of a larger set of possible criterion symptoms.

For example, a person would be diagnosed with schizophrenia by displaying

A. Any two of these five symptoms (delusions, hallucinations, disorganized speech, grossly disorganized or catatonic behavior, and negative symptoms such as flat emotions or extreme apathy) for at least a 1-month period

B. A marked deterioration in a major area of functioning such as work, interpersonal relations, or self-care

C. Continuous signs of disturbance for at least 6 months, including 1 month in which the symptoms in Criterion A are present

D. A ruling out of other conditions that might account for the aforementioned criteria.

In addition, schizophrenia would also be diagnosed as continuous, occurring in episodes, or as in remission. It would also be classified into one of five subtypes (paranoid type, disorganized type, catatonic type, undifferentiated type, or residual type), depending upon which of the Criterion A symptoms were most prominent.

Additional classification and description of the person would involve making appropriate decisions regarding the information relevant to Axes II, III, IV, and V.

Axis II now contains one category: Personality Disorders, of which there are 10 different examples.

Axes III, IV, and V contain, respectively, a description of physical conditions the person may be experiencing, the amount of stress encountered, and the level of overall functioning achieved by the person.

BOX 3–2

Classification of Mental Disorder Using *DSM-IV*

swer this criticism by pointing out that the criteria are merely guidelines for clinicians to use as they decide whether or how to diagnose a disorder (Frances et al., 1991).

Finally, Carson (1991) raises the surprising argument that too much attention has been devoted to issues of diagnostic reliability, at the expense of diagnostic validity. He suggests that the diagnostic criteria have been simplified to ensure good interrater agreement among clinicians but that because of this simplification the true nature of disorders has been lost or distorted. Clinicians may now be able to agree on diagnoses, but their diagnoses may not adequately reflect the core features or implications of a disorder.

Indeed, the practice of classification is probably doomed to a life of controversy. On the one hand, it should accurately reflect the reality of the phenomena it is intended to describe. On the other hand, it attempts to provide a simplified, shorthand version of reality that helps guide clinical decisions. These two goals are often at odds. As almost any type of classification system illustrates, the more one goal is accomplished, the less the other one is served.

2. Description. As clinical psychology developed a postwar identity independent of psychiatry, changes in assessment goals began to appear. Blind administration and interpretation of a few popular psychological tests to diagnose clients became increasingly distasteful to clinicians who were interested in conducting broader assessments that produced a fuller understanding and more elaborate description of the client (see Thorne, 1948; Watson, 1951).[3]

The desire to go beyond diagnosis to seek a wider view was based partly on clinical psychology's burgeoning self-confidence, but it was also due to the conviction that people cannot be understood simply on the basis of an interview or a Rorschach test. In addition, interest in the content of behavior was supplemented by a concern for its social, cultural, and physical context. The result was a movement by clinical psychologists toward assessment that described *person–environment interactions* and that concentrated on a full description of an individual's personality. This movement got its impetus in the 1930s and 1940s from the pioneering work of Henry Murray at the Harvard Psychological Clinic and David Rapaport at the Menninger Clinic. These men and their colleagues developed extensive batteries of interviews, tests, and observations designed to comprehensively assess "normal" people as well as those with psychological problems (Murray, 1938; Rapaport, Gill, & Schafer, 1945, 1946) and to take into account the external situational context of behavior as well as its internal determinants (Wiggins, 1973).

The desirability of description as opposed to classification as an assessment goal was increased by the disturbing results of the research conducted on the accuracy and meaning of diagnostic systems described in the previous section. Further, acceptance of the medical/psychodynamic model on which diagnosis was based began to wane in the 1960s as alternative theoretical models gained strength and as the stigma associated with being labeled was more clearly recognized (Goffman, 1961; Laing, 1967; Scheff, 1966; Szasz, 1960).

The rise of descriptive assessment prompted many clinicians to approach classification in less psychiatric ways. The result was proposals for classification systems that assign individuals to descriptive categories on the basis of factors such as motivation, intrapsychic functions, openness to therapy, test responses, potential for mental health, conditionability,

---

[3]Clinical psychologists were not alone in their recognition of the limited value of diagnostic labels. Adolf Meyer, one of America's most prominent psychiatrists of the early 20th century, is reported to have remarked, "We understand this case; we don't need any diagnosis" (Watson, 1951, p. 22).

subjective experience, relationship patterns, needs, functional relationships between behavior and the environment, behavioral excesses and deficits, and other factors (see Adams, Doster, & Calhoun, 1977; Borofsky, 1974; Goldfried & Davison, 1976; Mahrer, 1970; McLemore & Benjamin, 1979; and Tryon, 1976, for examples). Another alternative is to rate persons on various dimensions of personality (Widiger, Trull, Hurt, Clarkin, & Frances, 1987) or symptoms (Lorr, 1986) rather than assign them to any specific category. In dimensional approaches, a person receives scores on several dimensions which, taken together, produce a profile that describes the person's standing on the different dimensions. With categorical systems, like *DSM-IV,* the person is assigned to one or more categories that are considered qualitatively different from one another (McReynolds, 1989; Millon, 1987b).

Although the multiaxial system of *DSM-III* was a step toward a more descriptive approach, the overall logic of *DSM* classification has remained categorical despite clinical experience showing that mental disorders are not arranged nearly as neatly as *DSM* systems suggest (Carson, 1991). The categorical approach has been retained for at least three reasons: (a) The medical tradition from which it developed emphasizes discrete diseases, (b) categorical models are usually easier to use clinically, and (c) theorists have been unable to agree on the number of dimensions necessary to describe psychopathology adequately (Millon, 1991).

Description-oriented assessment makes it easier for the clinician to pay attention to clients' assets and adaptive functions as well as to weaknesses and problems. Descriptive assessment data are used to provide pretreatment measures of clients' behavior, to guide treatment planning, and to evaluate changes in behavior after treatment. They also are of value in research in clinical psychology. For example, in an investigation of the relative value of two treatments for depression, assessments that *describe* clients' posttreatment behaviors (e.g., job absenteeism, time spent alone, self-reports of sadness, and scores on tests of depression) would be of greater value than those that concentrate on labeling the clients (e.g., depressive versus nondepressive).

Despite the advantages of descriptive assessment, current practice, especially in inpatient psychiatric settings, is once again forcing clinicians to focus their assessments on classification (Sweeney, Clarkin, & Fitzgibbon, 1987). Skyrocketing health care costs have increased pressures to limit hospital stays by concentrating on short-term treatments. A thorough battery-based evaluation of a patient is time consuming and many of the data obtained are not structured for the purposes of diagnosis or treatment planning. Therefore, clinicians are currently being shaped into limiting their assessment to initial screening of patients, rapid measurement of symptoms, and differential diagnosis of disorders for treatment planning. These emphases have stimulated several other trends including increased use of computerized testing and structured interviews (see Chapters 4 and 5).

3. Prediction. The third goal of clinical assessment is to make predictions about human behavior. Will client X attempt suicide? Is client Y going to harm others if released from an institution? Questions of this kind constitute a severe test of clinical assessment, both because accurate prediction of what a given individual will do is extremely difficult and because the consequences of error can be socially and personally disastrous (see Box 3–3).

Prediction may be concerned with dangerous behavior, as described in Box 3–3, or may be aimed at less dramatic tasks involving selection of individuals who must meet some future performance standard. Instruments such as the Scholastic Aptitude Test (SAT) and the Graduate Record Examination (GRE) provide familiar examples of predictive assessment. Similar approaches have been adopted by business, industry, and the military to guide selection of their personnel.

The assessment goals of description and

The bottom-line question for clinical predictions is, "How accurate are they?" An answer to this question requires that clinicians or researchers keep track of the predictions they make for a group of people and later check the outcome for each person to see if the prediction was a hit or a miss.

Psychologists are often called on to predict two types of dangerous behavior of great societal concern—suicide and homicide. The question frequently takes the form, "Is this person a danger to himself or to others?" If clinicians are forced to make a yes or no reply (as they often are) and if we dichotomize the ultimate outcome for the person into "behaved dangerously–did not behave dangerously," then there are four possible results for the prediction. Take the example of predicting behavior dangerous to others. The clinician can predict the person will act dangerously and he or she does so (this is a *true positive*), or the clinician can predict the person won't act dangerously and he or she does not do so (*true negative*). The probability that a dangerous person is accurately predicted to be dangerous by a clinician is called the *sensitivity* of prediction, while the probability that a nondangerous person is accurately predicted to be nondangerous is called the *specificity* of prediction. If the clinician predicts the person won't act dangerously but he or she does so, a *false negative* has been committed; when the clinician predicts dangerous behavior will occur but the person commits no dangerous act, a *false positive* has been made.

Psychologists find it difficult to predict future dangerous behavior very accurately (Monahan, 1984, 1988). One reason for this problem is that the *base rate* or frequency with which dangerous acts are committed in any group of people is very low. When base rates for a behavior are either very low or

very high, prediction of that behavior will involve many errors (Meehl & Rosen, 1955). The following example shows why this is so.

Assume that a clinician is 80% accurate in predicting homicidal behavior. Further assume that the base rate for homicide in the population the clinician examines is 10 murders per 10,000 persons. As indicated in the table below, the clinician would correctly predict 8 of the 10 murders. However, these 8 true positives would be distributed among 1,998 false positives where the clinician incorrectly predicted a homicide would occur. Thus, of the 2,006 persons predicted to be homicidal, fewer than 1% would be correctly classified. The clinician's *positive predictive power* would be woefully low. However, the accuracy of predictions of nondangerousness, called *negative predictive power,* would be greater than 99.9%. Finally, if the clinician went with the low base rate and predicted that no one would commit a homicide, he or she would be 99.9% correct. However, all the errors would be false negatives, and society usually believes this type of mistake (i.e., murderers predicted to be safe) to be more serious than false positives. When base rates are closer to 50-50 for a behavior's occurence, clinical predictions have a better chance of improving over predictions founded solely on the base rate.

CLINICIAN'S PREDICTION	ULTIMATE OUTCOME	
	Homicide	*No Homicide*
Homicide	8 (True positives)	1,998 (False positives)
No homicide	2 (False negatives)	7,992 (True negatives)

BOX 3–3
Measuring the Accuracy of Clinical Predictions

prediction show their greatest overlap with respect to selection. Descriptive assessment data constitute part of the information from which predictions and selections are made. A classic example was Henry Murray's descriptive assessment approach (a combination of specialized tests, interviews, and observations) to select men for work as spies, saboteurs, and other behind-enemy-lines work during World War II (Office of Strategic Services, 1948). Along with a staff of other psychologists, Murray set up a comprehensive assessment program that took each man from 1 to 3 days to complete and measured everything from intelligence to ability at planning murder (see Chapter 6).

This hybrid goal of description for prediction for selection has continued in a variety of large-scale postwar screening programs. Some of these were focused on improving candidate selection for civilian and military jobs (Institute of Personality Assessment and Research, 1970) or for graduate training in clinical psychology and psychiatry (Holt & Luborsky, 1958; Kelly & Fiske, 1951), but perhaps the best-known descendant of the approach was the elaborate program for selecting Peace Corps volunteers (Colmen, Kaplan, & Boulger, 1964). Because these assessment programs influence socially important decisions affecting large numbers of people, they must be evaluated not only for their predictive validity, but also for their impact on the persons assessed and on the organizations in which they are used. One must be concerned with (a) the number of correct selections prompted by particular assessment procedures; (b) the cost of correct decisions in terms of money, time, and effort; and (c) the costs of selection errors (choosing inappropriate candidates or rejecting appropriate ones).

The Case Study Guide

The clinician's choice of particular questions and inquiry levels provides an outline of the assessment task's scope. Ideally, this outline is broad enough to give a general picture of the client on the basis of information from each of the levels listed in Box 3–1 and focused enough to allow intensive coverage of levels and questions relevant to the specific purpose of assessment.

The conceptual outline for a clinician's assessment task sometimes takes the form of a *case study guide*. The idea for such an outline comes to psychology from medicine and psychiatry (Bolgar, 1965), but it has been adopted as a means of organizing assessment by many clinicians. A major advantage of the case study approach is flexibility. Case study outlines can be tied to a theoretical model, or they can be open and eclectic.

One of the most comprehensive and theoretically neutral examples of a case study outline was composed by Sundberg, Taplin, and Tyler (1983). It is organized for interview procedures with adults, but much of the information could also apply to children and could be obtained through life records, tests, or observation. This outline is presented in Box 3–4. Although sufficiently problem oriented to be used in settings where persons are seeking psychological help, it also allows the assessor to consider broader and less problematic aspects of a client's life.

When case study guides are tied to a theoretical model, the clinician pursues different themes consistent with the model's main emphases. For example, psychodynamically oriented outlines (Korchin, 1976) include questions about unconscious motives and fantasies, ego functions, early developmental periods, and character structure. Behavioral case study outlines (Kanfer & Saslow, 1969) focus on the relationships between behaviors, the stimulus conditions that precede them, and the environmental-social consequences that follow them. Phenomenologically oriented clinicians are less likely to follow a set assessment outline; however, their practice of assessment is a collaborative process in which they seek to understand with the client how the client is "coauthoring" or perceiving "his or her environment, neurophysiology, culture,

1. *Identifying data,* including name, sex, occupation, income (of self or family), marital status, address, date and place of birth, religion, education, cultural identity.

2. *Reason for coming* to the agency, expectations for service.

3. *Present and recent situation,* including dwelling place, principal settings, daily round of activities, number and kind of life changes over several months, impending changes.

4. *Family constellation* (family of orientation) including descriptions of parents, siblings, other significant family figures, and respondent's role growing up.

5. *Early recollections,* descriptions of earliest clear happenings and the situation surrounding them.

6. *Birth and development,* including age of walking and talking, problems compared with other children, view of effects of early experiences.

7. *Health and physical condition,* including childhood and later diseases and injuries, current prescribed medications, current use of unprescribed drugs, cigarettes, or alcohol, comparison of own body with others, habits of eating and exercising.

8. *Education and training,* including subjects of special interest and achievement, out-of-school learning, areas of difficulty and pride, any cultural problems.

9. *Work record,* including reasons for changing jobs, attitudes toward work.

10. *Recreation, interests, and pleasures,* including volunteer work, reading, respondent's view of adequacy of self-expression and pleasures.

11. *Sexual development,* covering first awareness, kinds of sexual activities, and a view of adequacy of current sexual expressions.

12. *Marital and family data,* covering major events and what led to them, and comparison of present family with family of origin, ethnic or cultural factors.

13. *Social supports, communication network, and social interests,* including people talked with most frequently, people available for various kinds of help, amount and quality of interactions, sense of contribution to others and interest in community.

14. *Self-description,* including strengths, weaknesses, ability to use imagery, creativity, values, and ideals.

15. *Choices and turning points in life,* a review of the respondent's most important decisions and changes, including the single most important happening.

16. *Personal goals and view of the future,* including what the subject would like to see happen next year and in 5 or 10 years, and what is necessary for these events to happen, realism in time orientation, ability to set priorities.

17. Any further material the respondent may see as omitted from the history.

(From N. D. Sundberg, 1977, *Assessment of Persons,* pp. 97–98. Reprinted by permission of Prentice-Hall, Inc., Englewood Cliffs, New Jersey.)

BOX 3–4
Outline for a Case History Interview

community, and other persons" (Fischer, 1989).

Collecting Assessment Data

So far we have looked at ways clinicians answer the first of the primary assessment questions raised by McReynolds (1975): "What do we want to know?" Next we consider his second question: "How should we go about learning it?"

Sources of Assessment Data

Clinical psychologists collect assessment data from four sources: interviews, tests, observations, and life records. In this section we highlight the characteristics of these techniques and note the problems of each. These sketches preview the more detailed coverage of interviews, tests, and observations in the next three chapters.

1. Interviews. Kelly (1958, p. 330) succinctly characterized a straightforward approach to assessment: "If you don't know what is going on in a person's mind, ask him; he may tell you." This point explains why the interview is the most basic and widely employed source of psychological assessment data. It is popular for other reasons as well. Since the clinician talks with the client in a situation that mimics ordinary social interaction, interviews provide a way of collecting simultaneous samples of a person's verbal and nonverbal behavior. Second, the procedure can take place almost anywhere. Third, there is no more flexible assessment tool than the interview. Except in cases where research limitations prevail, the interviewer is free to adjust the inquiry and conversation to those issues that appear most important.

What about the quality of data collected through interviews? Peterson (1968, p. 13) comments that "the interview . . . must not be

regarded as the 'truth' about the individual and his environment, but as another form of data whose reliability, validity, and decisional utility must be subjected to the same kinds of scrutiny required for other modes of data collection." It may be distorted by (a) characteristics of interviewers and the questions they ask, (b) client characteristics such as memory and willingness to disclose accurate information, and (c) circumstances under which the interview takes place. The interview will be discussed in greater detail in Chapter 4.

2. Tests. Like interviews, tests provide a sample of behavior. However, the stimuli to which the client responds on a test are more standardized than in most interviews. A test exposes each client to the same stimuli under the same circumstances. Tests can be easy, economical, and convenient to administer; often, a professional need not even be present. Further, the standardized form of a test helps eliminate bias in the assessor's inquiries. Responses to most tests can be translated into scores, thus making quantitative summaries of a client's behavior possible.[4] In this way, test data facilitate communication between professionals about a client. Finally, test data allow the clinician to compare a client's behavior with that of hundreds or perhaps thousands of other individuals who have already taken the same test. The use of these reference scores, or *norms,* allows the clinician to compute percentile scores or standard scores which help establish a frame of reference for interpreting the meaning of a test score.

Assume, for instance, that on a word association test the first thing that pops into a client's mind when the tester says *house* is *pantyhose.* If the assessor had never head this association before, she might interpret it as in-

---

[4]Certain aspects of interview and observational data can be handled in this way as well, but may involve more cumbersome procedures.

dicative of some psychological problem. But if the tester has access to a book containing the associations of 12,000 subjects to the word *house,* it may turn out that *pantyhose* is a fairly popular response (it is not, by the way) and thus not worthy of concern.

All these advantages, along with the fact that for many years testing was the main activity for clinical psychologists, have led to the widespread use of tests as assessment devices.

Tests are not magical devices that always reveal the "truth" about people. They must be evaluated in terms of reliability and validity; like other assessment techniques, they are sometimes found wanting in important respects. Anything that is not standard about test stimuli, including the tester, the client, or the testing situation, can threaten the psychometric quality of the data obtained. These and other evaluative issues will be dealt with in Chapter 5.

3. Observations. The old adage "Actions speak louder than words" supports the clinician's desire to supplement interviews or tests with direct observation of a person's behavior in situations of interest. The goal here is to go beyond what a client *says* and find out what the person *does.* A notable example of how observational data can alter the impression left by self-report was given by Wicker (1969, p. 42; see also Dillehay, 1973).

In the 1930s when, according to studies of social distance, there was much anti-Chinese sentiment in the United States, LaPiere (1934) took several extensive automobile trips with a Chinese couple. Unknown to his companions, he took notes of how the travellers were treated, and he kept a list of hotels and restaurants where they were served. Only once were they denied service, and LaPiere judged their treatment to be above average in 40% of the restaurants visited. Later, LaPiere wrote to the 250 hotels and restaurants on his list, ask-

ing if they would accept Chinese guests. Over 90% of the 128 proprietors responding indicated they would not serve Chinese, in spite of the fact that all had previously accommodated LaPiere's companions.

Here, observational data provided different and perhaps more accurate views of the question of anti-Chinese prejudice than did the self-reports. Observation is considered by many to be the most valid form of clinical assessment because it is so direct and capable of circumventing problems of memory, motivation, response style, and situational bias that can reduce the value of interviews and tests. A smoker's self-report that five cigarettes were smoked in 1 day may be biased by ability to recall, a desire to appear moderate, or feelings about the assessor. An actual count of smoking frequency recorded by an observer would reflect none of these factors.

A second advantage of observation is its *relevance* to behaviors of greatest interest. A child's aggressiveness, for example, can be observed as it occurs in recess, where the problem has been most acute. This illustrates a related benefit of observation: Behavior is assessed in its social and situational context rather than in the abstract. In a mental hospital, observation of a long-term resident may reveal that the patient acts depressed only after meals. This information may be more valuable to a therapist than an affirmative response to the query, "Are you ever depressed?"

Finally, observations allow for description of behavior in specific terms and in great detail. For example, a person's sexual arousal in response to particular stimuli might be defined in terms of penile volume or vaginal blood flow, both of which can be measured with specially designed apparatus. Similarly, psychotic behavior can be observed by recording the frequency of explicitly defined behaviors such as "strikes own body," "speaks incoherently," or "kisses water fountain."

In spite of its advantages, observational assessment is not problem free. The degree to which one can rely on information from this source varies considerably, since the reliability and validity of observational data can be threatened by observer error or bias , inadvertent observer influence on the behavior under observation, and specific situational factors. These problems will be discussed in Chapter 6.

4. Life Records. As people pass through life, they leave a trail of behavior in many forms, including school, work, police, and medical records; credit ratings; letters; photographs; awards; income tax returns; diaries; and creative products like paintings or sculpture. Much can be learned about a person through such life records, and because this approach to assessment does not require the client to make any *new* responses (as do interviews, tests, and observations), there is little chance that memory, motivation, response style, or situational factors can distort the data obtained. Thus, a 10-minute review of a person's high school transcript may provide more specific and accurate academic information than a 30-minute interview asking questions like "How did you do in school?" Similarly, reading diaries written during significant periods in a client's life can reveal on-the-spot feelings, ideas, behaviors, and situational details that might be lost or distorted by imperfect recall.

Life records provide an inexpensive way of broadening one's working image of a client. They can summarize a great deal about a person's behavior over a long period of time and across a range of situations. Life records act like a wide-angle camera lens by bringing into view that which might otherwise be missed. Wide-angle lenses produce distortion, however; records can do the same. For one thing, they tend to be superficial. Records may show that a person was divorced at age 18, but say nothing of why or how the person felt about it. Records may be valuable, but are not usually complete. These and other shortcomings will be discussed in Chapter 6.

The Value of Multiple Assessment Sources

Clinical psychologists seldom rely on a single source of assessment data for their working image of a client, partly because there is a multiplicity of data available within each of the four assessment sources we have described. For example, it is virtually impossible not to observe a person's behavior in the course of an interview or a testing session; interview data may emerge as a client responds to written tests.

The availability of multiple channels of assessment provides distinct advantages for the clinician. To begin with, lies or distortions of fact can be cross-checked. The interviewer who is told by a mental hospital resident that he or she has been there "about 6 months" may discover via hospital records that the correct figure is 20 years. Indeed, the whole story of a client's problems is not clear until multiple assessment has been completed. Nietzel and Bernstein (1976) showed that college students who described themselves as socially unassertive were capable of strong assertive responses under the right conditions. In such cases, multiple assessment helps separate those individuals who *cannot* engage in certain behaviors from those who *do not* engage in them.

Another benefit of multiple assessment appears when the clinician evaluates the effects of a psychological intervention. Suppose a married couple comes to a therapist because they are considering divorce. If "marital happiness" based on interview data were the only measure employed, the couple's divorce following 3 months of clinical sessions would indicate that the marital problem was worsened by treatment. Other assessments, including observations, third-person reports, and life records might show, however, that one or both members of the former couple find their divorced status liberating as they begin to develop new interests and abilities. These satisfactions might not be reported to the therapist in an interview because the clients feel guilt over divorce, because fear of the future seems to be a more appropriate topic for a clinical session, or for other reasons.

Of course, multiple assessment can reveal the opposite situation as well. After a therapist helps a young man to stand up for his rights, he may report improved self-esteem and comfort in social situations. These interview data might not reveal the fact that the client has now become aggressive in his relations with others and that, in the long run, he is likely to suffer socially. Future social problems could be avoided by detecting inappropriate behavior through observational assessment.

Processing Assessment Data

Once assessment data have been collected, the clinician must determine what they mean. If the information is to be useful in reaching the goals of assessment, it will have to be transformed from raw form into interpretations and conclusions. For example, knowing that a young child cries at high intensities for precise lengths of time each evening when placed in its crib constitutes valuable assessment data. So does the observation that after the crying continues for varying periods, someone enters the baby's room to provide comfort. However, these data mean little in psychological terms until the clinician translates them into meaningful statements about the infant's behavior and interprets what psychological processes are involved. This crucial part of assessment is often referred to as data *processing* or *clinical judgment.* As Levy (1963, p. 8) put it: "Events . . . do not carry with them their own interpretation. They are innocent of any meaning except insofar as we impose it on them."

The processing task is formidable because a degree of *inference* is involved, and inference requires a leap from known data to what is assumed on the basis of those data. In general, as the jump from data to assumption gets longer, inference becomes more vulnerable to error.

Consider this: A young boy is observed sitting on a lawn, playing with an earthworm. At one point, he cuts the worm in half. It would be easy to infer from this incident that the child was cruel and aggressive and that more serious forms of aggression, perhaps toward other people, will appear in later life. These inferences would be off the mark, however, for "what the observer could not see . . . was what the boy—who happened to have few friends—thought as he cut the worm in half: 'There! Now you will have someone to play with'" (Goldfried & Sprafkin, 1974, p. 305).

Elaborate inference, especially when based on minimal data, can be dangerous. The only way to eliminate inference error is to eliminate inference, but doing so would also eliminate the meaning of most assessment data. Indeed, it may be impossible for human beings to avoid inferences, even in relation to the simplest stimuli. For example, the raw data of Figure 3–2 are a series of rectangles that gradually increase in size and angle on the page, and are displaced to the left as one looks from bottom to top. However, it is difficult to avoid *inferring* that the stack is about to fall over, or that the smallest box is about to be crushed.

The main questions about assessment data processing do not include *whether* inferences will be drawn, but center around what *kinds* of inferences to make, *how* clinicians go about making them, how *accurate* they are, and how inference error can be minimized.

Levels and Types of Clinical Inference

Clinical judgment or inferences can be characterized in terms of their *goals,* their underlying *models,* and their *levels of abstraction.* Remember, the goals of assessment in-

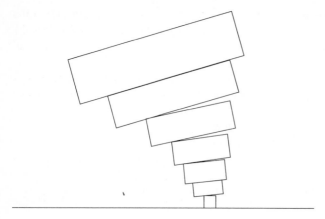

FIGURE 3–2 Can you look at this drawing without inferring anything about it?

clude classification ("the client suffers from an anxiety disorder"), description ("his symptoms worsen in the presence of women"), and prediction ("he will benefit from cognitive behavior therapy"). Inferences also tend to be tied to the assessor's model of clinical psychology. Learning that a client had attempted suicide would lead a behavioral clinician to the judgment that the client was reacting to a loss of reinforcers; a psychoanalyst might infer that the suicide attempt pointed to a conflicted identification with a parent who had abandoned the client at an early age; a phenomenological clinician would judge the suicide attempt to reflect the demoralization of a person whose tried-and-true assumptions about life no longer made sense. Finally, inferences vary in their level of abstraction. Clinicians can make cautious, low-level inferences that do not stray far from the original data or can attempt bolder statements that go beyond the hard data available but are supported by the assessor's experience, theoretical model, and intuitive hunches.

At the lowest inference level, assessment data are taken at face value, as when a test score determines whether a student is admitted to graduate school. At higher inference levels, assessment data are generalized beyond their original limits. Thus, behavior revealed through tests, interviews, observations, and records is thought to be characteristic of the person and may be used as the basis for applying trait terms like *anxious, depressed, hostile,* and *charming.*

At the highest inference level, assessment data are processed to form an overall picture of the client. Ideally, the whole story of the person is reconstructed, and the client's problems are viewed in light of this panorama. This level of clinical judgment ventures furthest from the original data, so the clinician depends on experience and a theoretical model to guide the statements and predictions that are made.

Three Views of Assessment Data

Clinicians tend to view assessment information in three main ways: as *samples, correlates,* or *signs* (Goodenough, 1949; Wiggins, 1973). Consider the following raw assessment data: "A person took 16 sleeping pills before going to bed at a hotel last night, but was saved after being discovered by a housekeeper and rushed to a hospital."

How can this event be viewed and what inferences would follow from each perspective? The incident could be seen as a *sample* of the client's behavior and the following judgments might result:

1. The client has access to potentially lethal medication.

2. The client did not wish to be saved because

no one knew about the suicide attempt before it occurred.

3. Under similar circumstances, the client may attempt suicide again.

Notice that looking at the client's behavior as a sample results in low-level inferences. The pill taking is seen as an *example* of what the client is capable of doing under certain circumstances. No attempt is made to infer *why* the individual tried suicide; more assessment would be required before specific causal statements would be justified.

The same incident could be viewed as a *correlate* of other aspects of the client's life. Even though no further information is available about the client, knowledge gained from similar cases might guide inferences of the following type:

1. The client is likely to be a middle-aged female who is single or divorced and lives alone (this is a common set of characteristics among attempted suicides).

2. The client is or has recently been depressed.

3. The client has little emotional support from family or friends.

Here, higher-level inferences are based on a combination of (a) known facts about the client's behavior, and (b) the clinician's knowledge of what tends to correlate with that behavior. These inferences go beyond the original data with the support of empirically demonstrated relationships among variables such as suicide, age, sex, marital status, and depression. In general, the stronger the known relationships between variables, the more accurate the inferences will be.

This correlate-oriented, or *psychometric,* approach is not tied to any theoretical orientation. As long as they can be quantified, assessment data of any kind (ego strength scores, reinforcer preferences, personality traits, perceptions of others) can be dealt with as correlates. As such, the psychometric approach to assessment data processing links individual-oriented clinical psychology to the general field of personality theories and research.

Finally, the pill taking may be thought of as a *sign* of other, less obvious qualities about the client. A sign-oriented view might result in the following inferences:

1. The client's aggressive impulses have been turned against the self.

2. The client's behavior reflects intrapsychic conflicts.

3. The pill taking represents an unconscious cry for help.

These statements go beyond the hard information in directions suggested by a particular theory of behavior. Assessment data provide the signs, a theory provides their meaning; the relationship between a sign and an inference may stem solely from theoretical speculation.

Models, Views, and Levels

Levels of inference, views of assessment data, and theoretical models are interrelated. When assessment information is viewed primarily as a behavior *sample,* inference is likely to be minimal and the guiding model will probably be behavioral. On the other hand, conceptualizing assessment data as *signs* usually results in higher levels of inference and often employs a psychodynamic or phenomenological model of behavior. In between, where assessment data are viewed as *correlates,* inferences are at low to moderate levels, and there is more emphasis on statistical analyses of relationships among variables representing a range of theories.

The primary characteristics of the three views of assessment data we have described are presented in Box 3–5. The right-hand column of Box 3–5 shows that assessment data processing may be based on formal statistical

Data Seen as	Level of Inference	Underlying Theory	Source of Data	Typical Data-Processing Procedures
Sign	High	Psychoanalytic or phenomenological	Interviews, tests, observations, life records	Informal; based on subjective judgments about assessment data
Sample	Low	Behavioral	Interviews, tests, observations, life records	Formal and informal; based on subjective judgments and functional analysis of client behavior
Correlate	Low to moderate	Various theories	Interviews, tests, observations, life records	Formal; based on statistical analysis of assessment data

BOX 3-5
Three Views of Assessment Data

procedures or informal, subjective means. The informal approach usually involves looking at assessment data as signs, while the formal approach typically sees such data as correlates.[5] Both alternatives are rooted in the history of clinical psychology. The informal, subjective, inferential approach is a reflection of Freud and his influence on clinicians' thinking. The formal, objective, statistical approach comes to clinicians through its ties with experimental psychology and through the work of Galton, Cattell, Binet, and other psychometrically oriented pioneers. In the next part of this chapter we examine the ways clinicians have followed both traditions as they make inferences about clinical assessment data.

The Process of Clinical Inference

The popular image of clinical psychologists is that they are primarily sign-oriented users of the informal approach to clinical inference. Clinicians are often portrayed as astute translators of obscure signs into accurate statements about a person's past, present, or future, a kind of psychological Sherlock Holmes who can tell much from very little.

A typical example of this appears in a 1949 film called *The Dark Past*. In it, a killer called "Mad Dog" (William Holden) and a gang of fellow prison escapees hold a psychologist, his family, and friends hostage in a remote cabin. The psychologist (Lee J. Cobb) saves the day by getting Mad Dog to talk about his life and dreams and by noticing that one of his hands is paralyzed. From these limited data, Cobb is guided by psychoanalytic theory to the correct conclusion: As a child, Mad Dog was responsible for his hated father's death, and now his crippled hand and murderous ways are symptoms of unconscious conflict about it. The hand immediately becomes normal after Mad Dog hears Cobb's interpretation.

---

[5]This rule of thumb has many exceptions. Prominent among them is that clinicians often use *informal* procedures with data they see as correlates. As we saw in our attempted suicide case, the psychologist must somehow mentally correlate current information about a client with everything else he or she knows about similar instances. This is a difficult task, as we shall see later.

Clinical Intuition. To a limited extent, such long-shot inferences have their counterparts in fact. The psychoanalyst Theodore Reik describes a well-known example involving a young woman who was upset about the dissolution of her intimate relationship with a medical doctor:

After a few sentences about the uneventful day, the patient fell into a long silence. She assured me that nothing was in her thoughts. Silence from me. After many minutes she complained about a toothache. She told me that she had been to the dentist yesterday. He had given her an injection and then had pulled a wisdom tooth. The spot was hurting again. New and longer silence. She pointed to my bookcase in the corner and said, "There's a book standing on its head."

Without the slightest hesitation and in a re-proachful voice I said, "But why did you not tell me that you had had an abortion?" The patient jumped up and looked at me as if I were a ghost. Nobody knew or could know that her lover, the physician, had performed an abortion on her. . . . (Reik, 1948, pp. 263–264)

Reik (1948) suggests that his correct inference from the data presented by the client (toothache, the injection by a dentist, the tooth extraction, the pain, the book "on its head") was based partly on an intuitive gift. It has long been supposed that clinical psychologists possess that same gift which, along with their past experience and their guiding theories, makes them superior at drawing high-level inferences from assessment data. While certain individuals seem better than others at correctly interpreting assessment data, this ability is not unique to clinicians.

Research contradicts the existence of special inferential capabilities among clinical psychologists. Peterson (1968, p. 105) makes this point forcefully: "The idea that clinicians have or can develop some special kinds of antennae with which they can detect otherwise subliminal interpersonal stimuli and read from these the intrapsychic condition of another person is a myth which ought to be demolished."

When an informal approach to assessment data processing is used, clinical psychologists (a) are not significantly better than non-clinicians at making judgments, and (b) do not make more accurate judgments than could be obtained through formal, statistical procedures. To illustrate, we review the research on the clinician versus nonclinician question and then look at evidence related to the informal versus statistical issue.

The Clinician as Inference Expert. A classic example of research on the clinician's alleged special inference capabilities is provided by Goldberg (1959). In his study, various types of judges attempted to infer the presence of organic brain damage from clients' responses to a psychological test widely used for such purposes. Half of the 30 clients suffered organic problems; the other half did not. Test results were judged by (a) four PhD clinical psychologists with 4 to 9 years' experience with the test, (b) 10 MA-level psychology trainees who had used the test for 1 to 4 years, and (c) eight VA hospital secretaries who had no psychology background and no experience with the test. Since the inference to be drawn in this case was simply "organic" or "not organic" (of which there were 15 cases each), the probability of being correct by chance on any given patient was .50. Only one of the four psychologists did better than chance; as shown in Box 3–6, the psychologists were no better than their students or their secretaries. Other studies of this type (Garner & Smith, 1976; Levenberg, 1975) present a basically similar picture.

The image of clinical psychologists as ordinary mortals has also been strengthened by research on their information-processing ability. Studies by Kostlan (1954), Sines (1959), Golden (1964), Oskamp (1965), and Weiss (1963) suggest that having larger amounts of assessment information may increase clinicians' *confi-*

Group	N	% Correct	% Exceeding Chance
Psychology staff	4	65	25
Psychology trainees	10	70	60
Secretaries	8	67	62
Total	22	68	54

Source: After Goldberg, 1959.

BOX 3-6
Inference Accuracy of Three Types of Judges

dence about inferences, but it does not necessarily improve their accuracy (see Einhorn & Hogarth, 1978; Garb, 1984; Kleinmuntz, 1984; Rock et al., 1987 for reviews of this issue).

While some studies show that trained clinicians can be more accurate judges than laypersons when they use the results of well-validated psychological tests (Garb, 1992), this advantage is neither large nor frequent. Many other studies find no superiority for trained clinicians' judgments. Why is this the case? Why don't clinicians make better clinical judgments? After years of training and experience, why don't they surpass the accuracy of non-professionals? There are two sets of answers to these questions.

One explanation criticizes the manner in which clinical judgment has been studied by researchers. This *ecological* response argues that the way researchers study clinical judgment is different from the way clinicians actually practice, thereby handicapping their performance (Holt, 1970; Rock et al., 1987). For example, researchers often ask clinicians to make judgments about events (e.g., grades in school) that they do not make in their practice and for which they have no training. Also, when making these judgments in research studies, clinicians are often not allowed to em-

ploy their usual assessment methods but must use the materials prescribed by the investigators.

The other answer to the question of why clinical judgment is so problematic is that clinical judgment tasks are full of traps that are difficult to avoid. Because there are limits to how much data any person can process and then combine, clinicians develop habits or tendencies for integrating assessment data. However, these organizing rules of thumb or *heuristics* turn out to be wrong in many cases (Faust & Ziskin, 1988). Clinicians, like other people, remember their successes better than their failures and they continue to employ methods they believe are valid even when they are not. We discuss examples of these problems next.

The psychologist may be inordinately impressed with the first few pieces of information available and then pay little attention to subsequent data, a tendency known as the *anchoring bias* (Dailey,1952; Meehl, 1960). Or the clinician may allow assessment information coming from certain sources (e.g., parents' report of a child's behavior) to outweigh other, contradictory information (McCoy, 1976). Clinicians often rely on vivid cases that stand out in their memory and guide their judgments. This *availability bias* (Tversky &

Kahneman, 1974, 1983) can lead to misjudgments because the clinician places too much confidence in familiar material and neglects potentially important information that is less available to memory. Personal bias can also distort inferences. The clinician may react differently to males and females, to different age groups, or to members of certain socioeconomic, racial, or political groups (Abramovitz, Abramovitz, Jackson, & Gomes, 1973; Broverman, Broverman, Clarkson, Rosenkrantz, & Vogel, 1970; DiNardo, 1975; Kaplan, 1983; Lee & Temerlin, 1970; Routh & King, 1972). Theoretical bias may also alter inference, since adherents to different models approach their clients with preconceptions about what behaviors to expect and what those behaviors mean (Langer & Abelson, 1974; Shoham-Salomon, 1985).

General folklore and misremembered past experiences can affect clinicians as strongly as anyone else. For example, a form of superstition called *illusory correlation* has been shown to affect clinical inference (Chapman & Chapman, 1967; Golding & Rorer, 1972). Just as one may falsely believe it rains every time she washes the car, many clinical psychologists have long believed that the presence of elaborated eyes on tests that involve drawing the human figure is related to paranoid behavior, even though no firm empirical evidence exists for this belief (see Fisher & Fisher, 1950). The fact that paranoid tendencies are still inferred from such cues by some clinicians illustrates a type of error to which many people are prone.

As we learned in Box 3–3, if clinicians ignore the base rates of events they are trying to predict, the accuracy of their predictions and judgments will suffer (Faust & Ziskin, 1988). Unfortunately, clinicians seldom have accurate knowledge of these base rates or do not consider them adequately. Other influences that can reduce inference accuracy include the situation in which inferences are made (e.g., school or mental hospital), the effects of fatigue, and the types of clients the clinician usually sees (Bieri et al., 1966; Hunt & Jones,

1962; Thorne, 1972). Another example of a troublesome bias is illustrated in Box 3–7.

Clinical training received in graduate school may provide clinicians with important information and experience, but there is little evidence that it improves their ability to make accurate inferences. Some data suggest that certain aspects of clinical training *decrease* inferential accuracy by prompting students to see problems where none exist. Soskin (1954) found that prior to taking a course on the Thematic Apperception Test (TAT), beginning graduate students tended to see a well-adjusted person as well adjusted. After the course, the students inaccurately saw such a client as somewhat troubled.

There is "little empirical evidence that justifies the granting of 'expert' status to the clinician on the basis of his training, experience, or information processing ability" (Wiggins, 1981). Despite this conclusion, attempts continue to show that, in principle at least, it is possible to train clinicians to avoid some of the more common sources of their inferential inaccuracies (see Arkes, 1981; Koriat, Lichtenstein, & Fischhoff, 1980). We summarize the results of this training later in this chapter.

There *are* clinicians who, for whatever reasons, appear to be superior to their colleagues and intelligent laypersons in inference accuracy. Is this some stable ability which these clinicians manifest in all cases, or is it more sporadic, depending on the client, situation, and judgment task involved? The answer is not clear. Some studies have shown greater inferential abilities in certain persons (Cline & Richards, 1961); other evidence suggests the opposite conclusion (Crow & Hammond, 1957). The truth may lie somewhere in between; a person's inference ability may be a joint function of general skill as it interacts with situational variables (Bieri et al., 1966; Taft, 1955). At this point, psychologists are beginning to prescribe specific training steps that may enable more clinicians to overcome some of the impediments to accurate clinical judgment (Arkes, 1981; Nisbett & Ross, 1980).

Clinicians often fall victim to another kind of inference error termed *representative thinking*. Representative thinking is the tendency to make decisions about the probability of an event or the implications of the event on the basis of the event representing some characteristic. Because the characteristic appears so important, we may neglect to consider more essential information and may consequently make incorrect judgments. Psychologist Robin Dawes (1986) has described this bias with a series of clever illustrations that show how easy it is to fall into representative thinking. Below are a couple of these examples with which you can test your own judgments.

Dawes quotes the following excerpt from a magazine article:

> Results of a recent survey of 74 chief executive officers indicate that there may be a link between childhood pet ownership and future career success.
>
> Fully 94% of the CEOs, all of them with Fortune 500 companies, had possessed a dog, cat, or both, as youngsters. . . .
>
> The respondents asserted that pet ownership had helped them to develop many of the positive character traits that make them good managers today, including responsibility, empathy, respect for other living beings, generosity, and good communication skills.

Do you see the problems with this logic linking pet ownership to business success? The 94% figure is impressively large, and it misleads us into thinking pet ownership is a childhood experience unique to future CEOs. The survey doesn't measure how many people, regardless of whether they ever became CEOs, had owned pets as children. It is entirely possible that more than 90% of firefighters, ministers, and salesclerks also were pet owners as children. The article ignores the high base rate of pet ownership.

Another illustration, somewhat closer to the concerns of a clinical psychologist, is drawn from research by Tversky and Kahneman (1983). Read the following description about a hypothetical person:

> Linda is 31 years old, single, outspoken, and very bright. She majored in philosophy. As a student, she was deeply concerned about issues of discrimination and social justice, and also participated in anti-nuclear demonstrations.

Based on this, decide which of the following two possibilities is the more likely description of Linda's current life:

1. She is a bank teller.
2. She is a bank teller and is active in the feminist movement.

If you are like the majority of subjects, you chose the second option. Your choice probably reflects the fact that even the limited information you were given about Linda helped you form an image of her as a person with feminist interests. However, it is logically impossible for the second possibility to be more probable than the first; Linda could always be a bank teller regardless of whether she was a feminist. If you chose the second possibility, you overestimated its probability relative to the first option because you ignored the basic rule that a special outcome (bank teller and feminist) can never be more likely than the general outcome (bank teller) of which it is only a part.

BOX 3–7
Examples of Clinical Judgment Errors

Inference by Formal Versus Informal Procedures. The image of the clinician as a sign-oriented expert who consistently makes accurate inferences has been badly tarnished by research on clinical training, experience, and data-processing ability. This sobering body of work was prompted by research on another question about clinicians' inference ability. Many investigators wondered whether clinicians' subjective, informal efforts to interpret assessment data as signs or to correlate those data mentally with other facts were more accurate than inferences based upon formal, statistical data processing in which the clinician plays no part at all.

Clinicians have traditionally been divided on the relative merits of clinical (subjective) and statistical (objective) inference procedures. Those who favor the informal, clinical approach see it as meaningful, organized, rich, deep, and genuine, while critics characterize it as mystical, vague, unscientific, sloppy, and muddleheaded. Proponents of formal, statistical inference think it is objective, reliable, precise, and empirical; opponents label it artificial, trivial, superficial, and rigid.

The statistical versus clinical data-processing issue is central to how clinicians (a) spend their time, (b) make decisions about clients, (c) shape their research, and (d) conceive of their professional identity. Clinicians who informally interpret assessment data, make recommendations based on their interpretations, and do research on such activities usually do so because they believe that they, or their profession, are good at these things. Thus it came as a shock when, in a 1954 monograph, University of Minnesota psychologist Paul Meehl reported his review of 20 studies comparing the accuracy of predictions based on informal, clinical procedures and formal, statistical procedures. He found that in all but one case, the accuracy of the statistical approach equaled or surpassed the clinical approach. Later, even the sole exception to this surprising conclusion was called a tie, and, as additional research became available, the superiority of the

statistical method of prediction was more firmly established (Dawes, Faust, & Meehl, 1989; Meehl, 1957, 1965). Box 3–8 shows the "box scores" and the kinds of variables predicted in studies covered by Meehl's reviews.

Meehl's review had a devastating impact on clinical psychologists. At least 18 responses to it were published in the years following its appearance, most of them critical. Detractors pointed out methodological defects in some of the studies that could have biased results in favor of statistical data-processing procedures. Similar to the ecological criticisms we described earlier, many clinicians felt that the variables being predicted (e.g., grades) were not like those typically dealt with by practicing psychologists, while others suggested that the clinicians in several studies were handicapped by inadequate or unfamiliar information about clients and what they were supposed to predict (Holt, 1958, 1978). Thorne (1972, p. 44) put it this way: "The question must not be what naive judges do with inappropriate tasks under questionable conditions of comparability with actual clinical situations, but what the most sophisticated judges can do with appropriate methods under ideal conditions."

The furor over Meehl's conclusions has not negated the fact that inference based on subjective, clinical methods is not as accurate as it was once assumed to be. However, this initially discouraging conclusion was not without positive aspects. Meehl's reviews, along with other reports on the clinician's limited capabilities, focused research on the problem and advanced knowledge, theory, and practice in assessment data processing (Kleinmuntz, 1984; Wiggins, 1981). Two major lines of work have appeared in this regard.

Improving Informal Inference. The first involves investigating how the best clinical inferences are made, how they can be improved, and how they can be taught. Thorne (1972, p. 44) suggests that "clinicians must become much more critical of the types of judg-

Source	Number of Studies Reviewed	Variables Predicted	OUTCOME		
			Clinical Better	Statistical Better	Tie
Meehl (1954)	20	Success in school or military; recidivism or parole violation; recovery from psychosis	1[a]	11	8
Meehl (1957)	27	Same as above, plus personality description; therapy outcome	0	17	10
Meehl (1965)	51	Same as above, plus response to shock treatment; diagnostic label; job success and satisfaction; medical diagnosis	1[b]	33	17

[a]Later called a tie.

[b]Later called a tie by Goldberg (1968).

Source: After Wiggins, 1973.

BOX 3-8
Summary of Outcomes of Studies
Comparing Clinical Versus Statistical Predictive Inference

ments they attempt to make, the selection of cues upon which judgments are based, and their modes of collecting and combining data." Work in these areas began in the 1960s as researchers attempted to analyze the logic of inference (Sarbin, Taft, & Bailey, 1960); relate it to social and physical judgment processes and errors (Bieri et al., 1966; Grossberg & Grant, 1978; Hunt & Jones, 1962); analyze the nature and influence of specific cues used by clinicians (Goldberg, 1968; Hoffman, 1960); optimize the amount of assessment data to be processed (e.g., Bartlett & Green, 1966); and identify the conditions under which inference can be most reliable and valid (e.g., Watley, 1968). These efforts are continuing.

In general, the results of training clinicians to avoid the common pitfalls of clinical judgments have been disappointing. Experienced clinicians tend to do no better at personality assessment than inexperienced clinicians or graduate students (Garb, 1989). Clinicians with training in specific assessment areas perform better than laypersons, but the size of their advantage is surprisingly small. Informing clinicians about their biases is also not very helpful, although there may be benefits from having clinicians keep a written record of the biases they show and the mistakes they make (Dawes, 1986).

Even though the accuracy of clinical inference can be improved over levels previously reported (Kahneman & Tversky, 1979), whether the improvement justifies the extra effort still remains a question. Even the most superior human judges operating under optimal conditions are variable enough in their accuracy to raise questions about their suitability for the data-processing task.

Consider a study by Kleinmuntz (1963) that involved describing the specific rules by which the very best clinical judges draw inferences. Knowing these rules could facilitate the training of less accurate, less experienced clinicians (Kagan, 1974). Kleinmuntz asked a recognized MMPI expert to think aloud while working with test results from 126 college-age subjects. The task was to decide whether each individual was adjusted or maladjusted. The decision rules that emerged were transformed into a computer program used to score future subjects' MMPI scores.

The study showed that a good clinician's inference processes can be objectified and taught, but also revealed that the most appropriate "student" may be a computer; the machine used the rules perfectly and consistently with each new set of data. It actually did better at subsequent inference tasks than the clinician who had "taught" it (Kleinmuntz, 1969).

Improving Formal Inference. The performance of formal inference procedures has provided the impetus for the other line of research in the "post-Meehl" era, namely the elaboration and improvement of techniques for statistical processing of assessment data. Though it may seem that this type of research might put clinicians out of a job, one of its by-products has been to map out the assessment tasks in which clinicians can be most effective.

Meehl (1954) and other researchers in this area (e.g., Sawyer, 1966) have distinguished between the clinical psychologist's roles in data *processing* versus data *collection*. They have highlighted the fact that, just as data processing can be formal or informal, collection of assessment data can be done mechanically (with objective tests and life records) or subjectively (through unstructured interviews and informal observations). Thus, in a given assessment sequence, many combinations of subjective and statistical procedures are possible for the clinician (see Box 3–9). When the studies reviewed by Meehl are reexamined in

this light, as Sawyer (1966) did, it is clear that though clinicians may be inferior to statistical formulae at *processing* assessment data, they can make unique contributions by *collecting* and reporting their subjective judgments. The most accurate inferences found by Sawyer (1966) were based on the formal, statistical processing of data collected by *both* mechanical and subjective techniques. "This suggests that the clinician may be able to contribute most not by direct prediction, but rather by providing, in objective form, judgments to be combined mechanically" (Sawyer, 1966, p. 193). These findings have by no means shut the clinician out of the assessment process. Although the clinician is not an accurate *combiner* of data, he can be an unsurpassed *source* of assessment data (Anastasi, 1988). Clinicians can use their interviewing skills to obtain information from clients not otherwise available. They can use their theoretical model to develop hypotheses about other aspects of the client that need exploration. Finally, clinicians can act as an interpersonal stimulus to which the client, in turn, responds, providing a controlled assessment of a sample of behavior.

Many clinicians and researchers now focus on upgrading observational and other data-*collection* skills to optimize their role in clinical assessment. As an example, clinical intuition has been recast as a skill in observing verbal and nonverbal cues coming from the client. As such, it can be developed, practiced, and improved (see Arkes, 1981; Dawes, 1986).

Other investigators have been studying the accuracy of statistical, usually computer-oriented, data-processing methods. Some of these methods are thoroughly mechanical and empirical; for example, a client's test scores are interpreted according to formulae that have been derived from statistical relationships between other clients' test scores and behavior (see category 1 in Box 3–9). In effect, the computer takes the client's test profile and looks up the characteristics of other people with similar profiles. Development of this type

Data-Collection Procedure	Data-Processing Procedure	Example
1 Formal	Formal	Psychological test scores processed by computer according to a statistical formula which predicts potential for behavior problems
2 Formal	Informal	Psychological test scores interpreted by clinician based on experience, theory, and hunches to establish psychiatric diagnosis
3 Informal	Formal	Clinician's subjective judgments (based on an interview) converted into quantitative ratings, which are then processed by a computer or statistical formula to describe client's personality
4 Informal	Informal	Subjective impressions and judgments (from interviews, projective tests, etc.) interpreted subjectively to decide whether client needs to be hospitalized
5 Formal and Informal	Formal	Psychological test scores and clinician's subjective impressions and judgments all fed into computer, which uses complex formula to describe client or make predictions about behavior
6 Formal and Informal	Informal	Psychological test scores and clinician's subjective impressions and judgments all scanned and interpreted by clinician to decide whether client is capable of standing trial for a crime

BOX 3–9
Some Combinations of Formal and Informal Procedures
for the Collection and Processing of Assessment Data

of purely actuarial program is expensive because it requires a large backlog of data from hundreds of previous clients.

To fill the gaps where appropriate statistical formulae are not yet available because there are no data on the relationship between predictors and criteria, a hybrid system of formal data processing has evolved. The Kleinmuntz (1963) study provides an example of this approach. In general, it involves having a computer interpret assessment data, not through use of a statistically derived formula but on the basis of clinicians' experience and theoretical beliefs, which have been transformed into de-

cision rules. Wiggins (1973) refers to this process as "automating clinical lore." The result of this procedure is often a *computerized narrative interpretation* or report generated by the computer as it links quantitative test scores with a series of interpretive statements. These computerized reports can only be as valid as the original actuarial or clinical rules upon which they are based, and many systems in use do not provide convincing data about the reliability or validity of their interpretations.

The use of hybrid computer programs for scoring and interpreting psychological tests has become a popular enterprise that can be quite lucrative (see Box 3–10). These programs vary considerably in their sophistication and quality. Many have been developed with the logic pioneered by Kleinmuntz (1963), although not all have been adequately concerned with assessment of reliability and validity (Matarazzo, 1983a; 1986). Several steps have been taken to regulate computer-based testing and interpretation. A special set of guidelines pertaining to computer testing has been developed (APA, 1986); *The Standards for Educational and Psychological Testing* (APA, 1985) includes several provisions about computerized testing; and a journal, *Computers in Human Behavior,* includes a section on computer software used to interpret tests such as the MMPI (see the December 1985 issue of the *Journal of Consulting and Clinical Psychology* for a special series of articles on computerized psychological assessment).

The following limitations and problems of computerized assessment have been raised by critics:

1. Actuarial techniques can be applied only where adequately developed, fully standardized assessment devices, inference norms, and formulae are available. At the moment, such devices and data are the exception, not the rule (Lanyon, 1984; Wiggins, 1981).

2. There is a certain amount of public distrust of decisions made about people on the basis of computer techniques. Part of this problem involves increased risks for invasion of privacy by using computerized assessment services. However, there are also data indicating that clients are very positive toward computerized assessment, especially when the subject matter is sensitive in nature (see Burke & Normand, 1987, for a review).

3. New discoveries about behavior are less likely to occur if clinicians become less involved in assessment data processing.

4. Relegation of clinicians to the data-collection role decreases the chances of future improvement of human data-processing skills (Matarazzo, 1986).

5. Exclusion of the clinician from the data-processing role reduces the probability that rare behavioral events and relationships will be noticed, since actuarial tables and statistical formulae may not be set up to handle them.

6. Certain kinds of assessment may be more appropriately dealt with by informal means. Levy (1963) suggests that specific, "bounded" questions (Will this person be likely to abuse children?) may most adequately be answered by formal data processing, while more general "unbounded" concerns (What is this person like?) are best handled through informal means.

7. Computerized testing may encourage poorly prepared testers to hold themselves out to the public as well-trained clinicians who provide impressive-sounding, but poorly conceived, assessment reports.

8. Computerized narratives usually focus on only one plausible interpretation of test results rather than considering and evaluating the merits of the several possible interpretations that a complete assessment battery almost always suggests (Matarazzo, 1986).

9. Studies of computerized test interpretations have often used poor research methods (Harris, 1987; Moreland, 1987) and have not adequately studied the various elements that go together to make up a computer-based interpretation (Snyder, Widiger, & Hoover, 1990).

These are important criticisms, and they focus attention on crucial assessment issues. One point that some critics of computer-based test interpretation seem to miss, however, is that many of their criticisms apply at least as well to the assessment reports of individual clinicians. The core research problem in clinical assessment is the lack of validation studies of all kinds of assessment reports whether computer generated or not (Ben-Porath & Butcher, 1991).

Though there is still disagreement over exactly what assessment questions and roles clinicians should handle, Wiggins's (1973, p.

Although the MMPI is the psychological test most often interpreted through computerized narratives, computerized interpretations are now available for more than 100 different psychological tests. One of the most carefully developed systems for this type of interpretation is Snyder's (1981) Marital Satisfaction Inventory (MSI), a 280-item, 11-scale test designed to assess several aspects of marital satisfaction. Below is an example of a computerized MSI report (Snyder, Lachar, & Wills, 1988) for a couple who had just begun marital therapy, complaining of increasing conflict around several relationship problems. While both Mr. and Mrs. D. completed an MSI independently, the interpretive report combines the results into one summary.

Marital Satisfaction Inventory (MSI) Computerized Interpretive Report for Mr. and Mrs. D. at Intake

Global Marital Affect

This husband and wife have described their marriage in a highly similar manner. Both spouses openly acknowledge serious difficulties in their marriage and dissatisfaction with their spouse; they may have a tendency to emphasize marital conflict to the exclusion of acknowledging more positive aspects of their relationship. Overall, they indicate extensive marital distress and feelings of alienation and anger toward one another. Relationship problems are likely to be of long duration and generalized across different areas of the marriage. Persons with similar profiles describe their marriage as a major source of disappointment; general inability to resolve even minor differences is characteristic. In response to marital difficulties, both respondents may have withdrawn emotionally from their marriage and be reluctant to confide in their spouse. They describe their marriage as having an uncertain future, and may express strong reservations regarding the potential for improvement in the relationship. Determination of specific steps either spouse has taken toward separation or divorce would be prudent.

Spousal Communication

Both spouses express dissatisfaction with the amount of affection shown by their partner, although the wife reports somewhat less distress in this regard. Women with similar scores often feel emotionally distant from their husbands, and may feel unappreciated or misunderstood. They may wish that their

BOX 3–10
An Example of a Computerized Narrative Interpretation

199) summary of the situation provides a positive concluding note:

Clinicians need not view themselves as second-rate IBM machines unless they choose to engage in activities that are more appropriately performed by such machines. In the realm of clinical observation and hypothesis formation, the IBM machine will never be more than a second-rate clinician.

The Behavioral Approach to Assessment

Clinical psychologists have traditionally been concerned with formal and informal processing of assessment data that are viewed as signs or correlates. In that tradition, assessment information is interpreted in terms of psychological traits or intrapsychic dynamics, and the clinician's goal is to predict something about the client or to describe the client's personality.

husband would be more open with their feelings, and often describe a reluctance, themselves, to confide in their mate. Depending on the amount of relationship distress in other areas, the wife may be motivated to pursue ways in which she and her husband can enhance intimacy and mutual self-disclosure.

In comparison, the husband describes extensive dissatisfaction with the quality of affective communication in the marriage. Men with similar scores typically describe their wives as emotionally distant and uncaring. The husband may describe his wife as withdrawn and unsupportive. Like his wife, the husband is likely to feel unappreciated and misunderstood by his spouse, and may be reluctant to confide in her. The husband's experience of disaffection from his wife is likely to limit the couple's effectiveness in resolving spousal differences.

Both the husband and wife describe difficulties in resolving disagreements, although the husband's dissatisfaction in this regard is somewhat less than his wife's. When differences arise, there may be a notable shift toward more negative forms of interaction including reciprocity of negative affect, failure to acknowledge each other's view, or attribution of negative intentions to the partner's behavior. There may exist a long accumulation of unresolved differences, such that even minor disagreements precipitate major arguments. The wife may describe her husband as being hurtful or verbally abusive at these times. Both spouses may perceive the other as being overly sensitive or critical, with certain areas of the relationship being "off limits" for discussion. Each partner is likely to regard the other as being entrenched in their own position and unresponsive to legitimate concerns or complaints.

Specific Areas of Interaction

Overall, the husband and wife have evaluated specific dimensions of spousal interaction in a somewhat different manner. They may identify different areas of their relationship as sources of distress, or may disagree on the extent of distress in these areas. This divergence in spouses' views of the marriage may hinder their collaboration in rank-ordering relationship concerns and identifying therapeutic goals. The couple may profit initially from interventions in areas of relative agreement noted below.

The husband and wife differ somewhat in their evaluation of leisure time spent together. The wife reports general satisfaction with the variety of interests and activities she and her husband share both in and outside the home. Any conflicts she experiences in this regard

---

BOX 3–10
Continued

Clinical psychologists who adopt a behavioral model disagree with many of these assessment concepts. Their main criticisms and alternative formulations are summarized in the following points:

1. The use of assessment data as *signs* of personality traits involves too much inference. Behaviorists do not see personality traits, psychological dispositions, or personality dynamics as useful concepts for learning about people. In their view, such dispositional constructs exist in the eye of the clinician who uses them (Shweder, 1982), and, real or not, these constructs have limited utility for describing people, predicting their behavior, or evaluating behavior change programs.

Many behaviorists argue that part of the reason for clinicians' poor showing as data processors is that they rely on vague trait concepts as the bases for inferences that stray too far from initial assessment information. When

may stem more from a lack of sufficient time toegehter than from a failure to enjoy mutual activities. In comparison, the husband reports few common interests with his wife and indicates that they engage in relatively few activities together. He may regard his spouse as somewhat withdrawn or lacking a desire for closer involvement in leisure activities.

The husband and wife both describe finances as an area of relative agreement. Fiscal responsibilities are likely to be shared by both spouses, with substantial consensus on financial priorities. The respondents may describe their partner as a good manager of financial resources, and as generous and trusting. If financial stresses are experienced by this couple, they may be confined to the adequacy of income and have little generalized impact on their marital relationship.

Both respondents indicate dissatisfaction with their sexual relationship, although the wife reports somewhat less distress in this area. Disagreements regarding the frequency or variety of sexual behaviors may be frequent; it is somewhat unlikely that sexual difficulties evolve exclusively from more general marital distress, and specific interventions in this area may be warranted. Both spouses may describe their mates as uncaring or uncommitted to a satisfying sexual relationship, and may complain of deficits in

nonsexual expressions of affection. The couple is likely to have difficulty in discussing sexual matters openly and effectively.

Concerns Regarding Children

The husband and wife both indicate significant conflict regarding childrearing issues, although the husband reports somewhat less distress in this respect. Conflicts around division of childcare responsibilities are likely, and spouses may experience frequent disagreements regarding discipline and their children's privileges and responsibilities. The couple could likely benefit from interventions aimed at clarifying their respective expectations for their children's behavior and identifying each spouse's responsibilities for various childrearing tasks.

The respondents have somewhat different evaluations of their own relationships with their children, with the wife reporting greater satisfaction in this regard. The wife describes herself, and may be perceived by her husband, as a good parent. She may view her children as contributing to her own investment in the marriage and to her own personal fulfillment. From her perspective, the children present few difficulties in behavioral management. In comparison, the husband describes disappointment with the

---

BOX 3–10
Continued

---

clinicians do not share common definitions for terms like *anxiety, aggression,* and *ego,* studies reporting low reliability and validity for personality traits are easier to understand. Trait concepts are seen by behavior assessors as adding confusing and ultimately superfluous labels to behavior that does not need them.

Accordingly, the behavioral model treats available data as *samples* of client capabilities rather than as bases for inference about per-

sonality traits or dynamic states. Mischel (1968, p. 10) notes that "the emphasis is on what a person *does* in situations rather than on inferences about what attributes he *has.*"

2. In spite of the early efforts of Murray (1938) and Rapaport (Rapaport et al., 1945), trait concepts have often isolated people's behavior from the environment in which it occurs. Since behavior is learned in a social context, one cannot describe or predict that behavior

children 's behavior or dissatisfaction with the general demands of childrearing. He may perceive one or more children as exhibiting significant emotional or behavioral problems. Any marital distress the husband experiences may evolve in part from childrearing difficulties. Given the respondents' somewhat different perceptions in this area, a careful assessment should be conducted of possible alliances of one or more children with one parent against the other; an in-depth evaluation of one or more children may be warranted.

Role Orientation and Family History

The husband and wife differ sharply in their role orientations, with the husband expressing a more traditional view toward marital and parental roles. He may believe that he ought to have somewhat more influence than his wife in decisions regarding family matters. The husband may prefer a traditional division of household and childrearing responsibilities, with his assuming the role as primary wage-earner and the wife investing herself more fully in her role as wife and mother at home. In

contrast, the wife describes a fairly nontraditional view of marital and parental roles. She is likely to prefer a more flexible division of household and childrearing tasks, with both spouses pursuing independent careers and sharing equally in decision making and in housework and childcare responsibilities at home. The couple's responses in this regard express their role values, and the extent to which these preferences are consistent with their actual role behaviors in the marriage should be carefully evaluated. Given their different attitudes in this domain, the potential for marital role conflict merits further examination.

Finally, both respondents report a history of moderate distress within their families of origin. They are likely to describe significant disruption of their relationships with either their siblings or parents. Their parents' marriages may have been characterized by difficulties in expressing affection or resolving differences. Maladaptive relationship patterns in both families of origin should be carefully examined to determine the extent to which they generalize to the couple's own marriage.

Source: Reprinted from Volume 14, Number 4, of the *Journal of Marital and Family Therapy*, Copyright 1988, American Association for Marriage and Family Therapy. Reprinted with permission.

BOX 3–10
Continued

accurately unless situational factors are taken into account: A woman who displays dominance on a psychological test may behave quite differently with her boss.

Two decades ago, behaviorists tended to concentrate on situational variables to the virtual exclusion of person variables, an imbalance that Eysenck, Wakefield, and Friedman (1983) termed "committed 'environmental-

ism.'" More modern behaviorists consider both the person and the environment as important in behavioral assessment, so the focus of data collection includes (a) client capabilities, (b) characteristics of the physical and social environment in which behavior occurs, and (c) the nature of *client–environment* interactions. This person–situation orientation in the behavioral view of assessment has emphasized *interactionism* or the *reciprocal relationship* between person and situational variables (Bandura, 1978; Mischel, 1984).

3. Traditional assessment practices promote separation between data collection and data use. Too often, assessment information is processed into descriptions or predictions that are not useful for planning or evaluating behavior-change techniques. Behaviorists document this point by citing research that shows that traditionally oriented therapists often pay little attention to the assessment data available (Dailey, 1953; Meehl, 1960).

From the behavioral perspective, clinical assessment must be tied to efforts at modifying behavior. Toward this end, clients, situations, and client-situation interactions are described on dimensions that (a) are as precise and data based as possible, (b) have direct implications for treatment planning, and (c) can be monitored during and after treatment. Rather than describing a particular child's problem in trait-oriented terms like *aggressiveness* or *hyperactivity,* assessment would focus on the *frequencies, durations,* or *intensities* with which specific acts (striking others, running around the room) occur, the settings in which these acts appear, and the environmental factors that appear to elicit and reinforce them. Goldfried and Sprafkin (1974) coined an acronym, SORC, or Stimulus-Organism-Response-Consequence, to indicate the types of variables that a thorough behavioral assessment must consider. The spirit of interactionism is suggested by this system's attention to environmental (the "C" and "S" components) and organismic (the "O" component) control of important responses ("R"). Behaviorists also study extended *chains* or sequences of interaction in an attempt to understand such complex behaviors as marital interaction or social deficits (Haynes, 1984).

In general, questions asked during behavioral assessment are not oriented toward *why* a person behaves in a particular way, but *what* she or he does, and *when, where,* and *under what circumstances* the activity occurs. When

behavior is described in this fashion, change tactics flow directly from assessment. If assessment suggests that Sam's high-frequency whining in the classroom is reinforced by teacher attention, a program to terminate reward of the maladaptive behavior and plan reinforcement of more appropriate behaviors might be instituted. As that program begins, its effect upon the variables identified in the initial assessment would be observed and used as a guide for continuing, altering, or terminating the intervention.

In recent years behavioral and traditional (trait-oriented) approaches have come closer together on several assessment principles. For their part, behaviorists increasingly stress the need to demonstrate the classic psychometric qualities of reliability and validity for their methods rather than simply assuming such qualities (see Cone, 1988, for a discussion of why such qualities may not be relevant to all forms of behavioral assessment). Behaviorists are also now more interested in assessing personal variables that give stability and unity to behavior across different situations (Mischel, 1984) than they were in the days when they severely criticized assessment of personality dispositions (Mischel, 1968).

At the same time, traditional emphases on trait assessment and psychiatric diagnosis have embraced some behavioral recommendations. The specific, criterion-based formulation of *DSM-IV* is an excellent example of how behavioral principles of assessment have influenced clinical practice. As a result, psychiatric diagnosis is no longer the heresy it was once considered to be by behaviorists. At a more theoretical level, increased attention to what personality theorists (Rorer & Widiger, 1983) call *ascription rules* (the implicit rules we use for describing people as possessing or not possessing certain qualities: "He is honest"; "She is friendly") reflects an awareness that situational variables play a major role in assigning trait names to an individual's behavior. Buss and Craik (1983, 1986) have attempted to tie trait concepts to multiple-behavior criteria by finding those behaviors that are the most important or *prototypic* for assigning trait descriptions like "dominant" or "submissive" to another person.

The behavioral approach to assessment is not without its critics. Many clinicians see objective assessment of overt behaviors in relation to specific environmental situations as too narrow and inadequate for tapping the various personality dimensions stressed in their own models. Other critiques have been advanced from within the behavioral camp itself.

Many concerns stem from the fact that the behavioral approach to assessment is still in a rather primitive stage of development. Its methods are often not well standardized or psychometrically sophisticated when compared to psychological tests like the MMPI (Franks, 1976; Wiggins, 1973). Behavioral assessments are still used inconsistently by different practitioners who, like other clinicians, operate without formal actuarial formulae and depend on their own subjective judgment to interpret the data they collect. Also, though behavioral assessment provides excellent descriptions of behavior that can be used as a guide for treatment planning, it has not resolved the question of what behaviors constitute a problem and who sets up the definitions (Mash, 1985; Morganstern, 1988). Further, it has not yet reached a level of sophistication that allows for a reliable, empirically determined choice of specific treatment techniques, especially in complex cases. More comprehensive presentations of the theory, practice, and problems of behavioral assessment are available in several recent volumes (Barlow, 1981; Bellack & Hersen, 1988; Ciminero, Calhoun, & Adams, 1986; Haynes, 1978; Mash & Terdal, 1988; Nelson & Hayes, 1986; Ollendick & Hersen, 1984).

Phenomenology and Assessment

Many objections raised by behavioral theorists to traditional assessment procedures relate not only to their apparent lack of clinical utility, but also to the belief that people should not be placed in a "one-down" status, exam-

ined apart from their physical and social environment, and burdened with labels that focus on problems and weaknesses to the exclusion of assets and strengths. In this respect the behavioral and phenomenological models are in accord. However, in line with their subjective, relationship-oriented approach, phenomenological clinicians have suggested assessment alternatives that differ substantially from those outlined in the last section (Brown, 1972; Dana & Leech, 1974; Fischer & Fischer, 1983).

Some of them (Rogers, 1951) have argued against assessment on the grounds that such procedures are dehumanizing, take responsibility away from clients, and threaten the quality of clinician–client relations. Advocates of this position are unlikely even to review assessment data collected and processed by others. Their assumption is that all necessary knowledge of the client will emerge during specially conducted interviews. The characteristics of these interviews will be described in Chapters 4 and 10.

Other phenomenologists raise the possibility that assessment data *collected* through traditional sources such as personality tests can be useful clinically if they are *processed* in line with humanistic principles (Fischer, 1985, 1989). For example, test data can be viewed as clues to how a client looks at the world. In the same vein, traditional assessment procedures can provide opportunities for the clinician and client to build their relationship. By discussing assessment data with the client and using these interactions as a starting point for further exploration, the clinician not only shares knowledge openly, but reveals personal reactions to it, thus helping to cement a lasting partnership (Dana & Leech, 1974; Fischer, 1985; Mosak & Gushurst, 1972).

Some phenomenologists who feel that traditional assessment devices do not facilitate growth of a relationship have developed specialized instruments that they believe do the job better. These tests include the Personal Orientation Inventory (Shostrom, 1968), the Purpose-in-Life Test (Crumbaugh, 1968) and the "Who-are-you?" Test (Bugental & Zelen, 1950).

Communicating Assessment Data

Raw data about a client's behavior must be interpreted before they become psychologically meaningful. However, the value of these interpretations may be limited unless they are presented in some coherent way. This organized presentation of assessment results is called a *psychological report.*

If the results of assessment are to have maximal value, they must be presented in a way that is *clear, relevant* to the goal of assessment, and *useful* to the intended consumer. Clinicians must guard against several problems that can make reports vague, irrelevant, and useless. To illustrate, consider the following personality sketch. It is not as extensive as most assessment reports, but many of its characteristics are relevant to our discussion:

> You are a person of varied interests, although you pour most of your energy into a few activities that mean the most to you. In general, you show a well-balanced outlook and disposition, but when frustrated you can display temper. With those you know well you are spontaneous and expressive, but often you keep your feelings very much to yourself. You have a few defects in personality that you are aware of, particularly in connection with dealing with people. You are persistent enough, however, to achieve success in dealing with these faults. There are times when you worry too much. You will find that it suits you better to take things as they come and to show more confidence in your own future. (Wallen, 1956, p. 42)

At first glance, this sketch appears clear, relevant to the person in question, and reasonably useful. However, closer examination will reveal that this is not the case. First, the terms ("balanced outlook" and "defects in personal-

ity") are vague and can mean different things to different readers. Second, the statements are so generally applicable to everyone that they are not relevant for the description of a particular individual. Careful examination of actual assessment reports often exposes the same problems. In fact, the tendency for people to accept general descriptions as accurate for them specifically is so well known that it has its own name: the "Barnum effect," so-called because of P. T. Barnum's famous, cynical claim that "there's a sucker born every minute." Let us briefly consider these problems and then discuss a few ideas for dealing with them.

Clarity of Reports

The first criterion for an assessment report is clarity. Without this basic attribute, relevance and usefulness cannot be evaluated. Lack of clarity in psychological reports is troublesome because misinterpretation of a report can lead to misguided decisions. Hammond and Allen (1953, p. v) cite a case in point:

> A young girl, mentally defective, was seen for testing by the psychologist, who reported to the social agency that the girl's test performance indicated moderate success and happiness for her in "doing things with her hands." Three months later, however, the social agency reported to the psychologist that the girl was not responding well. Although the social agency had followed the psychologist's recommendation, the girl was neither happy nor successful "doing things with her hands." When the psychologist inquired what kinds of things, specifically, the girl had been given to do he was told "We gave her music lessons—on the saxophone."

A related problem exists when the assessor uses jargon that the reader may not understand. Consider the following excerpt from a report on a 36-year-old man cited by Mischel (1968, p. 105):

Test results emphasize a basically character-ological problem with currently hysteroid defenses. Impairment of his ability to make adequate use of independent and creative fantasy, associated with emotional lability and naivete, are characteristic of him. . . . Due to markedly passive-aggressive character make-up, in which the infantile dependency needs are continually warring with his hostile tendencies, it is not difficult to understand this current conflict over sexual expression.

The writer may feel he understands the client, but does the reader understand the writer? Anyone not well versed in psychoanalytic terminology would find such a report mystifying. Professionals may not even agree on the meaning of the terms employed. Factors such as excessive length (or excessive brevity), large amounts of technical information (statistics or esoteric test scores), and lack of coherent organization also contribute to lack of communication clarity in assessment reports (Olive, 1972; Tallent & Reiss, 1959).

Relevance to Goals

The second requirement of a valuable assessment report is that it is *relevant* to the goal that prompted the assessment in the first place. If that goal was to classify the client's behavior, information relevant to classification should be highlighted. If description of the client's current psychological assets and liabilities was the purpose, the report should contain those descriptions. If predictions about a client are requested, these should appear, unless the clinician believes that no sound basis for them exists.

These are simple, almost self-evident prescriptions, but assessment objectives sometimes get lost, especially when explicit goals were never stated. Although the procedure is no longer as common as it once was, clinicians may still be asked for psychologicals (usually a standard test battery and interview) without being told why assessment is being

done. Under such circumstances, the chances of writing a relevant report are minimal.

Unfortunately, there are cases in which lack of relevance in psychological reports is due mainly to the clinician's failure to keep clearly stated objectives in mind. When this happens, the report may reflect the assessor's theoretical bias and personal style more than the client's behavior.

Usefulness of Reports

Finally, one must ask if an assessment report is useful. Does the information it contains add anything important to what we already know about the client? Reports frequently contain clear, relevant information that is already available through other sources. Or a report may *sound* useful at first, but contain little information of real value. These problems appear because the assessor has either (a) not collected useful information or (b) not made useful statements about the data available. In the former case, the clinician may have employed techniques low on what Sechrest (1963) called *incremental validity*. For example, a clinician may conclude on the basis of several psychological tests that a client "has strong hostile tendencies and weak control over them." If the client has already been convicted as an ax murderer, such information provides no increment in knowledge over what was already obvious.

In other instances, the assessor's report may have limited usefulness because it says nothing beyond what would be expected on the basis of general past experience and common sense. One example of this is the base-rate problem, one aspect of which we discussed in Box 3–3. It refers to the fact that some statements tend to be true about certain types of clients (e.g., college professors do a lot of reading) and that if an assessment report fails to provide information beyond these known base rates, its usefulness will be limited.

An example of how knowledge of base rates in a population can facilitate the creation of useless though impressive-sounding reports has been given by Sundberg, Tyler, and Taplin (1973, pp. 577–579). A clinician wrote the report that follows *without ever having seen the client*. The material contained in it is based entirely on two pieces of information: (a) The client is a new admission to a Veterans Administration hospital, and (b) the case was to be discussed at a convention session entitled "A Case Study of Schizophrenia." In edited form, the report said:

> This veteran approached the testing situation with some reluctance. He was cooperative with the clinician, but mildly evasive on some of the material. Both the tests and the past history suggest considerable inadequacy in interpersonal relations, particularly with members of his family. It is doubtful whether he has ever had very many close relationships with anyone. . . . He has never been able to sink his roots deeply. He is immature, egocentric, and irritable, and often he misperceives the good intentions of the people around him. . . . He tends to be basically passive and dependent, though there are occasional periods of resistance and rebellion against others. . . . Vocationally, his adjustment has been very poor. Mostly he has drifted from one job to another. His interests are shallow and he tends to have poor motivation for his work. Also he has had a hard time keeping his jobs because of diYculty in getting along with fellow employees. Although he has had some relations with women, his sex life has been unsatisfactory to him. At present, he is mildly depressed. . . . His intelligence is close to average, but he is functioning below his potential. . . . Test results and case history . . . suggest the diagnosis of schizophrenic reaction, chronic undifferentiated type. Prognosis for response to treatment appears to be poor.

In writing this report, the clinician relied heavily on knowledge of VA hospital residents and familiarity with hospital procedures. For example, since the case was to be discussed at a meeting on schizophrenia, and since schizophrenic diagnoses are common for VA residents, the correct diagnosis was easy to surmise. Also, the description given fits the "average" VA resident and thus is likely to be at least partially accurate.

This bogus document once again exemplifies a feature of assessment reports that reduces their usefulness: overgenerality, or the tendency to write in terms that are so ambiguous they can be true of almost anyone. Documents laden with overly general statements have been dubbed "Barnum Reports," "Aunt Fanny Reports," or "Madison Avenue Reports" (Klopfer, 1983; Meehl, 1956; Tallent, 1992). Overly general material has the dual disadvantages of spuriously increasing a report's impressiveness while actually decreasing its usefulness.

Presenting Assessment Data

While there is no single "right" way to present assessment data in all instances, several guidelines are worth noting.

First, the criteria of clarity, relevance, and usefulness may be more easily achieved by using an outline, organized around the issues the clinician believes to be most important to the goal of assessment. It would be impossible to give examples of all possible report outlines, so we shall consider just a few representatives of the main models of clinical psychology. Illustrations of the reports that might be based upon each outline will also be presented.

1. A Psychodynamic Report. The following dynamically oriented outline is an edited version of the one used by Tallent (1976, pp. 121–122) for reporting his assessment of a young man who had been in trouble with the law for bookie activities and assault:

I. Conflicts

  A. Self-perception

  B. Goals

  C. Frustrations

  D. Interpersonal relations

  E. Perception of environment

  F. Drives, dynamics

  G. Emotional cathexes

  H. Emotional controls

II. Social stimulus value

  A. Cognitive skills

  B. Conative factors

  C. Goals

  D. Social role

III. Cognitive functioning

  A. Deficit

  B. Psychopathology

IV. Defenses

  A. Denial

  B. Interpersonal tactics

  C. Fantasy

    2. Effects of medication

    3. Cognitive determinants of problems

  E. Dimensions of problems

    1. Duration

    2. Pervasiveness

    3. Frequency

    4. Magnitude

  F. Consequences of problems

    1. Positive

    2. Negative

III. Other problems (observed by assessor but not stated by client)

IV. Personal assets

V. Targets for change

VI. Recommended treatments

VII. Client motivation for treatment

VIII. Prognosis

IX. Priority for treatment

X. Client expectancies

  A. About solving specific problems

  B. About treatment enterprise in general

XI. Other comments

The report based on this outline is presented in Box 3–11.

2. A Behavioral Report. Pomeranz and Goldfried (1970) describe an assessment outline representative of the behavioral model. An edited version is as follows:

I. Description of client's physical appearance and behavior during assessment

II. Presenting problems

  A. Nature of Problems

  B. Historical background of problems

  C. Current situational determinants of problems

  D. Relevant organismic variables

    1. Physiological states

The use of this outline for summarizing assessment of a male college student produced the report contained in Box 3–12.

3. A Phenomenological Report. In line with their subjective approach and general distrust of formal assessment, phenomenologically oriented clinicians deemphasize specific outlines for guiding psychological reports. Reports may be based upon a general framework such as:

I. Client from own point of view

II. Client as reflected in tests

III. Client as seen by assessor

An example of a report organized in this phenomenological way is presented in Box 3–13. Although the clinician administered some

This man is most readily understood in terms of his unusually passive, dependent approach to life and his attempts to overcome the deeply unhappy state brought about by this personality limitation.

Mr. A does not feel very adequate as a person, an attitude which is developed through experiencing a continual sense of failure in terms of his own goals, and which apparently is reinforced by others. In fact, his relations with his father very likely are the basic reason for such feeling. This person is seen by the patient as cold, rejecting, punishing, and unapproachable. He has an urge to rebel and fight against this person—an urge which has been generalized to all society, but he is afraid to give vent to his impulses. Whatever emotional support he does get (got) seems to be from the mother.

As others see him, he seems to have the essential capacity to do well if only he would try. He scores at the average level on a test of intelligence (IQ: 106), he is able to learn readily, when he wants to, and on occasion can perform unusually fast and effectively.

Yet he does not typically follow through on this advantage. His willingness, sometimes even his desire, to do well fluctuates, so that in the long run he could not be regarded as a constructive or responsible person.

Other personality deficiencies also compromise his functioning. Under stress or when faced with difficult problems he becomes blocked, confused and indecisive. His thinking does not show sufficient flexibility to meet such situations so that he would be regarded as inadaptable and unspontaneous.

Mr. A's felt inadequacy causes him to feel that he is not as good as others. By way of reassuring himself on this matter he frequently during examination makes remarks that he is "like everybody else." The feeling that he is inferior includes also the sexual area where he is quite confused about his maleness. It is likely that one or more sex problems contribute to his sense of failure, although, quite understandably, he denies this and indicates a satisfactory sex life "like everybody else."

BOX 3-11
Example of an Assessment Report
Based on a Psychodynamically Oriented Outline

formal psychological tests, the data from them are reported in subjective terms.

More detailed discussions of the techniques and problems associated with writing clinical assessment reports are available in articles and books by Groth-Marnat (1984), Klopfer (1960; 1983), Sattler (1988), and Tallent (1992).

A Note on Ethics

The collection, processing, and communication of assessment data require that clinicians have access to sensitive information that the client might not ordinarily reveal. This places a heavy responsibility on the assessor to use and report this privileged information in a fashion that safeguards the client's welfare and dignity and shows concern for (1) how psychological assessment data are being used, (2) who may have access to confidential material, and (3) the possibility that improper or irresponsible interpretation of assessment information will have negative consequences for clients.

With these concerns in mind, clinicians must first be sure their inquiries do not comprise an unauthorized invasion of a client's privacy (see Bongar,1988, for suggestions on how to maintain privacy when using comput-

He hardly experiences the full effect of his failures, however. He protects himself by denying many events of reality, by keeping many facts about himself and other unconscious, by a general attitude of "not knowing"—an attitude of naiveness. He can hardly take corrective action about himself because he does not understand himself or his actions, or recognize the nature of his problems. Oddly enough, as already stated, this is an unhappy person, but he does not adequately recognize this fact nor does he appear to others as depressed. Yet on occasion this might be a factor in his behavior which could be personally or socially unfortunate.

This man's insecurity about himself forces him into a receptive orientation to other people. He must have friends to provide support. To achieve this he presents himself in a positive, correct light, tries to say the "right" things and even to be ingratiating and obsequious. It is important that he create the "right" effect and may resort to dramatic behavior to bring this about. "Friends" are so important to him that he sometimes must take abuse in order to hold them. He must always hold back hostile expression.

But it is perhaps in fantasy where the greatest satisfaction is derived. He dreams of being a "success" (his term)—accumulating enough money by the age of 35 so he can retire and effortlessly enjoy the comforts of the world. In his fantasy he is independent of authority, can openly express the aggression he ordinarily cannot, and flout society. He has no positive feelings about social rules (although he may profess to), but is concerned when apprehended for misconduct, possibly less for the real punishment than for how it "looks" to be known for doing what he is afraid to do. It is little wonder then that he is easy prey for an "easy money" scheme.

Source: Norman Tallent, *Psychological Report Writing,* © 1976, pp. 121–122. Reprinted by permission of Prentice-Hall, Inc., Englewood Cliffs, New Jersey.

BOX 3–11
Continued

ers in assessment). Next, care should be taken to assure that assessment goals are not socially or culturally biased so that certain clients (e.g., members of ethnic or racial minorities) are placed at a disadvantage. Some psychological tests have been alleged to be inappropriate for use with minority groups, leading to court decisions prohibiting their use for educational placement and other purposes (see Lambert, 1981 for discussion of the landmark *Larry P. V. Wilson Riles* case in California). Finally, clinicians must wrestle with the problem of who may have access to assessment data if they do not maintain sole control over them. When test scores, conclusions, predictions, and other information are communicated in a report, they may be misused by persons who see the report but are not qualified to interpret it. In such cases, not only is the client's privacy invaded, but the assessment may harm the client.

Minimizing these problems is a major concern of public officials, government agencies, citizens groups, and private individuals. Some of them advocate elimination of all psychological assessment (especially testing), while others urge safeguards to protect clients from assessment abuses. The latter option has been adopted by the American Psychological Association, whose *Ethical Principles of Psychologists* (APA, 1992), *General Guidelines for Providers of Psychological Services* (APA, 1987), and *Standards for Educational and Psychological Testing* (APA, 1985) contain extensive

Behavior During Interview and Physical Description:

James is a clean-shaven, long-haired young man who appeared for the intake interview in well-coordinated college garb: jeans, wide belt, open shirt, and sandals. He came across as shy and soft-spoken, with occasional minor speech blocks. Although uneasy during most of the session, he nonetheless spoke freely and candidly.

Presenting Problem:

A. *Nature of problem:* Anxiety in public speaking situations, and other situations in which he is being evaluated by others.

B. *Historical setting events:* James was born in France, and arrived in this country seven years ago, at which time he experienced both a social and language problem. His social contacts had been minimal until he entered college, at which time a socially aggressive friend of his helped him to break out of his shell. James describes his father as being an overly critical and perfectionistic person who would, on occasion, rip up his homework if it fell short of the mark. The client's mother is pictured as a controlling, overly affectionate person who was always showing concern about his welfare. His younger brother, who has always been a good student, was continually thrown up to James by his parents as being far better than he.

C. *Current situational determinants:* Interaction with his parents, examinations, family gatherings, participation in classes, initial social contacts.

D. *Relevant organismic variables:* The client appears to be approaching a number of situations with certain irrational expectations, primarily unrealistic strivings of perfection and an overwhelming desire to receive approval from others. He is not taking any medication at this time.

E. *Dimensions of problem:* The client's social and evaluative anxiety are long-standing and occur in a wide variety of day-to-day situations.

F. *Consequences of problem:* His chronic level of anxiety resulted in an ulcer operation at the age of 15. In addition, he has developed a skin rash on his hands and arms, apparently from excessive perspiration. He reports that his nervousness at one time caused him to stutter, but this appears to be less a problem in more recent years. His anxiety in examination situations has typically interfered with his ability to perform well.

Other Problems:

A. *Assertiveness:* Although obviously a shy and timid individual, James said that lack of assertiveness is no longer a problem with him. At one time in the past, his friends would take advantage of him, but he claims that this is no longer the case. This should be followed up further, as it is unclear what he means by assertiveness.

BOX 3–12

Example of an Assessment Summary Based on a Behavioral Outline

B. *Forgetfulness:* The client reports that he frequently misses appointments, misplaces items, locks himself out of his room, and generally is absent-minded.

Personal Assets:

The client is fairly bright and comes across as a warm, friendly, and sensitive individual.

Targets for Modification:

Unrealistic self-statements in social-evaluative situations; possibly behavioral deficits associated with unassertiveness; and forgetfulness.

Recommended Treatment:

It appears that relaxation training would be a good way to begin, especially in light of the client's high level of anxiety. Following this, the treatment should move along the lines of rational restructuring, and possibly behavior rehearsal. It is unclear as yet what would be the best strategy for dealing with forgetfulness.

Motivation for Treatment:

High.

Prognosis:

Very good.

Priority for Treatment:

High.

Expectancies:

On occasion, especially when going out on a date with a female, James would take half a sleeping pill to calm himself down. He wants to get away from this, and feels what he needs is to learn to cope with his anxieties by himself. It would appear that he will be very receptive to whatever treatment plan we finally decide on, especially if the emphasis is on self-control of anxiety.

Other Comments:

Considering the brief time available between now and the end of the semester, between-session homework assignments should be emphasized as playing a particularly important role in the behavior change process.

BOX 3–12
Continued

Referral: Last January 24-year-old Darrell and his partner were arrested in New Jersey for collecting funds on department store goods which they simply had picked up from the shelves. They collected $100 to $200 per day in this fashion for several months. Both young men were released on probation in March following a couple months in jail. Mr. and Mrs. Holderin are now seeking psychotherapy for their son in hopes that it will be of personal help to him and will preclude further lawbreaking.

The psychiatrist they contacted has in turn requested a general psychological assessment prior to deciding whether to begin psychotherapy. He is particularly concerned with the possibility of schizoid functioning, especially as it might appear in the Rorschach, and with Darrell's intellectual assets.

Date of assessment: 5-6-74

Date of report: 5-12-74

Assessment opportunities: Extended interview, Bender-Gestalt, Wechsler Adult Intelligence Scale (partial), Rorschach, Thematic Apperception Test, human drawings, and mutual discussion of my impressions.

First appearance: Darrell showed up at my office precisely on time. He was dressed in a fashionable doublebreasted suit, wide silk tie, and silk shirt with cufflinks. He carried these well, and indeed struck me as youthfully handsome. After waiting for me to indicate where we were to go, he comfortably explained that he needed change for $10 in order to feed a parking meter. Secretaries, students, and I all scurried around looking for change as he stood by politely and nonchalantly. When he wrote a check for my services, he added the forty cents I had offered him.

Once into my office, Darrell continued to seem at ease. In a casual way he asked permission to smoke, suggested that the window be opened, and took off his jacket. Except when doing pencil work, he seemed bodily relaxed. Later, he smilingly mentioned that his idol is Alexander Mundy of the T.V. program "To Catch a Thief"—boyish in handsome appearance, a lady-killer, mod dresser with expensive entertainment tastes, sports car enthusiast, conman with class, and thief extraordinaire. Darrell remarked both that such aspirations were "unrealistic" *and* that he had thoroughly enjoyed approximating them during his recent misadventure.

Toward the end of our meeting, this suave appearance was thown into relief as Darrell recounted his favorite horror stories, joked continuously, and drew cartoon figures complete with slapstick captions. He had also earnestly shared his educational ambitions

BOX 3-13
Example of an Assessment Summary
Based on a Phenomenological Outline

guidelines for assessors to follow as they go about the sensitive task of learning about their clients. Supervision of psychological assessment has not just been the responsibility of the profession. Federal legislation in the form of the Equal Employment Opportunity Act (part of the Civil Rights Act of 1964) prohibits discriminatory use of tests that have "adverse impact" on the selection of minority group job candidates. Ethical problems and standards associated with clinical psychology will be considered in greater detail in Chapter 14.

and sought advice from me. Altogether I found him consistently easy to be with and to like—something in the manner of a teacher shaking her head but enjoying a charmingly problematic student.

Darrell as he sees himself: As mentioned, the Alexander Mundy project is a powerful and often successful one for Darrell. When he has the money, he dresses well and wines and dines well. He even owns a sports car of sorts (a Karman Ghia). And like Mundy, he has only a few male friends, but is highly successful with having his way with women. Although he would "go to pieces" if he saw a girl cry because he had hurt her, he usually lies to get what he wants and sees nothing wrong with doing so. Girls are all phony anyway, except one whom he met since being released from jail. Darrell finds he can't put on airs with her and doesn't want to. She's honest and really likes him. She even invited him to come with her and her parents to Atlantic City—"nobody ever did that for me before!" But he won't get married for at least three years, until he's sure that his criminal conviction (which she doesn't know about yet) would not hurt either of them.

Back to the Mundy style. Even in grade school Darrell was often regarded as some sort of trouble maker who wasn't properly fulfilling his potential. Darrell wouldn't tell much about these years, but he did talk about a haunting memory of a woman principal chastising him about what was going to become of him. He was quite upset when he read a few years ago about her death. But mostly Darrell focuses on his triumphs. For example, he talks his way into job after job easily, and once was able to get an extended leave of absence by making up an intricate tale about having to go to the Mayo Clinic for critical surgery. And, not caring for the "hurry up and wait" routine of military service, and missing his friends and old life, Darrell waited out the requisite six months before applying for a psychiatric discharge that would formally be an honorable discharge. He feels he really put one over on the doctor, who wrote that Darrell was prone to "impulsive outbursts." Darrell acknowledges pride in these behaviors as well as in his recent thievery—if it weren't for his partner, they would never have been caught. But he emphasizes that he doesn't want anyone else to know about his lawbreaking, and he feels it would be stupid to run the risk of again doing something that he might get caught at. He also suspects that what he did was somewhat immature—an abhorrent thought.

BOX 3–13
Continued

Darrell through the tests: Darrell plunged right into whatever I asked of him, with the effect of partially masking what I took from his frequent sideways glances at me as discomfort and uncertainty about his ability. When asked to copy the *Bender* designs, he did so in about half the usual time. He started out carefully counting dots, asking for instructions, and so on, but wound up with the wrong number going in the wrong direction. As he noted my acceptance, he simply frowned at his mistakes and let them go. Not having planned ahead, he also ran out of space. When I mentioned these things to him and asked if they were similar to other events in his life, Darrell readily and amusedly agreed. Examples were getting arrested, not being further ahead in life at his age, and impatience with all his forms of employment (copyboy to clothes salesman).

On the *WAIS* information section, I noticed Darrell's rapid way of speaking—sort of nonstop, in this case with all kinds of qualifiers, protestations, quick approximations, and requests for feedback. Here, he earned an average score. He acknowledged that this style is typical when a task is not intrinsically interesting and/or when it leaves no room for him to make up his own answers. "I was never any good at math, chemistry, and languages." And sure enough, when he was asked to repeat a series of digits, Darrell failed to score beyond average; he tried to memorize the digits, but often blurted them out, seemingly hoping that they would fall into place. We agreed that he behaves in a similar fashion while working for his father. Moreover that situation becomes exaggerated when Darrell responds to his father's chidings with even more carelessness.

For the most part, Darrell raced through the Rorschach, giving rapid responses and elaborations, turning the cards, and stopping abruptly with about three responses to each card. Most of the percepts involved motion, e.g., "scorpions fighting, people dancing at a costume party, men racing to dance with this girl. Keystone cops—'I'm going first; no, I'm going first,' fighting a duel, violent fight, two roadrunners colliding—'beep-beep,' atomic bomb explosion, flying dinosaurs." In addition, these percepts were laced with enthusiastic rehashings of T.V. horror stories, movies, and science fiction stories. When I suggested that maybe Darrell is action-oriented, he readily agreed and gave more examples of having acted without thinking. Among these were what he called "instinctive" hitting back when physically pushed around. He denied other combativeness. When I pointed out that much of the Rorschach action seemed to be competitive, he saw no relation to his own life,

BOX 3–13
Continued

instead asserting that, for example, he doesn't have to compete because he's usually the first choice of the girls he wants. Nevertheless, I have a sense of his struggling in a vague way to be first in order not to be somehow put down—or squashed down.

Moving on to the *TAT* stories, I remarked to Darrell that his stories (again rapidly given) were usually straight adaptations of T.V. stories, novels, and movies. He denied that he watches these much anymore, and couldn't "go" with my observation that there were no real people, no involvements in the present, little interpersonal warmth. But he did reiterate that he has never had many friends and that girls are phony. With that, to the blank card he made up a picture of Annette (his new girl friend, 18 years old) and himself on a picnic in a beautiful meadow, just being alone together listening to music, and looking at the mountains. "Sounds childish, but I enjoy doing it."

Conclusion: In answer to the referral question, there is no evidence of autistic thinking. Although there is a general dysocial picture, it is definitely not of schizoid proportions. Moreover, Darrell has begun to let himself form closer relationships with at least Annette and his father, tentative as these may be. And under nonconfrontational circumstances, such as moments in our assessment session, he has been able to own and explore certain affects. Thus although there were certain similarities to "schizoid functioning," he can be viewed more productively as living an extended adolescence. I suspect that therapy would have to encourage him through some developmental sequences as well as current difficulties. As I see it, he could thus become more intimate with and sensitive to other persons.

For whatever it's worth, I might point out a problem I might have in an extended relation with Darrell, a problem which I think he's run into repeatedly. His charm and likeableness are likely to rally people to his side until he lets them down by running off or by not returning their care. Then he is either ignored or nagged, both of which demonstrate to him again that people are phony and there are no close friends. So off he goes to emulate Mundy with little concern for the consequences to others.

Source: Report by Constance T. Fischer, in Norman Tallent, *Psychological Report Writing,* © 1976, pp. 221–225. Reprinted by permission of Prentice-Hall, Inc., Englewood Cliffs, New Jersey.

BOX 3–13
Continued

CHAPTER 4

Interviewing
in
Clinical Psychology

The interview is the most widely employed tool in clinical psychology. It plays a prominent role in psychological treatment and is a major component of clinical assessment. Although much of the material in this chapter about assessment interviews applies to treatment interviews as well, later chapters will discuss treatment interviews more fully.

This chapter does not teach you how to interview. The material covered here is only a preliminary introduction to the interview as an assessment data source. Interviewing is a skill that requires practice and careful supervision. You cannot learn to be a good interviewer simply by reading about the subject, though there are excellent sources available (e.g., Bernstein, Bernstein, & Dana, 1974; Bingham, Moore, & Gustad, 1959; Cormier & Cormier, 1979; Deutsch & Murphy, 1955; Hersen & Turner, 1985; Shea, 1988; Sullivan, 1954).

WHAT IS AN INTERVIEW?

In simplest terms, an interview is a conversation with a purpose or goal (Matarazzo, 1965).

Consider the following interchange between A and B:

A: How did you spend the weekend?

B: Well, it was pretty quiet. I slept in on Saturday and then watched a football game in the afternoon. That night, my wife's brother came over with their 8-year-old boy. We sat around and talked most of the night. Drank a lot of beer.

A: Were you home on Sunday, too?

B: Most of it. I didn't feel too great so I just sat around. Later I watched the Packers game on TV. My wife kept griping about how we never go anywhere. Finally, I took her out to eat. We had a flat on the way home and I ruined a perfectly good shirt while I was changing the damn thing.

If A were B's co-worker and this interaction took place on the way to the office Monday morning, it would simply be a conversation like billions of others every day. But this same exchange could have been part of an interview in which A (a clinician) is gathering information about B and his lifestyle. The distinction between social conversations and interviews is based not so much on content as on whether they serve a particular purpose. Interviews have been a part of everyday life for centuries. It is important to recognize that clinicians adopted and refined the interview; they did not invent it.

CLINICAL INTERVIEW SITUATIONS

The fact that interviews resemble other forms of conversation makes them a natural source of clinical information about people, an easy means of communicating with them, and a convenient context for attempting to help them. Interviews are flexible, relatively inexpensive, and, perhaps most important, provide the clinician with simultaneous samples of clients' verbal and nonverbal behavior. These advantages make the interview useful in a variety of clinical situations, including the following:

1. Intake. The most common type of clinical interview is when a client comes to the clinician because of some problem in living. The psychologist may have little information about the client, so intake interviews are designed mainly to establish the nature of the problem. Information gathered in this situation may be used by interviewers to decide whether they are an appropriate source of help for the client. The interviewer must ask, "Can I work with this person? Is this problem within my area of expertise?" If, on the basis of one or more intake interviews, the answer to such questions is no, the clinician will refer the client to another professional or agency for alternative services. If further contact is seen as desirable, assessment or treatment is scheduled for future sessions. Most clinicians conduct their own intake interviews, but in some agencies and group practices, social workers or other personnel perform this function.

The intake interview is often critically important to successful treatment because almost half the clients who attend an intake interview fail to return for scheduled treatment (Baekeland & Lundwall, 1975). One variable that appears to affect this pattern is clients' perception of their intake interviewer. Clients are more likely to return for subsequent treatment after talking with an interviewer who treats them with warm friendliness as opposed to businesslike professionalism (Dembo, Weyant, & Warner, 1982).

2. Problem Identification. The decision to accept or refer a client on the basis of intake information rests, in part, on the nature of the client's problems. For this reason, intake interviews are also aimed at problem identification. In clinical situations where a decision to work with the client has already been made, an interview may focus entirely on identification or elaboration of the client's problems.

The interviewer is often asked for a *classification* or diagnosis of the problem (Wiens & Matarazzo, 1983). This can take the form of an Axis I label (e.g., Acute Paranoid Disorder), along with associated descriptions on the other four axes. Less psychiatrically oriented clinicians and those not required to classify people may use problem-identification interviews to develop descriptions of clients and the environmental context in which their behavior occurs.

This type of interview is sometimes known as a *psychiatric interview.* Originally patterned after the question-and-answer format of medical history taking, psychiatric interviews are usually structured according to a sequence of important topics, although there are those clinicians who, influenced by psychoanalytic or humanistic ideas, conduct them in a more indirect manner. According to Siassi (1984, p. 260), the purposes of psychiatric interviews are "to arrive at a diagnostic formulation and a rational treatment plan. . . . an attempt is made to discover the origin and evolution of the patient's mental disorder(s) by obtaining a biographical-historical account that can provide a psychological portrait of the patient." Many psychiatric interviews contain a *mental status examination,* which involves a planned set of direct, focused questions presented in a certain order. The mental status examination is analogous to the physical exam in a physician's assessment. It attempts to assess a client's functioning in a number of areas relating to mental functioning (see Box 4–1 for an example).

Interviews designed to *classify* client problems are most common in mental hospitals and other facilities where a diagnosis is required (see Hersen & Turner, 1985). Similar interviews may also occur when psychologists serve as diagnostic consultants to psychiatrists, courts, schools, or others interested in such questions as "Is Mr. P. competent to stand trial?" "Is Mrs. L. psychotic?" "Is Jimmy G. mentally retarded?"

Interviews focused on *describing* clients and their problems in more comprehensive terms usually occur in the context of the full-scale clinical exploration that precedes treatment by a mental health professional. Here, the interviewer elicits a detailed account of the client's strengths and weaknesses, current life situation, and social history, often following outlines such as those presented in the previous chapter.

3. Orientation. People receiving psychological assessment or treatment often do not know what to expect, let alone what is expected of them. This is especially true if they have had no previous contact with mental health professionals. To make these new experiences less mysterious and more comfortable, many clinicians conduct special interviews (or reserve segments of interviews) to acquaint the client with the assessment, treatment, or research procedures to come.

Orientation interviews are beneficial in at least two ways. First, because the client is encouraged to ask questions and make comments, misconceptions that might obstruct

subsequent sessions can be discussed and corrected. As an example, some clients may assume that whatever they say to a clinician will be repeated to other members of the family. Fears of this kind can be allayed during an orientation interview.

Orientation interviews also can communicate new expectations designed to facilitate later interactions. Often this is done by describing the kinds of things that "good" clients are expected to do in assessment or treatment. Thus, the client learns what is coming and what will be expected in the way of cooperation, effort, and self-disclosure. In most cases, clients are free to choose not to participate in the activities described. This freedom, along with accurate expectations by those who do participate, tends to make assessment and treatment sessions more efficient and effective (Goldstein, 1971; Heitler, 1976; Orne & Wender, 1968; Strupp & Bloxom, 1973).

4. Termination. Related to the problem of orienting clients to forthcoming clinical experiences is that of satisfactorily terminating those experiences. Persons who have just completed a series of assessment sessions involving extensive interviews, tests, and observations are understandably anxious to know "what the doctor found," how the information will be used, and who will have access to it. Such concerns are particularly acute when the assessor has acted as consultant to a school, court, or psychiatrist. An interview (or at least a portion of it) designed to explain the procedures and protections involved in transmission of privileged information, and to provide a summary and interpretation of assessment results, can help alleviate the distress that clients feel about assessment.

In research settings, a termination interview is referred to as *debriefing.* Debriefing includes an explanation of the project in which the subject has participated and discussion of the procedures employed in it. Debriefings permit subjects to ask questions and make comments about their research experiences. Debriefing

There are many guides on how to conduct the MSE and what information to include in it (MacKinnon, 1980; Spitzer, Fleiss, Burdock, & Hardesty, 1964). A typical outline of topics is the following organization recommended by Siassi (1984):

I. General apearance and behavior—client's level of activity, reaction to interviewer, grooming and clothing are assessed.

II. Speech and thought—is client's speech coherent and understandable; are there delusions present.

III. Consciousness—is the sensorium clear or clouded.

IV. Mood and affect—is client depressed, anxious, restless, is affect appropriate to situation.

V. Perception—does client experience hallucinations, depersonalization.

VI. Obsessions and compulsions—amount and quality of these behaviors are noted.

VII. Orientation—is client aware of correct time, place, and personal identity.

VIII. Memory—what is condition of short- and long-term memory.

IX. Attention and concentration—asking client to count backwards by 7's is a common strategy.

X. Fund of general information—questions like "Who is the President?"— or "What are some big cities in the U.S.?" are asked.

XI. Intelligence—estimated from educational achievement, reasoning ability, and fund of information.

XII. Insight and judgment—does patient understand probable outcomes of behavior.

XIII. Higher intellectual functioning—what is the quality of patient's form of thinking; is patient able to deal with abstraction.

The MSE attempts to gather information efficiently. The questioning is direct, as suggested by the following excerpt from an MSE:

CLINICIAN: Good morning. What is your name?

CLIENT: Randolph S———.

CLINICIAN: Well, Mr. S———, I would like to ask you some questions this morning. Is that all right?

CLIENT: Fine.

CLINICIAN: How long have you been here?

CLIENT: Since yesterday morning.

CLINICIAN: Why are you here?

CLIENT: I don't know. I think my wife called the police and here I am.

CLINICIAN: Well, what did you do to make her call the police?

CLIENT: I don't know.

CLINICIAN: What day is today?

CLIENT: Tuesday, the twelfth.

CLINICIAN: What year is it?

CLIENT: 1977.

CLINICIAN: What city are we in?

CLIENT: Chicago.

CLINICIAN: Who is the mayor of Chicago?

BOX 4–1
The Mental Status Examination (MSE)

of volunteers is aimed at assuring that no element of the research experience has left a harmful residue and is in keeping with the research ethics of the American Psychological Association (APA, 1990, see Chapter 14). Candid debriefings may also benefit the clinician, since they yield clues as to what variables determined volunteers' behavior in the laboratory (Orne, 1962).

Completion of treatment also requires some form of termination interview. Many loose ends need to be tied up: There is gratitude to be expressed and accepted, reminders to be given about the handling of future problems, plans to be made for follow-up contacts, and reassurance given to clients about their ability to go it alone. Termination interviews serve the purpose of making the transition from treatment to post-treatment as smooth and productive as possible.

5. Crises. When a person's problems are of an immediate and pressing nature, and normal problem-solving skills prove inadequate to deal with the situation, the person is said to be in a crisis. Often, people in crises appear for help at clinical facilities or call a hotline, suicide prevention center, or other crisis service. In such cases, the interviewer does not have the luxury of scheduling a series of assessment sessions followed by treatment. The crisis must be dealt with on the spot, requiring the combination of several interview goals that would otherwise be distributed over a number of sessions. The interviewer attempts to provide support, collect assessment data, and provide help. He or she must deal with the client in a calm and accepting fashion, ask relevant questions ("Have you ever tried to kill yourself?" "What kinds of pills do you have in the house?"), and work on the immediate problem directly or through referral to other services. One or two well-handled interviews during a crisis may be the beginning and the end of contact with a client whose need for assistance was temporary and situation specific. For others, the crisis interview leads to subsequent assessment and treatment sessions.

6. Observation. As already noted, interviews provide an opportunity to observe client behaviors. Clinicians sometimes conduct interviews to see how a person deals with certain circumstances. Here, the interview provides a context for observing the interviewee's reaction to stressful, ambiguous, or conflict-laden situations. This sort of interview will be more thoroughly described when we consider observational assessments in Chapter 6.

INTERVIEW STRUCTURE

The most basic variable in clinical interviews is *structure:* the degree to which the interviewer determines the content and course of the conversation. At one end of the structure continuum are *nondirective* interviews, in which the clinician does as little as possible to interfere with the natural flow of the client's speech and choice of topics. At the other end are *structured* interviews, which involve a carefully planned question-and-answer format. In between are many blends, usually referred to as *guided* or *semistructured* interviews.

Some excerpts from a few interviews may make the structure dimension clearer. Consider first this segment from a nondirective intake interview.

CLINICIAN: [Your relative] didn't go into much detail about what you wanted to talk about, so I wonder if you'd just start in at whatever you want to start in with, and tell me what kind of nervousness you have.

CLIENT: Well, it's, uh, I think if I were to put it in, in a few words, it seems to be a, a, a complete lack of self-confidence in, and an extreme degree of self-consciousness. Now, I have always been a very self-conscious person. I mean every, just about, since I was probably fourteen years old the first I remember of it. But for a long time I've realized that I was sort of using people as crutches. I mean I, a lot of things I felt I couldn't do myself I did all right if someone was along.

CLINICIAN: Um-hm.

CLIENT: And it's just progressed to the point where I'm actually using the four walls of the house as an escape from reality. I mean I don't, I don't care to go out. I, I certainly can't go out alone. . . . It's sort of a vicious circle. I find out I can't do it, and then I'm sure the next time I can't do it.

CLINICIAN: Um-hm.

CLIENT: And it just gets progressively worse. I think the first that I ever noticed it . . . (Wallen, 1956, p. 146)

The client continued a narrative about the problem's onset and duration, her occupation and marriage, her father's death, and other topics. Notice that the clinician hardly says a word, although as we shall see, there are things he could have done to nondirectively encourage client speech if necessary.

At the other extreme are highly structured interviews. We have already described the mental status exam as one example of a structured interview.

In some structured interviews, the format for questions is so tightly organized and the script for the interviewer so precisely worded that the resulting interview is more like an oral questionnaire than a free-flowing discussion. Most interviews are not this structured. Instead, they combine organization with flexibility and require the interviewer to exercise well-tuned listening skills and discretion in guiding the interview. These interviews are sometimes called *semistructured,* meaning that they follow a specific outline of topics, provide explicit rules for the interviewer to follow, but also require the interviewer to make independent decisions about the wording of questions and the interpretation of answers.

In the following excerpt, both nondirective and structured features appear; the interviewer encourages the client to express herself freely, but also places limits on the topic by asking a specific question.

CLINICIAN: You say that you are very jealous a lot of the time and this upsets you a great deal.

CLIENT: Well, I know it's stupid for me to feel that way, but I am hurt when I even *think* of Mike with another woman.

CLINICIAN: You don't want to feel jealous but you do.

CLIENT: I know that's not the way a "liberated" woman should be.

CLINICIAN: What is your idea of how a liberated woman should feel?

CLIENT: I don't know. In many ways I feel I have changed so much in the last year. I really don't believe you have the right to own another person—and yet, when it happens to me, I feel really hurt. I'm such a hypocrite.

CLINICIAN: You're unhappy because you are not responding the way you really would like to?

CLIENT: I'm not the person I want to be.

CLINICIAN: So there's really "double jeopardy." When Mike is with someone else, it really hurts you. And, when you feel jealous, you get down on yourself for being that way.

CLIENT: Yes, I guess I lose both ways. (Morganstern & Tevlin, 1981, p. 86)

While some clinicians adopt either a nondirective or structured interview approach under most circumstances, the majority adjust structure to accommodate the goals of the interview. For example, by their nature, crises demand more structure than might be needed during a routine intake interview. Structure may change during an interview; many problem-identification interviews begin in a nondirective way and become more structured as the interview continues.

Structure also depends on the theoretical orientation and personal preferences of the interviewer. In general, phenomenological clinicians provide the least interview structure.

Freudians usually provide more. Behavioral clinicians are likely to be the most verbally active and directive.

In recent years, the major development in psychological interviewing has been the proliferation of new structured and semistructured interviews to be used for a variety of purposes. The popularity of structured interviews can be traced to several sources. First, their use has been stimulated by increased reliance on operationally defined criteria for making psychiatric diagnoses via *DSM-III-R* and *DSM-IV* (Spiker & Ehler, 1984). Such criteria lend themselves well to being measured by structured questions. Second, the reliability of diagnoses appears to have improved greatly, a change that some experts (Matarazzo, 1983b) attribute, in part, to the increased use of structured interviews. Finally, structured interviews have proven valuable in clinical research. They are used to select subjects on the basis of criteria used in the research study, and, by providing a context where trust and rapport can be established, they enable researchers to conduct in-depth studies of sensitive topics such as drug abuse (Craig, 1988) or victimization experiences (Himelein, 1988). One other research area where structured interviews have become almost indispensable is *epidemiology,* the study of how disorders are distributed in the population and of the factors that affect this distribution (Williams & Poling, 1989).

Structured and semistructured interviews are designed according to several principles (Helzer, 1983; Morrison, 1988): (a) The interviewer asks specific questions that can be replicated by other interviewers; (b) the interview is conducted by a pre-established format in which the order of questions and the definition of terms used in the questions are standardized; and (c) consistent rules are provided for scoring the respondents' answers or for making additional probes that will obtain scorable responses. Structured interviews do not eliminate open-ended questions; neither do they prevent interviewers from formulating their own additional questions to clarify ambiguous responses. However, they do provide detailed rules (sometimes called "decision trees" or "branching rules") for informing the interviewer what to do in the event of certain responses ("if the respondent answers 'no' skip to question 32; if the respondent answers 'yes' inquire as to how many times it happened and continue to the next question").

The development of new structured interviews and revisions of existing ones are major research activities for some clinical psychologists. Box 4–2 lists a few of the structured interviews in use today and summarizes their intended purposes. Among structured interviews, the best-known instruments are those that enable the interviewer to arrive at a psychiatric diagnosis. Therefore, these interview formats are coordinated with *DSM* diagnostic criteria. Of this group of diagnostic interviews, the most commonly employed are the Schedule of Affective Disorders and Schizophrenia (SADS; Endicott & Spitzer, 1978), one of the earliest structured diagnostic interviews, intended to help differentially diagnose more than 20 mental disorders; the Diagnostic Interview Schedule (DIS; Robins, Helzer, Croughan, Williams, & Ratcliff, 1981), a highly structured interview designed to be given by nonprofessional interviewers in large-scale epidemiological surveys; and the Structured Clinical Interview for *DSM-III-R* (SCID; Spitzer, Williams, Gibbon, & First, 1988), an interview that comes in several slightly different forms for use with various client groups and enables clinicians to arrive at a *DSM* diagnosis. Box 4–3 presents an excerpt from the SCID that illustrates some features of structured interviews.

The increasing use of structured interviews has earlier parallels in the history of clinical psychology. As we discussed in Chapter 3, using formal, statistical rules for combining assessment data is consistently more effective than having clinicians subjectively integrate the data. A similar feature of structured interviews is that *some* clinical judgment is re-

Name of Interview	Reference	Purpose
1. The Schedule for Affective Disorders & Schizophrenia (SADS)	Endicott & Spitzer (1978)	Differential diagnosis of more than 20 categories of mental disorder.
2. Diagnostic Interview Schedule	Robins, Helzer, Croughan, Williams, & Ratcliff (1981)	Used by nonprofessionals in large-scale epidemiological studies of mental disorder.
3. Structured Clinical Interview for *DSM-III-R* (SCID)	Spitzer, Williams, Gibbon, & First (1988)	Broad-scale differential diagnoses tied to *DSM-III-R* criteria.
4. Diagnostic Interview Schedule for Children (DISC)	Costello, Edelbrock, Kalas, Kessler, & Klaric (1982)	Parallel formats for children and parents for making differential diagnoses of childhood disorders.
5. Anxiety Disorders Interview Schedule (ADIS)	DiNardo, O'Brien, Barlow, Waddel, & Blanchard (1983)	Differential diagnoses among anxiety disorders.
6. Structured Interview for *DSM-III* Personality Disorders	Stangl, Pfohl, Zimmerman, Bowers, & Corenthal (1985)	Differential diagnoses among *DSM-III* Personality Disorders.
7. The Referral Decision Scale (RDS)	Teplin & Schwartz (1989)	Preliminary screening of mental illness in jails.
8. Interdisciplinary Fitness Interview (IF)	Golding, Roesch, & Schreiber (1984)	Evaluation of competence to stand trial.
9. Rogers Criminal Responsibility Assessment Scale (RCRAS)	Rogers, Wasyliw, & Cavanaugh (1984)	Assess criminal responsibility against specific legal criteria.
10. Structured Interview (SI)	Rosenman (1978)	Assess major verbal and nonverbal components of Type A behavior pattern.
11. Structured Interview of Reported Symptoms (SIRS)	Rogers, Gillis, Dickens, & Bagby (1991)	Assess malingering in clinical populations.
12. Suicidal Behaviors Interview (SBI)	Reynolds (in press)	Assess current suicidal behavior in adolescents.

BOX 4–2
Structured Interviews Frequently Used in Clinical Psychology

placed or controlled by the interview's formal decision rules as a way of improving the consistency of the data obtained. As you will learn in Chapter 5, the increasing popularity of objective tests in clinical psychology in contrast to the declining use of the more subjective and unstructured projective tests is another example of the advantages of increased structure in assessment methods.

To summarize, the major advantages of structured interviews are increased reliability of the data obtained and the possibility of training nonprofessionals to conduct structured interviews or of designing computerized versions of the interviews (Farrell, Camplair, & McCullough, 1987) so that clinicians can use their skills for other more conceptually demanding tasks. Are there any limitations to structured interviews? One possible problem is that the structured interview depends too heavily on the memory and descriptive abilities of respondents. Therefore, while the reliability of what the respondent reports might be excellent, the validity or meaning of the reports might be questionable because of problems with a respondent's understanding of the question, motivation to answer truthfully, or ability to self-monitor.

Although theoretical models influence clinicians' approaches to interviews, there is similarity among experienced clinicians of varying theoretical persuasions in the way specific interview situations are handled (see, e.g., Bruinink & Schroeder, 1979; Fiedler, 1950). One suspects that this is due, in part, to the fact that although no one has developed one "right" way to interview, certain strategies have proven valuable in practice and have thus been adopted by skilled clinicians representing every model (Goldfried, 1980).

In the following sections, we will examine the interview techniques commonly employed by clinical psychologists. Selective emphasis on each of these procedures by proponents of various clinical models will be noted where appropriate.

STAGES IN THE INTERVIEW

Interviews are thought of as having a beginning, a middle, and an end. This is a considerable oversimplification, however, since such neat stages may not be discernible in all instances.

Intake or problem-identification interviews are most likely to pass through three segments. They usually begin with efforts at making the client comfortable and ready to speak freely (Stage 1); continue into a central information-gathering stage (Stage 2); and end with summary statements, client questions, and, if appropriate, plans for subsequent meetings (Stage 3). As the client gets to know the clinician, Stage 1 will probably grow shorter while Stage 2 gets longer. Similarly, Stage 3 may be brief until the final assessment interview, when it may take up most of the time available.

Treatment interviews follow a different three-stage format. A session may begin with the client's report of thoughts and events since the last meeting, continue with whatever treatment procedures are being employed, then conclude with a summary of current progress, plans for the next meeting, and/or "homework" assignments.

Interviews relating to crises, orientation, and termination may not be organized around a beginning-middle-end framework. Nevertheless, the three-stage model offers a convenient guide for organizing "typical" clinical interviews.

Stage 1: Beginning the Interview

During initial interviews, clinicians carefully attend to the first minutes of contact. The client is likely to be uncomfortable about talking to a stranger about personal matters, and this apprehension may be intensified by uncertainty about what the psychologist will be doing. As a result, many clients enter the interview with a wait-and-see attitude that prompts them to be careful about what they say. If this attitude continued throughout the conversation, little valuable assessment information would be generated.

Most clinicians see the establishment of *rapport*—a harmonious and comfortable working relationship—as their main task during the first part of initial interviews. Rapport can be gained in several ways, many of which involve common sense and courtesy. A client's anxiety and uncertainty can be eased by demystification of the interview. A warm smile, friendly greeting, and a handshake are excellent beginnings to an interview. Small talk about the weather or difficulty in finding the office also ease the client's transition into the interview but should not go on so long that the interview loses its distinctive quality.

Although interviews can occur anywhere, certain settings are especially conducive to building rapport for most clients. Except for those individuals whose cultural background might cause such surroundings to be threatening, interviews are best conducted in a comfortable, private office. This is because most people find it easier to relax when they can get comfortable physically. Also, it is easier to assure the client of the interview's confidential nature in such a setting.

Several other office characteristics can aid rapport. A reassuring equality is established when two people sit a few feet apart on similar chairs of equal height. If the clinician sits in a high-backed, massive chair behind a huge desk which is 6 feet from the client's smaller, lower seat, rapport may be impaired. A desk cleared of other work, along with precautions to hold phone calls and prevent other intrusions, lets the client know that she or he has the clinician's full attention and conveys sincere interest in what the client has to say.

This list of rapport-building techniques could be extended almost indefinitely; the point is that from the beginning, the clinician tries to create a warm, comfortable environment and a relationship that will encourage the client to speak freely and honestly about whatever topics are relevant to the interview.

Skilled clinicians can establish rapport during the first stage of an initial interview, but even for them, the process continues into the second and third stages and into subsequent contacts as well. Like other social relationships, the one between client and clinician takes time to grow. Once that relationship has taken root, the initial interview can move into its second, or information-gathering, stage.

BOX 4–3

Example of a Structured Interview:

Excerpt from the Structured Clinical Interview for *DSM-III-R* (SCID)

Designed to help clinicians make rapid, valid *DSM-III-R* diagnoses, the SCID is organized into several different modules. Each module is devoted to a major class of disturbance, such as mood disorders, anxiety disorders, or adjustment disorders. An advantage of this organization is that the SCID can be customized for specific research purposes by including only those modules relevant to the study. The excerpt below comes from a portion of the Mood Disorders module ad- dressed to the question of whether the patient has ever experienced a major depressive episode. In the left-hand column are the structured questions of the interview; notice that some of them are open ended, some call for a yes–no answer. In the middle column are the *DSM-III-R* criteria relevant to the interview questions. These are the criteria that interviewers (known as "SCID-ers") must judge, using the right-hand column ratings.

*PAST MAJOR DEPRESSIVE
SYNDROME*   MDS CRITERIA

-> IF NOT CURRENTLY DEPRESSED: A. At least 5 of the fol-   *
   Have you <u>ever</u> had a period   lowing symptoms have each   *
   when you were feeling de-   been present during the same   *
   pressed or down most of the   two-week period (and repre-   *
   day nearly every day? (What   sent a change from previous   *
   was that like?)   functioning); at least one of   *
                                        the symptoms was either   *
-> IF CURRENTLY DEPRESSED BUT   (1) depressed mood, or   *
   FAILED TO MEET FULL CRITERIA,   (2) loss of interest or   *
   SCREEN FOR PAST MDS: Has   pleasure.   *
   there ever been <u>another</u> time
   when you were depressed and   (1) depressed mood most of   ? 1 2 3   33
   had even more of the problems   the day, nearly every day,
   [SXS] that I just asked you   as indicated either by sub-
   about?   jective account or observa-
                                            tion by others
   IF YES: When was that? How
   long did it last (As long
   as two weeks?)

-> IF PAST DEPRESSED MOOD: (2) markedly diminished   ? 1 2 3 * 34
   During that time, were you   interest or pleasure in all,   *
   a lot less interested in most   or almost all, activities   *
   things or unable to enjoy the   most of the day, nearly   ┌──────────┐ *
   things you used to enjoy?   every day (as indicated   │IF NEITHER│ *
   (What was that like?)   either by subjective   │ITEM (1) │ *
                                            account or observation   │NOR (2) IS│ *
-> IF NO PAST DEPRESSED MOOD: by others of apathy most   │CODED "3,"│ *
   What about a time when you were   of the time)   │ GO TO   │ *
   a lot less interested in most   │*CURRENT │ *
   things or unable to enjoy the   │MANIC SYN-│ *
   things you used to enjoy?   │DROME,*   │ *
   (What was that like?)   │A. 10   │ *
                                                                           └──────────┘
   IF YES: When was that? Was
   it nearly every day? How
   long did it last? (As long as
   two weeks?)

Have you had more than one time
like that?
                                        NOTE: DO NOT INCLUDE SXS THAT
   IF MORE THAN ONE: Which time   ARE CLEARLY DUE TO A PHYSICAL
   was the worst?   CONDITION, MOOD-INCONGRUENT
                                        DELUSIONS OR HALLUCINATIONS,
                                        INCOHERENCE OR MARKED LOOSENING   *
                                        OF ASSOCIATIONS, OR SIMPLY   *
                                        PRODROMAL OR RESIDUAL SYMPTOMS   *
                                        OF SCHIZOPHRENIA.   *

?=inadequate information   1=absent or false   2-subthreshold   3=threshold or true

BOX 4-3
Continued

```
FOCUS ON THE WORST EPISODE
THAT THE SUBJECT CAN REMEMBER

During that time...
```

..did you loose or gain any weight? (How much?) (Were you trying to loose weight?) IF NO: How was your appetite? (What about compared to your usual appetite?) (Did you have to force yourself to eat?) (Eat [less/more] than usual?) (Was that nearly every day?)	(3) significant weight loss or weight gain when not dieting (e.g., more than 5% of body weight in a month) or decrease or increase in appetite nearly every day	?	1	2	3	35
..how were you sleeping? (Trouble falling asleep, waking frequently. trouble staying asleep, waking too early, OR sleeping too much? How many hours a night compared to usual? Was that nearly every night?)	(4) insomnia or hypersomnia nearly every day	?	1	2	3	36 * * *
..were you so fidgety or restless that you were unable to sit still? (Was it so bad that other people noticed it? Was that nearly every day?) IF NO: What about the opposite -- talking or moving more slowly than is normal for you? (Was it so bad that other people noticed it? Was that nearly every day?)	(5) psychomotor agitation or retardation nearly every day (observable by others and not merely subjective feelings of restlessness or being slowed down)	?	1	2	3	37 * * * *
..what was your energy like? (Tired all the time? Nearly every day?)	(6) fatigue or loss of energy nearly every day	?	1	2	3	38
..how did you feel about yourself? (Worthless?) (Nearly every day?) IF NO: What about feeling guilty about things you had done or not done? (Nearly every day?)	(7) feelings of worthlessness or excessive or inappropriate guilt (which may be delusional) nearly every day (not merely self-reproach or guilt about being sick) NOTE: CODE "1" OR "2" FOR LOW SELF-ESTEEM BUT NOT WORTHLESSNESS	?	1	2	3	39 * * *

```
?=inadequate information   1=absent or false    2=subthreshold    3=threshold or true
```

BOX 4–3
Continued

During that time...

..did you have trouble thinking or concentrating? (Nearly every day?)

   IF NO: Was it hard to make decisions about everyday things? (Nearly every day?)

..were things so bad that you were thinking a lot about death or that you would be better off dead? What about thinking of hurting yourself?

   IF YES: Did you do anything to hurt yourself?

(8) diminished ability to think or concentrate, or indecisiveness, nearly every day (either by subjective account or as observed by others)	?	1	2	3	40

(9) recurrent thoughts of death (not just fear of dying), recurrent suicidal ideation without a specific plan, or a suicide attempt or a specific plan for committing suicide	?	1	2	3	41

NOTE: CODE "1" FOR SELF-MUTI-LATION W/O SUICIDAL INTENT

AT LEAST FIVE OF THE ABOVE SXS [A(1-9)] ARE CODED "3" AND AT LEAST ONE OF THESE IS ITEM (1) or (2)   1   3   42

IF NOT ALREADY ASKED: Has there been any other time when you were (depressed/OWN EQUIV-ALANT) and had even more of the symptoms that I just asked you about?

  -> IF NO: GO TO "CURRENT MANIC SYNDROME,* A. 10.

  -> IF YES: RETURN TO "PAST MAJOR DEPRESSIVE SYNDROME,* A. 5, AND INQUIRE ABOUT WORST EPISODE.

?=inadequate information   1=absent or false   2=subthreshold   3=threshold or true

---

Source: R. L. Spitzer, J. B. Williams, M. Gibbon, and M. B. First, *Instruction Manual for the Structured Clinical Interview for DSM-III-R (SCID, 6/1/88 Revision)*. Biometrics Research Department, New York State Psychiatric Institute, 722 W. 168th St., New York, NY 10032.

BOX 4-3
Continued

Stage 2: The Middle of the Interview

Transition to the middle of an initial interview should be as smooth for the client as possible. The ways the clinician accomplishes this transition illustrate many major interview tactics.

Nondirective Techniques

In most cases interviewers begin the second stage with nondirective, *open-ended* questions. Common examples are: "What brings you here today?" or "Would you like to tell me about the problems you referred to on the telephone?" A major advantage of the open-ended approach is that it frees the client to begin in his or her own way. An open-ended invitation to talk allows the client to ease into painful or embarrassing topics without feeling pressed.[1] Relatively nonstressful beginnings of this type aid rapport because they communicate the clinician's willingness to listen to whatever the client has to say.

Contrast the open-ended initiations suggested earlier with binding statements like: "You said you thought there was a sex problem. Is it yours or your wife's?" or "What kind of work do you do?" Openings of this type prematurely focus the conversation on topics that may be threatening or irrelevant. An interview whose second stage employs binding tactics often degenerates into a question-and-answer session in which the client may feel put-upon, misunderstood, and frustrated. Accordingly, such interrogation procedures are usually reserved for situations in which the client's behavior indicates that spontaneous speech will not be forthcoming.[2]

Open-ended questions are used whenever the clinician wishes to prompt the client's verbal behavior while influencing its content as little as possible. Classic remarks like "Tell me a bit more about that" and "How did you feel about that?" exemplify a nondirective strategy. This strategy is supplemented by tactics designed to help clients express themselves fully and to enhance rapport by communicating the clinician's understanding and acceptance. The most general of these tactics is called *active listening*. Active listening involves responding to the client's speech in ways that indicate understanding and encouragement to go on. The clinician's "mm-hmms" in the nondirective interview excerpt presented earlier represent active listening. Others include comments such as "I see," "I understand," "I'm with you," or "Right."

A related strategy is called *paraphrasing,* in which the clinician restates what the client has said in order to (a) show that she or he has been listening closely, and (b) give the client a chance to correct the remark if it was misinterpreted. Carl Rogers called this *reflection* and emphasized not only restating content, but also highlighting client feelings. Let's consider some illustrations:

A.

CLIENT: Sometimes I get so mad at my husband, I could kill him.

CLINICIAN: You would just like to get rid of him altogether.

B.

CLIENT: Sometimes I get so mad at my husband, I could kill him.

CLINICIAN: He really upsets you sometimes.

In example A, the clinician merely reworded the client's remark. In example B, he or she reflected the *feeling* contained in the remark. Most clients respond to paraphrasing by con-

---

[1]Clients often begin with a "ticket of admission" problem which may not be the one of greatest concern to them. The real reason for the client's visit may appear only after varying amounts of diversionary conversation.

[2]This is not always the case. Rogers (1967) provides an example of continued, and ultimately fruitful, use of nondirective interviewing with a withdrawn institutionalized client (see Chapter 10).

PEANUTS *by Charles M. Schulz*

FIGURE 4-1   The effects of binding questions on rapport building can sometimes be difficult to repair. Reprinted by permission of United States Feature Syndicate, Inc.

tinuing to talk, usually along the same lines as before, often in greater detail. Paraphrasing often is preferable to a direct question because the latter might change or restrict the conversation. This is illustrated in the following interactions:

A.

CLIENT: What it comes down to is that life just doesn't seem worth living sometimes.

CLINICIAN: Sometimes it all just seems to be too much.

CLIENT: Yeah, and I don't know what to do when I feel that way. I don't really think I want to die, not really. But I also dread the thought of another day starting. For example. . . .

B.

CLIENT: What it comes down to is that life just doesn't seem worth living sometimes.

CLINICIAN: How often do you feel that way?

CLIENT: Oh, off and on.

There is a place for questions such as that asked in example B, but unless one knows enough to start pinpointing specifics, interrupt-

ing with such questions will limit the initial picture of the problem. Immediate use of direct queries can suggest to clients that they should simply wait for the next question. In general, this message does not promote rapport.

Paraphrasing can be used as a clarification device when the clinician is confused about what a client has said. Consider the following:

CLIENT: I told my husband that I didn't want to live with him anymore so he said "fine" and left. Well, when I got back, I found out that the son of a bitch kept all our furniture!

If, as is probably the case, the interviewer does not comprehend the sequence of events described, he or she could simply say "What?", but that might be interpreted by the client as an insult or as an indication that the clinician is a dunce. Instead, a combination of paraphrase and request for clarification serves nicely:

CLINICIAN: OK, let's see if I've got this straight. You told your husband you didn't want to live with him, so *he* left. You later came back to your house from somewhere else and found he had taken the furniture?

Ideally, the client will either confirm this interpretation or fill in the missing pieces. If not, the clinician may wish to use more direct questioning.

Directive Techniques

Most interviewers supplement nondirective tactics with more directive questions whose form, wording, and content are often the result of careful (though usually on-the-spot) planning. For example, the clinician wants to avoid asking binding questions which may (a) damage rapport and (b) bias assessment data by forcing the client to choose an artificial or inaccurate response supplied by the interviewer. Look at the following illustrative questions:

A. Do you feel better or worse when your husband is out of town?

B. How do you feel when your husband is out of town?

Example A offers a clear, but possibly irrelevant, two-choice situation. This is a "Do you walk to work or carry your lunch?" question, for which the most valid answer may be "Neither." Some clients are not assertive enough in the interview to ignore the choice, so they settle for one unsatisfactory response or the other. Unless there is a special reason for offering clients only a few response alternatives, skilled interviewers ask direct questions in a form that gets at specific information, but also leaves clients free to choose their own words (see example B above).

Experienced clinicians also avoid asking questions that suggest their own answers. Notice the implications contained in this query: "You've suffered with this problem a long time?" Questions such as this communicate what the interviewer expects to hear, and clients will oblige by biasing their response. "How long have you had this problem?" is a better alternative.

Along similar lines, inquiries based on unwarranted assumptions should be avoided in clinical interviews. Notice the hidden assumption in the example: "How bad is your insomnia when you are depressed?" If the client sleeps soundly when feeling low, this question cannot be answered without contradicting the clinician. A careful interviewer might explore that same issue with the following question: "You said you are often depressed. How do you feel during those times?"

Combining Interview Tactics

Because the interview is flexible, clinicians are free to combine the tactics we have described. They may facilitate the client's speech with open-ended requests, paraphrasing, prompts, and other active listening techniques, and then use more directive questions to zero in on topics of special importance.

However, directive procedures do not take over completely as the interview progresses. They continue to be mixed with less directive tactics. An example of this blending is provided by the concept of *repeated scanning and focusing*. Here the interviewer first scans a particular topic nondirectively, then focuses on it in more directive fashion:

CLINICIAN: You mentioned that your family is back East. Could you tell me something about them?

CLIENT: There's not much to tell. There's Dad, Mom, and the twins. They all seem to like it back there so I guess they'll stay forever.

CLINICIAN: What else can you say about them?

CLIENT: Well, Dad is a retired high school principal. Mom used to be strictly a housewife but, since us kids have grown, she's been working part time.

CLINICIAN: How did you get along with your folks when you lived at home?

CLIENT: Really fine. I've always thought they were great people and that's probably why they had so little trouble with me. Of course, now and then there would be a problem, but not often.

CLINICIAN: What kinds of problems were there?

The interviewer might go on to explore several specific issues about the client's relationship with both parents, then move on to another topic, again beginning with scanning procedures and progressing to more focused questions.

Clinicians who emphasize rapport and other relationship factors tend to conduct interviews heavily weighted toward the nondirective side. Behavioral interviewers also emphasize a good client–clinician relationship, but mainly as the context for assessment of specific information. Their tactics tend to be more directive (Morganstern, 1988).

Stage 3: Closing the Interview

The last stage of an interview can provide valuable assessment data as well as an opportunity to enhance rapport. The interviewer may initiate the third stage with a statement like this:

> We have been covering some very valuable information here and I appreciate your willingness to tell me about it. I know our session hasn't been easy for you. Since we're running out of time for today, I thought we could look back over what we've covered and then give you a chance to ask *me* some questions.

The clinician accomplishes several things here. First, the impending conclusion of the interview is signaled. Second, the client is praised for cooperativeness and reassured that the clinician understands that the interview has been stressful. Third, a plan for the final minutes is suggested; it invites the client to pose questions or make comments that may have been formed but were not verbalized for various reasons.

The clinician's recap of the session serves to summarize interview content and to check that

she or he has not misunderstood anything of importance. Comments from the client during this stage can be enlightening, especially when they disclose misconceptions or information gaps. This part of the interview (especially when it ends a first contact) becomes a miniature version of the termination interview described earlier. It usually concludes with leave-taking rituals ("It was good of you to come") and, when appropriate, confirmation of plans for future contact with the interviewer or other professional.

The last segment of interviews may evoke important client behavior. Clients sometimes drop bombshells during this period: "Oh gosh, look at the time. I have to hurry to a meeting with my physician or I won't be able to find out the results of my chest X-rays." A remark like this one illustrates that some clients will wait until the interview's end to reveal sensitive information. Other individuals disclose such information more or less inadvertently. They assume the interview is over and drop whatever protective cover they may have used earlier. For these reasons, the clinician devotes as much care to the final stage of the interview as to the stages that precede it.

COMMUNICATION IN THE INTERVIEW

Sensitive combination of the interview procedures we have described is necessary for effective rapport building and fruitful information gathering. However, other factors contribute significantly to interview quality. Chief among these is the clarity of communication between interviewer and interviewee. All the clinician's skill at posing good questions, encouraging the client to talk, or making smooth transitions between topics may be of little value if he or she does not understand what the client is saying and vice versa.

The basic problem in interview communication is message transmission. The speaker must put a message in transmittable form (words, gestures) and then send it. The listener must receive the message and interpret it within his or her own frame of reference. Communication lapses can occur at many points in both verbal and nonverbal channels.

Clinicians attempt to avoid communication problems by maximizing the clarity of the messages they send and by clarifying the meaning of the messages they receive. We consider an example of poor clinical communication and then look at some ways breakdowns of this type can be made less likely. In the following hypothetical exchange, the speakers' thoughts are in parentheses:

CLINICIAN: (I wonder what his teenage social life was like.) Tell me a little about the friends you had in high school.

CLIENT: (I had dozens of social acquaintances, but only one person who was a really close friend.) There was just one, a guy named Mike.

CLINICIAN: (So he was pretty much of a loner.) How did you feel about that?

CLIENT: (It was fine. I had a great time, went to lots of parties, had lots of dates, but knew I could always depend on Mike to talk with about really personal things.) I enjoyed it. Mike and I got along really well.

CLINICIAN: (Not only was he a social isolate, he claims to have liked it that way. I wonder if he is being honest with himself about that.) Did you ever wish you had more friends?

CLIENT: (For crying out loud, he makes it sound like it's a crime to have one really close friend. I think we've talked enough about this.) No.

Verbal Communication

In the preceding illustration, the clinician used *friend* to refer to casual as well as intimate acquaintances. Because this word had a different meaning for the client, it led to misunderstanding. The conversation could have gone on in this fruitless way for quite a while before the interviewer and the client straightened out their problem.

Although the client and clinician may technically be speaking the same language and thus assume they understand one another, the interviewer must be aware that educational, social, racial, cultural, economic, and religious factors can impair communication. Unless the clinician takes the client's background and frame of reference into account, and asks for clarification when verbal referents are unclear, the interview will suffer. Consider this example:

CLIENT: When I'm in such heavy situations, I just get real uptight.

CLINICIAN: What makes you uptight?

CLIENT: Well, the whole thing. Everybody kind of hanging out and running around. I can't seem to get it together with anybody, so I guess I freak out.

CLINICIAN: And then what happens?

CLIENT: I usually go home and go to sleep. But I'm usually pretty bummed out.

CLINICIAN: Are you saying that you don't fit in with these people and that's what makes you feel bummed out?

CLIENT: Well, I don't know. These are my friends, I guess—but it never seems to work out. (Morganstern & Tevlin, 1981, p. 91)

Do these people understand each other? We do not know for sure, and as long as the interview goes on this way, neither do they. This clinician will at some point need to request clarification of the client's words. She or he might say the following in order to clarify the information:

CLIENT: When I'm in such heavy situations, I just get real uptight. . . .

CLINICIAN: When you say that you're uptight in these situations, what does that mean to you?

CLIENT: Well, uptight, you know. Tense.

CLINICIAN: You mean your muscles get tense?

CLIENT: My neck gets very sore—and I get a head-ache lots of times.

CLINICIAN: What else happens?

CLIENT: Well, either because of my neck or my headache, I start sweating a lot.

CLINICIAN: When you say you're uptight you are really experiencing it physically. What are you thinking when this happens?

CLIENT: I'm thinking, man you are really paranoid. You just can't relax in any situation. You really are a loser. And then I want to get out of there fast. . . . (Morganstern & Tevlin, 1981, p. 91)

Clients can become as confused as clinicians, but if they are reluctant to appear stupid or to question a person in authority they may not reveal their dilemma. Some evidence on this point comes from a study conducted in a medical setting by Korsch and Negrete (1972). Their data showed that communication from doctors to patients' mothers in a pediatric clinic was obstructed by the use of medical terms and that client confusion and dissatisfaction often resulted. For example, a "lumbar puncture" (spinal tap) was sometimes assumed to be an operation for draining the child's lungs: "incubation period" was interpreted by one mother as the time during which her child had to be kept in bed.

Circumventing similar problems in interviewing can be facilitated by attention to certain guidelines. Skilled interviewers avoid jargon, ask questions in a straightforward way ("What experiences have you had with masturbation?", not "Do you ever touch yourself?"), and request feedback from their client ("Is all this making sense to you?"). In addition, clinicians try to assure that their verbal behavior conveys patience, concern, and acceptance. Expressions of impatience or pre-judgment by the interviewer are not desirable. Goldstein (1976) has summarized some conversational do's and don'ts from Wolberg (1967) illustrating the kinds of verbal communications clinicians prefer (and avoid). An example is presented in edited form:

CLIENT: I feel helpless and I think I ought to end it all.

Unsuitable Responses:

A. You better snap out of it soon.

B. Well, that's a nice attitude, I must say.

Suitable Responses:

A. I wonder what is behind this feeling.

B. You sound as if you think you're at the end of your rope.

Nonverbal Communication

As with all human beings, a constant stream of nonverbal behavior accompanies the client's and the interviewer's verbal behavior. Nonverbal communication channels usually remain open even when the verbal channel is shut down. This has been understood by perceptive individuals for centuries. King Solomon was wise on this matter: "He winketh with his eyes, he speaketh with his feet, he teacheth with his fingers" (Proverbs 6:13). In 1905 Freud summarized the point well: "He that has eyes to see and ears to hear may convince himself that no mortal can keep a secret. If his lips are silent, he chatters with his fingertips; betrayal oozes out of him at every pore" (pp. 77–78). Since both members of an interview dyad are sending and receiving nonverbal messages, the clinician must be sensitive to incoming signals as well as to those she or he may be transmitting.

A sample of nonverbal interview dimensions is summarized next:

1. Physical appearance—height, weight, grooming, style and condition of clothing, unusual characteristics, muscular development, hairstyle

2. Movements—gestures; repetitive arm, hand, head, leg, or foot motions; tics or other appar-

ently involuntary movements; pacing; handling of cigarettes, matches, or other objects

3. Posture—slouching, rigidity, crossed or uncrossed arms or legs, head in hands

4. Eye contact—constant, fleeting, none

5. Facial expressions—smiles, frowns, grimaces, raised eyebrows

6. Emotional arousal—tears, wet eyes, sweating, dryness of lips, frequent swallowing, blushing or paling, voice or hand tremor, rapid respiration, frequent shifts in body position, startle reactions, inappropriate laughter

7. Speech variables—tone of voice, speed, slurring, lisp, stuttering, blocking, accent, clarity, style, sudden shifts or omissions

In addition to picking up nonverbal client behaviors, clinicians also look for inconsistencies between the verbal and nonverbal channels. The statement "I feel pretty good today" is viewed differently if the speaker is on the verge of tears than if a happy smile is evident.

Interviewers also try to coordinate their own verbal and nonverbal behavior so as to give the client unambiguous messages. Telling a client "Take your time" will convey greater interest in the client if it is said slowly and quietly than if it is blurted out while tapping a foot. Friendly eye contact, some head nodding, an occasional smile, and an attentive posture lets the client know that the interviewer is listening closely. Overdoing it may backfire, however. A constant smile, a continuously knitted brow, sidelong glances, and other theatrics are more likely to convey interviewer anxiety or inexperience than concern.

Observation of nonverbal behavior begins when the client and clinician meet and continues until they part. Clinicians often differ, however, as to what nonverbal behavior means. Interviewers committed to a sign-oriented approach draw higher-level inferences from nonverbal behaviors than those adopting a sample-oriented stance.

For example, a behaviorist's interpretation of increased respiration, perspiration, and

fidgeting while a client talks about sex would probably be that emotional arousal is associated with that topic. Psychodynamic interviewers may go another step to postulate that nonverbal behaviors (e.g., twirling a ring on a finger) are symbolic representations of sexual activity or other unconscious impulses (Feldman, 1959; Garner, 1970). Adler interpreted where a client chose to sit: "One moves toward the desk; that is favorable. Another moves away; that is unfavorable" (Adler, 1933). Whatever level of inference stems from it, nonverbal behavior serves as a powerful communication channel and a valuable source of interview data.

A General Note

There are many aspects of clinical interviewing that we have not covered. Dealing with silences, how to address the client, the pros and cons of note taking, handling personal questions, and confronting a client's inconsistencies are a few of the additional issues that face clinicians in interviews. The reader interested in more detailed exploration of interviewing techniques should consult the references listed at the beginning of this chapter.

RESEARCH ON THE INTERVIEW

Social Interaction and Influence in the Interview

Until 1942, when Carl Rogers published the first transcripts from phonographic recordings of therapy interviews, the exact nature of clinical interactions had been unknown.[3] Afterward, interview research grew rapidly. At first it focused on such issues as the effects of re-

---

[3]Rogers's recordings were considered scandalous at the time, since tradition ruled out all but narrative case reports. The fact that he was a *psychologist* (not a psychiatrist) doing therapy with an adult made Rogers's revelations even more distasteful to those not yet accustomed to the expanding roles of postwar clinicians.

cording and the relative accuracy of clinicians' summaries versus electrical recordings of the same interview (Covner, 1944; Snyder, 1945). Later, when it was established that recording devices were not disruptive and provided the most complete account of the interview, researchers began several new areas of study.

Descriptive Research

One of these new directions involved descriptive research aimed at relating interview variables to rapport building, therapy effectiveness, and other interpersonal dimensions. Some studies focused on differences in interview tactics used by Rogerians and non-Rogerians (Porter, 1943; Seeman, 1949; Snyder, 1954; Strupp, 1960), while others tried to define interview variables like client resistance (Snyder, 1953), interviewer ambiguity (Bordin, 1955), and relationship warmth (Rausch & Bordin, 1957). Other investigators performed detailed analyses of the content of conversations as a means of better understanding the interview process (Auld & Murray, 1955; Leary & Gill, 1959; Mahl, 1959). One team of researchers devoted years to the content analysis of the first 5 minutes of a single interview (Pittenger, Hockett, & Danehy, 1960).

Researchers also sought to describe interviews in terms of *noncontent* variables. Specialized equipment was used to collect information about physiological arousal of interviewer and client (Greenblatt, 1959) and the stability, idiosyncrasies, and equilibrium of their speech and periods of silence (Lennard & Bernstein, 1960; Saslow & Matarazzo, 1959). It was suggested that such data could be used to define interview concepts like *empathy, transference,* and *insight* (Matarazzo, 1965).

Experimental Research

The research of the 1940s and 1950s generated large amounts of data about the interview, highlighting its complexity as a social event. An additional dimension of this complexity was revealed by experiments which confirmed that interviews are not only data-gathering contexts, but *social influence* situations as well. Research of this type was stimulated in large measure by Skinner's (1948, 1957) conceptualization of verbal behavior as a set of responses that can be modified by its consequences.

Dozens of *verbal conditioning* studies soon began to appear. They showed in general that not only can simple responses (like the use of plural nouns) be affected by reinforcement, but that more clinically relevant verbalizations (reports of family memories, expression of feelings, self-evaluations, and delusional speech) are alterable through contingent interviewer feedback (see reviews by Greenspoon, 1962; Kanfer, 1968; Krasner, 1965; Salzinger, 1959).

Other research indicated that noncontent variables in the interview could also be systematically influenced by the clinician. For example, duration of interviewee speech was increased when the interviewer nodded his head or said "mm-hmm" while listening (Kanfer & McBrearty, 1962; Matarazzo, 1965). Work by Matarazzo and his colleagues (Matarazzo, Weitman, Saslow, & Wiens, 1963) showed that when an interviewer increased and then decreased the duration of his own utterances over three parts of a conversation, interviewees did the same. When he decreased then increased his speech length, interviewees again followed suit. This is called *synchrony*.

A quick glance at this research might give the impression that interview assessment would always be facilitated by social reinforcement of client speech or by increasing the clinician's speech duration. Unfortunately, the problem is not that simple. For one thing, interviewers often avoid reinforcing specific types of statements, because they could bias the data generated. In addition, all the relationships described in published research do not hold universally. As an example, the use of "mm-hmms," especially when they are not contingent on specific responses, does not produce consistent effects (Siegman, 1972, 1974, 1976). Further, Dulany (1968) demonstrated that verbal conditioning may depend on subjects' awareness of the contingency in effect.

Some data on social influence in the interview are surprising. For example, "warm" interviewers do not always enhance interviewee speech (Heller, 1972; Heller, Davis, & Myers, 1966), and self-disclosure may be facilitated by interviewers who are reserved and who transmit messages that are somewhat ambiguous (Ganzer & Sarason, 1964; Heller, 1972). Perhaps under moderately stressful experimental circumstances some subjects feel they should try to please the interviewer by telling all. It is doubtful, however, that stress-producing interviewer behaviors aid client verbalization in actual clinical assessment interviews (Heller, 1972).

In summary, research on interview interaction and influence has shown these to be extremely complicated aspects of social behavior that are under the influence of interviewer, client, relationship, and situational factors. The data do not tell the individual clinician how to conduct interviews. Because there is not a single "right" way for all interviewers to talk to all clients under all circumstances, the greatest value of interview research is in providing scientific information about what is likely to happen when various combinations of people, tactics, and situations occur in clinical assessment.

Reliability and Validity of Interview Data

The degree to which an interviewee gives the same information on different occasions or to different interviewers (reliability) and the degree to which that information is accurate (validity) depend upon the clinician, the client, and the circumstances of the interview. How strongly these factors affect interview reliability and validity has been studied widely, so it is possible to give a general idea of the value of the interview as a data source.

Reliability

Some writers estimate interview reliability by looking at the degree to which different judges agree on the *inferences* (ratings, diagnoses, or personality trait descriptions) drawn from conversations with the same client (DiNardo et al., 1983; Matarazzo, 1965). This practice confounds the reliability of what the client said with the quality of the interviewer's inference system. For example, if a client tells two clinicians the same thing and they draw different conclusions from it, one might conclude that the interview was reliable, but the interviewers' inferences were not. On the other hand, if a client gives different answers to different interviewers, the interviews' reliability will suffer and the interviewers' inferences will probably also show decreased agreement. One strategy for isolating the reliability of interviewers' judgments is to videotape an interview and then play it for subsequent interviewers, who make ratings or other inferences from the tape. This approach is being used to assess clinicians' reliability in making *DSM-IV* diagnoses (Widiger, Frances, Pincus, Davis, & First, 1991).

An alternative approach is to ask about the reliability of interview data themselves. One would expect clients' responses to be similar from one interview to the next or from one interviewer to the next, but there is surprisingly little research on this point. The available data come mainly from survey research and indicate that when innocuous information (such as age) is requested, or, when interview intervals are short, reliability can be quite high (Sobell & Sobell, 1975; Vaughn & Reynolds, 1951). Reliability is also generally quite high with many of the structured interviews (Lesher & Whelihan, 1986; Vandiver & Sher, 1991) and with mental status interviews repeated over short periods of time (Fisk, Braha, Walker, & Gray, 1991). As the interval between mental status interviews increases, however, test–retest reliability sometimes decreases (Olin & Zelinski, 1991).

Other interview data are less reliable. Wenar and Coulter (1962) found that only 43% of the parents they talked to gave consistent information about their children's history (e.g., age at toilet training) when interviews were separated by 3 to 6 years. Other research on parents' reports about their children's behavioral history reveals that reliability tends to be particularly low on questions about issues such as temperament (Hubert, Wachs, Peters-Martin, & Gandour, 1982) or overactivity and quite high on more easily defined questions such as stuttering. Reports on child-rearing practices such as toilet training and weaning tend to change from interview to interview, usually in the direction of making the parents appear more up-to-date and in line with the latest trends (Robbins, 1963).

Validity

Interview data can be extremely accurate in absolute terms; in comparison to other assessment tools, it may be the best source of clinical information. In a study cited by Thorne (1972), for example, answers to the question, "Are you homosexual?" were more valid indicators of sexual orientation than any combination of psychological tests. Mischel (1968) cites evidence that what people say they will do is a better predictor of future behavior than test scores; but others (Nisbett & Wilson, 1977) disagree. The validity of interview responses can be reduced under certain circumstances. A client's response to "Tell me something about your marital problems" might be very different from his answer to the question, "Why can't you get along with your spouse?" (Heller, 1972; Thomas, 1973). Further, interviewer characteristics such as age, sex, or race may alter interviewee candor (Benney, Riesman, & Star, 1956; Grantham, 1973; Ledvinka, 1971).

Clients may also misremember or purposely distort various types of information. The prob-

ability of distortion is increased when the information sought is of an emotionally charged or sensitive nature, such as alcohol and drug use, criminal record, sexual behavior, behavior disorders, or instances of mental hospitalization. Clients may sometimes exaggerate or *malinger* complaints to give the false impression that they suffer a mental disorder. Concern about this kind of distortion has led to new techniques aimed at detecting malingering (Berry, Baer, & Harris, 1991; Rogers, Gillis, Dickens, & Bagby, 1991).

A person's overall emotional state can also affect his or her interview responses. For example, mothers' reports about their childrens' behavior are significantly influenced by the mothers' emotional adjustment, in particular by feelings of depression (Brody & Forehand, 1986; Webster-Stratton, 1988). Clients are often wary about what they will tell about themselves and to whom; a friend may laugh at tales of your vegetable imitations, but a psychologist might treat them more seriously. The desire to present oneself in a particular light to a mental health professional has been called "impression-management" (Braginsky, Braginsky, & Ring, 1969; Goffman, 1959), and it can lead to invalid interview data (Sherman, Trief, & Sprafkin, 1975). Situational factors of various kinds may also affect the validity of interview data. For example, self-disclosure may vary as a function of the topics discussed and whether candor and frankness are expected in the situation (Heller, 1971; Wilson & Rappaport, 1974).

In general, the validity of interviews has been studied less than their reliability. This problem arises for at least two reasons. First, psychologists have tended to believe that reliability should be studied and established before tackling validity problems. (In fact, validity can be studied simultaneously with reliability at the time any assessment tool is being constructed.) Second, finding trustworthy, meaningful criteria against which to measure diagnostic validity has been difficult (Pilkonis, Heape, Ruddy, & Serrao, 1991).

In clinical diagnosis, some structured interviews have achieved such high levels of reliability and (less often) validity that they are occasionally used as the criteria for judging the diagnostic validity of psychological tests, self-report interviews, or observational systems. Likewise, structured interviews have become the most widely accepted procedure for identifying homogeneous diagnostic groups of patients to be studied in research on the correlates and treatment of psychological disorders.

Interviewer Error and Bias

Reliable and valid interview data are of little value if they are distorted by the interviewer. Therefore, evaluation of the interview must consider its susceptibility to distortion.

Distortion may be accidental, as when the client's words are not reported accurately by the interviewer. Unless the interaction has been recorded, important information may be lost or misrepresented simply because the volume of incoming data is so large. Sometimes, "errors" are deliberate. Schwitzgebel and Kolb (1974) quoted an interviewer hired to conduct structured interviews as saying: "One of the questions asked for five reasons why parents had put their child in an institution. I found most people can't think of five reasons. I didn't want [the boss] to think I was goofing off, so I always filled in all five."

Personal biases, references, and prejudice may affect the conclusions reached by interviewers. In an early study by Rice (1929), social workers' judgments of why skid-row bums had become destitute were found to be related to personal views, not just to interview data. Thus, a prohibitionist interviewer saw drinking as the cause of poverty in 62% of the cases, while a socialist said the interviewees were poor mainly because of general economic conditions. In a similar fashion, psychoanalysts and behavior therapists differ in the explanations they prefer for various kinds of presenting clinical complaints (Plous & Zimbardo, 1986). Temerlin (1968) found that psychologists' and psychiatrists' diagnoses of a client may be determined by prejudicial information given to them before they ever hear the client speak.

One possible way around such problems would be to employ a mechanical interviewer, and computer interviewing is a part of some assessment procedures. Clients communicate with the computer through a television screen and a word processor; they appear to accept this type of interaction quite well. Although this approach eliminates error and bias in inquiry and response recording, computers are not likely to replace humans in interview-based assessment because the flexibility of a live clinician is an indispensable part of interviewing. However, computer interviewing saves time and energy in the gathering of routine information, is easily standardized, and is accepted well by most clients (Erdman, Klein, & Greist, 1985).

A Final Note

Research on the interview as an assessment tool does not justify one all-encompassing conclusion. As Garfield (1974, p. 90) put it, "The interview has been used in so many different ways for various purposes, by individuals with varying skills, that it is a difficult matter to make a final judgment concerning its values." The skill of the interviewer is very important, but the exact nature of what *skill* means is still not clear. Although the interview will continue to occupy a primary assessment role in clinical psychology, it must also remain the object of research. Any tendency to view interviews as primarily an art form practiced by gifted clinicians and therefore exempt from scientifically rigorous examinations of reliability and validity will ultimately result in the loss of the interview's utility as an important assessment tool.

CHAPTER 5

Testing
in
Clinical Psychology

The history of clinical psychology is intimately related to the development and use of psychological tests. Even though clinicians now perform many functions in addition to testing, tests remain an important part of clinical research and practice. It is therefore essential that we consider the nature of psychological tests, the ways they are constructed, and the research on their value as assessment tools.

WHAT IS A TEST?

A test is a systematic procedure for observing and describing a person's behavior in a standard situation (Cronbach, 1970). Tests present a set of planned stimuli (inkblots or true–false questions, for example) and ask the client to respond to them in some way. The client's reactions are recorded as the test's results or scores to be used as sample, sign, or correlate in the clinician's assessment strategy. Test data may lead to conservative, situation-specific statements ("The client appeared disoriented

during testing and was correct on 15 out of 60 items") or to sweeping, high-level inferences ("The client's ego boundaries are so ill defined as to make adequate functioning outside an institution very unlikely"). Most commonly, test results guide inferences that are between these extremes.

Tests are like highly structured interviews because they ask the person to respond to specific assessment stimuli presented in a predetermined sequence. They also share characteristics with observational assessments by providing an opportunity for the clinician to watch the client in the test situation. In some ways, however, tests are distinct from other assessment techniques. For example:

1. A test can be administered in a nonsocial context in which observational assessment does not supplement test data.

2. A client's test results can often be compared mathematically to the responses of hundreds or thousands of other persons who have taken the same test. These comparisons are

made through the use of *norms,* which are the scores obtained by other people taking the same test. These norms are established by giving the test to a large sample of persons under *standardized* conditions. Standardization means that the test is administered and scored using uniform procedures. Because differences in testing methods can influence test results, accurate interpretation of a test requires that it be given in the standardized fashion.

3. Tests can be administered in groups as well as individually. College entrance examinations provide a good example of how masses of people can be assessed at the same time through tests.

WHAT DO TESTS MEASURE?

There are thousands of psychological tests in existence today. They are administered to infants, children, adolescents, adults, senior citizens, students, soldiers, mental patients, office workers, prisoners, and every other imaginable group (see Mitchell, 1985). Further, tests appear in many *modes* or *styles.*

Some pose direct, specific questions ("Do you ever feel discouraged?"), while others ask for general reactions to less distinct stimuli ("Tell me what you see in this drawing"). Some are presented in paper-and-pencil form, while others are given orally. Some require use of verbal skills ("What is a chicken?"), and others ask the client to perform various tasks ("Please trace the correct path through this puzzle maze").

Despite the enormous variety of tests in existence, many have similar purposes and can be grouped into four general categories. The majority of tests seek to measure (a) *intellectual functioning,* (b) *personality characteristics,* (c) *attitudes, interests, preferences,* and *values,* or (d) *ability.* We shall consider each of these categories later. The tests most commonly used by clinical psychologists are those of intellectual functioning and personality (Lubin, Larsen, & Matarazzo, 1984). This is because clinicians are most interested in these areas in their own treatment and research, and because other people expect them to provide advice on these variables.

FIGURE 5–1 *Peanuts* reprinted by permission of UFS, Inc.

A major reason for the proliferation of tests is that testers continually hope to measure things in ever more reliable, valid, and sophisticated ways. For example, psychologist A may feel that the anxiety test developed by psychologist B does not really "get at" anxiety very well, so she or he constructs a new instrument. Psychologist C may argue that A and B are both "off base" with their tests and come up with yet another "more meaningful" device. This sequence has been especially noticeable in personality testing, but is evident in other test categories as well.

Another factor responsible for the increasing array of tests is that testers' interests become more specific, thus prompting the development of special-purpose tests. In intelligence testing, for example, instruments are available for use with infants, the physically handicapped, and persons not fluent in English or from specific cultural backgrounds. Similarly, surveys of general preferences or interests have been followed by special-purpose tests aimed at assessing the way adolescents spend leisure time or the things children find rewarding.

The number of psychological tests has increased so greatly that there are special publications that list tests in use and review these tests' reliability, validity, and utility. The best known and most authoritative of these references is the *Mental Measurements Yearbook,* first published in 1938 (Buros, 1938). This book is updated frequently; the 10th and latest edition appeared in 1989 (Conoley & Kramer, 1989), but a supplement to this edition was published in 1990. Other useful compendia of psychological tests and descriptions of testing principles include Anastasi (1988), Cohen, Swerdlik, and Smith (1992), Kaufman (1990), Newmark (1985), and Sattler (1988).

TEST CONSTRUCTION PROCEDURES

Members of the public often raise a basic question about psychological tests: "How do psychologists come up with these things?" The answer is that tests are constructed in three basic ways: the *analytic* approach, the *empirical* approach, and the *rational* or *sequential system* approach, which combines analytic and empirical principles (see Burisch, 1984; Golden, Sawicki, & Franzen, 1990; Jackson, 1975).[1]

The analytic technique begins by asking, "What are the qualities I want to measure?" "How do I define these qualities?" and "What kind of test and test items would make sense for assessing these qualities?" It then proceeds to build a test that answers the last question. It is a deductive approach to test construction. In its simplest form, the analytic approach relies on content validation—the test is designed to include items tapping all aspects of some domain. A more comprehensive analytic approach involves deriving test items from a theory of the characteristics to be measured.

The procedure can be illustrated through an extreme example. Suppose one wanted a test that could reliably and accurately identify adult humans as male or female. The analytic approach would involve theorizing about things that might differentiate the sexes. The clinician's view of what makes males and females different would shape the content of the tests, as would the opinions of other experts.

If physical characteristics are seen as crucial, and a true–false format is preferred, the test might contain items such as

1. I have a penis.

2. I have a vagina.

3. I once had a penis.

4. I once had a vagina.

5. I shave my face.

6. I have a beard.

_____

[1]Anastasi (1988) describes factor analytic methods of test construction as a fourth approach to test development.

Another clinician might believe that physical characteristics are only surface indicators of sex and that "real" maleness or femaleness must be measured by tapping the unconscious. The resulting test might look at unconscious themes by asking the client to fill in incomplete sentences such as:

1. A dependent person is _____.
2. Strength is _____.
3. The trouble with most men is _____.
4. Most women are _____.
5. I like to _____.
6. There is nothing worse than _____.

In either case, an analytically constructed test will reflect in large measure a specific theory of what should be tested and how.

The main alternative to analytic test construction is the empirical approach. Here, instead of deciding ahead of time what test content should be used to measure a particular construct, the tester lets the content "choose itself." Thus, in building a sex test, the clinician might amass a large number of self-report test items, performance tasks, or inkblots, and then administer all of them to a large group of people who have *already been identified* as males or females. Responses to all the test material would then be examined to see if any items, tasks, or other stimuli were consistently answered differently by men and women.

Such stimuli form the initial content of the test, *regardless of whether they make any sense rationally*. For example, "true" responses to items like "My nose runs a lot," "Coffee makes me sleepy," or "My shoes are too tight" might reliably discriminate males from females. The reasons *why* such items separate males from females may become the subject of additional theoretical research, but for practical purposes testers are usually willing to employ an empirically constructed test in spite of the fact that its individual items cannot be explained clearly.

How does the test constructor decide between analytic or empirical procedures? Several factors may be decisive. The analytic approach can be faster and less expensive because it does not require initial administration of many items to many people in order to settle on those that will comprise the test. These features make analytic procedures attractive to the clinician who does not have access to a large pool of test material and willing subjects or who is forced by circumstances to develop a test on short notice.

Analytic procedures will be favored by clinicians evaluating a particular theory. That theory may propose, for example, that people differ in terms of "nerdiness." Assuming no nerdiness test is available, the researcher who wishes to explore this hypothesis through testing will need an instrument that corresponds to what the theory says nerdiness is and how it should be measured. Development of a Nerd Test would thus likely proceed on analytic grounds.

On the other hand, clinicians who are less concerned with theoretical notions and who have time and other resources available may find the empirical approach more desirable, especially when attempting to make specific predictions about people. If the tester's task is to identify individuals likely to graduate from law school, for example, it makes sense to find out if graduates respond to the test in a way that is reliably different from dropouts.

Analytic and empirical techniques are combined in the *sequential system* approach to test construction. Here, data from analytically chosen items are examined statistically to determine those that are correlated and those that are not. Groups of correlated items are identified as *scales,* which are thought to be relatively pure measures of certain personality dimensions free of response biases (Maloney & Ward, 1976). Validity of the test is then assessed empirically.

Analytic-empirical combinations also appear in other contexts. For example, the person who wishes to construct a true–false test using empirical procedures is immediately faced with a problem: Of the millions of true–false items that could be included in the test, the tester must decide which ones to try. This decision is usually made on analytic grounds; items will be selected from older tests or might be those the clinician feels ought to be tried. Similarly, empirical procedures are often used in the development of analytically constructed tests. If administration of a new instrument reveals that certain items are better at discriminating between target groups (e.g., good versus poor typists), those items are more likely to be retained in the test than are items with little power.

Regardless of how a test is constructed initially, its value as an assessment instrument ultimately must be established through empirical research on its reliability and validity (see Chapter 3). Later we shall look at how various tests have fared when scrutinized by reliability/validity research. For now, let us examine the four psychological test categories identified earlier.

MAJOR TYPES OF TESTS

Intellectual Functioning

We begin our exploration of psychological tests with measures of intelligence, since, as noted in Chapter 1, the early history of clinical psychology is basically the early history of intelligence tests.

While everyone would agree that intelligence is a good thing to have, there is less consensus about what intelligence actually *is*. This state of affairs has generated the half-joking suggestion among clinicians that "intelligence is whatever intelligence tests measure." Indeed, the history of intelligence tests reveals that each tester proceeded initially on analytical grounds, and that each of the more than 200 assessment instruments that have resulted reflects its creator's view of how best to measure intellectual functioning.

Intelligence test builders have been influenced in their analytic approach by theories about the essential nature of intelligence. This is not the place to describe these theories (see Sternberg & Detterman, 1986), but to cite one major dimension, some theorists describe intelligence primarily as a *general* characteristic (called *g*) while others see it as made up of as many as 150 *specific* intellectual functions such as word fluency, reasoning, and memory. These specific abilities have been termed *s* by some psychologists. Weinberg (1989) calls the theorists who define intelligence as a general factor "lumpers"; he terms the theorists who see intelligence as composed of many separate abilities "splitters." The practical relevance of *g, s,* or other intelligence theories is limited, however, because none of the major intelligence tests described below reflects the *g* or *s* approach clearly enough to provide definitive validation of one theory or another (Kaufman & Harrison, 1991).

The Binet Scales

Alfred Binet was not the first person to develop a measure of intelligence, but his original test and the revisions based on it have been among the most influential means of assessing the mental ability of children. In its earliest form (1905), Binet's test consisted of 30 questions and tasks, including things like unwrapping a piece of candy, following a moving object with the eyes, comparing objects of differing weights, repeating numbers or sentences from memory, and recognizing familiar objects. The child's test score was simply the number of items passed.

Beginning with a 1908 revision, the tasks in Binet's test were *age graded*. The items were arranged so that younger children were expected to pass the earlier ones, while older children were expected to pass later ones. Binet and his collaborator, Theodore Simon, observed the test behavior of about 200 children and suggested, for example, that 3-year-olds ought to be able to identify their eyes, nose, and mouth; repeat a two-digit number and a six-syllable sentence; and give their last name. At 7 years, success at finding missing parts of drawings, copying simple geometric figures, and identifying denominations of coins was expected. Items to be passed at the 11th-year level included criticism of absurd sentences, definition of abstract concepts, and rearranging words to form a sentence. A child's *mental age* was the highest age level at which *all* test items were passed (plus credit for any correct responses at higher levels).

The 1908 scale covered ages 3 to 13; it was brought to America by Henry Goddard. Though popular, the Binet-Simon test had several shortcomings. Some users were dissatisfied because the test emphasized verbal skills more than the child's capacity for judgment. Others noted that the test was too easy at lower age levels and too difficult at the upper end. Binet attempted to correct some of these problems in a 1911 revision of his test, but a far more influential version was written in 1916 by Lewis Terman, a Stanford University psychologist.

Terman believed that expressing a child's intelligence in terms of "mental age" was imprecise and left too much room for misinterpretation: "If a child's mental age equalled his chronological age, he was considered 'regular' (average) in intelligence; if his mental age was higher, he was 'advanced'; if his mental age was lower, he was 'retarded'" (Reisman, 1976). Terman's edition of the Binet-Simon was called the Stanford-Binet; it soon became *the* intelligence test in American clinical psychology. The Stanford-Binet was standardized on a larger sample (1,400 white subjects) and across a wider age range (3 to 16) than had been used for Binet's 1911 revision.

More important was the fact that Terman adopted an idea suggested in 1912 by German psychologist William Stern for representing numerically the relationship between mental and chronological age. Stanford-Binet results were expressed as the *intelligence quotient* (or IQ) resulting when mental age (MA) is divided by chronological age (CA) and multiplied by

100. Thus, a 6-year-old whose mental age comes out as 8 on the Stanford-Binet would have an IQ of [(8 ÷ 6) × 100], or 133.

Terman suggested that various IQ ranges be given labels such as "average," "feeble-minded," and "genius." Today, the following categories are used: "very superior," "superior," "high average," "average," "low average," "borderline," and "mentally retarded." Similar systems are used to classify persons at the lower end of the IQ scale as "mildly," "moderately," "severely," or "profoundly retarded." The original intent of such labels was to provide a shorthand summary of a person's score relative to others of his or her age. However, IQ scores and the labels based upon them are often overemphasized and misused, especially by those unfamiliar with their meaning. For this reason, among others, the use of IQ data has become the center of considerable controversy, as we shall see later.

Terman and Merrill revised the Stanford-Binet in 1937, 1960, and again in 1973. The 1973 edition retained the same content as the 1960 edition but used larger, more diverse standardization samples consisting of 2,100 children representing diverse socioeconomic, geographical, racial, and cultural subgroups. In addition to being more representative, these norms showed a substantial increase in IQ estimates for children at all ages. This improvement has been attributed to several influences, including the effects of greater literacy among parents, the educational effects of mass media, and the fact that children stay in school longer now than they did in the 1930s (Flynn, 1984).

Beginning with the 1960 edition of the test, the mental age method of computing IQ scores was replaced by use of IQ tables which correct the MA/CA × 100 formula by taking into account the mean and variance in IQs at each age level in the standardization sample. Thus, if a 6-year-old girl scores a mental age of 9 (which is not only high relative to her chronological age, but also higher than most 6-year-olds in the standardization population), she would receive an IQ of 156 rather than the 150 that would have resulted from calculating MA/CA × 100. Such "corrected" scores were arrived at by setting up IQ tables in which the mean IQ at each age level is 100, with a standard deviation of 16. Thus, the deviation IQ score represents *degree of deviation* from the average of any level. An IQ of 100 is average for the age; 116 would be one standard deviation above average; 84 would be one standard deviation below average.

In spite of its widespread use with children, the Stanford-Binet continued to be criticized for its emphasis upon verbal aspects of intelligence, its outdated item content, and its reliance on one score rather than a pattern of different cognitive strengths and weaknesses.

The Fourth Edition of the Stanford-Binet. Published in 1986, the *Stanford-Binet Intelligence Scale: Fourth Edition* (Thorndike, Hagen, & Sattler, 1986) differs in many respects from earlier versions of the test. It is still an individually administered test, and it retains many of the same kinds of items as in earlier editions, but the organization and content have been dramatically changed.

Unlike previous editions, which grouped items according to age levels, items in the fourth edition are grouped into one of 15 tests. Within each test, the items (see Box 5–1) for examples) are arranged in increasing order of difficulty. The 15 tests are used to assess four major areas of functioning: verbal reasoning, abstract/visual reasoning, quantitative reasoning, and short-term memory. The organization of the 15 tests by the major content areas they measure is summarized in Box 5–2.

The 15 tests can be given in various combinations, increasing the flexibility of the Stanford-Binet and making it a more useful diagnostic tool for the assessment of cognitive skills and problems in individuals between the ages of two to adulthood. The choice of which tests to give and at what level of difficulty to begin each depends on the purpose of the evaluation, the child's age (not all of the tests are appropriate for children of certain ages), and initial test results that help route the examiner to the correct entry level for individual tests. Typically, the examiner would give somewhere between 8 to 13 tests, although a quick screening battery of four tests (vocabulary, bead memory, quantitative, and pattern analysis) is recommended when testing needs to be completed in less than 40 minutes.

A Standard Age Score (SAS) is determined for each test by using tables that convert raw scores to normalized standard scores with a mean of 50 and a standard deviation of 8 for each age group. For example, a SAS of 58 is one standard deviation above the mean for children of a given age and corresponds to

FIGURE 5–2 The Stanford-Binet being administered to a young child.

Vocabulary: Define words like train, wrench, letter, error, and encourage.

Comprehension: Answer questions like, "Why should people brush their teeth?" "Why should people be quiet in a library?" "What is one advantage and one disadvantage of living in a small town instead of a big city?"

Absurdities: Identify the mistakes or "silly" aspects of pictures in which, for example, a man is shown using the wrong end of a rake or a girl is shown putting a piece of clothing on incorrectly.

Copying: Arrange a set of blocks to match different designs; draw designs like those shown in pictures.

Memory for Objects: Choose the right order in which a series of pictures were presented.

Number Series: Determine which numbers come next in a series of numbers such as the following—32, 26, 20, 14, _____ , _____.

Verbal Relations: Indicate how three objects or words are alike but different from a fourth. For example, how are dog, cat, horse alike but different from boy.

Bead Memory: Arrange different colored and shaped beads to match pictures of the beads organized in different layouts.

BOX 5–1

Items Similar to Those Included in the Fourth Edition
of the Stanford-Binet

BOX 5–2

Organization of Tests by Content Areas on the Stanford-Binet,
Fourth Edition

4 Content Areas	Verbal Reasoning	Abstract/ Visual Reasoning	Quantitative Reasoning	Short-Term Memory
15 Individual Tests	Vocabulary	Pattern Analysis	Quantitative	Bead Memory
	Comprehension	Copying	Number Series	Memory for Sentences
	Absurdities	Matrices	Equation Building	Memory for Digits
	Verbal Relations	Paper Folding & Cutting		Memory for Objects

placement at the 84th percentile. SAS scores can also be calculated from the tables for each of the four content areas and for a composite for any combination of the four areas' scores. These area and composite scores are also normalized standard scores with means of 100 and standard deviations of 16, thereby allowing such summary scores to be expressed in the same units as the deviation IQ scores so familiar from the earlier versions of the test.

Because the fourth edition has been in use for only a few years, more research is required to evaluate its reliability, validity, and clinical utility. Initial results suggest very high internal consistency and test-retest reliability (generally, above .90 for both types of reliability). In addition, fourth edition scores correlate highly with other measures of intelligence and discriminate among samples of gifted, retarded, and learning disabled children (Anastasi, 1988).

Although the fourth edition of the Stanford-Binet was constructed to yield separate scores for four different cognitive abilities, it appears to measure only two basic abilities in young children—verbal reasoning and nonverbal intelligence. For children older than 6 years, a third ability—memory—emerges as an important component on the test (Laurent, Swerdlik, & Ryburn, 1992).

The Wechsler Scales

In the 1930s David Wechsler, chief psychologist at New York's Bellevue Psychiatric Hospital, began developing an intelligence test specifically for adults. The result of his efforts, the Wechsler-Bellevue (W-B) Intelligence Scale, was published in 1939. This test differed in several ways from the Stanford-Binet, even though some W-B tasks were borrowed or adapted from it. First, it was aimed at adults, age 17 and older. Second, it did not measure mental age, which Wechsler thought was not a useful concept. Instead, the W-B was a *point scale* in which the client receives credit for each correct answer. With this method, IQ

does not reflect the relationship between mental age and chronological age, but a comparison of points earned by the client to those earned by persons of equal age in the standardization sample.

Like the latest version of the Stanford-Binet, Wechsler-Bellevue items were arranged in groups or *subtests* based on similarity. Each subtest contained increasingly difficult items. For example, on the digit-span subtest, the client was asked to repeat numbers, starting with three digits and progressing to nine digits. The score on this subtest was determined by the maximum number of digits the client could repeat without error. The W-B contained six *verbal* subtests (information, comprehension, arithmetic, similarities, digit span, and vocabulary) and five *performance* subtests (digit symbol, picture completion, block design, picture arrangement, and object assembly).

The W-B had some deficiencies, the most serious of which was an inadequate standardization sample (1,700 white New Yorkers aged 7 to 70); in 1955 Wechsler revised and restandardized his test on a more representative sample of over 2,000 white and nonwhite individuals (aged 16 to 74) living in all parts of the United States. This revision was called the Wechsler Adult Intelligence Scale, or WAIS, and it soon became the most popular adult intelligence test in use. Like the W-B, the WAIS had six verbal and five performance subtests, and the client was given a Verbal IQ, a Performance IQ, and a Full Scale IQ (which combines the other two). Another revision, known as the WAIS-R, was published in 1981. It was restandardized on a sample of 1,880 U.S. adults whose age, race, and other demographic characteristics reflected 1970 census data. About 20% of the items on the WAIS-R are different from the 1955 version (Wechsler, 1981). Some examples of the types of items included on the WAIS-R are presented in Box 5–3.

The structure of the WAIS allows not only for IQ scores, but for the drawing of inferences from *patterns* of subtest scores (Kauf-

	(WAIS-R)
Information:	What does bread come from?
	What did Shakespeare do?
	What is the capital of France?
	What is the malleus malleficarum?
Comprehension:	What should you do with a wallet found in the street?
	Why do foreign cars cost more than domestic cars?
	What does "the squeaky wheel gets the grease" mean?
Arithmetic:	If you have four apples and give two away, how many do you have left?
	If four people can finish a job in six days, how many people would it take to do the job in two days?
Similarities:	Identify similar aspects of pairs like: hammer–screwdriver, portrait–short story, dog–flower.
Digit Symbol:	Copy designs that are associated with different numbers as quickly as possible.
Digit Span:	Repeat in forward and reverse order: two- to nine-digit numbers.
Vocabulary:	Define: chair, dime, lunch, paragraph, valley, asylum, modal, cutaneous.
Picture Completion:	Find missing objects in increasingly complex pictures.
Block Design:	Arrange blocks to match increasingly complex standard patterns.
Picture Arrangement:	Place increasing number of pictures together to make increasingly complex stories.
Object Assembly:	Arrange parts of puzzles to form recognizable objects (e.g., dog, flower, person).

BOX 5–3
Items of the Type Included in the Wechsler
Adult Intelligence Scale-Revised

man, 1990). Some clinicians use WAIS subtest patterns or "scatter" to help them diagnose the client, to assess the possibility of brain damage, or to describe personality dynamics (e.g., whether the person is impulsive or deliberate in problem solving).

After publication of the W-B, Wechsler be-

came interested in extending the point-scale test format for use with children. In 1949 the Wechsler Intelligence Scale for Children (WISC) appeared. The WISC was made up of 12 subtests (six verbal, six performance) of which only 10 were usually administered. The subtests were similar to those listed for the W-B, but easier. The WISC was standardized on 2,200 white children from all parts of the United States, but because they ranged in age from 5 to 15, the WISC was not useful for very young children. The Wechsler Preschool and Primary Scale of Intelligence (WPPSI) was developed later, but still only reached the 4-year-old level (Wechsler, 1967). A revision of this test (WPPSI-R) lowers the age limit to 3 years.

In 1974 a new version of the WISC was published. Called the WISC-R, it includes six verbal and six performance subtests; again, only five of each are usually administered. The content of the WISC-R items was changed to make it more representative of current social and cultural values, and the entire test was standardized on a new sample of 2,200 white and nonwhite children from varying socioeconomic levels and geographical locations.

The newest version of the WISC is the WISC-III, published in 1991 (Wechsler, 1991). Although the WISC-III retains the basic structure and format of its predecessors, its scoring is based on new norms collected on 2,200 children, ranging in age from 6 to 16, selected to be representative of 1988 U.S. census data. New items were added to the test to replace WISC-R items that were outdated, culturally unfair, too easy, or too difficult. In addition, a new subtest called Symbol Search was added as a supplementary test that can be substituted for the Coding subtest.

The WISC-III Manual (Wechsler, 1991) presents unusually thorough data about the test's reliability and validity, and additional research on the interpretation of WISC-III scores is in progress. Its basic scores are extremely stable over time and show very high correlations with the WISC-R, as well as appropriately strong correlations with criteria such as school grades, achievement test scores, and neuropsychological performance. In addition to Full Scale, Verbal, and Performance IQ scores, the WISC-III can be interpreted in terms of four other factors: Verbal Comprehension, Perceptual Organization (which are similar to, but not identical with, Verbal and Performance

IQ, respectively), Freedom from Distractibility (emphasizing memory and attention), and Processing Speed.

Other Intelligence Tests

Many other intelligence instruments are in use today, several designed to assess intelligence without emphasis on verbal or vocalization skills. It is important that such tests be available, since some clients may be too young or, for other reasons, unable to do well at verbal tasks. Tests such as the Peabody Picture Vocabulary Test-Revised and the Porteus Maze Test allow the clinician to assess intellectual functioning in clients of this type. They also provide a backup in cases where the clinician suspects that a client's performance on a standard IQ test may have been hampered by anxiety, specific verbal deficits, cultural disadvantages, or other situational factors. Prominent examples include the Leiter International Performance Scale, and the Raven's Progressive Matrices.

An intelligence test that has gained popularity over the past decade is the Kaufman Assessment Battery for Children (K-ABC; Kaufman & Kaufman, 1983). Suitable for children 2½ to 12½ years of age, the K-ABC was based on research and theory in cognitive psychology and neuropsychology. It defines intelligence as the ability to solve new problems (an ability sometimes referred to as *fluid intelligence*) rather than knowledge of facts (which has been termed *crystallized intelligence*). The standardization sample for the K-ABC was closely matched to the U.S. census on several demographic factors, and its psychometric qualities are excellent. In addition, several studies show that the K-ABC can be used to assess and study neuropsychological problems in children (Kaufman & Harrison, 1991).

Another relatively recent intelligence test is the 1989 revision of the Woodcock-Johnson Psycho-Educational Battery (Woodcock & Johnson, 1977, 1989). Although usually used with children, this test can also be employed with adults. A special feature of the Wood-cock-Johnson is that its 27 subtests cover cognitive ability, academic achievement, and individual interests. Scoring is more complex than for most other intelligence tests, and there is some evidence that the separate ability and achievement subtests are not as clearly differentiated as intended (Kaufman & Harrison, 1991). Additional intelligence tests for adults and children are described by Anastasi (1988), Lindemann and Matarazzo (1990), and Sattler (1988). Group intelligence tests are summarized by Vane and Motta (1990).

Ability Tests

Some clinicians think of intelligence as mental ability and refer to intelligence tests as general mental ability instruments. However, a number of other tests are designed to measure specific mental abilities. These include *aptitude* and *achievement* tests. Aptitude tests are designed to predict success in an occupation or an educational program. They measure the accumulated effects of many different educational and living experiences and attempt to forecast future performance on the basis of these effects. The Scholastic Aptitude Test (SAT), used to predict high school students' potential for college-level work, provides an example familiar to most undergraduates.

Achievement tests measure proficiency at certain tasks; that is, how much does the person know or how well can he or she do? The Wide Range Achievement Test-Revised is a well-known example. Somewhat in contrast to aptitude tests, achievement tests measure the effects of a more uniform set of learning or training experiences. Many psychologists argue that intelligence, aptitude, and achievement tests are more alike than different in that all attempt to measure "developed abilities" (Reschly, 1990; see also Fox & Zirkin, 1984).

Despite the overlap between intelligence and achievement, test-construction experts continue to develop intelligence test batteries that also contain achievement tests aimed at assessing strengths and weaknesses in academic areas. While the Wide Range Achievement Test-Revised remains the most popular of these achievement tests, three more sophisticated alternatives have been developed and may find increased use by clinicians: the achievement subtests of the Woodcock-Johnson, the Kaufman Test of Educational Achievement (K-TEA; Kaufman & Kaufman, 1985), and the newest addition, the Wechsler Individual Achievement Test (WIAT), which was introduced in 1992.

The more specific the ability or aptitude tested, the less familiar the test is likely to be. If you have never heard of the Seashore Measures of Musical Talents or the Crawford Small Parts Dexterity Test, it is probably because they are used to measure very specialized abilities. Ability testing is more often done by personnel officers and educational, vocational, and guidance counselors than by clinical psychologists. The reader interested in further information about ability testing should consult Conoley and Kramer (1989).

Clinicians' interest in ability testing is usually related to assessment of specific cognitive capabilities or deficits. Though clinicians may draw inferences about specific cognitive abilities, deficits, or even brain damage from the pattern of scores on the WAIS-R or the WISC-R, they may also utilize a variety of special-purpose tests, some of which emphasize perception and memory. For example, the Benton Visual Retention Test (Benton, 1974), the Bender Visual Motor Gestalt (or Bender-Gestalt; Bender, 1938) and the Memory-for-Designs Test (Graham & Kendall, 1960) ask the client to copy or draw from memory geometric figures or other designs. Other tests in this category assess the client's ability to form concepts and engage in other types of abstract thinking. The use of tests to detect brain damage or deterioration is known as neuropsychological assessment and is described in more detail in Chapter 13.

Attitudes, Interests, Preferences, and Values

Clinical psychologists often find it useful to assess a person's attitudes, interests, preferences, and values. For example, before beginning to work with a distressed couple, the clinician may wish to get some idea about each spouse's attitudes about marriage. Similarly, it may be instructive for the clinician to know that the interests of a client who is in severe conflict about entering the medical profession are totally unlike those of successful physicians. Finally, these instruments encourage clients to engage in their own self-exploration with respect to career decisions.

The many tests available to assess attitudes, interests, preferences, and values overlap a great deal, so there is little to be gained from labeling each instrument in this category. It is important, however, to be aware of some of the more commonly used tests, such as the Strong-Campbell Interest Inventory (Hansen & Campbell, 1985), the Kuder Occupational Interest Survey (Zytowski, 1985), the Career Assessment Inventory (Johansson, 1982), and the Self-Directed Search (Holland, 1985). These are paper-and-pencil instruments designed to assess clients' preferences for various pursuits, occupations, academic subjects, recreational activities, and people. Each results in an interest profile that can be compared with composite profiles gathered from members of occupational groups such as biologists, engineers, army officers, carpenters, police, ministers, accountants, salespeople, and lawyers.

Generalized life orientations can be assessed via the Allport-Vernon-Lindzey Study of Values (Allport, Vernon, & Lindzey, 1970), a paper-and-pencil instrument that asks the client to choose among alternatives about things like use of leisure time, interest in various news items, and the importance of various activities. The resulting profile of values shows the relative strength of six basic interests: theoretical ("intellectual"), economic, aesthetic, social, political, and religious. Other, more phenomenologically oriented, general value assessments include the Purpose-in-Life Test (Crumbaugh, 1968) and the Personal Orientation Inventory (Shostrom, 1968).

There are many tests designed to assess more specific interests and preferences (Hansen, 1984; Holland, 1986). For example, the behavioral model of clinical psychology has generated several tests aimed at illuminating client preferences and attitudes as a prelude to treatment. Among the most prominent of these is the Reinforcement Survey Schedule (Cautela & Kastenbaum, 1967), a list of situations and activities that the client rates in terms of their desirability. The Pleasant Events Schedule (MacPhillamy & Lewinsohn, 1976) provides an example of a behaviorally oriented preference assessment.

Many qualities assessed by tests described in this section are related to the client's personality. Indeed, attitudes, interests, values, and preferences make up a large part of personality. The overlap between these areas is well recognized, but there are a vast number of psychological tests whose goal is the measurement of many other aspects of personality, and it is to these instruments that we now turn our attention.

Personality Tests

Personality can be defined as the pattern of behavioral and psychological characteristics by which a person can be compared and contrasted with other people. When studying personality, clinicians examine the behavioral inconsistencies and similarities within the same person, as well as among different people. Some theorists see personality as an organized collection of traits, others hypothesize dynamic relationships among intrapsychic forces, while still others point to recurring patterns of behavior. As was the case with intelligence, the breadth of personality means that clinicians assess it in a multitude of ways, usually in accordance with their theoretical model of human behavior. This is probably why there are more tests in the personality category than in any other. We cannot begin to cover all of them here, so this section will be restricted to a brief look at the most prominent personality tests in clinical use. Readers interested in more detailed treatment of personality assessment should consult texts such as Anastasi (1988), Conoley and Kramer (1989), Goldstein and Hersen (1990), Kleinmuntz (1982), Lanyon and Goodstein (1982), a journal called *Journal of Personality Assessment,* and a series of books, *Advances in Personality Assessment,* edited by Butcher and Spielberger.

There are two major types of personality tests: *objective* and *projective.* Objective tests present relatively clear, specific stimuli such as questions ("Have you ever wanted to run away from home?") or statements ("I am never depressed") or concepts ("Myself" or "Large dogs") to which the client responds with direct answers, choices, or ratings. Most often, objective personality tests are of the paper-and-pencil variety and can be scored mathematically (often by computers), much like a multiple-choice or true–false test. Some objective tests focus on one aspect of personality such as anxiety, dependency, or ego strength, while others provide a comprehensive overview of many personality dimensions.

Although projective tests have been closely associated with psychodynamic models of clinical psychology over the years, they are used by clinicians of many different theoretical backgrounds. Beginning with Freud's notion that people defend themselves psychologically by attributing to others unacceptable aspects of their own personality, Frank (1939) broadened the concept of projection by suggesting that there is a "tendency of people to be influenced in the cognitive mediation of perceptual inputs by their needs, interests, and overall psychological organization" (Exner, 1976, p. 61). In other words, each individual's personality will determine, in part at least, the way she or he interprets things. Frank (1939) labeled tests that encourage clients to display this tendency as "projective methods." In general, these tests elicit reactions to ambiguous or unstructured stimuli (such as inkblots or in-

complete sentences), which are interpreted as a reflection of primarily unconscious personality structure and dynamics. Some projective tests use a paper-and-pencil format, but more often the client responds orally to each stimulus. These responses are transcribed or tape recorded for later scoring.

Compared to the answers given on objective tests, the stories, drawings, and associations that subjects give on projective tests are more difficult to translate into numerical scores. Scoring projective tests is more subjective than scoring objective tests. For many years, the primary guidelines for scoring projectives came from experts, who after administering hundreds of projective tests, summarized their experience into a long list of rules of thumb for interpreting different responses. This method of scoring often produced large discrepancies between examiners and led to severe criticism of projective methods. To remedy this problem, clinicians have developed more quantified scoring systems for some of the most popular projective tests, such as the Rorschach (Exner, 1986). These systems have improved the interrater reliability of projective tests and have helped to ensure their continued use by clinicians.

Objective Personality Tests

The first objective personality test developed by a psychologist was Woodworth's (1920) Personal Data Sheet, used during World War I to screen soldiers with psychological problems. It asked for yes or no answers to questions such as "Did you have a happy childhood?" "Does it make you uneasy to cross a bridge?" These items were selected because they reflected problems and symptoms reported at least twice as often by previously diagnosed neurotics as by "normals." No item was retained in the test if more than 25% of a normal sample answered it in an unfavorable manner. Item selection procedures such as these were a prelude to later, more sophisticated empirical test construction procedures (Butcher & Keller, 1984).

The MMPI.   Among the hundreds of objective personality measures that have appeared since Woodworth's early effort, the most influential and widely used is the Minnesota Multiphasic Personality Inventory (MMPI). This test was developed during the late 1930s at the University of Minnesota by Starke Hathaway (a psychologist) and J. C. McKinley (a psychiatrist) as an aid to psychiatric diagnosis of clinical patients. The MMPI was one of the first personality tests to be constructed empirically. Hathaway and McKinley took about 1,000 items from older personality tests and other sources and converted them into statements to which a client could respond "true," "false," or "cannot say." Approximately 500 of these items were administered to thousands of normal persons as well as to persons diagnosed with psychiatric disorders.

Certain response patterns appeared. When compared to normals, members of various diagnostic groups showed statistically different responses to many items. For example, a particular group of items tended to be answered in the same way by depressed persons, while another group of items was answered in a particular way by persons diagnosed as schizophrenic. Eight such item groups were identified as discriminating normals from non-normals and as being associated with a certain diagnostic category. These item groups were called *scales*. Later, two additional groupings were identified as being responded to differently by males and females and by shy, introverted college students. Thus, there are 10 *clinical scales* on the MMPI; their names and examples[2] of the kinds of items included in each are presented in Box 5–4.

---

[2]To avoid biasing the response of readers (or their friends) who might take the MMPI, its actual items are not presented. Incidentally, the MMPI item format has been widely parodied: A "Maryland Malpractice and Pandering Inventory" has circulated as a joke among clinicians for years. It contains items such as: "I used to tease vegetables," "The sight of blood no longer excites me," and "I use shoe polish to excess." (See also Walker & Walsh, 1969.)

Also included in the MMPI are four *validity scales*. These are groups of items designed to help detect various kinds of test-taking attitudes or distorted responses. The Cannot Say or ? scale is the number of items that the respondent does not answer. An elevated ? scale can be due to poor cooperation, failure to understand items, or defensiveness. The *L* (or *lie*) scale consists of statements which, if answered honestly, reveal mildly negative things about the client (such as the fact that he or she does not stay informed about world events every day). The assumption here is that if the client denies trivial negative behaviors or thoughts, she or he will probably not be honest about more serious problems covered on other items. The *F* (or *frequency*) scale contains items that are rarely endorsed by normals, but which are not associated with any particular diagnosed group. A high *F* score is interpreted as indicating carelessness in responding, a purposeful attempt to exaggerate symptoms, a very severe disorder, or some related factor. The *K* (or *correction*) scale is designed to detect a client's tendency to be overly defensive or overly disclosing about problems. A high *K* score is taken as evidence that the severity of problems revealed in the test was played down by the client. A low *K* score suggests that problems may have been overstated. In either case, the *K* scale is used as a guide for "correcting" scores on five of the clinical scales.

When people take the MMPI, their responses to the items are converted into clinical and validity scale scores. Originally, the MMPI clinical scales were taken literally; a person showing a high depression or schizophrenia score was given a corresponding diagnostic label. It soon became obvious, however, that elevation of a particular scale did not always mean that the individual belonged in the associated diagnostic category.

Recognition of this problem led to (a) calling the clinical scales by number (1–10) rather than by name, and (b) plotting all scale scores on a graph and analyzing the resulting profile

Validity (or Test-Taking Attitude) Scales

? (Cannot Say) Number of items left unanswered.

L (Lie) Fifteen items of overly good self-report, such as "I smile at everyone I meet." (answered True)

F (Frequency or Infrequency) Sixty items answered in the scored direction by 10% or less of normals, such as "There is an international plot against me." (True)

K (Correction) Thirty items reflecting defensiveness in admitting to problems, such as "I feel bad when others criticize me." (False)

Clinical Scales

1 or **Hs** (Hypochondriasis). Thirty-two items derived from patients showing abnormal concern with bodily functions, such as "I have chest pains several times a week." (True)

2 or **D** (Depression) Fifty-seven items derived from patients showing extreme pessimism, feelings of hopelessness, and slowing of thought and action, such as "I usually feel that life is interesting and worthwhile." (False)

3 or **Hy** (Conversion Hysteria) Sixty items from neurotic patients using physical or mental symptoms as a way of unconsciously avoiding difficult conflicts and responsibilities, such as "My heart frequently pounds so hard I can feel it." (True)

4 or **Pd** (Psychopathic Deviate) Fifty items from patients who show a repeated and flagrant disregard for social customs, an emotional shallowness, and an inability to learn from punishing experiences, such as "My activities and interests are often criticized by others." (True)

5 or **Mf** (Masculinity–Femininity) Fifty-six items from patients showing homoeroticism and items differentiating between men and women, such as "I like to arrange flowers." (True, scored for femininity)

6 or **Pa** (Paranoia) Forty items from patients showing abnormal suspiciousness and delusions of grandeur or persecution, such as "There are evil people trying to influence my mind." (True)

7 or **Pt** (Psychasthenia) Forty-eight items based on neurotic patients showing obsessions, compulsions, abnormal fears, and guilt and indecisiveness, such as "I save nearly everything I buy, even after I have no use for it." (True)

8 or **Sc** (Schizophrenia) Seventy-eight items from patients showing bizarre or unusual thoughts or behavior, who are often withdrawn and experiencing delusions and hallucinations, such as "Things around me do not seem real" (True) and "It makes me uncomfortable to have people close to me." (True)

9 or **Ma** (Hypomania) Forty-six items from patients characterized by emotional excitement, overactivity, and flight of ideas, such as "At times I feel very 'high' or very 'low' for no apparent reason." (True)

0 or **Si** (Social Introversion) Sixty-nine items from persons showing shyness, little interest in people, and insecurity, such as "I have the time of my life at parties." (False)

Source: Adapted from Norman Sundberg, *Assessment of Persons,* © 1977, p. 183. (Reprinted by permission of Prentice-Hall, Inc., Englewood Cliffs, New Jersey.)

BOX 5–4
MMPI-2 Scales and Simulated Items

(not just the highest score) and the relationships among its points.

The clinician conducts a profile analysis by comparing the client's MMPI with those of other clients. This can be done *clinically* by recalling previous clients, or *statistically* by reference to books containing sample profiles and the characteristics of the people who produced them (Archer, 1987; Butcher & Williams, 1992; Dahlstrom, Lachar, & Dahlstrom, 1986; Dahlstrom & Welsh, 1960; Dahlstrom, Welsh, & Dahlstrom, 1972; Gilberstadt & Duker, 1965; Graham, 1990). As noted in Chapter 3, several companies offer computerized scoring of the MMPI along with computer interpretations based upon actuarial formulae or previous clinical experience (sometimes called *automated clinical lore;* see Butcher, 1987).

In addition to being the most popular objective personality test in clinical use today, the MMPI spawned over 12,000 research reports and hundreds of other related tests and scales, many of which go beyond the test's original purpose of assessing "those traits that are commonly characteristic of disabling psychological abnormality" (Hathaway & McKinley, 1967, p. 1). For example, there are over 400 groupings of MMPI items, each of which tries to measure an aspect of personality such as ego strength, anxiety, dependency, dominance, social status, and prejudice. These new groupings or scales can be used in conjunction with the MMPI as a whole or as a separate test. Shorter versions of the MMPI have also been developed. Called the "Mini-Mult" or "Midi-Mult," these abbreviated editions are less comprehensive and designed for quick classification and screening purposes (see Stevens & Reilly, 1980, for a review).

Despite widespread use, the original MMPI had limitations. These involved the outdated and unrepresentative original standardization sample, deficiencies in coverage of some aspects of mental disorders, antiquated items, and inadequate reliabilities for some of the scales. In response to these problems, the publisher of the MMPI, the University of Minnesota Press, began an extensive revision of the MMPI in 1982. The revision focused on gathering new national norms using randomly selected samples of adults and adolescents in seven states, as well as gathering data on several clinical populations. The 2,600 restandardization subjects were comparable to 1980 U.S. census figures in terms of age, marital status, and ethnic group status. Also, 154 items were evaluated for possible addition to the test. Some were reworded examples of past items; most were new items intended to provide better coverage of topics and problems that had not been assessed with the original item pool. The result of these changes is the MMPI-2 (Butcher, Dahlstrom, Graham, Tellegen, & Kaemmer, 1989), made available for general clinical use in 1989. Although interpretation of this revised version is similar to the first edition of the test, changes in the wording and order of the items, as well as the introduction of new items, should allow clinicians to improve their assessment of areas such as substance abuse and certain personality patterns. A sample MMPI-2 profile is presented in Figure 5–3.

Among the major new developments contained in the MMPI-2, three are especially important:

1. A set of 15 new *content scales* are included. These scales allow supplementary assessment of personality factors not previously measurable with the basic clinical scales. These scales are summarized in Box 5–5.

2. New validity scales to be used in conjunction with ?, L, F, and K have been added. Two of these scales, abbreviated VRIN and TRIN, are designed to identify persons who have answered test items in an inconsistent or careless manner. Researchers are now studying the effectiveness of these scales (e.g., Berry et al., 1991).

3. Scoring is changed to equalize the clinical significance of similar scores on different scales; with the original MMPI, similar scores

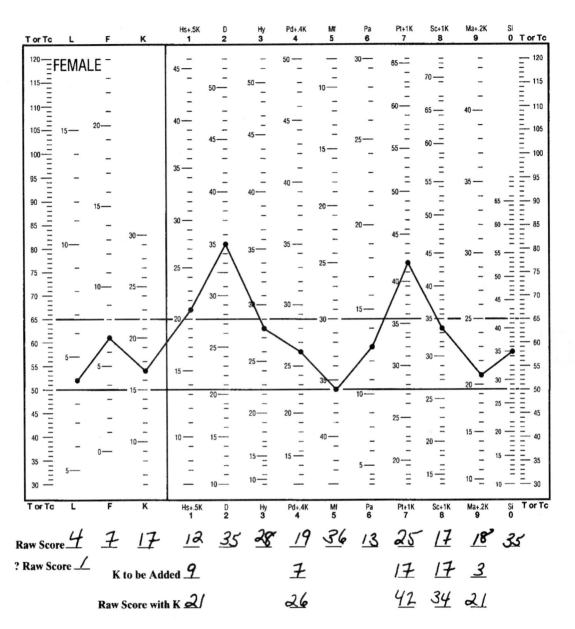

Raw Score 4 7 17 12 35 28 19 36 13 25 17 18 35

? Raw Score 1

K to be Added 9

Raw Score with K 21

7

26

17 17 3

42 34 21

FIGURE 5-3 This MMPI-2 profile was obtained from a 38-year-old woman who had suffered a sexual assault by a co-worker. The elevated scores on Scales 2 and 7 are typical of persons who are experiencing symptoms of depression, tension, anxiety, and general psychological distress. These two scales are often elevated for persons who have experienced a recent trauma. The high score on Scale 1 suggests that this woman is experiencing a fairly large number of physical complaints and is very concerned about her health. (Minnesota Multiphasic Personality Inventory-2, Copyright © by THE REGENTS OF THE UNIVERSITY OF MINNESOTA 1942, 1943 [renewed 1970], 1989. This Profile Form 1989.)

Among the changes appearing in the MMPI-2 are 15 new content scales. The developers of these new scales began by defining clinically relevant areas of personality that were not specifically measured by the MMPI. They then used sequential test construction procedures to create groups of items that clinical judgment and statistical analyses suggested would tap these areas. The names and targets of these new content scales are as follows:

SCALE NAME	DESCRIPTION OF CONTENT
Anxiety	Measures symptoms of anxiety including tension, physical complaints, sleep problems, worry, and/or concentration.
Fears	Assesses the presence of many specific fears such as fear of the dark, fire, leaving home, etc.
Obsessiveness	High scores on this scale indicate people who have trouble making decisions and ruminate excessively. They may also show some compulsive behaviors.
Depression	Measures symptoms of depression including sad mood, hopelessness, suicidal concerns, and despair.
Health Concerns	Measures frequent complaints about health, covering several different body systems. High scorers worry a lot about their health.
Bizarre Mentation	Persons who score high on this scale may show psychotic thinking. They may recognize that their thoughts are strange and peculiar.
Anger	Measures problems with controlling anger. High scorers on this scale report being irritable, grouchy, impatient, hotheaded, and stubborn.
Cynicism	High scorers on this scale see hidden, negative motives behind the acts of others. They are frequently distrustful of people.

BOX 5–5
The MMPI-2 Content Scales

on different scales signified different levels of disturbance (Tellegen & Ben-Porath, 1992). In addition, the definition of a clinical elevation has been lowered from 70 or higher on the MMPI to 65 or higher on the MMPI-2.

The CPI. The California Psychological Inventory is another prominent example of a broad-range, empirically constructed, objective personality test. Introduced in 1957, a 1987 revision (Gough, 1987) with updated content and reworded items is now available. In contrast to the MMPI, the CPI was developed specifically for assessing personality in the "normal" population. About half of its 462

true–false items come from the MMPI, but the CPI items are grouped into more diverse and positively oriented scales including sociability, self-acceptance, responsibility, dominance, self-control, and others. There are also three validity scales that serve basically the same purpose as those on the MMPI. The CPI was initially standardized on 13,000 males and females from all parts of the country and in all socioeconomic categories. Strengths of the CPI include the representativeness of its standardization sample and its relatively high reliability. The test has been used to predict delinquency, parole outcome, academic grades, and the likelihood of dropping out of high

SCALE NAME	DESCRIPTION OF CONTENT
Antisocial Practices	Measures a tendency toward mistrust as well as a pattern of such problem behaviors and antisocial practices as being in trouble with the law, stealing, or shoplifting.
Type A	High scorers on this scale are hard-driving, fast-moving individuals who are absorbed in their work and frequently become impatient, irritable, and annoyed.
Low Self-Esteem	Persons who score high on this scale hold low opinions of themselves. They feel that they are not liked by others and that they are not important.
Social Discomfort	Measures a tendency to be very uneasy around others and to prefer to be alone. High scorers feel shy and dislike group activities.
Family Problems	Assesses family discord. High scorers describe their families as quarrelsome, unpleasant, and lacking in love.
Work Interference	A high score on this scale indicates behaviors or attitudes likely to lead to poor work performance. The problems include low self-confidence, concentration problems, and difficulties in making decisions.
Negative Treatment	Measures the tendency to hold negative attitudes toward doctors and mental-health treatment. Persons scoring high on this scale are not comfortable discussing their problems with others.

BOX 5–5
Continued

school (Anastasi, 1988). Computerized scoring and interpretation services are available.

Other Objective Tests. Other objective personality inventories in clinical use include the Personality Research Form (PRF; Jackson, 1984), the Basic Personality Inventory (Jackson, 1989), the Personality Assessment Inventory (Morey, 1991), the Edwards Personal Preference Schedule (EPPS; Edwards, 1959), the Sixteen Personality Factors Questionnaire (16PF; Cattell, Eber, & Tatusoka, 1970), and the Millon Clinical Multiaxial Inventory (MCMI-II; Millon, 1987a). Among these tests, the PRF and MCMI deserve special attention. The PRF is one of the best examples of

the sequential system approach to test construction in which items were selected on theoretical grounds, combined into scales on empirical grounds, and then empirically validated against external criteria. It comes in five different forms, the most comprehensive of which contains 440 true–false items combined into 22 independent scales. In addition, the PRF was constructed to minimize certain response biases that can distort test results. The PRF is generally used with normal rather than clinical populations; its development was based on Henry Murray's (1938) *Variables of Personality*.

Millon's MCMI, first published in 1982, was also constructed using a combination of analytic and empirical methods. It reflects Millon's unique theory of personality (Millon, 1981), retains several positive features of the MMPI, and was designed to coordinate its interpretations with the diagnostic criteria in *DSM-III-R*. At 175 items, the MCMI is shorter than the MMPI. It is intended primarily for clinical diagnosis, though there are questions about its diagnostic utility (Widiger, 1985).

Factor Analysis and Psychological Testing

For much of the 20th century, psychologists have tried to determine the number of traits or characteristics necessary for an adequate description of human personality. At one extreme, if we measured every possible different trait, the hundreds of distinct characteristics would overwhelm our ability to organize the data into a meaningful pattern. At the other extreme, if we limited ourselves to one or two "super" traits, we would risk oversimplifying personality and ignoring essential characteristics.

One approach to this problem is to examine how much overlap different traits share with one another. Factor analysis is a mathematical procedure that helps us reduce the complexity of many different traits by grouping them into clusters or factors based on the pattern of correlations between the different traits. Using factor analysis to identify basic clusters, Cattell developed the 16PF, which we mentioned earlier as a prominent objective personality test.

The number and names of fundamental trait clusters have varied over the years. Hans Eysenck, the influential British psychologist, used factor analytic methods to arrive at three basic personality factors—Psychoticism, Introversion–Extraversion, and Emotionality–Stability. The Eysenck Personality Questionnaire (Eysenck & Eysenck, 1975) measures these three factors. Auge Tellegen (1982) used factor analytic methods to develop the Multidimensional Personality Questionnaire (MPQ), a 300-item personality inventory that yields three factors that Tellegen calls Positive Emotionality, Negative Emotionality, and Constraint.

A second group of psychologists focus on a five-factor organization of personality. The "big five" approach includes the following dimensions: (a) *neuroticism* (a tendency to feel anxious, angry, and depressed in many situations), (b) *extraversion* (a tendency to be assertive, active, and to prefer to be with other people), (c) *openness* (a quality indicating active imagination, curiosity, and receptiveness to many experiences), (d) *agreeableness* (an orientation toward positive, sympathetic, helpful interactions with others), and (e) *conscientiousness* (a tendency to be reliable and persistent in pursuing goals). The "big five" model of personality is associated with the NEO Personality Inventory-R (Costa & McCrae, 1992a). The first three letters in the title of this test refer to the factors of Neuroticism, Extraversion, and Openness to Experience. First introduced in 1985, the latest revision of this test consists of 243 items that measure the "big five" traits as well as six specific facets of each trait. Box 5–6 depicts the six facets for each "big five" trait. While the NEO PI-R was developed as a comprehensive measure of normal adult personality, its authors suggest that it can also be used in the diagnosis of psychological disorders, the prediction of psychotherapy progress, and the selection of optimal forms of treatment for some clients (Costa & McCrae, 1992b). This suggestion is challenged by other clinicians who are not convinced that instruments like the NEO PI-R add any clinically useful information beyond that provided by tests like the MMPI-2 (Ben-Porath & Waller, 1992).

Behavioral Tests

Proponents of the behavioral model of clinical psychology see personality as patterns of behavior and have therefore constructed objective tests which, unlike those described so far, gather behavior samples upon which only minimal inferences are based. These tests tend to be short and analytically constructed.

Probably the most frequently employed behavior "personality test" is the Fear Survey

Extraversion	*Neuroticism*	*Conscientiousness*
Warmth	Anxiety	Competence
Gregariousness	Angry Hostility	Order
Assertiveness	Depression	Dutifulness
Activity	Self-Consciousness	Achievement Striving
Excitement Seeking	Impulsiveness	Self-Discipline
Positive Emotions	Vulnerability	Deliberation

Openness to Experience	*Agreeableness*
Fantasy	Trust
Aesthetics	Straightforwardness
Feelings	Altruism
Actions	Compliance
Ideas	Modesty
Values	Tendermindedness

Source: Based on Costa and McCrae (1992a).

BOX 5-6
Facets of the Major Traits of Personality
as Measured by the NEO Personality Inventory-R

Schedule (FSS). It is simply a list of objects, persons, and situations that the client is asked to rate in terms of fearsomeness. The several editions of this test (e.g., Geer, 1965; Lawlis, 1971; Wolpe & Lang, 1969) contain from 50 to 122 items and use either 1-to-5 or 1-to-7 scales for the fear ratings. The FSS is used to assess the prevalence of various fears, to identify persons with specific fears, and to assess changes over the course of fear-reduction treatment. A few items from the FSS are presented in Box 5–7. There is also an FSS for children (Ollendick, 1983).

Among other behavioral objective tests focused upon anxiety, one finds the State-Trait Anxiety Inventory (Spielberger, Gorsuch, Lushene, Vagg, & Jacobs, 1983), the Social Avoidance and Distress Scale (Watson & Friend, 1969), the Social Phobia and Anxiety Inventory (SPAI; Turner, Beidel, Dancu, & Stanley, 1989), and the Trimodal Anxiety Symptom Questionnaire (Lehrer & Woolfolk, 1982). Behaviorally oriented clinicians have also developed tests that assess other features of behavior. These tests include the Beck Depression Inventory (Beck, Ward, Mendelson, Mock, & Erbaugh, 1961), the Multiple Affect Adjective Checklist (Zuckerman & Lubin, 1965), the Expanded Attributional Style Questionnaire (Peterson & Villanova, 1988), and The Maudsley Obsessional-Compulsive Inventory (Hodgson & Rachman, 1977). The reader interested in detailed material on behavioral tests should consult Bellack and Hersen (1988); Ciminero, Calhoun, and Adams (1986); or Mash and Terdal (1988).

1. Snakes	6. Arguing with parents	11. Being alone
2. Death of a loved one	7. Hypodermic needles	12. Heights
3. Seeing a fight	8. Swimming alone	13. Closed places
4. Being a passenger in a car	9. Making mistakes	14. Cemeteries
5. Failing a test	10. Strange dogs	15. Roller coasters

On Fear Survey Schedules, persons are asked to rate how much fear they feel in response to items like those above on a 1-to-5 or 1-to-7 scale.

Source: Geer, 1965.

BOX 5–7
Sample Items From a Fear Survey Schedule

Projective Personality Tests

Projective assessment goes back to the 1400s, when Leonardo da Vinci is said to have selected his pupils partly on the basis of the creativity they displayed while attempting to find shapes and patterns in ambiguous forms (Piotrowski, 1972). In the late 1800s Binet adapted a parlor game called "Blotto" to assess "passive imagination" by asking children to tell what they saw in inkblots (Exner, 1976). Galton constructed a word association test in 1879; Carl Jung was using a similar test for clinical assessment by 1910. These informal projective techniques evolved into projective *tests* when their content was standardized such that each client was exposed to the same stimuli in the same way.

Lindzey (1961) suggested a set of criteria that outline the general nature of projective tests[3] as follows:

1. They are sensitive to unconscious personality dimensions.

2. They permit the client a broad range of responses.

3. They are capable of measuring many different aspects of personality.

4. They leave the client unaware or at least unsure of the specific meaning of his or her responses.

5. They generate a large amount of complex assessment data.

6. They employ relatively ambiguous stimuli.

7. They can be interpreted to provide an integrated picture of the client's personality as a whole.

8. They are capable of evoking fantasy material from the client.

9. They have no right or wrong answers.

Projective methods can be classified according to the stimuli they use; the way the tests are constructed, interpreted, or administered; their designated purpose; and the kind of response they elicit. Classification by client response is the clearest strategy for our purposes, so the following sections will correspond to Lindzey's (1961) labeling of projective tests as evoking *associations, constructions,*

---

[3]Exner (1976, pp. 66–67) notes that answers to certain intelligence items may provide projective clues about personality: "The best answer to the question, 'why does the state require people to get a license in order to get married?' is that it is for purposes of record keeping. However, if a subject says, 'To prevent the scourge of VD from being inflicted on unsuspecting women,' then the answer . . . conveys something about the peculiar interests of the respondent."

completions, choices or *orderings,* and *expressions* from the respondent. We consider only a few examples in each group, but a vast quantity of more detailed information about these and other projectives is available in such references as Erdberg (1990), Exner (1978, 1986), Lindzey (1961), Schaefer (1967), Shneidman (1965), Sundberg (1977), and Zubin, Eron, and Schumer (1965).

Association Tests

These projective tests ask clients to look at an ambiguous stimulus and tell what they see in or associate with it. The most widely known and frequently employed projective of this type is the Rorschach Inkblot Test. It is a set of 10 colored and black-and-white inkblots created by Hermann Rorschach, a Swiss psychiatrist, between 1911 and 1921. Many researchers in Europe and America had previously employed inkblots to assess fantasy, imagination, and perception, but it was Rorschach who first attempted to use such stimuli for diagnosis and personality assessment.

Rorschach began with geometric figures cut from colored paper and later switched to inkblots, partly as a result of having read about an inkblot test of fantasy developed by Hens, a Polish medical student. When the inkblot test finally appeared in 1921, it was not well received. European test experts such as Stern "denounced it as faulty, arbitrary, artificial, and incapable . . . of understanding human personality. . . ." (Reisman, 1976). Rorschach's book, *Psychodiagnostik,* which described his test and its interpretation, sold few copies.

The Rorschach would have had an early demise if David Levy, an American psychiatrist studying in Switzerland in 1920–21, had not brought a copy of the test back to the United States and, in 1927, instructed a psychology trainee named Samuel Beck in its use. Beck published the first American report involving the Rorschach. In 1937 he provided a standardized procedure for administering and scoring the test. Another scoring manual appeared that same year (Klopfer & Kelley, 1937), and the Rorschach was on its way to wide popularity among American psychologists, who until then had no global test of personality available to them. The growing clinical use of the test was paralleled by an explosion of research on its reliability, validity, scoring, and interpretation.

The test itself is simple. The client is shown 10 cards, one at a time. An inkblot (similar to that pictured in Figure 5–4) is on each card; the client is asked to tell what she or he sees or what the blot could be. The tester records all responses verbatim and takes notes about response times, how the card was being held (e.g., upside down, sideways) while a response occurred, noticeable emotional reactions, and other behaviors. Next, the tester conducts an *inquiry* or systematic questioning of the client about the characteristics of each blot that prompted the responses.

The initial reactions to the blots and the comments made during the inquiry are then coded, using a special scoring system. Scoring involves the *location, determinants, content,* and *popularity* of the responses. *Location* refers to the area of the blot to which the client responds: The whole blot, a common detail, an unusual detail, white space, or some combination of these are location responses. The *determinants* of the response refer to the characteristic of the blot influencing a response; they include form, color, shading, and "movement." While there is no movement in the blot itself, the respondent's perception of the blot as a moving object is scored in this category. *Content* refers to the subject matter perceived in the blot. Content includes human figures, parts of human figures, animal figures, animal details, anatomical features, inanimate objects, art, clothing, clouds, blood, X-rays, sexual objects, and symbols. *Popularity* is scored on the basis of the relative frequency of different responses among people in general.

Assume that a client responded to Figure 5–4 by saying, "It looks like a bat" and during subsequent inquiry noted that "I saw the whole

FIGURE 5–4 Inkblot similar to those used in the Rorschach. (From Norman D. Sundberg, *Assessment of Persons*, © 1977, p. 207. Reprinted by permission of Prentice-Hall, Inc., Englewood Cliffs, New Jersey.)

blot as a bat because it is black and is just sort of bat shaped." If one of the popular scoring systems (e.g., that of Beck or Klopfer) were used, these responses would be coded as "WFC′ + AP," where W indicates that the whole blot was used (*location*); F means that the blot's form (F) was the main *determinant* of the response; and C′ means that achromatic color was also involved. The + shows that the form described corresponded well to the actual form of the blot; A means that there was animal *content* in the response; and P indicates that "bat" is a *popular* response to this particular card.[4]

The clinician may draw inferences from several aspects of Rorschach responses. Normative data exist to establish particular responses as common or unusual, and there have even been attempts to computerize interpretations (Fowler, 1985). For the most part, however, inference is based upon experience with the test and general interpretive guidelines. Sundberg (1977, p. 208) provides a summary of such guidelines that conveys the flavor of the inferences that stem from coded responses:

Using the whole blot suggests integration and organization; many small details indicate compulsiveness and over-control, and the use of white space suggests oppositional and negativistic tendencies. The presence of much poor form, uncommon responses, and confused thinking suggests a psychotic condition. Responsiveness to color is supposed to represent emotionality, and in the absence of good form, it suggests uncontrolled emotions and impulsivity. Responses mentioning human movement indicate imagination, intelligence, and a vivid inner life. . . . Content also has much potential for interpretation. . . . Knives, guns, mutilated bodies, and angry interactions suggest strong hostility.

---

[4]There are at least five reasonably distinct systems for scoring the Rorschach (Erdberg, 1990), so a given response may be coded in various ways; further, each scoring system is used somewhat differently by individual clinicians.

The clinician also looks for recurring patterns of responses across cards, and certain test statistics contained in a "structural summary" are interpreted. The overall number of responses (called *productivity),* the frequency of responses in certain categories, and various ratios and relationships between and among categories are seen as significant. For example, because most people tend to use form more often than color in determining their responses, a high proportion of color-dominated determinants may be taken as evidence of weak emotional control. In Exner's (1986) interpretive system, there are more than 20 response percentages and ratios available for interpretation.

The client's overt behavior in response to the Rorschach itself is also interpreted by the clinician. Evidence of tension, enjoyment, or confusion; attempts to impress the examiner; and other behavioral cues are an important part of Rorschach interpretation (e.g., Goldfried, Stricker, & Weiner, 1971).

A number of variants on the Rorschach have appeared since its 1921 publication. The most notable examples include techniques for administering the test to groups of subjects (Harrower & Steiner, 1945) and the development of new sets of blots (e.g., Harrower, 1945; Holtzman, Thorpe, Swartz, & Herron, 1961; Wheeler, 1938). With the possible exception of the Holtzman Inkblot Test, which was designed to improve the reliability and validity of the inkblot assessment method, none of these procedures has approached the popularity of the Rorschach.

Construction Tests

This type of projective asks the client to construct a story or other product on the basis of test stimuli. Among such tests, the Thematic Apperception Test (TAT) is the most popular, though interest in it appears to be declining somewhat (Polyson, Norris, & Ott, 1985). The TAT presents relatively recognizable stimuli consisting of 30 drawings of people, objects,

and landscapes (see Figure 5–5). In most cases, about 10 of these cards (one of them blank) are administered; the subset chosen is determined by the client's age and sex and by the clinician's interests. A separate set of cards depicting African Americans is also available. The examiner shows each picture and asks the client to make up a story about it, including what led up to the scene, what is now happening, and what is going to happen. The client is encouraged to say what the people in the drawings are thinking and feeling. For the blank card, the respondent is asked to imagine a drawing, describe it, and then construct a story about it.

The TAT was designed in 1935 by psychologists Christiana D. Morgan and Henry Murray at the Harvard Psychological Clinic (Murray, 1938, 1943). It was based on the general projection hypothesis and the assumption that, in telling a *story,* the client's needs and conflicts will be reflected in a character (usually the heroine or hero with whom the client identifies; Lindzey, 1952).

As with the Rorschach, there is no one "right" way to analyze clients' responses to TAT cards. As early as 1951, Shneidman found at least 20 systems for scoring and interpretation, and new methods have appeared since then (Harrison, 1965; Zubin, Eron, & Schumer, 1965). Analysis can focus upon both the *content* and the *structure* of the TAT stories. Content refers to *what* is described: the people, the feelings, the events, the outcomes. Structure involves *how* the story is told: the logic and organization, the use of language, the appearance of speech disfluencies, misunderstandings of instructions or stimuli in the drawings, and obvious emotional arousal.

The original interpretive scheme of Morgan and Murray (1935) takes a "hero-oriented" approach in which responses are read for the *needs* (e.g., achievement, aggression, affiliation) and *presses* (perceived environmental influences such as criticism, affection, or physical danger) associated with the main character. The frequency and intensity of each need and

FIGURE 5–5 Drawing of the type included in the TAT. (Reprinted by permission of the publishers from Henry A. Murray, *Thematic Appercep-tion Test,* Cambridge, MA: Harvard University Press, copyright © 1943 by the president and fellows of Harvard College, © 1971 by Henry A. Murray.)

press are scored on a 1-to-5 scale, and the themes and outcomes of each story are noted as well.

Other scoring approaches have used more formal quantitative procedures to describe TAT stories (e.g., Dana, 1959; McClelland, Atkin-son, Clark, & Lowell, 1953). These systems have resulted in the appearance of TAT response norms (Eron, 1950; Lindzey, Bradford, Tejessy, & Davids, 1959; Murstein, 1972; Rosenzweig &

Flemming, 1949), which clinicians can compare to stories told by their own clients (see Vane, 1981, for a review). Some interpretive systems make little use of formal scoring procedures (Henry, 1956), while others combine preliminary quantitative analysis with subjective interpretation of the resulting numbers (Bellak, 1986).

Most users of the TAT in clinical situations prefer scoring systems that are less structured and use response norms and formal scoring criteria only as general guides (Harrison, 1965; Sundberg, 1977). They may use Murray's need and press concepts and some psychoanalytic thinking, but more commonly they develop an idiosyncratic combination of principles derived from theory and clinical experience. An example of a TAT story and a clinician's interpretation of it are presented in Box 5–8. Other projective tests similar to the TAT are:

1. The Children's Apperception Test (CAT; Bellak, 1992), whose cards depict animal characters rather than human beings.

2. The Rosenzweig Picture-Frustration Study (Rosenzweig, 1949), which presents 24 cartoons showing one person frustrating another in some way (e.g., "I'm not going to invite you to my party"). The client's task is to say what the frustrated person's response would be.

3. The Roberts Apperception Test for Children (RATC; McArthur & Roberts, 1982), which consists of 27 cards showing children interacting with adults and other children. Scores on several scales are derived by comparing responses of a child to norms collected on 200 well-adjusted children. This test represents a combination of the logic of projective tests with the scoring of standardized, objective tests.

Completion Tests

These tests involve presenting the subject with part of a stimulus (usually a sentence) and asking the subject to complete it in his or her own way. The assumption is that the way the client finishes the sentence will reflect important personality dimensions. The incomplete sentence format had been used previously as a measure of intellect (Ebbinghaus, 1897, cited in Reisman, 1976). Its use as a projective technique dates from tests described by Payne (1928) and Tendler (1930), but more widely used versions did not appear until the 1940s.

Today, the most popular completion test is the Rotter Incomplete Sentences Blank (Rotter & Rafferty, 1950). It contains 40 sentence "stems" such as "I like . . . ," "My father . . . ," "I secretly . . . " Client responses are compared to extensive data provided in the test manual and are given a seven-point rating of adjustment or maladjustment depending upon the degree of deviation from established norms. Item ratings are totaled to provide an overall adjustment score.

These relatively objective scoring procedures are primarily associated with Rotter's test and a few other research-oriented sentence-completion instruments aimed at assessing specific aspects of personality (Lanyon & Lanyon, 1980).

Choice or Ordering Tests

These projective instruments ask the client to arrange test stimuli in some order or to make choices from an array of stimuli according to preference, attractiveness, or some other dimension. Such tests are now used infrequently by clinical psychologists, but in the 1940s and 1950s the now-obscure Szondi Test (pronounced "zon-dee"; Szondi, Moser, & Webb, 1959) was quite popular. This instrument was developed around 1947 by Lipot Szondi, a Hungarian psychiatrist who believed that liking or disliking a particular type of person was due in part to genetically determined traits shared with that person. The test required the client to choose the two most liked and the two most disliked persons from each of six groups of photographs. The choices supposedly revealed basic personality traits of the subject.

The following responses were given by a 25-year-old, unmarried male to a TAT card which shows a young boy looking at a violin which rests on a table in front of him.

This child is sick in bed. He has been given sheet music to study, but instead of the music, he has come across a novel that interests him more than the music. It is probably an adventure story. He evidently does not fear the chance that his parents will find him thusly occupied as he seems quite at ease. He seems to be quite a studious type and perhaps regrets missing school, but he seems quite occupied with the adventure in the story. Adventure has something to do with ocean or water. He is not too happy, though not too sad. His eyes are somewhat blank—coincidence of reading a book without any eyes or knowing what is in the book without reading it. He disregards the music and falls asleep reading the book.

A segment of a skilled TAT user's working notes on this story is presented below (Holt, 1978, pp. 166–167). After listing several indicators of psychosis (perceptual distortion, arbitrariness, peculiarities, delusional ideation, blandness, interpersonal isolation), he concludes:

On the basis of this story alone, I feel certain that there is a schizophrenic process present, even though not necessarily a pure schizophrenia. Slightly pretentious, facade tone, helped along with basic fact of perverse refusal to acknowledge presence of violin, strongly suggests that he *does*

see violin but consciously thinks that he's being "clever" or "original," or is out-tricking the examiner (whom he might see as trying to trick him) by ignoring it or seeing it as a book. That he is aware of it on some level is suggested by the fact that the basic theme, p Parental Imposed Task→n Auto Resis, passive Aggression, comes through. Consistent also is statement at the end: he *disregards* the music. Not a psychopath trying to act smart—too schizzy.

Sick in bed as a child may be an autobiographical theme. He's almost certainly "sick" (that is, psychotic) now, and so that may be enough explanation for it. But most psychotics don't [see the card this way]; therefore it becomes plausible that he may have had long illnesses as a child, cutting him off from other kids, and → to fantasy escape—dreams of travel and adventure.

Sentence 3 may also describe his overt behavior: nonchalant, seemingly "at ease," really frightened underneath.

Above are almost all hypotheses, to be confirmed or excluded by later stories.

Strong passivity throughout—especially in outcome. Also suggestion of *flight* and *avoidance* of very passive sort—drastic enough to include denial of threatening aspects of reality.

Nothing holds his interest long—not even adventure novel. Hero soon withdraws into his *own* fantasy, to conviction of knowing what's in book without reading it even though "took a chance" to read it, and finally withdraws into sleep.

Source: Robert R. Holt, *Methods in Clinical Psychology.* © 1978 by Plenum Press. New York. (Reprinted by permission.)

BOX 5–8
Examples of Inferences Based on the TAT

The Kahn Test of Symbol Arrangement (Kahn, 1955) exemplifies a choice/ordering projective still in use. The client is shown 16 plastic objects of various shapes (stars, animals, crosses) and asked to place them into categories such as "love," "hate," "bad," "good," "living," and "dead." The client is then asked to free-associate to each object in order to illuminate its symbolic meaning for her or him. The arrangements of objects are then interpreted in light of the meaning of each symbol and what it suggests about the client's unconscious personality processes.

Expressive Tests

These procedures ask clients to express themselves in some way, most commonly by drawing a picture. The most notable example is the Draw-a-Person Test (DAP; Machover, 1949) which, as its name implies, requires the client to draw a person. In the DAP, various aspects of personality are inferred from the drawings. Each client may be asked to make several drawings; the initial instructions to draw a person may be followed by requests to draw a person of the opposite sex, a family, self, mother, and so on. Some users of the test ask the client to answer questions or tell a story about their drawings, but the primary rationale is that the drawings themselves reveal significant personality data.

Machover (1949) suggested that the inclusion, exclusion, and characteristics of each body part, along with the placement, symmetry, organization, size, and other features of the drawing, were indicative of the client's self-image, conflicts, and perceptions of the world. A sample drawing and the inferences based upon it are presented in Figure 5–6.

FIGURE 5-6 DAP Drawings (done by an 18-year-old male who was caught stealing a television set) and Interpretations. (Reprinted from Emanuel Hammer, "Projective Drawings," in A. I. Rabin, ed., *Projective Techniques in Personality Assessment*, pp. 375–376. Copyright © 1968 by Springer Publishing Company, Inc., New York. Used by permission.)

Beneath the obvious attempts at an impressive figure of masculine prowess, there are more subtle trends of the opposite: of inadequacy and inconsequentiality. The muscles of the drawn figure have been inflated beyond the hard and sinewy, into a puffy softness as if it is a figure made of balloons; the legs taper down to insubstantiality and, finally, absent feet, and an incongruous hat is placed on the boxer making comical his lifting of one gloved hand in victory. . . On the one hand, emblematic of his defenses, his drawn achromatic person is the "twenty-year-old" boxer with muscles flexed and a weight-lifter's build. Beneath this inflated image, however, on the crayon drawing of a person—which, due to the impact of color, tends to tap the relatively deeper levels ot personality (Hammer, 1958)–he offers now only a "six-year-old boy" who then looks even more like an infant than a child: with one curlicue hair sticking up and the suggestion of diapers on (. . . shown here in black and white). The ears are rather ludicrous in their standing away from the head and, all in all, the total projection in this drawing is that of an infantile, laughable entity, rather than the impressive he-man he overstated on the achromatic version of a person. Beneath his attempts to demonstrate rugged masculinity (which may have culminated into the offense with which he is charged), the patient experiences himself as actually a little child, dependent and needing care, protection, and affection.

Buck's (1948) House-Tree-Person Test asks the client to draw each of those objects and then discuss them in an extended interview. The Bender-Gestalt Test, described earlier as a measure of ability and intellectual deterioration, has also been interpreted as a projective indicator of personality when the symbolic meaning of errors and distortions in the copied figures are focused upon.

THE STATUS OF TESTING IN CLINICAL PSYCHOLOGY

Although new psychological tests are introduced every year, clinicians tend to use the tests with which they are most familiar and on which the most research has been conducted. For these reasons, overall preferences for psychological tests have remained surprisingly stable over the past 40 years (see Box 5–9), despite differences in test usage among professionals working in different settings (counseling centers versus VA hospitals; Lubin, Larsen, Matarazzo, & Seever, 1985). As Box 5–9 shows, the most popular tests are "the old reliables": the MMPI, the Wechsler Scales, the Rorschach, and the TAT. These data demonstrate that clinicians are continuing to use projective techniques despite their limited predictive validity.

The role of testing in clinical psychology has undergone large shifts in popularity across the decades. Beginning in the 1930s and continuing through the mid-1960s, tests were touted as semimagical pathways to the "truth" about intelligence, personality, and ability (Reisman, 1976). During this time clinical psychology students were trained intensively in the use of tests. For example, Harrower (1965, p. 398) remarked, "It is hard to conceive . . . of anyone in the field of clinical psychology reaching the postdoctoral level without being thoroughly well-versed in the Rorschach."

From the late 1960s through the 1970s, testing lost much of its appeal and was deemphasized as a training goal and profes-

sional activity for clinicians. The decline of psychological testing during this time was brought about by several factors. For one thing, there was a shift away from traditional diagnostic assessment in clinical psychology, so the use of tests for that purpose decreased. Second, many clinicians do not like the "tester" role, which they see as subservient to psychiatry and potentially damaging to relationships with clients. More general concerns also emerged as clinical psychologists, the public, the government, and individual clients placed the testing process under more intense scrutiny than ever before. This increased criticism of psychological tests stemmed from (a) research on the reliability and validity of many instruments; (b) awareness of the susceptibility of tests to various biases; (c) recognition that tests, particularly those assessing intelligence, may place members of certain minority groups at a disadvantage; (d) concern that collection of test information may invade the respondents' privacy; and (e) worry that tests are too easily misused or misinterpreted.

Psychometric Properties of Tests

A fundamental criticism of psychological tests is that they do not do their job very well; that is, that they are unreliable, invalid, or both. While it is unfair to say that this is true about all tests under all circumstances, research on their psychometric properties has often been unfavorable. This research is too voluminous to be described on a test-by-test basis, but can be summarized as follows.

First, in general, the reliability of psychological tests tends to be fairly high but not uniformly so. Test-retest reliability coefficients for the MMPI and MMPI-2 scales range from .6 to .9, for example (Pope, Butcher, & Seelen, 1993). Parallel form, test-retest, and split-half reliabilities are commonly .80 to .96 for major intelligence tests. Similarly, aptitude and ability tests such as the GRE, the Miller Analogies Test (MAT), the Medical College Admission Test (MCAT), and the Law School Admission

Periodic surveys have been conducted to determine which tests are most often used by psychologists. In spite of using different definitions of test's popularity, these surveys confirm the claim that clinicians have retained remarkable loyalty to a small core of instruments over the past 5 decades. Consider the results of five surveys summarized in the table below.

Test	Louttit & Brown (1947)[a]	Sundberg (1961)[b]	Lubin, Wallis, & Paine (1971)[c]	Lubin, Larsen, & Matarazzo (1984)[d]	Sweeney, Clarkin, & Fitzgibbon (1987)[e]
WAIS	2*	6	1	1	4**
MMPI	15.5	7.5	6	2	2
Bender-Gestalt Visual Motor Test	54	4	3.5	3	5
Rorschach	5.5	1	2	4	1
TAT	3.5	2.5	3.5	5	3
WISC	—	10	7	6	4**
Peabody Picture Vocabulary Test	—	—	13	7.5	
Sentence Completion Tests (all kinds)	—	13.5	8.5	7.5	7
House-Tree-Person Test	—	12	9	9	6 (all kinds)
Draw-a-Person Test	—	2.5	5	10	

[a] Ranking of 43 respondents mentioning some use of test.
[b] Ranking of 185 respondents mentioning some use of test.
[c] Ranking of 251 respondents mentioning some use of test.
[d] Ranking of 221 respondents mentioning some use of test.
[e] Ranking of 107 Directors of Association of Psychology Internship Centers.
* Reported for Wechsler-Bellevue.
** Reported for WAIS and WISC.

BOX 5-9
Testing's Top Ten

Test (LSAT) display reliability coefficients ranging from .71 to .97. Tests of interests and values have produced reliabilities from the .70s to the low .90s.

Reliability is difficult to compute for projective tests because split-half, parallel form, and test-retest approaches often do not make sense with such instruments (see Atkinson, 1981). Attempts to determine reliability in the traditional sense for the Rorschach, the TAT, and other major projectives have produced mediocre results (Anastasi, 1988; Vane, 1981).

Projective test advocates point instead to the relatively high levels of agreement shown by different clinicians using similar scoring systems. For example, several surveys of reliability of the Rorschach have found interrater and intrarater reliabilities to average above .80, similar to WAIS and MMPI values (Parker, 1983; Parker, Hanson, & Hunsley, 1988).

Second, the validity of psychological tests has been less impressive than their reliability. To a certain extent this will be the case since, mathematically, a test's validity is limited by its reliability, but for most tests the discrepancy between reliability and validity is too high, in absolute terms. It is probably fair to say that the closer the test content or tasks are to the content or tasks being assessed (i.e., the criterion), the higher the validity will be.

For example, aptitude and ability tests that ask respondents to provide information or perform tasks directly related to academic skills are consistently among the most valid tests available. The major intelligence tests are next in terms of relative validity. These tests, especially their verbal sections, correlate with academic performance, specific skills (such as reading and arithmetic), and teacher ratings in the .17 to .75 range. When intelligence tests are used to draw inferences about a client's psychiatric disorder or personality characteristics, validity data have been disappointing (Cronbach, 1970).

Because their content is often remote from the criteria they aim to describe or predict, personality tests have been among the least valid assessment instruments. There are several other reasons for this pattern. Faking and distortion are usually more common in personality assessment than in intellectual testing. Temporary fluctuations in emotional behavior and other personality-relevant behavior is also likely, posing problems for reliability and validity of personality assessment.

There are many theoretical reasons for the problematic validity of personality tests. For example, the criteria these tests try to describe or predict are themselves often vague, multidi-

mensional, and variable, depending upon situational and other factors. In addition, the meaning of personality test items ("I enjoy people") or response alternatives ("often" or "rarely") may vary considerably among clients. Galton recognized this same problem when he invented the questionnaire: "There is hardly any more difficult task than that of framing questions which are not likely to be misunderstood, which admit of easy reply, and which cover the ground of inquiry" (Galton, 1883, p. 279). Finally, the basic question of whether to use test responses as samples or signs is still not resolved.

In general, the validity of objective personality tests is superior to that of projective tests (Anastasi, 1988). For example, despite a host of problems involving outdated and limited norms, development for a now obsolete diagnostic system, and high inter-correlations between scales (Helmes & Reddon, 1993), the original MMPI has proven to be a remarkably useful instrument for many different assessment purposes. Its predictive and concurrent validity coefficients are generally in the .30 to .50 range (Dahlstrom, Welsh, & Dahlstrom, 1975; Parker et al., 1988). Though some evidence suggests that when used in the manner for which it was intended and when used to evaluate theoretically or empirically derived hypotheses, the Rorschach does surprisingly well (Parker et al., 1988), the psychometric properties of most projective tests are inadequate. Accordingly, most researchers tend to avoid projective techniques in the study of personality. As noted earlier, however, many clinicians continue to use them because they believe that these measures offer special information about clients.

Distortion of Test Scores

Tests are designed to collect assessment data under standard conditions. When conditions are not standard, test scores may be distorted in ways that can mislead the clinician. A multitude of factors can alter the outcome of all types of tests. For example, Mussen and Scodel (1955) demonstrated that after having been sexually aroused by photographs of nude females, college men gave more sex-related responses to the TAT when it was administered by a young, informally dressed male graduate student than when given by a man who was older and more formal.

Test instructions can also influence client responses. As part of their investigations of impression-management tactics used by mental hospital residents, Braginsky, Grosse, and Ring (1966) gave a true–false psychological test accompanied by varying instructions. In one condition, the test was described as an index of mental illness on which "true" responses indicated pathology. Other patients were told that the test measured self-insight and that "true" responses were associated with readiness to leave the hospital. The "mental-illness" test prompted high scores from those who wished to stay in the hospital and lower scores from those who wanted to leave. The "self-insight" instructions prompted the opposite pattern: Patients wishing to leave scored higher than those wanting to stay. Instructional effects also appear on IQ tests (Engleman, 1974), personality tests such as the MMPI (Kroger & Turnbull, 1975), and projective tests (Stewart & Patterson, 1973).

On some tests, the structure of the items and response alternatives may influence results. Suppose a tester wants to know how parents feel about allowing their children to display aggression toward them. The tester may write an item that says "No child should be permitted to strike a parent" and ask the client to agree or disagree. In this case, the client must mentally construct an alternative such as "A child should be encouraged to strike a parent" to guide the decision to agree or disagree. Each person may construct different mental alternatives, however, thus making the psychological content of the items variable among clients.

The circumstances under which a test is given can be important. Sometimes the exam-

iner can produce emotional arousal which reduces the client's test score. Handler (1974) reports a case in which a child's IQ rose from 68 to 120 by eliminating the disruptive presence of the psychologist. When later IQ tests were administered with the examiner present, the child's score never surpassed 79.

Another source of test distortion stems from the fact that some clients tend to respond in particular ways to most items, regardless of item content. This tendency has been called response *set* (Cronbach, 1946), response *style* (Jackson & Messick, 1958), and response *bias* (Berg, 1955). Some clients exhibit *social desirability* responses, where they endorse statements that are socially acceptable and approved (honesty and fairness) and reject those that are less valued (Edwards, 1957). Clients have also been suspected of *acquiescent* response styles (Jackson & Messick, 1961), in which they tend to agree with virtually any self-descriptive test item. Defensive, deviant, and overly disclosing styles have also been postulated. The significance of response styles as influencers of test data has been a hotly debated matter. It is also not clear whether response tendencies represent stable client characteristics (McCrae & Costa, 1983) or temporary behavior patterns dictated and reinforced by the circumstances under which the test is taken (Linehan & Nielsen, 1983). In any case, the client's point of view while taking the test should not be ignored when evaluating test data.

Other client variables may also be important determinants of test data. Clients whose cultural background leaves them unfamiliar with the concepts and vocabulary of middle-class white America often perform poorly on psychological tests reflecting those ideas and terms. The influence of one's background on intelligence test scores is of great concern, especially to culturally distinct and racial minority groups within our society.

One approach to this problem has been to use culture-specific instruments such as the Black Intelligence Test of Cultural Homogeneity (BITCH; Williams, 1972) with persons thought to be discriminated against on standard tests, but this merely shifts cultural bias to another racial group. Another approach involves using intelligence tests that are not strongly influenced by culture-specific experience or particular verbal skills. Examples of some of these tests were given earlier. Unfortunately, hopes for culture-fair tests have been dampened by research which shows that cultural and environmental factors influence such tests as much or, in some cases, more than standard instruments (see Samuda, 1975, for a review and Bernardoni, 1964, for a parody of cross-cultural measures). Instead of ignoring IQ tests or attempting to *remove* their cultural and subcultural bias, some testers choose to *examine* the differential performance of certain groups in order to identify specific deficits and create corrective programs. Anastasi (1988, p. 66) summarizes this view:

Tests are designed to show what an individual can do at a given point in time. They cannot tell us *why* he performs as he does. To answer that question, we need to investigate his background, motivations, and other pertinent circumstances. Nor can tests tell how able a culturally or educationally disadvantaged child might have been if she had been reared in a more favorable environment. Moreover, tests cannot compensate for cultural deprivation by eliminating its effect from their scores. On the contrary, tests should reveal such effects, so that appropriate remedial steps can be taken. To conceal the effects of cultural disadvantages by rejecting tests or by trying to devise tests that are insensitive to such effects can only retard progress toward a genuine solution of social problems. Such reactions toward tests are equivalent to breaking a thermometer because it registers a body temperature of 101°. Test scores should be used constructively: by the individual in enhancing self-understanding and personal development and in educational and vocational planning; by teachers in improving instruction and in ad-

justing instructional content to individual needs; and by employers in achieving a better match between persons and jobs, recognizing that persons can be trained and jobs can be redesigned.

Other assessors make a related suggestion for reducing irrelevant cultural effects: When specific predictions are desired, use instruments that sample as directly as possible the particular behaviors and skills of interest. When this is done, the opportunity for extraneous characteristics to distort performance is greatly reduced.

The potential sources of test-score bias discussed here barely scratch the surface of the problem. Readers interested in more intensive study of this issue should consult Anastasi (1988), Bersoff (1981), Masling (1966), Reynolds (1982), Sattler (1988), Shepard (1982), and Wigdor and Garner (1982).

Abuse of Tests

Like all assessment procedures, tests involve entry by the clinician into the privacy of clients' thoughts and behaviors. The extent to which such entry is desirable or even legal is a matter of debate and litigation. Many observers contend that there are too many tests and too much testing. They also argue that testing is irrelevant, inaccurate, and too easily misused. Overdependence on IQ scores by ill-informed test consumers provides an excellent case in point.

During the mid-1960s, Congress conducted hearings on psychological testing, particularly as used in educational and vocational selection. These inquiries were prompted in part by serious, knowledgeable test critics and also by the appearance of nonexpert books with sensational titles like *The Brain Watchers* (Gross, 1962), *The Tyranny of Testing* (Hoffman, 1962), and *They've Got Your Number* (Wernick, 1956).

The concern over privacy and other issues produced restrictions on testing in certain settings. For example, personality tests have been eliminated from routine selection procedures for federal employees, and IQ tests are restricted in some school systems. Reschly (1984) and Cohen et al. (1992) review court cases and legislation that have attempted to regulate ability testing in educational settings.

As noted earlier, the APA is sensitive to these issues and has urged its members to reduce the possibility of abuse in the testing field by adhering to the *Standards for Educational and Psychological Tests*. These standards embody the pro-test argument that when developed, evaluated, administered, interpreted, and published with due regard for scientific principles and the rights and welfare of clients, psychological tests can make a positive contribution to society. The *Uniform Guidelines on Employee Selection Procedure* was developed by the Equal Employment Opportunity Commission to regulate the use of tests and other methods as selection techniques. For additional material on this highly sensitive set of issues, see Cronbach (1975), Wigdor and Garner (1982), Heller, Holtzman, and Messick (1982), Fremer, Diamond, and Camara (1989), Bersoff (1988), and special issues of *The American Psychologist* (November 1965 and October 1981).

Testing Today

One might anticipate that the many problems associated with testing would have a devastating impact on clinicians' use of tests. In fact, testing is still an active enterprise in this country, and clinical psychologists show no signs of abandoning even poorly validated instruments (Lubin et al., 1984; Reynolds, 1979; Wade & Baker, 1977). In fact, psychological testing enjoyed a comeback in the 1980s that has extended into the 1990s. Why? For one thing, psychologists have worked hard to improve the theoretical basis and psychometric quality of tests. This improvement in the quality of psychological testing is seen in five trends, recognized by Lanyon (1984):

1. The mutual influence of behavioral and traditional testing approaches on one another has improved several areas of assessment. This collaboration is best revealed in *DSM* developments involving behaviorally based rules for making psychiatric diagnoses. Clinicians are now less apologetic about their role in diagnostic classification and the use of new, criterion-based tests in making these diagnoses.

2. Assessment procedures are becoming more specific to the criteria they attempt to describe or predict. The days of giving a broad-based personality inventory such as the MMPI and then attempting, after the fact, to make sense out of whatever correlations emerge are giving way to focused tests designed on the basis of theory and prior findings to illuminate specific constructs or clinical conditions. Assessment of cognitive functioning in depressed persons (Kendall & Ingram, 1989), information processing as a component in intelligence (Anastasi, 1988), and interpersonal style in adult behavior (Lorr & Youniss, 1986) are prime examples of this development.

3. Greater attention is being given to psychometrically sound evaluation of children and adolescents. Prominent examples include the Personality Inventory for Children (PIC; Wirt, Lachar, Klinedinst, & Seat, 1984), which is completed by parents and provides clinically useful descriptions of the behavior and problems of children between the ages of 3 to 16; the Millon Adolescent Personality Inventory (MAPI; Millon, Green, & Meagher, 1982), which provides information on 20 scales particularly relevant for clients aged 13 to 19; and the Child Behavior Problem Checklist (CBCL; Achenbach, 1978), a widely used and researched test, completed by parents, which compares children against norms on several different dimensions of potentially problematic behavior.

4. There is increasing interest in developing well-constructed tests for the assessment of specific clinical targets such as marital distress

(Snyder, 1981), health problems (see Williamson, Davis, & Prather, 1988 for a review of tests used with different illnesses), and social support and coping resources (Cohen, Mermelstein, Kamarck, & Hoberman, 1985; Folkman & Lazarus, 1980).

5. There has been more careful theorizing about the nature and structure of intelligence, mental abilities, attitudes, and personality, leading in turn to increased attention to the *construct validity* of psychological tests. As noted in Chapter 3, construct validity refers to the ability of an instrument to measure a psychological quality in ways indicated by a theory of the quality in question. Construct validation of a test never stops; it is a continuing process of elaborating and testing theories about what a construct actually means (Hogan & Nicholson, 1988). An unwavering commitment to construct validation not only enhances test development, it also promotes a better understanding of fundamental psychological phenomena such as intelligence and personality.

Improved tests tend to fuel demand for psychological assessment, especially in educational, industrial, and medical settings. Testing can also be a profitable professional activity, and the increased availability of computer-based test scoring and interpretation has made it more efficient for clinicians. Indeed, most clinicians' strong personal interest in at least one specific type of testing prompts many of them to develop a testing specialty within their professional practice. Finally, as ordinary mortals, clinical psychologists form habits they find hard to break. Graduate training tends to set patterns of assessment practices to which clinical psychologists become personally attached. Clinicians do what they were taught to do and continue doing so because it is what they have always done.

Of course, such habits are not based entirely upon blind adherence. Many clinicians attend to data about their tests in selective ways. Further, negative *research* findings about a test may simply be seen as irrelevant to that test's use in *clinical* settings: "Published indexes of validity . . . are but rough guides, for the psychologist must reach his own judgments of clinical validity and meaningfulness in each particular case" (Tallent, 1976, p. 14).

It must also be recognized that certain clinicians, for reasons not clearly understood, are able to draw remarkably accurate inferences from test data. Almost every practitioner knows of at least one MMPI or Rorschach "ace" whose reputation shores up general confidence in particular tests. Most clinical psychologists are themselves reinforced for using even the least scientifically supported tests by the fact that, now and then, they make their own insightful inferences on the basis of test data.

When these factors are added to the traditional view of clinical psychologists as test experts and the societal demand for testing services, the continued popularity of psychological testing is not surprising. When important decisions about people must be made, a psychological test with even modest proof of validity will usually be accepted for use because it promises at least some increase in the accuracy of those decisions. Thus, though more stringent standards and limitations regarding the use of tests in many spheres appear likely, testing will continue to be a major contribution of clinical psychologists.

CHAPTER 6

Observation
in
Clinical Psychology

Observation of the behavior of other people is a fundamental aspect of assessment. We all base innumerable social judgments on the appearance and actions of others. Indeed, the notion that "seeing is believing" prompts us to emphasize observation of what people *do* as opposed to what they *say* they do.

Clinical psychologists also collect and analyze observational data as part of their assessment activities. The appeal of what Sundberg and Tyler (1962) term the "watch 'em" approach is that it provides a first-hand look at behaviors of clinical interest and yields many clues about the causes of those behaviors. In general, the goals of observation are to (a) collect information not available in any other way, and/or (b) supplement other data as part of a multiple assessment approach.

Consider a situation in which a teacher and a problem pupil give different reports of why they fail to get along: "He's a brat"; "She's mean." A less-biased picture may emerge from observations by neutral parties of relevant classroom interactions. In other instances,

knowing what a person can or will do is so important that only observation can suffice. For example, knowing that a mentally disturbed person feels better and wishes to leave the hospital may be less valuable than observing that person's ability to hold a job, use the bus system, and meet other demands of everyday life. In combination with other methods, observation can lead to a more comprehensive understanding of the client. This is particularly true when intermethod discrepancies or similarities are revealed. For example, observers' reports that a person claiming to have quit smoking is or is not lighting cigarettes in their presence can provide valuable information to the clinician interested in evaluating an antismoking program.

When administering tests or conducting interviews, the astute clinician also observes how the client handles the assessment situation. However, the way clinicians use observational information in assessment varies considerably. Some see the client's overt behavior as providing only supplementary clues to personality traits and dynamics that will be revealed more fully through tests or interviews. For others, observable behavior plays a larger role in assessing underlying personality or pathology; they may weight this behavior equivalently to self-reports or test scores. In both cases, observations are used as *signs* of more fundamental, unobservable constructs.

On the other hand, behaviorally oriented clinicians regard observational data as behavior *samples* that represent the most direct, important, and scientific assessment channel available. These clinicians use observation to describe person–situation interactions rather than to draw inferences about hypothesized underlying characteristics of clients.

The more importance clinicians attribute to observational data, the more systematic they are likely to be in gathering and analyzing such data. At one end of the spectrum are informal, anecdotal accounts of client behavior that often are by-products of other assessment efforts like testing and interviewing. The following excerpt from a report that followed administration of the Stanford-Binet to a 12-year-old boy provides a clear example:

> John's principal difficulties were on tests requiring precise operations, as in the use of numbers. With such tests he became insecure and often seemed confused with slips of memory and errors in simple calculations. He asked to have instructions repeated, was dependent on the examiner, and easily discouraged. Although cooperative and anxious to do well, it was extremely hard for him to master a task (such as "memory span") in which he was required to be exact by fixed standards. (Jones, 1943, p. 91)

Clinicians who place greater emphasis on overt behavior have improved on casual observation methods in at least two ways. First, they have developed more accurate and systematic methods for watching and quantifying behavior. Second, they have demonstrated the feasibility of collecting observational data in situations other than interviews or tests. Together, these developments have made it possible for modern clinicians and researchers to observe scientifically a wide range of human behavior in a multitude of settings. In this chapter we describe and evaluate some of the observational systems and techniques now in use.

SOME HISTORICAL NOTES

Overt behavior existed long before language, so observation was probably the first source of assessment data. In prehistoric times, one learned quickly how to judge the intentions of others on the basis of their actions (e.g., an offer of food; a raised club); the importance of observation did not diminish as language developed. In ancient Greek and Chinese civilizations, conclusions about an individual were sometimes drawn on the basis of physical and behavioral characteristics. In the Western world, the practice of interpreting physical features and behaviors came to be called *physiognomy* (McReynolds, 1975). Homer provides an early illustration of this in his *Iliad:*

> There is nothing like an ambush for bringing a man's worth to light and picking out the cowards from the brave. A coward changes color all the time; he cannot sit still for nervousness, but squats down, first on one heel, then on the other.... But the brave man never changes color at all and is not unduly perturbed from the moment when he takes his seat in ambush with the rest. (Translation by Rieu, 1950; quoted in McReynolds, 1975, p. 488)

Pythagoras, Hippocrates, Plato, Aristotle, and Galen elaborated on the relationship between overt behavior and personality characteristics. Even the Bible contains references to assessment via behavioral observation. In order to help Gideon defeat the Midianites with the smallest possible force, God tells how to identify the most able soldiers:

And the Lord said unto Gideon, The people are yet too many; bring them down unto the water, and I will try them for thee there. . . . So he brought down the people into the water; and the Lord said unto Gideon, Everyone that lappeth of the water with his tongue . . . him shalt thou set by himself; likewise everyone that boweth down upon his knees to drink. And the number of them that lapped, putting their hand to their mouth, were three hundred men; but all the rest of the people bowed down upon their knees to drink water. And the Lord said unto Gideon, By the three hundred men that lapped will I save you, and deliver the Midianites into thine hand. . . . (Judges 7:4–7)

Obviously, the best warriors were those who remained alert to danger, even when drinking. Thus, the foundations of observational assessment, content analysis of speech, gesture and movement analysis, and research on the relationship between facial expressions and emotion were laid down centuries ago. Like the test and the interview, clinical observation is the modern form of an old tradition (Ben-Porath & Butcher, 1991).

APPROACHES
TO CLINICAL OBSERVATION

Weick (1968) defined observational methods as "the *selection, provocation, recording,* and *encoding* of . . . behaviors" (italics added). This definition highlights the fundamental elements of nearly every type of observational system. The observer first *selects* persons, classes of behavior, events, situations, or time periods to be the focus of attention. Second, a decision is made about whether to *provoke* (i.e., artificially bring about) behaviors and situations of interest or to wait for them to happen naturally. Third, plans are made for observations to be *recorded:* Observer memory, audio or video recording devices, physiological monitoring systems, timers, and counters are all possible choices. Finally, a system for

encoding raw observations into usable dimensions must be developed. This translation is often the most difficult aspect of any observational procedure.

Differing assessment goals, unique client populations, specific environmental limitations, and other factors produce many approaches to clinical observation. The clearest way to organize this array is in terms of the *settings* employed. At one extreme there is *naturalistic* observation, where the assessor looks at behavior as it occurs in its natural context (e.g., in a home, school, or factory). *Controlled,* or *experimental,* observation lies at the other extreme, where the clinician or researcher sets up a special situation in which to observe behavior. These approaches can be blended to handle specific assessment needs so there are many subtypes of both naturalistic and controlled observation. Another important way these procedures differ involves the observers' role. *Participant* observers are visible to the clients being watched and may even interact with them. *Nonparticipant* observers are not visible, although in most cases the clients are aware that observation is taking place.

To present a reasonably complete picture of clinical observation, we describe naturalistic and controlled observational systems that focus on several kinds of behavior. The examples will illustrate the use of (a) participant and nonparticipant observers; (b) human, mechanical, and combined recording procedures; and (c) informal and formal encoding systems that deal with behavior as samples and signs. More comprehensive coverage of this material is available in Bellack and Hersen (1988), Ciminero, Calhoun, and Adams (1986), Cone and Hawkins (1977), Haynes (1990), Mash and Terdal (1988), Nelson and Hayes (1986), and Wiggins (1973).

Naturalistic Observation

Watching clients behave spontaneously in a natural setting such as their homes has several obvious advantages. Natural settings provide a background that is realistic and relevant for understanding the client's behavior and factors influencing that behavior. Additionally, naturalistic observation can be done in subtle ways that provide an accurate view of behavior, uncluttered by the client's self-consciousness or attempts to convey a particular impression.

The classic case of naturalistic observation is the anthropological field study in which a scientist joins a tribe, subculture, or other social unit to observe its characteristics and the behavior of the individuals within it (e.g., Mead, 1928; Williams, 1967). In such cases the observer is a participant in every sense of the term, and observations are usually recorded in anecdotal notes which later appear as a detailed account called an *ethnography*.

In psychology, the work of Roger G. Barker provides an example of naturalistic observation whose intensity approaches anthropological proportions. In an effort to understand the ecology of human behavior, Barker and his colleagues observed as much of it as possible to capture the richness and details of its relationship to the environment. This involved participant (but noninteractive) observation of children on a continuous basis from morning until night as they went about a normal day's activities in their home town (Barker, Schoggen, & Barker, 1955; Barker & Wright, 1951, 1955). No attempt was made to select particular behaviors, situations, or events for special attention. Observations were recorded in notebooks as narrative "day records" (see Box 6–1) and later encoded as "behavioral episodes."

BOX 6–1
Excerpt From a Day Record

5:39:

Raymond tilted the crate from side to side in a calm, rhythmical way.

Clifford's feet were endangered again. Steward came over and very protectively led Clifford out of the way. [Observer's opinion.]

Raymond slowly descended to the ground inside the crate.

When Stewart came back around the crate, Raymond reached out at him, and growled very gutturally, and said, "I'm a big gorilla." Growling very ferociously, he stamped around the "cage" with his arms hanging loosely.

He reached out with slow, gross movements.

Raymond reached toward Clifford but didn't really try to catch him. Then he grabbed Stewart by the shirt.

Imitating a very fierce gorilla, he pulled Stewart toward the crate.

Stewart was passive and allowed himself to be pulled in. He said, "Why don't you let go of me?" He spoke disgustedly and yet not disparagingly. Raymond released his grasp and ceased imitating a gorilla.

He tilted the crate so that he could crawl out of the open end. As he crawled out, he lost control of the crate and it fell over on its side with the open end perpendicular to the ground.

Steward said, "Well, how did you get out?"

Raymond said self-consciously, "I fell out," and forced a laugh.

He looked briefly at me as if wondering what I thought.

Source: Barker and Wright (1951).

When episodes involved other people, they were treated as signs representing "nurturance," "resistance," "appeal," "submission," "aggression," "avoidance," etc. Notice the amount of observer inference involved in the Box 6–1 narratives (e.g., "He looked briefly at me *as if wondering what I thought*").

The data generated by these procedures are staggering. For example, one 8-year-old girl had 969 behavioral episodes involving 571 objects in the course of a single day. Barker was aware that this full-scale ecological approach produced too much information, and he suggested more practical alternatives, including periodic rather than continuous observation. In current practice, most assessors collect their observational data intermittently, focusing on those aspects of behavior and behavior–environment interaction that are of special theoretical or practical importance (Haynes, 1984). Psychologists interested in child development, for example, have devised observation systems aimed at categories of behavior thought to indicate particular levels of physical, cognitive, and social functioning (Arrington, 1932; Bayley, 1965; Piaget, 1947). Similarly, social psychologists have developed observational tools to code the complex interplay of behaviors of people in groups (Bales, 1950).

The targets of naturalistic observation have included behaviors used to infer personality characteristics (Santostefano, 1962) or intelligence (Lambert, Cox, & Hartsough, 1970), but the primary focus has been on assessing problems that brought the client to the clinician. These include everything from nail biting, cigarette smoking, troublesome thoughts, maladaptive social interactions, and psychotic behavior to community problems such as crime and littering (Haynes, 1990).

In its early forms, naturalistic clinical observation required observers to draw inferences of many kinds: What were the meanings of a behavior; which behaviors should be observed, and which should not. As a result, the interobserver reliability of naturalistic observation suffered. For example, Box 6–2 contains the notes of four observers who watched the

same 10-minute film, *This Is Robert,* which showed a boy in classroom and playground situations. Notice the different images generated by each viewer. Cronbach (1960, p. 535) summarizes this problem well: "Observers interpret what they see. When they make an interpretation, they tend to overlook facts which do not fit the interpretation, and they may even invent facts needed to complete the event as interpreted."

Attempts to improve anecdotal accounts in naturalistic clinical observation have taken many forms. To reduce unsystematic reporting of client behaviors, most modern observation schemes focus the observer's attention on specific behaviors. These behaviors of interest are specified ahead of time, and observers rate their frequency or intensity using a predetermined checklist or rating scale. The observers are also trained to use their methods consistently so that interobserver reliability is as high as possible.

Another approach to naturalistic observation is to inspect the by-products of ongoing behavior. Examples include different types of life records that are routinely collected for most people. School grades, arrest records, and court files have been used to evaluate treatment of delinquent and predelinquent youth (Davidson, Redner, Blakely, Mitchell, & Emshoff, 1987); changes in academic grade point averages have served as indices of the reduction of test anxiety (Allen, 1971).

Maisto and Maisto (1983) refer to life records as *institutional measures;* Haynes (1990) calls them *product-of-behavior* measures. Actually, these measures are part of a broader observation approach called *nonreactive* or *unobtrusive* measurement that clinical psychologists and other behavioral scientists use to learn about people's behavior without altering it in the process. These techniques are fully illustrated in a fascinating, often humorous, book by Webb, Campbell, Schwartz, and Sechrest (1966).

In clinical research, unobtrusive measures may be used to test theories about the causes of behavior problems. For example, Barthell

BOX 6–2
Excerpts From Four Observers' Notes on the Same Film[a]

Observer A: (2) Robert reads word by word, using finger to follow place. (4) Observes girl in box with much preoccupation. (5) During singing, he in general doesn't participate too actively. Interest is part of time centered elsewhere. Appears to respond most actively to sections of song involving action. Has tendency for seemingly meaningless movement. Twitching of fingers, aimless thrusts with arms.

Observer B: (2) Looked at camera upon entering (seemed perplexed and interested). Smiled at camera. (2) Reads (with apparent interest and with a fair degree of facility). (3) Active in roughhouse play with girls. (4) Upon being kicked (unintentionally) by one girl he responded (angrily). (5) Talked with girl sitting next to him between singing periods. Participated in singing. (At times appeared enthusiastic). Didn't always sing with others. (6) Participated in a dispute in a game with others (appeared to stand up for his own rights). Aggressive behavior toward another boy. Turned pockets inside out while talking to teacher and other students. (7) Put on overshoes without assistance. Climbed to top of ladder rungs. Tried to get rung which was occupied by a girl but since she didn't give in, contented himself with another place.

Observer C: (1) Smiles into camera (curious). When group break up, he makes nervous gestures, throws arm out into air. (2) Attention to reading lesson. Reads with serious look on his face, has to use line marker. (3) Chases girls, teases. (4) Girl kicks when he puts hand on her leg. Robert makes face at her. (5) Singing. Sits with mouth open, knocks knees together, scratches leg, puts fingers in mouth (seems to have several nervous habits, though not emotionally overwrought or self-conscious). (6) In a dispute over parchesi, he stands up for his rights. (7) Short dispute because he wants rung on jungle gym.

Observer D: (2) Uses guide to follow words, reads slowly, fairly forced and with careful formation of sounds (perhaps unsure of self and fearful of mistakes). (3) Perhaps slightly aggressive as evidenced by pushing younger child to side when moving from a position to another. Plays with other children with obvious enjoyment, smiles, runs, seems especially associated with girls. This is noticeable in games and in seating in singing. (5) Takes little interest in singing, fidgets, moves hands and legs (perhaps shy and nervous). Seems in song to be unfamiliar with words of main part, and shows disinterest by fidgeting and twisting around. Not until chorus is reached does he pick up interest. His special friend seems to be a particular girl, as he is always seated by her.

---

[a]The observers were told to use parentheses to indicate inferences or interpretation. The numbers used refer to scenes in the film and were inserted to aid comparison.

and Holmes (1968) were interested in the hypothesis that social isolation early in life and particularly during adolescence was related to a later diagnosis of schizophrenia. As a partial test of this hypothesis, they inspected the high school yearbooks of people labeled "schizophrenic" or "neurotic" and compared the activities listed for these individuals with non-labeled students from the same schools. A similar use of life records is illustrated by research that relates factors such as age, marital status, employment history, and education to the development of schizophrenia and to chances for its improvement.

Unobtrusive measures are not problem free. They can be hard to obtain in comparison to asking subjects simply to report on their behavior. In addition, unobtrusive measures may not generalize well to other situations that differ from those in which the measures were originally collected. Accordingly, some researchers have experimented with embedding unobtrusive measures in a computer assisted instruction program that asks subjects about selected topics at the same time as it delivers instructional material. Meier and Wick (1991) used this approach to collect data on alcohol use and found that the data correlated well with self-report measures.

Most retrospective observation systems involve asking persons familiar with the client to report the frequency, intensity, duration, or form of specific categories of behavior displayed in the recent past. We will consider some examples as

they have been used in different observational settings.

Hospital Observations

An excellent example of a hospital observation system is the Inpatient Multidimensional Psychiatric Scales, or IMPS (Lorr, McNair, & Klett, 1966), used in hospital settings by ward personnel who observe and interview their clients. The IMPS contains 75 items, which are either rated by the observer/interviewer on five- or nine-point scales or responded to with a yes or no (see Box 6–3). These data are translated into scores on dimensions such as excitement, hostile belligerence, paranoid projection, grandiose expansiveness, disorientation, and conceptual disorganization. The scores can then be plotted as a profile that describes the client.

Many observation systems not only specify the targets to be observed, but also reduce the observer/coder inferences required. Raters observe a client's behavior and record that behavior as it occurs. When such observations are made at regular intervals (e.g., once per hour), the process is called *time sampling*. When only certain activities are observed (mealtime interactions, cigarette smoking), the method is called *event sampling*. Often both techniques are involved, as when observations are made once per minute during particular events such as mother–child interactions.

One of the first observation systems used

BOX 6–3

Samples From the Inpatient Multidimensional Psychiatric Scales (IMPS)

Compared to the normal person, to what degree does/is the client:

1. Exhibit an attitude of superiority
2. Ramble off the topic discussed
3. Assume bizarre positions
4. Unrestrained in showing feelings

5. Blame others for difficulty
6. Believe he has unusual abilities or talents
7. Believe people are against him
8. Make unusual facial grimaces

with inpatients was the Behavioral Study Form (BSF) developed by Schaefer and Martin (1975) at Patton State Hospital in California. The BSF requires ward personnel (usually nurses) to observe clients approximately every 30 minutes and to record specific behaviors. A list of these behaviors and a sample record are presented in Figure 6–1. At each observation point the nurse records a "mutually exclusive" behavior (which defines the client's general activity) and any concomitant behavior that accompanies that activity. The client's location and other relevant facts are also noted. The observation targets are clearly defined, thereby

FIGURE 6–1   Coding system and sample record from an early hospital observation system. (H. H. Schaefer and P. L. Martin, *Behavioral Therapy*, 2nd ed. © 1975 by McGraw-Hill Book Company, New York. Reprinted by permission.)

Watch Especially for:

19- head in hands. HH
18- Working - assigned
16- Talking to others

GENERAL CODE

Mutually Exclusive Behaviors
1. Walking   4. Sitting
2. Running   5. Lying down
3. Standing

Concomitant Behaviors
6   Drinking
7   Eating–meals
7a Eating–other than meals
8   Grooming (describe)
9   Group meeting
10 Medication
11 Reading
12 Receiving pay
13 Rocking
14 Pacing
15 Smoking
16 Talking to others
17 TV
18 Working–assigned
19 Other

Location
A   Dining room
B   Hall of lounge
C   Sleeping quarters
D   Lavatory
E   Outside

Patient   *Susan R.*

Admission _____

Followup:

① 2   3   4   5   6   7   8   9

Date: *August 24, 1967*

Time	Behavior	Location
0630	3-8	D
0700	3-6	B
0730	4-15	B
0800	3-10	A
0830	4-18	A
0900	9-18	A
0930		
1000	4-19 HH	B
1030	4-19 HH	B
1100	3-19 Buying item	B
1130	3-18	A
1200	4-7	A
1230	3-16 (Employer)	B
1300	4-11	A
1330	4-9	A
1400	4-9	A
1430	4-9	A
1500	Unavailable	
1530	1	E
1600	3-11	A
1630	3-18	A
1700	3-18	A
1730	4	D
1800	4-16	E
1830	3	C
1900	3-16	C
1930	3-17	B
2000	3-11	A
2030	2-19 (screaming)	B
2100	5	C

increasing the likelihood that different observers will use the system reliably.

The Behavioral Study Form served as the basis for more elaborate observation systems now used in psychiatric hospitals. The most sophisticated and well-researched observation system is the Time-Sample Behavioral Checklist (TSBC; Paul & Lentz, 1977), which was developed to assess a large number of behaviors by psychiatric patients using trained observers. It provides measurement of clinically relevant behavior in great detail (69 different behavioral characteristics are coded for a 2-second focus on one patient) and with great regularity (each patient is observed at least once every waking hour 7 days a week). Several TSBC index scores can be computed to summarize the overall quality of a patient's behavior. The TSBC Total Inappropriate Behavior Index gives a measure of "crazy" behaviors by indicating the presence of any one of 24 inappropriate behaviors. The TSBC Total Appropriate Behavior Index assesses amount of "normal" behavior by indicating the presence of any one of 27 appropriate behaviors. Other indices can be computed from the TSBC that indicate the frequency of different categories of clinically disturbed behavior. For example, Figure 6–2 compares the effects of two hospital programs (social-learning versus milieu) on three such indices—Schizophrenic Disorganization (bizarre behaviors like rocking and blank staring), Cognitive Distortion (bizarre verbal behaviors like incoherent speech, hallucinations), and Hostile-Belligerence (aggressive behaviors like screaming and cursing).

Barker-style ethological observations have also been used in hospital settings by clinicians interested in a detailed view of children's behavior problems. Rather than attempting to observe all aspects of the client's behavior, clinicians will focus on certain subcategories of it (e.g., social behavior). They will then concentrate on analyzing the long-term functional relationships between these behaviors and the stimuli that precede and follow them. Using this approach, Hutt and Hutt (1968) found that autistic children are more likely to engage in such bizarre motor behavior as hand flapping when new people or objects are introduced into their environment. Dunlap, Koegel, and O'Neill (1985) describe a very thorough observational system for assessing the behavior of autistic children in both treatment and natural settings.

School Observations

The desire to observe children's behavior for clinical purposes has spawned a number of systems for use in schools, playgrounds, and other relevant settings (Ollendick & Greene, 1990). In the tradition of early experimental sociologists (e.g., Dawe, 1934; Thomas, 1929), recording and coding systems designed by Bijou (Bijou, Peterson, & Ault, 1968) and O'Leary (O'Leary & Becker, 1967; O'Leary & O'Leary, 1972) use symbols to represent the behavior of children and the adults around them during time-sample observations. The symbols (and their definitions) described by Bijou, Peterson, and Ault (1968) in a study done in a nursery school are presented in Figure 6–3. Like other observation systems of this type, the data gathered can be summarized in quantitative form. In this case, percentages can be calculated to summarize how much time a child spends talking to or touching adults or other children. Classroom observation may focus on a single child and those with whom the child interacts, or, an observer can rotate his or her attention and assess the behavior of several target children or even of a whole class (Milich & Fitzgerald, 1985).

Home Observations

Observational assessment procedures are also available to measure clinically relevant behaviors in the client's home. As has been the case in other areas, early clinical observations in homes contained much inference and unsystematic target selection (e.g., Ackerman, 1958). More recently, more reliable home ob-

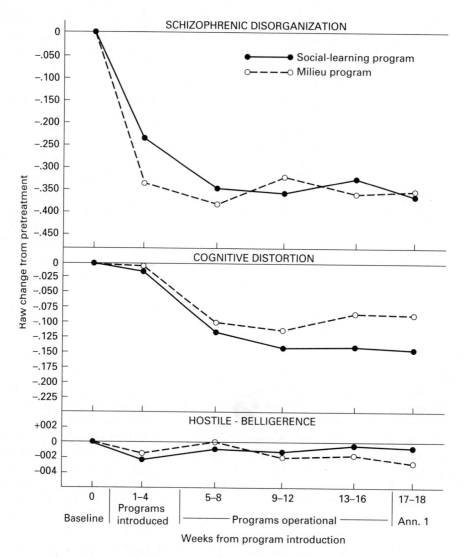

FIGURE 6–2 Effects of social-learning and milieu programs on three TSBC dimensions. (After G. Paul and R. Lentz, *Psychological Treatment of Chronic Mental Patients,* published by Harvard University Press, 1977. Reprinted by permission.)

servation systems have evolved. One of the first practical, scientific home observation packages was designed by Gerald Patterson (Patterson, Ray, Shaw, & Cobb, 1969) for use in the homes of conduct-disordered children. This system, known as the Family Interaction Coding System, places trained observers in the client's living area for an hour or two, usually just before dinner.[1] The observers avoid inter-

___

[1]This and most other observation procedures described in this chapter are set up only after the client or a person responsible for the client gives consent.

acting with the family and concentrate on recording the behavior of one member at a time
during successive 5-minute periods. Each type
of behavior observed (talking, crying, hitting,
laughing, ignoring) is summarized by one of
29 symbols similar in nature to those in Figure
6–3. Reid (1978) provides details of this system. Other systems are available as well (see
McIntyre et al., 1983 for a review of home observation systems), some of which have been
used not only to assess individual clients but
to gather data on how certain parental behaviors contribute to children's maladjustment
(e.g, Forehand, Lautenschlager, Faust, & Graziano, 1986).

When adult interactions at home are observed, more complex recording and encoding systems are usually needed. To measure
the at-home social skills of depressed clients,
for example, Lewinsohn and Shaffer (1971)
had observers record family interactions at
mealtimes on a time-sampling basis. The encoding system categorized verbal behavior as
self-initiated *actions* (questions, comments, requests for information, complaints) or positive
and negative *reactions* to the behavior of others (approval, laughter, criticism, disagreement). These dimensions were then used to
examine differences between depressed and
nondepressed persons (e.g., Libet & Lewinsohn, 1973) as well as changes in depressed
behavior as a function of treatment.

Gottman (1979) developed a complex coding system for the assessment of couple interactions called the Couples Interaction Coding
System (CISS, pronounced "kiss"). Each verbal
statement is categorized in terms of its (a) *content,* (b) *affect,* and (c) *context.* Two aspects of
Gottman's work merit special mention. The
first involves the use of sequential, or *time-
series,* analysis of the observational data (Gottman, Markman, & Notarius, 1977). This technique allows the assessor to look not only at
the influence of one person on the other at a
given point (as when a wife insults her husband), but also at the influence of previous interactions on later ones. Negative "spirals" and

other long-term social sequences can be discovered more easily with this technique than
with procedures that merely present "percent
of time spent" summaries. Clinicians can use
these observations to calculate the *conditional
probability* of a behavior—the likelihood that
a behavior will occur given the prior occurrence of another behavior or event. (For example, what is the probability that a husband
will criticize his wife if she has just insulted
him?). The second interesting feature of
Gottman's observational system is its use in
the study of emotion in couples. In addition to
developing a coding system devoted to the
study of emotions in marital interactions
(known as the Specific Affect Coding System;
Gottman & Krokoff, 1989), Gottman and his
colleagues have studied how couples' behavioral interactions are linked to physiological
indicators (heart rate, skin conductance) of
emotion in each member of a couple. One
finding from this research is that during emotional conflicts, couples reciprocate each
other's feelings not only at the behavioral
level, but also at the physiological level
(Levenson & Gottman, 1983). When a couple
are having an upsetting interaction with each
other, they also tend to experience a similar
sequence of physiological arousal associated
with their conflict. Levenson and Gottman
(1983) speculate that this linkage of physiological reactions contributes to the common feeling by intimate partners of being trapped or
locked into unpleasant interactions.

Observations by Insiders

So far, the naturalistic observation systems
we have described employ specially trained
personnel as participant or nonparticipant observers. Because some researchers question
whether these outsiders can do their job without inadvertently influencing the behavior
they are to watch, they arrange to have observational data collected by persons who are
part of the client's day-to-day world. The
IMPS, completed by nurses or other ward per-

Symbol	Definition
	First Row **(Social Contacts)** *S* verbalizes to himself. Any verbalization during which he does not look at an adult or child or does not use an adult's or child's name. Does not apply to group situation.
	S verbalizes to adult. *S* must look at adult while verbalizing or use adult's name.
	S verbalizes to child. *S* must look at child while verbalizing or use child's name. If in a group situation, any verbalization is recorded as verbalization to a child.
S	Child verbalizes to *S*. Child must look at *S* while verbalizing or use *S*'s name.
	Adult verbalizes to *S*. Adult must look at *S* while verbalizing or use *S*'s name.
s	Adult gives general instruction to class or asks question of class, or makes general statement. Includes storytelling.
	S touches adult. Physical contact with adult.
	S touches child with part of body or object. Physical contact with child.
V	Adult touches *S*. Physical contact with adult.
T	Child touches *S* with part of body or object. Physical contact with child.

Symbol	Definition
	Second Row **(Sustained Activity)** *Sustained activity in art.* *S* must be sitting in the chair, facing the material and responding to the material or teacher within the 10-sec interval. Responding to the material includes using pencil, paint brush, chalk, crayons, string, scissors or paste or any implement on paper, or working with clay with hands on clay or hands on implement which is used with clay, or folding or tearing paper. Responding to the teacher includes following a command made by an adult to make a specific response. The behavior must be completed (child sitting in his chair again) within two minutes.
	Sustained activity in storytime. *S* must be sitting, facing the material, or following a command given by the teacher or assistant. If the *S* initiates a verbalization to a peer, do not record sustained activity in the 10-sec interval.
	Sustained activity in show-and-tell. *S* must be sitting, facing the material, or following a command given by the teacher. If the *S* initiates a verbalization to a peer, do not record sustained activity in that 10-sec interval.
	Sustained activity in reading. *S* must be sitting in the chair, facing the material and responding to the material or the teacher within the 10-sec interval.
	Sustained activity in writing. *S* must be sitting in the chair, facing the material and responding to the material or the teacher within the 10-sec interval. Responding to the material includes using the pencil (making a mark), or holding the paper or folder. Responding to the teacher includes responding verbally to a cue given by the teacher.
	Sustained activity in arithmetic. *S* must be sitting in the chair, facing the material and responding to the material or the teacher within the 10-sec interval. Responding to the material or teacher includes using the pencil or eraser or holding the paper or folder or responding verbally to cue.
	Sustained activity did not occur in interval.

sonnel, is an example. Observation of children in classrooms and at home has been accomplished by training teachers, parents, and even other children to collect and record data regarding specific behaviors (e.g., Lyman, 1984).

The use of insiders as observers of adult behavior for clinical purposes is less common, but not unknown. For example, in helping clients quit smoking, a clinician may ask for corroborative reports of success or failure from family members or friends (e.g., Mermelstein, Lichtenstein, & McIntyre, 1983). Such reports may also be solicited as part of the assessment of alcoholics (e.g., Foy, Nunn, & Rychtarik, 1984), sexual activity (e.g., Rosen & Kopel, 1977), marital violence (Jouriles & O'Leary, 1985), and other adult behaviors (Margolin, Michelli, & Jacobson, 1988).

Self-Observation

Although insiders usually have a less-obstructed view of a client's behavior than would an outside observer, no one spends as much time with the client as the client does. Therefore, in many clinical and research settings, clients are asked to observe and record their own behavior. This procedure is called *self-monitoring*. It is usually done by adults, though children can be successful at it as well.

Self-monitoring requires clients to keep a written record of the frequency, duration, or intensity of their behavior. A chart may be used to record the occurrence of events such as exercise, headaches, pleasant thoughts, hair pulling, giving or receiving praise, pain, and so on.

Figure 6–4 illustrates a diary used for recording smoking behavior. Space is provided for noting the time at which each cigarette is lit as well as for information about the physical and social setting and the mood that preceded smoking. Similar diaries detailing specific behaviors, their antecedents, and their consequences are commonly used in research on eating habits (Brownell, 1981), sleep problems (Miller & DiPilato, 1983), anxiety disorders (Cooper & Clum, 1989), and other targets (Heinrich & Schag, 1985). As we discuss later in this chapter, self-monitoring is sometimes a *reactive* form of observation, meaning that the act of observation may modify the behavior being observed. This characteristic results in self-monitoring sometimes being used as a treatment method in itself. However, the direction of the reactivity is difficult to predict; self-monitoring sometimes increases, sometimes decreases the rate of a behavior. The value of the behaviors being self-monitored, the timing involved in the self-monitoring, and the contingencies for self-monitoring have been found to affect direction of reactive effects. For a review of self-monitoring procedures and applications, see Nelson (1977) and Kanfer and Gaelick (1986).

Observation Aids

Human sight and hearing are restricted in their ability to detect and discriminate what happens in the environment. To assist humans in their observation tasks, mechanical and/or electronic devices are often used. Mechanical devices sometimes assist in self-monitoring, especially when frequency or duration measures are of primary concern. The client may carry a counter that is pressed each time a target behavior occurs. Daily totals can then be

FIGURE 6–3 Part of a symbol-coding system for observation of children. (S. W. Bijou, R. F. Peterson, and M. H. Ault, "A method to integrate descriptive and experimental field studies at the level of data and empirical concepts," *Journal of Applied Behavior Analysis,* 1968, 1, 175–191. © 1968 by the Society for the Experimental Analysis of Behavior, Inc. Reprinted by permission.)

Name_____   Date_____

Time	Intensity of craving*	Was cigarette smoked? (✓)	Place	With whom	Mood
1.					
2.					
3.					
4.					
5.					
6.					
7.					
8.					
9.					
10.					
11.					
12.					
13.					
14.					
15.					
16.					
17.					
18.					
19.					
20.					

*indicate the intensity of your craving on a scale of 1 to 5: 1 = no perceptible craving; 2 = slight craving; 3 = moderate craving; 4 = fairly strong craving; 5 = intense craving.

Total number of cigarettes smoked_____

FIGURE 6–4 Behavioral diary for recording smoking behavior. (From O. F. Pomerleau & C. S. Pomerleau, *Break the Smoking Habit,* © Research Press, Champaign, Illinois, 1977. Reprinted by permission.)

read off the counter and recorded on a summary sheet. Commercially available counters can be used, or specially designed response counters are sometimes provided by the clinician.

Precise monitoring of the duration of target responses can be accomplished by timers. In many cases a clock can be turned into a cumulative timer. For example, the client is asked to set a clock to noon, plug it in each time she or he begins some activity (studying, exercising, sleeping), and unplug it each time the activity stops. The time on the clock face at the end of the day thus displays the duration of the target behavior for that day. Specially designed stopwatches that record time automatically can be used in the same way (Hoelscher, Lichstein, & Rosenthal, 1986).

A running record of behavior can be provided by mechanical devices (usually switches and counters) that are connected directly to the client. This is typified by systems that measure physical activity, which is a variable of interest with depressed, hyperactive, and other clients (see Milich, Loney, & Landau, 1982).

Electronic data collection devices have also played a role in naturalistic observation procedures. Audio and video tape recorders have been employed to gather larger amounts of continuous data than would be possible using human observers. The advent of tiny solid-state transmitters has allowed audio recordings of a client's verbal behavior to be made even when that client is nowhere near the tape recorder. This involves having the client wear a tiny microphone attached to a pocket-size wireless transmitter that sends a signal to a remote receiving point, where it is stored in a standard tape recorder. Telephones can be used as modems to collect data from clients in their homes. Miniaturization of recording devices has made it possible to use portable physiological monitors to collect data on heart rate in clients who have been treated for cardiac problems or carbon monoxide levels in clients who are enrolled in stop-smoking programs. Examples of how electronic and telemetric technology can be used in observational assessment abound in the clinical literature (Rugh, Gable, & Lemke, 1986).

Controlled Observation

The major appeal of naturalistic observation is that it yields large samples of spontaneous, real client behavior occurring under circumstances of relevance and interest to the clinician. The assets of naturalistic observation can become liabilities, however, especially when observation targets occur infrequently. Suppose, for example, that the clinician wants to observe a client's response to stress. Using naturalistic procedures, observers would have to monitor the client's behavior in settings where stressful events might occur. Because there is no guarantee that the client would actually encounter clinically relevant stress in a given situation, much time could be wasted.

Further, because naturalistic observation usually takes place in an uncontrolled environment, even if a stressor occurs, other events can complicate the assessment. The client may move out of the observer's line of vision or the client may get assistance in dealing with the stressor from a family member or friend. How would the client have reacted without help? The assessor would not know unless the same situation recurs when the client is alone and under observation.

The fact that the situation of interest may not soon recur points to another limitation of naturalistic observation: Repeated assessment of a client's reaction to low-probability events is difficult. This problem is important because comparison of the behavior of many people under identical conditions is a cornerstone of many experimental designs and assessment approaches.

One way of dealing with some difficulties of naturalistic observation is to set up special circumstances under which clients can be observed as they react to planned, standardized events. This is usually called *controlled observation* because the clinician maintains control over the assessment stimuli in much the same way as do users of the tests described in Chapter 5. Controlled observations are also referred to as *situation tests, analogue assessments,* and *contrived observations.*

As was true with early naturalistic observations, the first controlled observations involved a great deal of inference. For example, Barker, Dembo, and Lewin (1941) set up a frustration situation by first allowing nursery school children to play with highly desirable toys in a fenced area, then locking the youngsters out. The varying reactions to frustration displayed by each child were interpreted as evidence of maturity, constructiveness, regression, and other characteristics. Earlier, Hartshorne and May (1928) studied honesty by observing children in situations where they could steal money without fear of being detected.

During World War II, military psychologists devised controlled observations for assessing personality traits as well as behavioral capabilities. In the Operational Stress Test, for example, would-be pilots were placed in a flight simulator and asked to manipulate controls. The candidates did not know that the tester was purposely trying to frustrate them by giving increasingly complicated instructions accompanied by negative feedback (e.g., "You're making too many errors"; Melton, 1947). During the test, the assessor rated the candidate's reaction to criticism and stress, and these ratings supplemented objective data on skill with the simulator.

Traits of initiative, dominance, cooperation, and group leadership were inferred from observational assessments developed by the staff of the Office of Strategic Services (OSS; later to become the CIA) to help select espionage agents and other special personnel. One example was a construction test, in which a candidate was assigned to build a 5-foot cube-shaped frame out of large wooden poles and blocks resembling a giant Tinker Toy™ set. Because the test was supposed to measure the candidate's organizational and leadership ability, he was given two "assistants" (actually, psychologists) who called themselves Buster and Kippy.

> Kippy acted in a passive, sluggish manner. He did nothing at all unless specifically ordered to, but stood around, often getting in the way. . . . Buster, on the other hand, . . . was aggressive, forward in offering impractical suggestions, ready to express dissatisfaction, and quick to criticize what he suspected were the candidate's weakest points. . . . It was their function to present the candidate with as many obstructions and annoyances as possible in ten minutes. As it turned out, they succeeded in frustrating the candidates so thoroughly that the construction was never . . . completed in the allotted time. (OSS, 1948, p. 103)[2]

---

[2]The fact that Kippy and Buster were Army privates and often got to torment high-ranking officers "set an untouchable record for job satisfaction among psychologists" (Cronbach, 1960, p. 568).

Since World War II, milder versions of the OSS situational tests have been used for personnel selection. In current clinical and research settings controlled observations take many forms. In some cases, the "control" consists of asking clients (usually couples, families, or parent–child pairs) to come to a clinic or laboratory and have a discussion, attempt to solve a problem, or just talk while under observation by TV cameras, tape recorders, or human coders (e.g., Hahlweg, Revenstorf, & Schindler, 1984). In other instances clients are presented with a structured task or situation designed to elicit behaviors of relevance to clinical assessment (e.g., Humphrey, Apple, & Kirschenbaum, 1986).

Role-Playing Tests

Psychologists sometimes create make-believe situations in which the client is asked to *role play* his or her typical behavior. Role playing has been advocated by clinicians for many years (e.g., Borgatta, 1955) and serves as the cornerstone for several group, psychodynamic, and phenomenological treatments (e.g., Kelly, 1955; Moreno, 1946; Perls, 1969). However, it was not until the late 1960s that it became a part of systematic clinical assessment. The most common use of role playing in controlled observation has been in the assessment of social competency, self-expression, and assertiveness.

Sometimes the procedures are simple and structured, as in the Situation Test (ST) developed by Rehm and Marston (1968) to explore college males' social skills. In the ST, the client sits with a person of the opposite sex and listens to tape-recorded descriptions of scenes to be role played. The woman (an assistant to the clinician) then reads a question or statement such as "What would you like to do now?" or "I thought that was a lousy movie," and the client is asked to respond as if the situation were real. Another example is provided by Nelson, Hayes, Felton, and Jarrett (1985), who required subjects to respond to interpersonal situations such as the following: "You have been seeing this man/woman for about four months. He/she has been very demanding on you and he/she gets extremely jealous when he/she sees you just talking to another man/woman. He/she says he/she doesn't want to lose you but you want to end this relationship. So you say. . . . "

Role-playing tests have become a standard ingredient in the assessment of children's social and safety skills (Harbeck, Peterson, & Starr, 1992), parent–child interactions (Jouriles & Farris, 1992), social behavior in socially anxious persons (Turner, Beidel, & Long, 1992), behavior of depressed patients (Bellack, Hersen, & Himmelhoch, 1983), and conversational skills of chronically mentally ill persons (Kelly, 1982). In most role plays, the subjects' responses are videotaped and then rated by observers on a number of target criteria such as appropriateness of content, level of positive and refusal assertiveness, anxiety, latency to respond, response duration, speech dysfluencies, posture, eye contact, gaze, hand gestures, head movements, and voice loudness. This list is not exhaustive, but it illustrates the tremendous variability of measures that have been employed.

A major question about role-playing assessments is how valid and reliable they are. Do their results generalize to natural settings? Do they agree with other types of assessment such as self-report or peer evaluation? Are they correlated with important external criteria? In the early days of role-playing assessments, their use was based on their assumed, or face, validity. Today most investigators are not satisfied with face validity. They require demonstrations that results obtained from role playing are related to naturalistic behavior.

Although the results of research on the validity of role-playing methods are mixed, the basic conclusion is that with proper care they can yield moderately useful data. Role plays that increase the client's feelings of involvement and that are personally relevant appear to be the most useful (Kern, 1991). A large number of variables influence the way clients

and subjects respond to role-playing assessments. Instructions to behave as one naturally would versus instructions to behave as an assertive person would produce very different behavior in subjects (Kazdin, Esveldt-Dawson, & Matson, 1983; Rodriguez, Nietzel, & Berzins, 1980). The content of the scenes used in role plays (Nelson et al., 1985), their level of difficulty (Kolotkin, 1980), the responses of the experimenter to the subject (Kirchner & Draguns, 1979), and the social impact of role-played behavior (Kern, Cavell, & Beck, 1985) also influence role-played performance.

As investigators have learned about such variables, they have modified role-playing methods to make them more realistic and more specific to the problems of individual clients. For example, the Extended Interaction Test (McFall & Lillesand, 1971) assesses the generality of clients' behavior by using a tape that talks back to clients who are trying to be assertive. To assess the persistence of clients' ability to refuse unreasonable requests, the Extended Interaction Test requires clients to respond to a series of gradually escalating demands made by a taped antagonist (see Box 6–4). Presumably, a person who withstands repeated requests is more assertive than one who gives in after an initial refusal.

The Extended Interaction Test provides one example of assessing the generality of client behavior through controlled observation, but there are others. Some involve administration of different role-play items to measure the range of situations in which a client is skilled or assertive (e.g., Edelstein & Eisler, 1976), while others attempt to observe the client in naturalistic settings (e.g., Kazdin, Matson, & Esveldt-Dawson, 1984). Because the first strategy may not be realistic and because the second strategy is difficult to carry out, a third approach has appeared in recent years. It involves creating a *staged naturalistic event* (Gottman & Markman, 1978) consisting of controlled observational circumstances of which the client is unaware or about which he or she has been misin-

NARRATOR: You are feeling really pressed for study time because you have an exam on Friday afternoon. Now, you are studying at your desk, when a close friend comes in and says, "Hi, Guess what. My parents just called and offered to pay for a plane ticket so I can fly home this weekend. Great, huh!? The only problem is, I'll have to skip my Friday morning class, and I hate to miss out on those notes; I'm barely making it in there as it is. Look, I know you aren't in that class, but it'd really be a big help if you'd go to the class Friday and take notes for me so I could go home. Would you do that for me?"

SUBJECT: (responds; if refusal . . .)

N: "I guess it is kinda crazy to expect you to do it, but, gee, I've got so many things to do if I'm gonna get ready to leave, and I don't want to waste the time asking around. Come on, will you do it for me this once?"

S: (responds; if refusal . . .)

N: "Look, what're friends for if they don't help each other out of a bind? I'd do it for you if you asked. What do you say, will you?"

S: (responds; if refusal . . .)

N: "But I was *counting* on *you* to do it. I'd hate to have to call my folks back and tell them I'm not coming. Can't you spare just *one* hour to help me out?"

S: (responds; if refusal . . .)

N: (sarcastically) "Now look, I don't want to *impose* on your *precious* time. Just tell me. Will you do it or do I have to call my folks back?"

S: (responds)

Source: McFall and Lillesand, 1971.

BOX 6–4
Excerpt from the Extended Interaction Test

formed. The idea is to look at behavior in a *controlled* setting that appears *naturalistic* to the client.

For example, unobtrusive role-playing tests have been used to measure social skills in psychiatric inpatients (Goldsmith & McFall, 1975). The client is asked to meet and carry on a conversation with a total stranger (who is the clinician's confederate). The confederate had been instructed to confront the subject with three "critical moments": "not catching the subject's name, responding to a lunch invitation with an excuse that left open the possibility of lunch at another time, and saying 'Tell me about yourself' at the first convenient pause in the conversation." Similar contrived situations have been used in other psychiatric settings (Holmes, Hansen, & St. Lawrence, 1984) and with college students (Kern, 1982).

Observation that involves deception and possible invasion of privacy must be set up with care and with regard for client welfare and dignity. The proponents of unobtrusive controlled observation have sought to avoid its potential dangers and point out that its value may be limited to measuring specific behaviors (such as refusal) rather than more complex interactive social skills.

Performance Measures

In most of the controlled observations described in the previous section, the client is asked to act as if an event were taking place. There are other procedures, however, in which the client is actually faced with a clinically relevant situation so that her or his behavior can be observed.

Controlled observations of performance have focused on behaviors such as eating, drinking, or smoking. For example, the eating style (amount, speed, preferences) of normal or obese individuals has been recorded during a meal or snack in a controlled setting (Spiegel, Wadden, & Foster, 1991). Alcoholic and nonalcoholic drinkers have been observed in specially constructed cocktail lounges (see Figure 6–5) or living rooms located in hospitals (Collins, Parks, & Marlatt, 1985). The details of cigarette use (puff rate, depth of inhalation, number of puffs) have been scrutinized in volunteers smoking in simulated social settings (Ossip-Klein, Martin, Lomax, Prue, & Davis, 1983).

Another important type of performance measure in controlled settings is the physiological activity (heart rate, respiration, blood pressure, galvanic skin response, muscle tension, blood alcohol levels, and brain waves) that appears in relation to various stimuli. An early example is provided by Malmo, Shagass, and Davis (1950), who showed a film about headaches to a client with a severe headache problem and measured her forehead muscle tension while she watched.

Clinical psychologists have increased their use of physiological measures in recent years for at least two reasons. First, they have become much more involved in studying medical and psychological disorders that have physiological components. Insomnia, headaches, chronic pain, gastrointestinal disorders, and diabetes are a few examples of such disorders. Second, reliable measurement of physiological responses becomes crucial in evaluating new treatments for several of these disorders.

Physiological measures have become particularly important in the assessment of sexual arousal, wherein clinicians seek measures that subjects cannot voluntarily control. Typically, a male subject listens to or watches tapes that depict different types of erotic behavior, some of it deviant and some nondeviant. While the subject monitors the tape, a strain gauge attached to his penis records changes in penile circumference.

FIGURE 6–5 Simulated bar located in a hospital setting. (Courtesy of G. Alan Marlatt. Reprinted by permission.)

Greater erectile responses to the tape material are assumed to signal greater levels of sexual arousal. Several studies have shown sex offenders to have equal or greater arousal to rape stimuli than to scenes of consenting sexual activity (Hall, 1990). In contrast, nonrapists usually show less sexual excitation in response to scenes of rape. The expected patterns of arousal are not found consistently enough to ensure that physiological measures are valid measures of deviant sexual arousal; Figure 6–6 illustrates how rapists' and nonrapists' erections

FIGURE 6–6 This graph illustrates the differences between 20 rapists' and 20 non-sex-offenders' sexual responsiveness, as measured by penile responses, to 10 audiotaped descriptions of sexual activity. Note that the rapists showed more sexual arousal to depictions of rape and nonsexual violence with females than the control subjects. The control subjects showed more arousal to scenes involving consenting sexual activity. The groups did not differ in their responses to stories involving homosexual activity or heterosexual bondage and spanking. (From V. L. Quinsey, T. C. Chaplin, & D. Upfold, 1984. Copyright 1984 by the American Psychological Association. Reprinted by permission.)

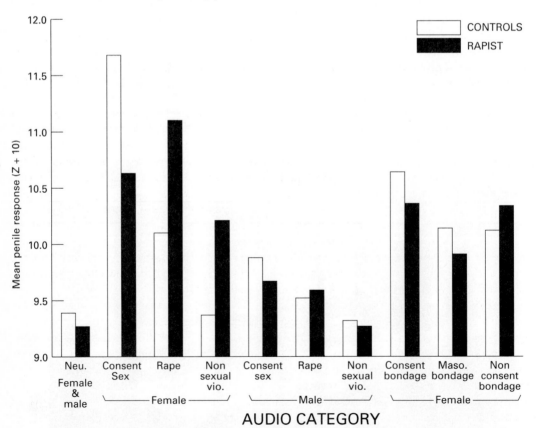

Figure 1. Average penile (z scores + 10) responses of rapists and control subjects to the stimulus categories. (Neu = neutral; vio = violence; maso = masochistic.)

to audiotaped sexual content showed clear differences in one study.

Assessment of the physiology of fear in controlled settings has also occupied many clinical researchers. In a classic study, Paul (1966) used measures of heart rate and sweating taken just before giving a talk to help identify speech-anxious clients. These measures were repeated following various anxiety-reduction treatments to aid in the evaluation of their effects. The wide range of physiological assessments of anxiety is reviewed by Nietzel, Bernstein, and Russell (1988).

Behavioral Avoidance Tests (BATs) are a popular performance measure in controlled observation. BATs are designed to assess overt anxiety in relation to specific objects and situations by confronting clients with the stimulus they fear and then having observers record the type and degree of avoidance displayed. Informal BATs had been conducted with children as early as the 1920s (e.g., Jones, 1924a and b), but it was not until the early 1960s that systematic avoidance-testing procedures became a common form of controlled observational assessment.

In a study of systematic desensitization (see Chapter 9) for snake phobia, Lang and Lazovik (1963) asked each client to enter a room that contained a harmless caged snake and to approach, touch, and pick up the animal. The clients were scored on whether they were able to look at, touch, or hold the snake. In subsequent versions of the BAT, many other fear stimuli (e.g., rats, spiders, cockroaches, dogs) have been used, and the "look-touch-hold" coding system for scoring responses has been replaced by more sophisticated measures. These include recording how close the client is able to come to the fear target, maximum amount of interaction achieved, length of time between entering the test room and making physical contact with the target, overt anxiety behaviors during the test, and changes in physiological arousal (heart rate, respiration, galvanic skin response). Usually, clients are asked to approach the feared target, but occasionally BATs are set up to measure how long clients can look

at a frightening stimulus or how close they will allow that stimulus to approach them.

Controlled performance tests have also been developed to assess fear of certain *situations*. Paul's (1966) use of contrived speeches to assess clients' discomfort about public speaking was an early example of this type of assessment. Others include asking persons who fear heights to climb fire escapes (Emmelkamp & Felten, 1985) or observe dental phobics as they wait for and receive treatment from a dentist (Getka & Glass, 1992).

EVALUATION OF OBSERVATIONAL ASSESSMENT

As noted in Chapter 3, direct observation of behavior can help avoid many inference problems that reduce the reliability and validity of some interview and test procedures. Behaviorally oriented psychologists, the most enthusiastic proponents of observational assessment, have argued that this approach provides the most realistic view of behaviors of clinical relevance.

Observations are sometimes thought of as being like photographs that provide an accurate picture of human behavior. But just as a photograph of a scene is a product of the scene itself, the equipment used, the photographer's techniques, and the developing process, data from observational procedures are determined by factors other than the behavior of the clients. Some of these factors can distort observational assessment. Observing human behavior does not automatically establish the resulting data as reliable and valid.

To illustrate, consider a hypothetical situation in which a clinician is working with a distressed married couple and decides to include observational procedures as part of an assessment battery. A controlled situation is set up in which the couple is videotaped as they talk about one of their problems and attempt to resolve it. Later, the videotape is scored by trained observers using a coding system. A summary of the couple's behavior would result ("couple spent 63% of the session in negative interaction") and might be accompanied by the suggestion that this is a sample of how the husband and wife related to one another. Such an observational procedure is direct and apparently objective, but is it reliable and valid?

Reliability in Observational Assessment

The first question that must be asked about observational data is, "Are they reliable?" To what extent do observers arrive at the same ratings or conclusions about the behavior they watch? If interobserver agreement is low, such that our hypothetical couple's interaction was scored in different ways by different individuals, one cannot place much confidence in the observation. The assessor would either have to believe one particular observer or average all observers' data in some way. Neither alternative is attractive because (a) there is usually an inadequate basis for trusting one observer above others, and (b) averages of widely discrepant scores represent a mathematical but not a behavioral reality (the couple's *average* scores from unreliable observers may not reflect their actual behavior at all).

The interobserver reliability of modern clinical observation systems that use trained observers is usually very high; coefficients in excess of .80 and .90 are not uncommon (Paul & Lentz, 1977). When clients observe their own behavior through self-monitoring, agreement between their data and those of external observers is sometimes in the .90s (Kazdin, 1974). Although such impressive figures do not always appear, when they do occur it is usually because the clinical assessor has avoided some of the pitfalls, caused by the following factors, that can threaten the reliability of observational data (see Cone & Foster, 1982, for a review).

Task Complexity

If observers must make many difficult discriminations in recording, coding, or rating behavior, reliability will probably be lower than if fewer, easier judgments are required (Mash & McElwee, 1974). In the case of our married couple, the clinician would be more likely to obtain reliable observations using a 15-category rather than a 100-category coding system. Observation will also be more reliable if clients do not engage in a large number of short-duration responses in quick succession.

Knowledge of Reliability Checks

Another factor that affects reliability is the observers' knowledge that their agreement is being monitored. When people are first trained to use an observation system, they work very hard during practice sessions and pay close attention to the task, partly because they are being evaluated. Later, when "real" data are being collected, the observers may become careless if they think no one is checking their reliability (Romanczyk, Kent, Diament, & O'Leary, 1973; Taplin & Reid, 1973). The same can be said for clients who self-monitor their behavior (Lipinski, Black, Nelson, & Ciminero, 1975). Of course, the relationship between reliability and observers' knowledge that their agreements are being checked can be viewed in another light. When observers know they are being checked for level of agreement, they might collaborate, either deliberately or coincidentally, to produce misleadingly high levels of interobserver agreement (see Foster, Bell-Dolan, & Burge, 1988, for a discussion of this issue). The best protection against this threat to reliability is unobtrusive or random checking of performance. Thus, our clinician should tell the observers that their agreement about the observed couple's behavior will be checked from time to time but that they will not be told when.

Observer Training

If the observers of our married couple are told to record laughter in their coding system but are not given a definition of laughter, one observer might count belly laughs but not giggles, while another would include everything from a quiet titter to violent guffaws. Obviously, when observers are left to define for themselves what is meant by specific coding categories or global constructs like "hostile" or "happy," the reliability of observational data drops dramatically.

High reliability coefficients do not always mean that an observation system is being used properly. Reliability estimates can be artificially inflated by several factors (Harris & Lahey, 1982a; Cone & Foster, 1982; Mitchell, 1979). To be blunt, observers sometimes cheat, especially when they want to please their employer and when they are unsupervised. Cheating usually takes the form of altering scores to enhance agreement. Obviously, our clinician should supervise the coding of the couple's behavior and arrange for reliability coefficients to be calculated by someone other than the observers.

Another situation in which high reliabilities may be misleading is when there is *observer drift* (Johnson & Bolstad, 1973; O'Leary & Kent, 1973). When observers work together in unchanging pairs or groups, they tend to form their own particular well-agreed-upon version of the rating system so that, over time, each pair or group "drifts" away from the others. Within each pair or group, reliability may be very high, but if new pairings are made or if between-pair reliabilities are calculated, interobserver agreement may be much lower. This problem can be combated by constant rotation of observer pairs and/or periodic retraining of all observers.

Interpreting Reliability Figures

Another question arises when high reliability figures are encountered: How were they calculated? There are many mathematical issues involved concerning questions of what a reliability coefficient means. For example, suppose that our clinician reported interobserver agreement 95% of the time. Depending on how this figure was calculated, it could either mean there was strong agreement about what the observers *saw* or about what they did *not* see. If agreement is registered only when two observers record the occurrence of the same behavior at the same time, 95% would be impressive indeed. However, if agreement also means that each of two observers did *not* record the occurrence of a particular behavior that seldom occurs, the agreement percentage could be inflated by chance associated with the base rate of that behavior. Agreeing about the nonoccurrence of a behavior that happens rarely is not a useful indicator of reliability.

Several mathematical procedures are available to control or correct problems of this type, but they are not used uniformly enough to warrant unequivocal faith in the reliability figures cited in observational assessment literature. To summarize, interobserver agreement in clinical observation can be high, but interpretation of what various reliability figures mean depends on how they were calculated (Foster et al., 1988; Mitchell, 1979).

Validity of Observational Assessment

The next questions one must ask about observational procedures concern validity: Are these procedures measuring what they are supposed to measure, and how well are they doing it? At first glance, observation of behavior would appear to rank highest in validity among all clinical assessment approaches. Instead of hearing about behavior in interviews or speculating about behavior through tests, the clinician using observation can actually watch the real thing.

To a certain extent, however, the directness or face validity of clinical observation has caused a deemphasis on proving its validity in traditional terms (Cone, 1988). After all, if we *observe* aggression in our married couple, are we not *measuring* aggression, and is that not enough to establish the validity of our technique? The answer is yes only if we can show

(a) that the behaviors coded (e.g., raised voices) constitute a satisfactory definition of aggression, (b) that the data faithfully reflect the nature and degree of aggression that occurred during observation, and (c) that the clients' behaviors while under observation would accurately represent their reactions in other, unobserved situations.

When a number of nonparticipant observers repeatedly see a child engaging in violent, unprovoked attacks on siblings and peers at home and in school, and when these data agree in detail with the verbal reports of parents and teachers, the validity of observational data would be difficult to question. In other instances, however, establishing the validity of observation is not as easy. Many issues must be dealt with before we can be confident we are getting a valid picture of client behavior.

Defining Observation Targets

A basic issue relating to the validity of observational assessment involves clarification of what is being measured. For example, when clinicians set out to develop an observation system for assertion, they typically use what we referred to in Chapter 5 as a rational approach. The assessor tells the observers what behaviors to look for and code, and the choice of these behaviors is based on how that assessor thinks assertion can be detected in behavior. Basic decisions, such as what aspects of behaviors to code (e.g., frequency, intensity, duration) and how these targets are defined, reflect the theory or preferences of individual investigators. For example, one clinician might assess assertiveness by observing clients' ability to refuse unreasonable requests, while another focuses on the direct expression of positive affect. This problem of definition may never be resolved to everyone's satisfaction, but it is important to ask on what behavioral features the observation system focuses.

One way to assess the validity of an observation is to ask, "What is it related to?" Does the ability to refuse unreasonable requests

occur more often in people judged to be assertive by their peers? If one is accurately observing part of a phenomenon of interest, meaningful relationships of this type should emerge (Foster et al., 1988). If, on the other hand, it is merely *assumed* that an observation system captures a valid picture of assertion, the clinician risks collecting samples of behavior with little importance outside the measurement situation. This problem has been given surprisingly little attention by users of observational assessment, partly because, as already noted, the validity of observation appears so obvious.

Some efforts toward formal validation of observational systems have been made. Jones, Reid, and Patterson (1975) summarize a series of studies designed to explore the relationship between certain categories in their Behavioral Coding System (BCS) and other variables. Their research shows that children who had been previously identified by others as aggressive were, in fact, aggressive when observed through the BCS.

Some researchers have approached the validity of their observations by designing their system empirically rather than rationally. Instead of deciding ahead of time what particular behaviors reflect anxiety, an assessor may code virtually all client behavior that occurs during observation. Patterns of behavior are then correlated with other data (self-reports, physiological arousal, third-party accounts) about the client's reaction to the observed situation and to other relevant situations. If a pattern of behavior, for example, shaking and whimpering, is strongly associated with high scores on other measures also designed to assess anxiety, that behavior pattern can be referred to as anxious with greater confidence than if the assessor had simply decreed that shaking and whimpering indicate anxiety. If, in addition, the anxious behavior increases under circumstances that are stressful of if it changes for the better following some form of treatment, evidence of the anxiety-related meaning of the behavior becomes stronger. Kleinknecht and Bernstein (1978) used this approach in developing an observation system for measuring patients' fear while in a dental office.

A more sophisticated strategy for building validity into an observation system is embodied in Goldfried and D'Zurilla's (1969) *behavior-analytic* model. Here, the assessor first carefully explores the construct to be measured and then custom tailors observations to that construct. An example of an observation system based on this strategy is the Taxonomy of Problematic Social Situations for Children (TOPS) developed by Dodge, McClaskey, and Feldman (1985). These researchers first asked teachers and psychologists to describe social situations in which peer problems might occur for school children. Sixty-four situations were described and classified into one of eight categories by undergraduate assistants. The categories involved activities such as responding to failures, attempting to join a peer group, being rejected or excluded by a peer group, etc. Next, the researchers asked teachers to use the TOPS to rate a group of children who frequently suffered rejection from peers as well as a group who enjoyed good peer relationships. In a related study, 39 clinic-referred children with a history of rejection and 34 socially adjusted children role played responses to a subsample of representative items from the TOPS. Socially rejected children were found to be less competent in several social situations whether measured by teacher ratings or their own role plays. Other behavior-analytic approaches to assessment have been used in the observation and treatment of social skill deficits in various populations such as delinquents (Gaffney & McFall, 1981), violent men (Holtzworth-Munroe, 1992), and rapists (Lipton, McDonel, & McFall, 1987).

Another contemporary approach to the validity of observational data is provided by Cone (1988), who suggests that the major criterion for observations is *accuracy*. Do observations, when made according to the rules provided by developers, correspond closely to an "incontrovertible index" of the behavior in question? An accurate observational system is sensitive to the occurrence of behavior, the repeated occurrence of the behavior in different situations, and relationships between that behavior and other behaviors. Cone (1988) argues that the best method for establishing accuracy is the intensive study of the individual subject. You will recall from Chapter 1 that this approach to assessment is known as the *idiographic* approach, in contrast to the *nomothetic* approach where the psychologist studies differences and similarities between groups of persons responding to standardized measures of psychological qualities. Cone's (1988) call for an idiographic-behavioral approach to clinical assessment is consistent with a revived interest in the close study of individuals by clinicians of various theoretical backgrounds (Harris, 1980; Lamiell & Trierweiler, 1986; Pervin, 1984).

Observer Effects

No matter how reliable observers are, they must also be accurate about what they see if their data are to be valid. The clinician or researcher has several worries with respect to observers' accuracy. First, there is the problem of observer error. Just as an interviewer may remember certain client responses more accurately than others, an observer can also make mistakes.

Second, the quality of observational data may be compromised by observer *bias*. Human beings may see things that are not objectively there to see, partly because, as the Gestalt school of psychology emphasized, there is a perceptual tendency in human beings to "complete" or "close" incomplete stimulus patterns. Thus, an observer may *see* a child raise a hand toward another child, but *record* the behavior as "striking" rather than "hand raising." In a paper called "Seeing's Believing," Johnson (1953) tells about a radiologist who concluded that a button revealed in an X-ray was on the patient's vest when, in fact, it had lodged in the patient's throat. The error probably occurred because, as Rosenthal (1966, p. 6) put it, "buttons occur more frequently on vests than in throats." Johnson (1953, p. 79) concluded: "Our assumptions define and limit what we see, i.e., we tend to see things in such a way that they will fit in with our assumptions even if this involves distortion or omission."

The effects of biasing information are stronger if observers make broad, general ratings about behavior. In a well-known example of this phenomenon, psychiatrists, psychologists, and graduate students listened to a taped interview in which an actor portrayed a well-adjusted man (Temerlin, 1968). When they listened under neutral conditions, 57% of the observers rated the "client" as "healthy," while 43% called him "neurotic." No one thought he was psychotic. However, ratings were biased if the tape was described as either that of a "perfectly healthy man" or a person who "looks neurotic but actually is psychotic." In the former case, 100% of the listeners rated the "client" as "healthy." In the latter, an average of nearly 30% diagnosed the man "psychotic," and over 60% called him "neurotic."

In a study involving observation and global descriptions (Rapp, 1965, cited by Johnson & Bolstad, 1973), eight pairs of observers watched a child in a nursery school. One member of each pair was told that the client was feeling "under par," while the other was told the child was feeling "above par." In seven of the eight pairs, the observers' descriptions differed significantly and corresponded with their implanted expectations. However, it is important to note that (a) when specific, well-defined behavioral coding systems rather than global ratings are used, observers are more immune to the effects of externally imposed bias (Foster et al., 1988); and (b) more recent, better-designed studies have failed to replicate the effects of bias on observation (Cone & Foster, 1982).

Reactivity of Observation

In addition to observer bias, the clinician utilizing observational assessment must be concerned about *reactivity:* Clients may react to being observed by intentionally or unintentionally altering the behaviors that are of greatest clinical interest. This problem parallels the issues of response bias and impression management in tests and interviews. The problem of reactivity can be illustrated by turning on a tape recorder at any social gathering. Noticeable changes in people's behavior usually occur immediately, and they last either until the machine is switched off or the novelty disappears. Awareness of the possible reactivity of clinical observation has a long history (e.g., Covner, 1942), but the dimensions of the problem are still unclear.

Some psychologists claim that observational procedures have only a minimal and short-term reactive influence on subjects, after which their behavior regains its natural spontaneity. For example, Mercatoris and Craighead (1974) found that the amount of appropriate behavior by retarded adult women did not change when they were watched by a visible observer as opposed to a hidden television camera. Other data suggest stronger reactive effects are associated with observation. For example, Zegiob, Arnold, and Forehand (1975) reported increases in mother's play, positive verbal statements, and other behaviors when mother–child interactions were overtly as opposed to covertly observed. In general, more research studies demonstrate reactive effects of observation than do not (Baum, Forehand, & Zegiob, 1979; Cone & Foster, 1982; Harris & Lahey, 1982b).

There is also evidence that self-monitoring can be reactive. For example, smoking usually decreases when smokers record each cigarette they light. Other behaviors such as eating, nail biting, hallucinating, alcohol intake, tics, child-management skills, and studying often change when self-observed (see Nelson, 1977, for a review). In fact, because self-monitoring usually produces *beneficial* changes in recorded behavior, it has been used as a form of therapy. Self-monitoring does not *always* alter behaviors it is meant to record. Little change in depression, obsessive ruminations, hair pulling, overeating, and other targets has been reported in clients who self-monitored these responses.

In light of this conflicting research, it is not easy for the clinician to reach firm conclusions about whether awareness of observations will alter clients' behavior. Kent and Foster (1977, p. 289) observed: "There seems little reason to doubt that the presence of an observer may, in fact, affect the behavior of those he observes. But the number of factors determining the magnitude and direction of behavior change may be so great that manifest reactivity is scattered and almost completely unpredictable."

The possibility of reactivity in clinical observation cannot be ignored. To be on the safe side, the clinician should observe clients as unobtrusively as possible (perhaps using two-way mirrors or video cameras to keep coders out of sight) and should schedule assessment sessions that are long enough to give clients ample time to get used to being observed.

Representativeness of Observed Behavior

Even after reactive effects have disappeared, observed behavior may not provide a *representative* or *ecologically valid* (Brunswick, 1947) picture of the client. The client may have a hangover on the day of an observation. A death in the family may have just occurred. Any number of factors can result in temporary patterns of depressed, euphoric, or hyperactive behavior that are atypical of the client.

Some features of the situation in which observation occurs exert an influence by suggesting to the client what behaviors are appropriate or expected. When this happens the observation is likely to produce specific behaviors through social cues called *demand characteristics* (Orne, 1962). If a clinician observes a married couple in a setting that contains strong social cues about how the clients should behave (e.g., "We would like to measure just how much fighting you two actually do"), she or he may learn more about

the effects of the situation than about the typical behavior of the couple.

Problems of situational bias occur most often in controlled settings, though they can appear in naturalistic observation as well. In most controlled observations, the client must go to some specially identified location to be observed and is thus aware of the purpose of assessment. Further, specific instructions about the observation are usually given to orient clients and to help them recognize when assessment begins and ends.

The social and situational cues in most observational assessments can alter client behavior radically. For example, Orne and Schiebe (1964) monitored male college students undergoing a period of isolation in a small, well-lighted room. Half the subjects were told that the room was a sensory deprivation chamber. In this condition, the experimenter wore a white coat, conducted a medical history interview, asked the subject to sign a medical release form, and displayed an "emergency tray" of drugs and equipment that were part of the "precautionary measures" in the laboratory. He also mentioned that release from the chamber was possible by pressing an emergency alarm if "the situation becomes difficult," and that a physician was available "if you should feel upset." The other subjects were told they were in a control group. There was no white coat, no interview, no "emergency tray," and no "emergency alarm." Once in the isolation room, the two groups differed markedly in behavior. Control subjects appeared relaxed and comfortable. They rested or slept, worked on various time-filling tasks, and said little. "Sensory deprivation" subjects, on the other hand, were restless, slept very little, expressed discomfort or feelings of disorientation, and "gave an impression of almost being tortured" (Orne & Schiebe, 1964, p. 11).

Similar situational effects operate in the assessment of social skills, fears, and other clinical targets. For example, in a study designed to measure assertiveness, Nietzel and Bernstein (1976) asked college students to respond

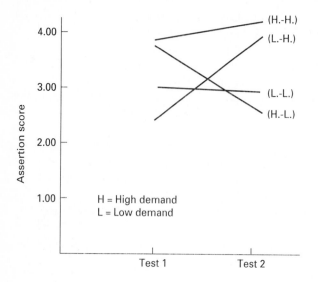

FIGURE 6–7 Instructions significantly increased or decreased subjects' rated assertiveness in this study of situational influence in observation. Subjects given consistent instructions did not change over time (Nietzel & Bernstein, 1976).

to tape-recorded social situations similar to those described earlier in this chapter. Subjects heard the tape twice, once in a "low demand" situation, when they were asked to give "your natural reaction," and once under "high demand," when responses were to be "as assertive as you think the most assertive and forceful person could be." Other subjects heard low- or high-demand instructions twice. The assertiveness of subjects in each condition was scored on a five-point scale. The results are summarized in Figure 6–7. Obviously, these instructions not only had an initial effect, but were capable of significantly altering subjects' behavior from test to test.

In anxiety assessment, the instructions given, the presence or absence of an experimenter, the characteristics of the physical setting, and other situational variables influence the amount of fear clients display during BATs (e.g., Bernstein, 1973; Bernstein & Nietzel, 1977). As another example, the behavior of children under observation in their own homes can be made to look "good" or "bad" depending upon what their parents think the assessor wants to see (Johnson & Lobitz, 1974).

Various strategies have been suggested to minimize situational bias in observational as-

sessment (Bernstein & Nietzel, 1977; Borkovec & O'Brien, 1976), but the problem cannot be entirely eliminated. As long as the stimuli present when the subject's behavior is being observed differ from the stimuli that are present when the client is not being observed, we cannot be sure that the behavior displayed during formal observation will generalize to other situations. The best a clinician can do is minimize any cues that might influence client behavior. The use of completely naturalistic or unobtrusive observations is a solution in theory, but from a practical point of view, psychologists will often have to rely on contrived, analogue observations.

A Final Word

Like interviews and tests, observation is not a perfect clinical assessment tool. Nevertheless, it has many advantages that make it a valuable source of data. The challenge for the clinician or researcher is to use observation in a way that minimizes the influence of the various distorting factors we have discussed, so that the data generated can have maximum value in an overall assessment plan.

CHAPTER 7

Clinical Intervention: Overview

All kinds of people try to change your behavior. Politicians work for your vote. Advertisers persuade you to buy their product. Parents encourage children to abide by their wishes. Almost every human interaction involves an attempt by one party to influence another to behave in a certain fashion. Some people are strong influencers who move us to behave in entirely novel ways. Others are ineffective influencers with an insignificant impact on us.

Behavior influence is not always interpersonal. Our behavior is affected by the physical as well as the social environment (Krasner & Ullmann, 1973). Consider the effect the weather has on your conduct: When was the last time you went swimming in a sleetstorm? Behavior influence can also be a private matter. Our memories of the past affect the way we live in the present, our internal conversations with ourselves lead us to react differently to others, and our fantasies about the future inspire or deter current activities.

In this chapter we concentrate on the behavior influence exerted by clinical psycholo-

gists. When a psychologist, in a professional capacity, seeks to influence someone's behavior, we describe the activity as an *intervention.* Depending on the qualities of the intervention, we could describe it as *prevention, consultation, education, psychotherapy, counseling, group therapy, family therapy,* or *play therapy.* If we knew more about the training and theoretical leanings of the clinician, we could qualify the nature of the intervention even further, using such terms as *primary prevention, crisis intervention, gestalt therapy, client-centered therapy, rational-emotive therapy,* or *behavior therapy.* In this chapter, *clinical intervention* is the umbrella term we use to describe deliberate attempts by psychologists to change behavior in a desirable direction.

To intervene means "to come between in action; to intercede or interfere." When we speak of a psychologist's intervention, we could be referring to many types of "coming between": *consultation* and *education,* where the psychologist comes between some audience and its needs for specific knowledge;

program development, where the psychologist comes between a social problem and the need for an innovative solution; or *psychotherapy,* where the psychologist comes between an individual and the individual's personal problems in living. In this chapter, we focus on psychotherapy (including group therapy, family therapy, and marital therapy), the most traditional type of "coming between" practiced by clinical psychologists. We pay special attention to the common features of most therapeutic approaches, the core assumptions shared by most psychotherapists, and the means by which psychotherapy is evaluated. Later in this chapter we consider other types of intervention, such as prevention, consultation, and program development, that are used by psychologists. In Chapters 8, 9, and 10 we present the three dominant perspectives on psychotherapy: psychodynamic, behavioral, and phenomenological.

WHAT IS PSYCHOTHERAPY?

The literal translation of *psychotherapy* would be "treatment of the psyche." While this is not a sufficient definition of the activity, it suggests several implications that will help us understand the fundamentals of psychotherapy.

The Participants

To speak of "treating psyches" suggests that psyches or personalities are in distress. The extent to which an individual feels disturbed can vary a great deal. In some, the disturbance is great. Employment may be terminated; suicide may be attempted; hospitalization may occur. In others, the disturbance may be less extreme, but still very upsetting. An unhappy marriage, a lack of self-confidence, a nagging fear, an identity crisis, depression, sexual problems, and insomnia are just a few of the problems that motivate people to enter psy-

chotherapy. The essential feature is that a person has become disturbed enough that she or he seeks the help of a professional. The individual is suffering. The help of friends, the long-awaited vacation, and the understanding of the family are no longer sufficient antidotes. When the point is reached where the problem is seen as requiring the intervention of a professional, we have the first participant in psychotherapy: the *client.*

The second participant is the *therapist.* By special training and experience the therapist is prepared to help the client overcome the disturbance that motivated the desire for treatment. Therapists should possess skills that will enable them to understand clients' disturbance and then interact with these clients to help them cope more effectively with their problems.

In addition to advanced training, the psychotherapist is expected to possess personal characteristics that contribute to therapy. The ability to listen to clients and convey a sense of understanding and sensitivity without being judgmental is one important quality of the therapist. Combining warmth and support for troubled clients with a resolve to confront them with their own ability and responsibility for change is another vital attribute. Clinicians often cite the need for the therapist to project *genuineness, empathy,* and *unconditioned positive regard.* These are called *Rogerian qualities* because Carl Rogers claimed that they are the necessary and sufficient conditions for bringing about therapeutic change.

This emphasis on personal characteristics has sometimes led to the suggestion that natural ability is more important than professional training in making a good therapist. In fact, a current controversy in the field is whether professional therapists are more effective than nonprofessional helpers. This is an important question because if untrained helpers are equal to or better than professional therapists, as Durlak (1979) and others (Dawes, 1992) have claimed, it would be difficult to justify the extensive training of therapists or the great expense of professional treatment. Although Durlak's conclusion has been criticized on several grounds (Nietzel & Fisher, 1981), the evidence has yet to prove that professional therapists achieve better outcomes than nonprofessionals in most cases (Berman & Norton, 1985). There is need for more well-designed research on this topic, and clearly the burden of proof is on professionals, who must show that they possess a special ability to help persons with psychological problems.

A related question is whether experienced therapists achieve superior treatment outcomes compared to therapists with less experience. Auerbach and Johnson (1977) conclude that there is a modest positive relationship between therapist experience and better outcomes. Others (Stein & Lambert, 1984) suggest that whatever benefits are associated with more therapist experience may be due to two facts: (a) Clients of less-experienced therapists are more likely to drop out of treatment prematurely, and (b) as the difference in experience level widens, the probability of more positive outcomes for experienced therapists increases.

Beyond the question of whether psychologists' training or experience improves their therapeutic effectiveness is the question of whether clinical psychologists can lay unique claims to their status as therapists. The answer to this question is "No!" Clinical psychologists are but one of many types of professionals who provide therapy and counseling to the public. Psychiatrists, counseling psychologists, social workers, psychiatric nurses, family counselors, and pastoral counselors deliver psychotherapy, and there is no consistent evidence that psychologists are better therapists than other mental health professionals (Beutler, Crago, & Arizmendi, 1986).

Finally, mental health professionals of all types are not the most frequent sources of help for persons experiencing problems in living (Gurin, Veroff, & Feld, 1960). Informal, nonprofessional caregivers counsel far more people about psychological problems than do members of the mental health professions. Included in the category of informal caregivers are friends, physicians, ministers, teachers, police officers, lawyers, family members, and neighbors. Cowen (1982) examined the help given by four groups of natural caregivers—hairdressers, divorce lawyers, bartenders, and industrial supervisors—and found that they used many helping strategies, some that resembled professionals' techniques (e.g., proposing alternative solutions) and some that did not (e.g., telling people to count their blessings). The important point is that psychotherapy is nobody's exclusive property. It would be arrogant for clinical psychologists to believe that psychotherapy is their activity, just as it would be foolish for mental health professionals of any type to claim that helping people change is exclusively their business.

While there is a vast literature on the importance of "good" therapist qualities (e.g., Gurman & Razin, 1977) the characteristics of the "good" psychotherapy client have also been studied (Garfield, 1986). The type of person likely to benefit most from psychotherapy is verbal, intelligent, motivated, moderately anxious about the need to change, able to communicate with the therapist, capable of becoming personally involved at early stages of therapy, and psychologically minded, a characteristic that means the person appreciates the importance of psychological factors in determining behavior. As some cynics point out, the ideal psychotherapy client is someone who would probably be successful whether or not he or she received therapy. However, this criticism ignores that psychotherapy is seldom practiced under conditions involving either the ideal client or the ideal therapist.

Interest in therapist and client characteristics has progressed past a focus on the personal attributes of the therapist or client in isolation to a concern for their interactive quality. This perspective has given rise to the concept of therapist–client *matching,* which Berzins (1977) defined as

> the idea that certain therapist-patient pairings are more desirable than others. Empirical study of this problem requires an understanding of the conditions under which, regardless of the characteristics of therapists and patients considered separately, the *interaction of these characteristics proves decisive for the processes or outcomes of psychotherapy.* (p. 222)

Since there is little research on various matching strategies, most clinicians rely on such stereotypes as "opposites attract" or "like cures like." Also, in many clinical settings assignment of clients to therapists is a haphazard affair accomplished through a glance at the calendar or the intuitions of a receptionist. Proper matching of clients to therapists faces two other large obstacles. First, the number of possible combinations of different client and therapist characteristics (e.g., race, gender, religion) is so large that it would be impractical to study all of them. There is not even sufficient knowledge at this point to guide selection of the most potentially important combinations (Steketee & Chambless, 1992). Further, even if good and bad matches were discovered, we are not convinced that professional therapists would necessarily tailor their practices to conform to the recommended matches given the financial implications of turning away some types of clients.

The Therapeutic Relationship

The uniqueness of psychotherapy stems not from its cast of characters, but from the special relationship that develops between therapist and client. What are the characteristics that make the therapeutic relationship unique?

First, the relationship is one in which both parties should be aware of why they are there and what the rules and goals of their interaction should be. The relationship should be a voluntary one initiated by the client and accepted by the therapist.[1]

Psychotherapy often begins with a therapeutic contract that specifies the goals of treatment, the procedures to be employed, the potential risks, and the individual responsibilities of client and therapist. In many instances the contract is negotiated informally, with both parties providing information about what they expect therapy to accomplish. In other instances the contract takes the form of a signed document, which states the obligations of each participant. In either case, contracts should help the therapeutic relationship become one in which clients are active decision makers, not passive recipients of help (Blau, 1988; Orlinsky & Howard, 1986).

Although the therapist may be friendly and sympathetic, the therapeutic relationship involves more than compassion (Waterhouse & Strupp, 1984). Therapy sometimes requires the clinician to be an objective assessor of clients and at other times an insistent observer who helps clients overcome their own resistances. Therapists give psychological support even when they challenge clients to give up old ways of behaving in exchange for new, more adaptive behaviors.

The intensity of the therapeutic relationship may tempt the therapist to discard a professional orientation toward clients in favor of more spontaneous, "natural" reactions such as sexual attraction, pity, frustration, hostility, and boredom. Most therapists try to stay alert to the way in which their personal needs intrude upon therapy. Learning to detect these needs and deal with them are major reasons why some therapists undergo therapy themselves. The ethical obligations of psycholo-

---

[1]In many cases the client is not a voluntary participant. A client sometimes enters therapy when someone (a parent, judge, or spouse) becomes distressed by the client's behavior and compels the individual to seek help. Therapy may proceed very differently and is usually less effective when the client is not a voluntary participant.

gists, which are discussed more fully in Chapter 14, require them to avoid any romantic involvement with their current clients.

The therapist attempts to form an attentive relationship with the client without losing sight of the fact that the relationship must advance the client's attempt to change. The therapeutic relationship requires a "balance of attachment and detachment" (Korchin, 1976). With some clients, a therapeutic relationship develops easily; with others, the "capacity for collaboration" is lacking and therapy suffers as a result (Strupp & Hadley, 1979).

The relationship between client and therapist imposes several commitments on the therapist's part that function to insulate the relationship from the heat of outside forces. Confidentiality is the most essential of these commitments. The therapist protects the client's privacy and does not reveal information that the client shares in therapy. In addition, therapists are obligated to regard the welfare of their clients as their main priority.[2] With very few exceptions, the therapist's actions must be directed by a singular concern: "What is best for my client?"

How can a therapist nurture the therapeutic bond? What qualities on the part of a client promote a positive alliance with a therapist? These questions have been studied extensively and, in general, the research suggests that therapeutic relationships flourish when both parties are capable of bringing three elements to their relationship (Orlinsky & Howard, 1986): *role investment* (the personal effort both parties commit to therapy), *empathic resonance* (the degree to which both parties are "on the same wavelength"), and *mutual affirmation* (the extent to which both parties care for each other's well-being).

Strupp (1989, p. 723) provides the following eloquent recipe for therapists' contributions to the therapeutic relationship:

> Patients reasonably expect a therapist to be human—keenly attentive, interested, caring, respectful, and empathic. His or her manner should be natural and unstudied; there should be a willingness to respond to patients' questions and concerns; a therapist should never criticize, never diminish the patient's self-esteem and self-worth, and should leave no doubt about his or her commitment and willingness to help. There may be occasions when reassurance and even advice are appropriate. The patient should never feel that he or she is "just another patient." The therapeutic relationship should be experienced as a "real" relationship rather than an artificial or contrived one. This should be possible even though its "professional" aspects are observed. A good therapist should obviously refrain from fueling power struggles or reciprocating angry provocations. The therapist's language should be simple, straightforward, and understandable. The patient should feel that the therapist understands his or her feelings, at least a good part of the time.

The Techniques of Psychotherapy

There are dozens of psychotherapeutic techniques. Every system of psychotherapy has its preferred procedures, and every therapist has a unique style of employing those procedures. The therapist's methods are usually based on some formal theory of personality and psychopathology in general and the client's problem in particular (see Chapter 2). Although therapists remain flexible, their therapeutic methods are usually guided by personal preferences and the general principles which they believe underlie effective treatment. These general principles should be grounded in empirical research, but too many therapists employ methods whose effectiveness is not well supported.

---

[2]There are, of course, some exceptions. See Chapter 14 for a fuller discussion of situations that compel the psychologist to break confidentiality.

Psychotherapeutic approaches differ in the extent to which their theories of personality and disorder are related to specific techniques. For example, psychoanalysts have developed a complex theory of personality but are less specific about what procedures should be used in applying this theory to a given case. Many behavior theorists, on the other hand, specify in great detail the procedures to be employed in treatment.

Treatment approaches also vary in terms of the changes they are designed to produce (Andrews, 1989; Messer & Winokur, 1980). (Refer again to the case of Mr. A., in Chapter 2.) Behavior therapists are likely to deal directly with the problem as the client initially presents it (along with other difficulties that might contribute to the primary complaint). For example, a mother who reports depression and fears that she will kill her children might be assigned a variety of "homework assignments" involving her relationship with her husband, disciplinary methods for her children, or the development of new, out-of-the-house activities for herself. By contrast, the psychoanalyst would work on underlying causes of the mother's depression. Therapy might be aimed at helping the woman understand how her current symptoms are due to feelings of inadequacy as a mother because of failure to meet her own mother's rigid and unrealistic standards. Finally, a phenomenological therapist might deal with the problem by helping the mother discover her potential for creating alternatives that would free her from the one-sided way of life in which she now feels trapped.

Notwithstanding these theoretical differences, several techniques are common to most therapeutic approaches. These so-called common factors are mostly psychological in nature. They may take different forms when implemented by individual therapists, but they are similar enough to be seen as common strategies. In addition, they are all delivered in the context of a special relationship which is believed to enhance their effectiveness (Grencavage & Norcross, 1990). We now describe a few of these common-factor techniques of psychotherapy.

1. Fostering Insight. Insight into psychological problems was a chief objective of Freud, who described it as "re-education in overcoming internal resistances" (Freud, 1904, p. 73). While Freud was interested in a particular type of insight—analysis of unconscious influences—most therapists aim for insight in the general sense of greater self-knowledge. Clients are expected to benefit from learning why they behave in certain ways, because such knowledge is presumed to contribute to new behavior. The psychotherapist's rationale for fostering a client's insight is like the well-known justification for studying history: to know the errors of the past in order to avoid repeating them in the future.

Therapists of all theoretical persuasions seek to promote self-examination and self-knowledge in their clients. There are numerous approaches to this goal. Some procedures deal with a specific type of content; dream analysis would be an example. Other therapists try to promote insight by asking their clients to examine the implications of certain behaviors (e.g., "What relationship do you see between your troubles with your boss and the dislike you express for your father?"). Behavior therapists stress the importance of helping the client understand how behavior is functionally related to past learning and current environmental factors.

A common technique for developing insight is for the therapist to *interpret* the client's behavior. The purpose of interpretation is not to convince clients that the therapist is right about the significance of some event, but to motivate them to examine carefully their own behavior and draw new conclusions about its meaning. Interpretation comes in many forms, as Jerome Frank (1973) noted in his influential book, *Persuasion and Healing:*

The simplest form of interpretation consists of repeating something the patient has said, perhaps with some change in emphasis, so that he becomes more clearly aware of it. In a roughly ascending scale of degree of inference and amount of complexity, other forms of interpretation are summarizing, in order to coordinate and emphasize certain aspects, verbalizing the feelings that seem to lie behind the patient's utterances, and confronting him sharply with attitudes implied by his statements that he had not recognized. Complex interpretations may indicate similarities between a patient's feelings toward important contemporaries, including the therapist. They may also suggest symbolic meanings of his statements or link them to a theoretical scheme. (pp. 222–223)

Although interpretation remains a mainstay technique of many psychotherapists (Crits-Christoph, Cooper, & Luborsky, 1988), some clinicians caution against the dangers of interpretations that are too confrontive or challenging (Strupp, 1989). Particularly when working with very disturbed clients, therapists who minimize their use of interpretation in favor of being actively supportive, emotionally soothing, and directly reassuring tend to achieve the best outcomes (Jones, Cumming, & Horowitz, 1988). Conversely, less-disturbed clients benefit more from therapy experiences in which the therapist interprets connections between their behavior in therapy with their relationships outside of therapy (Jones et al., 1988).

2. Reducing Emotional Discomfort. Clients sometimes come to a therapist in such emotional anguish it is difficult for them to participate actively in therapy. In such instances, the therapist will try to reduce the client's distress enough to allow the person to begin working on the problem. Therapists do not strive to eliminate all discomfort; in so doing, they might also eliminate motivation for working toward more lasting change. The challenge is to diminish extreme distress without sapping the client's desire to deal with enduring problems.

A common method for reducing client discomfort is to use the therapeutic relationship to boost the client's emotional strength. Clients

gain emotional stability and renewed confidence by knowing that the therapist is a personal ally, a buffer against the onslaughts of a hostile world. Some therapists offer direct reassurances like "I know things seem almost hopeless right now, but I think you will be able to make some important changes in your life."

3. Encouraging Catharsis. Clients are usually encouraged to express emotions freely in the protective presence of the therapist. This technique is known as *catharsis,* and involves the release of pent-up emotions that the client has not acknowledged for a long time, if ever. The therapist encourages the client to give voice to those emotions, believing that through their release they will be eased. At the least, catharsis may help the client become less frightened of certain emotions.

Although therapists have always been concerned with their clients' emotional experiences, empirical research on the value of emotion-focused techniques has been slower to accumulate. Recent research points to the value of emotion-focused interventions in at least five areas (Greenberg & Safran, 1989): (a) synthesizing or getting in touch with emotions so they can be understood and expressed in acceptable, even constructive ways; (b) intensifying certain emotions, often through nonverbal, expressive methods, so they can instigate useful behavior; (c) restructuring emotions by giving new information that allows emotions to be modified in desired directions; (d) evoking emotions so that thoughts and behaviors strongly and specifically bound up with these emotions can be reexamined; and (e) modifying directly those emotions that have become so maladaptive that the client's functioning is impaired.

4. Providing New Information. Psychotherapy is often educational. The therapist provides new information to correct gaps or distortions in a client's knowledge. Certain areas of adjustment are plagued by misinformation, sexual functioning being a notable example.

All therapists attribute considerable importance to the therapeutic relationship and work carefully to establish a good one. In general, therapists of all theoretical stripes believe that a helping alliance between client and therapist is formed when the therapist responds with consistent empathy to the needs of the client. When an accepting atmosphere is provided by the therapist, the client will be able to feel securely attached to another person (perhaps in a manner not previously experienced), will have a model for clear interpersonal communication, and will feel strong enough to attempt new solutions to old personal problems. Beyond these general goals, the different schools of psychotherapy have specific views of the ideal therapeutic relationship and the role it plays in therapy.

Phenomenologically oriented therapists regard the therapeutic relationship as the essential element in therapy. Carl Rogers, the founder of client-centered therapy, took the position that the client–therapist relationship was the crucible in which all the necessary and sufficient ingredients for therapeutic change were generated. According to Rogers (1951):

> The process of therapy is . . . synonymous with the experiential relationship between client and therapist. Therapy consists in experiencing the self in a wide range of ways in an emotionally meaningful relationship with the therapist. The words—of either client or counselor—are seen as having minimal importance compared with the present emotional relationship which exists between the two. (pp. 172–173)

In classical psychoanalysis, the relationship between client and therapist is a means to the goal of insight. The therapist–client relationship is an instrument for achieving a specific purpose, which is to show the client how his or her present behavior is determined by experiences in earlier periods of life. Psychoanalysts speak of the *transference relationship,* or simply *transference* to refer to the fact that after a period of therapy the client begins to attach to the therapist the friendly, hostile, and ambivalent attitudes and feelings the client formerly felt in relationship to parents or other significant persons. As a consequence, the original conflicts of early familial relationships are repeated in relation to the therapist. To encourage transference, the analyst remains a passive and detached figure. In psychoanalysis, the relationship is not as typically human as it is for the Rogerian therapist. The analyst's detachment is a strategic calm, a studied technique for encouraging transference. The following bits of advice from Freud reveal his view of the therapeutic relationship:

BOX 7–1

Four Views of the Therapeutic Relationship

Some therapists offer direct advice to their clients, adopting a teacherlike role. Others suggest reading material about a topic, a process known as *bibliotherapy* (Marx, Gyorky, Royalty, & Stern, 1992). Still others rely on more indirect maneuvers—a shrug of the shoulder or a skeptical facial expression—to suggest to clients that there are other ways of perceiving the world. New information gives clients an added perspective on their

I cannot recommend my colleagues emphatically enough to take as a model in psychoanalytic treatment the surgeon who puts aside all his own feelings, including that of human sympathy, and concentrates his mind on one single purpose, that of performing the operation as skillfully as possible. (Freud, 1912, p. 121)

The analytic technique requires the physician to deny the patient who is longing for love the satisfaction she craves. The treatment must be carried through in a state of abstinence; I do not mean merely corporal abstinence, nor yet deprivation of everything desired, for this could perhaps not be tolerated by any sick person. But I would state as a fundamental principle that the patient's desire and longing are to be allowed to remain, to serve as driving forces for the work and for the changes to be wrought. (Freud, 1915, p. 173)

Modern-day psychoanalysts are likely to take a more humanistic view of the therapist–client relationship than Freud did. They recommend that the analyst not be so detached or neutral about the client's human needs that the client comes to lose faith in the analyst as a helper. In this view the therapeutic relationship can offer clients a second chance to correct interpersonal problems that linger from the past.

Interpersonal therapists regard the therapeutic relationship as the means by which the client can learn alternative styles of interacting with other people that are more productive and satisfying than the narrow, one-sided security maneuvers in which the client has become entrenched. This view of the relationship requires the therapist to be active in assessing and evoking specific types of interpersonal behavior, reacting to it in prescribed ways, and monitoring the effects of his or her own interpersonal style on clients. Because of these requirements, interpersonal therapists take a more provocative, strategic approach to the therapeutic relationship than do other therapists.

Behavior therapists tend to view the therapy relationship as an important but not sufficient condition of therapy (Sweet, 1984). It is seen as a useful context in which more specific behavior-change techniques are introduced. Alan Goldstein (1973) reveals a typical behavioral view that a good relationship is an important preface to subsequent and more vital techniques.

In most cases, it is required that an atmosphere of trust be established if any therapeutic intervention is to be effective. This usually is accomplished quickly by the therapist through his establishing that (1) he understands and accepts the patient, (2) that the two of them are working together, (3) and that the therapist has at his disposal the means to be of help in the direction desired by the patient. (Goldstein, 1973, p. 221)

BOX 7–1
Continued

problems that makes them seem less unusual as well as more solvable.

5. Assigning Extratherapy Tasks. Therapists often ask clients to perform tasks outside of therapy for the purpose of encouraging the transfer of positive changes to the "real world." This is known as therapy "homework." Harper (1959) describes homework as follows:

One paradox of the proliferation of psychotherapeutic approaches is that the majority of therapists pledge allegiance to no single system, preferring instead to select from several theoretical models the one approach that best fits a given client. This orientation is known as eclecticism or *eclectic psychotherapy*. Eclectics do not consider themselves to be anti- or atheoretical clinicians who simply reach into a grab bag and yank out a technique. Their choice of techniques is a principled one, based on the exigencies of each individual case rather than on the dictates of a general theoretical system. Increasingly, the term *integrationism* is being used to describe a style of psychotherapy that draws on the combined and complementary wisdom of different theoretical approaches.

In one survey (Garfield & Kurtz, 1976), the majority of clinicians contacted identified themselves as eclectics, and in almost all other surveys of clinicians, the eclectic approach to therapy is the most popular choice (Norcross, Prochaska, & Gallagher, 1989b). There is also an *International Journal of Eclectic Psychotherapy* and a Society for the Exploration of Psychotherapy Integration, two more indicators that integrationism is thriving among today's clinicians. As a result any investigation of psychotherapy that concentrates on specific theoretical orientations is studying a minority of those engaged in the practice of psychotherapy.

Because it is not a school of psychotherapy, eclecticism has not attracted a large number of vocal adherents, nor has it been popularized by many famous founders. Frederick Thorne (1967, 1973) is a well-known advocate of an eclectic approach, and even he appears to be a somewhat reluctant spokesman: "Eclecticism carries with it none of the special advantages of uniqueness, newness or proprietorship of special knowledge implicit in the special schools whose adherents often turn such attributes to personal advantage" (Thorne, 1973, p. 449). Other champions of eclecticism are James Prochaska, who has attempted to identify the common therapy processes in any effective psychotherapy (Prochaska & DiClemente, 1984), and Arnold Lazarus (1981), whose therapy approach we discuss more thoroughly in Chapter 9.

What combination of general strategies or specific techniques are integrated into an eclectic psychotherapy package? In a recent national survey of psychotherapists (Jensen, Bergin, & Greaves, 1990), 68% of the respondents were classified as eclectic, the highest percentage of any survey conducted on this question in 30 years. Among those eclectic therapists surveyed by Jensen et al. (1990), 72% reported using psychodynamic principles within their version of eclectic therapy, 54% reported cognitive approaches, and 45% reported using behavioral methods as part of their eclecticism. Blends including humanistic approaches were the fourth most likely combination. Eclectic therapy therefore does not come in only one form; there are analytic eclectics and behavioral eclectics and humanistic eclectics. Eclectic psychotherapy is a diverse orientation that embraces many different combinations that have yet to be carefully compared or studied.

BOX 7–2
Eclectic Psychotherapy

The therapist and the patient agree on certain actions (based on the patient's changed conceptions of himself and his environment) with which he is to experiment between one psychotherapeutic session and the next. The patient reports on his successes and failures regarding these attempted changes in his behavior, and then he and the therapist make plans for additional changes. As the patient experiences gratification from successful accomplishments in new modes of behavior, his self-esteem grows. This, in turn, enables him to execute still more improvements in his behavior.

Behavior therapists are enthusiastic advocates of homework assignments, believing them to be an effective way to promote the generalization of new skills learned in the therapist's office.

6. Developing Faith, Hope, and Expectancy for Change.

Of all the procedures common to different systems of therapy, raising clients' faith and expectancy for change is the ingredient most frequently mentioned as a crucial contributor to therapeutic improvement. In fact, many scholars attribute the success of psychotherapy not to specific techniques, but to its ability to arouse clients' belief that they can be helped. The curative power of faith is not restricted to psychotherapy. The effects are well known in medicine; the "history of medical treatment can be characterized largely as the history of the placebo effect" (Shapiro, 1971, p. 442). Some therapy techniques may be particularly potent in motivating these beliefs because they appear dramatic or technical or because they tap into ingrained cultural norms associated with the best ways to achieve personal change.

Clinicians are so accustomed to thinking about placebo effects in psychotherapy that they have coined additional terms to designate their influence. The most popular of these have been *demand characteristics* (Orne, 1962), *common factors* (Critelli & Neuman, 1984), and *expectancies* (Wilkins, 1979). These designations refer to various aspects of the same theme: Psychotherapy achieves its successes, in part, because of its capacity to generate clients' expectancy for improvement.

Frank (1973) equated expectancy for improvement with such concepts as optimism, hope, and faith, all of which involve "the perceived probability of achieving a goal" (p. 136). An emphasis on placebo effects in psychotherapy does not eliminate the importance of the specific techniques that distinguish one therapeutic approach from another. It does mean, however, that one important element (some might say the *most* important element) of any effective therapy is that it causes clients to believe that positive changes are attainable (Wilkins, 1984).

Part art and part science, psychotherapy profits from the mystique that surrounds both fields. Clients often begin psychotherapy with the belief that they are about to engage in a unique, powerful experience conducted by an expert who can work miracles. The perceived potency of psychotherapy is further enhanced by the fact that clients usually begin therapy after having fretted for a long time about whether they really need treatment. By the time this internal debate is resolved, the client has a large emotional investment in making the most of a treatment that is regarded with a mixture of fear, hope, and relief.

For their part, therapists attempt to maximize the client's faith in the power of psychotherapy, providing assurance that she or he understands the problem and is confident that, by working together, they will be able to achieve desired changes. The perception by a client that "I have been heard and understood and can be helped" can be as important as the soothing effect a physician produces when he or she conveys a calm attitude about the mysterious physical symptoms you have been experiencing. The procedures that encourage this perception are embodied in the general techniques already described—the formation of a therapeutic relationship, interpretations, catharsis, and the alleviation of emotional panic. Most therapists also offer a *rationale* for why psychotherapy will be effective. In place of the client's uncertainty about what therapy will involve, the therapist structures the experience so that the client understands why beneficial change should occur.

Having structured therapy to increase the client's motivation and expectancies for treatment, the therapist attempts to ensure that the client experiences early success. The success might be a small one—a minor insight after a simple interpretation by the therapist or the successful completion of a not-too-difficult homework assignment. Whatever the means, the objective is to bring about the kind of change the client expects.

There is a cumulative impact to the small changes in the initial stages of therapy. Clients begin to believe that they can control their lives and that their problems are understandable. A sense of despair begins to be replaced by a growing feeling of capability as the client glimpses the possibility of a new self-image.

Expectancies can exert a circular effect. At the beginning of therapy, the client's faith in treatment is strengthened to the point that he or she believes improvement is possible. When changes, regardless of their magnitude, are experienced, the client's expectancies are confirmed and they grow. As a result, the client believes that more meaningful changes can be attained, and she or he pursues them with reinforced expectations. Meanwhile, the therapist can enhance the client's self-esteem by pointing out that changes are the result of the client's own effort (Bandura, 1982).

Returning now to the question "What is psychotherapy?" our answer emphasizes the following:

1. Psychotherapy consists of a relationship between at least two participants, one of whom has special training and expertise in handling psychological problems and one of whom is experiencing a problem in adjustment and

has entered the relationship to alleviate this problem.

2. The psychotherapeutic relationship is a nurturant but purposeful alliance in which several methods, largely psychological in nature, are employed to bring about the changes desired by the client.

3. These methods are based on some theory regarding psychological problems in general and the specific complaint of the client in particular.

4. Regardless of theoretical preferences, most therapists employ several of the following techniques: fostering insight, reducing emotional discomfort, encouraging catharsis, providing new information, assigning extra-therapy tasks, and raising clients' expectancy for change.

MODES OF THERAPY

So far, we have described psychotherapy in its most popular mode—individual, or one-to-one, treatment. This classic arrangement forms the backbone of most clinical treatment. However, therapy is also undertaken with *groups* of clients. These groups may consist of unrelated individuals or may be composed of family members. In the former case, the treatment is usually called *group therapy;* in the latter, it is called *marital* or *family therapy.*

Group Therapy

Group therapy is more than simultaneous therapy for several individuals. First practiced at the turn of the 20th century in Boston by Joseph Pratt, and later stimulated by the shortage of professional personnel around World War II, group therapy has progressed to the point that it is now regarded as a valuable intervention in its own right (Klein, 1983).

Every major model of clinical psychology offers group treatment. There are analytic groups, client-centered groups, transactional analysis groups, encounter groups, gestalt groups, and behavioral groups. Groups are also popular with many nonprofessional self-help organizations (Jacobs & Goodman, 1989). Weight-control groups, assertiveness groups, consciousness-raising groups, and Alcoholics Anonymous are common examples. Certain groups assume a special identity because of one idiosyncratic quality. Marathon groups which run for long, uninterrupted periods of time provide a good illustration.

This wide range of theory and practice makes it difficult to talk about any uniform process of group therapy. However, most group therapists emphasize the importance of interpersonal relationships and assume that personal maladjustment involves difficulties in interpersonal relations. Like individual psychotherapy, many forms of group therapy share common curative factors. Some of these factors are similar to those found in one-to-one treatment, but most of them are unique to groups. A full discussion of the curative factors in group therapy is contained in Yalom's (1985) authoritative text, *The Theory and Practice of Group Psychotherapy*. In summary, these factors include the following:

1. Sharing New Information. New information is imparted from two sources in groups: The group leader may offer advice, and direct advice also comes from other members of the group who share their own experiences from the past. The multiple perspectives of the group constitute a richer store of information than would usually be the case with a single therapist. A major feature of group information and feedback is its *consensuality*. The impact of new information is magnified by the agreement on which it is based. While it may be tempting to discount feedback from one therapist, it becomes more difficult to dismiss the similar opinions of 8 or 10 observers as biased or inaccurate. In numbers there is strength, especially when the numbers all agree.

2. Instilling Hope. As with individual psychotherapy, confidence in the therapist and an expectancy that treatment can be helpful are important features of groups. Group therapy can be introduced with a rationale that buoys the hope of new members, but there are also special features of groups that increase the positive expectancies of their members. One of these features is the opportunity for group members to observe positive changes in others. An individual client might become impatient about an exasperatingly slow pace of improvement. However, detecting positive changes in others may lead to the recognition that everyone grows at about the same pace; this may sustain faith in the group.

3. Universality. Groups dramatize that everyone struggles with problems in living. Group members learn that they are not alone in their fear or their disappointment. This discovery is important because many persons are secretive about their problems, which restricts their ability to find out they are not unique. As group members share their problems they derive comfort from knowing "there are others just like me." Learning about the universality of one's problems also soothes anxiety about "going crazy" or "losing control."

4. Altruism. Groups give clients a chance to find out they can help other people. Just as group therapy produces new insights into interpersonal weaknesses, it confirms the presence of interpersonal strengths. In addition to being clients, group therapy members serve as one another's therapists. Clinicians refer to the positive emotions that follow altruistic behavior as "feelings of self-worth," an outcome that should be promoted by effective group therapy.

5. Interpersonal Learning. When a group first forms, the interpersonal contacts between members are usually hesitant and guarded. As group members come to know one another, their contacts become more spontaneous and direct. A properly conducted therapy group is an ideal setting to learn new interpersonal skills. It presents repeated opportunities to practice fundamental social skills with different types of people and with immediate feedback on performance. Groups also contain numerous models for imitative learning, one of the most efficient ways to learn novel behaviors.

6. Recapitulation of the Primary Family. Some group therapists regard the therapy group as a "reincarnation" of clients' primary families. This *family reenactment* is thought to be a curative factor because it allows clients to deal with those early family experiences that still confuse their current functioning. Recapitulation of the family is group therapy's counterpart to the transference relationship in individual psychodynamic therapy. Yalom (1985) suggests that there is value in exploring past family "spirits" as long as the primary focus of the group remains in the here and now.

7. Group Cohesiveness. Cohesiveness is the "attractiveness of a group for its members" (Frank, 1957). Members of cohesive groups are accepting of one another; they are willing to listen to and be influenced by the group. They participate in the group readily, feel secure in it, and are relatively immune to outside disruption of the group's progress. Cohesive groups also permit the expression of hostility, provided such conflicts do not violate the norms of the group. Attendance is more reliable in cohesive groups, and premature termination of treatment is less of a problem (Yalom, 1985).

Group cohesiveness is often regarded as the most important of the curative factors. Yalom (1985) considers cohesiveness to be a "necessary precondition" for effective group treatment that enhances development of other curative factors. The *acceptance* that members receive from the group may counteract their own feelings of worthlessness. The *public es-*

teem of the group serves as a reference point that increases members' own *self-esteem* because groups tend to evaluate individual members more favorably than the individuals evaluate themselves. Group members, in turn, will try to change in order to confirm the group's impression. The effect is something like a *group fulfilling prophecy,* where members are motivated to not let the group down. Behaviors once thought by the individual to be impossible may be performed because of the group's supportive demand that they at least be attempted.

The Practice of Group Therapy

Group Composition. Therapy groups usually consist of 6 to 12 members. If a group is too small, the advantages of universality and cohesiveness may be jeopardized. With larger groups, feedback may become too mechanical and superficial. There may also be less sensitive exploration of others' viewpoints. Another problem with larger groups is that isolates (members who make infrequent contributions) are more likely.

An important question for the group leader is what type of client should be accepted into a group. Initial assessment of group candidates is often not as structured as one encounters in individual psychotherapy. Many group therapists exclude brain-damaged individuals or those who are paranoid, hypochondriacal, suicidal, extremely narcissistic, sociopathic, drug or alcohol addicted, or psychotic.

Group leaders disagree on whether groups should be *homogeneous,* consisting of members who are similar in age, sex, and type of problem, or *heterogeneous,* in which there is a mix of different types of clients. Heterogeneous groups are easier to form. They also have the advantage of exposing members to a wider range of people and perspectives. The major advantage of homogeneous groups is that they facilitate a more direct focus on symptom improvement. This emphasis is understandable, since the group's identity is

This brief excerpt describes the beginning of a group therapy session. This particular group follows a cognitive-behavioral orientation and therefore concentrates on helping its members improve their coping skills and interpersonal relationships.

The group consisted of five women and three men in their late 20s and 30s. All were unmarried or separated. This was the fifth session of the group designed to help singles cope more effectively with their unique stresses. As the group settled into places on the floor or on chairs, Harriet, the group therapist, welcomed them and asked each member to review what he or she had done throughout the week to complete the assignment of the previous week. One at a time, members described their social achievements, their success in coping with anxiety, and the frequency with which they used the relaxation exercise. Several also related unusually stressful situations they had experienced during the week.

After each had summarized her or his experiences, amid a great deal of praise and support from group members for achievements, Delores volunteered to describe in some detail her situation in which her ever-present feelings of helplessness were intensified. Her supervisor at her office, she stated, was always giving her instructions on the least little thing. "It was as if she thought I was stupid and, frankly, I'm beginning to believe it." The other members inquired as to the nature of her job, which was quite complicated. They noted that she did receive good feedback from her peers, who often consulted with her with various problems. She also noted that in a previous job no one gave her more than the briefest instructions, and she did fine. Charles wondered whether she couldn't conclude that there was a problem between her and her supervisor and not with her as a person. There was just no evidence that she was dumb in any way; in fact, she appeared to be uniquely qualified to do the job. The others agreed.

Delores said she guessed they were right, but she didn't know what to do about it, and it was making her miserable. She had thought about quitting, but it was in other ways a good job; and besides, she added, "good jobs were hard to get these days."

After careful questioning by the other clients in order to have a clear picture of what was going on, they then provided her with a number of strategies she could employ to deal with the situation and suggested what she could specifically say to herself and to her supervisor. She evaluated and selected several from among these for practice in the group (Rose & LeCroy, 1991).

BOX 7–3
An Example of Group Therapy

often defined by a common problem that motivated treatment.

Group Duration. How long does group therapy last? What is the length of the usual group session? Questions about time are important in group therapy because the quality of group interactions is influenced by the amount and the nature of time that members spend together.

Some groups, like old soldiers, never die. These groups function over long time periods, adding new members as old ones depart. Other groups last only a specific number of sessions. These groups may be open to new members, but more often they continue only with the initial participants.

Group sessions are typically longer than sessions of individual psychotherapy. Two hours is a common length. Group sessions are longer because it takes more time for eight clients to talk than for one. It also tends to take more time for a group to reach a meaningful level of dialogue.

Lengthy sessions are a defining characteristic of marathon groups. While there is no clear demarcation between marathon and other group approaches, it is generally assumed that a marathon session lasts from 6 to 48 hours or more. The rationale for marathon length is that as people become tired, they also become less defensive. As social facades erode, people are assumed to be more willing to express their true feelings. Little, if any, empirical evidence exists to justify this rationale; in fact, one might just as reasonably suggest that fatigue reduces motivation and makes one more hostile toward other members of the group.

The Group Therapist. The group therapist must walk a narrow line between exerting too much control over the group and allowing it to run free without a focus. The effective group therapist is a first among equals who is responsible for keeping the group on course. The group therapist usually assumes the role of a guide who steers the group process in constructive directions and prevents individual members from getting lost or becoming disruptive along the way.

Marital and Family Therapy

Marital and family discord are two of the most common problems encountered by clinical psychologists. More than one of every three marriages ends in divorce. The tragedy of family breakdowns is revealed by frightening increases in rates of child abuse, adolescent suicide, runaways, substance abuse within families, and parental desertion. A burgeoning professional literature on the theory and treatment of disturbed families and marriages has appeared (Gurman, 1985; Gurman & Kniskern, 1981; Jacobson & Gurman, 1986; Lederer & Jackson, 1968; Minuchin, 1974; Satir, 1967); these topics are also discussed in Chapter 11.

Marital Therapy

In marital therapy the client is the marriage or the married couple. (Because of the changing nature of living arrangements in our culture, marital therapy is often called couples therapy in order to reflect the fact that it is intended for persons involved in long-term, intimate relationships, not just those who are legally married.) This treatment is also described as conjoint therapy, which means that both members of the couple see the same therapist(s) within the same sessions.

Marital therapy can be preceded, followed, or accompanied by individual psychotherapy for either or both of the spouses. Individual psychotherapy in addition to marital therapy is recommended when one member of the couple is suffering from a problem largely unrelated to the relationship.

In marital therapy the focus is on a *disturbed relationship*. This emphasis is different from working with a *disturbed individual in a relationship,* which would be a goal for individual psychotherapy. The need for marital therapy usually arises out of the conflicting expectations and needs of the couple. A wife who was initially attracted to her husband because of his dashing charm and playboy image now finds these qualities to be obstacles to the emotional security she currently needs from their relationship. A husband comes to feel that what he once admired as spunkiness in his wife is now a threat to his dominance in the marriage. Intimate relationships are frequently beset by problems in the areas of sexual satisfaction, personal autonomy, dominance–

submission, responsibility for child rearing, communication, intimacy, money management, fidelity, and the expression of disagreement and hostility. The goals and techniques of marital therapy depend on which of these conflicts is the most pressing for any given couple. Although the theoretical orientation of marital therapists will influence their choice of procedures, the differences between practitioners of marital therapy are probably smaller than those that exist between the same people practicing their version of individual psychotherapy.

A common theme among marital therapists is their emphasis on *problem solving*. Problem solving involves teaching the couple how to solve their own problems more constructively. It does not mean that the therapist solves the couple's problems for them or even that the therapist advises the couple how to solve their problems. The therapist's task is to facilitate the couple's working together so that they can learn new ways to handle the inevitable problems of a close relationship. The touchstone of problem solving is teaching the couple how to communicate and negotiate more effectively with each other. Improving communications is such a basic ingredient in couple therapy that it runs the risk of becoming a cliché; yet its role in marital therapy is central.

Working with communication involves changing not only the way a couple talks to each other but also how they think about their relationship (Baucom, Epstein, Sayers, & Sher, 1989). When there is a problem in a relationship, the couple often becomes preoccupied with deciding whose fault it is. They devote their energies to blaming each other, to thinking about the past, to stating demands in a way that ensures they will not be met, and, finally, to withdrawing and avoiding one another. Among the multiple tasks of improved communications are teaching the couple to accept mutual responsibility for working on problems, maintaining focus on the here and now of their relationship, fostering expression of preferences rather than demands for obedience,

and negotiating compromises to problems the couple had decided couldn't be solved.

Regardless of their theoretical orientation, most marital therapists attempt to help distressed couples improve their ability to collaborate in solving problems. The following brief excerpt, from a book on marital therapy by Ables and Brandsma (1977), illustrates an attempt by the therapist (T) to help a wife (W) learn new ways of communicating some of her negative feelings to her husband:

T: I do think that what Pete is saying is an important point. There are things that are going to be different about you and each of you is going to think the things you do maybe make more sense than the other person's, and that's probably going to be pretty much of a reality. You're not going to be able to change all those. You may not be able to change very many of them. And everybody is different. They have their own predilections to do things a certain way and again what's coming through from you is sort of like damning those and saying those are wrong; they're silly, they don't make sense, I don't understand them or whatever. You may not understand them but they are a reality of each of you. That's something you have to learn how to deal with in some way. Otherwise, you . . . the reason I'm stressing this is I think it plays a large part in your criticalness.

W: Well, I do find it difficult to cater to, I guess that's the word, cater to some idiosyncrasies that I find or think are totally foolish. I am intolerant. I am, and I find it very difficult. I find it almost impossible to do it agreeably and without coming on as "Oh, you're ridiculous."

T: I guess what would be helpful would be if you could come on honestly enough to say "I don't like them" or "It doesn't sit well with me" without having to add the additional value judgment of whether they're foolish or ridiculous or whatever. That's the part that hurts. It's when you damn him because of these things—that's gonna hurt. I'm sure from Pete's point of view they make sense for his total economy of functioning. There's some sense to why he does things the way he does, just as there is for why you do things the way you do. It's not that they're foolish. They make sense in terms of where you are, what you're struggling with, and what's the best way you can deal with right now. I'm not trying to say that means you have to like them, but when you come across and say "It's ridiculous or foolish"—that's the part that makes it hurt.

W: Well, tell me again how to say it, because I find it hard to say anything except "That's really stupid—that's silly." I know you said it a minute ago but I lost it.

T: Well, anytime you can say it in terms of how it affects you and say with it, like "It's hard—I find it hard to take," that doesn't say "I find you're an ass for wanting to do that such and such a way. It's just that, I find it hard to take—I get upset in this circumstance" or whatever. Stay with what your feelings are rather than trying to evaluate Pete. (pp. 92–94)

Family Therapy

Although similar in some respects, marital therapy and family therapy evolved for different reasons. Marital therapy was the natural outgrowth of the fact that many clients complained of marital problems. The roots of family therapy stem from the fact that individuals who made large improvements during individual therapy or institutional treatment often had a relapse when they returned to their families. This observation, along with other clinical insights and research, led to several early theories of psychopathology that emphasized the family environment and parent-child interactions as causes of maladaptive behavior (Bateson, Jackson, Haley, & Weakland, 1956; Lidz & Lidz, 1949; Sullivan, 1953). In addition, the basic concepts of family therapy differ from those of individual psychotherapy. Family

therapy is grounded in systems theory (von Bertalanffy, 1968), which includes the principles of (a) circular causality—events are interrelated and mutually dependent rather than fixed in a simple cause–effect sequence; (b) ecology—systems can only be understood as integrated patterns, not component parts; and (c) subjectivity—there are no objective views of events, only subjective perceptions filtered by the experiences of perceivers in a system.

Family therapy can be defined as a psychotherapeutic focus on changing interactions between or among family members with the goal of improving the functioning of the family or the functioning of individual members of the family (Gurman, Kniskern, & Pinsof, 1986). Family therapy often begins with a focus on one member of the family who is having problems. Therapists speak of the identified client as the person in the family who has been singled out as the one with the problem. Typically, the identified client is a male child (often of adolescent age) whom the parents label as a behavior problem or as unmanageable. While family therapy may begin with a focus on this individual, the therapist will try to reframe the problem in terms of disturbed family processes or faulty family communication. The family therapist will encourage all family members to see their own contributions to the problem as well as the positive changes each member can make.

As with marital therapy, a common goal of family therapy is improved communications. Disturbed families often rely on coercion as their major means of communication (Patterson, 1982). The message from both parents and children is, "Do what I want or you'll be sorry." The therapist tries to teach family members noncoercive ways of communicating their needs. The therapist might also focus on teaching parents consistency in discipline, encouraging each member of the family to communicate clearly with one another, minimizing scapegoating of the identified client, and helping the family members examine the appropriateness of what they expect from the rest of the family.

Virginia Satir (1967), a well-known practitioner of family therapy, offers the following example of how the family therapist tries to help parents and children communicate better with one another. In the first example the therapist helps a parent understand her son and receive feedback from him.

MOTHER: His pleasure is doing things he knows will get me up in the air. Every minute he's in the house . . . constantly.

THERAPIST: There's no pleasure to that, my dear.

MOTHER: Well, there is to him.

THERAPIST: No, you can't see his thoughts. You can't get inside his skin. All you can talk about is what you see and hear. You can say it looks as though it's for pleasure.

MOTHER: All right. Well, it looks as though, and that's just what it looks like constantly.

THERAPIST: He could be trying to keep your attention, you know. It is very important to Johnny what Mother thinks.

The therapist also helps the child express frustration and anger and specify situations which precipitate anger:

THERAPIST: Do you kind of get mad at Daddy when he gets mad at you?

SON: Yeah, and sometimes he gets real mad and pinches my ear.

THERAPIST: He pinches your ear. Do you feel like hitting him back?

SON: Yeah, I get real mad sometimes.

THERAPIST: So what keeps you from hitting him?

SON: Well he's, uh, he's bigger than me. (pp. 151–152)

EVALUATION
OF THERAPEUTIC INTERVENTION

The evaluation of psychological treatment is a major concern for three different audiences. Each audience has its own values, which influence its definition of mental health and the criteria used to assess it (Strupp & Hadley, 1977). First, there is the client, who has an obvious interest in the success of an activity in which personal effort, time, and money have been invested. The client asks two questions of therapy: "Did it help me?" and "Was it worth the expense?" The second source of evaluation is the therapist, who needs to know if her or his efforts are worthwhile or if they need to be modified in some way. The final evaluative audience for psychotherapy is society, which means any third party having an interest in therapy's outcome. A third party can be a spouse, parent, friend, lover, teacher, judge—anyone who is concerned about the changes that psychotherapy produces in a client. Third parties can take on a cumulative quality; if we add together all the third parties with an interest in psychotherapy, we can speak of society in the traditional sense of an organized, cooperative social group concerned that psychotherapy produce desirable effects for the community at large. Third-party evaluation of psychotherapy provides an assessment independent of the participants in psychotherapy, whose judgments about effectiveness may be biased by their personal investments in the treatment.

Evaluating therapy is a dominant research activity in clinical psychology. For a long time the basic question posed by clinical researchers was: "Is psychotherapy effective?" Clinicians gradually discovered that this question was too broad to be answered meaningfully, and they abandoned it in favor of Paul's (1969a) famous reformulation: "What treatment, by whom, is most effective for this individual with that specific problem, under which set of circumstances, and how does it come about?" (p. 44). Kazdin (1982b) organized Paul's "ultimate question" into several possible research goals including (a) determine the efficacy of a specific treatment; (b) compare the relative effectiveness of different treatments; and (c) assess the individual components of treatment that are responsible for particular changes. Other important criteria for measuring the effects of psychotherapy include how durable or long-lasting the changes are, what negative side-effects are associated with the treatment, how acceptable the treatment is to a range of consumers, how efficient and cost-effective the treatment is, and how socially meaningful or useful are the improvements achieved (Kazdin & Wilson, 1978).

To answer these questions the psychotherapy researcher must design and conduct an evaluation in such a way that the results can be interpreted unambiguously. Deceptively easy to describe, this obligation is exasperatingly difficult to execute. It is impossible to perform an evaluation that yields completely unambiguous results for the simple reason that any human activity is a fallible effort. Despite this fallibility, researchers strive to conduct the best evaluations they can by evaluating psychotherapy through scientific experiments. A scientific experiment is a complex activity, the true meaning of which evokes heated debate among philosophers as well as scientists. We describe an experiment as *an attempt to discover the causes of specific events by making systematic changes in certain factors and then observing changes that occur in other factors.* Researchers call the factors they manipulate the *independent variables,* while the factors in which resulting changes are observed are termed the *dependent variables.*

In psychotherapy research there are two experimental strategies. One is called *within-subject* research; the other is known as *between-subject* research. Both approaches examine the effects of varying conditions (independent variables) on the performance of a participant or group of participants; however, each approach uses different methods.

Within-Subject Research

In within-subject designs, the comparisons are made on the same subjects at different points in time. The within-subject experiment requires that the dependent variables be measured on several occasions in sequence. The experiment is begun by observing the dependent measures before any independent variables are manipulated. This period is the *baseline;* it provides an estimate of the preintervention, or existing, level of the dependent measure. Following the baseline, the *intervention* phase of the experiment is introduced. In this phase the independent variable is manipulated by the experimenter, and the dependent measures are observed to detect any changes from their baseline levels. In evaluating the effects of psychotherapy, the baseline period would involve observing the client's behavior for several days before treatment was initiated. The intervention phase would correspond to the active treatment, during which regular assessments of the client's progress would be made.

Although there are several types of within-subject experimental designs (Hayes, 1983; Kazdin, 1982a), the two used in the majority of cases deserve special comment. The best-known of this pair is the *ABAB,* or *reversal,* design, in which the no-treatment baseline (A) is alternated with a treatment intervention (B). The length of each phase is determined by many factors, but usually each phase is continued until the client's behavior (the dependent measure) becomes relatively stable. If behavior changes reliably and substantially in conjunction with the sequential experimental phases, the experimenter gains confidence that treatment is responsible. An example of an ABAB evaluation of a clinical intervention is provided in Figure 7–1.

The other major within-subject approach is the *multiple-baseline* design, which evaluates an intervention without withdrawing treatment as in the reversal design. This is a major advantage, because there are clinical and ethical objections to interrupting treatment at arbitrary times. Multiple-baseline designs allow the researcher to observe simultaneously several dependent measures while applying the intervention to only one of them. In other

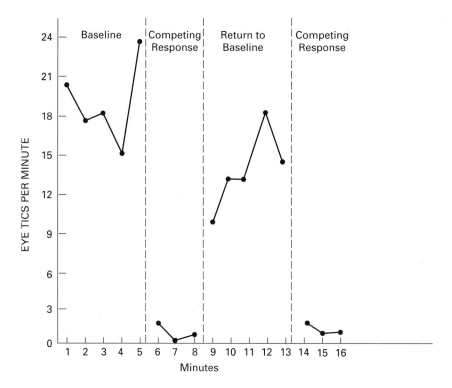

FIGURE 7-1 An example of a reversal or ABAB design. The client in this study was a 9-year old girl with a severe eye tic. The frequency of tics observed under the initial baseline declined dramatically when the intervention, consisting of teaching the girl to blink softly every 5 seconds as a competing response to the tic, was introduced. Notice that when the baseline condition was returned, the eye tics again increased. When the competing response intervention was resumed, eye tics decreased to low levels again. (From N. H. Azrin & A. L. Peterson, 1989, Reduction of an eye tic by controlled blinking. *Behavior Therapy, 20,* 467–473.)

words, baseline conditions are maintained for all dependent variables except one. This procedure is continued so that the treatment is applied to different variables, one at a time, while all other measures continue under baseline conditions. The experimenter gains confidence in the effects of a given treatment if a dependent measure changes only when the intervention is being applied to it. A cause-effect relationship is strengthened if this finding is repeated, or *replicated,* on each of the measures.

The need for different baselines can be filled in a number of ways. The experimenter can focus on several behaviors in the same individual, applying treatment to one behavior while the others remain at baseline. Imagine a study that evaluated the effects of social praise by hospital staff on the behavior of psychotic patients. In this hypothetical experiment, three behaviors are examined—grooming, attending occupational therapy, and socializing on the ward. The intervention (social praise) is introduced at different points in time for each behavior. Each "new" intervention begins on the day following the termination of the baseline phase for each behavior.

As Figure 7–2 shows, each behavior improved when, *and only when,* "its" intervention was introduced. The fact that each behavior changed only when social praise was given for it makes it unlikely that some other factor (e.g., the influence of other patients) could account for such a specific pattern of results.

Within-subject research can be done with a small number of subjects. In fact, the logic of within-subject designs permits the use of only one subject, in which case it is called "single subject" or "N = 1" research (Barlow & Hersen, 1984). "N = 1" research is a popular psychotherapy research strategy for several reasons. First, it permits the intensive study of clinical phenomena such as multiple personality that are too rare to allow large-group designs. Second, it encourages an integration of research and clinical practice because it gives clinicians a way to evaluate empirically the treatment they deliver to individual clients (Hayes, 1983). Third, it brings together process and outcome questions through its fine-grained study of how critical events in therapy are followed by particular changes in the client (Rice & Greenberg, 1984). The intensive study of how interactions, events, or sequences within a psychotherapy session are related to important changes in a client has become a major focus of psychotherapy research (Greenberg, 1986; Mahrer, 1988). One goal of this research is to discover *how* psychotherapy produces change in a client so that therapists can learn how to bring about more therapeutic "good moments" (Mahrer & Nadler, 1986) where clients show change or improvement. This type of discovery-oriented research is not tied to any one school of therapy. Therefore, its recommendations, derived primarily from empirical observations, should encourage more integrative tendencies among therapists with different theoretical leanings.

FIGURE 7–2   Data from a multiple-baseline design. (From A. E. Kazdin & S. A. Kopel, "On resolving ambiguities of the multiple baseline design: Problems and recommendations," *Behavior Therapy,* 1975, *6,* 601–608. © 1975 by Academic Press, New York. Reprinted by permission.)

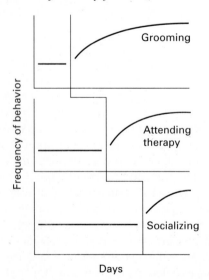

Between-Subject Research

Between-subject research compares groups of subjects that are exposed to different interventions. The simplest example of this approach is an experiment including an *experimental* group and a *control* group. Subjects are randomly assigned to the experimental group and are given some special experience (in psychotherapy research this would be treatment), while the control group subjects are left alone. Dependent measures are collected for both groups prior to the experiment (the *pretest*) and shortly after it is over (the *posttest*). These same measures may also be repeated at longer posttreatment intervals (a *follow-up*). Once the pretest equivalence of the experimental and control groups is established, differences between the groups, at either the posttest or follow-up, are attributed to the treatment that only the experimental group received.

One difference between within-subject and between-subject research is that in the latter case statistical analyses are usually used to assess the magnitude and *significance* of differences between treated and untreated subjects. A mean score and a measure of variability are computed for each group, and statistical tests are applied to determine whether the between-group differences are likely to have occurred by chance. In single-subject research, such statistics are usually not used because the researcher is more interested in demonstrating that the behavior of a subject is reliably related to manipulations of the independent variable. The single-subject researcher believes that statistics are not necessary to demonstrate such control; a person can look at a graph of the subjects' performance and see the differences. Within-subjects designs, involving a group of subjects as opposed to a single subject, often do rely on statistical techniques that measure the magnitude of change across time periods (Kraemer & Thiemann, 1989; Kratochwill, Mott, & Dodson, 1984).

Psychotherapy outcome research has progressed to the point where the two-group (experimental versus control) design is not adequate for the questions researchers now seek to answer. Even if large differences appear between a treatment and a no-treatment group, little is learned about the effects of psychotherapy except, perhaps, that it is more effective than doing nothing at all. This type of design cannot reveal whether treated subjects' improvement is due to specific therapeutic techniques, characteristics of the therapist, or the capacity of therapy to generate expectancy for improvement. This design is also unable to answer the question of whether the particular treatment tested would be more effective than some alternative approach.

One way of answering such questions is to build the factors of interest, along with the appropriate controls, into the experimental design. The advantage of such *factorial designs* is that they compare several factors that might be responsible for therapeutic change. Thus,

one group of subjects might receive a complete treatment package, while another gets only that part of treatment thought to be most important to its effectiveness. Another group might be exposed to procedures impressive enough to generate hope for improvement but not hypothesized to be helpful. A fourth group might get no treatment at all.

By comparing the results of all these groups, the experimenter begins to determine whether the complete treatment package is (a) better than no treatment, (b) better than what could be gained from placebo effects, and (c) better than a streamlined version of treatment. If another group of subjects had been given a completely different form of treatment, the experimenter could also compare the first approach with that alternative.

Between-subject research has been popular among psychotherapy researchers because it allows them to manipulate several variables simultaneously rather than sequentially, as required by within-subject designs. In addition, between-subject research allows the researcher to address questions for which within-subject designs are ill suited. It is difficult to evaluate whether a certain treatment is more effective with a specific type of client in a within-subject design because the same participants are involved in all the conditions of the experiment. In general, it is necessary to use between-group designs when the researcher wants to study selected aspects of a treatment and their unique contribution to therapeutic change. Between-subject designs are expensive, however; it usually takes many subjects and a large research staff to compose and treat the groups necessary for the statistical analyses used. In addition, between-subject designs are not as suitable for evaluating the effects a *sequence* of interventions has on clients. This type of question is better addressed by within-subject designs.

The major priority for both within-subject and between-subject designs is that they demonstrate *internal validity* (Cook & Campbell, 1979). Internal validity is the degree to which the design of an experiment allows one to be confident that the results are due to the specific factor(s) manipulated rather than to some unintended factor. In addition to internal validity, researchers also try to conduct experiments that have *external validity* (the results of a specific experiment can be generalized to other situations); *construct validity* (the effects of an independent variable are correctly attributed to the influential properties of the independent variable); and *statistical validity* (the relationship between the independent and dependent variables is analyzed with the correct statistical techniques using a sample of subjects that is large enough to allow any real relationship to be detected).

PRACTICAL PROBLEMS IN PSYCHOTHERAPY RESEARCH

Most researchers agree that the best way to assess the outcome of psychotherapy is to conduct research on actual therapy offered by trained clinicians to bona fide clients in real treatment settings. The ideal experimental study would be to select a large sample of clients seeking treatment for a certain problem, assign them randomly to different treatments and control conditions, use trained therapists, and measure outcome on several indices of therapeutic change collected by persons blind to the conditions under which clients had been treated. Unfortunately, this ideal is achieved so seldom as to be almost nonexistent in the outcome literature. One approximation is the outcome study of Sloane, Staples, Cristol, Yorkston, and Whipple (1975), which compared behavior therapy with psychoanalytically oriented therapy delivered by experienced therapists to 90 adult outpatients randomly assigned to one of the two treatments or to a waiting list control group. Despite its many admirable qualities, this study, whose conclusions are quite complicated (both treatment groups improved about equally by the end of treatment, but the control group also improved markedly during a follow-up period), has been criticized on several grounds (see Agras, Kazdin, & Wilson, 1979).

Obstacles to ideal psychotherapy evaluations are numerous (Kraemer, 1981). In most cases, the requirements of an adequate experimental design cannot be met in a real-life clinical context. For example, both clinical and ethical considerations prevent random assignment of clients to different treatment and control conditions. Few clients will tolerate being put into a no-treatment group simply for the sake of good science. For their part, therapists also are reluctant to allow clients to be assigned to conditions that have little probability of bringing about constructive changes. These problems are accompanied by a more basic impediment to research on psychotherapy: There are few clinical situations in which the researcher can obtain a sufficient number of clients who meet the criteria for inclusion. It is also almost impossible to control for external factors that may influence clients' behavior such as additional treatment, advice from friends, or major life changes.

Add to these obstacles the practical problems of enlisting experienced therapists to participate in a study, convincing agency administrators to invest resources in the research, preventing subjects from prematurely dropping out of the research, and collecting meaningful long-term outcome measures from clients, and you can sympathize with the psychotherapy researcher's sense of futility in conducting real-life evaluations of treatment outcome.

There are two approaches to solving these psychotherapy outcome research problems. One is for researchers to summon all their creativity and tenacity and conduct the best clinical research they can while at the same time recognizing that certain questions cannot be answered with certainty in a nonlaboratory study. The fine-grained study of psychotherapy's "good moments" is a strategy we have already described for conducting real-world psychotherapy research. One can also link treatment with the assessment of an individual client, develop a specific treatment formulation for each client, and then assess the therapy's effects for the client (Kazdin, 1993). This case-study model of research on psychotherapy (Persons, 1991) would increase the external validity of psychotherapy research, but it would make internal validity more difficult to achieve. Investigators can also conduct cooperative outcome studies in which they pool similar types of subjects from several clinical centers, thereby increasing the power of their research.

The other approach is to bring psychotherapy research questions into the laboratory. In doing so, the researcher "buys" the control afforded by the laboratory but sacrifices the realism inherent in actual clinical settings. This second approach, in which clinical variables are approximated in a controlled experimental setting, is called *analogue research*. Psychotherapy analogue research (a) allows control of extraneous variables that cannot be controlled in the clinic, (b) makes possible a greater number of participants, (c) permits replication of results, (d) allows selection of subjects and research personnel on several dimensions, and (e) allows variables such as the number and length of treatment sessions to be held constant for all subjects.

Analogue research should resemble actual clinical conditions as much as possible. To the extent that the analogy is a close one, the external validity of the research is enhanced.

There are four dimensions along which the similarity between clinical and analogue settings are assessed (Bernstein & Paul, 1971). The first is *subject characteristics* and *recruitment*. The degree to which an analogue experiment's results can be generalized to a clinical population depends on the extent to which the subjects are similar to clients who seek treatment.

The second dimension is the nature of the *target problem*. Certain target problems selected for analogue study, such as the fear of small animals or insects, bear such little resemblance to the personal anguish and problems of actual clients that they may distort our understanding of the potency of therapeutic techniques.

The third dimension of interest is *therapist characteristics*. In most analogues the "therapists" are graduate students in clinical psychology who have limited clinical experience. It is doubtful that they possess the general clinical skills and specific treatment techniques that ideally characterize the competent, practicing clinician.

The final dimension on which to compare clinical and analogue activities is the *treatment techniques* themselves. Most analogue treatments are standardized on several dimensions, which means that these dimensions are specified and held constant across all participants. Standardization is seldom encountered in psychotherapy. Instead, the intervention is tailored to the unique needs of each client. In many analogues, treatment techniques are simplified, altered, shortened, or even omitted. Such modifications may so change a technique that it misrepresents the clinical procedure it was intended to approximate.

Standardization of treatments for research purposes often takes the form of writing manuals that specify how a treatment should be conducted during a research study (Moncher & Prinz, 1991). *Manualization* of therapy has been accomplished for behavioral (Linehan, 1984), interpersonal (Safran & Segal, 1990), and psychoanalytic (Luborsky, 1984) treatments. Manuals provide comprehensive guides for conducting therapy from a specific theoretical point of view, but by themselves manuals will not guarantee that treatments will be conducted in a consistent manner.

Analogue designs pose a trade-off in research priorities. The gains in internal validity analogues provide must be balanced against the sacrifices in external validity they require. The objection is not to analogy per se. The objection is to *rigorless* analogy brought about by merely substituting the language of one domain for the terminology of another.

The ultimate outcome question ("What treatment, by whom, is most effective for this individual, with that specific problem, under which set of circumstances, and how does it come about?") cannot be answered in any single investigation. The maximum knowledge about therapy outcome, whether it be from an uncontrolled case study, a factorial experiment in a clinical setting, or an experimental analogue, is achieved by integrating individual investigations into a program of related studies. Paul (1969a) noted that

> All levels and approaches to the ultimate question may be expected to continue. It is to be hoped, however, that each approach will be seen in perspective, in its relationships both to other approaches and to the actual level of product obtained, so that future generations may view the field as a composition of "artisans" or "scientists," rather than as cultists bound by historical inheritance. (p. 61)

The Effectiveness of Psychotherapy

Although therapists have studied the outcomes of psychotherapy for many years, the modern era of outcome research began in 1952 when Hans J. Eysenck, a British psychologist, reviewed several studies and concluded that the recovery rate is about the same for patients who receive therapy as for those who do not. Eysenck argued that the rate of "spontaneous remission" (improvement within any special treatment) was 72% over 2 years compared to improvement rates of 44% for psychoanalysis and 64% for eclectic therapy (Eysenck, 1952). In later reviews, Eysenck (1966) evaluated more studies, persisted in his pessimism about the effectiveness of traditional therapy, but claimed that behavior therapy produced superior outcomes.

Eysenck's conclusions sparked heated debate among clinicians. Many critics attacked his thoroughness, fairness, and statistical analyses. Other reviewers surveyed the outcome literature and reached more optimistic opinions about the effectiveness of psychotherapy. For example, Bergin (1971) concluded that

"psychotherapy on the average has modestly positive effects" (p. 228), a belief he later amended to "clearly positive results" (Bergin & Lambert, 1978). Meltzoff and Kornreich (1970) reported that more than 80% of psychotherapy outcome studies produced positive results. Indeed, most reviewers have concluded that most forms of psychotherapy produce better outcomes than no treatment and that different types of therapy are equally effective with most clients (e.g., Lambert, Shapiro, & Bergin, 1986; Luborsky, Singer, & Luborsky, 1975; Stiles, Shapiro, & Elliott, 1986). Other reviewers have supported Eysenck's claim that traditional psychotherapy has not proven to be superior to no treatment, but that for several kinds of problems behavior therapy *is* effective (Kazdin & Wilson, 1978; Rachman & Wilson, 1980). Although there are many reasons for this disagreement, a major source of the problem has been that different reviewers use varying standards in (a) selecting the outcome studies they survey, (b) evaluating the quality of these studies, (c) interpreting the magnitude of therapy effects, and (d) combining the results of many studies into an integrated conclusion.

The traditional approach to summarizing outcome research has been the *narrative* or *box score* review.[3] Reviewers who use this method have been criticized for being subjective and unsystematic in the way they integrate research studies, causing inevitable disagreements. Another problem with narrative reviews is that the sheer number of outcome studies makes it difficult for reviewers to weigh properly the merits and results of each study.

An alternative to narrative reviews is *meta-analysis,* a quantitative technique for combining the results of many studies. Meta-analysis standardizes the outcomes of a large number of studies so they can be compared or com-

---

[3]In a box score review, the reviewer makes categorical judgments about whether a study yielded positive or negative results and then tallies the number of positive and negative outcomes.

bined (see Rosenthal, 1983, for discussion of various meta-analytic strategies). The first application of meta-analysis to psychotherapy research was the monumental effort of Smith, Glass, and Miller (1980), in which 475 psychotherapy outcome studies were analyzed.

Smith et al. (1980) evaluated therapy effectiveness by computing *effect sizes* for all the treatments used in all the studies. An effect size was defined as the treatment group mean on a dependent measure minus the control group mean on the same measure divided by the standard deviation of the control group. Thus, an effect size indicates how many standard deviations above or below the control group mean the average treated client falls. There can be as many effect sizes for a treatment as there are measures on which that treatment is evaluated, although there are statistical reasons why it might be better to derive just one average or composite effect size for each treatment evaluated (Hedges & Olkin, 1982).

On the basis of their meta-analysis, Smith et al. (1980) concluded the following:

1. The average effect size for psychotherapy was .85 standard deviations, which Glass and Kliegl (1983) interpreted as meaning that "the average person receiving psychotherapy was better off at the end of it than 80% of the persons who do not" (p. 29).

2. Only 9% of the effect sizes were negative, indicating that deterioration due to psychotherapy was not frequent.

3. Different types of therapy (behavioral versus insight oriented) were not associated with significantly larger effect sizes, leading to a conclusion that different therapies were about equally effective.

4. Larger effect sizes were related to (a) more reactive methods of measuring outcome, (b) allegiance of experimenters to the therapy they were evaluating, and (c) immediate versus follow-up evaluation of outcomes.

Following Smith et al. (1980), several other researchers performed meta-analyses using different statistical methods or applying the method to selected sets of studies (e.g., Andrews & Harvey, 1981; Landman & Dawes, 1982; Shapiro & Shapiro, 1982). In general, these analyses have confirmed the Smith et al. (1980) conclusion that psychotherapy is an effective intervention for several varieties of psychological disorder. In addition, this second generation of meta-analyses has led to additional conclusions about the effects of psychotherapy. Some important findings are summarized next.

1. In general, better-designed research studies yield larger estimates for the effectiveness of psychotherapy (Landman & Dawes, 1982).

2. The effects of psychotherapy are well maintained over time periods of 6 to 18 months (Nicholson & Berman, 1983). Despite fears that gains due to psychotherapy might be short lived, the overall evidence is more encouraging—client improvement appears to be fairly durable as measured in most outcome studies.

3. A small percentage of clients become worse after psychotherapy. The causes and course of deterioration or negative change are not well understood. In addition, about 10% of effect sizes in major meta-analytic studies of psychotherapy have been negative (Shapiro & Shapiro, 1982; Smith et al., 1980).

4. Although the consensus of most meta-analyses is that the school or brand of psychotherapy does not make a major difference in overall estimates of effectiveness, if there is any advantage it would go to cognitive and behavioral therapies. With certain kinds of specific target problems, cognitive and behavioral methods have shown a small but consistent advantage over other methods (see Lambert et al., 1986, pp. 165–171, for a discussion of the meta-analytic studies of this issue).

Despite its recent popularity, meta-analysis has been severely criticized (e.g., Eysenck, 1978; Wilson, 1985; Wilson & Rachman, 1983). Most objections fall into one of the following categories: (a) Meta-analysis is subject to the same biases and arbitrariness encountered in narrative reviews; that is, certain studies are omitted and others are combined into categories that may not be reliably defined; (b) meta-analysis involves an "apples-and-oranges" approach to evaluation (combining different treatments for varying purposes on a wide range of clients) that obscures important distinctions in treatments and outcomes; (c) meta-analysis pays insufficient attention to the research quality of individual studies of psychotherapy; and (d) meta-analysis is based on several statistical assumptions that, if violated, can invalidate the results of the analysis.

Each of these criticisms has been answered by proponents of meta-analysis who argue that (a) meta-analysis makes explicit the rules for selecting and combining studies (in narrative reviews, these rules are often not explicitly defined); (b) if one is interested in evaluating psychotherapy as a general intervention, combining different treatments is not an error (just as it is not an error to combine apples and oranges if one is evaluating fruit); (c) the research quality of individual studies can be coded and analyzed to determine if the quality of the studies is related to their effect sizes; and (d) corrections are available for remedying most of the statistical problems that can threaten a meta-analysis.

Clinical Significance

Many psychotherapy outcome studies focus on the following question: Does a specific treatment produce significantly larger effects than control conditions or other types of treatment? This is an important question, but it is not the only one with which clinician-researchers are concerned. A related and equally important question is whether psychotherapy produces outcomes of *clinical significance.*

Clinical significance can be defined as the extent to which treatment outcomes achieve *meaningful* change. Clinical significance involves measuring whether psychotherapy produces practically important improvements.

How one defines *meaningful* is no small problem. Kazdin (1982b) proposed two methods: (a) *subjective evaluation,* in which individuals who interact with the client or who are in a special position to judge changes evaluate whether those changes have led to important qualitative differences; and (b) *social or normative comparisons,* in which clients' behavior before and after treatment is compared to the behavior of nondisturbed, "normal" peers. Using this second method, one can quantitatively define clinical significance in terms of the standard deviation units that separate treated clients from the mean of some normative group (Jacobson & Truax, 1991; Kendall, 1984). This method uses the same logic as the meta-analysis of effect sizes. Quantitative social comparisons have been reported for treatments for impulsivity (Kendall & Zupan, 1981), depression (Nietzel, Russell, Hemmings, & Gretter, 1987), anxiety disorders (Nietzel & Trull, 1988), marital problems (Snyder & Wills, 1989), and schizophrenia (Hansen, St. Lawrence, & Christoff, 1985) (Figure 7–3).

COMMUNITY PSYCHOLOGY

Not all psychologists believe that psychotherapy (or couple therapy, group therapy, and family therapy) is the best intervention for psychological problems. Despite often being originally trained as clinicians, many psychologists have become convinced that different strategies based on a different model of human behavior are necessary to produce meaningful improvements in people's lives. These interventions and their accompanying theoretical principles are known as *community psychology.*

In the remainder of this chapter we acquaint you with the history, principles, and current status of community psychology. Although there are large differences between the community psychologist and the clinician, there also are fundamental similarities be-

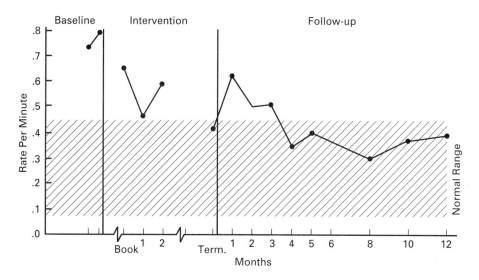

FIGURE 7-3 The shaded area shows the normal range of deviant behavior per minute in home settings. The solid line shows the average deviant behavior for a group of boys before, during, and after receiving treatment for their conduct problems. By comparing the shaded area with the treatment line, one can determine the degree to which the boys approximated the behavior of "normal" children after treatment. (From G. R. Patterson, "Intervention for boys with conduct problems: Multiple settings, treatments, and criteria," *Journal of Consulting and Clinical Psychology,* 1974, *42,* 471–481. Copyright 1974 by the American Psychological Association. Reprinted by permission.)

tween them. Each emphasizes a *psychological perspective* on human behavior and applies this perspective to change behavior and promote human welfare. Each also champions the scientific study of human behavior.

What Is Community Psychology?

Community psychology applies psychological principles to (a) the understanding of individual and social problems, (b) the prevention of behavioral dysfunction, and (c) the creation of lasting social change. Various community psychologists emphasize different characteristics in their definition of this field (e.g., Heller, Price, Reinharz, Riger, & Wandersman, 1984; Iscoe & Harris, 1984; Mann, 1978; Sarason, 1974), but a common ingredient in all the de-

finitions is that human behavior develops out of interactions between people and all aspects of their environment—physical, social, political, and economic. This idea requires that efforts to alleviate individual and social problems must entail *changes in both environmental settings and individual competencies,* not just changes at the individual level (which is the goal of psychotherapy). In his influential text on community psychology, Rappaport (1977) refers to this emphasis on person–environment interactions as the *ecological perspective*—"an orientation emphasizing relationships among persons and their social and physical environment [and implying] that there are neither inadequate persons nor inadequate environments, but rather the fit between persons and environments may be in relative accord or disaccord" (Rappaport, 1977, p. 2).

Along with an emphasis on environmental factors community psychologists have shown great concern for underserved, "underprivileged" populations (Snowden, 1982) who often have not been seen as appropriate recipients for psychotherapy or whose problems have been viewed as more social than psychological in nature and as requiring social rather than individual change.

The History of Community Psychology

Early Contributions

Several early developments in the history of the mental health professions form the basis of community psychology. For example, the Moral Era's emphasis on environmental determinants of disorder and its reformist fervor (see Chapter 1) were early inspirations for community psychology. Other precursors are presented below in a roughly chronological order.

1. The Advent of Clinical Psychology. Community psychology is embedded in clinical psychology. The majority of community psychologists were trained in clinical psychology programs. The early history of clinical psychology is thus relevant to community psychology. As Chapter 1 indicated, early clinical psychology was psychoeducational, and its emphasis on children reflected a belief that the treatment of early problems could prevent them from growing into major disabilities.

2. The Mental Hygiene Movement. In 1908 a former mental patient, Clifford Whittingham Beers, published *A Mind That Found Itself,* a moving book that described Beers's experiences as a mental patient and called public attention to the deplorable conditions in mental institutions. The book spurred several reforms in the treatment of the mentally ill and led in 1909 to the founding of the National Committee for Mental Hygiene, the organization that initiated the *mental hygiene* and *child guidance* movements. The mental hygienists

preferred to promote health rather than combat illness. Impressed by the success of public health's aggressive attack on contagious illnesses, they called for preventive programs and public education efforts to "inoculate" people against mental illness. The mental hygiene movement received a major boost when Beers enlisted William James, America's leading psychologist, and Adolf Meyer, the foremost American psychiatrist of the day, as spokesmen for his organization and its enlightened views on the treatment of mental disorders.

3. The Child Guidance Movement. The 1920s saw the growth of the child guidance movement, an offspring of mental hygiene, which concentrated on the delivery of clinical services to children, especially those who were severely emotionally disturbed. The child guidance movement furthered the philosophy of the mental hygienists and solidified the *team approach* to treatment, an idea anticipated by Witmer.

4. World Wars I and II. Two aspects of World Wars I and II were relevant to community psychology. First, both wars stimulated the growth of clinical psychology. Second, the two wars dramatically reshaped clinical psychology to make it more adult oriented, more concerned with psychopathology, more enamored with psychotherapy, and more often housed in hospital settings. These postwar attributes of clinical psychology were criticized by some clinicians who became disenchanted with the profession's course. In the soil of this disenchantment community psychology took root.

Recent Contributions

In the 1950s and 1960s a concentrated array of influences came together to accelerate the development of community psychology, leading to its formal birth in the mid-1960s. Two sets of developments were crucial. One set was internal to psychology itself; the other entailed extensive social and political changes taking place throughout America during this period.

Within psychology the following issues were the most prominent: (a) disenchantment with a clinical psychology that was dominated by intrapsychic models of psychopathology (Rappaport, 1977); (b) skepticism about the positive effects of psychotherapy (Eysenck, 1952, 1966) as well as the reliability and validity of psychological diagnosis and evaluation (Rosenhan, 1973); (c) prophecies of personnel shortages given the prevalent one-to-one style of delivering mental health services (Albee, 1959); and (d) dissatisfaction with the training models and role expectations for clinical psychologists (Korman, 1974; Peterson, 1968).

Several forces external to the profession nurtured the growth of community psychology. Social and political activism during the 1960s dramatically affected many who experienced these forces, including psychologists. The civil rights movement, black separatist ideology, urban crises, the war on poverty, and the unrest and demonstrations of university students prompted many psychologists to broaden their conceptions of what the helping professions should do in the interest of social change.

Another external force was legislative. The Mental Health Study Act of 1955 established the Joint Commission on Mental Health and Illness. This commission's final report in 1961 was a direct impetus for the community mental health and community psychology movements because it recommended the construction of multiservice comprehensive care centers to serve the mental health needs of local communities.

The joint commission's final report was followed in 1963 by the Community Mental Health Centers Act, which had the vigorous support of President John F. Kennedy. This bill provided funds for the construction of a network of comprehensive mental health centers that could cover service areas of not less than 75,000 nor more than 200,000 people. Comprehensive care was defined by this legis-

FIGURE 7–4 There are several ways of handling the shortage of mental health personnel. This is not one of them. (© 1972, Punch/Rothco.)

"Yes, what is it? I'm very busy . . . ."

lation to include 10 types of services. Five of these services were *essential,* meaning that they were required for centers seeking federal funds; five other services were *desirable,* indicating that they were important but not required for funding.

The five essential services were inpatient care, partial hospitalization, outpatient treatment for adults and children, 24-hour emergency services, and consultation and education programs. The five desirable services were diagnostic services, social and vocational rehabilitation, precare and aftercare, training of mental health personnel, and research and evaluation of program effectiveness and the problems of mental illness.

Finally, in 1965, legislation was passed that mandated funds for the personnel to be employed in these "comp care" centers. These staffing grants were to provide funding for the first several years of operation, after which financial responsibility would be shifted to the individual states, health insurance, direct fees, and other sources.

The comprehensive care system continues to be an important ingredient in this country's mental health effort, although its role is not as prominent as originally intended. The system's major achievement was that, with the help of antipsychotic drugs, it reduced the patient population in mental institutions. It also opened up mental health services by including paraprofessionals on treatment staffs and by offering community supervision or aftercare as an alternative to custodial confinement. A final accomplishment was that it made mental health services available to people who had not typically been served by the mental health system.

Since the late 1960s the federal government's commitment to mental health financing has been very weak. As a consequence, only a minority of the planned centers were actually constructed, and very few are adequately funded. In addition, many centers suffered severe reductions in staff after the original federal staffing grants ran out and were not replaced.

The community mental health movement also has been criticized at a philosophical level. Many critics argued that it merely placed the old wine of the medical model in the new bottle of community centers, while leaving intact a medical view of mental health services. A second objection concerned the fact that comprehensive care centers are not oriented toward *prevention* of human distress (Cowen, 1973). Another criticism has been that comprehensive care centers' services are still not sought by persons who may be in need of them because of financial limitations, cultural barriers, geographic isolation, bureaucratic red tape, and the fear of being stigmatized. A related point stressed by almost all critics is what they view as insufficient community participation in the planning and direction of the centers.

The current skepticism surrounding comprehensive care centers is due in part to the unrealistic optimism that greeted their creation. Great expectations run the risk of becoming great disappointments. But disappointments have an educational value: They can point us in new directions. Disappointments about community mental health have forced psychologists to reconsider and extend the innovations that led to the modern community mental health movement. The remainder of this chapter concentrates on such extensions, because they comprise an important part of community psychology.

Community Psychology's Formal Beginning

The birth of community psychology was in the spring of 1965 in Swampscott, Massachusetts, where more than 30 psychologists, many employed in community mental health centers, issued a call for community psychologists who would be "change agents, social system analysts, consultants in community affairs, and students generally of the whole man in relation to all his environments" (Bennett, 1965, p.

833). The community psychologist was to be a *participant conceptualizer.* Someone who tries to change social conditions as much as understand them.

This conference stressed three principles for the new profession. First, community psychology should not be limited to combating mental illness. Rather, it must work for "community well-being" and "furthering normal development" (Bennett, 1965). Second, community psychologists should promote community growth through planned social action and the scientific method. Finally, community psychology must be broader than community mental health, which, as we have seen, retained trappings of the medical model.

Today, community psychology is in its fourth decade. Its accomplishments are recorded in several professional journals *(The American Journal of Community Psychology, The Community Mental Health Journal,* and *The Journal of Community Psychology).* It has been surveyed and evaluated in several textbooks (e.g., Glenwick & Jason, 1980; Heller et al., 1984; Rappaport, 1977; Seidman, 1983; Tolan, Keys, Chertok, & Jason, 1991). Since 1967 there has been a division of community psychology within the American Psychological Association, and several thousand psychologists are now members.

The training of community psychologists has also become an important activity of graduate psychology programs. In 1962 there was one program offering an MA or PhD in community psychology and community mental health. By the late 1980s, there were about 100 programs in the United States with some graduate training in community psychology (Elias, Dalton, & Godin, 1987).

Principles of Community Psychology

Any model of mental health service has two basic components—a *conceptual component* and a *style of delivery component* (Rappaport & Chinsky, 1974). According to Rappaport (1977), the conceptual component "dictates the empirical data base, theoretical notions and basic assumptions for understanding human behavior" (p. 72). The style of delivery component, on the other hand, "dictates how the service called for by the conceptual component will be offered to the target population" (Rappaport, 1977, pp. 72–73).

Community psychology can be analyzed from this perspective if we realize that it involves several principles that can be organized under either the conceptual or style of delivery headings. Taken together, these ideas form the nucleus of the field and differentiate it from clinical psychology.

Conceptual Principles

1. The Ecological Perspective. The community psychologist believes that behavior cannot be explained solely through individual factors. Change in individuals often needs to be preceded by change in social institutions. The community psychologist views social, environmental, and political factors as important determinants of behavior and will seek changes in the communities into which individuals must fit.

The ecological perspective means that the psychologist must look for causes of behavior at several nonpsychological levels. For example, the child whose constant misbehavior in the classroom leads her to be labeled hyperactive may have a neurological impairment. But the behavior may also be due to a classroom whose organization rewards underachievement, a curriculum whose subject matter is too easy for her level of development, or a peer culture that devalues academic achievement. The ecological perspective directs attention to the role that social and environmental forces play in the development of this problem.

2. Social-System Change. The change implied by the ecological perspective is often termed *social-system-level change,* as distinguished from *person-oriented change.* Social-system changes are intended to make the social institutions in our lives more growth enhancing. Changes in social systems can occur at a low level, when one classroom in a school system begins to use a token economy to increase class participation. Social changes also can occur at a higher level, when a group of parents, dissatisfied with the quality of public education, begins its own alternative school. This is not to say that community psychologists never use person-oriented interventions. They do, often with the belief that they can be successful, but their preference is for social-system changes because these changes present the greatest opportunity to bring about important improvements for large numbers of people.

3. Prevention. The quest for prevention is the cardinal feature of community psychology. Caplan (1964) identified three types of prevention. *Tertiary prevention* aims to minimize the severity of illness, reduce the short- and long-term consequences of the disorder, and contain the disturbance so that personal effectiveness is retained. Tertiary prevention is prevention in name only. Almost any treatment can claim to being tertiary prevention.

Secondary prevention aims for a reduction in the prevalence of illness through coordinated early detection and effective intervention, or, as a cab driver was quoted as saying, "getting to people before they go nuts" (Schaar, 1978). Instruments that allow reliable and valid diagnosis early in the course of a problem are essential for secondary prevention. Secondary prevention is often directed at elementary school children because of the relationship between early school maladaptation and later adjustment problems and because schools can be a vehicle for optimizing personal as well as educational growth.

An example of this approach is the Primary Mental Health Project (PMHP) of Cowen and his colleagues at the University of Rochester (Cowen, Gesten, & Wilson, 1979; Weissberg, Cowen, Lotyczewski, & Gesten, 1983). The PMHP uses quick-screening techniques to identify primary schoolers having educational and behavioral problems. At-risk children are then seen by trained, nonprofessional child aides, who help the children cope with their difficulties and build new skills. Outcome data on the PMHP suggest that the participants experience both behavioral and educational improvements (Cowen et al., 1979), but Stein and Polyson (1984) offer a more skeptical view. The majority of preventive programs in community psychology have taken place at this secondary level (see Edelstein & Michelson, 1986; Felner, Jason, Moritsugu, & Farber, 1983; Hermalin & Morell, 1987; Rickel & Allen, 1987 for reviews of psychology's attempts at prevention).

Primary prevention involves the reduction and elimination of disorders by either modifying the pathogenic qualities of the environment or bolstering individuals' resources to the point where disorder will not occur. Primary prevention can be accomplished by *social action,* where changes in community institutions are made to reduce problems, or through *interpersonal action,* in which the goal is to enhance individuals' competencies at dealing with certain problems. Urban renewal, legal reforms, and social welfare are examples of the first type of prevention. Family intervention, parent education, and the training of coping skills are examples of prevention through interpersonal action.

4. Crisis Intervention. *Crisis intervention* plays a prominent role in the work of many community psychologists (Auerbach & Kilmann, 1977). People face many crises in their lives. There are the predictable crises of development, such as beginning school and finding a job. As personality theorists have emphasized, maturation also involves a series of psychological problems that must be resolved for optimal personality growth to occur. Other crises are less predictable and occur before the person is prepared for them: Serious illness, the death of a loved one, and natural disasters like fires or floods are examples.

In most cases, individuals confronted by a crisis are able to cope with the situation. In some cases, however, the crisis remains unsolved because the person has limited resources for coping or because the problem is especially difficult. As a result, the individual suffers emotional upset. If the crisis continues for a long time, serious personality disturbances may ensue.

Crisis intervention is a technique for helping people deal effectively with problems at the time they are occurring. The most influential contribution to crisis intervention was the work of Erich Lindemann (1944) and his associate Gerald Caplan (1961). Lindemann's notions of crisis therapy were based on his work with relatives of victims of the tragic 1943 fire at the Coconut Grove, a Boston nightclub. Lindemann concluded that there were stages of grief people must go through in order to adjust to the loss of a loved one. He further demonstrated that grieving people could be helped in working through the stages of bereavement by therapy aimed at the crisis itself, rather than at the person's personality.

The goals of crisis intervention are usually more limited than those pursued in psychotherapy. Butcher and Koss (1978) list the following common objectives of crisis intervention: (a) relief of the client's primary symptoms as rapidly as possible, (b) prompt reestablishment of the client's previous emotional stability, and (c) development of the client's understanding of the current disturbance and its precipitating factors, as well as an enhanced ability to cope with crises in the future.

Crisis intervention can also be distinguished from psychotherapy on the basis of the techniques used. Crisis intervention is usually brief. In most cases, it would not be expected to exceed 6 weeks. The crisis intervener is more likely than the average therapist to focus on the primary problem, to be interested in the here and now rather than past reasons for the problem, and to offer direct advice and information about alternative behavior. In crisis intervention, a premium is placed on gathering assessment information as efficiently as possible, preferably in the initial session. The development of a therapeutic relationship is considered important, but a compromise must be struck between the evolution of this relationship and the limited time available for treatment.

5. Promoting a "Psychological Sense of Community." Beyond solving immediate problems, the community psychologist is concerned with strengthening the ability of a community to plan and create its own change. This emphasis is what Sarason (1974) has called the "psychological sense of community":

> I have never met anyone—young or old, rich or poor, black or white, male or female, educated or not—to whom I have had any great difficulty explaining what I meant by the psychological sense of community. My explanation or language varied, of course, depending on whom I was talking with, but it never took long for them to comprehend that what I was getting at was the sense that one was part of a readily available, mutually supportive network of relationships upon which one could depend and as a result of which one did not experience sustained feelings of loneliness that impel one to actions or to adopting a style of living masking anxiety and setting the stage for later and more destructive anguish. It is not merely a matter of how many people one knows, or how many close friends one has, or even the number of loved ones—if they are scattered all over the country or world, if they are not part of the structure of one's everyday living, and if they are not available to one in a "give and get" way, they can have little effect on one's immediate or daily sense of community. Indeed, for many people these treasured but only occasionally available relationships accentuate the lack of a feeling of community. . . . (p. 351)

Community psychologists try to create this sense of community by developing people's strengths rather than eliminating their weaknesses. They try to encourage collective action by people with common needs or interests and then seek to help these coalitions maintain their commitment to mutual problem solving. This goal involves the development of collective power mobilized for the purpose of specific reforms. Increasing a community's competence and shared sense of purpose requires that community psychologists tolerate or even increase the positive diversity of the people they encounter. The ways in which a community insures its safety, educates its children, protects its environment, promotes its health, and establishes a sense of vitality in its citizens usually represent a small portion of available means to desired ends. The successful community psychologist helps people create effective alternatives to existing social institutions by treating their cultural preferences and differences as assets rather than liabilities, a strategy that has been termed *empowerment* (Rappaport, 1981).

The idea of empowerment is connected with two other recent developments in the thinking of community psychologists. One theme, which we will return to later in Chapter 12, is the role that social support can play in helping people cope better with stressful experiences and crises. A large number of studies have suggested that people with high levels of perceived support from others suffer fewer psychological and physical symptoms of distress in times of crisis than people who are not embedded in a helpful social network (House, Landis, & Umberson, 1988; Jemmott & Magloire, 1988). This discovery suggests the value of interventions that increase persons' chances for helpful interaction with a social network of friends, neighbors, or relatives.

The second empowerment-related theme involves the concepts of resilience and invulnerability. Despite a host of social disadvantages, personal tragedies, and environmental obstacles, some people manage not only to overcome adversity, they actually seem to thrive or prosper. How they do it becomes a question that, if studied carefully, could lead psychologists to understand and then promote effective coping in others (Cowen & Work, 1988; Garmezy, 1985).

Style of Delivery

The second way of defining a model of mental health service concerns the *style of service delivery*. The following are three principles of delivery style from the perspective of community psychology.

1. Expansion of Professional Roles. Clinical psychologists usually offer *direct services* to clients who, because they have some psychological complaint, are willing to pay for them. Community psychologists, on the other hand, emphasize *indirect services* that have no single target client, but which are expected to achieve benefits because the social-system changes they produce radiate to the intended target groups.

Consultation is a common activity for the community psychologist. Community psychologists have placed greater reliance on this type of intervention than have clinical psychologists (see O'Neill & Trickett, 1982, for a review of consultation within community psychology).

Another example of expanding roles for community psychologists is the preparation of *volunteers, paraprofessionals,* and *nonprofessionals* for behavior-change functions typically reserved for the professional. These include child care workers, mental health workers, self-help group leaders, peer counselors, and abortion counselors. The nonprofessional movement creates meaningful careers for people, provides troubled people with help from persons with whom they share a cultural heritage, and provides a new source of workers necessary for adequate delivery of mental health services.

In many cases, helpers are drawn directly

from the groups that will receive the services. These workers have been called *indigenous nonprofessionals,* and their cultural rootedness within a consumer group is one of their fundamental assets. In other instances paraprofessionals are drawn from groups with a high commitment to service but with a cheap price tag for their labor. College students and homemakers are often volunteers, and they have been used as mental health workers in many settings. Community psychologists may also train relatives (Guerney, 1969), peers (Harris & Sherman, 1973), teachers (Meyers, 1975), and friends (Sulzer, 1965) to initiate behavior-change conditions or to maintain conditions that had been introduced during a professional intervention.

Related to the nonprofessional movement is the increasing use of self-help groups (Jacobs & Goodman, 1989) and advocacy groups comprised primarily of relatives of mentally ill persons (Backer & Richardson, 1989). The growth of these programs stems in part from citizens' dissatisfaction with professionals' failure to provide them with the support and practical advice so necessary for coping with the stress of living with a chronically mentally ill relative (see Box 7–4).

2. Use of Activism. Social action has been considered both an essential contribution and an unnecessary evil in community psychology. Advocates of activist tactics claim that professionals' willingness to provoke, agitate, and confront accounts for a large measure of their effectiveness. Opponents of professional social action argue that such activity is incompatible with the objective empiricism that is the scientist's defining characteristic.

In the present context, social activism refers to the use of *power* to accomplish social reform. This power may be economic, it may be political, or it may be the coercive power of civil disobedience. Power can be manipulated through publicity, and it is for this reason that community psychologists cultivate media contacts to spread their influence. Finally, power

resides in positions of leadership. Psychologists may seek employment where they have access to the formation of social policy. A member of an urban planning team, a consultant to the city council, an advisor to legislators, a director of a citizen's advocate group, the head of a social-service agency—these are all jobs with the potential to influence social change.

3. Use of Research as a Form of Intervention. Community psychologists view research as a way of producing change. This is particularly true in the case of *evaluation research,* which compares the effects of a new program against existing programs or against no intervention at all. In the event that an innovative procedure is associated with greater benefits than alternative programs, the researcher can argue that the procedure should be implemented on a more permanent basis.

Experimentation from this perspective is a technique of demonstration and persuasion. George Fairweather, a psychologist at Michigan State University, coined the phrase *experimental social innovation* to describe research which, after demonstrating the value of a new program, can be used to support that program's implementation. Research as intervention is also exemplified by what is called *dissemination research.* This is experimentation designed to evaluate alternative methods of implementing those programs that initial evaluation research has shown to be successful. In the course of finding the most effective means of persuading other communities to adopt a given program, that program is, by necessity, adopted. The best example of dissemination research is Fairweather's experimental project on the effectiveness of different approaches to persuading mental hospitals to adopt an outpatient "lodge program" designed for chronic mental patients (Fairweather, Sanders, & Tornatzky, 1974). The research investigated what techniques were most effective in activating the lodge program once a decision to adopt it had been made and explored the procedures used in spreading the lodge

Although estimates vary, about 6 to 7 million Americans belong to self-help groups (SHGs) of some kind (Jacobs & Goodman, 1989). This number rivals the number of clients in psychotherapy and suggests that SHGs have become a major method for mental health care in the 1990s.

SHGs have been described as miniature mental health democracies that have the following characteristics (Jacobs & Goodman, 1989):

1. Group members share a relatively well-defined, common problem or set of life experiences.

2. Groups concentrate on three activities—exchanging information, providing social support, and discussing mutual problems.

3. Groups charge low or no fees.

4. Groups are largely member governed, but some may use professionals as consultants.

5. Groups rely on fellow members as their primary mental health care givers.

SHGs range in size, organization, and goals. Power (1987) described five different types of SHGs. *Habit disturbance* groups emphasize a specific change in behavior; examples include Alcoholics Anonymous and Gamblers Anonymous. *General-purpose* groups address a wide range of difficulties such as dealing with the death of a child (Compassionate Friends) or helping psychiatric patients cope with crises (GROW, Recovery, Inc.). *Lifestyle organizations* support individuals who feel they are not receiving fair treatment in society, such as single parents (Parents Without Partners) or the elderly (Gray Panthers). Significant-other organizations provide advocacy, education, support, and partnership for relatives of disturbed persons; examples include Gam-Anon (relatives of compulsive gamblers) and Al-Anon (relatives of alcoholics). Finally, several *physical handicap organizations* support persons with disorders like heart surgery patients (Mended Hearts) or cerebral palsy (Cerebral Palsy Association).

The effects of SHGs have seldom been evaluated empirically. Most members of SHGs are convinced of their value and see formal studies of their effects as unnecessary. The goals of SHGs are often hard to describe precisely, making their evaluation more difficult. Those evaluation studies that have been performed produced mixed results (Nietzel, Guthrie, & Susman, 1991); generally, it appears that active members experience moderate improvements in some areas of their lives.

BOX 7–4
Self-Help Groups and Mental Health

approach to other mental health programs (Fairweather, 1980).

An Evaluation of Community Psychology

Critiques of community psychology have been aimed at what it has accomplished as well as what it has failed to accomplish.

Rhetoric Versus Results

The most general criticism of community psychology is that its tenets are oversold and its accomplishments exaggerated. Community psychologists have been prolific in pointing out what is wrong with society and the mental health professions, but they have been less adept at coming up with a technology that produces specific, durable changes. This criticism claims that the rhetoric of the community psychology camp has not been matched by results.

The Status of Prevention

Primary prevention is the one promise community psychology must keep if it is to remain a viable intervention strategy. What accomplishments from primary prevention can community psychologists claim? Historically, aspirations for prevention have outdistanced achievements. Novaco and Monahan (1980) classified the research published in the first six volumes of the *American Journal of Community Psychology*. They found that only 2.4% of the articles dealt with primary prevention; only 10.2% dealt with secondary prevention. Novaco and Monahan (1980) concluded that "the majority of research published in the field's leading journal has little to do with the stated objectives of the discipline" (p. 143).

Effective prevention is difficult for several reasons. First, good prevention requires good theories of etiology and vulnerability. Generally, we cannot prevent problems if we do not understand what causes them. Second, prevention is often very expensive, and unless legislators are convinced that the effects of a prevention program justify the initial outlay of funds, they are usually reluctant to appropriate the money. In the long run, prevention may be more economical than direct-service treatment, but the long run is a difficult perspective for most politicians (and many psychologists) to maintain.

Another challenge to prevention is the contention that prevention is not the best way to conceptualize community psychology, because even if effective, it carries sufficient negative implications as a way of solving problems that we should resist institutionalizing it as the best approach to intervention.

What are the negative implications of prevention? Rappaport (1981) warns against the dangers of pursuing any "one-sided" intervention, whether it be psychotherapy or prevention. In Rappaport's (1981) words:

Partly because institutions have a tendency to become one-sided many social problems are ironically and inadvertently created by the so-called helping systems . . . and often "solutions" create more problems than they solve. (p. 8)

That social institutions and professions create as well as solve problems is *not* a call for working harder to find the single best technique or lamenting the failure of our best minds to be creative. Quite the opposite. It *is a problem to be understood as contained in the basic nature of the subject matter of our field*. It will always be this way. There can never be a now and for all time single scientific "breakthrough" which settles and solves the puzzles of our discipline. Today's solution must be tomorrow's problem. (p. 9; italics in original)

Typically enacted by experts, preventive programs run the risk of overpowering the natural strengths and coping abilities in any population. As a result, recipients may lose actual and perceived control over their own lives as they yield to the myth that mental health professionals know best how to solve problems.

A related problem is the "psychologicalizing" of problems to the point where prevention is legitimized as an intervention even though it may be unnecessary. Rappaport (1981) describes this "overreach" problem as "a new arena for colonization" that "underlies much of what is called prevention: find so-called high-risk people and save them from themselves, if they like it or not, by giving them, or even better, their children, programs which we develop, package, sell, operate, or otherwise control" (p. 13).

While fundamental questions about primary prevention are debated, many psychologists are still developing preventive programs, and there are indications that prevention of certain social problems may be attainable. Cowen (1980) points to five promising areas in the field of prevention: mental health education, social-system analysis and modification, competence building, stress reduction and coping, and fortification of support systems. Reviews of successful preventive programs can be found in several comprehensive handbooks on prevention by Burchard and Burchard (1987), Edelstein and Michelson (1986), Felner, Jason, Moritsugu, and Farber (1983), and Rickel and Allen (1987). A special 1982 issue of the *American Journal of Community Psychology* presents some high-quality studies of primary prevention.

Community psychologists have increased their study of social problems such as crime, drug addiction, and poverty while shifting away from research on community mental health, a former mainstay for community researchers (Speer et al., 1992). This shift has been accompanied by an increase in research on prevention programs, perhaps because as investigators focus on specific problems they also home in on particular causal variables that must be addressed for true primary prevention to be accomplished.

Prevention has also made inroads into traditional clinical psychology (Levy, 1984; Watkins, 1985) as clinicians have become more interested in the promotion of physical and psychological health (see Chapter 12). The ideas of stress and coping provide a common ground for clinicians and community psychologists to understand dysfunction and to develop interventions for protecting vulnerable persons against effects of stress.

Another theoretical framework that integrates the philosophy of community psychologists with the techniques of clinicians is *behavioral community psychology* (Glenwick & Jason, 1980; Nietzel, Winett, MacDonald, & Davidson, 1977). This field involves a synthesis of behavior modification techniques with the philosophy and style of community psychology. The advantages of this alliance are to be found in the complementary strengths the two areas provide each other. Behavioral interventions have been effectively used in

one-to-one treatment of moderately distressed individuals or in institutional settings with chronically disturbed patients. They have not usually been used preventively or with an intention to produce large-scale changes in society. On the other hand, community psychologists have lacked effective techniques for bringing about the changes in environments or persons that they desire. Joining the ecological perspective of community psychologists with the efficacious techniques of behavior modifiers is a merger that may make possible an empirically based science of social change.

Overreach

Community psychology has been accused of losing sight of appropriate and realistic objectives. For example, the idea that communities, not individuals, are the clients in need of modification elicited a well-known critique from Warren Dunham (1965), a sociologist who labeled the community movement the "newest therapeutic bandwagon," claiming that interest in the community is a compensation for the frustration many clinicians have experienced in their unsuccessful attempts to treat chronic mental disorders.

Ethical Objections

Community psychology has evoked ethical concerns. A common fear is that community programs, particularly those aimed at prevention, may threaten individual freedoms and rights. Halleck (1969) expressed concern that the community movement would encroach on privacy and the right to live our lives the way we please.

There are at least two reasons why this fear may be exaggerated. First, Americans are notably resistant to controls and coercion. Our mistrust of undue regulation from any source, whether it is political, military, or medical, has been effective protection against most excesses of control. At present, this quality appears sufficiently strong to prevent abuses by the overly zealous community psychologist.

Second, we must return to the issue of community psychology's record of accomplishment. Outside the area of delivering traditional mental health services to larger segments of the population, the community movement has not produced many preventive programs or social-system-level changes. Community psychology's most pressing ethical dilemma is not so much the threat of doing too much to communities as doing too little.

Other critics fear that increasing the emphasis on prevention will distract professionals from offering the intensive treatment severely disturbed clients require (Lamb & Zusman, 1981). This is unlikely, since the mental health fields suffered from an insufficiency of professional personnel long before community psychology came along. Another objection is to the early identification and treatment associated with secondary prevention. By being too aggressive in finding at-risk persons, the psychologist may damage them with premature labels. Two decades ago, Ullmann and Krasner (1975) warned that "case finding" should not turn into "case making."

Finally, there is uncertainty about exactly who in a community decides the goals of community interventions. Is it the psychologist, the recipients of the program, the majority of the community, or only influential leaders? Community psychologists assure us that the aims of their interventions are directed by the people they serve. Zax and Specter (1974) claim: "The notion of a community psychology would be impossible were it not for the fact that, because of the unity of social problems, need is felt for it at a grass roots level" (p. 325). This may be true, but the notion of community participation is a complex ideal made all the more difficult by the frequent value conflicts between community residents and professional psychologists.

Final Thoughts on Community Psychology

Community psychology's emphasis on prevention, its attention to stressful environments, and its concern with well-being (as opposed to pathology) have been incorporated into other applied areas of psychology, particularly clinical psychology and health psychology. Because of these achievements, community psychologists continue to struggle with their sense of identity and purpose. As prevention is absorbed into other subfields of psychology, community psychology is threatened with a loss of distinctiveness. Felner (1985) suggests that community psychology has a special role as the base of prevention knowledge and research, and that its future contributions will best be realized in those areas. Iscoe and Harris (1984) also recommend that it is in research and consultation that community psychologists can make their most decisive impact.

CHAPTER 8

Clinical Intervention: Psychodynamic Models

The most influential figure in the development of psychotherapy was Sigmund Freud. His *psychoanalysis,* which was a method of treatment, a theory of personality, and a means of studying human behavior, revolutionized psychiatry and altered forever the ways people think about themselves. Freud's voluminous writings stimulated many followers and opponents to extend and revise his ideas. Today there is a spectrum of psychodynamically oriented theories ranging from classical or orthodox psychoanalysis (which closely follows Freud's tenets) to systems that not only reject some of Freud's basic beliefs, but actually overlap with phenomenological, interpersonal, or behavioral models. There is a corresponding array of psychodynamic treatment approaches, and in this chapter we describe the techniques and the effectiveness of a few prominent examples. We begin with Freud.

PSYCHOANALYTIC TREATMENT

Sigmund Freud was the founder of psychotherapy as we know it today. His one-to-one method of studying and helping people; systematic search for relationships between a person's history and current problems; emphasis on conflict, thoughts, and emotions; and focus on the therapist–patient relationship pervade all modern treatment modalities. Where did Freud's ideas come from?

It will not be possible to provide a complete account of Freud's life or the evolution to his thought; a brief sketch will have to suffice. More complete coverage can be found in Fancher (1973) as well as in several other sources (e.g., Ford & Urban, 1963; Munroe, 1955). Those seeking detailed material should consult Ernest Jones's monumental three-volume biography, *The Life and Work of Sigmund Freud* (1953, 1955, 1957), Clark's *Freud:*

The Man and the Cause (1980), Peter Gay's *Freud: A Life For Our Time* (1988), or translations of Freud's own works (e.g., Brill, 1938; Freud, 1953–1964).

The Beginnings of Psychoanalytic Treatment

Freud was born in Freiberg, Moravia (Czechoslovakia), on May 6, 1856, the son of a Jewish wool merchant. His family moved to Vienna, Austria, where at the age of nine, Freud entered Gymnasium, a sort of advanced high school. He was originally interested in law or politics, but prior to graduation, an essay on nature by the poet Goethe prompted him to concentrate on natural science instead. In 1873, at the age of 17, Freud entered the University of Vienna medical school. Research interested him more than routine course work, and he spent most of his time on research projects in the university's Institute of Physiology. As a result, it took Freud eight years to complete his medical degree.

His efforts during this period led to his discovering the location of the sex organs in the male eel and the accumulation of a great deal of new information about neurology. More important than these studies themselves was Freud's introduction to the concept of neurological *mechanism*. This view held that the activity of the nervous system was based on electrochemical factors that obeyed laws of physics and chemistry. An implication of mechanistic theory was that human behavior could be explained in *physical* terms and that lawful relationships about human behavior were possible. These notions had a profound effect on Freud's later work.

In the 1880s it was virtually impossible to make a living as a research scientist. This fact, coupled with Freud's desire to marry his sweetheart, Martha Bernays, caused him to change his career to the more lucrative field of medical practice. In 1882 Freud began 3 years of clinical training at Vienna General Hospital. This was an era when the medical model of behavior disorder was resurgent; there was a diligent search for the organic causes presumed to underlie all mental illness. The director of the Vienna Hospital psychiatric clinic was Theodor Meynert, an authority on brain anatomy and pathology whose work impressed Freud. Meynert believed, for example, that patterns of neural activity in the brain correspond to various thoughts or memories, and that psychological phenomena are due to nerve cell activity which, in turn, is based on electrochemical events.

This psychological extension of mechanistic theory led Freud to believe that the best way to blend his research interests in neurology with his clinical work was to study and treat diseases of the nervous system in humans. By 1886 Freud had enough background (and money) to begin the private practice of medicine. He also married in that year. One of the people who helped Freud begin his private practice was Joseph Breuer, a senior medical colleague and close friend. Breuer's early attempts to cure certain unusual symptoms in his patients ultimately led Freud to the development of psychoanalysis.

Freud often saw patients with symptoms of neurological damage for which no organic cause could be found. These cases displayed what Freud called "neurological nonsense." For example, patients sometimes complained of paralysis that affected their entire hand, but not their arm. Others suffered paralysis of the legs during the day, but walked in their sleep. Patients of this type were called *neurotics*. Since the cause, let alone the cure, for their problems was unknown, most physicians ignored them, assuming that neurotic symptoms were either phony or the result of character defects.

Freud often dealt with the most common type of neurotic patients: those displaying *hysterical* (i.e., nonorganic) paralyses, amnesia, anesthesia, blindness, and speech loss. Treat-

FIGURE 8–1   Sigmund Freud (1856–1939). (Courtesy of Historical Pictures Service, Inc., Chicago, Illinois. Reprinted by permission.)

ment for hysteria mainly involved the use of "wet packs" and baths (hydrotherapy) or electrically generated heat (electrotherapy), neither of which was effective. Freud became convinced that whatever benefits patients received from these procedures were due to suggestion. Accordingly, he began to experiment with techniques that maximized the benefits of suggestion, foremost among which was *hypnosis.*

In Freud's time hypnosis was generally regarded as a magician's trick, beneath the dignity of serious physicians and scientists. This view was prompted mainly by the theatrics and bizarre theories of Anton Mesmer, the first promoter of hypnosis or *mesmerism.* Nevertheless, hypnosis was studied seriously by a few individuals who used it to cure hysterical disorders.

Freud's familiarity with hypnosis began when he spent 6 months studying in Paris with Jean Charcot, director of the neurology clinic at the Salpetriere asylum. Charcot showed that hysterical symptoms could be created and temporarily removed through a hypnotic trance and thus that hysteria and hypnosis were related phenomena. In fact, Charcot believed that only hysterics could be hypnotized. Later, in the French city of Nancy, Freud visited a clinic organized by Ambrose-August Liebault and Hippolyte Bernheim. These two physicians believed that the ability to be hypnotized was not a symptom of nervous disorder, but a routine phenomenon attainable with normal individuals. Liebault and Bernheim used hypnotic suggestions to remove hysterical symptoms, with limited, often temporary, success. Freud's use of hypnotic suggestion produced equally mediocre results, but around 1890 he began to combine hypnosis with a new technique he learned from Joseph Breuer.

Breuer had stumbled on this technique, called the *cathartic method,* while attempting to relieve the hysterical symptoms of a wealthy young woman, Anna O. These symptoms included headaches, a severe cough, neck and arm paralyses, involuntary squinting, anesthesia in both elbows, and other problems. Her difficulties began during her father's

illness and intensified following his death. She began to display extremes of mood which went from agitation and hallucinations during the day to calm, trancelike states in the evenings. Breuer was struck by the fact that these "trances" resembled hypnosis. Fancher (1973, p. 48) describes what happened next:

> Breuer discovered that if Anna were permitted while in the hypnotic state to recite the contents of all her hallucinations from the day, then she invariably would leave the trance state and enjoy a period of almost normal tranquility and lucidity during the following late night hours. . . . Anna came to refer to the exercise of reciting her hallucinations as the "talking cure," or . . . "chimney sweeping."

This "talking cure" did not eliminate Anna's daytime disorders, however. To Breuer's dismay, new symptoms began to appear. In attempting to cure one of these, an inability to drink liquids, Breuer made the discovery that would later start Freud on the road to psychoanalysis:

> During one of Anna's hypnotic states . . . she began describing to Breuer an Englishwoman whom she knew but did not especially like. The woman had a dog that Anna particularly despised. Anna described how on one occasion she entered the woman's room and observed the dog drinking water from a glass. When the event occurred, Anna was filled with strong feelings of disgust and loathing, but out of politeness she was unable to express them. As she recited this account to Breuer, she for the first time permitted herself the luxury of expressing fully and animatedly her negative feelings about the dog's drinking. When she emerged from the trance she immediately asked for a glass of water, which she . . . drank without the slightest difficulty. (Fancher, 1973, p. 49)

Removal of Anna's fear of drinking was apparently brought about by her vivid recollection of a forgotten event while in a trance. It occurred to Breuer that other hysterical symptoms might be caused by forgotten memories and that their recall might cure them. He began hypnotizing Anna and asking her to remember everything she could about her symptoms.

> (H)e discovered that every symptom could be traced to a traumatic or unpleasant situation for which all memory was absent in the waking state. Breuer found that whenever he could induce Anna to recall those unpleasant scenes and, more importantly, to *express the emotions* they had caused her to feel, the symptoms would disappear. (Fancher, 1973, pp. 49–50; italics added)[1]

Freud also found the cathartic method successful, but he encountered serious drawbacks as well. Not all his patients could be hypnotized. In addition, Freud found that recall of memories and expression of the emotions associated with them are most beneficial when the patient remembers what happened after hypnosis is removed. To facilitate *conscious* recognition of early memories, Freud began to look for nonhypnotic means of helping patients locate lost memories.

He first tried a pressure technique he had seen Bernheim use at Nancy. This technique involved pressing a hand against the patient's forehead and suggesting that she or he could remember. Freud's adaptation of this method consisted of having the patient relax with eyes closed and recite memories that came to mind. Recall was often helped by having the patient

lie on a couch, but Freud found that significant memories did not always appear immediately, no matter how strongly he suggested that they would. Freud ultimately abandoned the laying on of hands and simply instructed his patients to report whatever thoughts, feelings, or memories came to mind. This procedure later became known as *free association,* a mainstay among psychoanalytic techniques to be described later.[2]

Freud's early treatment of "neurotic" patients focused on helping them remember important, usually unpleasant, memories and emotions they had repressed and protected from recall by various *defense mechanisms* (see Chapter 2). He also constructed a model of nervous-system functioning that could not only explain the development and cure of neurotic symptoms, but of normal, everyday behavior as well. Freud called this work the "Project for a Scientific Psychology." Its specific features included nerve energy called "Q" which could "fill up" or *cathect* a given nerve cell and could be discharged by that cell. Freud also suggested a force he called "ego" which inhibited the discharge of various neurons. Where ego energy was strong, nervous activity adjusted to the requirements of the external environment. Where ego energy was weak, neural discharge was less inhibited. Thus, controlled or impulsive behavior was determined by natural forces and factors in the person's nervous system.

The project reflected Freud's neurological sophistication and objective, scientific view of human behavior. Unfortunately, he was never able to construct his neurological model so that it could explain why painful memories

---

[1] Anna's case has been a controversial one in the history of psychoanalysis. Several scholars (e.g., Ellenberger, 1972; Thornton, 1983) have claimed that Anna's illness was not hysterical but was in fact a case of meningitis, that she continued to suffer from the illness, and that although Freud was aware of her suffering he did not publicly acknowledge it. This incident, along with others in Freud's career, has led to frequent allegations (e.g., Eysenck, 1985; Masson, 1983; Zwang, 1985) that Freud was an insincere, sometimes dishonest man.

[2] Incidentally, Freud may have hit upon this technique through a lost memory of his own. Fancher (1973) reports that when Freud was a teenager, he read an essay by Ludwig Borne called "The Art of Becoming an Original Writer in Three Days." In that essay Borne suggested that the would-be writer should spend 3 days writing down everything that comes to mind "without any falsification or hypocrisy" and that amazingly new and surprising thoughts would appear.

should be automatically repressed by the nervous system. In 1896 Freud abandoned his efforts at explaining neurotic behavior on neurological grounds and concentrated instead on *psychological* explanations.

Freud became convinced that the causes of neurotic problems were more complex than he had initially supposed. For example, many of his patients recalled early memories of sexual trauma, usually molestation by a parent or other relative. Freud assumed that such events were the basis for most hysterical symptoms. By the turn of the century, however, Freud was convinced that this "seduction theory" was incorrect and that there were more important causal factors to be considered (see also Chapter 2). For one thing, he simply could not believe that seduction and sexual abuse of children were as widespread as indicated by his patients' reports. Second, Freud began to pay attention to *dreams* (his patients' and his own) and concluded that they represented the fulfillment of *wishes*. He found that many of these fantasies are socially unacceptable and thus appear in disguised form only when defenses are relaxed during sleep. Freud then suggested that, like dreams, hysterical symptoms were based on unconscious wishes and fantasies, not just on memories of actual events. Thus, a patient's "memory" of childhood seduction by a parent might be a *fantasy* or *wish* about such an encounter.

The implications of this new theory led Freud to develop his most controversial concepts: infantile sexuality, the Oedipus conflict, and the instinctual basis of human behavior. It altered his approach to therapy as well. Psychoanalytic treatment of neurosis shifted from the recovery of memories to the illumination of the unconscious.

The Goals of Psychoanalytic Treatment

The basic goal of classical psychoanalytic therapy is to help patients think and behave in more adaptive ways by understanding themselves better. In theory, when patients understand the real, often unconscious, reasons why they act in maladaptive ways and see that those reasons are no longer valid, they will not have to continue behaving in those ways. The analogy comes to mind of the Japanese soldier left on a remote Pacific island during World War II with orders never to surrender. Decades after the war, the soldier is still hiding, holding out against an enemy that no longer exists except in his own mind. When someone finally helps him understand that his original orders no longer apply, he can stop acting like a hunted animal and start living productively.

In psychoanalytic treatment, it is not enough for the therapist to say "the war is over" by simply describing the unconscious material that he or she thinks is at the root of the patient's problems. Patients must make these discoveries for themselves, with guidance from the therapist. This process of self-understanding includes *intellectual* recognition of one's innermost wishes and conflicts, *emotional* involvement in discoveries about oneself, and the *systematic tracing* of how unconscious factors have determined past and present behaviors and affected relations with other people.

Freud described the basic psychoanalytic situation in the following terms:

> The ego has been weakened by the internal conflict; we must come to its aid. The position is like a civil war which can only be decided by the help of an ally from without. The analytical physician and the weakened ego of the patient, basing themselves upon the real external world, are to combine against the enemies, the instinctual demands of the id, and the moral demands of the superego. We form a pact with each other. The patient's sick ego promises us the most complete candor, promises, that is, to put at our disposal all of the material which his self-perception provides; we, on the other hand, assure him of the strictest discretion and put at his service our experience in interpreting material that has

been influenced by the unconscious. Our knowledge shall compensate for his ignorance and shall give his ego once more mastery over the lost provinces of his mental life. This pact constitutes the analytic situation. (Freud, 1938)

Thus, the main goals of psychoanalytic treatment are (a) intellectual and emotional *insight* into the underlying causes of the patient's behavior problems, (b) *working through* or fully exploring the implications of those insights, and (c) strengthening the ego's control over the id and the superego. One myth about psychoanalysis is that insight about one's life comes in a sudden flash, accompanied by the explosive release (or "abreaction") of pent-up emotions from the past, and followed by the permanent disappearance of the patient's problems. Although his patients were often relieved of a symptom following recovery of repressed memories, Freud believed that symptom removal (no matter how dramatically it occurs) was only part of therapy. If more important unconscious material were not unearthed through a process of "benevolent scrutiny," new symptoms would appear. Thus, "making the unconscious conscious" (Freud, 1901) is a gradual process that takes place over many analytic sessions. This self-exploration is slowed by dead ends, false leads, and psychological defenses thrown up by the patient to prevent conscious awareness of long-hidden truths.

Even after these truths are revealed, the therapist must promote the *working through* of insights and the defenses that kept them from consciousness for so long. The patient needs to understand how pervasive the unconscious conflicts and defenses are so that he or she can learn to recognize them and prevent their return. It would do little good for a patient to know that she had unconscious feelings of anger toward her mother if she did not also see that she deals with women in the present as if they were her mother, and that her problems in relation to these women are based on unconscious hostility and/or at-

tempts to defend against it. Insight provides the outline of a patient's story; working through fills in the details.

Reaching the ambitious goals set by classical psychoanalysis involves the dissection and gradual reconstruction of the patient's personality. This process requires a lot of time (three to five sessions each week for 2 to 15 years), a lot of money (fees exceed $100 per hour), and a great deal of therapist skill. The ways psychoanalysts work at this formidable task are described in the next section.

Psychoanalytic Treatment Techniques

An assumption of psychoanalytic theory is that the patient's most important feelings and conflicts are unconscious and protected by psychological defenses. No matter how hard the patient tries, it is unlikely that he or she alone can penetrate the depths that have been avoided for so long. The therapist must create an atmosphere where the patient can engage in real self-exploration. The therapist must show the patient how and where to look for important material and help the patient understand the things that emerge.

The specific ways these tasks are accomplished differ for each analyst and for each patient, but a few techniques and strategies are common. We shall discuss each of them separately, but in practice they are interwoven in multiple combinations rather than performed in a certain order.

Free Association

As noted earlier, free association evolved from the search for a nonhypnotic way to recover past memories. It involves asking the patient to follow a single fundamental rule: to say everything that comes to mind without editing or censorship.

The patient is . . . asked to verbalize everything that occurs to him in the original sequence and form without any modification or omission. He is asked to assure a passive attitude toward his train of thought; in other words, to eliminate all conscious control over his mental processes to which he gives free rein. . . . (Alexander, 1937, pp. 40–41)

The rationale for free association is that by removing the constraints of logic, social amenities, and other rules, unconscious material will surface.

The most common approach is to have the patient free associate while lying on a couch. The analyst sits out of the patient's view in order to avoid interfering with the associative process. In early analytic sessions the therapist may give some instructions ("Just say whatever occurs to you regardless of how unimportant it may seem"), but later the patient becomes familiar enough with the role to begin free associating without a prompt:

PATIENT: God, it's been a long day. I haven't worked this hard since I was in high school. Back then I used to work part time on my uncle's farm and part time in a drugstore. The farm work was really hard. I thought I was going to die out in those fields. It was a lot nicer when I visited the farm as a small child. Dad and Mom used to take me and my sister to the farm on weekends and us kids would play all day. We used to go in the barn a lot and it seems like we played some secret game or something. (pause) Now I remember! We played doctor and my sister and my two cousins and I would take turns being the doctor and examining each other's genitals. We knew we weren't supposed to do it though and I remember being scared to death that we'd be caught. . . .

Because of defenses, the unconscious bases for the patient's current problems are seldom clearly revealed in memories, feelings and wishes. More often, free association merely gives glimpses of the underlying causes of distress. It is the therapist's task to try to make sense of the bits and pieces that emerge. *Patterns of association* are often important:

PATIENT: My dad called long distance last night. It was nice to hear from him, but I never quite feel comfortable when we talk. Once we get through the usual "hello; how are you" part, there just doesn't seem to be anything to say. (long silence) I almost fell asleep there for a minute. I used to do that a lot in college. I must have slept through half my classes. Once I woke up and saw the professor standing over me, shaking me, and the whole class was laughing.

The fact that thoughts about father led to memories about a threatening authority figure could have significance, especially if this pattern is repeated in other sessions. It could mean that the patient still has unresolved feelings of fear and hatred toward his father, feelings that will need to be clarified and dealt with.

What the patient says during free association may be defensive in nature. The patient whose mind goes blank or who comes up with only trivial details of the day is throwing up barriers to self-exploration. The following excerpt from an analytic-style session with S (Murray, 1938, quoted in White & Watt, 1973, pp. 257–258) provides an example of a patient's defenses (the analyst is denoted as E):

S: The thing uppermost in my mind at present is the hour exam I just had. Rather easy exam. I wasn't feeling particularly brilliant this morning. I don't know whether I made any mistakes or not. Quite a bit hinges on this exam because I want to get a scholarship for the second semester. If I get it, I will be able to carry through my work to my master's degree. If I don't, I don't believe I'll be able to make it. It's hard to borrow money these days. I would like to keep on at college though because with the kind of work I get here I will get the kind of job I want. I am particularly interested in research work and this course that I am taking fits me for that.

E: I am afraid you are telling me a story rather than telling me what is coming into your mind. (After the first few sentences S has been giving a reasoned statement of his financial position. This is contrary to instruction and hence constitutes the first manifestation of resistance.)

S: I have an experiment this afternoon and I'm darned if I know what it is about. (This remark may contain a double meaning: S is wondering what the present session is about, as well as the afternoon's experiment. But he has abandoned his first form of resistance, the next topic being a good example of free associations.)

S: I wonder how my dad is getting along. He is on his last legs, so to speak. Dad and I never got along very well. I remember one time when I was a youngster I was supposed to be watching some cows that were grazing near an orchard. I got so interested in reading that I forgot about the cows and they entered the orchard and ate some of the fruit off the trees. Dad was angry as the devil. He came around the corner and made a beeline for me and I ran and he, being the old backwoods type, took a healthy swing at me with his foot as I went by and he slipped and nearly broke his arm on the wet grass. (At this point S turned around on the couch to look at E.)

E: What did you think when you turned around?

S: The reason I turned around was to look directly at you.

E: Why did you want to look directly at me?

S: If you are trying to put over a point and look directly at the person it is generally better. In sales work, for instance . . . (Again S has departed completely from free association to the idea of making a point and selling an argument. This is another form of resistance, similar to the first. At the same time he has dramatized his feeling toward E. Doubtless

annoyed because E corrected him on account of his first lapse from the fundamental rule, he thinks of an earlier incident in which he lapsed from duty but eluded his father's wrath, and indeed turned the tables by being the cause of his father's hurting himself. This line of thought, however, awakens so much anxiety that he has to turn around to make sure that E is not getting angry. At this point E again reminds S of the fundamental rule.)

According to analytic theory, the therapist initially will be faced with resistance and other forms of defense in free-associative material. These defenses must be recognized by the analyst and made clear to the patient in the process of analytic probing. (We shall return to this point later.)

The Use of Dreams

Because they are viewed as expressions of wishes usually kept from consciousness, dreams play an important role in psychoanalysis. Freud once called them "the royal road to the unconscious." However, there is difficulty faced by the analyst in using dream material: While the patient's defenses are relaxed during sleep, they are not totally absent. Some defenses still operate. Psychoanalysts believe that dreams express unconscious wishes in versions that are sufficiently well disguised to avoid traumatizing (and waking) the sleeper. Because unconscious material is believed to be closer to the surface in dreams than during waking hours, great importance is attached to them in psychoanalysis. A series of sessions may be consumed in recounting and discussing a single dream.

The patient's description of a dream reveals its *manifest content* or obvious features. If a person dreams that he or she is running through the woods and suddenly falls into a lake, this story is the manifest content. Manifest content often contains features associated with the dreamer's activities that day (called "day residue") or may merely supply convenient ways of satisfying temporary wishes without the dreamer having to waken. A hungry person may dream of food, for example.

For psychoanalytic purposes, the most interesting aspect of dreams is their *latent content:* the unconscious ideas and impulses that appear in the form of a safe compromise between repression and expression. The process of transforming unacceptable material into acceptable manifest content is called *dream work.* The many forms that dream work takes have been the subject of extensive writing, beginning with Freud's own *Interpretation of Dreams* (1900).

Most manifest dream content is viewed as *symbols* of something else. In spite of the popular belief that certain dream content (e.g., a snake) always means something specific (e.g., a penis), Freud did not believe dreams could be understood in this inflexible fashion (he is said to have pointed out that "sometimes a cigar is just a cigar"). Most analysts assume, however, that manifest content has symbolic significance, the specifics of which may differ for each person or even from dream to dream.

For example, a meaningful unconscious impulse (e.g., the desire to have extramarital sex) might be *displaced* to a position of minor importance in the dream (a massage parlor advertisement glimpsed from a moving car). In some cases, an innocuous dream event (such as one's brother leaving for a vacation) may *substitute* for taboo wishes (e.g., the brother's death). Dream work may also *devalue* significant material. Munroe (1955) tells of a prudish woman who often dreamed of being partly clothed or naked in public without feeling embarrassed. Presumably, she defended against unconscious sexual wishes by making them seem unimportant.

Unconscious material may be expressed by dreams in *condensed* form. Munroe (1955) provides an excellent example of a dream in which the patient reports: "I am afraid of the dog." To the analyst, this may mean (a) the patient is afraid of God (which is *dog* spelled backward), (b) the patient seeks to hide his fear, even from himself, and (c) by equating God with a dog, the patient expresses contempt for a Supreme Being. Similar shortcuts also appear in dreams as *alogical sequences* (e.g., when there is a sudden shift of time or place) or as *dramatizations* (two people fighting may represent conflicting tendencies within the dreamer).

In addition to dream work, waking defense mechanisms hamper the analyst's attempts to uncover latent content. Usually, the patient is asked to describe the dream as accurately as possible, but the report may be unconsciously organized more logically than was the case in the dream itself. Freud called this process *secondary revision.* To identify those aspects of a dream with the greatest unconscious significance, some analysts ask their patients to repeat a dream two or more times. Later versions will usually differ from the initial story, and the analyst assumes that changes reflect unconscious efforts to disguise or defend against highly charged material.

A common procedure is to ask the patient to free associate to a dream's manifest content. In the process, unconscious material may be revealed. Consider this dream reported to Dr. Robert Lindner by a female patient whose father and mother (who was confined to a wheelchair by paralysis) had a violently unhappy marriage:

I was in what appeared to be a ballroom or dance hall, but I knew it was really a hospital. A man came up to me and told me to undress, take all my clothes off. He was going to give me a gynecological examination. I did as I was told but I was very frightened. While I was undressing, I noticed that he was doing something to a woman at the other end of the room. She was sitting or lying in a funny kind of contraption with all kinds of levers and gears and pulleys attached to it. I knew that I was supposed to be next, that I would have to sit in that thing while he examined me. Suddenly he called my name and I found myself running to him. The chair or table—whatever

Freud claimed that the *Interpretation of Dreams,* first published in 1900 but revised several times thereafter, contained the "most valuable of all the discoveries it has been my good fortune to make." He believed that unless a person understood the origins of his or her dreams, the person would not be able to understand the meaning and source of his or her neurosis.

To give you a flavor of Freud's approach to dreams, we include a few excerpts about the meaning and interpretation of specific dreams, and more general dream themes. First, an illustration of the idea that dreams derive from wishes:

> I do not myself know what animals dream of. But a proverb, to which my attention was drawn by one of my students, does claim to know. 'What,' asks the proverb, 'do geese dream of?' And it replies: 'Of maize.' The whole theory that dreams are wish-fulfillments is contained in these two phrases. (p. 165)

The next passage reports a dream of Freud's youngest daughter, Anna, who went on to become an influential psychoanalyst. It also reveals a wish as the source of a dream:

> My youngest daughter, then nineteen months old, had had an attack of vomiting one morning and had consequently been kept without food all day. During the night after this day of starvation she was heard calling out excitedly in her sleep: 'Anna Fweud, stwawbewwies, wild stwawbewwies, omblet, pudden!' at that time she was in the habit of using her own name to express the idea of taking possession of something. The menu included pretty well everything that must have seemed to her to make up a desirable meal. The fact that strawberries appeared in it in two varieties was a demonstration against the domestic health regulations. It was based upon the circumstance, which she had no doubt observed, that her nurse had attributed her indisposition to a surfeit of strawberries. She was thus retaliating in her dream against this unwelcome verdict. (p. 163)

Freud was convinced that no dream was totally "innocent" of psychological significance—"we do not allow our sleep to be disturbed by trifles." The following dream, simple in its details, reveals how Freud invested importance in the most mundane manifest content:

BOX 8–1

Freud and the Analysis of Dreams

---

it was—was now empty, and he told me to get on it. I refused and began to cry. It started to rain—great big drops of rain. He pushed me to the floor and spread my legs for examination. I turned over on my stomach and began to scream. I woke myself up screaming. (Lindner, 1954, pp. 134–135)

Lindner describes how this manifest content is used as raw material for free association:

"Well," she said after a brief, expectant silence, "What does it mean?"

"Laura," I admonished, "you know better than that. Associate and we'll find out."

"The first thing I think of is Ben," she began. "He's an intern at the University, you know. I guess that's the doctor in the dream—or maybe it was you. Anyhow, whoever it was, I wouldn't let him examine me."

"Why not?"

He dreamt that he was putting on his winter overcoat once more, which was a dreadful thing. The ostensible reason for this dream was a sudden return of cold weather. If we look more closely, however, we shall notice that the two short pieces that make up the dream are not in complete harmony. For what could there be 'dreadful' about putting on a heavy or thick overcoat in cold weather? Moreover, the innocence of the dream was decidedly upset by the first association that occurred to the dreamer in the analysis. He recalled that a lady confided to him the day before that her youngest child owed its existence to a torn condom. On that basis he was able to reconstruct his thought. A thin condom was dangerous, but a thick one was bad. The condom was suitably represented as an overcoat, since one slips into both of them. But an occurrence such as the lady described to him would certainly be 'dreadful' for an unmarried man. (p 219)

Finally, we turn to a category of dream that almost all students report having experienced—the dream that one has missed a crucial test or has forgotten to prepare for it until it is too late:

The ineradicable memories of the punishment that we suffered for our evil deeds in childhood become active within us once more and attach themselves to the two crucial points in our studies. . . . The 'examination anxiety' of neurotics owes its intensification to these same childhood fears. After we have ceased to be schoolchildren, our punishments are no longer inflicted on us by our parents or by those who brought us up or later by our schoolmasters. The relentless causal chains of real life take charge of our further education, and now we dream of Matriculation or Finals (and who has not trembled on those occasions, even if he has well-prepared for the examination?) whenever, having done something wrong or failed to do something properly, we expect to be punished by the event—whenever, in short, we feel the burden of responsibility. (p. 308)

Source: S. Freud, *The Interpretation of Dreams* (1900). New York: Avon Books, 1965.

BOX 8–1
Continued

"I've always been afraid of doctors . . . afraid they might hurt me."

"How will they hurt you?"

"I don't know. By jabbing me with a needle, I guess. That's funny, never thought of it before. When I go to the dentist I don't mind getting a needle; but with a doctor it's different . . . I shudder when I think of having my veins punctured. I'm always afraid that's what the doctor will do to me."

"Has it ever been done?"

She nodded. "Once, in college, for a blood test, I passed out cold."

"What about gynecological examinations?"

"I've never had one. I can't bear to think of someone poking around inside me." Again silence; then, "Oh," she said, "I see it now. It's sex. I'm afraid the doctor in the dream *is* Ben. He wants me to have intercourse, but it scares me and I turn away from him." (Lindner, 1954, p. 135)

This "insight" seems to have come too easily and was too obvious. The analyst feels sure there is more to it.

" . . . Other men have made love to you."

"Yes," she said, sobbing now, "but I only let them as a last resort, as a way of holding on to them a little longer . . . I'd do anything to keep them from getting inside me—poking into me . . . like the needle, I guess."

"But why, Laura?"

"I don't know," she cried "I don't know. Tell me."

"I think the dream tells you," I said.

"The dream I just told you?"

"Yes . . . There's a part of it you haven't considered. What comes to your mind when you think of the other woman in your dream, the woman the doctor was examining before you?"

"The contraption she was sitting in," Laura exclaimed, "It was like a—like a wheel chair—my mother's wheel chair—my mother's wheel chair! Is that right?"

"Very likely," I said.

"But why would he be examining *her?* What would that mean?"

"Well, think of what that kind of examination signifies for you."

"Sex," she said. "Intercourse—that's what it means. So that's what it is—that's what it means! Intercourse put my mother in the wheel chair. It paralyzed her. And I'm afraid that's what it will do to me. So I avoid it—because I'm scared it will do the same thing to me. . . . Where did I ever get such a crazy idea?" (Lindner, 1954, pp. 136–137)

Notice how free association to dream content led the patient to an insight that will provoke further exploration of unconscious material not yet revealed.

The first dream reported to the analyst may contain a summary of all major problems (Blanck, 1976). Frequently, a series of dreams is used in analysis. Attention to multiple dreams reveals patterns of latent content and helps to avoid errors that occur when too much emphasis is placed on a single dream.

Dreams provide ideas for further probing more often than they provide final answers. The caution with which one must analyze even obvious dream content, symbols, and association is spelled out by Bonime (1962):

If a woman were dreaming of a snake which associatively became established as a penis, it would still be necessary, if one is to achieve insight into her personality through her dream symbol, to establish the quality of experience with a penis which was symbolized by that snake. If she were a professional dancer largely preoccupied by a desire to be seductive, and if she had performed the dance of a snake charmer, then the penile snake could symbolize her desire to charm men or control them by her sexual allure. . . .

If a woman had been made pregnant before a promised marriage by a man who later deserted her, the penile snake in her dream might represent the quality of deceit or poisonousness, or both, not only in men but also in any human being who offered intimacy. If she had had a puritanical upbringing and yet indulged in a sexual affair, the penile snake might represent hidden "sinful" desires or actual secret activities of a sexual nature. . . . By still further extension, the snake could refer . . . to yearnings for other types of self-indulgence [or] self-gratification. . . . (p. 36)

Attention to Everyday Behavior

One of Freud's primary concepts was *psychic determinism,* the notion that human behavior is caused by conscious and unconscious mental processes. An obvious consequence of this view, spelled out in *The Psychopathology of Everyday Life* (1901), is that our day-to-day behavior reflects unconscious wishes, fantasies, and defenses.

Accordingly, the psychoanalyst is consistently sensitive to all of a patient's behavior, whether in treatment sessions or in their reports of activities between sessions. The analyst tries to maintain an "evenly divided" or "free-floating" attention to trivial as well as momentous events, to purposeful acts and accidental happenings, to body language as well as spoken language. These processes expose habitual defense tactics and the secrets they are assumed to protect. Psychoanalytic theory has generated numerous examples of potentially meaningful everyday behaviors. Two of the better-known categories, *mistakes* and *humor,* are discussed next.

Mistakes. In the midst of the Watergate scandal, former President Nixon made the following statement in a speech to Congress: " . . . Join me in mounting a new effort to replace the discredited president. . . . " He actually meant to say " . . . to replace the discredited present welfare system . . . ," but other problems on his mind may have been revealed in this slip of the tongue. Such Freudian slips, or *parapraxes,* are thought to indicate the speaker's actual, often unconscious feelings. Slips of the pen may also reflect feelings: "Dear Madeline: Your party was just divine. Thanks so much for inviting us. We can wait to see you again. . . . "

While analysts use parapraxes to help the patient's self-exploration, they also focus on more subtle errors that reflect carefully protected unconscious material that has slipped out. Brenner (1974) mentions a case in which a young male patient who was interested in body building referred to "physical culture" as "physible culture." This "accidental" mistake had no immediate meaning for either patient or therapist. However, the patient was asked to free associate to the word *physible*. His first association was the word *visible* and from there he continued until he revealed an un-

conscious wish to exhibit his nude body (and to see others naked).

"Accidental" events, especially those in which the patient has at least partial responsibility, may also be seen as wishful. The waiter who spills hot soup on an elderly male customer might be asked in analysis to free associate to various elements in this "accident." The result might be an inference that the waiter was attempting to execute a father substitute.

Forgetfulness is a prime example of a motivated error. We are not talking about cases in which a person purposely "forgets" a dental appointment, but about instances in which a memory lapse occurs without obvious cause. If a patient forgets the manifest content of the dream she or he had planned to describe, the analyst may suspect that the dream contained material too threatening to remember. Sometimes a patient achieves an important insight into an unconscious wish and forgets what it was, apparently as a defense against acknowledging unflattering personal characteristics.

Brenner (1974) tells of a patient who inexplicably forgot the name of a familiar friend at a party. As the patient free associated to this event, it came to have important unconscious meaning:

> As he talked about it, it developed that the name of the acquaintance was the same as that of another man whom he knew and toward whom he had strong feelings of hatred which made him feel very guilty. . . . In addition he mentioned that the acquaintance was crippled, which reminded him of some of his wishes to hurt and injure the namesake whom he hated. . . . In order to avoid becoming conscious of his destructive fantasies . . . he repressed the name which would have made the connection between the two. (p. 130)

Although psychoanalytic theory seems to leave no room for real accidents or innocent mistakes, events over which a person has no control (e.g., being injured when a plane crashes through one's roof) are seen as genuine accidents. However, if the victim can be seen as in any way responsible for the mishap, there is a potential for unconscious significance. The authors know of a woman who returned from the grocery store on a snowy day and, in the process of carrying several bags of groceries into the house, fell on the ice and broke her leg. Upon hearing the commotion, her psychiatrist husband ran outside, saw her writhing in pain, and shouted, "Why did you do this to me?" Using analytic logic, the husband presumed that, though the fall was probably due to snow and ice, his wife's failure to ask for help or to carry only one bag at a time expressed an unconscious desire to get more loving attention from him or to punish him by adding the nursing of an invalid to his daily responsibilities.

Humor. Freud noted that humor usually contains expressions of *hostility* or *aggression*. The transformation of angry feelings into humor is called *wit work,* which can take several forms. Puns are good examples of *condensation,* in which multiple meanings are conveyed by a single word: "The elephant circumcisor told me his job had good and bad points. The pay is lousy but the tips are big." Here, in addition to condensation in the word *tips,* there may be some *displacement* of aggression toward persons symbolized by the elephant. When one considers how many jokes present situations in which a person or group is made to look foolish or is injured or killed, it is easy to see how Freud reached his conclusions.

According to psychoanalytic theory, jokes provide a safe outlet for anger which, if ex-

---

BOX 8–2

Freud's Analysis of a Slip of the Tongue

In *The Psychopathology of Everyday Life,* Freud (1901) describes his analysis of a slip of the tongue made by a young male acquaintance. It reveals how, according to psychoanalytic theory, significant material emerges in extremely subtle ways.

In the course of his conversation with Freud, the young man quotes, in Latin, Virgil's *Aeneid:* "Exoriare aliquis nostris ex ossibus ultor" ("Let someone arise from my bones as an avenger"). In doing so, he left out *aliquis* ("someone"). To help the man find the meaning of his error, Freud asked him to free associate to *aliquis.*

The associations included dividing the word into *a* and *liquous* as well as other words like *reliquien* (meaning "relics"), *liquefying, fluidity,* and *fluid.* He then thought of the relics of Simon of Trent which he had seen 2 years earlier, then of blood sacrifices, then of a newspaper article called "What St. Augustine Says about Women." Later, he thought of St. Januaris and the miracle of his blood

(which is supposed to liquefy on a certain holy day each year) and the fact that the miracle was once delayed.

The young man then became disturbed and he stopped associating. Freud asked what was wrong and was told that the new association was too intimate to reveal and involved a young lady from whom he was expecting some news. At this point, Freud said that the news involved the possibility that the woman was pregnant.

The man's astonishment at having his secret (which was far more shocking in 1900 than it is now) uncovered was relieved somewhat as Freud explained his method. The references in free association to liquid, blood, calendar saints, regularly occurring miracles of flowing blood, concern over a delay in the miracle, and the like all led Freud to see the man's conscious and unconscious preoccupation with menstruation and possible pregnancy.

pressed directly, might bring retaliation or feelings of guilt. Because the joke disguises the aggressive impulse, the psychic energy that would have been used to repress that impulse becomes unnecessary and is released in the form of laughter. Thus, the jokes a person makes or finds funny may be examined by the analyst in helping that person toward self-understanding. Freud's theory of humor is covered in his *Jokes and Their Relation to the Unconscious* (1905) and in Grotjahn (1957).

Analysis of Resistance

The psychoanalyst assumes that the patient will display various forms of *resistance* in the course of treatment. We have discussed resistance in the context of free association and dream analysis, but there are other forms as well. All are important because (a) they highlight the topics and time periods about which the patient is most defensive, and (b) they provide current examples of habitual defenses the patient can recognize and finally abandon. Because ultimate improvement can only be made in the absence of resistance, psychoanalysis is fundamentally involved with removing it.

The ways resistance can appear are too numerous to catalog here. We give a few examples to illustrate the possibilities (see Fine, 1971, especially Chapters 8–10, for more detailed coverage). Obvious resistance is inferred from a patient's repeated absence from or lateness for treatment sessions. Unwillingness to speak about certain topics,[3] refusal to lie on the couch, falling asleep, or failure to pay the therapist's bill are often interpreted in the same way.

Depression or expression of hopelessness when a breakthrough is about to occur is sometimes viewed as the patient's way of delaying painful insights. "At the point where

feelings of hopelessness arise, many therapists are tempted to switch to some other technique, convinced that the standard analytic approach has failed. This is precisely what the patient is trying to get them to do. ... His hopelessness has a manipulative purpose, to drive other people away, and allow him to wallow in his misery" (Fine, 1971, pp. 123–124).

A similar interpretation may be made of other patient behaviors. A common example is *intellectualization*. Here, important emotions are repressed, but the patient does not appear uncooperative. Instead, she or he simply substitutes logic and reason for feelings that may be present. In discussing a parent's death, the patient might calmly say something like "Well, yes, I was sad, but actually we had all been expecting this to happen so there was no shock. Besides, I was responsible for making all the arrangements and that took up all my energy." Other patients avoid their problems by attempting to engage the analyst in scholarly debates about the effectiveness of various therapeutic techniques.

When threatened by analytic probing, some patients develop physical symptoms for which there is no organic cause. A chronic cough, a lingering cold, or other "physical" problems may make conversation difficult during sessions or may prevent sessions from taking place. Resistance is suspected by analysts when other, more severe, behavior patterns appear. *Regression,* in which the patient goes backward in development by remaining in bed, abandoning good grooming, crying, and requiring constant care, may be potentially permanent obstacles to analysis.

Other resistant behaviors involve *acting out*. Substance abuse, participation in dangerous activities, or other dramatic life changes may be the patient's way of escaping anxiety brought about by the possible uncovering of repressed material. As dangerous as these tactics are for the patient, acting out can be hazardous to the therapist as well. Analytic patients have, on rare occasions, attempted to

___
[3]Or refusal to speak at all. There is a case on record of a patient who said nothing in therapy for 2 years (Fine, 1971).

injure or kill their therapists, perhaps as part of a desperate attempt to avoid recognizing the truth about themselves.

A final form of resistance, probably the most difficult for nonanalytic observers to accept, is when the patient feels that (a) external rather than intrapsychic factors are primarily responsible for problems, (b) problems are getting worse, or (c) he or she has a right as a consumer to be given evidence of the value of the psychoanalytic approach. In each instance, the patient makes a reasonable statement or request, but the therapist interprets it as diverting attention from the dynamics presumed to underlie problems. Therefore, if the analyst focuses attention on *why* the patient wants to know about the analysis or the reason for slow progress, instead of giving a straightforward answer, the goal is not to evade the issue but to follow psychoanalytic principles. Those principles dictate that any patient behavior that interferes with the analytic process should be dealt with as a defense so that, ultimately, the unconscious material that underlies the patient's problems can be made conscious.

Analysis of the Transference

In psychoanalysis, the therapist–client relationship is an important source of raw material for probing the unconscious and its defenses. The patient's feelings toward and relationship with the therapist are called the *transference*.[4] It is thought to develop on at least two levels. The first involves realistic, mostly conscious feelings, as when the patient expresses gratitude for the therapist's help. At this level, there is a *therapeutic alliance* that facilitates treatment.

At an unconscious level, however, the transference contains attitudes and reactions

related to the patient's unconscious conflicts, many of which go back to childhood and lie at the root of current symptoms. The patient may have reactions to or feelings about the analyst determined not by the therapist's actual characteristics or behavior, but by the ways the patient related to significant people in the past. The transference is a dramatic example of how current relationships are built from past blueprints.

This assumption is based on Freud's belief that time does not exist in the unconscious. The earliest unconscious conflicts are always active (unless made conscious and worked through) no matter how much time goes by, and they make their presence known in many problematic ways, including disrupted interpersonal relationships.

Unconscious factors color the patient's interactions with anyone who evokes childhood conflicts. The therapist is an especially likely transference candidate for several reasons. First, the analyst is in a position of high status in relation to the patient who comes for help in time of trouble. This identifies the therapist as an *authority* and brings to mind images of a parental figure. These images are intensified by the therapist conveying a *caring attitude*. The patient may associate this attitude with actual or wished-for attributes of her or his parents. In addition, the therapist tries to be non-judgmental and to accept with equanimity whatever the patient reveals. This tends to foster feelings of trust, again reminiscent of real or fantasized attitudes toward parents or other valued persons from the past. Finally, because the analyst maintains an "analytic incognito" by revealing little about herself or himself, she or he becomes a sort of blank screen onto which the patient can project all sorts of attributes and motives.

While the patient may sometimes unconsciously see the therapist as a loving parent, he or she may also react as though the therapist were a vengeful father, a seductive mother, a jealous lover, or one of many other figures. The specifics depend on the patient's

---

[4]The therapist's feelings about the patient are referred to as *countertransference*. They distort the therapeutic process; therefore, therapists must be keenly alert to their own countertransference tendencies.

particular unconscious difficulties. When the patient–therapist relationship creates a miniature version of the patient's overall problems, it is referred to as the *transference neurosis* and becomes the central focus of analytic work. Freud noted that the appearance of the transference and transference neurosis often took the form of female patients' erotic fantasies about him. He concluded that these women were expressing childhood wishes about their fathers, for whom he had been symbolically substituted.

The reproduction of early unconscious conflicts is remarkably convenient because it allows the analyst to work with important problems from the past as they occur in the present through the transference. For this reason, most of an analyst's attention is centered on events occurring during treatment sessions themselves.

Patients display transference and transference neurosis in many ways. Among the more obvious is *dependence* on the therapist. The patient may show up early for every session,[5] express reluctance to leave at the end of the hour, telephone for advice at all hours, or make demands on the analyst. The development of intense feelings of love for the analyst may reach dramatic proportions. Some patients become so caught up in fantasizing about a love affair with the analyst that nothing else seems important to them. When the therapist fails to reciprocate, strong feelings of disappointment and/or anger often appear. The patient may become depressed and may even attempt suicide.

Negative feelings about the therapist also reflect transference. The patient may decide that the analyst is incompetent. Although these sentiments are repeatedly expressed in no uncertain terms, the patient may not terminate therapy. To the therapist, this means that the

patient is not simply an unhappy customer, but one who is using the therapeutic relationship to express feelings intended for a parent or other significant person. Negative transference may also appear in less direct, more childish ways. Fine (1971) tells of a 16-year-old patient who attempted to annoy the analyst by calling him on the telephone 15 or 20 times an hour, sometimes identifying himself as Christopher Columbus.

Transference and transference neuroses must be handled with care. The analyst tries to decode the meaning of the patient's positive or negative feelings. If the analyst responded "normally" to a confession of love or a verbal attack, the patient would not learn much and a premature termination of therapy could occur. The transference must be kept active without forcing the patient out of therapy. If this can be done, unconscious material can be made conscious and worked through. The transference neurosis is thereby resolved. When all these goals are accomplished, the patient's analysis is usually seen as complete.

Working through the transference takes much longer than working through a specific symptom. Thus, while psychoanalysis may begin because of a particular complaint (e.g., anxiety attacks), it is likely to continue long after that problem disappears because the patient's real difficulties are believed to be revealed in the transference.

Making Analytic Interpretations

So far, we have outlined major sources of unconscious material and the psychoanalytic techniques used to tap them. We have also seen that defense mechanisms make it unlikely that the patient will understand this material, because unconsciously he or she does not want to.

The analyst, on the other hand, is trained to look for hidden meanings and, because she or he is an objective observer, the significance of the patient's behavior should be easier for the analyst to detect. The problem, of course, is how

---

[5]It has jokingly been pointed out that you cannot win in analysis because you are dependent if you show up early, resistant if you show up late, and compulsive if you are right on time.

to help patients accept material that might be threatening, while at the same time not overwhelming them with too much insight before they are ready to handle it. This is where *analytic interpretation* comes in. Through questions and comments about verbal and nonverbal behaviors, free associations, dreams, and the like, the analyst guides the patient's self-exploration. When the patient is resistant or when she or he is unable to see the potential meaning of some event, the therapist points this out and offers suggestions for new ways to look at things.

Interpretations are not simply statements of how the analyst construes the patient's problems. The interpretive process is tentative and continuous, a constant encouragement of the patient to consider alternative views, to reject obvious explanations, to search for deeper meanings. Interpretations move analysis along by promoting insight and the working through of those insights.

The analyst does not interpret everything of unconscious significance for the patient as soon as he or she detects it. Therapists face three important questions as they work at the delicate task of giving valid and usable interpretations: What could this dream (or association or response) mean? Is it related to important unconscious content? Is now the time to say something to the patient about it?

A correctly timed interpretation can result in a step forward; it " . . . stirs up the patient in one way or another. It brings his whole personality into the office of the analyst and provides a kind of emotional reeducation on the spot" (Munroe, 1955, p. 307). When an interpretation is accurate, important, and well timed, it will evoke positive (or negative) feelings in the patient that promote insight. On the other hand, most analysts feel that a correct interpretation of important material can arouse too much emotion or strong defenses if it is given before the patient is ready to use it.

As a rule of thumb, an interpretation is best delivered at the point where the patient is nearly aware of something important, but has not yet verbalized it. Ideally, " . . . one 'tells' a patient

what the patient *almost* sees for himself and one tells him in such a way that the patient—not the analyst—takes 'credit' for the discovery" (Menninger, 1958, p. 134). The therapist tries to say just the right things at just the right times. When he or she succeeds, the analytic interpretation becomes a tool like the surgeon's scalpel.

The analyst's interpretations can reflect narrow hypotheses about specific relationships, or they can deal with broader conceptualizations. Some interpretations are made directly, especially when the patient is thought to be ready for a straightforward presentation. In other instances the analyst will merely hint at hypotheses so that the patient can deal with the new idea gradually. Several illustrations of analytic interpretations are presented next.

Interpreting Resistance. The analyst's first job (besides establishing a good working relationship) usually involves identifying and overcoming resistance to the analytic process. The patient can be made aware of resistance in many ways.

PATIENT: I've been thinking; we've spent five sessions together and have gotten nowhere. How long does it take for me to start seeing some changes?

If the analyst were sure that this was resistance, a direct interpretation might be offered:

THERAPIST: I don't know the answer to that question, but it seems to me that by bringing it up, you could be attempting to avoid talking about other things.

A less direct interpretation could also be used:

THERAPIST: I don't know the answer to that question, but I wonder why you asked it.

After an analyst has had time to observe continuing patterns of resistance, a more elaborate interpretation might be ventured:

PATIENT: I'm sorry to be late, but I got a long-distance call from my brother-in-law just as I was leaving the house. He told me that my sister has gotten sick and wanted to know if I had some cash to spare to help with the medical bills. I don't know how I can afford to do it and still keep coming to see you. Sometimes everything falls on me at once.

THERAPIST: You know, last session we began to see that your feelings toward your parents were not all positive. I think we are on to something important in that area. Today you start off by saying that, through no fault of your own, you may not be able to continue therapy. This seems to be a recurring thing. Whenever you are threatened by what you learn about yourself, a disaster seems to occur that diverts your attention. You got out of trouble this way as a child, too. Whenever your parents became angry with you, you found a way to show that someone else had prevented you from doing what you should have done. Has this ever occurred to you?

Interpreting Other Analytic Productions. Dreams also produce raw material for analytic interpretations. The wheelchair dream illustrated how an analyst might lead a patient to an understanding of latent content. Here is another example of interpretation based on various analytic products:

You know, it's very interesting that whenever you say something that is a little bit nasty to anyone you smile. After you've been a little bit aggressive, you become *very* agreeable and nice, and I notice it here. I wonder if when you were with your father you discovered that the only way to keep him from attacking you was to become more sociable, amiable, in this kind of smiling, passive way. . . . (Barton, 1974, p. 33)

Interpreting the Transference. Because it is thought to be intimately related to the patient's early intrapsychic conflicts, the transference is a prime target for analytic interpretation. After observing a patient's dependence, the analyst might remark: "I notice that you often deal with me in the same way you dealt with your parents as a child. You want me to protect you and help you through the difficulties you are facing." The same interpretation could be couched in less obvious terms: "I get the feeling that you would like me to magically solve all your problems, and I wonder if you have ever felt that way about anyone else."

Accurate interpretation of transference sometimes provokes a negative reaction from the client. This reaction must itself be interpreted. For example:

PATIENT: I have a confession to make. I never could have come through these last 2 months without your help. I love you.

THERAPIST: If we examine why you feel that way about me, we might discover who I represent to you when I provide psychological support.

PATIENT: Can't you even take a compliment like a human being? I was trying to tell you how I feel about *you*; I wasn't saying anything about me! Can't you come off your analytic throne for even 1 minute?

THERAPIST: You expressed love for me. That has been very hard for you to do. It is important to understand why you do it in relation to me now when you couldn't before. It is also important to understand why you got so angry just now when I did not respond as you wanted me to.

This exchange is likely to lead to exploration of the patient's problems in expressing tender feelings toward others, particularly toward parents, and may uncover a strong need to be reassured about self-worth. In the process, the patient may find that unreturned love does not mean one is worthless. It may also become clear that his or her parents were not able to be loving and that nothing he or she could have done as a child would have changed that fact. Insight about this discovery may be worked through in later sessions as the analyst and patient consider implications of the transference.

As interpretations help the patient understand and work through the transference, the therapist–patient relationship changes. The patient not only sees how defenses and unconscious conflicts caused problems, she or he learns to deal differently with the world, beginning with the therapist. The patient learns that the forces of the past no longer need dictate the behavior of the present. The analyst is not the patient's parent, and neither is the patient's boss or spouse. Ideally, this emotional understanding will liberate the patient to deal with life in a more realistic and satisfying manner.

Our outline of classic psychoanalytic techniques has left out many details and oversimplified others. More complete coverage of the approach is contained in Munroe (1955), Menninger (1958), Kernberg (1976), and, of course, Freud (e.g., 1949).

Applications

In its original form, psychoanalysis was used in one-to-one treatment of "neurotic" adults over a period of several years. This classical approach has been varied to make it shorter and more applicable to groups, families, and younger patients, but the typical recipient of psychoanalytic treatment remains a relatively intelligent adult who has the time and financial resources to embark on an extended intellectual and emotional adventure.

A "good" analytic patient should be motivated to work at solving problems. She or he must be capable of free association and must be able to form an interpersonal relationship with the therapist. Further, the patient should be able to think logically about the world, including her or his own behavior, and to maintain contact with reality. Finally, the patient must have enough courage to focus on his or

her problems. These requirements rule out, for the most part, the use of orthodox psychoanalysis with psychotic patients.

VARIATIONS OF PSYCHOANALYSIS

Freud attracted many followers. Some sought to preserve his ideas and techniques in their original form; others advocated changes ranging from minor alteration to wholesale rejection of fundamental principles. These changes suggested a broader range of therapeutic techniques than had been "legal" under orthodox Freudian rules. In this section we describe a few of these treatment innovations, beginning with those that are least distinct from the original model and progressing to those incorporating more radical changes.

Psychoanalytically Oriented Psychotherapy

Many therapists employ psychoanalytic procedures that depart somewhat from the guidelines set down by Freud. Although these individuals see themselves as practicing psychoanalysis, traditional Freudians refer to such treatments as *psychoanalytically oriented psychotherapy*. This phrase encompasses a number of nonorthodox analytic procedures, but it is most closely associated with the approach developed by Franz Alexander and his colleagues at the Chicago Psychoanalytic Institute during the 1930s and 1940s.

The treatment philosophy of the Chicago group (e.g., Alexander, 1956, 1963; Alexander & French, 1946) grew out of doubts about traditional therapeutic practices. For example, the Alexander group questioned the belief that treatment must be intense, extended, and fundamentally similar in all cases. They also sought to apply psychoanalysis to two previously excluded patient groups: the young and the more severely disturbed.

Alexander (1963, p. 273) summarized his

views this way: "Psychoanalytic principles lend themselves to different therapeutic procedures which vary according to the nature of the case and may be variably applied during the treatment of the same patient." In psychoanalytically oriented psychotherapy, not every patient is seen for the traditional five sessions each week because some people may not benefit from such intense effort. Daily sessions may foster too much dependence on the analyst or may become so routine that the patient pays too little attention to them.

In a given case, the frequency of sessions varies as circumstances dictate. Early in treatment the patient may be seen every day. Later, the sessions may take place less often. Alexander even suggested that temporary interruptions in treatment could be beneficial by testing the patient's ability to live without therapy and to reduce reliance on the therapist.

Traditional psychoanalysis is lengthy due to the perceived need for fully exploring and working through resistance, insights, and the transference. Alexander suggested that persons whose problems are relatively mild, who are well adjusted except for a particular difficulty, or who are more seriously disturbed than the usual analytic patient are candidates for less extensive treatment aimed at support rather than at the uncovering and reconstruction associated with classic analysis.

Alexander emphasized *corrective emotional experiences* in therapy. The idea is to help the patient see that old conflicts need no longer run her or his life, and to use the transference to let the patient resolve those old conflicts in a better way. "Re-experiencing the old, unsettled conflict *but with a new ending* is the secret of every penetrating therapeutic result . . . " (Alexander & French, 1946, p. 338).

Modern-day practitioners of psychodynamically oriented therapy (e.g., Strupp, 1989; Strupp & Blinder, 1984) try to create an empathic and supportive atmosphere where the patient feels cared for and understood. In this context, the patient begins to reenact conflicts from the past with the therapist (the transference). The therapist becomes, at least for a time, part of the reenacted conflict. The therapist strives to respond to this in a way that suggests to the client that his or her struggles are understandable, that they can be confronted safely, and that they can be changed. How the therapist responds to the troublesome reenactments is crucial; psychodynamically oriented therapists are likely to be more empathically supportive and less prone to interpretation than classic psychoanalysts at this juncture. In other words, in this version of psychoanalysis, transference is not only analyzed, it may be manipulated; countertransference is not only a complicating reaction that the analyst comes to understand through self-analysis, it is also a potential treatment tool.

A general rule in Freudian analysis is that the patient should not make major life decisions while treatment is underway in order to prevent bad decisions caused by maladaptive impulses, false insights, or neurotic defenses. In contrast, the analytically oriented therapist may encourage life changes that the patient and analyst agree make sense. This procedure is based on the assumption that the therapeutic relationship is a good stage on which to rehearse ideas for progress that are then tested in real life. The changes sometimes involve manipulation of the patient's environment and are often initiated by the therapist. A patient who is unhappy about an unsatisfying job might be encouraged to look for a better position. Here, the therapist performs a guidance function that is more active and direct than in orthodox analysis.[6]

At various points in treatment, psychoanalytically oriented therapists use a number of unorthodox techniques, including the following:

---

[6] In spite of their theoretical restrictions, orthodox analysts also give advice (Munroe, 1955; Strupp, 1972).

1. The patient may sit up and face the analyst rather than lie on a couch.

2. Normal conversation may be substituted for free association.

3. Hypnosis may be used to promote self-exploration.

4. The nature of current problems and their solution is emphasized.

5. The patient's family may be consulted (or even offered treatment) as part of a total effort at helping the client.

The Ego Analysts

Psychoanalytically oriented psychotherapists accept most of Freud's basic tenets but revise his procedures. Another group of therapists, usually referred to as *ego analysts,* stray from the strict Freudian path by arguing that the psychoanalytic preoccupation with sexual and aggressive instincts as the bases of behavior is too narrow. Wolberg's (1967) summary of the ego-analytic position is presented in edited form:

1. Behavior is determined by forces other than instinct. These include responses encompassed under the concept of ego.

2. The ego has an autonomy separate from both instinct (id) and reality.

3. The ego prompts drives for environmental mastery and adaptive learning that are separate from sexual and aggressive instincts.

4. Female sexuality is on a par with, rather than inferior to, male sexuality.

5. The classical topography (id, ego, superego) does not explain the structure of personality.

6. Therapy is more than a means of exploring and working through early childhood experiences. It is a relationship experience that contains positive growth potential that can lead to self-actualization.

7. Activity and flexibility are essential to therapy.

8. An optimistic rather than a pessimistic viewpoint is justified with regard to the human potential for creativity and love.

These views led the ego analysts "to explore the complexity in behavior that each person develops and with which he *directs his own activity and deals constructively with his environment"* (Ford & Urban, 1963, p. 181; italics added). People are presumed to be capable of using ego functions to control their behavior and organize that behavior in positive as well as negative ways. This more optimistic view of human beings has much in common with the phenomenological approach (see Chapters 2 and 10). It led analysts such as Heinz Hartmann (1958), David Rapaport (1951), Melanie Klein (1960), Freud's daughter Anna Freud (1946), and Erik Erikson (1946) to use psychoanalytic techniques to explore patients' adaptive ego functions as well as their basic id instincts. For more on the theory and practice of ego analysis, see Munroe (1955), Ford and Urban (1963), Guntrip (1973), Eagle (1984), or Slipp (1981).

Psychoanalytically oriented psychotherapy and ego analysis are *revisions* of Freudian concepts and techniques, not outright revolts against them. However, other therapists moved further from Freud. These therapists retained a psychodynamic orientation, but deemphasized Freud's theory of instincts, infantile sexuality, and the unconscious determination of behavior. The treatment techniques developed by this group are our next topic.

Alfred Adler's Individual Psychology

Alfred Adler, an early follower of Freud, was the first to defect from the ranks of orthodox psychoanalysis. The reasons for his departure and the alternative theory he formulated are outlined in Chapter 2.

Adler believed that people's problematic lifestyles were based largely on misconceptions they held. His treatment methods focused on exploring and altering those misconceptions. Where a strict Freudian might see a student's vomiting before school each day as a defense of some kind, the Adlerian analyst would suggest that the problem was a manifestation of general tension brought about by some misconception ("I must do better than anyone else" or "The teachers are out to make me look bad") on which the student bases his or her lifestyle. In Freudian analysis, this vomiting might be explored through free association or other means to understand its defensive function. In Adler's Individual Psychology, the symptom would be discussed as one illustration of the patient's mistaken attitudes and maladaptive lifestyle. The patient would then be helped to form more appropriate attitudes and given encouragement to change his or her style in the direction of what Adler (1963) called *social interest, courage,* and *common sense.*

Mosak and Dreikurs (1973) have outlined the goals of Adlerian psychotherapy:

1. To establish and maintain a good therapeutic relationship (i.e., a therapeutic alliance, in Freudian terms)

2. To uncover the patient's lifestyle and goals, as well as to explore how they affect him or her in daily life

3. To give interpretations that lead the patient to gain insight into his or her lifestyle and its consequences

4. To reorient the patient's attitudes so that they support a more adaptive lifestyle; to translate the patient's insight into constructive action.

Adlerian Treatment Techniques

Patient–Therapist Relationship. Adlerians' goal is to create a cooperative relationship between equals. Accordingly, the patient and therapist normally sit face to face in similar chairs. The feelings and reactions expressed toward the therapist (transference) are not seen as reflecting unconscious childhood conflicts, but are interpreted as the patient's habitual style of dealing with people like the therapist. "The patient ... expects from the therapist the kind of response he has trained himself from childhood to believe that people or certain people will give him" (Mosak & Dreikurs, 1973, p. 55).

The therapist also watches for lifestyle clues in the scripts, or standard interpersonal ploys, that the patient creates in treatment. Usually, the therapist is expected to play a particular part. For example, the patient may repeatedly enact the "poor soul" role intended to bring a nurturant response from the therapist. This style may be typical of the patient's maladaptive way of getting love and attention.

Handling Resistance. Adlerians view resistance as a sample of the patient's usual way of avoiding unpleasant material. In addition, resistance may reflect the fact that the patient and therapist have different goals. The therapist's goal is to explore the patient's basic lifestyle and misconceptions, but, because clinging to one's misconceptions maintains feelings of security, the patient will protect those misconceptions from exposure. When the patient's goal is to maintain the status quo, he or she will appear resistant ("I can't understand what you are talking about"; "I'm too upset to talk about this now"). The therapist may handle such resistance by interpreting its meaning and by pointing out its consequences. A discussion of goals may then result which, for the moment at least, reestablishes therapist–patient cooperation.

Dreams. Adler did not interpret dreams in treatment as the compromised fulfillment of wishes from the past, but rather as a rehearsal of how the patient might deal with problems in the future. The moods in a dream are seen as setting the stage for the next day's activities. "If we wish to postpone action, we forget the dream. If we wish to dissuade ourselves from some action, we frighten ourselves with a nightmare" (Mosak & Dreikurs, 1973, p. 58).

Adler also used dreams as an indication of therapeutic progress. For example, short dreams with little action might reflect a passive approach to dealing with problems. As treatment proceeds and the patient begins to experiment with a more active lifestyle, her or his dreams should become more active as well. Some Adlerians use the patient's dreams to guide them in deciding when to terminate therapy (Rosenthal, 1959).

The Lifestyle Investigation. In addition to attending to dreams, resistance, the transference, nonverbal behavior, and other material, Adlerians (e.g., Dreikurs, 1954) explore the patient's lifestyle in a more systematic way. They focus on the patient's family and his or her position in it, the earliest memories the patient can recall (because they reflect the lifestyle), basic mistakes or misconceptions, and the assets and strengths the patient possesses. The summary of a lifestyle investigation is presented in Box 8–3.

Interpretation. In Adlerian therapy, resistance and transference are usually interpreted as examples of the patient's maladaptive lifestyle. Interpretation is also used to promote insight about the lifestyle meaning of the patient's dreams, interpersonal relationships, and other behavior. Where Freud interpreted in order to promote insight into *past causes* of current problems, Adler interpreted in order to promote insight into the patient's current lifestyle.

Instead of using it as a scalpel, Adlerians employ interpretation as a mirror in which patients can see how they cope with life. Adler often phrased his interpretations as questions, such as, "Could it be that your unhappiness with your work is related to your insistence that everything must go perfectly for you, and that if it doesn't, you are a failure?" This style of interpretation emphasizes the purpose of the patient's behavior rather than its cause, and it encourages the patient to be an active collaborator in the search for this purpose. When patients see what it is they are doing, it

becomes harder to maintain maladaptive ideas and behaviors.

Advice and Encouragement. While Freud pointed out that patients must sometimes be encouraged to do things they have been afraid of in the past, the strict psychoanalyst generally remains objective and detached most of the time. By comparison, the Adlerian therapist is more involved in advising and encouraging the patient. As long as the patient does not become dependent on the therapist for advice, it is seen as an essential part of translating insight into action.

For example, once a patient realizes that her dependence on her husband is part of her overall style of seeking protection (and controlling others), the therapist might point out several alternative ways she might start to change. In other cases, the therapist might offer more direct advice (e.g., "Get a part-time job"), especially when the patient needs help to get started toward a more adaptive lifestyle.

Other Treatment Procedures. Adlerians use other techniques to help patients become aware of their lifestyle and to prompt them to change. Many of these are similar to tactics employed by proponents of behavioral and phenomenological treatment (see Chapters 9 and 10):

1. *Modeling.* The therapist exemplifies attitudes and behaviors that the patient might wish to emulate. "The Adlerian therapist presents himself as 'being for real,' fallible, unconcerned with prestige considerations, able to laugh at himself, possessing courage, caring— a model for social interest" (Mosak & Dreikurs, 1973, p. 60).

2. *Task setting.* Adler advocated prompting patients to do new things, which would help the treatment process. "Acting as if" was one favorite method. When patients express a longing to be different than they are, the therapist may suggest that they act *as if* they really were the way they want to be. The patient also may

Summary of Family Constellation

John is the younger of two children, the only boy, who grew up fatherless after age 9. His sister was so accomplished at almost everything that, early in life, John became discouraged. Since he felt he would never become famous, he decided perhaps he could at least be notorious, and through negative traits brought himself forcefully to the attention of others. He acquired the reputation that he was pretty obnoxious and a "holy terror." He was going to do everything his way, and nobody was going to stop him. He followed the guiding lines of a strong, masculine father from whom he learned that the toughest man wins. Since notoriety came with doing the disapproved thing, John early became interested in and engaged in sex. This also reinforced his feelings of masculinity. Since both parents were handicapped and still "made it," John apparently decided that without any physical handicaps, the sky would be the limit for him.

Summary of Early Recollections

"I run scared in life, and even when people tell me there's nothing to be scared of, I'm still scared. Women give men a hard time. They betray men, they punish them, and they interfere with what men want to do. A real man takes no crap from anybody. But victory is hard to come by because somebody always interferes. I am not going to do what others want me to do. Others call that 'bad' and want to punish me for it but I don't see it that way. Doing what I want is merely part of being a man, and why should anyone want to interfere with my being a man?"

"Basic Mistakes"

1. He exaggerates the significance of real masculinity and equates it with doing what he pleases.
2. He is not on the same wavelength as women. They see his behavior as "bad"; he sees it as only "natural" for a man.
3. He is too ready to fight, many times, just to preserve his sense of masculinity, and not because of the issue he is allegedly fighting over.
4. He perceives women as the enemy, even though he looks to them for comfort.
5. Like Moses, victory is snatched from him at the last moment.

Assets

1. He is a driver. When he puts his mind to things, he makes them work.
2. He engages in creative problem solving.
3. He knows how to get what he wants.
4. He knows how to keep the world busy with him.
5. He knows how to ask a woman "nicely."

Source: H. H. Mosak & R. Dreikurs, "Adlerian Psychotherapy," in R. J. Corsini (ed.), *Current Psychotherapies*. © 1973 by Peacock Publishers, Inc., Itasca, Illinois, p. 57. (Reprinted by permission.)

BOX 8–3
A Sample Lifestyle Summary

be asked to *try* to perform the very behaviors he or she wishes to stop (a technique known as *paradoxical intention*). An insomniac might try to stay up all night; a person who always seems to be crying might try to cry constantly. By not fighting against these behaviors, the patient often finds that they disappear.

3. *Creating images*. The patient is sometimes given a summary image of his or her lifestyle. This image can then be used as a day-to-day reminder of the style she or he is trying to alter. "Superman," "The Beggar King," and "Miss Perfection" are a few examples of lifestyle images.

4. *The push-button technique*. When patients believe themselves to be at the mercy of their emotions, the therapist might help them learn that this is a misconception. The patient is asked to imagine some past unpleasant experience and notice the negative emotional feelings that result. The patient is then told to "push a button" and switch attention to some past pleasant event. The appearance of accompanying positive emotions and the possibility of switching back and forth between affective states illustrate the degree of control over emotion that the patient has.

BOX 8–4
An Example of Adler's Task Setting

Adler often employed task setting as a means of helping depressed people. In the example below, note the charming combination of good humor and practical advice.

To return to the indirect method of treatment: I recommend it especially in melancholia. After establishing a sympathetic relation I give suggestions for a change of conduct in two stages. In the first stage my suggestion is "Only do what is agreeable to you." The patient usually answers, "Nothing is agreeable." "Then at least," I respond, "do not exert yourself to do what is disagreeable." The patient, who has usually been exhorted to do various uncongenial things to remedy this condition, finds a rather flattering novelty in my advice, and may improve in behavior. Later I insinuate the second rule of conduct, saying that "it is much more difficult and I do not know if you can follow it." After saying this I am silent, and look doubtfully at the patient. In this way I excite his curiosity and ensure his attention, and then proceed, "If you could follow this second rule you would be cured in fourteen days. It is—to consider from time to time how you can give another person pleasure. It would very soon enable you to sleep and would chase away all your sad thoughts. You would feel yourself to be useful and worthwhile."

I receive various replies to my suggestion, but every patient thinks it is too difficult to act upon. If the answer is, "How can I give pleasure to others when I have none myself?" I relieve the prospect by saying, "Then you will need four weeks." The more transparent response, "Who gives me pleasure?" I encounter with what is probably the strongest move in the game, by saying, "Perhaps you had better train yourself a little thus: do not actually do anything to please anyone else, but just think out how you could do it!"

Source: Adler, 1964, pp. 25–26.

Applications

Adlerian therapy is appropriate for one-to-one treatment with the kinds of patients who might be seen in Freudian psychoanalysis, but it can also be applied with other types of patients in individual, group, and family contexts. Adler also worked with "normal" individuals because he believed that one can have problems in living due to misconceptions and a maladaptive lifestyle without being a diagnosed patient. This view resulted in the establishment of community education centers designed to prevent behavior disorders by providing parents and teachers with information and advice about child rearing and family relations. These centers anticipated the community psychology movement of the 1960s and 1970s (see Chapter 7).

Other Psychodynamic Therapies

In discussing psychoanalytically oriented psychotherapy, the ego analysts, and Adler, we have merely scratched the surface of the variations on Freud's model of treatment. Box 8–5 lists additional systems. The work of many of the therapists and theorists included in that table (Stekel, Ferenczi, Reich, Federn) paralleled the effort of the Chicago group and the ego analysts to expand the techniques, patients, treatment settings, and presenting problems associated with psychoanalysis. Others (Horney, Sullivan, Fromm) used psychoanalytic concepts in treatments that emphasized the cultural and interpersonal environment of the patient. Still others (Jung and Rank) followed in Adler's footsteps by breaking with Freudian principles and founding distinct treatments.

One of the most important developments in modern psychoanalysis is *object-relations theory,* a movement associated with a group of influential British analysts, including Ronald Fairbairn (1952), Donald Winnicott (1965), Melanie Klein (1975), and Margaret Mahler (Mahler, Pine, & Bergman, 1975) as well as Otto Kernberg (1976) and Heinz Kohut (1971,

1977, 1983). Object-relations theory studies the nature and origin of interpersonal relationships as they are built from very early infant–mother interactions and the nature of present personality structures as they are derived from reactivated internalizations of these interactions (see Blatt & Lerner, 1983; or Eagle, 1984, for descriptions of object-relations theory).

Object-relations theorists emphasize preoedipal development, particularly the quality of the mother–infant relationship and its effect on the structure and strength of the ego. In Kohut's *Self-Psychology,* for example, the analyst's task is to provide the type of empathic responding and nurturing that the patient is assumed to have missed as an infant. When parental inadequacies do not allow an infant to realize his or her "mirroring," "idealizing," and "twinship" needs (see below), the child is unable to achieve a unified self.

Defective aspects of the self have a tendency to emerge in later life in the form of personality disorders such as narcissism and the borderline personality. In treating such patients, the analyst's task is to be a responsive, warm, emphatic *selfobject* who allows the patient's self to be completed by encouraging expression of the self's earliest needs. Kohut (1983) described three types of *selfobject transferences* essential to self-completion: (a) the *mirror transference,* where exhibitionistic and grandiose needs are recognized and admired by an empathic selfobject; (b) the *idealizing transference,* where needs for protection and soothing are answered by a powerful selfobject; and (c) the *twinship transference,* where needs for closeness to another person like oneself are answered by an alter ego selfobject.

A fundamental difference between object-relations therapists and classic psychoanalysts is their approach to the therapeutic relationship. The object-relations theorists view this relationship as a "second chance" for the client to obtain in a close relationship the gratification that was neglected during infancy. They therefore stress providing a need-gratifying re-

I. Alternate systems of analytic psychotherapy based on theoretical or ideological differences from Freudian classical analysis.

   1. The non-Freudian systems.

      a. The *individual psychology* of Alfred Adler.

      b. The *analytical psychology* of Carl Jung.

      c. The *will therapy* of Otto Rank.

   2. Neo-Freudian systems based on the cultural emphasis.

      a. The *holistic* approach of Karen Horney.

      b. The *interpersonal relations* school of Harry Stack Sullivan.

      c. The *cultural* approach of Erich Fromm.

II. Attempts to streamline, abbreviate, and speed up the process of psychoanalytic therapy.

   1. Stekel's *active analytic* psychotherapy.

   2. Ferenczi's experiments with *active* techniques.

   3. The Chicago school of *brief* psychoanalytic therapy.

III. Expansions of Freudian classical analysis in various directions.

   1. The "object-relations approach" of Guntrip, Winnicott, Fairbairn, and the British school.

   2. The "eight stages of man" and Erikson's extension of Freud's theory of character development.

   3. Character analysis of Wilhelm Reich.

   4. Kohut's approach to the treatment of narcissistic character disorders.

IV. Modifications based on the shift in emphasis to ego psychology.

   1. Federn's ego psychology and the psychotherapy of the ego boundaries.

   2. Wolman's interactional psychoanalytic therapy.

Source: Kutash, 1976, pp. 89–90.

BOX 8–5
Modifications in Psychoanalytic Therapy

lationship to the client, rather than analyzing the historical sources of the client's desperately felt needs. The object-relations theorists are interested primarily in the psychological trauma caused by early emotional deprivations and how current personality conflicts have originated from these deprivations.

Object-relations therapists extend a special type of parenting to their patients to give them a second chance for the development of a coherent self. Their emphasis on ego support, acceptance, and psychological "holding" of

damaged selves is similar to many of Carl Rogers's ideas about psychotherapy (Kahn, 1985; see Chapter 10). For this and other reasons, classic psychoanalysts have been skeptical about such treatments, claiming that they owe less to Freud than to existentialism and humanism (Levine, 1985). Freud himself seemed to anticipate self-enhancement treatments, referring to them somewhat disparagingly as the "cure through love."

Currently, the object-relations approach is one of the most popular versions of psychoanalysis. Its popularity stems from several sources. First, its descriptions of psychopathology, often stated in bold metaphorical terms such as "empty selves," "safe anchorage," and "fragmented selves," have a contemporary sound to them that seems to tap the emotional experience of modern men and women better than the original Freudian terms (Eagle, 1984). Second, object-relations theory allows a friendly, naturally human stance toward the therapeutic relationship which many therapists prefer to traditional Freudian neutrality. Finally, object-relations therapy seems more compatible with other approaches to therapy than does classical analysis, an asset in this era of integration and eclecticism (Westen, 1991).

Other variants on psychoanalysis helped lay the groundwork for procedures associated with behavioral and phenomenological models. For example, when Otto Rank broke with Freud, he developed a therapeutic approach that deemphasized the unconscious and the detailed exploration of the past. Instead, Rank employed the patient's innate *will to health* as a vehicle for promoting mature independence. Rank treated his patients as responsible individuals and emphasized the therapy relationship as a major growth experience. He saw the therapist as a *facilitator* of the patient's inherent potential for growth, not as a relentless prober of the unconscious. These concepts provided part of the base upon which Carl Rogers would later build his phenomenologically oriented client-centered therapy (see Chapter 10).

Similarly, Harry Stack Sullivan, discussed in Chapter 2 as the father of the interpersonal perspective, employed methods that anticipated later cognitive-behavioral approaches to psychotherapy (see Chapter 9; Wachtel, 1977). Sullivan believed the therapist needed to be an expert observer of interpersonal relationships who could clarify for clients how their typical cognitions and accompanying style of behavior interfered with successful living. Clients would then be able to use this information to develop more adaptive ways of living.

Ford and Urban's (1963) outline of the usual sequence of events in Sullivanian therapy (Box 8–6) shows the systematic attention to behavior that is a hallmark of behavioral interventions.

BOX 8–6
Summary of the Therapeutic Sequence in Sullivanian Therapy

a. Initial review of the problem.

b. Reconnaissance of the behaviors relevant to the problem.

c. Decision as to general outlines of the difficulty and the course therapy shall pursue.

d. Careful and detailed study of the subject's response repertoire.

e. Identification of the anxieties, avoidance patterns, and the interpersonal situations in which they occur.

f. Rendering these patterns explicit to the subject.

g. Making explicit the fact of intervening anxiety.

h. Drawing out the effects of these anxiety patterns on the remainder of the subject's behavior.

i. All of the foregoing reduces the intensity of anxiety and permits the operation of other responses in its stead.

Source: D. H. Ford, and H. B. Urban, *Systems of Psychotherapy*. © 1963 by John Wiley & Sons, New York. (Reprinted by permission.)

EFFECTIVENESS
AND OTHER RESEARCH ISSUES
IN PSYCHODYNAMIC THERAPY

When people think of psychotherapy, they imagine a pipe-smoking therapist and a patient on a couch. This image was once reasonably accurate, because psychodynamic treatment was the first systematic psychological treatment for psychological problems. For many years it dominated clinical interventions and controlled professional ideas about how therapy should be conducted. Today, its dominance is reduced because its underlying theoretical model has been challenged by phenomenological, interpersonal, and behavioral alternatives and because, in spite of modern revisions, it is still too expensive and lengthy to be useful with many problems. Critics have also questioned the effectiveness of psychodynamic therapy.

A frequent argument is that the psychodynamic approach has seldom been evaluated by quantitative, empirical research. Analysts are frequently depicted as suspicious of, or even hostile to, controlled studies of therapy outcome. Indeed, some advocates of the psychodynamic model have argued that their treatment methods are too complex, too multifaceted, and too subjective to be evaluated fairly by quantitative methods.

Nevertheless, there is considerable quantitative research on psychodynamic treatments, which many psychologists either ignore or remain uninformed about. This research has been summarized by Wallerstein and Sampson (1971), Masling (1982), Gill and Hoffman (1982), and Fisher and Greenberg (1977). A thorough review of research on psychoanalysis is also provided by Luborsky and Spence (1978).

The research questions asked about psychodynamic treatment are similar to the questions posed about other forms of therapy by Luborsky & Spence (1978): (a) What kinds of clients are best suited for psychoanalysis? (b) What kinds of therapists are best suited to perform it? (c) What outcomes are produced by psychoanalysis? and (d) What is the nature of change throughout the course of treatment?

Questions concerning outcome have received the least attention in the psychoanalytic literature. Most studies have focused only on a group of treated clients who, at the end of treatment, are rated by their therapists on some sort of improvement scale. Control groups are usually not included. Psychoanalysis has rarely been compared directly to other forms of psychotherapy. Cartwright's (1966) study is well known, but its importance is diminished by the fact that there were only four patients. Piper, Debbane, Bienvenu, and Garant (1984) conducted a well-designed evaluation of short- and long-term psychoanalytically oriented therapy delivered in either a group or individual context. The most influential investigations have included the Sloane, Staples, Christol, Yorkston, and Whipple (1975) outcome study previously described in Chapter 7, and Cross, Sheehan, and Khan's (1980) comparison of behavior therapy and "insight-oriented therapy." Brief, psychodynamically oriented therapy has been compared to behavior therapy for treatment of adults with various phobias (Klein, Zitrin, Woerner, & Ross, 1983). The overall outcomes between the two treatments (both of which were also supplemented with chemotherapy) did not differ, a finding that is somewhat surprising given the supposed advantages of behavioral treatments for phobic disorders.

Psychoanalysts have also compared the processes and outcomes of classic psychoanalysis and psychodynamically oriented psychotherapy. The best-known example of this research is the Psychotherapy Research Project of the Menninger Foundation, in which 42 patients were studied over several years (Wallerstein, 1986, 1989). Twenty-one of the patients received standard psychoanalysis; 21 received psychodynamically oriented treatment. The patients were not randomly assigned to these treatments; rather, each patient received the treatment the Menninger staff believed was more appropriate for that patient. The results of this study were consistent with the opinions of other psychodynamic practitioners (Strupp, 1989) that the supportive aspects of the therapeutic relationship accounted for the most change in the patients. This finding, which was true for both types of psychoanalysis, also supports Alexander and French's (1946) emphasis on corrective emotional experience, as opposed to interpretation, as the central therapeutic mechanism in psychoanalysis.

A meta-analysis of 19 studies evaluating the effects of short-term psychodynamically oriented psychotherapy (Svartberg & Stiles, 1991) found that this type of treatment achieved a small superiority over no treatment at all but was inferior to other types of psychotherapy, particularly at longer follow-up periods. The case for psychodynamic treatments was further weakened in this meta-analysis by the discovery that the better the design of the study, the smaller the positive effects for psychodynamic therapy.

Research on the process of psychoanalysis has been more frequent and of generally higher quality. For example, considerable research has been performed on the effects of therapists' interpretations. Accuracy of interpretation, the nature of transference, and level of empathy have been investigated in several studies (e.g., Crits-Christoph, Cooper, & Luborsky, 1988; Luborsky, Crits-Christoph, & Mellon, 1986).

Despite the increasing sophistication of research on psychoanalysis, most analysts would probably agree with Luborsky and Spence's (1978) judgment: "Quantitative research on psychoanalytic therapy presents itself, so far, as an unreliable support to clinical practice. More is known now through clinical wisdom than is known through quantitative objective studies" (p. 358). Later, they add that "few, if any, quantitative research findings have changed the style or outcome of psychoanalytic practice" (Luborsky & Spence, 1978, p. 360). Without disparaging the value of clinical wisdom, we believe that no form of psychotherapy should remain too long isolated from the findings of well-controlled research. The ultimate scientific status of psychoanalysis, or any other therapy, depends on empirical investigation of its methods rather than on the consensual approval of its practitioners.

CHAPTER 9

Clinical Intervention: Behavioral Models

The definition of behavior therapy has undergone considerable revision over the years (Farkas, 1980; Follette & Houts, 1992; Kazdin, 1978; Masters, Burish, Hollon, & Rimm, 1987; Ross, 1985; Wilson, 1978). Considering these changes, we believe the essential principles of behavior therapy are the following:

1. The basic laws of learning apply to all behaviors. Maladaptive behaviors are acquired through the same psychological processes as any other behaviors.

2. Therapeutic techniques are based on the empirical findings and theoretical foundations of experimental psychology. In its early years, behavior therapy relied on the findings of learning theory, but today its empirical foundations are much broader.

3. Therapy is aimed at the modification of overt, maladaptive behaviors. The cognitions, physical changes, and emotions that accompany overt behavior are also dealt with, but in a more direct manner than in many other therapeutic approaches.

4. There is a focus on the client's present problems. This here-and-now emphasis results in less attention to early childhood experiences or historical material than in psychoanalysis.

5. There is a commitment to the experimental evaluation of treatment. The behavior therapist attempts to employ techniques that have been scientifically investigated through experimental group designs or single-subject methodology.

6. Emphasis on problem-focused techniques and empirical validation of treatment does not reduce the need for behavior therapists to be sensitive clinicians who are concerned for the welfare of their clients and who exercise good clinical judgments and sound ethical practices when providing their services.

While at one time the public's stereotype of psychologists was of professionals who practiced Freud's brand of therapy, behavioral techniques now augment or have replaced psychodynamic images in the popular conception of psychology. This new stereotype misses the target only a little: Most clinicians, regardless of their theoretical background, *are* familiar with behavior therapy[1] and employ its techniques on many occasions.

The term *behavior therapy* first appeared in a 1953 paper by Lindsley, Skinner, and Solomon that described operant conditioning with psychotics. Though these authors did not continue to use the term, Eysenck (1959) did, and he is often given credit for introducing it. Arnold Lazarus was the second person to use the term in print, publishing a 1958 article on behavior therapy in the *South African Medical Journal*.

Behavior therapy has become one of the most popular research areas in clinical psychology. Thirty years ago there was not a single professional journal devoted exclusively to research on behavioral approaches in clinical psychology. Now there are more than a dozen, the most influential of which are *Behaviour Research and Therapy, Journal of Applied Behavior Analysis, Behavior Therapy, Journal of Behavior Therapy and Experimental Psychiatry, Behavior Modification, Cognitive Therapy and Research, Behavioral Assessment,* and *European Journal of Behavior Analysis and Modification*.

Similar growth has occurred in the publication of textbooks and handbooks dealing with behavior modification. The first book with "behavior therapy" in the title was Eysenck's *Behavior Therapy and the Neuroses,* published in 1960 (Kazdin, 1978). Today there are hundreds of books about behavior modification, and many of them are updated each year. Several behaviorally oriented interest groups have been formed, the most influential of which is the Association for Advancement of Behavior Therapy (AABT). There are at least a score of behavioral newsletters, catalogs of equipment for behavior modifiers, and special bibliographies of behavioral publications. There is even a special code of ethics for behavior modifiers (AABT, 1977).

The increasing complexity of the area is also illustrated by the proliferation of behavioral splinter groups. Thus, we have *broad spectrum behavior therapy, cognitive behavior therapy, rational behavior therapy,* and *psychodynamic behavior therapy* (Wilson, 1978). We doubt that much is to be gained by inventing new brand names or by trying to acquaint you with the subtle differences they represent. More valuable lessons can be learned from studying the origins of behavior modification and understanding those developments that shaped modern behavioral interventions.

Alan Kazdin (1978) has discussed several scientific and professional foundations of behavior modification. In this chapter we focus on six of these areas: early Russian research on conditioning, comparative psychology, Watsonian behaviorism, learning theory, B. F. Skinner and operant conditioning, and applications of learning therapy to human behavior and psychotherapy. For more elaborate coverage of these topics and several others, consult Kazdin (1978, especially pp. 49–185).

FOUNDATIONS OF BEHAVIOR MODIFICATION

Conditioning Research in Russia

The impact of Russian conditioning research on behavior modification was transmitted through the early 20th-century work of three men: Ivan Sechenov, Ivan Pavlov, and Vladimir Bekhterev. Each of these scientists was trained in medicine, and each advocated objective mechanistic explanations of behavior,

---

[1]Throughout this chapter we use the terms *behavior modification* and *behavior therapy* interchangeably, even though some writers insist that the two are not synonymous. Among those psychologists who emphasize the difference between the two concepts, those with an operant or Skinnerian orientation prefer the name *behavior modification,* leaving *behavior therapy* to clinicians who operate from a social learning and/or cognitive framework. These theoretical differences will become more meaningful as we progress through this chapter.

including those human behaviors considered to be highly subjective. Of greatest importance, each insisted that behavior be studied through scientific, empirical methods.

Aside from championing the empirical method, Sechenov made two important contributions to a behavioristic psychology. First, he claimed that all behavior was composed of reflexes elicited by the environment. Thus, he saw the ultimate cause of behavior as external. Second, Sechenov believed that the reflexes that formed complex human behavior were acquired through associative learning; that is, responses are learned when they are associated repeatedly with certain stimuli.

Pavlov's work on conditioning salivation in dogs led him to the discovery that if an *unconditioned stimulus* that elicits a reflex (*or unconditioned response*) is paired repeatedly with a neutral stimulus, the previously neutral stimulus becomes a *conditioned stimulus* which will elicit a response (*the conditioned response*) that resembles the original reflex. A diagram of this process is presented in Figure 9–1.

In his famous experiments with dogs, Pavlov demonstrated that food would elicit salivation and that after pairing a tone with the food several times, the tone itself would elicit salivation. Pavlov discovered *higher-order conditioning* when he noticed that, after many associations with the tone and food, his own presence also elicited the dog's salivation. Pavlov's greatest contributions were his study of the conditions under which one form of learning (often called *Pavlovian, classical,* or *respondent conditioning*) took place and his demonstration of the effects that changes in those conditions would have on the conditioning process.

Bekhterev studied motor reflexes in humans, using mild electric shock to the hands and feet as the unconditioned stimulus. He argued that psychology would be replaced by a more objective discipline, which he termed *reflexology.* Bekhterev used conditioning to treat several disorders, including hysterical deafness and sexual deviations.

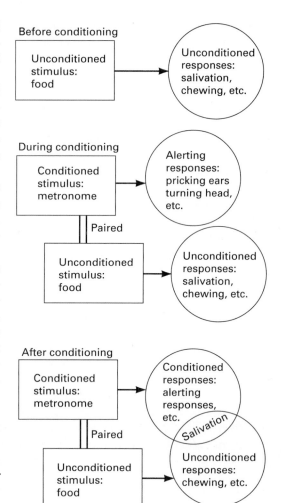

FIGURE 9–1 The course of Pavlovian conditioning. Before conditioning, food, an unconditioned stimulus, elicits unconditioned responses like salivation and chewing. During conditioning, a metronome, the potential conditioned stimulus, comes on a few moments before the food is given. The food still elicits various responses, while the metronome elicits only the usual alertness to a new sound. After a number of conditioning trials, the metronome elicits a new set of responses that include some overlap (for example, salivation) with the original unconditioned responses. (From R. Brown and R. J. Hernstein, *Psychology.* Reprinted by permission of the authors.)

Comparative Psychology

Comparative psychology involves the study of animal behavior. It is important to the development of behavior modification because it gave support to Darwin's claim that there was a continuity in the behavior of humans and animals. Because of this continuity, the laws of animal learning being discovered in the late 19th and early 20th centuries were thought to apply to humans as well.

Watsonian Behaviorism

John B. Watson "was responsible for crystallizing an existing trend toward objectivism" in psychology (Kazdin, 1978, p. 63). Watson received his PhD in 1903 from the University of Chicago, where the orientation to psychology was *functional* (psychologists studied how human consciousness operated through the method of introspection). Watson was also exposed to the methods of physiology and biology at Chicago, and he became dissatisfied with functionalist psychology which, by comparison to the "hard" sciences, was too subjective for his tastes.

Watson's vision for a more objective psychology was first published in 1913 in a paper called "Psychology As the Behaviorist Views It." In this article Watson described two essential qualities of behaviorism. First, introspection as a method was to be replaced with observation, the method used by the animal psychologists. Second, psychologists must abandon the study of consciousness and focus instead on overt behavior and its relation to environmental stimuli. Watson's system came to be known as S–R psychology because of his emphasis on stimulus–response bonds, through which all behavior could be explained. For example, thinking was seen as small movements of the vocal cords, and emotions were the product of physiological changes in certain organs.

Watson popularized behaviorism and claimed that it could be used to solve human problems. His most extravagant allegation was that if he were given one dozen healthy infants,

> well-formed, and my own specified world to bring them up in . . . I'll guarantee to take any one at random and train him to become any type of specialist I might select—doctor, lawyer, artist, merchant, chief, and yes, even beggarman and thief, regardless of his talents, penchants, tendencies, abilities, vocations and race of his ancestors. (Watson, 1930, p. 104)

Partly as a result of this kind of enthusiasm, the literature of the 1920s contained many articles describing how behaviorism could solve the problems of education, abnormal behavior, and society in general (Willis & Giles, 1978).

Learning Theory

By the 1930s the major topic of research in American psychology had become the psychology of learning and the construction of theoretical systems that explained learning processes. These learning theories attempted to explain a wider range of behavior (including speech) than earlier conditioning theories, which were concerned with more discrete responses (eye blinks, startle responses).

Edward L. Thorndike, one of America's first learning theorists, was interested in the voluntary behavior of animals. For example, how does a cat learn to escape from a cage? Thorndike believed the most important factor in the development of a new response was the consequence of that response. Responses are strengthened or weakened according to the *law of effect*, which held that

> Of several responses made to the same situation, those which are accompanied or closely followed by satisfaction to the animal will, other things being equal, be more firmly connected with the situation, so that, when it recurs, they will be more likely to recur; those

which are accompanied or closely followed by discomfort to the animal will, other things being equal, have their connections with that situation weakened, so that, when it recurs, they will be less likely to occur. (Thorndike, 1911, p. 244)

This law of effect was the theoretical forerunner of B. F. Skinner's concepts of reinforcement and operant conditioning, of which more will be said later.

Another early learning theorist was Edwin Guthrie, whose major statement on learning was his 1935 book, *The Psychology of Learning*. Guthrie's theory was similar to Watson's: Learning occurs as a result of contiguity or close association between stimuli and responses. Unlike Thorndike, Guthrie did not believe that reinforcement played a major role in learning. According to Guthrie, reinforcement simply prevents the organism from performing new behavior that could break up the previously formed associations between a stimulus and response.

Other important learning theorists were Clark Hull and Edward Tolman. Hull attempted to synthesize the classical conditioning of Pavlov and the instrumental conditioning of Thorndike under a single theoretical system. His work influenced the later learning theories of such eminent psychologists as Kenneth Spence (1956), O. Hobart Mowrer (1960), and Neal Miller (1951). Hull's theory has been cited as a theoretical foundation for several modern behavior therapy techniques, most notably systematic desensitization.

Tolman emphasized the role of such intervening variables as *expectancy, cognition,* and *meaning* in his learning theory. He distinguished between learning and performance: An organism could learn the correct behavior in some situation without necessarily performing that behavior. Tolman suggested that reinforcement *regulates* overt performance but does not "teach" us which responses are correct. As you shall see, Tolman's ideas were similar to those expressed by modern social-learning theorists and cognitive behavior therapists.

Skinner and Operant Conditioning

The most important figure in the application of operant conditioning to human conduct was B. F. Skinner, whose *Science and Human Behavior* (1953) is one of the foundations of modern behavior therapy. The basic premise of operant conditioning is deceptively simple: Behavior is learned and strengthened as a result of its consequences. The term *operant* suggests a behavior that operates or acts upon the environment to produce consequences. In turn, these consequences influence the probability that the behaviors that preceded them will recur.

The main effect of operant conditioning is that randomly emitted, trial-and-error behaviors are progressively shaped into meaningful patterns of activity as a result of their outcomes. Positive consequences (reinforcers) strengthen the likelihood of previous operants, while aversive consequences weaken the probability of similar future responses.

Five principles define the core of operant conditioning. Four of these are represented in Figure 9–2. Presenting a positive reinforcer following some behavior is *positive reinforcement* (Cell I), a process that strengthens the behavior. Having a beer after a study session is a common form of positive reinforcement. Cell II describes one type of *punishment,* in which a negative consequence presented after some behavior results in a decrease in that behavior's future probability.

Cell III represents a second form of *punishment,* which occurs when a previously available positive event is removed following some behavior. For example, having one's car stolen while unlocked would probably decrease the future probability of such careless behavior. *Negative reinforcement* (Cell IV) results in an *increase* in the probability of a behavior's future occurrence by removing something unpleasant following that behavior. The relief of headache pain after taking aspirin tends to strengthen future aspirin taking. Positive and negative reinforcement strengthen behavior, while both

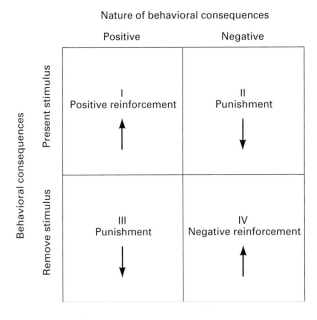

Nature of behavioral consequences

FIGURE 9–2 Techniques and effects of operant conditioning. The arrows in each cell indicate that behavior preceding various consequences will be strengthened (↑) or weakened (↓).

kinds of punishment decrease the future probability of the behaviors preceding them.

The fifth operant principle is *extinction,* which refers to the weakening of behavior as a result of the absence of both positive *and* negative consequences. A simple example of this process would be giving up telephoning someone after repeatedly failing to get an answer. Of course, many other concepts and principles are associated with operant conditioning. For more extensive coverage of this material, see Martin and Pear (1983) or Leahey and Harris (1989).

Applications of Learning Theory to Human Behavior and Psychotherapy

Within the first quarter of the 20th century, psychologists had become interested in applying the laws of conditioning and learning to the investigation and treatment of behavior disorders. An illustration of this trend was the discovery that emotional responses resembling human neuroses could be experimentally induced in laboratory animals. Pavlov observed *experimental neuroses* in his dogs after exposing them to electric shock or requiring them to make difficult sensory discriminations. The dogs' symptoms included agitation, barking, biting the equipment, and forgetting things they had previously learned. In the 1940s Jules Masserman of Northwestern University studied the conditioning and deconditioning of experimental neuroses in cats. Investigation of experimental neuroses in a variety of animal species quickly became a popular research topic. Kazdin (1978) reports that W. Horsely Gantt, another early researcher of experimental neuroses, had a dog named Nick whom Gantt claimed remained neurotic for more than 12 years.

The discovery of experimental neuroses in animals led to research on similar problems in humans. The most famous of these studies was a classic experiment in 1920 by John B. Watson and his graduate student, Rosalie Rayner. A 9-month-old-infant, Albert B., was presented with several stimuli such as a white rat, a dog, a rabbit, a monkey, masks, and a burning newspaper. He showed no fear toward any of these objects, but he did become very upset when a loud noise was sounded by striking a steel bar with a hammer. He was startled by the noise, his breathing was affected, and he trembled and cried during later presentations of the noise.

To see whether Albert's fear could be conditioned to formerly nonfrightening objects, Watson and Rayner associated the loud noise with a white rat. The rat was brought to Albert and, as soon as he began to reach for it, the noise was sounded. After several pairings over a 1-week period, the rat elicited a strong emotional reaction in Albert—"the instant the rat was shown the baby began to cry. Almost instantly he turned sharply to the left, fell over on his left side, raised himself on all fours and began to crawl away so rapidly that he was caught with difficulty before reaching the edge of the table" (Watson & Rayner, 1920, p. 5). The investigators were interested in whether this conditioned fear had generalized to other objects, so they presented several stimuli which only two months earlier had not upset Albert. This time the effects were different. Albert was squeamish when confronted with a rabbit, a fur coat, Watson's own hair, and even a Santa Claus mask. Albert's fear persisted in less extreme form during assessments conducted over a 1-month period.

The child was removed from the research setting before anything could be done to completely remove his fears, but a few years later, Mary Cover Jones, another of Watson's students, investigated several techniques for reducing fear in institutionalized children. Two methods were most successful: *direct conditioning,* in which a fear stimulus was associated with some pleasant activity like eating, and *social imitation,* where the fearful child watched other children who were not afraid of the object in question (Jones, 1924a).

These two methods were investigated more carefully in Jones's (1924b) work with a 3-year-old named Peter. Peter was afraid of many things, particularly rabbits. Social imitation was used first. "Each day Peter and three other children were brought to the laboratory for a play period. The other children

were selected carefully because of their entirely fearless attitude toward the rabbit. . . . " (Jones, 1924b, p. 310). The rabbit was present during these play periods, and, with the fearless examples of the other children, Peter became more comfortable as he gradually came closer to the animal. At this point, Peter's treatment was interrupted by a bout with scarlet fever, and his progress was jeopardized by a frightening encounter with a big dog.

When treatment resumed, it included direct conditioning. Peter was placed in a high chair and fed his favorite food while a caged rabbit was placed gradually closer to him at each session. Sometimes other children were present during the sessions. This procedure eliminated Peter's fear of rabbits, and this effect generalized to other stimuli. For example, he showed no fear toward a mass of angleworms or a box of frogs. Peter himself summed up the results of this case by announcing one fateful day, "I like the rabbit."

These case histories had a major impact on behavior modification because they suggested that conditioning could account for both the acquisition and treatment of fear. The range of problems to which conditioning was applied during the 1920s and 1930s was wide, covering children's fears, sexual disorders, substance abuse, and several neurotic conditions. Interest in the clinical use of conditioning persisted despite the failure of some investigators to replicate initial results. O'Leary and Wilson (1987) reviewed a case reported by English (1929), who attempted to condition a 14-month-old girl to be afraid of a large wooden duck by banging a metal bar each time the girl reached for the duck. After 50 pairings the child's enthusiasm for the duck was unabated, so English used a noisier hammer. Still the child remained unafraid, although several professionals in the building complained about the racket. Amazed by the little tyke's nerves of steel, English theorized that the usual rambunctiousness of the girl's three older brothers had made her immune to the aversive properties of noise.

The Recent History of Behavior Therapy

Official recognition of behavior therapy occurred in the late 1950s and early 1960s, a time when clinical psychology had become unusually receptive to behavioral approaches to treatment. Eysenck's challenges to the effectiveness of psychotherapy, widespread dissatisfaction with clinical assessment, and discontent with the medical model of behavior disorder caused clinicians to view behavioral approaches as attractive alternatives to traditional forms of psychotherapy.

Behavior therapy was formally initiated in South Africa, England, and the United States. Developments in each country were independent of the others to a degree, but collaboration existed also. In South Africa, psychiatrist Joseph Wolpe was conducting research that culminated in the publication of his book, *Psychotherapy by Reciprocal Inhibition* (1958). The work of two of his psychology students, Stanley Rachman and Arnold Lazarus, was to receive worldwide attention as well.

In England, the two most important influences on behavior therapy were Hans Eysenck and M. B. Shapiro, both affiliated with the Institute of Psychiatry at the University of London and Maudsley Hospital. England's "Maudsley group" (which also included Rachman, Isaac Marks, and Michael Gelder) included prolific researchers who investigated the effectiveness of many behavioral techniques, such as flooding, aversion therapy, and desensitization (all to be discussed later).

The clinical use of behavioral techniques was pioneered in the United States by several individuals, including Knight Dunlap, who in the 1930s used the method of *negative practice* to eliminate bad habits. Voegtlin and Lemere used chemical aversion to treat alcoholics at the Shadel Sanitarium in Seattle, Washington (Shadel, 1944), and Andrew Salter (1949) employed a therapeutic strategy he called "conditioned reflex therapy" to increase emotional expressiveness. Throughout the 1950s and 1960s operant conditioning was used increasingly in the treatment of psychotic patients and troubled children.

The crystallization of behavior therapy in America was the result of two factors: (a) a recognition of the behavior-therapy movement in England, particularly the work of Eysenck, and (b) the publication of several books in this country that provided a unified framework for behavior modification. In this latter category are Skinner's (1953) *Science and Human Behavior; Conditioning Techniques in Clinical Practice and Research* (Franks, 1964); *Case Studies in Behavior Modification* (Ullmann & Krasner, 1965); *Research in Behavior Modification* (Krasner & Ullmann, 1965); Wolpe's 1958 book; and *Behavior Therapy Techniques: A Guide to the Treatment of Neuroses* (Wolpe & Lazarus, 1966).

CONTEMPORARY BEHAVIOR-THERAPY TECHNIQUES

In the remainder of this chapter we describe some techniques used in behavior therapy. We trace the development of each procedure, describe its current applications, and discuss empirical evidence for its effectiveness.

Systematic Desensitization

Systematic desensitization (SD) is one of the best-known and most thoroughly researched techniques in behavior therapy. It is used to reduce certain anxiety disorders, particularly phobias, but has also been applied to many other clinical problems.

Background

The demonstrations by Watson and Rayner that fear could be learned through conditioning, and by Mary Cover Jones that it could be unlearned through the same mechanism, were early examples of how learning principles could be applied to anxiety problems. In addition, Guthrie (1935) proposed several techniques for breaking maladaptive habits, including fearfulness. For instance, he suggested presenting phobic persons with an example of the frightening stimulus that is so weak it does not elicit anxiety, then gradually increasing the stimulus until it can be tolerated fearlessly at full strength. During the 1920s Johannes Schultz, a German psychologist, developed a technique called "autogenic training." It involved a combination of hypnosis, relaxation, and autosuggestion with which clients themselves induced states incompatible with anxiety (Pikoff, 1984).

Systematic desensitization was first described in Joseph Wolpe's (1958) *Psychotherapy by Reciprocal Inhibition*. Wolpe had been studying how cats develop "experimental neuroses" and found that after animals had been repeatedly shocked while eating, they resisted being put in the feeding cages, acted emotionally, and refused to eat while there.

Wolpe reasoned that if conditioned anxiety could inhibit eating, the reverse might be true; eating might inhibit conditioned anxiety. Luckily for the cats, Wolpe was right. Relying on a principle called *reciprocal inhibition,* he hand-fed fearful cats in the cages where their anxiety had been learned. According to Wolpe (1958): "If a response antagonistic to anxiety can be made to occur in the presence of anxiety-evoking stimuli so that it is accompanied by a complete or partial suppression of the anxiety responses, the bond between these stimuli and the anxiety responses will be weakened" (p. 71).

Many animals benefited from this procedure, and their emotional behaviors were reduced. Those cats remaining "neurotic" were moved into a room unlike the conditioning room. After they ate there without anxiety, Wolpe moved the animals to a room more like the feared environment. He continued feeding the cats in places more and more like the original conditioning setting until they were able to eat in the feared cage itself.

Desensitization Procedures

Wolpe (1958) later extended his methods to humans who suffered maladaptive anxiety. He first needed to find a response incompatible with anxiety. He selected three inhibitors: deep muscle relaxation, interpersonal assertion, and sexual arousal. In each instance the principle was the same: People cannot be anxious while they are relaxed or assertive or sexually aroused. Deep muscle relaxation has become the standard anxiety inhibitor in systematic desensitization. However, assertion or sexual arousal may also be employed, especially when the anxiety to be inhibited relates to interpersonal or sexual problems.

The most common relaxation technique is *progressive relaxation training* (e.g., Bernstein & Borkovec, 1973), a shorter version of a method pioneered by Jacobson in 1938. The client is taught to become physically and mentally relaxed by going through a series of exercises in which groups of muscles are tensed for a few seconds and then released, while the client focuses on the sensations of relaxation that follow. You can get some idea of what these exercises feel like by clenching your fist for about 5 seconds and then abruptly releasing the tension. The resulting flow of relaxation is a mild version of what can be experienced by tensing and relaxing muscles throughout the body.

Relaxation training initially takes approximately 40 minutes per session. After four to six sessions and practice at combining the exercises, the client may be able to relax in less than 10 minutes. Relaxation may be attained through other methods if the client is unable to perform the exercises or if the therapist has a preference for another technique. Hypnosis is used on occasion, as are drugs, stretching exercises, biofeedback, and meditation (Bernstein & Carlson, 1993).

The next step in desensitization is to introduce anxiety-arousing situations in a gradual hierarchy. There are *in vivo* hierarchies, where clients are actually exposed to gradually more threatening versions of what they fear, and *imaginal* hierarchies, in which clients imagine or visualize a series of increasingly frightening scenes. The order of scenes is determined by the client so that each scene elicits just a bit more anxiety than the one before it. Too large an increase in arousal between items will make progress difficult, while too small an increase may lengthen treatment needlessly. An imaginal desensitization hierarchy is presented in Box 9–1.

After training in relaxation and the construction of the hierarchy, desensitization itself is begun. In imaginal procedures, the client is relaxed and asked to visualize the easiest item on the hierarchy. If the client can imagine the scene without anxiety for 10 seconds, the next scene is presented. If any anxiety is felt, however, the client signals the therapist and stops visualizing the scene. After regaining complete relaxation, the client again pictures the item for a shorter duration. Visualization times for that scene are gradually increased until the client can comfortably imagine it twice for 10 seconds. This sequence is continued until the client can handle all the items.

Reduction of anxiety to imaginal scenes may gradually transfer to their real-life equivalents, but the client is also urged to seek out real-world counterparts of the visualized scenes in order to reinforce progress and to assess the generality of the treatment effects. Completion of a hierarchy typically takes three to five sessions, though it is possible to finish a short hierarchy in a single meeting.

Applications

Systematic desensitization has been applied to fears of almost everything, including high and low places, closed and open spaces; an ark's worth of mammals, reptiles, birds, insects, and fish; encounters with women, with men, with strangers and with noise, dirt, and death. Desensitization has been used to relieve such uncommon phobias as the fear of balloons, wind, the year 1952, feathers, violins, sanitary napkins, dirty shirts, and short people.

Desensitization is also used in cases where

anxiety is not immediately obvious. For example, when anxiety causes complex patterns of behavior to break down, clients may focus on the disruption itself, not the anxiety causing it. Inability to concentrate, poor memory, confusion, speech disfluency, sexual dysfunction, or impairment of motor skills (e.g., typing) can be treated with desensitization. Similarly, certain maladaptive or bizarre behaviors such as amnesia, obsessions, compulsions, delusions, hysterical paralysis, drug abuse, alcoholism, or unusual sexual practices are sometimes motivated by efforts to avoid certain anxiety-provoking stimuli.

Prolonged anxiety may cause *physical damage* to organ systems and result in psychosomatic or psychophysiological disorders (e.g., ulcers) or in symptoms such as headaches, high blood pressure, or chronic fatigue. Where actual tissue damage has occurred, medical treatment is of course required, but anxiety reduction through desensitization may help eliminate one of the factors causing these problems.

Variations on Desensitization

The popularity of desensitization has led to a proliferation of methods based upon it. In *group desensitization* with several clients who share a common fear, a single hierarchy is used; progress up the hierarchy is geared to the pace of the slowest individual.

In vivo desensitization is the most popular variant. As noted earlier, the client is actually exposed to anxiety-arousing objects or situations, presented in a gradual fashion, and often in real-life settings. As an alternative to deep muscle relaxation, therapists themselves may act as anxiety inhibitors by accompanying their clients on *in vivo* "field trips." Sometimes the client is asked to engage in behavior that is incompatible with strong anxiety. This approach was used to treat a severe elevator phobia by having the client eat a multicourse gourmet meal while seated in a moving elevator (Bryntwick & Solyom, 1973).

Below is a desensitization hierarchy used by James Geer (1965) in his treatment of a 17-year-old high school girl who had a "morbid fear of contracting a case of nits in her hair." The numbers in parentheses indicate the session(s) of desensitization during which that item was presented.

1. Writing the words *bug* and *lice*. (1)
2. While reading in school you notice a small bug on your book. (1)
3. While walking down the sidewalk you notice a comb in the gutter. (1)
4. You are at home watching television when an ad concerning a dandruff-removing shampoo comes on. (2)
5. You are reading a *Reader's Digest* article that goes into detail concerning the catching and curing of a case of lice. (2)
6. You look at your desktop and notice several bobby pins and clips upon it. (3)
7. You are in a department store, and the saleslady is fitting a hat on you. (3)
8. At a store you are asked to try on a wig and you comply. (3)
9. You are watching a movie and they show a scene where people are being deloused. (4, 5, and 6)
10. At school, in hygiene class, the teacher lectures on lice and bugs in people's hair. (4 and 5)
11. A girl puts her scarf on your lap. (5)
12. In a public washroom you touch the seat of a commode. (6)
13. You are in a beauty shop having your hair set. (6)
14. A girl sitting in front of you in school leans her head back on your books. (6 and 7)
15. While sitting at home with your sister, she tells you that she used someone else's comb today. (7 and 8)
16. While sitting in the local snack bar a friend tells you of her experiences when she had a case of lice. (8 and 9)
17. You are combing your hair in the washroom when someone asks to borrow your comb. (9)
18. A stranger asks to use your comb and continues to ask why not when you say no. (9)
19. While standing looking at an ad in a store window, someone comes up beside you and puts their head near yours to see too. (10)
20. A stranger in the washroom at school hands you her comb and asks you to hold it for her. (10)
21. Your sister is fixing your hair when she drops the curlers on the floor, picks them up, and uses them in your hair. (11)
22. A stranger notices a tangle in your hair and tries to help you by combing it out with her comb. (11)

BOX 9–1
An Example of a Desensitization Hierarchy

Cue-controlled relaxation is another means of inhibiting anxiety in real-life settings, either as part of *in vivo* desensitization or various stress management procedures. The technique involves learning standard progressive relaxation, then repeatedly subvocalizing a cue word like *calm* or *relax* with each exhalation. This procedure is designed to condition relaxing properties to the cue word. After a few weeks of practice, the client is presented with some frightening (real or imagined) stimulus in the office and told to take a deep breath and subvocalize the cue word upon exhalation. If relaxation is achieved, the client is encouraged to use the cue to prevent maladaptive anxiety in real-life encounters.

Effectiveness and Other Research Issues

Regarding the effectiveness of desensitization, Paul concluded that "for the first time in the history of psychological treatments, a specific therapeutic package reliably produced measurable benefits for clients across a broad range of distressing problems in which anxiety was of fundamental importance" (Paul, 1969b, p. 159). Paul's conclusion has been extended over the years, with the result that behavior therapists are confident about the efficacy of desensitization, especially when it is applied to its most appropriate target: conditioned, maladaptive anxiety.

The major research questions surrounding desensitization are (a) Why is it effective? and (b) With what types of anxiety problems is it less effective than alternative treatments? Wolpe's original counterconditioning explanation has been challenged by a vast amount of research, and many behavior therapists no longer subscribe to it (Kazdin & Wilcoxon, 1976; McGlynn, Mealiea, & Landau, 1981). Several mechanisms have been proposed as alternative explanations for the success of desensitization. Among the most popular are the following:

1. Desensitization depends on changing the way the client thinks about a feared object (Wil-

kins, 1971). For example, the technique may produce a strong *expectancy* that a fear can be overcome.

2. The therapist acts as *social reinforcer* for the client's nonfearful responses (Leitenberg, Agras, Barlow, & Oliveau, 1969).

3. As the client recognizes progress up the hierarchy, further nonphobic behavior is supported through increased confidence that bolder behavior is now possible (Bandura, 1986).

4. Clients learn to *shift their attention* from threatening to nonthreatening properties of phobic situations (Wilkins, 1971).

5. Anxiety is *extinguished* or *habituated* via the presentation of conditioned emotional stimuli (hierarchy scenes) without any aversive consequences (Marks, 1975).

Hundreds of research investigations have yet to resolve the question of how desensitization produces its effects. Whether future research will be any more conclusive is uncertain. In any event, systematic desensitization still stands as one of the best-validated treatment techniques available to the clinical psychologist.

There are some anxiety-related problems for which systematic desensitization has been less successful. In general, anxiety problems that do not have well-defined stimulus elicitors and/or that have more components than simple phobias are less responsive to desensitization. Included in this group are agoraphobia, panic attacks, obsessive-compulsive disorder, and certain types of social anxiety. Behavioral clinicians have found that treatments involving direct exposure of the client to feared stimuli may be the treatment of choice for many of these disorders (Barlow & Wolfe, 1981).

Exposure Techniques

Most exposure treatments entail direct or *in vivo* exposure to frightening stimuli rather than imaginal presentations, as does desensitization. Second, most exposure treatments require a longer duration of exposure so the anxiety will dissipate or wear out, giving clients the opportunity to learn that they need not be afraid of their own fear. In desensitization, exposure times are abbreviated so intense anxiety is not experienced. Finally, most exposure treatments do not attempt to induce a state of relaxation, as is the practice in desensitization.

Exposure treatments are formulated and practiced in many different ways. Some therapists favor intense, prolonged, *in vivo* exposures; others prefer more gradual, self-paced, indirect exposures (see Barlow & Waddell, 1985, for a discussion of this issue). However, the major component of all exposure treatments requires the fearful person to confront the situations that are frightening so that she or he can learn that these situations lack actual danger.

One version of exposure-based treatments is *flooding;* this involves extended exposure of a client to anxiety-eliciting stimuli. It is based on the principle of extinction, whereby conditioned stimuli lose their aversive qualities when no harmful consequences follow them. In flooding, clients are prevented from avoiding or escaping stimuli they fear in order to learn that the stimuli are not objectively threatening.

Implosion or implosive therapy is similar to flooding, but implosive stimuli are more intense than those actually found in life and sometimes include material that psychoanalytic theory suggests would be important in causing a certain fear (Stampfl & Levis, 1973).

Implosion has steadily lost favor among behavior therapists since the 1970s. Its decline is related to the fact that research has not consistently shown it to be effective and to the increasing belief that the psychoanalytic material often incorporated into visualized exposure scenes is unnecessary (Masters et al., 1987).

Background

Flooding had its modern origin in two types of experiments. The first was Masserman's work on experimental neurosis, which demonstrated that an animal's experimentally induced anxiety could be eliminated by forcing the animal back into the feared setting. Experiments on avoidance learning also suggested the therapeutic value of forced exposure (Solomon, Kamin, & Wynne, 1953).

Although there are few references to techniques resembling flooding in early clinical literature, similar methods have been employed nonsystematically for many years. Aphorisms such as "Face your fears," "The only thing to fear is fear itself," and "When you fall off a horse, get right back on it" are all supported by the same rationale as flooding.

Flooding Procedures

Flooding can be conducted imaginally or it can be done *in vivo*. In either instance, exposure times must be long enough for anxiety to dissipate. Exposure should not be terminated while the client is still anxious, as this would reinforce avoidance behavior. Flooding sessions may last 45 minutes to an hour, although they sometimes last 2 hours or more before a decrease in anxiety is noted. Another component in many exposure treatments is *response prevention,* which involves requiring the client to stop performing various rituals or avoidance behaviors used in the past to reduce anxiety.

Applications

One problem for which flooding is especially popular is obsessive-compulsive disorder which includes both *obsessions* (persistent ideas or worries that the client cannot stop from running through his or her mind), and *compulsions* (behaviors that are repeatedly performed in response to obsessions to neutralize or undo the fears associated with the obsessions). One of the most highly publicized cases of obsessive-compulsive disorder was that of the billionaire recluse Howard Hughes, whose life apparently came to be controlled by a serious obsession-compulsion

Howard Hughes was one of America's richest and most colorful tycoons. During the last half of his life, Hughes was apparently afflicted with a severe obsessive-compulsive disorder about infection. He lived as a recluse, but unlike most obsessives, he was rich enough to hire a retinue of servants to carry out his rituals for him, rather than doing them himself. Hughes's fear of germs and contamination dominated his life. He wrote numerous memos in which he explained in detail what he wanted done to prevent the "back transmission" of germs to him. For example, in a three-page memo, he explained how he wanted a can of fruit opened to prevent "fallout" of germs. He required that special equipment be used to open the can, writing, "The equipment used in connection with this operation will consist of the following items: 1 unopened newspaper; 1 sterile can opener; 1 large sterile plate; 1 sterile fork; 1 sterile spoon; 2 sterile brushes; 2 bars of soap; sterile paper towels." The ritual he devised for opening the can had nine steps: "preparing a table, procuring of fruit can, washing of can, drying the can, processing the hands, opening the can, re-moving fruit from can, fallout rules while around can, and conclusion of operation." He worked out complicated procedures for each step of the operation; for example, to wash the can, he wrote:

> The man in charge then turns the valve in the bathtub on, using his bare hands to do so. He also adjusts the water temperature so that it is not too hot nor too cold. He then takes one of the brushes, and using one of the bars of soap, creates a good lather, and then scrubs the can from a point two inches below the top of the can. He should first soak and remove the label, and then brush the cylindrical part of the can over and over until all particles of dust, pieces of paper label, and in general, all sources of contamination have been removed. Holding the can in the center at all times, he then processes the bottom of the can in the same manner, being very sure that all the bristles of the brush have thoroughly cleaned all the small indentations on the perimeter of the bottom of the can. He then rinses the soap from the cylindrical sides and the bottom of the can.

Source: Bartlett and Steel, 1979, p. 233, as cited in Rosenhan and Seligman, 1989.

BOX 9–2
An Example of an Obsessive-Compulsive Disorder

involving fears of dirt and contamination (see Box 9–2). A brief excerpt of an *in-vivo* exposure treatment for an obsessive-compulsive disorder is presented in Box 9–3.

Exposure treatments are also used extensively with *agoraphobia* (literally translated from the Greek, meaning "fear of the market place"), an often severe anxiety disorder involving fear of being separated from a safe place, such as one's home, or of being trapped in a place from which escape might be difficult. Exposure treatments are also used for panic attacks, which are intense, unexpected episodes of terror manifested by physical symptoms such as trembling, sweating, flushes or chills, dizziness, and nausea. Agoraphobics often develop an intense fear of having a panic attack in a place where they cannot get help. They come to suffer a fear of their own fear and become increas-

Below is an brief excerpt from a session in which a client suffering an obsessive-compulsive disorder about contamination and subsequent cleaning rituals is treated with *in vivo* exposure methods. This interaction illustrates how the therapist guides and encourages the client to confront a frightening situation (a dead animal by the side of a road) and stick with it until the fear begins to subside.

THERAPIST: (*Outside the office.*) There it is, behind the car. Let's go and touch the curb and street next to it. I won't insist that you touch it directly because it'a a bit smelly, but I want you to step next to it and touch the sole of your shoe.

PATIENT: Yuck! It's really dead. It's gross!

T: Yeah, it is a bit gross, but it's also just a dead cat if you think about it plainly. What harm can it cause?

P: I don't know. Suppose I got germs on my hand?

T: What sort of germs?

P: Dead cat germs.

T: What kind are they?

P: I don't know. Just germs.

T: Like the bathroom germs that we've already handled?

P: Sort of. People don't go around touching dead cats.

T: They also don't go running home to shower or alcoholing the inside of their car. It's time to get over this. Now, come on over and I'll do it first. (*Patient follows.*) OK. Touch the curb and the street, here's a stone you can carry with you and a piece of paper from under its tail. Go ahead, take it.

P: (*Looking quite uncomfortable.*) Ugh!

T: We'll both hold them. Now, touch it to your front and your skirt and your face and hair. Like this. That's good. What's your anxiety level?

P: Ick! Ninety-nine. I'd say 100 but it's just short of panic. If you weren't here, it'd be 100.

T: You know from past experience that this will be much easier in a while. Just stay with it and we'll wait here. You're doing fine.

P: (*A few minutes pass in which she looks*

BOX 9–3

An Excerpt From a Session of *in vivo* Exposure Treatment

ingly avoidant of situations associated with a possible panic attack. Therefore, successful treatment usually must help clients learn that anxiety itself is not as dangerous as they have come to believe (Foa, Rothbaum, & Kozak, 1989).

Effectiveness and Other Research Issues

Although empirical research has not yet isolated the exact mechanism responsible for exposure treatment's effectiveness, major research efforts have (a) evaluated the clinical conditions for which it is effective, or more effective than alternative treatments (Jansson & Ost, 1982); (b) investigated the extent to which its efficacy is improved by combining it with medication (Mavissakalian & Michelson, 1986), spouse involvement in therapy (Barlow, O'Brien, & Last, 1984), or assertion training (Emmelkamp, Van Der Hout, & De Vries, 1983); and (c) studied what forms and length of exposure treatments are most effective (see Foa, Rothbaum, & Kozak, 1989, for a review).

very upset.) Would you do this if it wasn't for me?

T: Yes, if this were my car and I dropped my keys here, I'd just pick them up and go on.

P: You wouldn't have to wash them?

T: No. Dead animals aren't delightful but they're part of the world we live in. What are the odds that we'll get ill from this?

P: Very small I guess. . . . I feel a little bit better than at first. It's about 90 now.

T: Good! Just stay with it now.

The session continues for another 45 minutes or until anxiety decreases substantially. During this period conversation focuses generally on the feared situations and the patient's reactions to it. The therapist inquires about the patient's anxiety level approximately every 10 minutes.

THERAPIST: How do you feel now?

PATIENT: Well , it is easier, but I sure don't feel great.

T: Can you put a number on it?

P: About 55 or 60 I'd say.

T: You worked hard today. You must be tired. Let's stop now. I want you to take this stick and pebble with you so that you continue to be contaminated. You can keep them in your pocket and touch them frequently during the day. I want you to contaminate your office at work and your apartment with them. Touch them to everything around, including everything in the kitchen, chairs, your bed, and the clothes in your dresser. Oh, also, I'd like you to drive your car past this spot on your way to and from work. Can you do that?

P: I suppose so. The trouble is going home with all this dirt.

T: Why don't you call Ken and plan to get home after he does so he can be around to help you. Remember, you can always call me if you have any trouble.

P: Yeah. That's a good idea. I'll just leave work after he does. OK. See you tomorrow.

Source: Steketee and Foa, 1985.

BOX 9–3
Continued

Social Skills Training

A collection of treatment techniques, known generally as *social skills training,* has been used by behavior therapists for several disorders including depression (Bellack, Hersen, & Himmelhoch, 1983), anxiety disorders (Ost, Jerremalm, & Johansson, 1981), antisocial and delinquent behavior (Stumphauzer, 1986), and social withdrawal and isolation, often with children and adolescents. The rationale for this type of treatment is that psychological disorders can develop as a result of deficits in the social skills necessary for participating in satisfying interpersonal relationships and for gaining other reinforcers. If these deficits are too severe, the person can become demoralized, anxious, angry, and/or alienated. Self-esteem is lowered, and psychological symptoms may appear.

Although social skills training encompasses many techniques, its most common target when used with adults is unassertiveness. Unassertiveness is thought to contribute to psychological problems in several ways: Unassertive persons are often unable to express their wishes in a manner that improves the chances of their desires being met; they are frequently dissatisfied with themselves because of their timidity; and they often grow resentful of others, who they blame for taking advantage of their "weakness."

Assertiveness is *the appropriate expression of feeling in ways that do not infringe upon the rights of others* (Alberti & Emmons, 1974; Wolpe & Lazarus, 1966). Thus, telling your boss that you will not agree to some unreasonable request requires assertion, but so does telling your friends that you were moved by their recent expression of sympathy. Assertion is not the same as aggression. Responding to the person who pushes ahead of you in a supermarket check-out line by saying "Pardon me, there is a line here; please wait your turn" is assertive. Saying "Get your ass out of here before I hit you with my pot roast" is aggressive and not a goal of assertion training. Finally, assertiveness does not preclude politeness or altruism. An assertive individual may make sacrifices to help others ("Why don't you check out first; I'm not in a hurry"), but *only* because he or she wishes to do so, not because of fear of expressing objections.

All too often, people know what they would like to say and do in a difficult social situation (and chide themselves later for not having said or done it) but, because of thoughts like "I have no right to make a fuss" or "He won't like me if I object," they suffer in silence. Increased social awkwardness, continual self-blame, and varying degrees of depression are common results. Assertion training is designed to (a) teach clients how to express themselves appropriately if they do not already have the skills, and/or (b) eliminate cognitive obstacles to clear self-expression.

Background

Assertion training was anticipated by several therapeutic procedures. Moreno's (1946) psychodrama used role-playing techniques that encouraged participants to act spontaneously and express feelings freely. George Kelly's (1955) *fixed-role therapy* asked clients to assume the role of some model whose outlook on the world and actual behavior were less constricted than their own. Through this type of identification, the client was expected to learn the benefits of more assertive behavior.

The first systematic description of assertion training was Andrew Salter's *Conditioned Reflex Therapy* (1949). Salter prescribed a number of *excitatory* techniques for "inhibited" clients. Among these methods were use of "feeling talk" ("I absolutely despise crows"), expression of contradictory opinions, "facial talk" (making facial expressions consistent with emotions), improvisation, acknowledging and accepting compliments, and using the word *I* in conversation.[2]

An influential figure in assertion training was Joseph Wolpe, who advocated using assertive behavior as an anxiety inhibitor as early as 1949. Wolpe found assertive responses to be particularly effective in inhibiting interpersonal anxiety and trained his clients in specific assertion skills.

Assertion Training Procedures

Assertion training has not been standardized into a specific set of procedures. A wide assortment of methods is employed. Though it can be done on a one-to-one basis, assertion training often takes place in groups and usually includes four components: (a) defining assertion and distinguishing it from aggression and submissiveness, (b) discussing client's rights and the rights of others in a variety of social situations, (c) identifying and eliminating cognitive obstacles to assertion, and (d) practicing assertive behavior.

---

[2]These techniques are also part of gestalt therapy and other phenomenologically oriented treatment approaches discussed in Chapter 10.

This last component usually begins with role playing or rehearsal of various social interactions, with the therapist taking the client's role and modeling appropriate assertiveness. Next, the client tries the same behavior. This effort is reinforced and suggestions are made for further improvement. After more refined rehearsals, the client is asked to try the new thoughts and actions in real-life settings. Successes and failures are then analyzed at subsequent sessions, where new or slightly adjusted skills are practiced. This sequence continues until the need for further training disappears.

Applications

Many types of clients can benefit from assertion training, although few enter a therapist's office and request it specifically. Couples suffering marital discord, college students who have interpersonal problems, shy and introverted adults, alcoholics, drug abusers, socially awkward adolescents, and people who rely on aggression to coerce others are often helped by assertion training as part of an overall clinical intervention.

Effectiveness and Other Research Issues

Research on the effects of assertion training has been popular among behavioral clinicians. Most of this work has been done with college students or psychiatric inpatients and has attempted to ascertain the relative effectiveness of the modeling, behavioral rehearsal, and feedback components of assertion training. While the results are complex and difficult to summarize, it would seem that with college students, almost any training technique is sufficient to produce behavioral changes. Psychiatric patients require a more elaborate treatment package, in which modeling may be especially important.

Although most research demonstrates that subjects receiving training do significantly better than those who receive either a placebo or

no treatment, it has been difficult to show that new assertive behavior transfers to *in vivo* contexts. Few studies have examined the generalization of treatment effects. Those that have often discover a disappointingly small amount of transfer of recently developed assertiveness (see Bellack, 1983, for a review of assessment issues in measuring social skills).

Assertion research has received considerable criticism. Most studies have been limited only to negative or refusal assertion, which involves expression of dissatisfaction and saying no to unreasonable requests. Assertion in which the client communicates positive affect, gives and receives compliments, or expresses tender feelings has largely been neglected by researchers. In recent years, a specific focus on training assertive behaviors has been replaced by a broader concern with those social skills believed to be essential to effective interpersonal functioning. These targets include conversational skills (Hansen, St. Lawrence, & Christoff, 1989), social problem solving (Kazdin, Esveldt-Dawson, French, & Unis, 1987), and responding appropriately to emotionally provocative encounters (Tisdelle & St. Lawrence, 1988).

Modeling

A very important mechanism in social-learning theory is *modeling,* or observational learning. Bandura (1969) claimed that "virtually all learning phenomena resulting from direct experiences can occur on a vicarious basis through observation of other persons' behavior and its consequences for them" (p. 118). Learning through modeling is usually more efficient than learning through direct reinforcement. Observation of competent models can eliminate the hazards of unguided trial-and-error behavior. (Imagine the problems if everyone had to be hit by a car before knowing how to cross streets safely!) Highly sophisticated behaviors such as speech require appropriate models, as do complex chains of motor behavior such as driving. Of course, many behaviors *can* be developed through direct experience and reinforcement, but the process of learning is often shortened by the opportunity to observe models.

In addition to developing new behaviors, modeling has other effects. Observation of the consequences of a model's behavior may either *inhibit* or *disinhibit* imitative behavior in an observer. (Would you pet a dog that just bit your friend?) Observing the behavior of others can also *facilitate* the performance of similar responses already present in the repertoire of the observer (a pedestrian who crosses the street against a red light after watching someone else do it first is a good example).

Historical Background

Modeling has long been recognized as an important influence on behavior. Gabriel Tarde (1903), the French judge and sociologist, developed a theory of criminality based on the idea that crime is acquired through imitation. Early theorists viewed imitation as an innate characteristic of humans. Later, psychologists began to explain modeling in terms of conditioning (Allport, 1924) and reinforcement (Miller & Dollard, 1941) principles.

One of the earliest therapeutic examples of modeling was Jones's (1924a,b) use of *social imitation* to overcome conditioned fear in children. Bandura (1969) also credits Masserman (1943) with using modeling to remediate experimental neuroses produced in laboratory animals. According to Bandura, the opportunity for Masserman's inhibited animals to observe a fearless cagemate was sufficient to reduce avoidance behavior in some of them.

Modeling Procedures

Modeling has been used to treat many clinical problems, including social withdrawal among adults and children, obsessive-compulsive behaviors, unassertiveness, antisocial conduct, physical aggressiveness, and early infantile

autism (Rosenthal & Steffek, 1991). Probably its most common use, however, is in the reduction of fears.

In its simplest form, a modeling approach to the elimination of fearful avoidance involves having a client observe live or videotaped models who perform the behavior that the client avoids. The observable consequences for the models should be positive, or at least not negative.

Several variations on the basic modeling package have been developed. The most common of these is *participant modeling*. In this procedure, live modeling is supplemented by giving the client an opportunity to make guided, gradual contact with the feared object under controlled or protected circumstances.

Another innovation in modeling techniques is *covert modeling*. Here, clients "observe" the activities of *imagined* therapeutic models rather than watching live or videotaped displays. Covert modeling involves three components: imagination of situations where fear is expected to occur, imagination of one or more persons comfortably dealing with these situations, and imagination of favorable consequences for the model.

Effectiveness and Other Research Issues

For the most part, outcome research on modeling for fear reduction and other goals has shown it to be effective in producing beneficial changes, especially when combined with other techniques (Bandura, 1986; Rosenthal, 1982). Many questions remain unanswered, however.

A primary concern of modeling research is the investigation of several procedural variations intended to bolster the effectiveness of modeling. Participant and covert modeling are two important examples. Other research has shown that observers are especially influenced by models with whom they share characteristics, by models who are prestigious, by models who

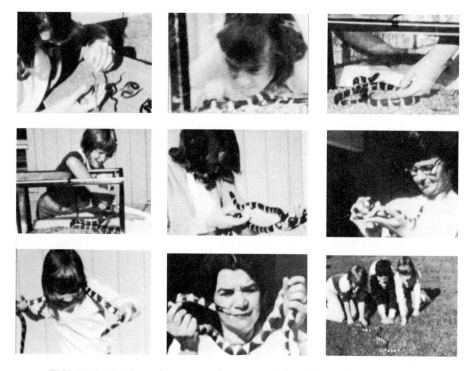

FIGURE 9-3 These frames are from a modeling film used to treat snake phobics. The film depicts children and adults in progressively more threatening interactions with a king snake. (From A. Bandura, E. B. Blanchard, & B. Ritter, The relative efficacy of desensitization and modeling approaches for inducing behavioral, affective and attitudinal changes. *Journal of Personality and Social Psychology,* 1969, *13,* 173–199. Copyright by the American Psychological Association. Reprinted by permission.)

are rewarded for their acts, and by multiple models (Bandura, 1986).

In an interesting variation on the customary modeling procedure, Meichenbaum (1971) proposed that the display of some fearful behavior by models could enhance modeling effects if presented as the initial part of a more complete demonstration in which the model ultimately copes with and overcomes the fear. He termed this technique *coping modeling* and suggested that it could strengthen treatment because it enhances observer–model similarity and provides useful information on how to deal successfully with a fear. While not universally supported, some studies have replicated the finding that coping models produce stronger effects than *mastery models,* who display total fearlessness and competence (e.g., Kazdin, 1973).

The effects of modeling treatments have increasingly been linked to their ability to increase a sense of self-efficacy, which is a person's belief that he or she can successfully perform important behaviors. When a client lacks skills in critical behaviors, modeling methods that quickly promote mastery or proficiency and thereby give the client a basis for increased self-efficacy might be the best therapeutic strategy. In fact, recent research has shown that modeling by a therapist who provides direct guidance on how to achieve masterful performance is a particularly effective treatment for agoraphobics (Williams & Zane, 1989).

Aversion Therapy

Aversion therapy is a set of techniques using painful or unpleasant stimuli to decrease the probability of some unwanted behavior. Drug abuse, alcoholism, overeating, smoking, and disturbing sexual practices are typical targets of aversion therapy. Most aversion methods are based on classical conditioning. Stimuli that elicit problem behavior are paired with a noxious stimulus (a person is shocked as he sits at a simulated bar by a bottle of Scotch). Continuation of this sequence should result in a decrease in the positive value of the eliciting stimuli until the unwanted behavior is reduced, if not eliminated.

Aversion therapy may also employ punishment. In such cases, the aversive stimulus is delivered just after the client performs the problematic behavior (shock would occur immediately after taking a drink of alcohol).

Historical Background

Aversion techniques have been used for centuries. Ullmann and Krasner (1975) report that the Romans encouraged sobriety by placing an eel in the wine cups of intemperate drinkers. Early in the 20th century, Bekhterev and Pavlov suggested the clinical utility of conditioning aversions to previously positive stimuli. Another Russian, Nikolai Kantorovich, was the first person to use aversion conditioning (electric shock to the hands) for the treatment of alcohol abuse. As noted earlier, one of the first applications of aversion therapy in the United States was by Voegtlin and his associates at the Shadel Sanatorium in Seattle.

Aversion Therapy Procedures

The noxious stimuli used in aversion therapy usually involve electric shock (to the hands, feet, or legs) or drugs which either induce nausea or temporarily suppress breathing. Substances with a foul taste or smell have also been used.

In an early example of electrical aversion, Blake (1965) used shocks along with relaxation training and instructions about the negative consequences of drinking to treat a group of alcoholics. Participants were shocked on half the occasions they sipped alcohol. Termination of the shock occurred only when subjects spat out the alcohol, a procedure known as *aversion relief*. Follow-up interviews indicated a 54% rate of abstinence over 6 months and 52% abstinence after 1 year.

Raymond (1956) successfully used chemical aversion with a hospitalized 33-year-old male fetishist charged with numerous malicious attacks on and damage to prams (baby carriages) and handbags. (One prosecutor was moved to label the patient "a menace to any woman with a pram.") Treatment involved repeatedly pairing the fetish objects with apomorphine-induced nausea. After several sessions over a period of days, the patient claimed to be repulsed by the objects of his former affections and even relinquished some pram photos he had been hiding.

One controversy in aversion therapy is whether there is a basis for preferring chemical or electrical events as the noxious stimuli. For a time, clinicians appeared to favor electrical methods. Davidson (1974) described seven advantages associated with electrical methods: (a) greater temporal precision, (b) greater suitability for frequent repetitions, (c) fewer medical complications, (d) fewer apparatus requirements, (e) fewer staff needed, (f) less traumatic implementations for staff, and (g) wider applicability. Others (e.g., Elkins, 1975) suggest that the positive effects of chemical aversion were underestimated in early investigations because the procedures were often incorrectly applied. Certain types of aversion may be more appropriate for behaviors that involve a particular sensorimotor system (Garcia, McGowan, & Green, 1972). For example, associations between nausea and overeating or overdrinking might be biologically and psychologically easier to establish than connections between, say, overeating and pain. On the other hand, shock may be more easily associated with sexual or aggressive misbehaviors than would chemically induced sickness.

A form of aversion therapy called *covert sensitization* requires the client to visualize or imagine aversive consequences that could accompany unwanted behavior. According to Little and Curran (1978), covert sensitization usually proceeds as follows:

> The covert sensitization client, after receiving several sessions of relaxation training, is asked to relax and imagine a sequence of events leading up to a hypothetical problematic performance. The client is then asked to imagine a series of aversive events (typically, nausea and vomiting) just as the point in the imaginal sequence is reached when initial reinforcement is about to be received. The aversion trial is concluded with a suggestion to the client that relief is experienced coincident with an imaginal turning away from the target stimulus. Escape trials are alternated with aversion trials. In the escape trials, the client successively imagines that he or she has an urge to commit the target behavior, begins to experience aversive consequences (typically, nausea), resists the undesired urge, and consequently feels fit and self-satisfied. The therapist attempts to facilitate the client's visualization by describing both types of scenes and by providing an especially detailed and exaggerated description of the aversive consequence. (p. 513)

Joseph Cautela, the originator of covert sensitization, describes the following scene to be visualized by an alcoholic client:

> You are walking into a bar. You decide to have a glass of beer. You are now walking toward the bar. As you are approaching the bar you have a funny feeling in the pit of your stomach. Your stomach feels all queasy and nauseous. Some liquid comes up your throat and it is very sour. You try to swallow it back down, but as you do this, food particles start

coming up your throat to your mouth. You are now reaching the bar and you order a beer. As the bartender is pouring the beer, puke comes up into your mouth. You try to keep your mouth closed and swallow it down. You reach for the glass of beer to wash it down. As soon as your hand touches the glass, you can't hold it down any longer. You have to open your mouth and you puke. It goes all over your hand, all over the glass and the beer. You can see it floating around in the beer. Snots and mucus come out of your nose. Your shirt and pants are full of vomit. The bartender has some on his shirt. You notice people looking at you. You get sick again and you vomit some more and more. You turn away from the beer and immediately you start to feel better and better. When you get out into the clean fresh air you feel wonderful. You go home and clean up. (Cautela, 1966, p. 37)

Covert sensitization offers advantages over shock or chemically induced aversion (Cautela & Kearney, 1986): Few side effects have been noted; special equipment or medical personnel are not required; and the procedure can be applied repeatedly in many different kinds of settings. Because the client's own experiences are used, a wider variety of stimuli are available which, when presented in imagery, may better approximate those encountered in the natural environment. These advantages are reduced by the fact that some patients report difficulty maintaining clear visualizations, which necessitates extensive imagery training.

Effectiveness and Other Research Issues

As researchers have continued to study aversion therapy, they have learned how to increase its effectiveness in treating undesirable behaviors. One commentator recently summarized the effects of this research as follows: "in many quarters and in spite of the continuing controversies, aversion therapy is rapidly achieving the status of respectability in the total range of services to be considered by professionals concerned with behavior change objectives" (Sandler & Steele, 1991, p. 241).

Professional debate about the use of aversion methods tends to focus on two broad concerns. First, how extensive, durable, and generalizable are the changes produced by aversion therapy? Many clinicians are skeptical that aversion therapy produces long-lasting, extensive changes. Indeed, aversion therapy, by itself, does not teach clients alternative behaviors that can replace their maladaptive ones. This is important in the treatment of problems such as overeating, smoking, drug abuse, or sexual deviations. In the sexual area, for example, problems usually reappear if clients do not develop other sexual outlets that are satisfying to them and acceptable to society.

The data on covert sensitization are mixed. Its practical advantages (flexibility, ease of administration) are numerous, but the existing literature is based on studies that lack necessary controls. Little and Curran (1978) concluded that covert sensitization may be effective in producing desired changes in sexual preferences, but that there was little support for its effectiveness with alcoholism, smoking, or obesity.

The second major concern about aversion therapy is that, even if it is effective, do its advantages outweigh clinicians' personal qualms and ethical misgivings about using it? Many therapists find aversion techniques to be offensive, and a small number of clinicians have called for the abolition of aversion techniques. These concerns stem from at least four sources (Masters et al., 1987): (a) evidence that the changes produced by aversive techniques are often not stable, (b) evidence that aversive techniques by themselves seldom increase appropriate alternative behavior, (c) society's general distaste for the intentional infliction of pain, and (d) the possibility of several unwanted side effects, including increases in generalized fear or aggressiveness in recipients, disruption of other nonproblematic behaviors, and an increased willingness by frustrated therapists to use the techniques because they can bring about quick (but temporary) changes.

When aversive methods are used, it is usually as a last resort to control some dangerous behavior (like self-abuse) that has not been controlled by any nonaversive method, or as part of a collection of techniques with demonstrated effectiveness as a treatment package. Even under these circumstances, clinicians have tried to use as mild an aversive stimulus as possible to minimize harm and potential side effects. One strategy is to use naturally occurring aversive events rather than artificial ones like shock. For example, in reducing cigarette smoking, clients can be instructed to smoke much more rapidly than usual so as to increase immediately the nasty consequences of breathing tobacco smoke. Another alternative is *overcorrection,* a procedure in which a person is forced to undo or correct some problem behavior, often by repetitively performing some action that is its opposite. Brief physical restraint of persons who are trying to injure themselves or others is another relatively mild aversive method sometimes used in institutional settings.

Contingency Management

Contingency management is a generic term for any operant technique that modifies a behavior by controlling its consequences. *Shaping, time out, contingency contracting, response cost,* and *token economies* constitute types of contingency management. In practice, contingency management refers to the contingent presentation and/or withdrawal of reinforcers and aversive stimuli following certain behaviors. *Contingent* means that a consequence occurs *if and only if* the behavior to be strengthened or weakened has occurred.

Historical Background

Psychologists did not discover reward and punishment. The Old Testament depicts God as an effective contingency manager who practiced extinction (responding to the provocation of his sons and daughters, "I will hide my face from them," Deuteronomy 32:19–20) as well as time out and punishment (when the Israelites disobeyed God, He sent them to the wilderness for 40 years).

The same principles were used by correctional workers during the 1800s. For example, Alexander Maconochie, governor of a British penal colony, wanted to reform the prison's deplorable conditions. He developed a plan by which a prisoner could gain early release by earning a sufficient number of "marks" through industry and good conduct. Another important feature of the system was its organization into graduated phases like those of contemporary token economies. The five phases were (a) rigid discipline and absolute confinement, (b) labor on a chain gang, (c) limited freedom within certain areas, (d) "ticket-of-leave" or conditional freedom, and (e) total freedom.

Applications

Contingency management has been applied to a broader range of problems than any other behavioral technique. Autism, temper tantrums, learning difficulties, hyperactivity, retardation, juvenile delinquency, aggression, hallucinations, delusions, depression, phobias, sexual disorders, and physical and psychosomatic complaints are a few of the targets that have been dealt with through contingency management.

A special advantage of contingency management is its flexibility. It is suitable for the very young and the very old. It can be tailored to the unique complaints of an individual or applied to the common needs of a group or even a community. Its principles are easy to learn, making it possible to train friends, relatives, teachers, and peers to employ contingency management in real-life settings.

Contingency management can also be used by an individual to modify his or her own behavior. This process is known as *self-control;* it can be thought of as the ability to regulate personal behaviors by arranging appropriate reinforcement contingencies. The overweight person who permits herself or himself to eat only at specified times, only in the kitchen, and

only in the presence of family is practicing a form of self-control. Specific components of self-control include self-instruction, self-monitoring, self-reinforcement, and self-evaluation, each of which has been shown to have some clinical utility (Rehm et al., 1981).

Contingency Management Procedures

Complete accounts of the wide range of contingency management techniques are available in many texts (Kazdin, 1984; Masters et al., 1987). Here are just five examples:

1. Shaping. Also called *successive approximation,* shaping is a procedure for developing new behaviors by initially reinforcing any act that remotely resembles the ultimately desired behavior. Gradually the criterion for reinforcement is made more stringent until only those responses matching the final standard are rewarded. Shaping is useful for instigating behaviors that appear to exceed the person's present capacities. It has been used to teach speech to children who are mute, toilet habits to those who are incontinent, and self-help and occupational skills to the retarded.

2. Time Out. Time out is a special example of extinction that reduces the frequency of an unwanted behavior by temporarily removing the person from a setting where reinforcers exist for that behavior. The most common example is sending a child to a quiet, boring room for a short time following some act of mischief. Time out is based on the principle that ignoring a child's "bad" behavior will decrease it, especially if alternative "good" behavior is also reinforced.

3. Contingency Contracting. Contracting is a form of contingency management where a formal, often written, agreement between therapist and client spells out the consequences of certain behaviors on the part of both parties. It thus organizes the use of many behavior-change methods.

Behavioral contracting has been applied to

diverse clinical targets, including marital distress (Wood & Jacobson, 1985), family disruptions (Alexander & Parsons, 1973), drug abuse (Boudin, 1972), obesity (Brownell & Foreyt, 1985), and other problems (Walker, Hedberg, Clement, & Wright, 1981). The typical contract involves five components which were suggested first by Stuart (1971): (a) responsibilities of each of the parties to the contract, (b) rewards for fulfilling the contract, (c) a system for monitoring compliance with the provisions of the contract, (d) bonuses for unusual accomplishments, and (e) penalties for failures.

Therapy contracts have also become popular with some nonbehaviorally oriented clinicians as a means of informing clients about the ethical requirements and limitations of psychotherapy, facilitating the client's participation in decision making during therapy, and specifying possible risks and benefits of therapy (Handelsman & Galvin, 1988). However, not all clinicians agree that therapy contracts are a necessary or even desirable prelude to ethical treatment; some therapists believe that contracts are incompatible with certain types

of intervention (Widiger & Rorer, 1984). A final use of therapeutic contracts is to prevent dangerous or suicidal behavior by clients by developing a formal contract that forbids violent behavior by the client and requires the client to take specific precautionary actions (calling the therapist, turning over weapons to the therapist) should he or she consider acting dangerously (Bongar, 1991).

4. Response Cost. Response cost is a punishment contingency that involves the loss of a reward or privilege when some undesirable behavior is performed. Fines for traffic and parking violations are good examples of response cost. Another example is the loss of TV privileges imposed on a child who has misbehaved (see Figure 9–4).

Response cost methods have been used to decrease the frequency of many clinical problems, including smoking, self-abuse, overeating, academic problems, and a range of aggressive behaviors. Two major advantages of response cost methods are that (a) behaviors decreased through response cost remain sup-

---

FIGURE 9–4 Percentage of noncompliance across baseline and treatment conditions. The graphs show the effects of response cost treatments used by three different mothers to decrease the rates at which their children refused to comply with reasonable requests for appropriate behavior. Notice that during the baseline sessions all three children were noncompliant with their mothers' request more than 50% of the time. The response cost procedures consisted of taking away points that had been awarded at the beginning of each session each time the child disobeyed an instruction. Once the child had lost 50% of the points awarded for a session, a privilege such as watching TV or playing a game with a parent was taken away for that session. Across the treatment period, this 50% criterion was gradually made more stringent—e.g., the child would lose privileges if 20% of their points were taken away. Not only was noncompliance dramatically decreased during treatment for the children, it stayed decreased across a six-week follow-up. Reproduced from L. M. Little and M. L. Kelley (1989). The efficacy of response cost procedures for reducing children's noncompliance to parental instructions. *Behavior Therapy, 20,* 525–534. Copyright © 1989 by Association for Advancement of Behavior Therapy.

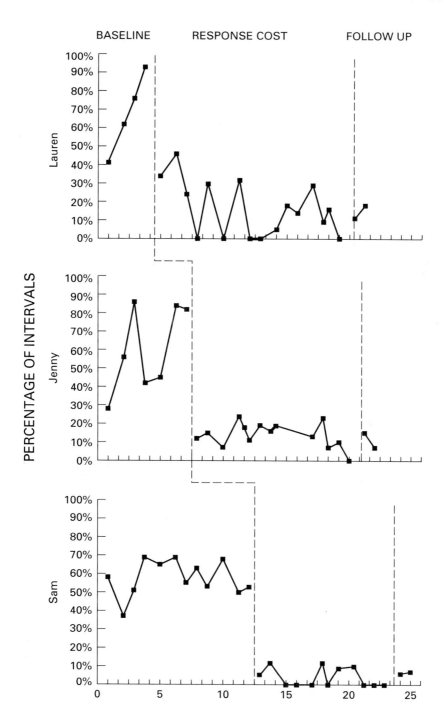

pressed longer than when other types of punishment are employed and (b) response cost does not carry as many unwanted side effects as other, more aversive, forms of punishment (Kazdin, 1972).

5. Token Economies. A token economy is a procedure for implementing the principles of contingency management to alter a variety of behaviors in a group of people. You might think of it as a scaled-down monetary system in which people are paid in a special currency (tokens) for performing designated behaviors. A token economy operates on the principle of being compensated for one's labors in institutional settings where residents have become accustomed to receiving rewards on a noncontingent basis.

The token economy usually consists of four components. First, *target behaviors* are specified. This means that the staff and often the clients designate the behaviors to be changed. Social interaction, self-help skills, and physical exercise are common target behaviors for institutionalized mental patients. Second, there must be a *token* or other medium of exchange which participants earn by performing the desired target behaviors. Gold stars and colored stickers are popular among children. Adults' tastes run toward poker chips or "coins." Third, there must be *backup reinforcers:* goods or services for which tokens may be exchanged. Food, recreational privileges, "vacations" from the hospital, and more luxurious living conditions are common backups. Finally, there must be *rules of exchange* governing the number of tokens to be earned by performing given target behaviors as well as the number of tokens necessary to purchase any backup. Exchange rules are often altered over the course of a token economy to avoid "inflation" or "deflation" of the currency.

The first report of a token economy in a psychiatric institution was published by Ayllon and Azrin (1965), who increased the rate of self-care behaviors and completed work assignments in a group of chronic female patients. Following Ayllon and Azrin's study, token economies in psychiatric hospitals increased at a rapid rate. There was also a dramatic increase in the application of token economy procedures to other populations. Several investigators used token systems to control delinquent and antisocial behavior (Burchard, 1967; Cohen, 1968), and token programs were soon introduced to elementary school classrooms for purposes of reducing disruptions and promoting learning (O'Leary & Becker, 1967). Special programs for Head Start participants, retarded persons, alcoholics, drug addicts, and autistic children were developed according to token economy principles.

Token economies have also been introduced directly into the community. For example, Miller and Miller (1970) increased the rate of community organization activities among poor people through a token economy. A variety of conservation and environmental protection efforts have also been promoted through token programs applied either to large geographical areas or large populations (Nietzel, Winett, MacDonald, & Davidson, 1977).

Effectiveness and Other Research Issues

In terms of sheer frequency, research on contingency management is unmatched by any other behavioral technique. A remarkable feature of this research is the consistency with which it finds operant methods to be effective in modifying specific behaviors in desired directions. There are exceptions to this pattern, of course, but they are few in number.

The most troublesome aspect of contingency management is the problem of generalization. The question is not whether the techniques produce change, but whether the changes are durable and generalizable (Woods, Higson, & Tannahill, 1984). The principal research goals in the field at this time are (a) development and evaluation of procedures designed to promote the transfer of new behaviors to natural settings, and (b) demonstration of the continuation of improved behaviors over time (Sullivan & O'Leary, 1990).

Another major trend in contemporary research on applied operant methods is the investigation of their success with problems that go beyond mental health. Several broad social problems, such as energy conservation, racial discrimination, crime and juvenile delinquency, unemployment, and mass transportation, have all been approached from an operant perspective (Morris & Braukmann, 1987; Nietzel et al., 1977). At the other extreme, behavioral and psychological events that underlie various physical illnesses have also been modified by contingent reinforcement (see Chapter 12 for a thorough discussion of health-related applications of behavior therapy).

Biofeedback

The use of behavioral methods to control internal, autonomic responses is known as *biofeedback*. Biofeedback is a unique version of contingency management because first, the behaviors to be changed are internal, autonomic responses such as heart rate and blood pressure, once thought to be involuntary, or they are responses which are normally easily controlled but have, as a result of disease or injury, become out of control. Second, biofeedback requires special equipment that monitors the activity of interest and then provides feedback on this activity to the client. Feedback is transmitted either through a visual display (a meter or graph) or an auditory stimulus (a varying tone).

Historical Background

K. M. Bykov demonstrated in the mid-1950s that physiological responses could be *classically* conditioned to previously neutral stimuli, but Neal Miller (1969) showed that visceral activity was also subject to the principles of *operant* conditioning. Miller demonstrated that rats could learn to increase and decrease autonomic func-

tions on the basis of contingent reinforcement (direct brain stimulation). The fact that the animals were immobilized with the drug curare ruled out the possibility that the autonomic changes were caused by muscular movement.

Despite the fact that Miller and several other researchers had difficulty replicating the results of the early animal studies, many investigators throughout the 1960s and 1970s began to show that humans could control such activity as brain waves and heart rate.

Applications and Procedures

Biofeedback has been used to treat several kinds of disorders, including essential hypertension (high blood pressure), migraine headaches, Raynaud's disease (a problem of reduced blood flow that can lead to gangrene in the hands or feet), and cardiac arrhythmias (irregular heart beats). EEG (electroencephalogram) conditioning can increase the percentage of alpha wave production and is often used as a special form of relaxation or meditation training. A recent use of biofeedback is for nocturnal bruxism, which is the clenching and grinding of teeth during sleep that can result in headaches, facial pain, and dental problems. This condition has been treated effectively with a device that monitors muscular tension in the face (EMG) while the patient is asleep. When the EMG rate reaches a critical level, it sets off a buzzer that awakens the patient and interrupts the bruxing episode (Cassisi & McGlynn, 1988). Urinary incontinence, breathing irregularities, and neuromuscular disorders are other problems that have recently been effectively treated via biofeedback.

In each of these applications the procedure is fundamentally the same. A monitor and feedback apparatus are attached to the client, who then uses some mental or physical strategy to change the internal response in a desired direction. In most cases the reinforcer for change is simply the knowledge of results provided by the feedback, but praise or monetary rewards may also be used.

Effectiveness and Other Research Issues

In spite of extravagant claims by some proponents, there is not enough evidence at this point to conclude that biofeedback is a clinically useful technique. Miller (1983) himself has observed that while biofeedback (if practiced "conscientiously") can be a useful treatment or part of treatment for several physical ailments including newer targets such as hemiplegias, fecal incontinence, and seizure disorders,

> much of the evidence is of the case-history type, and most of the better . . . studies still involve rather small numbers of cases. . . . Furthermore, there does not seem to be much evidence on the differential effects of different [techniques] or combinations of these techniques, and such evidence as there is indicates that these effects are approximately equal, so that there appears to be a practical advantage in trying the simpler ones, at least as the first step in a step-care procedure. (p. 23)

Even more crucial to the status of biofeedback are questions about the magnitude and permanence of the changes it produces. It is one thing to condition decreases in blood pressure levels already within normal limits, but it is much more difficult to establish changes large enough to make a significant difference in clinical hypertension. Further, if large changes can be produced in the lab or clinic, can they be maintained when the client is no longer attached to the special monitoring equipment? Finally, consistent with Miller's (1983) observations, simpler procedures like relaxation training may produce changes that equal or exceed those made through biofeedback (Reed, Katkin, & Goldband, 1986).

Cognitive-Behavior Therapy

One can no more expect a client to participate in psychotherapy without thinking about the experience than one can expect a sprinter to run a race without moving his or her legs. Any therapy technique, behavioral or otherwise, stimulates a multitude of cognitions: Will this treatment work? Why will it work? What if it doesn't work? Why didn't I think of trying this? When will I start to notice some improvement? In addition to thinking about these questions, clients depend on cognitive processes to understand a therapist's communications, to visualize material in procedures like desensitization or covert modeling, and to reflect on the changes they make or fail to make in therapy.

All therapeutic interventions involve cognitive processes, but some procedures are specifically directed toward changing maladaptive cognitions. These techniques compose what is known as *cognitive-behavior therapy* or simply *cognitive therapy*. Cognitive therapy can be defined as a treatment approach that attempts to modify maladaptive behavior by influencing a client's cognitions (beliefs, schemas, self-statements, and problem-solving strategies). Cognitive-behavior therapists attach special, causal status to cognitions that strict behaviorists avoid. They assume that emotional problems are largely due to irrational or improper thinking and that restructuring these cognitions will be therapeutic.

Another assumption of cognitive therapists is that some type of cognitions, particularly thoughts about the self, are especially important in the development of disorders (Salovey & Singer, 1991). These thoughts are usually connected to emotions; they affect how we feel about ourselves and our relationships with others. Self-cognitions influence our outlook on the future and our confidence that we will be able to cope with new demands. They also color how we think about the past and the way we explain events that have happened to us.

Cognitive therapy techniques take many different forms and have been described by several different names (Ledwidge, 1978). Recently, cognitive therapists have explored ways to integrate cognitive-behavioral techniques into other therapeutic approaches such as interpersonal therapy (Safran, 1990a, b) and psychoanalysis (Westen, 1991). Cognitive versions of behavior therapy have surged in popularity in the past 10 years. Detailed descriptions of these techniques can be found in the following sources: Dryden and Trower (1989), Freeman, Simon, Beutler, and Arkowitz (1989), Kendall and Braswell (1985), Ingram (1986), Mahoney and Freeman (1985), and Meichenbaum (1977).

One of the most influential types of cognitive therapy is Aaron Beck's approach to the treatment of depression. Because depression is a frequent clinical disorder and because evaluations of cognitive therapy have shown it to be a particularly effective intervention (Kovacs, Rush, Beck, & Hollon, 1981; Rush, Beck, Kovacs, & Hollon, 1977), Beck's treatment has earned a reputation as one of the most powerful forms of cognitive treatment. Cognitive therapy for depression is based on the assumption that emotions are determined by the way people think about their experiences. Depressive symptoms reflect logical errors and distortions that clients consistently make about the events in their lives. These illogical schemas lead individuals to perceive themselves, their world, and their future in pessimistic, self-deprecating ways. Beck termed this set of mistaken schemas the "cognitive triad" and pointed out several forms of distorted thinking in depressed persons. For example, *arbitrary inference* involves drawing conclusions about oneself on the basis of insufficient or irrelevant information (a woman believes she is worthless because she is not invited to a particular party). *Magnification* enlarges small events to a point of great significance (a man decides his record collection is ruined because one record has a scratch on it), while *minimization* does the opposite (a student believes that a good grade was the result of luck and that he is still basically stupid).

Cognitive therapists work to identify and correct their client's distorted beliefs. Five related strategies are emphasized: (a) recogniz-

ing the connections between cognitions, affect, and behavior; (b) monitoring occurrences of the negative cognitive triad; (c) examining the evidence for and against these distortions; (d) substituting more realistic interpretations for dysfunctional cognitions; and (e) completing "homework assignments" wherein the client can practice these new thinking strategies and cope with problems more effectively.

Although cognitive therapy is an effective treatment for nonpsychotic depression, its practitioners' claims that distorted cognitions *cause* depression is not well supported (Haaga, Dyck, & Ernst, 1991). Depressed persons do feel more hopeless and have more negative thoughts than nondepressed persons, but these differences appear to accompany or even follow depression rather than to precede it, which would be required for the cognitions to be a causal force. Further, the fact that depressed people hold more negative beliefs about themselves and the world does not necessarily mean they are distorting reality. Considerable evidence suggests an alternative: Nondepressed persons may be distorting their beliefs and perceptions in a slightly positive or "rosy" direction (Taylor & Brown, 1988; see Ackerman & DeRubeis, 1991, for a more cautious interpretation of depressive realism research).

Another cognitive therapy is Albert Ellis's rational-emotive therapy, or RET. Ellis (1973) stated the core principles of RET as follows:

> When a highly charged emotional Consequence (C) follows a significant Activating Event (A), A may seem to but actually does not cause C. Instead emotional Consequences are largely created by B—the individual's Belief System. When, therefore, an undesirable Consequence occurs, such as severe anxiety, this can usually be quickly traced to the person's irrational Beliefs, and when these Beliefs are effectively Disputed (at point D), by challenging them rationally, the disturbed Consequences disappear and eventually cease to reoccur. (p. 167)

To illustrate these principles, Ellis (1973) provides the following example. Suppose a man has a bad day at work. He arrives late, forgets his office keys, spills coffee on his desk, and misses two important appointments. He may think to himself, "I was lousy at my job today." He is correct; he did do a bad job. That is what Ellis called the activating event (A), a happening that is undesirable. Next the man may think, "This is horrible, what a schmuck I am; if I don't get with it I'll get fired which will serve me right for being so worthless." These ideas reflect the person's belief system (B), and according to Ellis, *they* may produce the emotional consequences (C) of anxiety, depression, and worthlessness.

To summarize the ABCs of RET: Psychological problems result not from external stress but from the irrational ideas people hold, which lead them to insist that their wishes must be met for them to be happy. Thus the task in RET is to attack these irrational, unrealistic, self-damaging beliefs and to instruct clients in more rational or logical thinking patterns that will not upset them.

Background

Ellis (1973) acknowledges numerous precursors to RET, which he began to practice in the mid-1950s. Among early philosophers, the Stoics, particularly Epictetus, believed that "men are disturbed not by things, but by the view they take of them." Shakespeare had Hamlet observe: "There is nothing either good or bad but thinking makes it so."

Ellis also notes that several early psychotherapists influenced RET. Chief among these was Alfred Adler, whose motto, "Everything depends on opinion," is a keystone of RET philosophy. Several therapists who employed a forceful, directive, active therapeutic style (Andrew Salter, Frederick Thorne, Alexander Herzberg, and Wilhelm Stekel) also anticipated RET. The most complete and informative presentations of Ellis's ideas are contained in his *Reason and Emotion in Psychotherapy* (1962), the *Handbook of Rational-Emotive Therapy* (Ellis & Grieger, 1977), and *The Practice of Rational-Emotive Therapy* (Ellis & Dryden, 1987).

RET Procedures

The RET therapist is active, challenging, demonstrative, and often abrasive. Ellis advocates the use of strong, direct communication in order to persuade clients to give up the irrational ideas with which they indoctrinate themselves into misery. Here is a brief excerpt from an initial RET session between a therapist (T) and a young woman (C) who presented several problems, among them the abuse of alcohol.

C: . . . my tendency is to say *everything*. I want to change everything; I'm depressed about everything; et cetera.

T: Give me a couple of things, for example.

C: What I'm depressed about? I, uh, don't know that I have any purpose in life. I don't know what I—what I am. And I don't know in what direction I'm going.

T: Yeah, but that's—so you're saying, "I'm ignorant!" (client nods) Well what's so awful about being ignorant? It's too bad you're ignorant. It would be nicer if you weren't—if you *had* a purpose and *knew* where you were going. But just let's suppose the worst: for the rest of your life you didn't have a purpose, and you stayed this way. Let's suppose that. Now why would you be so bad?

C: Because everyone *should* have a purpose!

T: Where did you get the *should?*

C: 'Cause it's what I believe in. (silence for a while)

T: I know. But think about it for a minute. You're obviously a bright woman; now, where did that *should* come from?

C: I, I don't know! I'm not thinking clearly at the moment. I'm too nervous! I'm sorry.

T: Well, but you *can* think clearly. Are you now saying, "Oh, it's hopeless! I can't think clearly.

What a shit I am for not thinking clearly!" You see: You're blaming yourself for *that.*

C: (visibly upset; can't seem to say anything; then nods)

T: Now you're perfectly *able* to think.

C: Not at the moment!

T: Yes you are! Want to bet?

C: (begins to sob)

T: What are you crying about now?

C: Because I feel so stupid! And I'm afraid!

T: Yeah, but "stupid" means "I'm putting myself down for acting stupidly."

C: All right! I didn't expect to be put on so *fast.* I expected a moment to catch my breath and see who you *were;* and to establish some different kind of rapport.

T: Yeah. And that would be nice and easier; but we would really waste our time.

C: Yes, I guess we would.

T: But you're really upset because you're not giving the right answers—and isn't that *awful!*

C: Yes. And I don't think that anybody likes to be made a fool, a fool of!

T: You *can't* be made a fool of!

C: (chokes a little)

T: You see, that's the *point:* That's impossible. Now why *can't* you be made a fool of?

C: (angry outburst) Why don't you stop asking me?

T: (interrupting) No! You'll never get better unless you *think.* And you're saying, "Can't we do something *magical* to get me better? And the answer is "No!"

The therapist's frontal assault on the client's irrational beliefs is not restricted to cognitive interventions. Role playing, sensory-awareness exercises, desensitization, assertion training, and

FIGURE 9–5 (Courtesy of the Western Psychological Association)

"Why doesn't she call? I don't understand. She said she'd call at 5:00. It's 5:15 already. Maybe she's been in accident. Maybe she's lying in a ditch somewhere. I'd better call her and make sure she's OK. No, what if she's not hurt. What if she's with a MAN. I can't call her. She'll think I'm too pushy. They never like pushy men. But it's 5:20 already, and she SAID she'd call— I didn't make her say that. She might really be hurt and bleeding somewhere. But what if I call her and she doesn't want to talk to me? God-damned women."

specific homework assignments also will be employed by the RET therapist in an attempt to provide behavioral complements to cognitive change. Applications of RET to special clinical problems have been described by Ellis and Bernard (1985), and Huber and Baruth (1989).

Effectiveness and Other Research Issues

A series of meta-analyses has found cognitive behavioral treatments to be an effective form of psychotherapy. Miller and Berman (1983) reported a mean posttreatment effect size of .83 for cognitive treatments compared to no treatment, and a mean effect size of .21 for cognitive treatments compared to other therapies; these advantages were fairly well maintained at follow-up. A meta-analysis of Beck's cognitive therapy for depression concluded that it was more effective than other therapeutic approaches for this specific problem (Dobson, 1989). Analyzing treatments that emphasized what they termed "self-statement

---

BOX 9–4
Multimodal Behavior Therapy

One innovative form of behavior therapy is *multimodal behavior therapy* as formulated and practiced by Arnold A. Lazarus of Rutgers University. Lazarus (1976, 1981, 1985) advocates "technical eclecticism" in his therapeutic approach, meaning that therapists should use whatever techniques are most appropriate for given problems regardless of the theoretical system from which the techniques are derived. Behavioral techniques might be appropriate for one type of difficulty, while Gestalt or psychoanalytic procedures would be preferred for another problem. While Lazarus would feel free to use any or all of these techniques, it is probably fair to say that his basic approach is eclectic, albeit with a strong behavioral emphasis.

Lazarus organizes his treatment around seven areas of functioning summarized by the acronym BASIC ID, which stands for Behavior, Affect, Sensation, Imagery, Cognition, Interpersonal Relations, and Drugs. Each of these areas of functioning (with the exception of drugs, which is a form of treatment) may call for different techniques, ranging across several schools of therapy, although Lazarus (1977) acknowledges that about 28% of multimodal therapy is devoted

to behavioral and interpersonal factors, with the rest of the time split among the other five areas.

Multimodal therapy has been sharply criticized by staunch behaviorists like Wolpe (Lazarus's former mentor) and Eysenck for straying too far from behavioristic principles and diluting the strength of pure behavior therapy (Wolpe, 1984). For his part, Lazarus (1977) claims that his treatment approach is committed to "behavioral principles," which he defines as

due regard for scientific objectivity, extreme caution in the face of conjecture and speculation, a rigorous process of deduction from testable theories, and a fitting indifference toward persuasion and hearsay. (pp. 550–551)

Multimodal behavior therapy is part of the trend toward eclecticism and integration of different schools of therapy that we previously described (see Chapter 7). Eclecticism remains a controversial issue, however, despite the fact that many clinicians claim it as their orientation (see Arkowitz & Messer, 1984; Haaga, 1986).

modification," Dush, Hirt, and Schroeder (1983) reported a healthy average effect size of .74 in comparison to no-treatment controls. Shapiro and Shapiro (1982) reported a "modest but undeniable superiority of behavioral and cognitive methods" in relation to other treatments (p. 596).

In several recent empirical studies that have directly compared cognitive and cognitive-behavior therapy to alternative treatments, cognitive methods have fared well. For example, cognitive therapies have been shown to be as effective as medication in treating bulimia nervosa (Leitenberg & Rosen, 1988) and tension headaches (Holroyd, Nash, Pingel, Cordingly, & Jerome, 1991) and more effective than behavior therapy in treating generalized anxiety disorder (Butler, Fennell, Robson, & Gelder, 1991).

The evaluative research on the effectiveness of rational-emotive therapy is not as methodologically elegant as that for other cognitive methods (Zettle & Hayes, 1980) but its results are positive. Ellis (1973) reported more than 25 experimental studies and a greater number of case histories that supported the positive effects of RET, and the basic principles of RET and its theory of emotional distress have received favorable evaluations (DiGiuseppe & Miller, 1977; Ellis & Greiger, 1977).

A meta-analysis of 70 RET outcome studies (Lyons & Woods, 1991) found that RET produced substantial improvements in clients compared to various control conditions, especially when more experienced therapists delivered the treatment and when treatment lasted longer. RET was not generally superior to various forms of behavior therapy. One recent review of RET research (Haaga & Davison, 1989) reached the following conclusions: (a) RET can be useful in the treatment of hostility, stress, depression, and antisocial conduct; (b) RET decreases self-reported anxiety; (c) in combination with other techniques, RET has some benefit for certain sexual problems; and (d) RET is not as effective as other methods for the treatment of simple phobias or agoraphobia.

In addition to research on effectiveness, there is a need to investigate more carefully the theoretical foundations of cognitive behavior therapy. Beidel and Turner (1986) have reviewed several problems in the conceptualization of cognitive behavior therapy that cognitive therapists need to take seriously. Difficulties exist in at least three areas: (a) definitions of cognitions are inconsistent—sometimes cognition is viewed as a process, sometimes it is viewed as an outcome; (b) distorted cognitions have not been proven to be the cause of various emotional disturbances as most cognitive therapies imply; and (c) distinctions between traditional behavior therapy and cognitive-behavior therapy are difficult because most cognitive-behavior therapists use several noncognitive techniques (e.g., role playing and assigned homework tasks) that could account for treatment effectiveness. Other theoretical critiques of cognitive-behavior therapy are presented by Haaga and Davison (1991), Muran (1991), and Rude and Rehm (1991).

A Final Note

In describing contemporary behavior therapy we have concentrated on specific techniques such as desensitization, flooding, contingency management, and cognitive techniques. This emphasis does not mean that behavior therapists are simply technicians who match problems with specific treatment methods in an automatic way. Behavior therapists, like other clinicians, are committed to the welfare of the people they treat; they attempt to convey a sense of support and caring during therapy. Technical proficiency is not a substitute for the special therapeutic relationship that a client and clinician can share.

Having developed so rapidly since the 1960s, behavior therapy now faces important challenges that it must meet in order to sustain its positive impact on clinical psychology. First, behavior therapy's tradition of integrating research findings with clinical practice has been endangered recently, a trend that Barlow (1980) identified as a widening "scientist-practitioner gap." Researchers must ask clinically meaningful questions and attempt to answer them in externally valid ways; clinicians must collect evaluative data as they practice. A related problem is what Ross (1985) called a "technological drift" manifested by clinicians' and researchers' greater interests in applications and techniques at the expense of basic research, conceptual advancements, and knowledge from biological, developmental, and social psychology. This problem is partly reflected by the finding that research published in the last 2 decades in one of clinical psychology's premier journals—the *Journal of Consulting and Clinical Psychology*—has be-

come progressively less guided by theory and more concerned with clinical pragmatics (Omer & Dar, 1992).

Finally, several content/research areas promise to be blue-chip investments in behavior therapy's future development. Fine-grained analyses of psychopathology (Hersen, 1981), more direct research on affect (Wilson, 1982; Zajonc, 1980), extension of behavioral principles to clinical problems that have not been priorities for behavior therapists such as the personality disorders (Linehan, 1987; Turner, 1989), and posttraumatic disorders (Foa, Steketee, & Rothbaum, 1989), and greater biological sophistication (Ross, 1985) are important needs that must be addressed by future behavior therapists.

CHAPTER 10

Clinical Intervention: Phenomenological Models

In Chapters 8 and 9 we described clinical interventions that assume human behavior to be a product of either intrapsychic conflicts or learning influences. However, a third force in clinical psychology deemphasizes these factors and focuses instead on *conscious experience* as the basis for human behavior. This *phenomenological* approach views humans as creative, growing beings who, if all goes well, consciously guide their own behavior in an attempt to realize their fullest potential as unique individuals. When behavior disorders arise, they are usually seen as stemming from disturbances in awareness or restrictions on existence that can be eliminated through various therapeutic experiences (Fischer & Fischer, 1983).

Working on behavior problems by increasing clients' conscious awareness reflects some psychodynamic principles on which phenomenological treatments are partly based. In addition, approaching each client as a unique individual guided by her or his own thoughts is similar to cognitive versions of behavior therapy. Nevertheless, many of the goals and techniques of phenomenologically oriented treatments are distinct. In this chapter we describe the background, procedures, and effectiveness of prominent phenomenological interventions.

Several themes unify the goals and techniques associated with phenomenological treatments. To set the stage for our discussion, we review some of these commonalities:

1. There is an emphasis on promoting the client's *growth* as a person rather than on facilitating the skill of "playing the game of life." Phenomenological therapists help clients become aware of and reach their own unique potential. The underlying assumption is that when clients approach their full potential, they will be capable of finding solutions to problems of living without help from anyone else. In fact, actively helping a client solve particular problems is viewed as counterproductive: If the client uses the *therapist's* solution, the opportunity will be missed to let her or his own feelings and ideas be a guide. In addition, the client may become dependent

on the therapist and less inclined to seek independent resolutions of future difficulties.

2. Because clients are viewed by phenomenological therapists as responsible individuals who are capable of handling their own lives, the roles of the client and therapist are considered to be comparable in status. If in psychodynamic therapy there is a doctor–patient relationship and in behavioral interventions there is a teacher–student relationship, in phenomenological treatment the clinician and client are more like gardener and flower. The therapist facilitates growth that is inherent in the client, but both may grow and benefit from the relationship.

3. The relationship between the client and the therapist is the primary vehicle through which growth takes place. The immediate, moment-to-moment experience of therapy is what helps the client. Thus, for an insecure client, insight into the past or making plans for handling future problems would be viewed as less helpful than being in a relationship where another person nonjudgmentally *accepts* and *values* the client despite his or her own lack of self-assurance. This experience prompts the client to perceive himself or herself in more positive terms. In phenomenological treatment, the client–therapist relationship is not a special, isolated context for talking about early conflicts, how those conflicts appear in the present, or possible new responses to the environment. It is a *real interpersonal relationship* which, apart from the topics discussed or the techniques used, gives the client human *experiences* which themselves promote growth.

4. Because the immediate experience of the therapy relationship is so important, the focus of phenomenological treatment seldom strays from what is going on between client and therapist in the session. The assumption is that the past cannot be changed and is not as important for the client's future as is the present.

5. Phenomenological clinicians assume that most clients are not sick, disordered, or differ-

ent from "normal" people, no matter how bizarre those clients appear to be. Phenomenologists see their clients as behaving in line with their unique perceptions of the world. Therefore, the therapist seeks to understand the client's problems by trying to look at the world through the client's eyes. It is hoped that in the process of revealing her or his perceptions to the therapist, the client will become more aware of how those perceptions guide behavior.

With these themes in mind, we examine examples of phenomenological treatment.

THE CLIENT-CENTERED THERAPY OF CARL ROGERS

The most influential phenomenological approach to intervention is the *client-centered therapy* of Carl Rogers (1942, 1951, 1954, 1959, 1961, 1970, 1980). Rogers's initial training as a psychologist was in a psychodynamic tradition, but he ultimately rejected that tradition and founded an approach to treatment which, by the 1940s, provided clinical psychology with its first systematic alternative to Freud. As we shall see, Rogers also established a tradition of doing research on the process and outcome of psychotherapy.

Some Background on Client-Centered Therapy

Carl Rogers was born on January 8, 1902, the fourth of six children in a close-knit, conservative Protestant family. Religion, self-reliance, and hard work were important early influences. "There was no drinking, dancing, card playing, theatre going, and little social life" in Rogers's youth (Sollod, 1978, p. 95); in fact, he reportedly had only two dates during high school (Reisman, 1976). His family moved to a farm when Rogers was 12 and he became interested in agriculture. By the age of 14, Rogers had become a student of agriculture and learned "how experiments were conducted, how control groups were matched with experimental groups, how conditions were held constant by randomizing procedures . . ." (Rogers, 1961, p. 6).

Rogers became an agriculture major at the University of Wisconsin; because of his family background, however, he leaned toward becoming a minister. In his junior year he spent 6 months at a World Student Christian Federation conference in China, where he began to question the religious views of his parents and became inclined toward more liberal forms of Christianity. After graduation he enrolled in New York City's Union Theological Seminary, an institution whose liberal orientation fit Rogers's developing religious views.

While at the seminary, Rogers and some of his fellow students formed an independent seminar group whose aim was to search for truth through discussion about personal ideas and doubts. There was no instructor. "The majority of the members of that group, in thinking their way through the questions they raised, thought themselves right out of religious work. I was one" (Rogers, 1961, p. 8). In 1925, after 2 years at Union, Rogers enrolled in Teachers College at Columbia University to study psychology.

At least as early as his China trip, Rogers had been wrestling with the concept of authority. In religion, in education, and in family life, he had learned that those "in authority" want to tell people what to do, how to think, and what values to adopt. Yet he began to question the wisdom of this approach, not only for his own life, but for the lives of others. At Teachers College, Rogers learned about *progressive education* and the notion that education should enhance the growth of students by pacing lessons to the student's level of reading and by tailoring material to student needs. Progressive education advocates such as John Dewey also used *guided discussion* to help students find things out for themselves

rather than depending on others to tell students the right answers.

Rogers's training in child therapy at Columbia began under Leta Hollingsworth and continued during a year-long internship at the Institute for Child Guidance in New York. Child-guidance clinics at this time were run primarily by psychiatrists, so Rogers was exposed to the Freudian model. Though he learned much from this experience, Rogers became as uncomfortable with the concept of therapist as authority as he had been with the notion of teacher as authority. Thus, after he took his first job as a psychologist in the child study department of the Rochester (New York) Society for the Prevention of Cruelty to Children, Rogers grew unhappy with the psychodynamic approach. By the early 1930s, Rogers was not sure what alternative to pursue, but he felt that there had to be a better way to go about clinical work.

An alternative appeared when Rogers discovered Otto Rank's approach to therapy, mainly through Rankian social workers at Rochester, and through Jessie Taft, a Philadelphia psychologist-social worker. Taft had developed *relationship therapy,* "which can take place only when divorced from all hint of control" (Taft, 1951, p. 94). Taft's procedures reflected the basic tenets advanced by Rank:

> The individual client . . . is a moving cause, containing constructive forces within, which constitute a will to health. The therapist guides the individual to self-understanding, self-acceptance. It is the therapist *as a human being* who is the remedy, not his technical skill. . . . The spontaneity and uniqueness of therapy lived in the present carry the patient toward health. (Meador & Rogers, 1973, p. 121; italics added)

These ideas meshed with the principles of progressive education that had impressed Rogers in graduate school, they reflected his distrust of authoritarian treatment, and they evoked ideals from his childhood: " . . . the in-

FIGURE 10–1 Carl Rogers (1902–1987) by John T. Wood (courtesy of Carl Rogers).

dividualism of the American frontier, the belief in self-reliance, the conviction that the individual could learn to do what was necessary for him to learn and do" (Meador & Rogers, 1973, p. 120).

In the 1930s, Rogers became increasingly aware of the shortcomings of traditional assessment and psychotherapy. For example, after using a psychoanalytic approach to help a fire-setting youngster see that his maladaptive behavior was based on unconscious conflicts over masturbation, Rogers was jolted to discover that the client did not improve. At another point Rogers reread the transcript of an interview with a mother that, years earlier, he had thought was excellent:

> I was appalled. Now it seemed to me to be a clever legalistic type of questioning by the interviewer which convicted this parent of her unconscious motives, and wrung from her an

admission of her guilt. I now knew from my experience that such an interview would not be of any lasting help to the parent or the child. It made me realize that I was moving away from any approach which was coercive or pushing in clinical relationship. . . . (Rogers, 1961, p. 11)

As a result of experiences like these, Rogers began to incorporate ideas about non-authoritarianism and the value of a good human relationship into his therapy. Rogers began to think that "it is the *client* who knows what hurts, what directions to go, what problems are crucial, what experiences have been deeply buried. It began to occur to me that unless I had a need to demonstrate my own cleverness and learning, I would do better to rely upon the client for the direction of movement. . . . " (Rogers, 1961, pp. 11–12).

Rogers's first book, *The Clinical Treatment of the Problem Child,* was published in 1939. It contained two noteworthy features. First, Rogers's preference for relationship therapy was obvious. Second, his orientation toward experimental research, which came from his early experiences in agriculture and from the experimental psychologists at Teachers College, became evident. He was among the first to recognize the need for scientific research to substantiate the alleged value of any treatment technique, including his own. Rogers pointed out, for example, that although many therapists extol the value of relationship therapy, "since their criteria are largely intangible measures such as the freedom from minor tensions and the greater degree of personal comfort achieved, any measurement of success is difficult indeed. From those who are most interested in relationship therapy, we find no mention of the degree or proportion of success . . . " (Rogers, 1939, p. 200). The same year his book was published, Rogers left his first job to become director of the Rochester Child Guidance Center.

By 1940 Rogers was developing a systematic approach to treatment that incorporated his ideas and those of the people who had influenced him. Three important things happened that year. First, Rogers participated in a symposium on therapy organized by Goodwin Watson, a Columbia University psychology professor. At that meeting, Rogers described the virtues of relationship therapy, but also heard Watson endorse similar ideas which shaped Rogers's thinking (Sollod, 1978). Second, Rogers moved from his clinical job in Rochester to his first academic position as a full professor at Ohio State University. The academic setting helped Rogers elaborate his views. "It was in trying to teach what I had learned about treatment and counseling to graduate students . . . that I first began to realize that I had perhaps developed a distinctive point of view of my own . . . " (Rogers, 1961, p. 13).

He became sure of this because of the third major event of 1940. On December 11 Rogers gave an invited talk to the Psi Chi[1] chapter at the University of Minnesota. In that talk, entitled "Some Newer Concepts in Psychotherapy," Rogers presented his notions about a *nondirective* approach, which allows clients to solve their own problems without judgments from the clinician. He stressed (a) relying on the client's drive toward growth, health, and adjustment rather than on treatment techniques to produce benefits; (b) emphasizing the *present moment* in therapy rather than the past as a key to change; and (c) focusing on the therapeutic relationship as a promoter of client growth (Rogers, 1974). The reaction to the "birth" of nondirective therapy was intense. "I was totally unprepared for the furor the talk aroused. I was criticized, I was praised, I was attacked, I was looked on with puzzlement" (Rogers, 1974, p. 8). Rogers's ideas appealed to some clinicians as an excellent alternative to the "all-knowing expert" approach of psychoanalysis. Freudians and other traditionalists were critical, for obvious reasons.

In 1942 Rogers published a full-length account of nondirective therapy, *Counseling and Psychotherapy.* In this book Rogers advocated

> a counseling relationship whose characteristics were the warmth and responsiveness of the therapist, a permissive climate in which the feelings of the client could be freely expressed, and a freedom for the client from all coercion or pressure. A client in such a relationship would gain understanding of himself

which then allows him or her to take positive steps toward self-help (Meador & Rogers, 1973, p. 122). Rogers's research orientation continued to be evident in this book. He reported the content analyses of clinical inter-

---

[1] A national psychology honorary organization that is still active today.

views which, for the first time, had been pho-nographically recorded.

In 1945 Rogers organized and became ex-ecutive secretary of the University of Chicago Counseling Center. During the next 12 years Rogers continued to develop and evaluate his treatment approach which, by 1946, he was calling *client-centered* rather than nondirective therapy. This change emphasized the primary role of the client's inherent potential for growth, and was formalized in Rogers's 1951 book, *Client-Centered Therapy*.

Over the years, Carl Rogers continued to practice and research psychotherapy and to apply his views in an ever-broadening range of contexts. After leaving Chicago, he spent 4 years at the University of Wisconsin and then moved to the Western Behavioral Sciences In-stitute in La Jolla, California. He started the Center for Studies of the Person in La Jolla. A distinguished series of books has resulted from his clinical experience. These include *On Becoming a Person* (1961), *Freedom to Learn* (an application of his concepts to education, 1969), *Carl Rogers on Encounter Groups* (1970), *On Becoming Partners: Marriage and Its Alternatives* (1972), and *A Way of Being* (1980). Rogers remained active in clinical psy-chology until his death in 1987.

The Client-Centered Approach

Rogers argued that therapy is a *process,* not a set of techniques. He advocated that a thera-pist cannot solve clients' problems by *telling* or by *teaching* them anything:

> No approach which relies upon knowledge, upon training, upon the acceptance of some-thing that is *taught,* is of any use. . . . such methods are, in my experience, futile and in-consequential. The most they can accomplish is some temporary change, which soon disap-pears, leaving the individual more than ever convinced of his inadequacy. (Rogers, 1961, pp. 32–33)

The *real* process of therapy is an "if . . . then" proposition: If the correct circumstances are created by the therapist, the client will sponta-neously change and grow. The therapeutic process will take place on its own, driven by the client's growth potential, but only when the proper atmosphere is present and regard-less of specific techniques or content.

This approach is related to Rogers's self-the-ory, which we sketched in Chapter 2. This the-ory assumes that people are thwarted in their growth by judgments imposed on them by oth-ers. These *conditions of worth* force people to distort their real feelings. When this happens, symptoms appear. Thus, if an accountant really wanted to be an artist but had to ignore those feelings due to family pressure, depression might result. Growth would stop as the person's behavior (e.g., professing satisfaction with ac-counting) became increasingly discrepant, or *in-congruent,* with real feelings.

Client-centered therapy is aimed at provid-ing the client with *new experiences* that will restart the growth process. These new experi-ences involve the therapist's responding to the client in ways that do not sustain conditions of worth, which accept the client as he or she is, and which value the client as a person. If such characteristics had been present in the client's past relationships, they would have prevented psychological problems; their appearance in the present can still be helpful, however. For this reason, the Rogerian therapist tries to pro-vide *an interpersonal relationship that the cli-ent can use to further personal growth.*

This relationship cannot be manufactured; phoniness would be detected by the client and would not be beneficial. For Rogers, the only way to generate a growth-enhancing relationship was for the therapist to experience and express three interrelated attitudes. These are *unconditional positive regard, empathy,* and *congruence.*

Unconditional Positive Regard

The basic therapeutic attitude in Rogers's system is unconditional positive regard. It conveys three messages: The therapist (a) *cares about* the client as a person, (b) *accepts* her or him, and (c) *trusts* the client's ability to change. This seems to be an easily adopted stance (after all, any good therapist cares about clients), but in practice it is often difficult to accomplish.

For example, there are many ways to care about someone. One can be superficial about it, as when ending a conversation with words like "Have a nice day." The recipient of messages like these probably does not attach much importance to them, and the person who uttered the words will not be automatically counted as a close friend. Rogerians wish to go beyond this kind of routine caring.

At the other extreme, a caring attitude can be so strong and possessive as to be incapacitating to the person who is cared for. A child who is constantly *told* how much his or her parents care and how that caring resulted in painful self-sacrifice ("Your mother and I went without so you could go to college") may feel burdened with guilt. Similarly, a young man who dotes on his fiancée and never lets her be away from him may cause her to feel stifled by the intensity of his caring. Rogerians try to avoid crippling their clients with caring.

The ideal regard is *nonpossessive caring,* in which genuine positive feelings are expressed in a way that is liberating, not limiting. There are many ways this can be done. The simplest involves *telling* the client, "I care about you." This straightforward statement has an important place in therapy but can become superficial, especially if overused. Therefore, Rogerians also try to *show* the client that they care.[2]

The therapist's *willingness to listen* is an important manifestation of this attitude. Patient, warm, and interested in what the client has to say, the therapist does not interrupt the client or change the subject or give other signs that

she or he would rather be doing something else. In addition to merely listening, the therapist seeks to *understand* the client's feelings from the client's point of view (this is discussed in more detail in the section on empathy, later in this chapter). For many clients, talking to someone who is willing to listen and who wants to understand is an exhilarating experience that provides the impetus for greater self-expression.

The unconditional aspect of the therapist's unconditional positive regard is manifested in a willingness to accept the client as he or she is, without judgment. Rogers believed that the experience of being prized as a human being, regardless of one's feelings or behaviors, can be a growth-producing experience, especially for clients whose development has been hampered by conditions of worth and other evaluative pressures.

Acceptance of the client means that the therapist refrains from many activities associated with the therapist role. For one thing, she or he avoids interpretations. When the client expresses a feeling (e.g., "I love my children very much"), the Rogerian views that feeling as reflecting the client's perception at that moment. To interpret the statement as a defense against unconscious hostile feelings would not convey an accepting attitude. If the client's stated feelings are inaccurate, the assumption is that he or she will eventually discover the more genuine emotion as self-expression continues.

Rogerians also try to avoid *evaluative judgments* about their clients. For example, the therapist will not summarize the client with a diagnostic label. The therapist tries to accept the client's reported feelings and behaviors as those of a valued person, no matter what those feelings and behaviors involve. This is not an easily attained goal. Consider your reaction to a person who says, "It doesn't really bother me to cheat on my husband; he's so dumb he'll never find out anyway" or "I never wanted any of my children, and I plan to kick them out of the house as soon as they are of legal age."

---

[2] If the therapist really does *not* care about the client, Rogers suggested that a different therapist be brought in rather than attempting to fake a positive attitude.

Unconditional positive regard does not require the therapist to *approve* of feelings like these. The goal is neither to approve nor to disapprove, but to *accept* these feelings as a real part of a person whom the therapist cares about. While the therapist might dislike the client's thoughts or actions, he or she can be nonjudgmental about the fact that they occurred and can still prize the client as an individual. This ideal is illustrated in the following interaction:

CLIENT: That was the semester my brother died and everything seemed to be going down the tubes. I knew how important it was to my parents that I get into medical school, but I also knew that my grades would be lousy that year unless I did something. To make a long story short, I bought a term paper and cheated on almost every exam that semester.

THERAPIST: It was a really rough time for you.

The therapist focuses on the client's feelings in the situation, not on the ethics of the behavior. A major aspect of unconditional positive regard involves the separation of a client's worth *as a person* from the worth of the client's *behavior*. Rogers believed that psychological problems would be less prevalent if a similar distinction were more common outside of therapy.

The positive component of unconditional positive regard is the therapist's *trust* in the client's potential for growth and problem solving. Rogers believed that if clients perceive a therapist's lack of trust in them, they may become dependent. On the other hand, "the more sincerely the therapist relies on the client to discover himself and to follow his own processes of change, the more freely the client will do just that" (Meador & Rogers, 1973, p. 138). The therapist must not be the expert who tells the client what is wrong or guides the client toward better ways of thinking and behaving. Rogerians try not to (a) give advice,

(b) take responsibility for clients, or (c) make decisions for clients.

These are difficult rules to follow, especially in cases where the therapist feels that he or she knows what is best for the client. However, the client must be allowed to make bad decisions or experience problems, even if they could have been averted through advice by the therapist. While advice might have solved some problems, others would be created: The therapist would become a superior, the client would become more dependent, and, most important, both client and therapist would have less faith in the client's ability to deal independently with problems.

Rogers believed so strongly in the importance of trusting the client that he held to his view even in the face of possibly tragic actions. This is illustrated in the following excerpt from the treatment of a depressed young woman:

CLIENT: I wish I'd never started this therapy. I was happy when I was living in my dream world. There I could be the kind of person I wanted to be—But now there is such a wide, wide gap—between my ideal—and what I am . . .

THERAPIST: It's really a tough struggle—digging into this like you are—and at times the shelter of your dream world looks more attractive and comfortable.

CLIENT: My dream world or suicide . . . So I don't see why I should waste your time—coming in twice a week—I'm not worth it—What do you think?

THERAPIST: It's up to you . . . It isn't wasting my time—I'd be glad to see you whenever you come—but it's how you feel about it—if you don't want to come twice a week—or if you do want to come twice a week?—once a week?—It's up to you.

CLIENT: You're not going to suggest that I come in oftener? You're not alarmed and think I ought to come in—everyday—until I get out of this?

THERAPIST: I believe you are able to make your

own decision. I'll see you whenever you want to come.

CLIENT: (note of awe in her voice) I don't believe you are alarmed about—I see—I may be afraid of myself—but you aren't afraid of me.

THERAPIST: You say you may be afraid of yourself—and are wondering why I don't seem to be afraid for you?

CLIENT: You have more confidence in me than I have. I'll see you next week—maybe. (Rogers, 1951, pp. 46–47)

The client's concluding statement is accurate. The therapist *does* have more confidence in the client than she has in herself. Ideally, this will be a temporary situation, for presumably, she will begin to share that confidence. Rogers pointed out, however, that the therapist cannot half-heartedly adopt a trusting attitude and expect the client to grow: "To me it appears that only as the therapist is completely willing that *any* outcome, *any* direction, may be chosen—only then does he realize the vital strength of the capacity and potentiality of the individual for constructive action" (Rogers, 1951, p. 48). This does not mean that Rogers expected the worst from clients. Quite the contrary. "It is as [the therapist] is willing for death to be the choice, that life is chosen; for neuroticism to be the choice, that a healthy normality is chosen" (Rogers, 1951, p. 49).

Empathy

To understand a client's behavior and help the client understand it as well, the therapist must try to see the world as the client sees it. When the therapist lets the client know that she or he understands (or at least wants to understand) what the client feels, the chances for a therapeutic relationship are enhanced. In Rogerian terms, this involves striving for *accurate empathy* or *emphatic understanding*.

Empathy requires that the therapist be immersed in an effort to *perceive* the client's feelings, but it does not dictate that the therapist

experience those feelings (Rogers, 1951). If a therapist actually felt the client's fear, the therapy session could become nothing but a place for two people to be frightened together! Empathy is not achieved by *sympathizing* with the client. A comment like "I'm sorry that you feel so depressed" reflects sympathy, not empathy.

Similarly, a therapist who merely *tells* the client that he or she empathizes will not convey an empathic attitude. It is common to hear people say "I really know how you feel" or "I understand what you are going through." If, as phenomenologists believe, each person's perceptions are unique, it takes more work by the therapist to approximate a genuine understanding of what it feels like to be any particular client. In fact, when people use an easy phrase such as "I know how you feel," they actually convey a *lack* of real understanding. Imagine your own reaction if, after giving someone a lengthy account of your complex feelings about a grandparent's death, she or he simply says, "Right, I've felt the very same way." It would be easy to question the degree to which she or he knows how you feel or even wants to know how you feel.

To illustrate the problems of conveying empathy, we present an excerpt from the beginning of a therapy session with a young male client. As you read the excerpt, try to be aware of your reactions to it.

CLIENT: I don't feel very normal, but I want to feel that way. . . . I thought I'd have something to talk about—then it all goes around in circles. I was trying to think what I was going to say. I tell you, I just can't make a decision; I don't know what I want. I've tried to reason this thing out logically—tried to figure out which things are important to me. I thought that there are maybe two things a man might do; he might get married and raise a family. But if he was just a bachelor, just making a living—that isn't very good. I find myself and my thoughts getting back to the days when I was a kid and I cry very easily. The dam would break through. I've been in the Army four and a half years. I had no problems then, no hopes, no wishes. My only thought was to get out when peace would come. My problems, now that I'm out, are as ever. I tell you, they go back to a long time before I was in the Army. . . . I love children. When I was in the Philippines—I tell you, when I was young I swore I'd never forget my unhappy childhood—so when I saw these children in the Philippines, I treated them very nicely. I used to give them ice cream cones and movies. It was just a period—I'd reverted back—and that awakened some emotions in me I thought I had long buried. (A pause. He seems very near tears.) (Rogers, 1951, pp. 32–33)

Many therapists would react to such material with sympathy and with a wish to understand the client intellectually. They would use what Rogers called an *external frame of reference*. They attempt to understand by being an outside observer and applying their values to what the client says. Examples of therapist thought based on an external frame of reference are presented on the left side of Box 10–1. On the other hand, the therapist could adopt an *internal* frame of reference, which reflects a desire to understand what it must be

BOX 10–1

Some Therapist Thoughts That Reflect
Internal Versus External Frames of Reference

External	*Internal*
I wonder if I should get him started talking.	You're wanting to struggle toward normality, aren't you?
Is this inability to get under way a type of dependence?	It's really hard for you to get started.
Why this indecisiveness? What could be its cause?	Decision making just seems impossible for you.
What is meant by this focus on marriage and family?	You want marriage, but it doesn't seem to you to be much of a possibility.
The crying, the "dam" sound as though there must be a great deal of regression.	You feel yourself brimming over with childish feelings.
He's a veteran. Could he have been a psychiatric case? I feel sorry for anybody who spent four and one-half years in the service.	To you the Army represented stagnation.

What is this interest in children?
    Identification?
    Vague homosexuality?
	Being very nice to children somehow has meaning for you; but it was—and is—a disturbing experience for you.

Source: Rogers, 1951, pp. 33–34.

like to be this client. The right side of Box 10–1 contains therapist thoughts that might result from an internal reference.

Rogerian therapists must not only *adopt* an empathic attitude; they must *communicate* it to clients. This is done through the active listening we described in Chapter 4. Of particular value in conveying empathy is *reflection,* which serves the dual purpose of (a) communicating the therapist's desire for emotional understanding and (b) making clients more aware of their own feelings.

Reflection is one of the most misunderstood aspects of client-centered therapy because, to an outside observer, the therapist appears to be stating the obvious or merely repeating what the client has said. In a famous joke about this approach, Rogers is supposed to have responded to a livid fellow duck hunter who threatens to shoot Rogers if he doesn't relinquish a disputed kill: "You feel this is your duck."

Reflection is not just repetition or paraphrasing. It involves distillation and playback of the client's feelings. Here are some examples.

CLIENT: This has been such a bad day. I've had to keep myself from crying three or four times. I'm not even sure what's wrong!

The therapist's response could be externally oriented (e.g., "Well what exactly happened?), but a reaction that communicates empathy would be along these lines:

THERAPIST: You really do feel bad. The tears just well up inside. And it must be scary to not even know why you feel this way.

At first glance, the clinician may seem to be a parrot, but look more closely. The client never *said* she felt bad; the therapist inferred it by taking the client's point of view. Similarly, the client never said her sadness frightened her—the clinician felt that this might be the case if she or he were in the client's shoes. If

the therapist is wrong about these points, the client can correct the reflection. Right or wrong, the clinician has let the client know that he or she wants to understand.

When communicating empathy through reflection, the therapist's nonverbal message is as important as what is said (see Chapter 4). Tone of voice, facial expression, posture, and other cues can add to (or detract from) an empathic attitude. Rogers (1951, p. 28) provided an example:

Here is a client statement: "I feel as though my mother is always watching me and criticizing what I do. It gets me all stirred up inside. I try not to let that happen, but you know, there are times when I feel her eagle eye on me that I just boil inwardly."

A response on the counselor's part might be: "You resent her criticism."

This response may be given empathically, with the tone of voice such as would be used if it were worded, "If I understand you correctly, you feel pretty resentful toward her criticism. Is that right?" If this is the attitude and tone which is used, it would probably be experienced by the client as aiding him in self-expression. Yet we have learned, from the fumblings of counselors-in-training, that "You resent her criticism" may be given with the same attitude and tone with which one might announce "You have the measles," or . . . "You are sitting on my hat."

The best way to get a feel for this nonverbal dimension of empathy is to watch and listen to a skilled Rogerian in action. An opportunity to do this is provided by a well-known film in which Rogers interviews "Gloria" as a demonstration of his approach (Rogers, 1965). Similar material is contained in other films and on tapes distributed by the American Academy of Psychotherapists (see footnote 3).

Communicating empathy is a slow process. The therapist's use of reflection may not get anywhere in a single session, but Rogers believed that over time, the empathic attitude gives even the most aloof or withdrawn client a sense that the therapist understands her or him. The *continuous experiencing* of this understanding attitude will ultimately lead to client growth.

Congruence

Rogers believed that the more *genuine* the therapist is in his or her relations with the client, the more helpful the therapist will be. The therapist's feelings and actions should be *congruent,* or consistent, with one another. "This means that I need to be aware of my own feelings . . . [and willing] to express, in my words and my behavior, the various feelings and attitudes which exist in me" (Rogers, 1961, p. 33). According to Rogers, when the therapist is congruent, she or he sets up a *real* human relationship. Rogers argued:

> It does not help to act as though I know the answers when I do not. . . . I have not found it to be helpful or effective in my relationships with other people to try to maintain a facade; to act in one way on the surface when I am experiencing something quite different underneath. (Rogers, 1961, pp. 16–17)

Congruence is often difficult for a clinician to achieve. The therapist must abandon the notion that expressing a particular reaction would not be good for the client and just go ahead and be genuine. In so doing, the therapist expresses confidence in the client's ability to handle the therapist's feelings, and, if those feelings are negative, shows a willingness to risk a temporary setback in the relationship. The hope is that, in the long run, the client's awareness that the therapist is for real (not just someone who is paid to be nice) will aid self-actualization.

To get an idea of how congruence promotes trust, think of a close friend. Chances are that friend has told you things you might not have wanted to hear, perhaps that you were wrong about something. Once you know your friend will say what he or she really feels (i.e., is congruent with you), even if it does not make you happy, it may be easier for you to trust what that person may say next week. However, if you know your friend tells you only what you want to hear, your faith in that person's reactions ("You really look great") might be reduced.

Consider a therapist–client interaction that illustrates how congruence can be displayed:

CLIENT: I have been feeling better since we started seeing each other. If my father had been as warm as you are, my childhood would have been a lot easier. (pause) It sounds silly to say it, but I wish you could be my father.

THERAPIST: I think it would be nice to have you for a son.

This client's statement could have prompted a Freudian to analyze the transference; the Rogerian's response was a reflection of how he *felt*.

Consider another example:

CLIENT: You really look tired, doctor. Don't you feel well today?

THERAPIST: (who really feels rotten) Oh no, I'm fine. Anyway, how you feel is more important.

Here is a case of therapist incongruence. The client is likely to see through the therapist's facade, and will probably feel guilty for making a sick person work when that person would rather be at home. The clinician could have said, "I do feel pretty sick, but I wanted to have our session today." If this actually reflects the therapist's feelings, it will strengthen the therapeutic relationship.

Finally, imagine this interchange:

CLIENT: I just feel so hopeless. Tell me what I'm doing wrong in my life.

THERAPIST: I guess when you are feeling this bad it would be nice if someone could come along and tell you what is going wrong and how you can put everything right again. I wish I could do all that, but I can't. I don't think anyone else can either.

Notice the therapist's reflection of client feeling plus the direct expression of (a) a genuine wish to understand and solve the client's problems, and (b) an admission that he or she is not capable of such a feat. A therapist who does not have all the answers but who says "Don't you think it would be better if you figured that out for yourself?" would, according to Rogers, show incongruence by suggesting that he or she *knows* what is wrong but won't tell. Such a message might promote client inferiority, not growth.

The Nature of Change in Client-Centered Therapy

Client-centered therapy represents an "if ... then" assumption: If the right conditions are created by the therapist, then the client will change. It is now time to describe the dimensions along which, according to Rogers, change takes place.

Increased Awareness

Therapy should bring clients in closer contact with their own feelings, many of which have been previously denied or kept out of awareness. Further, awareness should focus on the immediate present: how the client is feeling here and now. This new awareness usually is directed toward the *self* rather than toward specific symptoms.

Increased Self-Acceptance

Over time, clients become less self-critical and more self-accepting. They are more likely to take responsibility for their feelings and behavior and less likely to blame circumstances or other people. The client spends less time denying parts of the self that are not ideal. The client may decide to change some of these

things, but they are no longer disowned. Some of the increase in self-acceptance is thought to be based on the discovery that, in spite of things that may be less than admirable, the client is a basically good person.

Increased Interpersonal Comfort

As therapy progresses, the client becomes more comfortable in relationships. Defensive interpersonal games designed to keep other people at a distance are abandoned and the client experiences the pleasure of letting others know him or her as he or she really is.

Increased Cognitive Flexibility

As noted by Kelly (1955) and others, people have problems when they see the world in rigid, black-and-white terms ("all men are despicable," "all teachers are uncaring"). Successful client-centered therapy results in a loosening up of limited (and limiting) views of the world such that the client perceives the endless variability that exists. The cognitions that result ("the behavior of *some* men is despicable") are likely to promote less problematic behavior.

Increased Self-Reliance

A growing client becomes less dependent on the reactions of other people as a barometer of self-worth and more oriented toward internal evaluations. Clients may become less fearful in social-evaluative situations (speeches, tests, parties) because they come to feel that what they think is as important as what others think. These changes result from a shift in the client's *valuing process*. The client becomes less concerned with "shoulds" and "oughts" (e.g., "I should love being a student") and more concerned with how he or she actually feels (see Box 10–2). The growing client separates (as the therapist does) her or his worth as a *person* from the quality of her or his *behavior*.

Rogers believed that changes along these dimensions over the course of successful ther-

Here are some examples of thoughts based upon concern over evaluation by others (left column) and those based upon a greater focus on self-evaluation (right column).

1. I should never be angry at anyone.	1. I should be angry at a person when I deeply feel angry because this leaves less residual effect than bottling up the feeling, and actually makes for a better and more realistic relationship.
2. I should always be a loving mother.	2. I should be a loving mother when I feel that way, but I need not be fearful of other attitudes when they exist.
3. I should be successful in my courses.	3. I should be successful in my courses only if they have long-range meaning to me.
4. I have homosexual impulses, which is very bad.	4. I have homosexual impulses, and these are capable of expressions which enhance self and others, and expressions which achieve the reverse.

Source: After Rogers, 1951, pp. 149 and 151.

BOX 10–2
Self-Evaluation Versus Evaluation by Others

apy are relatively consistent from one client to the next. He has summarized these changes in a *therapy process scale,* which is presented in edited form in Box 10–3.

Improved Functioning

In addition to the psychological changes just described, Rogers noted that overt benefits also follow successful client-centered therapy.

The client's behavior changes in these ways: he considers, and reports putting into effect, behavior which is more mature, self-directing, and responsible than the behavior he has shown heretofore; his behavior becomes less defensive, more firmly based on an objec-

tive view of self and reality; his behavior shows a decreasing amount of psychological tension; he tends to make a more comfortable and more effective adjustment to school and to job; he meets new stress situations with an increased degree of inner calm, a calm which is reflected in less physiological upset . . . than would have been true if they had occurred prior to therapy. (Rogers, 1951, p. 186)

An Illustration of Client-Centered Therapy

Because client-centered therapy focuses more on processes than techniques, the preceding material may leave the reader aware of the principles that guide Rogerian therapy but un-

Stage 1: Communication is about externals. There is an unwillingness to communicate self. Feelings and personal meanings are neither recognized as such nor owned. Constructs are extremely rigid. Close relationships are construed as dangerous.

Stage 2: Feelings are *sometimes* described but as unowned past *objects* external to self.

Stage 3: There is much description of feelings and personal meanings which are not now present. These distant feelings are often pictured as unacceptable or bad. . . . There is a beginning recognition that any problems that exist are inside the individual rather than external.

Stage 4: Feelings and personal meanings are freely described as present objects owned by the self. . . . There is a beginning loosening of personal constructs. . . . There

is some expression of self-responsibility for problems.

Stage 5: Many feelings are expressed in the moment of their occurrence and are thus experienced in the immediate present. These feelings are owned or accepted.

There is a questioning of the validity of many personal constructs. The person has a definite responsibility for the problems which exist in him.

Stage 6: Feelings previously denied are now experienced both with immediacy and acceptance.

Stage 7: The individual lives comfortably in the flowing process of his experiencing. New feelings are experienced with richness and immediacy, and this inner experiencing is a clear referent for behavior. Incongruence is minimal and temporary.

Excerpts from "Person-centered therapy," by Betty D. Meador and Carl R. Rogers, in R. J. Corsini, ed., *Current Psychotherapies*, Itasca, IL: F E Peacock Publishers. Copyright 1984 by Peacock Publishers. (Reprinted by permission.)

BOX 10–3
Seven Stages in the Process of Therapeutic Change

---

clear about how these principles are translated into clinical practice. To provide a brief idea of what goes on in client-centered therapy, we present below some edited excerpts from Rogers's (1967) case of the "Silent Young Man," as described by Meador and Rogers (1973, pp. 139–144).[3]

The client in this case was a 28-year-old

man hospitalized as a "simple schizophrenic." During 11 months of therapy, "Jim" had made some progress but was still withdrawn and inarticulate. Rather than giving up on his client, Rogers continued the therapeutic attitudes he believed would ultimately bring about growth.

THERAPIST: I see there are some cigarettes here in the drawer. Hm? Yeah, it is hot out. (silence of 25 seconds)

THERAPIST: Do you look kind of angry this morning, or is that my imagination? (client shakes his head slightly) Not angry, huh? (silence of 1 minute, 26 seconds)

---

[3]A tape recording of two complete interviews with this client is available for professional use from the American Academy of Psychotherapists, 6420 City Line Avenue, Philadelphia, PA 19151. Its designation is the case of "Mr. VAC."

THERAPIST: Feel like letting me in on whatever is going on? (silence of 12 minutes, 52 seconds)

THERAPIST: I kind of feel like saying that "If it would be of any help at all I'd like to come in." On the other hand if it's something you'd rather—if you just feel more like being within yourself, why that's OK too—I guess another thing I'm saying, really, in saying that is, "I do care. I'm not just sitting here like a stick." (silence of 1 minute, 11 seconds)

THERAPIST: And I guess your silence is saying to me either you don't want to or can't come out right now and that's OK. So I won't pester you but I just want you to know, I'm here. (silence of 17 minutes, 41 seconds)

[After two more unanswered comments over the next minute or so, Rogers continues.]

THERAPIST: Maybe this morning you just wish I'd shut up—and maybe I should, but I just keep feeling I'd like to—I don't know, be in touch with you in some way. (silence of 2 minutes, 21 seconds)

[Client yawns.]

THERAPIST: Sounds discouraged or tired. (silence of 41 seconds)

CLIENT: [at last!] No. Just lousy.

THERAPIST: Everything's lousy, huh? You feel lousy? . . .

CLIENT: No.

THERAPIST: No? (silence of 20 seconds)

CLIENT: No. I just ain't no good to nobody, never was, and never will be.

THERAPIST: Feeling that now, hm? That you're just no good to yourself, no good to anybody. Just that you're completely worthless, huh? . . .

CLIENT: Yeah. That's what this guy I went to town with just the other day told me. . . .

THERAPIST: I guess the meaning of that, if I get it right, is that here's somebody that—meant something to you and what does he think of

you? Why, he's told you that he thinks you're no good at all. And that really knocks the props out from under you. [Jim weeps quietly] It just brings the tears.

CLIENT: I don't care though.

THERAPIST: You tell yourself you don't care at all, but somehow I guess some part of you cares because some part of you weeps over it. . . .

CLIENT: I guess I always knew it.

THERAPIST: If I'm getting that right, it is that what makes it hurt worst of all is that when he tells you you're no good, well shucks, that's what you've always felt about yourself. Is that—the meaning of what you're saying? [Jim nods in agreement] . . . So that between his saying so and your perhaps feeling it underneath, you just feel about as no-good as anybody could feel.

[The client continues to cry and, after several more minutes of reflecting the sad, hopeless feelings being expressed, Rogers ends the interview. Three days later another session takes place. After some initial comments by the therapist, the client breaks in:]

CLIENT: I'm gonna take off.

THERAPIST: You're going to take off? Really run away from here? . . . I know you don't like the place but it must be something special came up or something?

CLIENT: I just want to run away and die.

THERAPIST: M-hm, m-hm, m-hm. It isn't even that you want to get away from here *to* something. You just want to leave here and go away and die in a corner, hm? . . . Can't help but wonder whether it's still true that some things this friend said to you—are those still part of the thing that makes you feel so awful?

CLIENT: In general, yes.

[The next 30 minutes or so are taken up in further reflection of the client's negative feelings and in silences of up to 13 minutes.]

CLIENT: I might go today. Where, I don't know, but I don't care.

THERAPIST: Just feel your mind is made up and that you're going to leave. (silence of 53 seconds)

CLIENT: That's why I want to go, 'cause I don't care what happens.

THERAPIST: M-hm, m-hm. That's why you want to go, because you really don't care about yourself. You just don't care *what* happens. And I guess I'd just like to say—I care about you. And I care what happens.

After a 30-second silence, the client bursts into violent sobs. For the next 15 minutes or so, Rogers reflects the intense emotions that pour forth.

According to Rogers, this is an important moment of therapeutic change. "Jim Brown, who sees himself as stubborn, bitter, mistreated, worthless, useless, hopeless, unloved, unlovable, *experiences* my caring. In that moment his defensive shell cracks wide open, and can never again be quite the same" (Meador & Rogers, 1973, p. 145). The client in this case left the hospital after several more months of treatment; 8 years later he reported to Rogers that he was happy, employed, and living on his own.[4]

THE GESTALT THERAPY OF FRITZ PERLS

After Rogers's client-centered approach, the gestalt theory of Friedrich S. (Fritz) Perls is probably the best-known phenomenologically oriented treatment. Like Rogers, Perls believed that human development depends on self-awareness, and gestalt therapy aims at en-

hancing clients' awareness in order to free them to grow in their own consciously guided ways. The methods of the gestalt therapist differ from the Rogerian mode. Gestalt therapy requires a more active therapist and utilizes more dramatic procedures. Before describing the process itself, we will take a brief look at the origins of Perls's approach.

Some Background on Gestalt Therapy

Fritz Perls was born in Berlin, Germany, in 1893. He earned both an MD (specializing in psychiatry) and a PhD in psychology. His psychiatric training was at the Psychoanalytic Institutes in Berlin and Vienna. His *psychological* orientation, however, was that of the gestaltists. Perls thought of the human organism as a unified whole, rather than a fragmented set of warring components, and he believed that active perceptual and organizational processes, not instincts, were central to the development of human behavior.

Perls described himself as a Wandering Jew. When Hitler came to power in Germany, Perls went first to Johannesburg, South Africa (where he established the South African Institute for Psychoanalysis), and then, in 1946, to New York. By this time Perls's ideas about therapy had reached the stage that he founded the New York Institute for Gestalt Therapy. In the mid-1960s, Perls moved to Big Sur, California, where he became associate psychiatrist at the Esalen Institute. Just before his death in 1970 Perls moved to Vancouver, British Columbia (Canada), where he founded another institute for gestalt therapy.

Perls's discomfort with Freudian concepts first appeared in his book, *Ego, Hunger and Aggresson: A Revision of Freud's Theory and Method* (1947). In this book he focused on the vital role played by *awareness* in the development of "normal" human behavior, and he argued that disordered behavior indicated that psychological growth was obstructed by gaps or distortions in awareness. These ideas ulti-

---

[4]Rogers (1951) mentioned another case in which the therapist and client said almost nothing to one another during months of sessions. Yet the experience of genuine, caring relationship appeared to produce benefits.

mately led to an alternative clinical treatment which Perls called gestalt therapy (Perls, 1969, 1970; Perls, Hefferline, & Goodman, 1951).

Perls noted that disturbances in awareness and the problems that accompany them take many forms, including the neurotic symptoms and defense mechanisms described by Freud. Like Adler and Sullivan, however, Perls focused on symptoms and defenses manifested in interpersonal spheres. He noted that people who find it uncomfortable to experience and express certain needs (such as for love) develop manipulative games or roles to satisfy those needs in *indirect* ways. The person devotes more energy to these games and roles, with the result that less energy is available for adaptive growth. Indeed, a person's growth gets stuck as he or she clings to the problematic games by creating additional symptoms and defenses. The individual whose interactions with others are based on seemingly endless illnesses provides a familiar illustration. Roles of this type force other people to play along by being solicitous, but, because people are being manipulated, the game becomes burdensome and ends in rejection. The client must then find someone else to "play with."

To make matters worse, distorted or suppressed awareness creates an impression that one is *not responsible* for one's problems. The blame is placed on other people ("My problem is my wife"), environmental circumstances ("There are no interesting people in this city"), or on internal forces over which the client has no influence ("I can't control my anger"). This type of client looks to the therapist to solve problems *for* him or her. Perls emphasized that most clients enter therapy ostensibly to understand themselves and solve their problems, when in fact they really want to play their neurotic games better. An illustration of this phenomenon is the man who wants to be taken care of (but cannot tolerate awareness of this need) and who encourages nurturance indirectly by telling others of his struggle toward self-understanding through therapy.

The Goals of Gestalt Therapy

Above all, the gestalt therapist seeks to reestablish the stalled process of client growth. This is achieved by helping clients (a) become aware of those feelings that they have *disowned* but which are a part of them, and (b) recognize those feelings and values that they *think* are a genuine part of themselves, but which in fact are borrowed from other people.

The client is encouraged to assimilate or "re-own" those genuine aspects of self that have been rejected and to reject those features that do not belong. Ideally, when one assimilates and integrates all aspects of the personality (both the desirable and the undesirable), one can take responsibility for oneself as one really is, instead of being attached to and defensive of a partially phony, internally conflicted self-image.

For example, a person who feels superior to others but who has forced this feeling out of awareness in favor of a more socially acceptable air of humility will become aware of and express both sides of the conflict ("I'm great" versus "I shouldn't brag"). Once both *poles* of this conflict confront each other, the client may find a resolution ("It's OK to express my feelings of competence, but I need to take the feelings of others into account as well"). As long as one side of the conflict is out of awareness, such resolution is impossible. According to Perls, when conflict resolutions occur with full awareness of both poles, the person begins to grow again.

The Gestalt Therapy Approach

The therapist–client relationship in gestalt therapy should be a coequal one involving mutual growth. As Kempler (1973, p. 266) put it, "the therapist is like a composing maestro facing an accomplished musician. The maestro expects that between them new and beautiful tunes will be created."

Focus on the Here and Now

Perls believed that therapeutic progress is made by keeping clients in contact with their feelings as they occur in the here and now. He expressed this belief in a conceptual equation where "Now = experience = awareness = reality" (Perls, 1970, p. 14). Any attempt by the client to recount the past or anticipate the future obstructs therapy goals. It is an escape from reality.

Instead of *reflecting* (as a Rogerian might) the client's nostalgia or desire to look to the future, a gestalt therapist will point out the avoidance and insist that it be terminated. This method was illustrated by Perls in his filmed interview with "Gloria" (Perls, 1965). At one point Gloria says that what is happening in the interview reminds her of when she was a little girl. Perls immediately asks, "Are you a little girl?" to which Gloria answers, "Well, no, but it's the same feeling." Again Perls asks, "Are you a little girl?" Gloria says, "The feeling reminds me of it." Perls explodes: "Are you a little girl?" The client finally says, "No."

Keeping the client in touch with the immediate present helps the client see that the past or the future may be important in the present. Talking about the past or the future in the abstract gets the client nowhere, but *experiencing* past feelings or future fears as they occur in therapy may be helpful. For example, consider this statement:

CLIENT: My sister and I used to fight an awful lot when we were kids, but we seemed closer somehow then than we are now.

Instead of reflecting the feelings expressed here, the gestalt therapist would try to prevent the client from talking about his feelings as "things" that used to exist and get in touch with how he feels right now. The client might be asked to "talk" to his sister as if she were there and express his immediate feelings:

THERAPIST: Can you say this to your sister now?

CLIENT: OK. I feel so far away from you now, Janie. I want to have that feeling of being in a family again.

By asking a client to "speak" directly to a person from the past, the therapist promotes an immediate present feeling rather than a general, *intellectualized report* of feelings. The focus on the present is also evident in the language of gestalt therapy. Clients are encouraged to speak in the present tense. A statement like "I wish I could have talked to you last night" is less expressive of present feelings than "I really want to talk to you."

Handling Resistance

Perls realized that once clients find symptoms, games, and defenses that protect them from conflict and self-awareness, they will resist efforts to break through them. However, Perls believed that instead of viewing resistance as a barrier to growth which the client must put aside, the client should explore the resistance.

To help the client do this, Perls used *role playing* or part taking. A client who displays resistance is asked to "become" that resistance in order to gain an *experiential* awareness of what the resistance is doing *for* and *to* her or him. Polster and Polster (1973, pp. 53–54) present an example of this technique. John, a member of a gestalt therapy group, finds it difficult to talk to another group member, Mary, because he says there is a "wall" between them. The therapist asks John to "play" the wall:[5]

JOHN: (as the wall) I am here to protect you against predatory women who will eat you alive if you open yourself up to them.

The therapist asks John to "converse" with his resistance to experience both sides of the

_____

[5]Perls expressed his distrust of intellectual analysis as opposed to sensory awareness with the oft-quoted phrase, "Lose your mind and come to your senses."

conflict that prevents him from relating to others in an intimate way:

JOHN: (to the wall) Aren't you exaggerating? She looks pretty safe to me. In fact, she looks more scared than anything.

JOHN: (as the wall) Sure she's scared. I'm responsible for that. I'm a very severe wall and I make a lot of people scared. That's how I want it and I have even affected you that way too. You're scared of me even though I'm really on your side.

JOHN: (to the wall) I *am* scared of you and I even feel you inside me, like I have become like you. I feel my chest as though it were iron and I'm really getting mad about that.

JOHN: (as the wall) Mad—at what? I'm your strength and you don't even know it. Feel how strong you are inside.

JOHN: (to the wall) Sure I feel the strength but I also feel rigid when my chest feels like iron. I'd like to beat on you, knock you over, and go over to Mary.

Here, the gestalt therapist urges the client to *do* what he *feels* and resolve the conflict in a growthful way.

THERAPIST: Beat on your iron.

JOHN: (beats his chest and shouts) Get out of my way—get *out* of my *way!* (silence of a few moments) My chest feels strong—but not like it's made of iron. (after another silence, John begins to cry and talks to Mary) I don't feel any wall between us anymore and I really want to talk to you.

Of course it is not always this easy for the client to become aware of hidden feelings. Perls used a battery of methods for self-exploration, several of which are described in the following sections.

Frustrating the Client

Perls believed that most clients come to therapy hoping to feel better without having to give up their maladaptive roles. Since he felt that allowing clients to use their customary styles in therapy would waste everyone's time, Perls set out to frustrate clients' efforts to relate to him as they normally would to others. Perls put his clients on the "hot seat." Attention was focused on them, and their symptoms, games, or resistances were pointed out and explored.

Assume that a client begins a session by saying "I've really been looking forward to having this session. I hope you can help me." Instead of reflecting this feeling or asking *why* the client feels this way, a gestalt therapist would focus on the manipulative aspect of the statement, which seems to contain the message, "I expect you to help me without my having to do much." The therapist might say, "How do you think I could help you?" The client (somewhat taken aback) might respond, "Well, I was hoping you could help me understand why I'm so unhappy." From here, the therapist would continue to frustrate the client's attempt to get the therapist to take responsibility for solving the client's problems and, in the process, would help the client experience his real feelings.

THERAPIST: Tell me what you mean when you say "unhappy." (One gestalt therapy principle, not unlike certain behavioral tenets, is to go from the general problem to its specific manifestations.)

CLIENT: Oh, I don't know, it's just that I don't ever feel satisfied with myself. I never seem to be able to ... I don't know—it's very complicated and hard for me to express.

THERAPIST: How old are you?

CLIENT: Thirty-six.

THERAPIST: And as a 36-year-old person, you can't tell me what makes you unhappy?

CLIENT: I wish I could, but I'm too confused about it myself.

THERAPIST: (who infers that the client is "playing stupid" in order to avoid responsibility for problems) Can you play me trying to help you? What would I say and what would I do?

CLIENT: Well, you might say "Don't worry, I'll figure out what your problems are and help you get on the right track."

THERAPIST: OK, tell me how you expect me to do all this *for* you.

CLIENT: OK, I see. I guess I hope you have some magic pill or something.

At this point the therapist might again request a statement of the client's problems and, this time, might get a more mature answer.

Use of Nonverbal Cues

Nonverbal behavior is important material in gestalt therapy. The therapist must attend to what the client says *and* does. The nonverbal channel often contradicts the client's words. Here is an illustration:

CLIENT: I wish I wasn't so nervous with people.

THERAPIST: Who are you nervous with?

CLIENT: With everyone.

THERAPIST: With me, here, now?

CLIENT: Yes, very.

THERAPIST: That's funny, because you don't look nervous to me.

CLIENT: (suddenly clasping his hands) Well I am!

THERAPIST: What are you doing with your hands?

CLIENT: Nothing, I just clasped them together. It's just a gesture.

THERAPIST: Do the gesture again. (client reclasps his hands) And again, clasp them again, harder. (client clasps hands harder) How does that feel?

CLIENT: It feels tight, kind of constricted.

THERAPIST: Can you become that tightness? Can you get in touch with what that tightness might say to you?

CLIENT: OK, ah, I'm tight. I'm holding everything together. I'm keeping the lid on you so that you don't let too much out.

The therapist wondered what the clasped hands meant. Instead of asking *why* the client clasped them, she pointed out *what* the client did. She then asked him to concentrate on the associated feelings by repeating and exaggerating the gesture. Once the feelings brought on by the gesture are expressed, the client is asked to elaborate on them. The result is that the client expresses a defensive feeling about being in therapy that had originally been described vaguely as nervousness.

The Use of Dreams

In gestalt therapy, dreams are seen as messages from the person to himself or herself. After recounting a dream, the client is encouraged to "read" it by playing the part of some dream features and characters. In the process, the client may become aware of and assimilate disowned parts of the self. Here is an example of Perls's use of dream material:

LINDA: I dreamed that I watch . . . a lake . . . drying up, and there is a small island in the middle of the lake, and a circle of . . . porpoises—they're like porpoises except that they can stand up, so they're like porpoises that are like people, and they're in a circle, sort of like a religious ceremony, and it's very sad—I feel very sad because they can breathe, they are sort of dancing around the circle, but the water, their element, is drying up. So it's like a dying—like watching a race of people, or a race of creatures, dying. And they are mostly females but a few of them have a small male organ, so there are a few males there, but they won't live long enough to reproduce, and their element is drying up. And there is one that is sitting over here near me and I'm talking to this porpoise and he has prickles on his tummy, sort of like a porcupine, and they don't seem to be a part of him. And I think that there's one good point about the water drying up, I think—well, at least at the bottom, when all the water dries up, there will probably be some sort of treasure there, because at the bottom of the lake there should be things that have fallen in, like coins or something, but I look carefully and all that I can find is an old license plate . . . That's the dream.

PERLS: Will you please play the license plate?

LINDA: I am an old license plate, thrown in the bottom of a lake. I have no use because I'm of no value—although I'm not rusted—I'm outdated, so I can't be used as a license plate . . . and I'm just thrown on the rubbish heap. That's what I did with a license plate, I threw it on a rubbish heap.

PERLS: Well how do you feel about this?

LINDA: (quietly) I don't like it. I don't like being a license plate—useless.

PERLS: Could you talk about this? That was such a long dream until you came to find a license plate; I'm sure this must be of great importance.

LINDA: (sighs) Useless. Outdated . . . the use of a license plate is to allow—give a car permission to go . . . and I can't give anyone permission to do anything because I'm outdated . . . In California, they just paste a little—you buy a sticker—and stick it on the car, on the old license plate. (faint attempt at humor) So maybe someone could put me on their car and stick this sticker on me. I don't know . . .

PERLS: OK, now play the lake.

PERLS: I'm a lake . . . I'm drying up, and disappearing, soaking into the earth . . . (with a touch of surprise) *dying* . . . But when I soak into the earth, I become a part of the earth—so maybe I water the surrounding area, so . . . even in the lake, even in my bed, flowers can grow (sighs). New life can grow. . . from me (cries) . . .

PERLS: You get the existential message?

LINDA: Yes. (sadly, but with conviction) I can paint—I can create—I can create beauty. I can no longer reproduce, I'm like the porpoise—but I—I'm . . . I . . . keep wanting to say I'm food . . . I . . . as water becomes . . . I water the earth, and give life—growing things, the water—they need both the earth and water, and the . . . and the air and the sun, but as the water from the lake, I can play a part in something, and producing—feeding.

PERLS: You see the contrast: On the surface, you find something, some artifact—the license plate, the artificial you—but then when you go deeper, you find the apparent death of the lake is actually fertility . . .

LINDA: And I don't need a license plate, or a permission, a license in order to . . .

PERLS: (gently) Nature doesn't need a license plate to grow. You don't have to be useless, if you are organismically creative, which means if you are involved.

LINDA: And I don't need permission to be creative . . . Thank you. (Perls, 1969, pp. 81–82)

Other Methods

The gestalt therapist uses other methods to help clients increase awareness and to promote "re-owning" of alienated aspects of personality. We briefly mention a few of them here:

1. Use of Direct and Immediate Messages. Direct communication is encouraged for helping clients take responsibility for their feelings. In group therapy, the client who points to another client and says "She really makes me uncomfortable" would be asked to repeat the message directly to the person involved: "You make me uncomfortable." "I" language is preferred over "it" language. "It makes me furious to hear that" contains the message that "it" is responsible for the client's anger. A restatement (e.g., "I am angry at you") would be encouraged. Gossiping about people who are not present is prohibited because one evades responsibility for feelings if the target is absent. Finally, clients are asked to convert indirect *questions* into direct *statements*. The message behind the question "Do you think I'll ever feel any better than I do now?" may be "I am terrified that I'll always be depressed and maybe kill myself." If so, it is important for the client to be aware of and to express the fear.

2. Prohibition of Intellectual Discussion. The client in gestalt therapy is prevented from using intellectual analyses to avoid here-and-now awareness. The person who expounds a theory of a problem (e.g., "I think all this goes back to a time when I felt rejected by my parents") would be asked to identify with and "become" the nonconfident self in the present. Or, some nonverbal behavior that accompanied the theoretical analysis might be focused on by the therapist, who would request an exaggeration of the particular movement to bring its message into the foreground.

3. Use of Internal Dialogues and Related Techniques. Clients in gestalt therapy are often asked to "become" some of their characteristics and resistances. In group work, this technique includes extended "conversations" not only between parts of the person, but between the client and persons from the past with whom the client has unfinished business. Internal dialogues are also held between the client's superego (called "topdog") and the part that is suppressed by "shoulds" and "oughts" (the "underdog").

A related gestalt method is the *empty chair* technique, a strategy sometimes employed by other types of therapists as well. To increase clients' awareness of their conflicts and feelings about people or objects, the therapist asks them to imagine the person or object sitting in a nearby chair, and then to voice their true feelings to the unoccupied chair. The assumption is that this activity promotes here-and-now awareness of strong emotions in a safe environment and, in the process, allows the

person to master these feelings rather than be intimidated by them. Some therapists also use a comparable procedure that we call the *unmailed letter* technique. As a way of helping the client clarify and ventilate feelings toward a significant person in his or her life, the client is asked to write a letter in which he or she expresses important, but heretofore unspoken, feelings toward that person. The client writes the letter but does not mail it. The letter not only helps express feelings, but it serves as material for discussion in subsequent therapy sessions. The empty chair and unmailed letter techniques are presumed to promote catharsis. They assume that problematic emotions are analogous to the problem of dirty bath water—the quickest way to get rid of them is to pull the plug and let them drain away.

Reversals also are used to achieve awareness. Assume that a person denies feelings of tenderness toward others and conveys an image of coldness and self-sufficiency. This individual might be asked to play a warm, loving person. In the process, the client may get in touch with those feelings she or he has been suppressing.

An Illustration of Gestalt Therapy

The following edited excerpt from a gestalt group provides an idea of the way the aforementioned methods are integrated in practice. In this case the setting is a workshop run by Perls in which each group member was placed in turn on the "hot seat" (Perls, 1969). The client, "Jane," had worked with Perls before and thus shows more familiarity with the method than would a new client; otherwise, the procedures are representative.

JANE: I can't say that I'm really aware of what I'm doing. Except physically. I'm aware of what's happening physically to me but—I don't really know what I'm doing.

PERLS: I noticed one thing: When you come up

on the hot seat, you stop playing the silly goose.

JANE: Hum. I get frightened when I'm up here.

PERLS: You get dead.

JANE: ... I'm wondering whether or not I'm dead. I notice that my legs are cold and my feet are cold. I feel—I feel strange. ... I notice that my attention is concentrated on that little matchbox on the floor.

PERLS: OK. Have an encounter with the matchbox.

JANE: [as the matchbox] I don't care if you tell the truth or not. It doesn't matter to me. I'm just a matchbox.

PERLS: Try this for size. Tell us, "I'm just a matchbox."

JANE: I'm just a matchbox and I feel silly saying that. I feel kind of dumb, being a matchbox. ... A little bit useful, but not very useful. There's a million like me. And you can look at me, and you can like me, and when I'm all used up, you can throw me away. I never liked being a matchbox. ... I don't know if that's the truth when I say I don't know what I'm doing. I know there's one part of me that knows what I'm doing. ... She's saying (with authority) well, *you* know where you're at. You're playing dumb. You're playing stupid. You're doing this and you're doing that. ... She's saying (briskly) now when you get in the chair, you have to be in the here-and-now, you have to do it *right,* you have to be turned on, you have to know everything—

PERLS: "You have to do your job."

JANE: You have to do your job, and you have to do it *right.* And you have to—become totally self-actualized, and you have to get rid of all your hangups. ... [Now Jane spontaneously returns to being her frightened self again and talks to her demanding self:] You really make it hard for me. ... You're really putting a lot of demands on me. ... I don't know everything, and on top of that, I don't know what I'm doing half the time. ...

PERLS: So be your topdog again.

JANE: Is that—

PERLS: Your topdog. That's the famous topdog. The righteous topdog. This is where the power is.

JANE: Yeah. Well—uh—I'm your topdog. You can't live without me. I'm the one that—I keep you noticed, Jane. If it weren't for me, nobody would notice you. [Jane now responds to "topdog"] Well, I don't want to be noticed, *you* do ... I don't really want to be noticed, as much as you do.

PERLS: I would like you to attack the righteous side of that topdog.

JANE: Attack—the righteous side?

PERLS: The topdog is always righteous. Topdog *knows* what you've got to do, has all the right to criticize, and so on.

JANE: Yeah. ... You're a bitch! Like my mother. You know what's good for me. You make life hard for me. ...

PERLS: Now please don't change what your hands are doing, but tell us what's going on in your hands. ... Let them talk to each other.

JANE: My left hand. I'm shaking, and I'm in a fist, straining forward ... the fist is very tight, pushing my fingernails into my hand. It doesn't feel good, but I do it all the time. I feel tight.

PERLS: And the right hand?

JANE: I'm holding you back around the wrist.

PERLS: Tell it why you hold it back.

JANE: If I let you go you're gonna hit something. I don't know what you're gonna hit, but I have to—I have to hold back 'cause you can't do that. Can't go around hitting things.

PERLS: Now hit your topdog.

JANE: [gives short, harsh yells]

PERLS: Now talk to your topdog. "Stop nagging—"

JANE: [yells at "topdog"] Leave me alone!

PERLS: Again.

JANE: Leave me alone!

PERLS: Again.

JANE: [screaming and crying] *Leave me alone!*

PERLS: Again.

JANE: [screams and cries): LEAVE ME ALONE! I DON'T HAVE TO DO WHAT YOU SAY! (still crying) I don't have to be that good! . . . I don't have to be in this chair! You make me! You make me come here! . . . I'd like to kill you.

PERLS: Say this again.

JANE: I'd like to kill you.

PERLS: Again.

JANE: I'd like to *kill* you.

PERLS: Can you squash it in your left hand?

JANE: It's as big as me . . . I'm strangling it. [Perls gives Jane a pillow which she strangles while making choking noises and crying]

PERLS: OK. Relax, close your eyes. (long silence) OK, come back to us.

[Later in the session, Perls asks Jane to turn her perfectionist "topdog" into an "underdog" and to talk down to it.]

JANE: [to her perfectionist "topdog"] . . . You don't have to do anything, you don't have to prove anything. (cries) You're only twenty years old! You don't have to be the queen. . . .

JANE: [as her perfectionist "topdog"] OK, I understand that. I know that. I'm just in a *hurry*. . . . You have to keep hurrying and the days slip by and you think you're losing time, or something. I'm *much* too hard on you. I have to leave you alone.

PERLS: . . . Let your topdog say "I'll be a bit more patient with you."

JANE: [as topdog] . . . I'll be a bit more patient with you.

PERLS: Say this again.

JANE: It's very hard for me to be patient. . . . But I'll try to be a bit more patient with you. . . . As I say that, I'm stomping my foot, and shaking my head.

PERLS: OK. Say, "I won't be patient with you." [Perls asks Jane to repeat this and to take responsibility for the feeling by repeating the statement to several group members.]

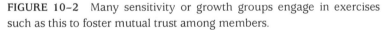

FIGURE 10–2 Many sensitivity or growth groups engage in exercises such as this to foster mutual trust among members.

PERLS: OK, how do you feel now?

JANE: OK.

PERLS: You understand, topdog and underdog are not yet together. But at least the conflict is clear, in the open, maybe a little less violent. (Perls, 1969, pp. 264–272)

Other case examples of gestalt therapy are available in Perls (1970), Polster and Polster (1973), and Rosenblatt (1975).

OTHER PHENOMENOLOGICAL THERAPIES

Rogers's and Perls's methods of treatment represent only two examples of phenomenological approaches to therapy. Many therapists blend psychodynamic, Rogerian, or gestalt methods with principles from humanistic or existential psychology (Kahn, 1985; Maslow, 1967, 1968; May, 1969; May, Angel, & Ellenberger, 1958). The *logotherapy* of Viktor Frankl (1963, 1965, 1967) is based on existential philosophy and is oriented toward helping clients (a) take responsibility for their feelings and actions, and (b) find meaning and purpose in their lives. Frankl believed that people can feel a lack of meaning and purpose without displaying neurotic or psychotic behaviors. He saw his approach as applicable to nonpatients as well as to "official" clients. Therapeutic procedures associated with humanistic and existential points of view are described in Bugental (1978), Fischer and Fischer (1983), Ford and Urban (1963), and Patterson (1973).

A phenomenologically oriented treatment that shares several features with social learning theory is the *fixed-role therapy* of George Kelly. On the basis of his personal-construct theory (see Chapter 2), Kelly (1955) developed treatment methods for helping clients become aware of and change the assumptions they use to guide their behavior. Usually this means helping clients adopt more flexible, elaborate constructs to replace the narrow,

rigid ones that Kelly believed were at the root of psychological disorders.

The subjective orientation of Kelly's theory places it partially in the phenomenological camp, but several of his methods are more at home elsewhere. Unlike phenomenologists who minimize diagnostic procedures, Kelly advocated systematic assessment of the problems and the personal constructs of the client. He advocated use of certain psychological tests to clarify the ways clients conceive of the world. Chief among these was Kelly's Role Construct Repertory Test.

Kelly encouraged clients to experiment with specific alternative constructs. To assist in this enterprise, the therapist asks the client to write a *fixed-role sketch,* a third-person account of what the client wishes to be like and how he or she feels. The client is helped to restart personal growth by temporarily (for several weeks) role playing the person described in the sketch. Role playing takes place both in therapy sessions and in the real world. The therapist treats the client as if she or he were the person in the sketch. Over time, the client may become comfortable with aspects of the adopted role and assimilate them. Other aspects may be unacceptable and will be dropped.

An Evaluation of Phenomenological Therapies

Phenomenological therapies and their counterparts (e.g., sensitivity and personal growth groups) have had a significant impact on clinical psychology. They provide a third choice for those who are not satisfied with the other models. This third choice is attractive because it generates faith in each client's ability to find meaning and self-actualization in life without having to exorcise unconscious, intrapsychic demons, extinguish bad habits, or learn new skills. Phenomenological approaches do not dwell on pathology, but focus instead on what the client can become. Finally, the phenomenological emphasis on the therapeutic relationship and a corresponding de-emphasis on therapy techniques appeal to clinicians who feel uncomfortable trying to do things *to* their clients.

Phenomenological approaches have received their share of criticism. Critics of phenomenological therapies make the following points:

1. *The Language of Phenomenology Is Often Esoteric and Unclear*. Terms like *B-values, Dasein, Eigenwelt, organismic experiencing, peak experiences,* and the like may stand in the way of understanding the treatments to which they apply. One client put it this way in a letter to Perls: "I tried reading your book, *Gestalt Therapy,* but I wish somebody . . . would write a book in very simple language . . . , explaining these same theories so that the average person . . . could maybe really get something more out of it" (Perls, 1970, p. 214). Some writers have made fun of gestalt therapy language without straying too far from reality. Compare the following satire by Hoffman (1973, p. 76) with the quote from Kempler (1973) in Chapter 2:

CLIENT: Sorry I'm late today.

THERAPIST: Can you get more in touch with that sorrow?

CLIENT: I hope it didn't inconvenience you.

THERAPIST: Let's focus on your capacity for choice rather than on my expectations.

CLIENT: But I didn't mean to be late.

THERAPIST: I hear you, and I don't put it down. But where we need to be is the immanence of the I-thou relationship . . . emanating from the here-and-now, and from there into a consciousness of the tension between be-ing and non-be-ing, and eventually into the transcendence of be-ing itself, through to a cosmic awareness of the oceanic I-dentity of self and the space-time continuum.

CLIENT: Gotcha.

Phenomenologists describe their goals as *humanistic,* and include among them client growth, creativity, fulfillment, joy, self-actualization, and individuality. Similarly, they describe their treatment as noncoercive, nonjudgmental, and nondirective. These qualities are not the sole property of phenomenology. Most psychodynamic and behavioral therapists also see themselves as committed to humanistic values. In fact, it would be difficult to find therapists who do not believe in the *ideals* of phenomenological therapy even though their methods of reaching them differ.

2. *Phenomenological Treatment Procedures Are Incomplete.* By deemphasizing assessment, phenomenological therapists may miss diagnostic signs or background factors that could be important to treatment. Trusting clients to tell about these things is seen as naive and as potentially dangerous as the abuses associated with traditional diagnosis. It is also suggested that while a good client–therapist relationship may be a *necessary* condition for effective treatment, it may not be a *sufficient* condition. The problems of some clients may be beyond their ability to solve; they need more in the way of help than an empathic relationship.

3. *Phenomenological Treatments Are Vague and Unrealistic.* Phenomenological methods are usually described as processes that are not translated into specific therapist behaviors. Further, many writers question the processes themselves. For example, can a person *really* know what it is like to be another person? Can any therapist *really* be nondirective and nonjudgmental? Nye (1975, p. 135) points out that

> client-centered therapists, despite themselves, bring about changes in the client's behaviors through inadvertent, subtle reinforcements (for example, nodding their heads or changing their facial expressions when clients speak about "interesting" things and remaining more

passive when clients speak about "uninteresting" things).

4. The Beneficial Effects of Phenomenological Treatments Have Not Been Established.

A number of phenomenological therapists have maintained a skeptical stance toward empirical evaluations of psychotherapy. They insist that only the client and therapist can evaluate therapy, and even then only in subjective terms, not in the language of science. This attitude has caused observers to reject some phenomenological treatments as viable approaches to changing human behavior. (However, see Fischer & Fischer, 1983, for a description of empirical phenomenological studies.)

Still, it is important to remember that Carl Rogers pioneered the first systematic research program on psychotherapy. His recordings of therapy sessions revolutionized psychotherapy research by creating the chance to study the moment-to-moment changes and interactions that occur in psychotherapy. This focus on specific client–therapist exchanges continues to be as important today as it was when Rogers introduced it (Orlinsky, 1989).

Decades of psychotherapy research have consistently indicated that the quality of the relationship between therapist and client is the aspect of therapy most strongly related to beneficial outcome (Orlinsky & Howard, 1986). Rogers's contention that the therapeutic relationship is more important than specific treatment techniques appears to have been well supported.

A few therapeutic techniques associated with gestalt therapy have been studied empirically. For example, in one study (Conoley, Conoley, McConnell, & Kimzey, 1983), researchers investigated a version of the empty chair technique by asking college students to spend 20 minutes expressing to an empty chair their feelings about an event that had angered them. Subjects' blood pressure and self-reports of anger were collected before and after this experience. Compared to a group of

subjects who experienced 20 minutes of "reflective listening" by the experimenter, the empty chair subjects achieved lower blood pressure and reported reduced feelings of anger after their therapy.

Indirect support for the effectiveness of the unmailed letter technique comes from research by James Pennebacker and his associates (Pennebacker & Beall, 1986; Pennebacker, Kiecolt-Glaser, & Glaser, 1988). These researchers assigned 25 undergraduate students to write for 20 minutes on each of four consecutive days about traumatic events in their lives; 25 other students wrote for the same amount of time about nontraumatic, somewhat trivial activities (e.g., recent social events). Before and after they had completed their writing assignments each day, the subjects rated their mood and reported any symptoms of physical illness. In addition, the researchers measured the subjects' immune system functioning and the number of visits subjects made to the health center during the course of the study. Those students who wrote about personal traumas showed better immune system functioning, made fewer visits to the health center, and reported less subjective distress than did the subjects who wrote about trivial matters. Perhaps writing about upsetting experiences in therapy via the unmailed letter also gives clients a way to confront and lessen emotional problems.

On the other hand, when outcomes of psychotherapy are considered, client-centered therapy and gestalt therapy have not fared particularly well. The average effect size for all types of psychotherapy in the Smith, Glass, and Miller (1980) meta-analysis was .85 of a standard deviation at treatment completion; the effect size for gestalt therapy was .64 while for client-centered therapy it was .62.

The claim by some phenomenologists (e.g., Rogers) that their treatments result in a similar pattern of change from client to client has also been attacked by critics. They suggest that the pattern is due not to spontaneous growth, but to direct therapist influences such as modeling and reinforcement of certain client behaviors. A participant in a gestalt therapy group once raised this possibility with Perls:

Dr. Perls, . . . as you've been formulating and experiencing what has come out as gestalt therapy, I want to be reassured, I want to hear you say it, it seems like a process of discovery. Yet I think that people can arrange themselves to fit the expectations of the therapist, like, I sit here and watch person after person have a polarity, a conflict of forces, and I think I can do it too. But I don't know how spontaneous it would be, although I think I would feel spontaneous. You've experienced people over a long time; are we fitting you or have you discovered us? (Perls, 1969, pp. 214–215)

Perls's answer was, "I don't know."

5. Because Phenomenological Approaches Are Often Applied in Short-Term Group Contexts That Fall Outside the Range of Formal Therapy, Some Unscreened Participants Are Inappropriately Included in the Process. The danger of client deterioration and other negative consequences may not be as critical as some people fear, and they are not restricted to phenomenological treatments, but phenomenological group experiences can produce "casualties." Casualties occur most often among participants who were unstable to begin with, a fact that further emphasizes the danger of inadequate screening of group members.

6. Phenomenological Approaches Are Applicable Mainly to Intelligent, Introspective Individuals. Despite the view that anyone can benefit from growth experiences, it has been argued that these experiences may be helpful only to relatively well-integrated people. The value of phenomenological therapies for more severe behavior problems, children, and the retarded is probably minimal.

Still, phenomenological methods provide an excellent set of therapeutic strategies. Rogers's techniques are among the most productive interviewing procedures available, and many gestalt exercises (e.g., empty-chair exercises) encourage clients to report on feelings that might otherwise require many interviews to reveal. Of greatest importance to the practicing clinician, however, is phenomenological-existential therapy's emphasis on the uniqueness of human experience in all its forms—thought, emotion, and action. This perspective encourages therapists to focus less on techniques and more on the client's "lived world" (Fischer & Fischer, 1983).

CHAPTER 11

Clinical
Child
Psychology

As we noted in Chapter 1, clinical psychology had its roots in the assessment and treatment of childhood disorders. Binet's development of mental ability measures to identify retarded children was one of the first examples of systematic psychological assessment. Similarly, the first psychological clinic in the United States was established by Witmer to treat children's academic and behavior problems. Given this background, it is surprising that for much of this century the study of childhood psychopathology was largely ignored, with primary attention concentrated on adult disorders. When childhood problems were considered, it was usually in the form of what has been called "adultomorphism"—the tendency to see children as miniature adults. As Garber (1984, p. 30) describes it, historically, ". . . the study of psychopathology in children has been simply a downward extension and extrapolation from the study of psychopathology in adults." Only within the last 3 decades has attention been focused on the unique nature of childhood disorders.

The delayed recognition of the unique nature of childhood disorders parallels the history of the entire concept of childhood. Only recently have children been considered and treated as something other than miniature adults, but there are indications that we may be reverting to that earlier view. For example, Elkind (1981) bemoans the fact that we force children to grow up quickly and enroll them in classes and activities at increasingly earlier ages.

Prior versions of the *Diagnostic and Statistical Manuals* illustrate this adult-oriented approach to childhood disorders (Gelfand & Peterson, 1985). *DSM-I,* with few exceptions (e.g., adjustment reactions), ignored childhood disorders. *DSM-II* (American Psychiatric Association, 1968) added only a few more disorders that were unique to childhood (e.g., hyperkinesis reaction).

A primary explanation for this adult perspective on childhood disorders relates to the two theories that have, until recently, dominated treatment approaches in this century.

Both psychoanalysis and behavior therapy downplayed the unique nature of childhood problems (Gelfand & Peterson, 1985).[1] It may seem paradoxical to accuse psychoanalysis of adultomorphism, because Freud's theory is recognized as a major contribution to our understanding of child development. However, children are not considered ideal candidates for psychoanalysis, and " . . . many analysts' formulations of patients' problems seem remarkably little affected by their patients' ages" (Gelfand & Peterson, 1985, p. 41).

In similar fashion, radical behavior therapy, so influential in the 1960s and 1970s, ignored the unique nature of childhood disorders. The guiding principle was "an organism is an organism," be it a rat, a child, or an adult. Because all organisms are subject to the same laws of learning, developmental level became an irrelevant issue in planning treatment interventions (Baer, 1973).

Within the last 3 decades this adult-oriented approach to child behavior problems has given way to a child-centered approach that recognizes that adult models of psychopathology ignore several important characteristics of childhood. In addition, clinicians are discovering that traditional methods of classification, assessment, and intervention may have limited relevance for childhood disorders. Several developments document this shift in approach to childhood disorders. *DSM-III* was the first version of *DSM* to make specific recommendations concerning developmental considerations in the diagnostic criteria for childhood disorders. *DSM-IV* contains more than two dozen Axis 1 disorders specific to children.

Since 1970 several major psychology journals have appeared (*Journal of Abnormal Child Psychology, Journal of Clinical Child Psychology*) that are devoted entirely to research on childhood behavior problems. Simi-

larly, there are now two sections of Division 12 (Clinical Psychology) of APA devoted to children (section 1: clinical child and section 5: pediatric). Finally, a new field of study, *developmental psychopathology,* has been introduced, and a new journal, *Development and Psychopathology,* has been published. Developmental psychopathology is the study of childhood disorders from a developmental perspective; it focuses on how various adaptive and maladaptive patterns of behavior are manifested during different stages of development (Sroufe & Rutter, 1984). In addition, developmental psychopathologists stress that understanding how children develop competencies may be as important as understanding the development of maladaptive behaviors (Masterpasqua, 1989; Strayhorn, 1988).

In the remainder of this chapter we discuss several issues that differentiate clinical child psychology from the general field of clinical psychology. First, we give an overview of clinical child psychology, paying special attention to referral processes, developmental considerations, infant temperament, parent-child interactions, and childhood stressors. The remaining sections of the chapter focus on the classification, assessment, and treatment of childhood disorders.

ISSUES UNIQUE TO CLINICAL CHILD PSYCHOLOGY

Referral Issues

Clinical contacts are set in motion with a referral, and immediately we see important distinctions between childhood and adult disorders. When adults feel distressed they can seek professional help. Children do not have this option; they do not refer themselves for help. They depend on significant others (parents, teachers) to determine whether they need intervention.

A child may be suffering considerable distress, but if the parents are indifferent to this

---

[1] Psychoanalysis and behavior therapy also shared a tendency to blame parents (primarily mothers) for children's behavior problems (Peterson & Roberts, 1991).

problem, the child does not receive the help he or she needs. Conversely, children may be referred for help for reasons that have little to do with how they are feeling or behaving, but instead reflect parent or family problems. Several parental factors influence whether children will be referred for psychological interventions, regardless of the children's actual behavioral or emotional state (Christensen, Margolin, & Sullaway, 1992). One factor is the parents' level of tolerance for the behavior; parents who perceive a given behavior (e.g., noncompliance) as being temporary and manageable are less likely to seek help for their child than are parents who perceive the same behavior as more permanent and unmanageable (Shepherd, Oppenheim, & Mitchell, 1971).

A widely investigated factor influencing the referral of children is maternal depression. Research has consistently shown a significant positive relationship between mothers' depression and their perception of maladjustment in their children; mothers who feel more depressed see their children as more behaviorally disordered (Griest, Wells, & Forehand, 1979; Webster-Stratton, 1988). For example, Griest et al. (1979) compared observations of inappropriate child behavior and maternal self-ratings of depression in predicting the mothers' perceptions of maladjustment in their clinic-referred children. Children's noncompliance and deviant behavior were not significantly related to the mothers' ratings of their children's behavior, but the self-ratings of depression showed that the more depressed the mothers, the worse they rated their children's behavior. Given the correlational nature of these findings, several explanations for this relationship are possible (Richters, 1992). It may be, as the authors argue, that maternal depression leads mothers to view their children as behaviorally disordered because depressed individuals see many aspects of their world as undesirable. Conversely, unmanageable child behavior may produce a sense of helplessness and depression in the mothers. It is even pos-

sible that a third factor, such as a father's indifference, accounts for both the mother's depression and the child's behavior problems. Whatever the explanation, results such as these suggest that mothers' emotional states, although not necessarily fathers' (Webster-Stratton, 1988), may influence how mothers perceive both their children's behavior and their own capacity to cope with their children. These influences determine, to a large degree, which children are referred for professional help.

Developmental Considerations

One obvious way in which children differ from adults is that children are in a period of rapid growth and development.[2] Besides the physical changes associated with this maturation, there are important social, cognitive, and behavioral changes that have profound implications for clinical child psychology. At the most basic level, the clinician must evaluate the appropriateness of a child's behavior relative to developmental norms. Behavior considered symptomatic at one age may be viewed as developmentally normal at an earlier (e.g., bedwetting, fears) or later (e.g., sexual activity) age (Campbell, 1989). In fact, most symptoms of childhood disorders are appropriate, or at least typical, behavior at an earlier stage of development. This is obvious for behaviors such as bedwetting, but it is also true for symptoms such as overactivity, restlessness, and even aggression (Campbell, 1989). For example, epidemiological studies of nonreferred, school-age children find parents reporting that approximately half the sample

---

[2]Of course, the developmental process does not stop when individuals reach adulthood. This is reflected in many developmental psychology courses that no longer focus exclusively on children, but instead discuss life-span development. The developmental considerations discussed in this section may also be relevant for the study of psychopathology among the elderly.

of children are restless, overactive, and distractible, the hallmark symptoms of attention-deficit hyperactivity disorder (Lapouse & Monk, 1958; Werry & Quay, 1971). The obvious implication of these developmental changes in behavior is that, with few exceptions, the appropriateness of a given child's behavior must be evaluated in light of his or her developmental stage. The main exceptions to this conclusion are symptoms associated with severe disorders, such as autism and mental retardation.

In addition to age, there are other, less obvious implications of a developmental perspective on childhood behavior disorders. For one, the conceptual models used to explain children's problems must take into account their developmental stage. With adults, a popular model for explaining depression is learned helplessness, the belief that outcomes are not contingent on one's actions. Individuals susceptible to such beliefs tend to make stable and internal attributions for failures ("I failed the test because I am stupid"), whereas a psychologically healthier response would be to make external or unstable attributions ("the test was unfair"; "I did not study enough this time"). The major premise of this model is that failures produce a sense of helplessness when individuals perceive there is nothing they can do to alter outcomes. However, a developmental study of the causal attributions made by children (Rholes, Blackwell, Jordan, & Walters, 1980) found that younger children (kindergarten, first, third graders) were less susceptible to helpless attributions following failure than were older children (fifth graders). One reason for this is that the younger children did not see ability as a stable attribute, so failures did not imply stable limitations on their likelihood of future successes. This attributional style of younger children may protect them against the onset of perceived helplessness. This argument is consistent with the claim that young children are not capable of manifesting clinical depression because of cognitive limitations. With increasing age, children may become more realistic and perhaps more pessimistic about their capabilities (Ruble & Rholes, 1981).

Unfortunately, numerous examples of the failure of clinicians to adopt a developmental perspective when working with children can be found in the behavioral literature (see Furman, 1980), as well as in areas such as pediatric psychology (see Burbach & Peterson, 1986; Whitt, Dykstra, & Taylor, 1979).

Infant Temperament

If you ask parents with several children to describe their experiences with these children, one common reaction is surprise about how different their children were, even in infancy. Consider the comments offered by a mother of a 5-year-old boy and a 3-year-old girl.

> He's a challenging kid (is it a parental sin to admit that you have a difficult child?), and Steve [the father] and I are learning the necessity of becoming consistent, and for Greg, strict disciplinarians. Jane is doing well—and to date is a pretty easy-going child. *It's mind-boggling sometimes to see the differences between the two of them.* (italics added)

These parental observations are well supported by empirical investigations. In a series of landmark studies, Thomas, Chess, and Birch (1968; Thomas & Chess, 1977; see also, Chess & Thomas, 1986) discovered reliable temperamental differences among infants in the first few months of life, differences that appear at birth and have both short-term and long-term implications. *Temperament* refers to the infant's behavioral style, how the infant reacts to and even produces environmental events. Thomas et al. (1968) rated the infants in their New York Longitudinal Study along nine dimensions, including activity level, response to new stimuli, intensity of reactions, disposition, and distractibility. Ratings along these nine dimensions revealed that many of the infants could be classified into one of three groups—the "easy" child; the "difficult" child; and the "slow-to-warm-up" child.

Easy children adapt well to new situations, they do not become upset easily, they are regular in biological functions such as feeding and sleeping, and they pose few problems for their parents. Parents whose first child displays this temperamental style wonder why others are always complaining about the problems of parenting. The difficult child, in contrast, is easily upset, irregular in biological functioning, shows intense and often negative reactions to environmental changes, and is quite trying for the parents. Parents whose first child falls in the difficult category may wonder at times whether they want to have another child. The slow-to-warm-up child falls somewhere between the easy and difficult types. Follow-up studies show that infants initially classified as difficult are at increased risk for behavior, learning, and peer difficulties when entering first grade 6 years later. For example, 70% of the difficult infants, versus only 18% of the easy infants, developed behavior problems by the time they entered school (Thomas et al., 1968).

The findings regarding infant temperament pose important implications for clinical child psychology. First, they suggest that subsequent behavior problems are partly a function of innate or biological characteristics of the child. These findings have created a renewed interest in the *diathesis-stress model* of psychopathology (see Kagan, 1989). This model emphasizes the interaction between a biological predisposition and environmental stressors (e.g., parenting and school characteristics) in determining subsequent behavior problems (see Chapter 12).

A second outgrowth of the work on infant temperament was a new conceptualization of parent–child interactions, with more attention paid to what the child brings to the relationship (Bell & Harper, 1977). Whereas traditional psychodynamic theory stressed the parents' influence on the child's subsequent development, findings from follow-up studies on temperament suggested that the child's be-

havior influences the parents just as much (Thomas & Chess, 1977). Specifically, there were few differences in parent–child interactions across the three temperamental categories during initial assessments. However, during subsequent assessments the parents of the earlier-identified difficult infants differed from the other parents; they issued more controlling statements and engaged in more punitive interactions with their children.

These results suggest that it is the child's difficult behavior that is producing the inappropriate reactions of the parents. Because the infant's difficult style precedes the faulty parenting, parenting style cannot be producing the child's behavioral difficulties. This interpretation contrasts with the traditional view that child psychopathology is a result of faulty parenting.

There are numerous examples of blaming parents for their child's behavior problems. Perhaps the clearest case is the theory that the social withdrawal and bizarre behavior associated with childhood autism are partially the result of having cold, indifferent (so-called refrigerator) mothers (Bettleheim, 1967; Kanner, 1943). This idea was derived from observations of mothers with their autistic children. This theory illustrates the danger of drawing causal conclusions from correlational data: When mother–child interactions are observed at a single point in time, it is fallacious to assume that the mother's emotional indifference caused the child's autism. An alternative explanation for these observations is that continued interaction with a child who does not communicate and respond in a normal fashion produces emotional withdrawal in the mother.[3]

Since the publication of the New York Lon-

---

[3]Although it may appear ludicrous to argue that such a severe disorder as childhood autism could result from an emotionally cold and indifferent mother, we are all subject to this type of fallacious thinking. Think of what you said to yourself the last time you witnessed a mother yelling at her child. You may well have drawn conclusions about the mother's causal role in producing the child's misbehavior.

gitudinal Study, increased attention has been devoted to examining how children affect parent–child interactions. For example, in the area of hyperactivity, clinician-researchers have learned that parents are often punitive toward their disordered child. However, as Barkley and Cunningham (1979) demonstrated, if the children are given medication that improves their behavior, the parents immediately behave more positively toward them. Similar evidence exists for teacher (Whalen, Henker, & Dotemoto, 1980) and peer (Cunningham, Siegel, & Offord, 1985) interactions with hyperactive children.

A dramatic example of the powerful effects of child behavior on adults is a study by Lang, Pelham, Johnston, and Gelernter (1989), who investigated the relationship between adult alcohol consumption and child behavior problems. There is convincing evidence that parental alcohol problems can contribute to child behavior disorders. However, Lang et al. (1989) addressed the reciprocal question: Can child behavior disorders contribute to adult alcohol consumption? In an ingenious investigation, the authors had 16 male and 16 female undergraduate students interact with either a normal child or a boy trained to act like a hyperactive child. The subjects were told that the purpose of the study was to examine the effects of adult alcohol consumption on child behavior. After this initial, baseline interaction, the subjects were allowed to drink as much beer as they wanted before going back for a second interaction. However, no second interaction took place. The dependent variables in the study were the amount of beer consumed, and how distressed the subjects reported feeling. Subjects who interacted with the hyperactive confederate were significantly more distressed than those who interacted with the normal child. Moreover, the males in the hyperactive condition also consumed significantly more alcohol than males in the normal condition. There were no differences for the females. At least for males, having a distressing interaction with a difficult-to-manage child can signifi-

cantly increase one's alcohol consumption, even among individuals who do not have an identified alcohol problem.

Thus, it is overly simplistic to believe that all children's behavior problems are due to faulty parenting. But it is equally unlikely that all child psychopathology can be understood exclusively in terms of what the child brings to the relationship. Parent-child interactions, like all dyadic interactions, are reciprocal in nature; the child's temperament and behavior affect the parents, and parents' tolerance and response in turn alter the child's behavior. Thomas and Chess (1977) used the term *goodness-of-fit* to capture the idea that whether a child develops a behavior problem is partially a function of the degree to which the child's temperament and the parental response style are concordant. The greater the mismatch (e.g., rigid parents with a difficult infant), the greater the likelihood that the child will be at risk for subsequent problems. Within the last 3 decades the major advances in understanding and treating childhood behavior disorders have been made by theorists who take a reciprocal or bidirectional view of parent-child interactions (see Box 11–1).

Childhood Stressors

Many childhood disorders result from the interaction between dispositional (e.g., temperamental) factors and environmental stressors. There are many environmental stressors to which children can be exposed, including multiple hospitalizations, having a psychiatrically or physically impaired parent, loss of a parent by divorce or death, birth of a sibling, and poverty (Garmezy, 1983). Even war is a stressor that has received attention, as documented by the classic studies of children in England during World War II (Freud & Burlingham, 1943) and the recent work with children in Belfast (Lyons, 1971). In this section we focus on three childhood stressors that affect many children—mandatory school attendance, marital conflict, and abuse.

The clearest example of reciprocal parent–child interactions and the impact they have on childhood disorders is Gerald Patterson's (1976, 1982) work with aggressive children and their parents. Starting from a social learning perspective, Patterson documented through the use of detailed and systematic observations in the home (Patterson et al., 1969) the reciprocal nature of parent-child interactions, both for normal and disordered families. Changes in parental behavior alter the probability of certain child responses, just as changes in the child's behavior alter the likelihood of a given parental response. Further, Patterson found important differences between normal and aggressive families in these *conditional probabilities.* For example, aggressive children are twice as likely as nonaggressive children to persist in their aversive behavior following parental punishment. The probability of aggressive children persisting in their hostile behavior following parental punishment was .41; this probability was only .23 for the nonproblem sample (Patterson, 1976).

Besides stressing the reciprocal nature of parent-child interactions, Patterson (1976) also suggested that aggressive families tend to operate through aversive control (negative reinforcement) procedures. In this model, coercive control by one member of the dyad (the mother threatens the child) produces an escalated, coercive response from the other member (the child screams louder). One member eventually finds this coercive escalation intolerable and terminates the interaction. This termination of an aversive response thereby reinforces the coercive escalation of the other member, who becomes more likely to respond in the future with a more extreme aversive response. The following scenario demonstrates both the reciprocal and coercive nature of parent-child interactions.

Mrs. Smith has just gotten off work and has picked up her son, Billy, at the day-care center. Before going home she has to stop at the grocery store to buy food for dinner. With her shopping cart half-full she passes the ice cream counter, at which point Billy indicates he wants an ice cream cone. Like any good mother, Mrs. Smith says, "No, you'll spoil your dinner." Like some young children, Billy responds with a temper tantrum in the middle of the aisle. This creates a problem for Mrs. Smith. Besides the social embarassment of having her child act out-of-control in public, she is worried about

BOX 11–1

Patterson's Coercion-Escalation Hypothesis of Aggressive Behavior

Mandatory School Attendance. From the perspective of an adult, it may seem unusual to consider school attendance as a stressor, but for several reasons, school is probably the single biggest stressor to which children are exposed. First, school attendance is required of all children so even if this policy adversely affected only a small percentage of children, it would still affect a large number of children. Second, the majority of referrals for childhood problems stem from problems in school. Learning disabilities, attention-deficit hyperactivity disorder, conduct and oppositional disorders, as well as peer difficulties are exacerbated by mandatory school attendance. One piece of evidence for the contributory role of the school environment is that age 6, the point when most children enter first grade, is the peak referral period for childhood disorders.

getting home to make dinner. Mrs. Smith solves this dilemma by giving in to Billy's request, but with the admonition that this is the last time he will get an ice cream cone before dinner. Billy stops screaming, and they proceed on their way.

This behavioral sequence can be graphically depicted as follows:

Child	Mother	Child	Mother	Child
Asks for ice cream	No!	Temper tantrum	Gives in	Stops tantrum
↑	↑	↑	↑	
First chain	(Stimulus)	(Behavior)	(Consequence)	
Second chain----------------------		Temper tantrum	Gives in	Stops tantrum
		↑	↑	↑
		(Stimulus)	(Behavior)	(Consequence)

If we examine the first stimulus–behavior–consequence chain, we see that Billy is learning that if he throws a temper tantrum when his mom says "No," he can get his way—he is positively reinforced for this behavior. Thus, Mrs. Smith is inadvertently teaching Billy that throwing a temper tantrum will get him what he wants. Consider what Mrs. Smith is "learning" from this interaction. As the second behavioral chain indicates, she is being negatively reinforced for giving Billy an ice cream cone when he throws a tantrum in a public place—this terminates his aversive (and humiliating) behavior. From learning theory we know that in the future Mrs. Smith is likely to respond in the same way when confronted with a similar situation, despite her admonitions to Billy to the contrary. She has fallen into what Patterson (1982) has called the "reinforcement trap"—she obtains a short-term benefit at the expense of unpleasant long-term consequences.

Not only has Patterson's work helped us understand aggressive behavior in the home, he also has developed the most systematic and most frequently employed behavioral intervention program for such families (see Patterson, 1975). We discuss this program more extensively in the section on treatment.

BOX 11–1
Continued

What is it about school that makes it such a potent stressor? Consider what is required of children when they enter the first grade. They must sit quietly for long periods of time while focusing their attention on schoolwork. They must master new and complex skills (e.g., reading, math) which make major demands on children's cognitive resources. Social skills are required in order for children to succeed with their peers. Finally, children must consistently comply with teacher requests. The skills just listed as crucial to adequate performance in school are also involved in the primary behavior problems in childhood (learning problems, noncompliance, peer difficulties, and attention problems).

What are the implications of considering school as a major childhood stressor? First, because most child referrals involve school-related difficulties, clinicians will routinely collect data directly from the school (teacher ratings, school observations) or at least gather school-related measures (e.g., achievement tests; see the section on assessment issues). Thus, child clinicians need to be knowledgeable about issues relating to school functioning, such as the diagnosis and assessment of learning disabilities. Second, clinical interventions often take place in the school setting and may involve training teachers in classroom management procedures (O'Leary & O'Leary, 1972) or helping teachers develop social skills training groups. Third, clinicians may find themselves mediating between the wishes of the school system (e.g., placing a child in a special class) and the concerns of the parents (avoiding the stigma associated with such placement). Finally, clinical child psychologists need to understand how school environments can either increase or decrease the likelihood of behavior and learning disorders (Rutter, Maugham, Mortimore, Ouston, & Smith, 1979). As such, the school environment is a fertile ground for primary prevention projects.

Marital Conflict and Divorce. By 1990, approximately 45% of children were not living with both their natural parents. This figure does not begin to represent all the children who are exposed to severe marital conflict, because many discordant marriages are not dissolved (Emery, 1982). Thus, there is increasing concern with the effects of marital conflict and divorce on children's psychological functioning.

Besides the obvious psychological distress associated with the disruption of family life, other aspects of divorce make it a potent stressor for children: (a) There is often a change in the standard of living associated with maintaining two households; (b) children may be caught in the middle of a custody battle between parents; (c) children are often exposed to high levels of parental conflict, and must adapt to two different living environments and inconsistent parenting practices; (d)

parenting skills often deteriorate, partly because there is only one parent in the home, and partly because the parents often are experiencing depression, anger, and other psychological problems that detract from their effectiveness as parents; and (e) when remarriage occurs, issues associated with stepparenting and blended families arise (Hetherington & Arasteh, 1988), not to mention the fact that remarried parents are at increased risk for subsequent separations and divorce (Hetherington, Stanley-Hagan, & Anderson, 1989).

When children are exposed to multiple stressors, the likelihood of mental health problems increases dramatically (Rutter, 1981). This increased risk seems to be the case for children of divorce. Especially among boys, in the 2 years following divorce there are marked increases in the rates of aggressive and noncompliant behavior, as well as disruptions in their school work and peer relations. The findings for girls are not as dramatic or clearcut. If girls do exhibit problems, they tend to be less severe and to disappear by the end of the first year after the divorce. Several explanations have been offered for these gender differences. First, boys tend to act out their problems whereas girls may internalize them, making them less obvious to others. Second, recent research by Hetherington (1989) suggests that the girls may experience delayed problems, especially regarding heterosexual relations.

A number of individual differences can moderate the effects of divorce. Not surprisingly, temperamentally difficult children show more adverse effects of divorce than do easy children (Hetherington, 1989). Similarly, children's reactions to divorce depend on their developmental stage (Wallerstein, Corbin, & Lewis, 1988). For example, preschool children often respond to divorce with regression and separation anxiety, whereas the most striking response of older children is intense anger at one or both parents (Wallerstein, Corbin, & Lewis, 1988). Finally, as Block, Block, and Gjerde (1986) suggest in a provocative study, certain early childhood characteristics, such as aggression (in boys), may actually predispose parents to a divorce.

One major question about divorce is how it produces negative consequences in children. One possibility is parental separation; the children now live with only one of the parents and see the other one (usually the father) much less frequently, if at all. However, the consensus among clinical child psychologists is that separation *per se* does not produce the adverse behavioral consequences associated with divorce (see Emery, 1982). Instead, the active component appears to be the degree of marital conflict, both prior to and following the divorce. Separations that are relatively amicable produce much less disturbance in children than those that are hostile.[4] Thus, when parents ask whether they should stay together for the benefit of the children, a common response is, "not if there is a high degree of marital conflict."

Given that divorce is a potent stressor, increasing attention is being directed toward helping both parents and children cope with this difficult transition (Grych & Fincham, 1992). For example, Pedro-Carroll and Cowen (1985) evaluated a program designed to help children cope with separation and divorce. The treatment program emphasized three goals: (a) social support, whereby the children were taught to share their feelings with others in a similar situation; (b) self-statement modifications, in which the children were trained to identify those problem areas over which they had some control and those they did not; and (c) anger control training, in which the children learned appropriate means of expressing anger. Intervention programs have also been created for parents going through the divorce

process (Bloom, Hodges, & Caldwell, 1982). The goals of these programs include teaching parents how to cope with their own feelings, as well as to help their children adjust to the disruption in their lives. (See Grych & Fincham, 1992, for a discussion of different types of interventions and their effectiveness for children of divorce.)

Child Abuse

Signaled by the publication of *The Battered Child Syndrome* by Helfer and Kempe (1968), the scope and seriousness of child abuse only came to the public's attention in the late 1960s and early 1970s. In 1974, Congress passed the Federal Child Abuse Prevention and Treatment Act. Since then the number of reported cases of abuse has increased dramatically. Between 1976 and 1984, the rate of reported abuse rose approximately 10% per year (Wicks-Nelson & Israel, 1991). It is now estimated that child abuse results in 50,000 deaths a year (Peterson & Roberts, 1991), a figure comparable to yearly automobile fatalities. What is not clear is whether the actual rate of abuse has risen, or whether public and professional sensitivity and awareness have increased. There are certainly reasons to believe that increased reports of abuse reflect changes in reporting practices. First, the public's awareness of the nature of the problem has risen dramatically. Only 10% of the population thought abuse was a serious problem in 1976; 90% of the population thought so 10 years later (Wicks-Nelson & Israel, 1991). In addition, all states have made it a legal requirement that any teacher, physician, psychologist, or other health professional who suspects abuse must report the case to the appropriate social agencies. Thus, professionals who come in contact with children now must be aware of the indicators of possible abuse as well as the mechanisms necessary to report suspected cases.

When Helfer and Kempe (1968) first described the battered child syndrome, attention focused on major physical abuse of children.

---

[4]Obviously, a major confound in these studies is that discordant separations are more probable in families that have had higher rates of discord and aggression all along. Thus, as the Block et al. (1986) study suggests, these children may have been predisposed to aggressive and noncompliant behavior.

The essential diagnostic signs included inexplicable or repeated injuries, and the primary assessment tools included X-rays and physical exams. However, the definition of abuse has now broadened to include neglect, psychological abuse, sexual abuse, and exploitation. *Neglect* refers to children whose physical and/or emotional needs are not being sufficiently met. *Psychological abuse* has proven more difficult to define; it consists of verbal and emotional assaults against the child, including rejection, degradation, and terrorizing (Hart & Brassard, 1987). Today the battered child now makes up only a minority of reported abuse cases. Not surprisingly, parents are the primary perpetrators of physical abuse, sexual abuse, and neglect, although other individuals (e.g., siblings, other relatives, and day-care workers) can also be responsible.

It is a common misconception among the public and professionals alike that if you were abused as a child, you are doomed to perpetuate the cycle by becoming an abusing parent. According to Kaufman and Zigler (1987), there is only a 30% chance of abused children becoming abusive parents. Although this figure exceeds the rate for non-abused children, it still means that the majority of abused children do not become abusive parents. Another misconception is that the vast majority of abusive parents are psychologically disturbed. In fact, most such parents do not meet diagnostic criteria for any psychiatric disorder and are not usually like the monsters whose extreme brutality occasionally captures media attention.

What causes parents to abuse their children? Three general factors have been identified (Wicks-Nelson & Israel, 1991): (a) social and cultural influences, including poverty, stress, and a tolerance for violence and harsh disciplinary procedures; (b) parents' personal characteristics, including a history of abuse, low frustration tolerance, and aggressiveness; and (c) characteristics of the parent–child interaction, including a difficult child, inappropriate expectations or explanations for the child's behavior by the parents, and ineffective disciplinary practices.

Twentyman and his colleagues examined the role of faulty parental expectations about a child's behavior in child abuse. Twentyman, Rohrbeck, and Amish (1984) propose a four-stage cognitive-behavioral sequence for abusive incidents: (a) The parent initially sets unrealistic expectations for the child; (b) the child fails to meet these expectations; (c) the parent misattributes the child's inappropriate behavior to intentional characteristics (e.g., deliberate spitefulness); and (d) the parent overreacts to the child's willful disobedience and becomes abusive. This vicious cycle is exacerbated by children who are prone to misbehavior and parents who overreact to environmental stresses.

What happens to abused children as they grow older? Research suggests that these children are at increased risk for behavioral and emotional problems but not for any specific disorder. Abused children are prone to later school failure, aggressiveness, depression, peer problems, and impaired sexual and marital relationships.

Treatment of abuse has focused on two components: helping the parents and helping the child victim (Wolfe, 1987). Work with the parents usually concentrates on helping parents improve their disciplinary practices so as to reduce out-of-control incidents, educating parents about realistic expectations for their child's behavior, training parents in anger control and stress management, and providing social support for parents who feel insulated and isolated. Direct intervention may also be provided for parental problems (e.g., marital discord, depression) that contribute to the abusive situation.

Much less attention has been directed toward the victims of abuse (Azar & Wolfe, 1989). Historically, the primary intervention for abused children was to remove them from the home and place them in foster care. The goals of this intervention were to remove children from dangerous environments and provide them with a stable and therapeutic setting. However, foster care has come under criticism for several reasons. First, it is expensive. Second, although it was designed to be short term in nature, it is not uncommon for abused children to spend many years in one foster home after another. Similarly, foster care placement was meant to provide a respite for abusing parents during which time they could learn more appropriate parenting skills, but little training was undertaken and the separation periods were often so long that it was difficult to reintegrate the child into the home.

A second broad category of intervention for abused children involves working directly with the child. This may involve an environmental enrichment program for children who exhibit developmental delays due to neglect or abuse. Alternatively, the intervention may be directed at the specific behavioral or emotional problems that arise from the abusive environment. For example, social skills training may be offered to socially withdrawn children, while impulse (or anger) control training or supportive therapy may be used with children experiencing emotional problems.

CLASSIFICATION

Classification of childhood disorders has followed a different path than adult disorders, even though they both have the same objectives (see Chapter 1). There has been a greater emphasis on *empirically derived* classification systems for children, while adult disorders have mainly been classified into *clinically derived* diagnostic categories. Empirically derived systems rely on statistical analyses of large amounts of data to determine the symptoms that make up a diagnostic category. In contrast, clinically derived systems rely on the judgments of experts, who use their clinical and research experience to determine the diagnostic criteria. There are at least two reasons for the emphasis on the empirical approach

among childhood researchers. First, as we noted earlier, the initial versions of the clinically derived *DSM* systems virtually ignored the unique aspects of childhood disorders. *DSM-I* (American Psychiatric Association, 1952) had only two categories specifically associated with childhood disorders, and one of these, Adjustment Reaction, was so nonspecific as to be virtually useless. *DSM-II* was little better. It was only with *DSM-III* (and *DSM-III-R*) that childhood disorders were given serious attention, but even versions as recent as *DSM-IV* retain several of the shortcomings typical of their predecessors.

The empirical approach to classification of childhood disorders arises also from the nature of the referral process discussed earlier. Because children do not refer themselves for help, standard assessment procedures rely on information from significant others in the child's environment (i.e., parents and teachers). The most common procedure for gathering this information is to have knowledgeable adults complete behavior rating scales on the referred child. These scales assess a wide variety of behavioral problems that children may exhibit, and the adults are asked to indicate whether a specific behavior is a problem for that child and, if so, to what degree. Child psychiatry clinics routinely collect such data on large numbers of children. The advent of high-speed computers made it possible to analyze these data to determine the symptoms that tend to cluster together.[5]

In this section we discuss both the empirical and clinical approaches to the classification of childhood disorders, as well as the similarities and differences in the derived category systems.

---

[5]In fact, the first empirical classification of childhood disorders was undertaken by Jenkins and his colleagues in the 1940s, without the aid of a computer (Hewitt & Jenkins, 1946). However, the widespread availability of computers has been a driving force behind the popularity of the empirical approach.

Empirically Derived Systems

In contrast to the clinical approach, the empirical approach to classification makes no initial assumptions about which symptoms are interrelated, or what diagnostic categories may exist, although *a priori* decisions are involved in determining which behavioral symptoms to enter into the statistical analyses. Basically, the data are allowed to "speak" for themselves about the extent to which they are interrelated. The primary statistical technique for determining the interrelationship among behavioral symptoms is *factor analysis*. This procedure involves examining the correlations among all symptoms and determining which behaviors tend to occur together. Those symptoms with the highest correlations among themselves form factors or dimensions. This dimensional approach to psychopathology assumes that all children possess these behaviors, but to varying degrees. Children who score high on the unique factors are considered to suffer the corresponding problems more severely. This approach contrasts with clinically derived systems, which assume that one either does or does not have a given disorder.

As an example of the empirical approach to the diagnosis of childhood psychopathology, Achenbach (1978; Achenbach & Edelbrock, 1979, 1981) developed rating scales for parents and teachers that assessed over 100 of the most common problems of childhood. He then administered these scales to thousands of parents and teachers of both referred and non-referred boys and girls ranging in age from 4 to 16. Although the results differed somewhat depending on the child's age and gender, all of them produced at least eight factors, reflecting a variety of childhood behavior problems. Figure 11–1 offers examples of factors that typically arise from such analyses, along with the characteristics associated with each.

Factor analytic studies have consistently identified two general factors that encompass the majority of childhood behavior disorders

(Achenbach & Edelbrock, 1978; Quay, 1986). One of these factors includes *externalizing* or *undercontrolled* problems (see Box 11–2); the other, *internalizing* or *overcontrolled* problems (see Box 11–3). The former dimension refers to acting-out behavior that is aversive to others in the child's environment, and frequently includes hyperactivity, aggression, and delinquency. The internalizing dimension includes problems where the child experiences greater discomfort but this distress may not be evident or aversive to others. Examples include depression, anxiety, and somatic problems.

Besides being reliable, these two broad dimensions offer a valid differentiation of childhood behavior problems. Children identified by these two factors differ significantly in symptomatology, sex ratio, academic performance, parental characteristics and long-term outcome. Generally, children with externalizing problems, compared to those with internalizing disorders, tend to be male, to have a poorer academic record, and to show a poorer prognosis. Given the aversive nature of the externalizing disorders, as well as their more negative prognosis, it is not surprising that until recently more attention has been devoted to these problems than to the internalizing disorders.

What are the strengths of empirical classification? First, this approach avoids the biases in judgment that may be associated with the clinical approach. As we saw in Chapter 3, clinicians sometimes misperceive associations among symptoms. Thus, in formulating diagnostic categories, clinicians sometimes perceive correlations that do not exist. Achenbach (1985) cites bedwetting and firesetting as examples of how clinicians' biases in judgment can lead them to perceive a relationship between two symptoms when there is, in fact, no association. This problem is compounded when clinicians are asked to perceive associations among numerous symptoms and disorders. In contrast, the empirical approach is not subject to these judgmental biases, and com-

Conduct Disorder
  Fighting, hitting
  Disobedient, defiant
  Temper tantrums
  Destructiveness
  Impertinent, imprudent
  Uncooperative, resistant

Attention Problems
  Poor concentration, short attention span
  Daydreaming
  Clumsy, poor coordination
  Preoccupied, stares into space
  Fails to finish, lacks perseverance
  Impulsive

Motor Overactivity
  Restless, overactive
  Excitable, impulsive
  Squirmy, jittery
  Overtalkative
  Hums and makes other odd noises

Social Ineptness
  Poor peer relations
  Likes to be alone
  Is teased, picked on
  Prefers younger children
  Shy, timid, lacks self-confidence
  Stays with adults, ignored by peers

Somatic Complaints
  Headaches
  Vomiting, nausea
  Stomach aches
  Muscle aches and pains
  Elimination problems

Socialized Aggression
  Has "bad" companions
  Truant from home
  Truant from school
  Steals in company with others
  Loyal to delinquent friends
  Belongs to a gang

Anxious-Depressed Withdrawal
  Anxious, fearful, tense
  Shy, timid, bashful
  Withdrawn, seclusive
  Depressed, sad, disturbed
  Hypersensitive, easily hurt
  Feels inferior, worthless

Schizoid Unresponsive
  Won't talk
  Withdrawn
  Sad
  Stares blankly
  Confused

Psychotic Disorder
  Visual hallucinations
  Auditory hallucinations
  Bizarre, odd, peculiar
  Strange ideas and behavior
  Incoherent speech
  Repetitive speech

This table lists nine factors typically obtained from factor analyses of behavior rating scales. The behavioral items that frequently load on that factor are listed under the factor name.
Source: Quay (1986).

FIGURE 11–1
Factors Typically Derived From Factor Analyses of Rating Scales,
Along with the Characteristics Frequently Associated with Each

Attention-deficit hyperactivity disorder (ADHD) is the most common childhood behavior disorder, affecting approximately 5 percent of school-age children. This represents on the average one child per classroom, which, as teachers will tell you, is enough to seriously disrupt the learning environment. ADHD primarily affects boys, with the boy-to-girl ratio ranging from 5:1 to 10:1. The disorder has an onset prior to first grade, although the problems are exacerbated by the demands made by the school environment (see section on childhood stressors).

ADHD has three core features: inattention, impulsivity, and overactivity. The attention problems consist primarily of children having difficulty sustaining attention to tasks; they fail to finish school assignments, and they do not stay on task in the classroom. Observations of these children in the classroom document that they are looking at their school work less often than are their classmates (Abikoff, Gittelman-Klein, & Klein, 1977).

Impulsivity refers to the fact that these children act before they think. Although it is agreed that ADHD children are impulsive, operationally defining this construct is difficult (Milich & Kramer, 1984). Behaviors typical of this problem include difficulty waiting in turn, interrupting, and being impatient.

ADHD children exhibit both gross motor and fine motor overactivity. Gross motor activity refers to behaviors such as running around the room, standing on chairs, and always being on the go. Fine motor activity refers to fidgeting and squirming, restlessness, and playing with objects.

In addition to the three core features, ADHD children display a myriad of other behavior and learning problems. These include aggressive and delinquent behavior, oppositional and noncompliant reactions to adult requests, and problems in social interactions. Peers, parents, and teachers all note that such children are difficult partners with whom to interact, and ADHD children consistently elicit from their partners negative, controlling behaviors. Merely telling a child that he is about to interact with an ADHD boy will adversely affect the subsequent interaction, even when the partner in fact does not have a behavior problem (Harris, Milich, Johnston, & Hoover, 1990).

As hyperactive children grow older, the primary features of the disorder lessen. ADHD adolescents do not run around the room as they did in grade school. Nevertheless, as a group they are still at significant risk for academic, social, and emotional problems. Long-term follow-up studies suggest that in adulthood ADHD children can expect one of three outcomes. One group has a relatively benign outcome, showing few residual problems. A second group adjusts relatively well, but shows residual effects of earlier academic and social difficulties. For example, they work at jobs below what their socioeconomic background would predict, and they report having fewer friends and being less happy than agemates (Weiss & Hechtman, 1986). A final group will have serious legal or psychiatric complications. For example, anywhere from one third to one half of ADHD children will be arrested at least once for a serious offense, compared to 10% of a non-ADHD control group (Satterfield, Hoppe, & Schell, 1982). Having a stable family background, a high IQ, and low levels of aggression in childhood seem to protect ADHD children against this last outcome.

BOX 11–2

An Externalizing Disorder: Attention-Deficit Hyperactivity Disorder

Only recently have internalizing disorders, such as childhood depression, received the attention given the externalizing disorders. Several reasons explain this neglect. First, internalizing disorders create little discomfort for parents and teachers, who are responsible for initiating referrals. Second, early follow-up studies suggested that children with internalizing disorders were not at risk for subsequent psychiatric problems. Third, some clinicians insisted that clinical depression simply did not, or could not, occur among children. Psychoanalysts believed that children did not have sufficient superego development to internalize the anger necessary for clinical depression (Cantwell, 1983). Others argued that depressive symptoms in childhood merely reflected temporary developmental phenomena (Lefkowitz & Burton, 1978). (See also our earlier discussion of learned helplessness in children.) Finally, other clinicians argued that depression exists among children, but manifests itself indirectly through other problems, such as aggression, school difficulties, and somatic complaints (Kaslow & Rehm, 1985). This concept of *masked depression* has now been discredited, primarily because it could not be falsified; any behavior could be a symptom of an underlying depression.

Childhood depression is similar to adult depression in terms of its emotional, cognitive, behavioral, and physical manifestations, although the specific symptom picture may differ depending on the child's developmental stage (Kaslow & Rehm, 1985). However, the debate still continues about whether the criteria for adult depression are appropriate for children. This problem is compounded by difficulty in assessing young children's feelings and beliefs.

Given its late start, research on childhood depression has had to play catch-up, simultaneously addressing all aspects of assessment, conceptualization, and treatment. Assessment has focused on the reliability and validity of children's self-reports (Saylor, Finch, Baskins, Furey, & Kelly, 1984), as well as the validation of behavioral observation measures (Kazdin, Esveldt-Dawson, Sherick, & Colbus, 1985). Conceptual issues include the question of whether adult models, such as learned helplessness, apply to childhood depression (Kaslow, Rehm, & Siegel, 1984). One study found that a depressive attributional style among children predicted depressive symptoms 6 months later, suggesting that it may be a risk factor for depression (Seligman et al., 1984).

Similar to adult depression, treatment of childhood depression has focused on antidepressant medication and cognitive-behavioral approaches. Medication is effective with depressed children, although it is less likely to be prescribed for children. However, unlike adult depression, evidence for the effectiveness of cognitive-behavioral approaches is still lacking for children. As Braswell and Kendall (1988, p. 193) conclude, "The development and evaluation of cognitive-behavioral treatments for children experiencing anxiety, depression, and other types of internalizing symptomatology lags far behind the existing work with adults experiencing these disorders." This conclusion applies to all aspects of childhood depression.

BOX 11–3
An Internalizing Disorder: Childhood Depression

puters have no problem identifying the relationships among multiple symptoms.

A second strength of empirical classification systems is their quantitative approach to decision making. Objective, operational rules can be generated to define inclusion and exclusion criteria for specific syndromes, based on large-scale normative investigations. For example, Achenbach and Edelbrock (1981) collected data from 1,300 parents of nonreferred children ranging in age from 4 to 16. The authors calculated the means and standard deviations for several factors for children of different ages and both sexes. With such information, a child's score on a specific dimension can be compared to children of the same age and sex. For example, Figure 11–2 presents a profile of a boy's scores on the mother version of the Child Behavior Checklist (CBCL). Scores falling above the dotted line occur in less than 2% of nonreferred boys that age and can be considered especially problematic. This type of profile resembles those generated by the MMPI, and offers many of the same diagnostic features.

A final strength of the empirical approach is that it allows evaluation of differing perspectives on childhood disorders. It is common practice to collect rating scales from both teachers and mothers and, to a lesser degree, from fathers. Factor analyses of these separate ratings indicate that the derived dimensions usually differ. Certain behaviors are more salient in some situations than others, and the different factors that result reflect these differences. For example, teachers may be less aware of delinquency problems than mothers, but the converse may be true for issues of social popularity.

A major problem with the empirical approach relates to the data used in the analyses. Most factor analytic studies employ parent or teacher ratings. Although clinicians' judgments can also be factor analyzed (Milich, Loney, & Landau, 1982), it is much easier to collect the large number of ratings needed for the factor analyses from parents and teachers. Thus,

most of the conclusions about the dimensions underlying childhood disorders have been based on symptoms as seen by parents and teachers. These persons offer a valuable perspective on childhood problems, but there are several problems with relying exclusively on their perceptions.

First, as noted earlier, parental ratings may be biased by personal factors, such as depression, that have little to do with the child's behavior. Second, parents and teachers have limited opportunities to observe certain behaviors (e.g., teacher ratings may not yield a delinquency factor since teachers do not routinely observe such behaviors). Third, the factor on which an item loads depends on how the parents and teachers interpret that item. For example, *DSM-IV* includes "often doesn't seem to listen" as an example of inattention. However, mothers associate this item more with oppositional or conduct disorders (Milich, Widiger, & Landau, 1987). They interpret "doesn't seem to listen" to mean active noncompliance rather than inattention.

Another problem with the empirical approach is that it does not identify rare disorders. For example, factor analytic studies almost never generate factors similar to the childhood disorder of infantile autism, yet almost all clinicians agree that this disorder does exist.

Clinically Derived Systems

The classification of adult disorders has relied on clinically derived systems, such as *DSM*. Clinical systems are developed by panels of experts who identify appropriate diagnostic categories, as well as the specific symptoms most typical of each disorder. These experts rely on their clinical experience with a variety of disorders, as well as their reading of the research literature, to arrive at an agreed-upon classification system. Even if experts observe similar patients and read the same empirical reports, they still do not always agree on the diagnostic criteria for a given disorder.

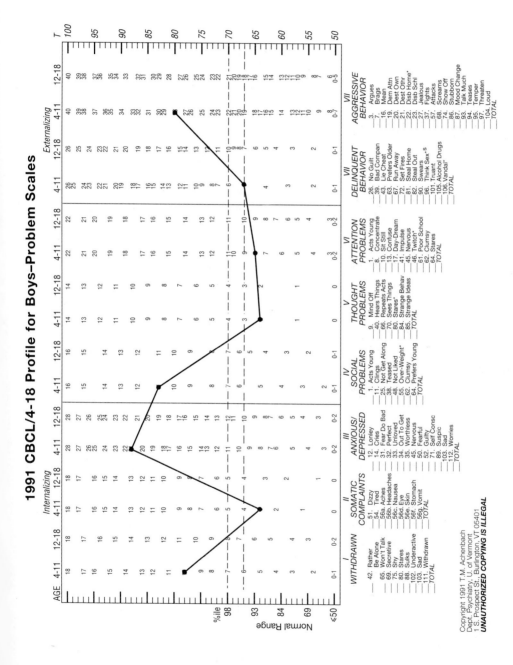

FIGURE 11–2 An example of a profile from the 1991 Child Behavior Checklist (CBCL). The CBCL contains scales for two age groups: 4–11 and 12–18. This profile is typical of what would be obtained for a 6-year-old boy having problems with aggression, peer difficulties, and depression. Adopted from Achenbach (1991).

Thus, reaching a consensus on these decisions often involves compromise, just as legislators must amend proposed legislation to produce a bill that will receive sufficient support.

Clinicians and researchers interested in childhood disorders have had mixed responses to the way in which these disorders have been classified in the various *DSM* systems that have appeared over recent years. Many felt satisfaction that childhood problems were finally recognized as unique disorders warranting clinical attention. Others questioned whether the revisions were a step forward or backward in terms of classifying child-

FIGURE 11–3

A Comparison of the Diagnostic Criteria for *DSM-II*, *DSM-III*, and *DSM-III-R* for Childhood Hyperactivity

DSM-II: Hyperkinetic Reaction of Childhood (or Adolescence)[a]

This disorder is characterized by overactivity, restlessness, distractibility, and short attention span, especially in young children; the behavior usually diminishes in adolescence.

If this behavior is caused by organic brain damage, it should be diagnosed under the appropriate non-psychotic *organic brain syndrome* (q.v.).

DSM-III: Attention Deficit Disorder with Hyperactivity[b]

A. *Inattention. At least three of the following:*

1. Often fails to finish things he or she starts
2. Often doesn't seem to listen
3. Easily distracted
4. Has difficulty concentrating on schoolwork or other tasks requiring sustained attention
5. Has difficulty sticking to a play activity

B. *Impulsivity. At least three of the following:*

1. Often acts before thinking
2. Shifts excessively from one activity to another

3. Has difficulty organizing work (this not being due to cognitive impairment)
4. Needs a lot of supervision
5. Frequently calls out in class
6. Has difficulty awaiting turn in games or group situations

C. *Hyperactivity. At least two of the following:*

1. Excessively runs about or climbs on things
2. Has difficulty sitting still or fidgets excessively
3. Has difficulty staying seated
4. Moves about excessively during sleep
5. Is always "on the go" or acts as if "driven by a motor"

D. *Onset before the age of seven.*

E. *Duration of at least six months.*

F. Not due to schizophrenia, affective disorder, or severe or profound mental retardation.

DSM-III-R: Attention-Deficit Hyperactivity Disorder[c]

Note: Consider a criterion met only if the behavior is considerably more frequent than that of most people of the same mental age.

hood disorders (Rutter & Shaffer, 1980). In this section we examine *DSM-III* and *DSM-III-R* classifications of childhood disorders, focusing on their improvements over the earlier versions, as well as their shortcomings. (*DSM-IV* appeared so recently and has been in use for such a short time that it is difficult to judge

how it will be received among clinicians and researchers.)

One improvement was greater breadth of coverage; the more recent versions had over four times as many childhood categories as did *DSM-II* (Bemporad & Schwab, 1986). The categories reflected five domains of function-

FIGURE 11–3
Continued

A. A disturbance of at least six months during which at least eight of the following are present:

1. often fidgets with hands or feet or squirms in seat (in adolescents, may be limited to subjective feelings of restlessness)

2. has difficulty remaining seated when required to do so

3. is easily distracted by extraneous stimuli

4. has difficulty awaiting turn in games or group situations

5. often blurts out answers to questions before they have been completed

6. has difficulty following through on instructions from others (not due to oppositional behavior or failure of comprehension), e.g., fails to finish chores

7. has difficulty sustaining attention in tasks or play activities

8. often shifts from one uncompleted activity to another

9. has difficulty playing quietly

10. often talks excessively

11. often interrupts or intrudes on others, e.g., butts into other children's games

12. often does not seem to listen to what is being said to him or her

13. often loses things necessary for tasks or activities at school or at home (e.g., toys, pencils, books, assignments)

14. often engages in physically dangerous activities without considering possible consequences (not for the purpose of thrill-seeking), e.g., runs into street without looking

Note: The above items are listed in descending order of discriminating power based on data from a national field trial for the *DSM-III-R* criteria for Disruptive Behavior Disorders.

B. Onset before the age of seven.

C. Does not meet the criteria for a Pervasive Developmental Disorder.

The three sets of diagnostic criteria highlight the changes in the child categories from *DSM-II* to *DSM-III-R*. Note especially the increased specificity of the symptoms from *DSM-II* to *DSM-III*.
[a]Source: American Psychiatric Association (1968)
[b]Source: American Psychiatric Association (1980)
[c]Source: American Psychiatric Association (1987)

ing: intellectual problems (e.g., mental retardation), behavioral problems (e.g., conduct disorders), emotional problems (e.g., anxiety disorders), physical problems (e.g., enuresis), and developmental problems (e.g., autism). On the other hand, some clinicians criticized this increased breadth of coverage as ". . . an over-reaching effort" (Garmezy, 1978, p. 4). They argued that disorders such as mental retardation and learning disabilities, which are included in both *DSM-III* and *DSM-III-R,* are educational problems rather than psychiatric disorders and therefore should not be included in a psychiatric classification system (Rutter & Shaffer, 1980). Finally, some psychologists feared this broad coverage was an attempt by psychiatrists to assume control of problems outside their expertise (Garmezy, 1978).

A second improvement of *DSM-III* and *DSM-III-R* was their use of operational criteria to define disorders. Figure 11–3 compares the diagnostic criteria of *DSM-II, DSM-III,* and *DSM-III-R* for hyperactivity. Whereas *DSM-II* contained one sentence listing the possible symptoms of the disorder, *DSM-III* included explicit diagnostic criteria about the number and types of specific symptoms necessary to fulfill each symptom category. *DSM-III-R* no longer distinguished among the three core features of inattention, impulsivity, and overactivity. Instead, it required a threshold level of symptoms. The latest versions offer information about onset and duration of the disorder, as well as exclusionary criteria. Finally, contrary to *DSM-II, DSM-III* and *DSM-III-R* did not consider possible etiology of the disorder as a criterion, an approach that even critics of the revised versions applaud (Rutter & Shaffer, 1980). Likewise, *DSM-IV* does not consider etiology as a criterion for the diagnosis. Its list of criteria is organized around two core features of the disorder—problems with inattention and symptoms of hyperactivity-impulsivity. This organization essentially represents a compromise between the three-feature emphasis of *DSM-III* and the undivided list of symptoms presented in *DSM-III-R.*

Any of the DSM classification systems still fall short of using fully operational criteria. They do not specify how to measure criterion behaviors, and terms such as *often* and *easily* are used without guidance about the severity of problems they represent. Similarly, no rationale is given for placement of some behaviors in the specific symptom categories (e.g., "needs a lot of supervision" under impulsivity).

The primary reason for operational criteria is to increase reliability of diagnostic categories (Cantwell, 1980). However, *DSM-III* failed to achieve this goal. The child categories in *DSM-III* exhibit lower levels of interrater reliability than do the adult disorders (Appendix F of *DSM-III*), and some studies even found *DSM-III* to be no more reliable than *DSM-II* (Mezzich, Mezzich, & Coffman, 1985). Generally, the broader diagnostic categories (e.g., conduct disorders) have acceptable reliabilities, but the finer distinctions often come up short.

A major goal of the more recent *DSM* systems was to introduce a developmental framework to the classification of the childhood disorders (Cantwell, 1980). Unfortunately, in *DSM-III* and *DSM-III-R,* the only consistent developmental data offered are age of onset and course of the disorder. The criteria are not adjusted to reflect developmental differences for any disorder.

ASSESSMENT

Clinical assessment of childhood and adult disorders share several features. Both are concerned with reliability, validity, and utility. In addition, many of the same assessment procedures are used with children and adults (e.g., interviewing, intelligence testing). Nevertheless, there are important differences between child and adult assessment questions (see Figure 11–4). These differences involve the issues of referral, developmental considerations, mandatory school attendance, and social/familial factors discussed at the beginning of this

1. Why is this child being referred for help at this time?

2. Are there differences between the parents, or between the parents and teachers, in how they perceive this child?

3. Is the child having academic or behavior problems in school?

4. Is the child having problems at home, either with parents or siblings?

5. Are there family factors (e.g., marital discord) that may exacerbate the problem?

6. How does the child get along with his or her peers? Does he or she make social overtures? Are they accepted or are they rejected?

7. Does the child acknowledge that he or she has a problem; what symptoms are admitted?

8. How does the child feel about the referral? What are the child's explanations for the referral problem?

9. Is this a long-standing problem or a stage through which the child is going?

FIGURE 11–4

Questions Routinely Addressed in the Assessment of Children

chapter. These issues influence our understanding of childhood disorders, and they determine the evaluation questions that are addressed and the data we collect, as the following examples demonstrate:

1. *Referral issues:* Because parents and teachers refer children for mental health services, paramount attention is given to information supplied by these adults. This information comes primarily from behavioral rating scales and clinical interviews.

2. *Developmental considerations:* Children's cognitive maturation limits the utility of their self-report data. For example, limitations in memory may produce unreliable self-reports while concrete thinking may undermine the use of projective testing. Thus, these assessment procedures, which are a standard part of the adult battery, have less utility in assessing children.

3. *Mandatory school attendance:* The majority of child referrals pertain to school-based problems. Thus, clinical assessment of children routinely includes an evaluation of school performance, including teacher reports of behavior as well as intelligence and achievement testing.

4. *Social/familial factors:* Children's emotional and behavioral states depend, in part, on their family life. Therefore, assessment of children will include measures of the child's behavior within the family (e.g., observations of mother–child interactions), as well as assessment of parental functioning (e.g., maternal depression, marital discord).

Because of the unique aspects of childhood disorders, assessment of children requires multiple assessment methods and multiple sources of information (Achenbach, 1988). A standard assessment battery for children includes behavioral rating scales, structured observations, clinical interviews, intelligence and achievement testing, and family assessment. The sources of data include parents, teachers, peers, and the children themselves. We briefly review each of these assessment procedures in the following sections.

Behavior Rating Scales

Behavior rating scales are inexpensive and easy to administer. Because they do not require professional training, they represent the only assessment procedure that does not require involvement of the clinician. The forms can be completed and returned in advance of a clinic appointment so the information can be evaluated before the formal assessment begins, or parents can complete the forms while they are in the waiting room. Recent versions of the Child Behavior Checklist (CBCL; Achenbach & Edelbrock, 1981) have computer scoring procedures to further minimize clinicians' time investment.

Standard rating scales cover most childhood behavior problems, so clinicians can obtain an overview of the child's functioning, including externalizing and internalizing problems, as well as social relations and school functioning. In addition, rating scales such as the CBCL have large-scale normative data that allow the child's problems to be evaluated relative to children of the same age and gender. Finally, because they are easy to administer, rating scales are excellent for repeated assessments, such as monitoring the effectiveness of an ongoing intervention. They also allow standardized collection of follow-up data after families have moved and are no longer accessible to the clinician.

In addition to these practical issues, it is necessary to evaluate the reliability and validity of rating scales. These data are encouraging. The most frequently used instruments show high test-retest reliability and good validity (Achenbach, 1988). For example, scores on the Conners (1973) 10-item Teacher Rating Scale differentiate ADHD children from children with other behavior problems, as well as ADHD children on medication from those on placebo. These ratings can even detect behavioral changes associated with different dosages of medication (Ross & Ross, 1982).

What are the limitations of behavior rating scales? First, ratings are subject to the information-processing biases we discussed earlier, as well as idiosyncratic characteristics of the rater (Cairns & Green, 1979). Parents' tolerance, their desire to make their child look "good" or "bad," and mothers' moods, all can influence ratings (Webster-Stratton, 1988).

A second limitation is that ratings represent global impressions of children's behavior. Raters tend to discount situational factors that may be responsible for the child's behavior. Instead, they focus on overall impressions of relatively stable characteristics of the child (Cairns & Green, 1979). Although such global information may be helpful in diagnosing a child's problems, it gives little information about factors that may elicit or maintain the behavior.

Clinical Interviews

Clinical interviews are crucial for assessment of childhood disorders. The clinician will usually interview the parents, as well as the referred child. However, the goals of the parent and child interviews differ. When interviewing the parents, the clinician has the following goals in mind (Achenbach, 1988):

1. Establish rapport so the parents will reveal personal information about the child and the family. The parents may later become the focus of therapy (see Box 11–8), so it is important for the clinician to establish a therapeutic alliance, even though the child is the initially identified client;

2. Obtain specific details about the child's problem (What is it? When does it occur? How do the parents and siblings respond?). Interviews allow the clinician to follow up rating scale responses by obtaining specific examples of problematic behaviors and situations.

3. Chart the course of the problem (When did it start? Did anything occur that triggered the problem? Has it been a continuous problem or does it come and go?).

4. Gather a developmental history of the child, including information on major developmental milestones, transition periods (e.g., starting school), and factors that may have disrupted normal development (e.g., hospitalizations, divorce).

5. Explore family factors that may exacerbate the child's problem. These factors might include

marital discord, sibling rivalry, and parental psychiatric problems. If both parents are being interviewed, clinicians will evaluate the degree to which the parents agree about the child's problems, how they developed, and the parents' resources to deal with the problems (e.g., ability to supervise the child).

When interviewing parents, clinicians must remember several limitations. First, human memory is fallible, especially for parents who are describing previous problems in their child's life. Second, parents do not have a normative basis for judging the appropriateness of their child's behavior. Third, parents' own emotional problems may distort their responses to the interview. Finally, parents may be motivated to present their child in either a positive or negative light (e.g., evaluations in custody battles or for school placement services).

Clinicians do not usually rely on interviews with the referred child for determining degree of behavioral symptomatology or making a diagnosis. Child interviews, especially with children under the age of 10, have low retest reliabilities. As one study concluded, ". . . our findings suggest that symptoms reported by young children should not be taken at face value for purposes of diagnosis, treatment selection, or treatment evaluation" (Edelbrock, Costello, Dulcan, Kalas, & Conover, 1985, p. 273). The reliability of child interviews increases with age of the child, so that adolescents are as reliable as parents in reporting their symptomatology. In fact, with increasing age of the child, the reliability of the parental reports decreases as the reliability of the child responses increases.

Because children can offer valuable information about themselves and their social environment (La Greca, 1990; Mash & Terdal, 1988), child interviews have several distinct goals.

1. As with parent interviews, the clinician must first establish rapport with the child. Children often do not know why they are being evaluated and may have misunderstood what the parents told them about the evaluation. Often, the parents do not tell the child anything about the clinic visit, or they present misleading information (e.g., you are going to the doctor's office). It is important that the clinician corrects misconceptions the child may have.

2. The clinician needs to evaluate the child's understanding of the referral problems; does the child feel he or she has a problem, and if so, what accounts for these difficulties?

3. Clinicians may evaluate the explanations a child gives for behavior to determine the attributional style employed. For example, does the child make hostile attributions in response to presumed threats (see Box 11–4), or helpless attributions in response to failure (Diener & Dweck, 1978)?

4. There has been an increased interest in children's internalizing disorders, especially depression and anxiety, and children are the best informants when describing these internal feelings (fears, sadness, anxiety, anger, low self-esteem).

5. By observing the child during the interview, clinicians confirm impressions formed from the parent interview. They can assess the child's cognitive maturity, activity level, or degree of compliance (Edelbrock et al., 1985). However, such informal assessments have limited validity. For example, one study found that 80% of hyperactive children did not exhibit any signs of overactivity in the physician's office (Sleator & Ullmann, 1981).

Intelligence and Achievement Tests

If you only had one session to evaluate a child, your time would probably be best spent administering IQ and academic achievement (e.g., reading, math, spelling) tests. The following reasons justify this decision (Sattler, 1988):

1. Compared to any other test or interview procedure, IQ and achievement tests have the best normative data available, allowing for

Imagine the following scenario: You are a third grader eating lunch in a school cafeteria. You look away and the next thing you know, milk is spilt all over your tray. You look at the boy next to you and he is laughing. How would you explain the milk getting onto your tray?

According to Dodge (1986), there are important differences between how aggressive and nonaggressive children explain this ambiguous event. Nonaggressive children would assume it was done by accident, while aggressive children would claim it was done on purpose. This tendency of the aggressive children to assume hostile intent in ambiguous situations (a *hostile attributional bias*) perpetuates their aggressive behavior and exacerbates their social difficulties. By assuming hostile intent, aggressive children feel more justified in retaliating. However, peers see this retaliation as unjustified, given the event was accidental. This retaliation therefore reinforces the peers' belief that these children are inappropriately aggressive and should be avoided. Thus, a vicious cycle is created in which the aggressive children think their peers are out to get them. They respond to this perceived threat by retaliating, which increases the likelihood that they will continue to have social difficulties.

BOX 11-4
The Hostile Attributional Biases of Aggressive Children

precise statements about the child's functioning relative to other children of the same age.

2. Excellent reliability and validity data exist for both types of tests. IQ scores are the single best predictor of children's current and future academic and occupational functioning.

3. The majority of child referrals involve academic and/or behavioral difficulties in the classroom. It is necessary to determine what contribution learning problems, low intelligence, or inappropriate parent or teacher expectations may make to these problems (see Box 11–6).

4. These tests assess specific strengths and weaknesses in the child's academic and cognitive functioning (e.g., memory or visual-spatial deficits). This information is used to make recommendations concerning treatment, special school placement or remediation.

5. Testing gives the clinician a standardized situation in which to observe the child's activity level, ability to follow instructions, speed of responding, distractibility and attention span, friendliness, flexibility in thinking, anxiety, and the child's response to success and failure feedback.

Although intelligence and achievement testing are crucial components of the assessment battery, their limitations must be kept in mind (Sattler, 1988).

1. The test environment is artificial and may yield an inaccurate representation of the child's performance in the classroom. For example, test anxiety may impair performance for some children. With others (e.g., ADHD children), the structured nature of testing may improve performance, compared to functioning in the classroom.

2. IQ and achievement tests may be biased against minority children or children for whom English is a second language.

3. Too much credence can be given to a single IQ score, so that lowered expectations about a child's ability become self-fulfilling prophesies leading to poorer performance (Rosenthal & Rubin, 1978). Factors other than intelligence influence success in the classroom.

Probably no area regarding children's self-reports is as controversial as that of their eyewitness testimony in trials involving charges of physical and sexual abuse. The controversy centers on whether (a) children can accurately testify in the courtroom about abuse they have allegedly suffered or observed and (b) whether testifying in court might have a negative impact on children's psychological well-being (Saywitz, 1990).

Trials can be an unnerving experience for anyone, and they can be especially distressing for children. As Saywitz (1990, p. 330) describes the process, "When children come in contact with the [legal] system, they typically follow a path of repeated contacts with strangers, in strange situations, governed by a set of unfamiliar rules." In addition, children do not usually testify against strangers. In most cases, it is a parent who is charged with the abuse, a situation that generates conflicting pressure on the child. One or both parents may employ subtle suggestions or even outright coercion to alter the child's testimony, and it is not unusual for child witnesses to be told repeatedly that their testimony may result in the parent being sent to prison for a long time. Summit (1983) has described the *sexual abuse accommodation syndrome* to account for children's delayed disclosures, recantations, or other alterations in testimony that may result from these pressures.

Testifying in abuse cases can also be traumatic for children because they may not be believed. Historically, judges and juries have been skeptical of child witnesses. Most of their concerns focus on limitations in children's cognitive development that may impair their ability to testify accurately to the events that transpired. Specifically, they worry about children's ability to differentiate truth from fantasy, limitations on children's memory skills, and children's susceptibility to suggestion.

Although the debate about whether children are competent to offer testimony in abuse cases is far from resolved (Ceci & Bruck, 1987), both researchers and courts appear to be moving toward the conclusion that children's testimony, although not perfect, is "good enough" to be relied upon in the courtroom (Wrightsman, Nietzel, & Fortune, 1994). In other words, children's memory capacity may be less than adults, and they may not offer as many details in recalling events as adults do. However, the research also indicates that children are able to describe accurately the basic events that occurred. Further, when children do make errors in recall, they are likely to be errors of omission rather than errors of commission. That is, they are more likely to leave out information than to add erroneous events or details.

The tendency to accept children as witnesses has been accompanied by recognition that special procedures may be needed to ensure the accuracy of their testimony and to minimize the stress it may create. Thus, children sometimes testify in another room so that they do not have to confront the accused, or they may be allowed to demonstrate the alleged acts of abuse through puppets or other play materials. The development and evaluation of such procedures provide examples of the roles that clinical child psychologists have played, and will continue to play, in helping the courts balance the rights of the accused and the accuser.

BOX 11–5
Children's Eyewitness Testimony in Abuse Cases

Some clinicians consider learning disabilities to be the most common childhood disorder, while others question whether they are a disorder at all. Instead, they argue that learning disabled children experience achievement problems that we do not understand and cannot explain. This controversy results in part from the definition of this disorder, an area in which the federal government has become involved. Federal Public Law 94-142 (1977) guarantees that all handicapped children receive a free public education designed to meet their unique needs. According to the law,

> Children with special learning disabilities exhibit a disorder in one or more of the basic psychological processes involved in understanding or in using spoken or written language. . . . They do not include learning problems which are due primarily to visual, hearing, or motor handicaps, to mental retardation, emotional disturbance, or to environmental disadvantage. (Cited in Taylor, 1988, pp. 403–404)

This definition is vague, and many states have had to develop means of operationally defining learning disabilities to comply with the law. Most laws consist of three basic features. First, there must be a significant discrepancy between a child's potential and his or her actual performance. States have usually required a discrepancy between scores on an intelligence test and scores on achievement tests (e.g., obtaining a reading achievement score 1.5 standard deviations below the predicted level of performance). This part of the definition is easily operationalized, and many states have detailed guidelines indicating which tests to use and statistical formulas to determine whether a child's scores fall within the learning disabled category.

The final two features of the definition are more difficult. First, the child's deficit must be due to "basic psychological processes." These deficits must be inferred from the child's performance on tests. However, no tests exist that can offer reliable and valid assessments of such processing deficits (Wong, 1986). Thus, attention has shifted to the third feature of the definition—the exclusionary criteria. If we can rule out all obvious causes for the child's aptitude/achievement discrepancy, then we can assume the problem is due to a deficit in a basic psychological process. However, it is impossible to rule out many of these causes (e.g., emotional disturbance or educational disadvantage). The result is that many states, fearing litigation, have relied exclusively on a significant aptitude/achievement discrepancy to define learning disabilities. Such a definition is easily quantifiable and thus less subject to dispute.

Other issues complicate this field. For example, courts have limited the use of intelligence testing to place minority children in special classes. In addition, because federal law requires special services for those identified as learning disabled, local school boards and administrators have attempted to limit the number of children receiving this diagnosis (Wong, 1986). Finally, even among those who agree that learning disabilities exist, the many differences among children with this diagnosis produce disagreements about the identification of valid subgroups.

BOX 11–6
Problems in the Definition of Learning Disabilities

Projective Tests

Clinicians continue to employ the Rorschach and other projective tests specifically designed for children in their assessment batteries. These include story-telling procedures, such as the Children's Apperception Test (Bellak, 1954) and the Mutual Story-Telling Technique (Gardner, 1971), as well as drawing techniques (see Figure 11–5) such as the Draw-A-Person (Koppitz, 1968) and House-Tree-Person (Buck, 1948). Despite this, re-

FIGURE 11–5 An example of a drawing and interpretations from the House-Tree-Person technique. This drawing is from a 15-year-old male who was referred for motivational problems regarding his school performance, as well as rule violations resulting in frequent suspensions. The following are his spontaneous comments about the drawing, as well as his responses to inquiries (Q): "I just drew a house. It's standing alone" . . . (Q) "It's 50 years old." (Q) "Old people live in the house—two grandparents—and the kids live far away." (Q) "It wishes it could be kept up more." (Q) (No response to question about how the house feels.) (Q) "It's wintertime," The boy's therapist made the following interpretations of the drawing: Doesn't see his house as a place of/for psychological warmth. Feelings of frustration due to a restricting environment. Weak ego strength. Fantasy satisfactions prominent. Concern over interpersonal relationships. Perceives home as prison-like. Adapted from Cummings (1986).

search suggests that projective tests have little to offer to the valid assessment of children.

Little systematic research on use of projective tests with children has been undertaken, and many of the available studies are of such poor quality that findings are uninterpretable (Martin, 1988). Retest- and interrater reliabilities are often unacceptably low for tests such as the Rorschach and Draw-A-Person (Gelfand, Jenson, & Drew, 1982; Gittelman, 1980), and there is little evidence that the tests are valid— that they measure what they purport to measure (Gittelman, 1980). Finally, there is no evidence for the *incremental validity* of the projective tests. Even if they were found to be valid (e.g., aggression scores on the TAT predicting aggressive behavior), this same information could be obtained more readily through other means. Projective tests with children, "sometimes . . . tell us poorly something we already know" (Gittelman, 1980, p. 434).

Given this dismal track record, why do projective tests remain popular in the assessment of children? The answer may be that drawing people or telling stories are excellent means for children to express themselves. As Piaget (1962) pointed out, the nonverbal aspects of play allow children to create and understand their world, given their cognitive limitations. In discussing children's drawings, Goodenough (1931, p. 505) captured the sentiment of many child clinicians: "They [drawings] must be looked upon as a universal language of childhood whereby children of all races and cultures express their ideas of the world about them." The courts also recognize the importance of nonverbal means of expression for children—they routinely allow child witnesses to use anatomically correct dolls when describing incidents of sexual abuse (Haugaard & Reppucci, 1988). Similarly, clinicians who work with children know that, often, the best way to break the ice and build rapport is to ask the child to draw a picture or tell a story. However, the evidence does not support interpreting these pictures or stories for insights into the child's personality, or using them to predict behavior outside the testing situation.

Behavioral Observations

Behavioral observations are an integral part of the assessment of childhood disorders. Because children's problems usually occur in the home or school, observations in these settings give clinicians the opportunity to validate parent and teacher concerns expressed through rating scales and interviews. In addition, behavioral techniques have become the treatment of choice for many childhood disorders. Behavioral approaches require systematic observation of target behaviors, as well as the stimuli that elicit and the consequences that maintain them.

Clinical observations of children occur in one of three places: the home, the school, and the clinic. Patterson and his colleagues pioneered the development of a home observation system (see Chapter 6). Several steps were involved in building this system. First, they recorded the rate of noxious child behaviors (e.g., noncompliance, teasing, whining). Second, they compared the rates of appropriate and inappropriate behaviors between deviant and nonreferred children to discover the characteristics of disturbed family interactions. Third, they tried to isolate which parent or sibling behaviors elicited the noxious child responses. For example, an important finding was that "sib teases" was a powerful stimulus for deviant responses. Patterson and his colleagues then developed a theoretical model that described how children's aggressive behavior began and was maintained (see Box 11–1). They also developed an intervention program to alter disturbed familial interactions (see Box 11–8).

School observation systems focus primarily on classroom behavior (Abikoff et al., 1977), although occasionally playground behavior will be observed (Pelham & Bender, 1982). In the classroom, the observations have concentrated on behaviors associated with attention-deficit hyperactivity disorder.

Home and school observations allow a naturalistic assessment of the child's behavior. They provide real-world information that interviews and tests cannot. Unlike rating scales, which offer global impressions, observations allow fine-grained analyses of stimulus–behavior–consequences relationships (Cairns & Green, 1979). From such data, individually tailored treatment interventions can be developed.

Despite these benefits, many factors discourage clinicians from undertaking home and school observations. First, they are expensive. Besides the time needed to obtain reliable observations, there is the added expense of travel time. In addition, if estimates of interrater reliability are desired, a second observer is needed. Further, home observations usually require visits during the evening, when the entire family is present. Even if paraprofessionals serve as observers, it is still a very expensive and time-consuming process.

Another problem with home observations is that they can create an unnatural environment, undermining one of their intended primary benefits. Patterson's (1982) system requires several ground rules for the observations (e.g., all of the family members in sight, no television or telephone conversations). Add to this the presence of one or more observers in a confined space, and the naturalism of the observation becomes more compromised.

To overcome these problems, clinicians often arrange for observations to be made in the clinic. There are several benefits to these observations (Mash & Barkley, 1986). Expense is diminished. Observations can be videotaped, so that trained observers are not needed precisely when a clinic family is seen. These videotapes can be evaluated at a later time or used for research purposes.

Standardized procedures can be employed. Home and school environments differ dramatically, making it difficult to compare behaviors across different children. Standardized clinic observations can structure procedures so that all children are exposed to identical situations. For example, clinic observation procedures simulating a classroom environment have been used to measure behaviors related to ADHD (Milich et al., 1982).

Social-Emotional and Familial Measures

Children live in several social worlds (e.g., home, school). Therefore, clinicians will often attempt to assess the impact of these multiple social environments on children. Unfortunately, many of these measures do not have the necessary reliability and validity data to justify their use (Achenbach, 1988). In addition, these measures are used unsystematically by clinicians, so they cannot be considered a standard part of an assessment battery.

To measure the child's social environment in school, the clinician can collect peer sociometric data (see Box 11–7). This is a very reliable and valid procedure, but it is difficult to implement. In addition, ethical concerns have been raised about this procedure (Hayvren & Hymel, 1984). Therefore, clinicians have turned to other means of obtaining relevant data, including teacher ratings (Greenwood, Walker, Todd, & Hops, 1979), and children's self-reports of their social anxiety (La Greca, Dandes, Wick, Shaw, & Stone, 1988), loneliness (Asher & Wheeler, 1985) and social goals (Renshaw & Asher, 1983).

The assessment of the family's social environment has a long and controversial history (Jacob & Tennenbaum, 1988). Early work was guided by the belief that faulty parental communications produced child psychopathology (Mishler & Waxler, 1968). This view was replaced by one that saw parent–child interactions as reciprocal in nature (Bell & Harper, 1977), and the primary assessment procedure involved observations of parent–child interactions (Patterson, 1982). Recently, there has been renewed interest in familial communication patterns (Alexander & Parsons, 1982; Foster & Robin, 1988). For example, parental communications that are critical, hostile, or emotionally overinvolved may exacerbate a child's psychopathology (Brown, Bone, Dalison, & Wing, 1966), even if they do not play a causal role. The next decade should see a further refinement of these assessment procedures.

The last 3 decades have seen a renewed clinical interest in the assessment of children's peer relations (Landau & Milich, 1990). If you think back to your own childhood you will better appreciate how children's social and emotional development are intimately related to how effectively they get along with their peers (Hartup, 1983). Puttalaz and Gottman (1983, p. 13) provide a poignant example (with spelling errors present) of this relationship.

> I can hide. i am a little boy. i don't have friends but i have som friends but win i wait at the busstop som people haet me and some like me . . . one day i was moving so people would not tesz me in ne mor but again they tesz me.

There are other reasons for the clinical interest in children's peer relations. Many developmental skills (e.g., sharing equally) are learned best through peer interactions. In addition, disturbed peer relations are one of the strongest predictors of later behavioral and psychiatric problems. In one follow-up study, negative evaluations made by third-grade peers predicted later psychiatric disturbance better than any other measure collected (Cowen, Pederson, Babigian, Izzo, & Trost, 1973).

Although mothers, teachers, or the individual child can offer information about peer relations, the child's peer group offers the most reliable and valid data. This procedure, known as *peer sociometics*, consists of asking children to evaluate their classmates. Two simple questions ("Whom do you like?" "Whom don't you like?") are sufficient. From these two questions a child receives two scores: a *popularity* index, which is the total number of classmates indicating they like this child; and a *rejection* index, which is the total number who dislike this child. Isolated children (low on both popularity and rejection) differ in important ways from rejected (low on popularity and high on rejection) and popular (high on popularity, low on rejection) children. Isolated children make few social overtures, whereas both rejected and popular children initiate many social interactions. However, the overtures of the popular children are successful, whereas those of the rejected children are rebuffed.

This interest in children's peer relations coincides with the development of social skills training programs to help children who are having peer difficulties. These interventions have proven to be more effective in helping isolated than rejected children (Krehbiel & Milich, 1986), although efforts to develop programs for the socially rejected child are continuing (Bierman, Miller, & Stabb, 1987).

BOX 11–7
Assessment of Children's Peer Relations

Regardless of their theoretical orientation, clinicians recognize that parental factors, such as marital discord, maternal depression, or paternal substance abuse, can influence a child's functioning, as well as determine the focus of intervention strategies. Thus, measures of these characteristics are becoming a standard part of the assessment of referred children.

TREATMENT

Treatment of childhood disorders differs in important ways from interventions for adults. Therapy with children poses a special challenge for clinicians because children do not self-evaluate or self-report effectively. Because children do not refer themselves for help, their

Because many childhood behavioral disorders reflect problems in the home, behavioral parent training procedures focus on systematically teaching parents how to manage their children better (Polster & Dangel, 1984). A variety of approaches have been proposed, although those developed by Patterson (1975) and Forehand and McMahon (1981) are the most widely implemented. Whatever the specific orientation, all behavioral parent training procedures include the following five steps.

1. *Pinpoint the target behavior.* Parents must define the problem behavior explicitly so that it can be measured. Often, parents present vague or global complaints about their child's behavior ("He won't mind," "He's got a bad attitude") that make it difficult for the clinician to design the intervention. Parents are encouraged to identify inappropriate behaviors to be decreased as well as appropriate behaviors to be increased.

2. *Chart the target behavior.* Parents are then asked to keep records of the target behaviors. There are two purposes to this data collection. First, these data offer a baseline against which subsequent interventions can be assessed. Second, merely by observing their child's behavior more systematically, parents begin to note the stimuli and consequences that elicit or reinforce the undesirable behavior ("When-

ever his sister teases him he hits her and she starts crying").

3. *Develop an intervention.* Behavioral parent training employs an operant perspective, which assumes that behaviors are elicited by the stimuli that precede them and maintained by the consequences that follow. Separating where two children sit at the dinner table is an example of altering antecedents to decrease the rate of fighting during dinner. Giving the children extra TV time for each 5 minutes of dinner that passes without fighting is an example of altering the consequences to modify the same behavior.

4. *Assess the intervention.* Throughout the intervention, the parents keep records of the target behaviors. These data indicate whether the intervention is effective or whether changes need to be made. For example, if a shaping procedure is employed, the data indicate when the parents should increase the behavior criterion required to earn reinforcement.

5. *Fade out the program.* The ultimate goal of all behavioral interventions is that naturally occurring antecedents and consequences will elicit and maintain the desired behaviors. Therefore, if an intervention is successful, the therapist will help the parents fade out the program so that the treatment gains can be maintained after the treatment has ended.

BOX 11–8
Behavioral Parent Training

client status and ensuing therapy depend on parent motivation and cooperation. The significance of these and related issues is apparent as we examine the major therapies for childhood disorders.

1. Psychoanalytic therapy. For many reasons, children are usually not appropriate

candidates for traditional psychoanalytic therapies (Johnson, Rasbury, & Siegel, 1986). Children are seldom motivated for an intensive therapy experience. In addition, they are unlikely to understand the need for introspection and the active role they must play in therapy. Their immature language and cognitive development may hamper verbal reasoning and abstract problem solving, thus limiting their ability to profit from interpretations.[6] Also, psychoanalysis requires established defenses and a relatively stable personality structure. Because of changes associated with development, children do not exhibit the consistency in personality required for this therapeutic approach. Finally, many childhood problems appear to result from environmental forces (e.g., school, parents) rather than intrapsychic conflicts.

For these reasons, traditional psychoanalytic therapy is rarely undertaken with children (Johnson et al., 1986). Variations on usual procedures—such as using play rather than verbalizations as the communication medium—have been introduced. Different treatment goals—helping the child successfully pass through a crucial stage of development rather than focusing on prior fixations—have also been pursued (Gelfand & Peterson, 1985). Nevertheless, both research (Achenbach, 1982) and clinical practice (Johnson et al., 1986) suggest that psychoanalytic therapies are not well suited for children.

2. Play therapy. Other interventions focus on helping children resolve their conflicts without relying on verbal skills. A popular intervention, especially in the 1950s and 1960s, was play therapy. Modeled after Rogers's client-centered therapy, play therapy allows children to express their inner concerns. Instead of expressing these feelings verbally, however, the child uses play materials, such as puppets, dolls, and clay. The play therapist conveys an accepting and empathic atmosphere in which children can feel secure to explore their feelings (Axline, 1976). The therapist does not direct the child's actions or conversations, but instead follows the child's lead.

Play therapy is still employed today, and although its popularity has waned, it remains an attractive intervention to clinical child psychologists for several reasons. First, as we discussed earlier, play encourages children to express their feelings and concerns. Second, the therapy's optimistic orientation about individuals' potential for self-actualization appeals to many clinicians. Third, the treatment is relatively easy to understand and implement (Johnson et al., 1986).

3. Behavior therapy. In the last 3 decades, behavior therapies, especially operant procedures, have been the most frequently employed interventions for childhood problems. These interventions often involve training parents (Dangel & Polster, 1984) or teachers (O'Leary & O'Leary, 1972) in behavior management procedures (see Box 11–8). The rationale behind these interventions is that environmental antecedents and consequences maintain problem behaviors. Parents and teachers are in a better position than therapists to manipulate the relevant environmental stimuli and consequences to modify the child's behavior.

Several reasons account for behavioral interventions becoming the treatment of choice for many childhood disorders. First, the community mental health movement of the 1960s emphasized preventive interventions, including training nonprofessionals as change agents. Behaviorally oriented parent and teacher training programs fit well with these goals. Second, there was dissatisfaction with traditional therapeutic approaches, especially for children with externalizing disorders or children with severe psychopathology (e.g., autism). Operant procedures gave parents and teachers concrete solutions for previously intractable child behavior problems. Third, in the late 1970s the federal government began to stress accountability in the treatment of handicapped children in school. Public Law 94–142 requires Individual Education Plans (IEPs) for all special education children. For

---

[6]It is ironic that in the case of Little Hans, which was so important in the development of Freud's theory, Freud talked only to the father, never to Hans.

every identified handicapped child, schools must develop an IEP, indicating what the treatment goals are for the child, how they are to be obtained, and whether they are reached. Behavioral interventions, with their clearly defined targets and treatment strategies, as well as their systematic data collection, lend themselves to such an accounting.

Behavior therapies have documented effectiveness for a wide range of childhood disorders, especially for externalizing disorders involving aggression (Patterson, 1976), stealing (Reid & Patterson, 1976), and hyperactivity (Pelham & Murphy, 1986). Behavioral procedures have also proven effective for a number of internalizing problems, including bedwetting (Doleys, 1983), fears (Morris & Kratochwill, 1983), and school avoidance (Last & Francis, 1988). Finally, operant approaches are the treatment of choice for the most severely disturbed children (e.g., mentally retarded, autistic).

Behavioral interventions are cost effective; most interventions can be completed in less than 20 sessions. In addition, by training parents and teachers as change agents in the natural environment, clinicians increase the likelihood that positive changes will be maintained after therapy is terminated, and that positive effects may generalize to other, nonreferred children (siblings, classmates).

Finally, the theory behind the behavioral approach is easy to understand, and the treatments are relatively straightforward to implement (Weisz, Weiss, Alicke, & Klotz, 1987). In addition, the quantifiable nature of the therapy permits parents and teachers to document, and thereby appreciate, improvements in the child's behavior.

Despite its popularity and proven effectiveness, the behavioral approach has limitations. It does not help everyone. Patterson (1982), in his treatment of aggressive children, reports that he is unable to help at least one-third of the families he treats. These families often are suffering serious parental psychopathology (e.g., maternal depression) or powerful environmental stressors (e.g., divorce). Be-

haviorally oriented therapists have recently recognized that simple parent training may not be sufficient for *insular* families (those with few social resources), and that a multimodal approach, addressing parental as well as child problems, may be necessary (Griest et al., 1982).

A second limitation of the behavioral approach is that although generalization of effects is a goal of the intervention, documenting such effects is difficult. Initial successes often are not maintained, or successes in one setting (e.g., the school) do not carry over to another setting (e.g., the home). Behavior therapists have struggled with this problem for some time (Stokes & Baer, 1977), but solutions remain elusive.

Finally, many childhood problems do not lend themselves to behavioral interventions. Depression and some anxiety disorders are prime examples. For these disorders clinicians are now turning to cognitive-behavioral interventions. Similarly, although behavioral approaches are useful for abusive parents (Reid, 1985) and marital problems (Epstein & Baucom, 1989), they may neglect the emotional problems of children who are victims of abuse or divorce.

Cognitive-Behavioral Interventions

Among adults, the cognitive-behavioral approach has focused on the treatment of anxiety disorders and depression, where it has had significant success (see Chapter 9). In contrast, with children cognitive-behavioral approaches have been applied almost exclusively to the externalizing disorders, especially impulsivity (Meichenbaum & Goodman, 1971), hyperactivity (Abikoff & Gittelman, 1985), and conduct disorders (Kazdin, Esveldt-Dawson, French, & Unis, 1987; Lochman, 1992).

The cognitive-behavioral approach to externalizing disorders involves training children to improve their problem-solving behaviors and to engage in careful planning before responding (Johnson et al., 1986). The rationale behind these procedures is that children with behavior disorders are cognitively delayed. Therefore, they need to learn to make the internal assessments and self-statements that adults routinely make before responding. In other words, they need to bring their inappropriate behavior under cognitive (rational) control. Several techniques are employed in these interventions, including:

1. Problem-solving training (Spivak & Shure, 1974). The child is taught to assess the problem (Billy just teased me); generate possible responses (ignore him, hit him, discuss the problem with him); and evaluate consequences of the alternative responses (if I hit him, I may get in trouble).

2. Impulse control training. This approach involves training hyperactive or impulsive children to slow down and evaluate response alternatives before responding—to "stop, look, and listen" (Douglas, 1972).

3. Perspective taking. Children are trained to evaluate the effects of their misbehavior (e.g., stealing, lying) on others, and to be sensitive to the thoughts and feelings of others. This approach is frequently employed with delinquent (Chandler, 1973) and aggressive (Kazdin et al., 1987) children.

Initially, cognitive-behavioral approaches were heralded as a clinical breakthrough for treatment of externalizing disorders. Training children to think, and to think more appropriately, before they act was assumed to produce the treatment generalization missing with traditional operant interventions. Whereas operant approaches require an adult (parent, teacher) to elicit and reinforce the desired behavior, cognitive interventions train children to carry this change strategy within themselves. Thus, the effects of the intervention should generalize to situations where adults were not present. Unfortunately, this initial optimism has not always been justified. A review of cognitive behavioral interventions

with ADHD children led to the conclusion that, "The expectation that the development of internalized self-regulation skills would facilitate generalization and maintenance has not been realized" (Abikoff, 1985, p. 508). Although other reviews are less pessimistic (Dush, Hirt, & Shroeder, 1989), the general conclusion is that these interventions are not very effective with seriously disturbed children (Baer & Nietzel, 1990).

One promising lead comes from recent work by Kazdin and his colleagues, employing cognitive behavioral therapy to treat severely conduct disordered children (Kazdin et al., 1987; Kazdin, Bass, Siegel, & Thomas, 1989). In both studies, intensive problem-solving training (compared to social-relationship therapy) improved the children's behavior, as reported by parent and teacher ratings. Even more noteworthy, the significant improvements were maintained at 1-year follow-up. These studies are some of the first to document long-term beneficial effects with seriously disturbed children. They offer a promising treatment technique for what has proven to be a most intractable problem.

Biological Interventions

Drug treatment is not widely employed with childhood disorders. This pattern is very different from treatment of adults, for whom drugs like Valium and Xanax are among the most widely prescribed (Julien, 1988). In contrast, antianxiety drugs have not been widely used to treat childhood disorders (Campbell, Green, & Deutsch, 1985). Similarly, while antidepressants are widely used for adults, when prescribed for children it is for problems other than depression (bedwetting, school avoidance, hyperactivity). The medication most frequently used for children's problems is stimulant medication in the treatment of attention-deficit hyperactivity disorder (see Box 11–9). Hundreds of studies have examined the effectiveness of this medication.

Why are drug treatments used less frequently

The most common and controversial form of treatment for attention-deficit hyperactivity disordered children is stimulant medication (e.g., methylphenidate or Ritalin). As many as 1 million school-age children in this country are currently being treated with such medications for their behavior or learning problems. Hundreds of careful studies have repeatedly shown that stimulant medication dramatically improves the behavior of ADHD children: They remain seated longer, finish more academic work, answer more school items correctly, and have better social interactions with their peers, parents, and teachers. ADHD boys even attend better while playing baseball when on medication than on placebo (Pelham et al., 1990).

Despite widespread recognition by clinicians and researchers that stimulant medication is effective for ADHD children, controversy continues to surround its use. Newspaper articles and television news segments publicize this topic, and a number of lawsuits have been filed, claiming that stimulant medication is responsible for a variety of negative outcomes, including suicides and homicides.

Most professionals dismiss these claims as sensationalistic, but many questions about stimulant medication have not been resolved. For example, even though medication may produce behavioral improvements, it may also convey to the children the message that such improvements are out of their control, that they are entirely due to the medication. If children conclude this is the case, they may exert less effort on tasks when they are not medicated.

A recent study examined the impact of medication on ADHD boys' self-evaluations, self-esteem, and mood, as well as on the explanations they offer for their improved performance (Pelham et al., 1992). On medication days, as compared to placebo days, boys were significantly more likely to report positive behavioral changes, including increased compliance and fewer rule violations. In addition, on medication days, as compared to placebo days, they reported feeling happier and liking themselves better. Finally, when asked to account for their good performance on medication days, the boys were more likely to say that they tried hard, rather than that the pill helped them.

These results indicate that ADHD children recognize the behavioral improvements due to medication, but they are willing to take credit for these improvements by indicating that they were trying harder on those days. In addition, these behavioral improvements made the children feel happier and like themselves better. Thus, the medication did not have a detrimental impact on the children's self-esteem or emotional state.

BOX 11–9
Stimulant Medication Treatment of ADHD Children

with children than with adults? First, psychoactive drugs are potentially dangerous, and because children are still developing, they are especially vulnerable to adverse effects. For example, stimulants decrease appetite, a side-effect that could adversely affect children's growth. Second, the adult disorders for which drug treatments are most frequently used (schizophrenia, depression, mania) do not usually appear until after puberty. Finally, development of interventions for child disorders has consistently lagged behind those designed for adults; the use of psychoactive drugs is one further example.

Besides medication, the major biological intervention for children involves dietary modifications. Food substances, such as food additives (Feingold, 1975) and refined sugar

(Charlton-Seifert, Stratton, & Williams, 1980) have been blamed for causing or exacerbating childhood behavior problems, especially hyperactivity. Reducing or even eliminating these substances from a child's diet has been proposed as an intervention for these disorders. However, carefully controlled studies suggest that these food substances have little or no impact on children's behavior (Harley et al., 1978; Milich, Wolraich, & Lindgren, 1986). Nevertheless, many parents and teachers continue to be convinced that eating a candy bar makes children overactive and out of control.

An Integrative Approach to Child Therapy

A variety of treatment approaches have been employed to treat a large range of childhood disorders. Although these interventions achieve short-term effectiveness (Casey & Berman, 1985), most serious childhood problems (attention-deficit hyperactivity disorder, conduct disorder, and delinquency) have proven resistant to long-term improvement (Pelham & Murphy, 1986; Zigler, Taussig, & Black, 1992).

Why have psychological interventions so consistently failed to demonstrate long-term gains? First, interventions for serious childhood disorders tend to be reactive rather than proactive. Regardless of whether the problem is delinquency, school failure, or child abuse, there is a tendency to wait until the problem is well established before intervening. A more effective approach would be to identify at-risk children and then try to intervene before the problem has become entrenched and resistant to treatment.

The second problem with childhood treatment, as currently conceptualized, is that it is not comprehensive enough. Zigler et al. (1992) argue that serious childhood disorders such as delinquency are caused by a multitude of economic, social, and psychological factors, and that for interventions to be effective, they must address as many of these factors as possible. Current treatments usually address only one or two causal factors. In delinquency, for example, a large number of causal factors have been identified, including the child's temperament, inhibitory control problems, faulty or abusive parenting, school failure, poverty, marital discord, and peer difficulties (Zigler et al., 1992). A comprehensive treatment package for this disorder would need to include treatments that focus on many, if not all, of these factors. It might consist of medication to decrease the child's inhibitory problems, academic tutoring to lessen the risk of school failure, training in problem solving to improve peer interactions, anger control training to decrease inappropriate responding to frustration, marital therapy to decrease discord in the home, parent training to improve the disciplinary procedures, and early childhood education to decrease the adverse effects of poverty.

The third factor limiting the long-term effectiveness of psychosocial treatments for serious childhood disorders is their relatively brief nature. For example, the typical parent training program lasts from 8 to 20 weeks. However, as Kazdin (1985) persuasively argues, chronic disorders need continual treatment. Using an analogy from medicine, he notes that a physician treating diabetes would not discontinue insulin treatment after diabetes comes under control. Similarly, psychosocial interventions should not be stopped once the problem shows initial improvement.

Serious childhood disorders require early, comprehensive, and long-term interventions. Unfortunately, the expense of psychosocial treatments makes it difficult to fund early prevention strategies, even though the initial expenditures would save money in the long run. Insurance companies generally do not reimburse the cost of treating children who are at risk for problems. Similarly, while governments will spend $40,000 a year to incarcerate a juvenile offender (Zigler et al., 1992), they have tended to refuse to spend a fraction of that amount on programs to prevent delinquent behavior.

This short-sighted perspective may be changing, however. The federal government has recently awarded a major grant to fund a pilot project designed to evaluate the long-term effectiveness of comprehensive treatments for at-risk conduct-disordered children. These treatments include many of the procedures described earlier (the intervention even pays for telephones to be installed in the homes of the children to help decrease their mothers' social isolation). If this pilot project proves effective in decreasing delinquency risk among these children, the government may decide to support such programs, even though they require funding mechanisms that are not tied to the usual service-provider system.

THE FUTURE OF CLINICAL CHILD PSYCHOLOGY

Predicting the future is a hazardous business. However, the history of clinical child psychology reflects that advancements have lagged several decades behind comparable developments in the adult area. Therefore, in order to forecast the future of clinical child psychology, we can examine recent adult developments. Based on this analysis, we predict the following areas will see dramatic growth in the near future (see also Kazdin, 1989): child neuropsychology, pediatric psychology, and cognitive behavioral interventions, especially for internalizing disorders.

In child neuropsychology, recent advancements in the assessment of adult functioning are now being applied in the evaluation of children (Hynd, Snow, & Becker, 1986). Health psychologists are developing programs to help children cope with chronic illnesses, such as diabetes (Delameter, 1986). During the late 1980s, clinicians recognized that children can be infected with the AIDS virus, producing profound social and psychological problems for the children and their families.

Interventions are needed to help children cope with the prolonged hospitalization, social stigma, and physical disabilities associated with this disease (Task Force on Pediatric AIDS, 1989). In the area of cognitive behavior therapy, several studies suggest that children at risk for learned helplessness can be trained to make more appropriate attributions, so that they persist to a greater degree in the face of failure experiences (Licht & Kistner, 1986).

Societal changes also will shape the future of clinical child psychology (Kazdin, 1989). For example, the dramatic rise in rates of divorce and remarriage will increase the need to help children cope with these significant stressors (Hetherington & Arasteh, 1988). Teenage pregnancy is epidemic, and the children of teenage mothers are at greater risk for behavior and learning problems (Furstenberg, Brooks-Gunn & Chase-Lansdale, 1989). Similarly, the increased number of mothers who are working outside the home is producing a generation of "latchkey" children, for whom effective child-care strategies need to be developed (Peterson, 1989). Finally, promising leads are now being explored in the prevention of drug and alcohol use among children (Christiansen, Smith, Roehling, & Goldman, 1989).

In this chapter we have discussed many factors that make the study of child behavior disorders unique. A clinician who works with children needs to be knowledgeable about children's social and cognitive development, family functioning, educational and social functioning in the school, academic remediation, and the various therapies available for children. Advancements in clinical child psychology have lagged behind progress in the assessment and treatment of adult disorders. This gap is especially unfortunate, because if we are ever to fulfill the goal of primary prevention, identifying and assisting at-risk children before problems emerge will become a necessity.

CHAPTER 12

Biological Factors
in
Clinical Psychology

Some of the questions first addressed by ancient philosophers were "What is mind?" "What is body?" and "Are mind and body related? If so, how?" This *mind-body problem* has been an issue psychology has struggled with since the field's beginning. This struggle may amuse those who take for granted that both mind and body exist and constantly affect each other.

In the history of medicine, cures of illnesses and improvement in physical functioning have often been attributed to the effects of positive thinking, faith, and a belief that a given medical treatment will work. This placebo effect is so well-known that physicians often present medical treatments to patients so as to maximize expectancies that the treatments will be effective. In psychology, the notion of psychosomatic disorders (physical diseases that have psychological causes) also has a long history, reflecting clinicians' observations that emotional problems sometimes lead to physical illnesses.

As a result of this history and research about the ways in which psychological factors can affect physical health, clinical psychologists believe that mind and body interact in a reciprocal fashion. In fact, anyone familiar with the topics in this chapter would find it difficult to deny the mutual influences between psychological and biological processes. As we indicated in Chapter 2, however, some clinicians fear that too much attention to biological variables amounts to a form of reductionism that ultimately will rob psychology of its status as an independent science. On the other hand, advocates of strict biochemical causation seem to believe that psychological explanations are little more than camouflaged ignorance that will be replaced by biological or physical explanations as soon as they become available.

In this chapter and the next, we discuss three aspects of clinical psychology—health psychology, biological factors in psychopathology, and neuropsychology—that demonstrate how important it is for psychologists to study relationships between psychological and biological factors. We have selected these three topics because they have been some of clinical psychology's best "growth stocks" in the past 20 years. New research discoveries and expanding professional roles for clinicians have increasingly attracted psychologists to these areas. In this chapter we discuss health psychology (along with its close companion, behavioral medicine) and biological factors as causes of psychopathology. In Chapter 13, we concentrate on the field of neuropsychology.

HEALTH PSYCHOLOGY

Health psychology is a specialty that emerged in the late 1970s and has enjoyed rapid growth ever since. It now has its own division in APA (Division 38) and its own journal (*Health Psychology*). Health psychology research is also often published in the *Journal of Behavioral Medicine* and *Psychological Medicine.* Related professional organizations include the Society of Behavioral Medicine and the American Psychosomatic Society. Many clinical psychology training programs now include a "track" that specializes in the training of health psychologists, and some programs have developed health psychology as their major focus.

Joseph Matarazzo, a pioneer of the field, defined health psychology as "the collective activities of psychologists who work as scientists, health professionals and teachers in the interdisciplinary field of behavioral medicine" (Matarazzo & Carmody, 1983, p. 658). Health psychologists are involved in the treatment and prevention of illness, the promotion and maintenance of health, the study of etiology and diagnosis of illness, and the improvement of systems of health care. A closely related field is *behavioral medicine,* which involves the integration of behavioral science and biomedical knowledge into an interdisciplinary science focused on the understanding and treatment of all types of medical disorders.

Health psychology and behavioral medicine follow a *biopsychosocial* model which holds that physical illness is the result of biological, psychological, and social disruptions.

They study how psychological conditions and behavioral processes are linked to illness and good health. For example, two important risk factors in the development of certain cancers are faulty diet and cigarette smoking, both of which are behavioral patterns that health psychologists study and attempt to modify in order to prevent some cancers.

In addition to studying how psychological and social factors contribute to diseases, health psychologists emphasize that concepts like illness and health are not just physiological conditions. Diseases are important primarily because they influence behavior. The behavioral outcomes of illnesses include symptoms and other experiences of dysfunction, a lowering of a patient's quality of life, and shortened life expectancy (Kaplan, 1990). As we will discuss shortly, behavior can also be a major contributor to some illnesses.

The history of health psychology has been traced from Hellenic scholars' attention to the mind–body problem to modern-day concerns about how to encourage healthy personal behavior and build health-supporting environments. Several books and chapters are available that review the research foundations and recent accomplishments of health psychology (Blechman & Brownell, 1986; Gross & Drabman, 1990; Rodin & Salovey, 1989).

In the remainder of this section, we discuss four examples of the topics that health psychologists study.

1. The effects of stress and stress coping on physical illness

2. The relationship between harmful or risky behaviors and health

3. The use of psychological techniques in the treatment or prevention of disease

4. The use of psychological techniques to increase patients' compliance with treatment methods

These four topics cover only some of the activities of health psychologists. The politics and economics of health care, the psychological adjustment of patients suffering chronic illness, and the search for disease-predisposing personality traits are other areas of study that are vital to health psychologists.

Effects of Stress on Health

Although there are many definitions of stress, one of the most influential is that it is an imbalance between the coping resources of an individual and the social, personal, and environmental threats perceived by that individual. These threats may be unpredictable, isolated events that are traumatic and will temporarily exceed the coping capacities of most people. Physical disasters are the prototype of this type of event, but financial reversals and educational failures are also examples. Other experiences are more predictable because they involve the milestone transitions that come with maturation and aging. Marriage, child rearing, starting school, occupational challenges, hospitalization, death of loved ones, and aging are examples. Even relatively minor events like having to wait in line or having your car stall in traffic can be stressful, especially when a number of such daily hassles accumulate in a short period of time.

One of the clearest explanations of how stress contributes to physical illness or psychological disorder is the following four-step model by Barbara Dohrenwend (1978):

1. Stressful life events occur. They may be introduced either by the environment (a person is laid off from work) or by the individual (inadequate job skills lead to unsatisfactory performance).

2. A transient stress reaction follows the stressful life event. Some temporary physical or psychological problems may occur as part of this transient reaction.

3. The transient stress reaction is mediated by environmental and psychological characteristics. Environmental mediators include material supports (wealth), material handicaps (poverty), so-

cial supports (advice from friends), and social handicaps (isolation). Psychological characteristics include cognitive abilities, self-esteem, social skills, and coping abilities and disabilities.

4. The transient stress reaction interacts with the moderators and proceeds to one of three outcomes. First, the moderators can nullify the impact of the event so that only the transient reaction is experienced. Second, supports may be so strong that the event is mastered and ultimately experienced as positive change. Finally, the transient reaction can persist and become a physical or psychopathological condition when environmental or psychological supports are inadequate buffers or when environmental hazards and/or psychological variables actually magnify stressful events.

To study the relationship between stress and illness, it is necessary to measure stress in an accurate way. Psychologists have tried to quantify stress in several ways. An early attempt was the Schedule of Recent Experiences (SRE), which was also entitled the Recent Life Changes Questionnaire (RLCQ; Rahe, 1975). The SRE (Amundson, Hart, & Holmes, 1986), which contains a list of 42 events involving health, family, personal, occupational, and financial matters, is summarized in Box 12–1. Subjects check the events that have happened to them in a particular period of time. Each event is given a weight based on the amount of adjustment needed to handle the events (1 = very little adjustment; 100 = maximal adjustment). These weights are summed to give an index of stress experienced in a given time period. The resulting Subjective Life Change Unit score has been found to be moderately correlated with a variety of illnesses (Holmes & Masuda, 1974; Marx, Garrity, & Bowers, 1975).

The RLCQ has been criticized on several grounds, and other researchers have developed their own instruments for measuring stress that differ in the ways they weight the occurrence of an event, the time periods surveyed, and the content of the events themselves. Zimmerman

In the Schedule of Recent Experiences (Amundson, Hart, & Holmes, 1986) subjects indicate which of 42 stressful events have happened to them in the past 6-, 12-, 24-, and 36-month periods. After subjects check the events that have occurred, the amount of adjustment each event requires is assigned a value on a 100-point scale. The stressful events are organized into five categories. Examples from each category are listed below.

A. Health
   A major change in eating habits
   A major change in sleepintg habits

B. Work
   Changed to a new line of work
   Experienced being fired from work
   Changed work hours or conditions

C. Home and family
   A change in family "get togethers"
   Death of a close friend
   A divorce
   Gaining a new family member

D. Personal and Social
   Sexual difficulties
   A minor violation of the law
   A vacation
   A major change in church activities

E. Financial
   Major business readjustment
   Foreclosure on a mortgage or loan
   Taking out a mortgage or loan for a major purchase, such as a home, business, property, etc.

BOX 12–1
Measuring Stress

(1983) reviews 18 different life event inventories, including the *Life Experiences Survey* (Sarason, Johnson, & Siegel, 1978), the *Interview Schedule for Events and Difficulties* (Brown & Harris, 1978), and the *Psychiatric Epidemiology Research Interview* (Dohrenwend, Krasnoff, Askenasy, & Dohrenwend, 1978).

Some researchers have concluded that stress should not be equated with the occurrence of major traumatic events, but should be examined in terms of chronic stress that involves "small" events occurring on a daily basis. One of the best-known of these chronic strain inventories is the Hassles Scale (Kanner, Coyne, Schaefer, & Lazarus, 1981).[1] On this scale subjects indicate how severely they have been hassled in the past month by events such

as "misplacing or losing things," "unexpected company," "auto maintenance," "too many meetings," and "filling out forms." Another approach to measuring stress involves examining the effects of specific life crises such as crime victimization (e.g., Burnam et al., 1988) on later adjustment. Extensive discussion of these methods and alternative ways of measuring stress can be found in Kessler, Price, and Wortman (1985), Dohrenwend and Dohrenwend (1981), and Thoits (1982).

How stress might contribute to illness is not clearly understood. There are several physiological reactions to stress (see Selye, 1956), including increased heart rate and blood pressure and greater gastrointestinal activity which, if sustained over long periods, can lead to illness. One mechanism that has been implicated recently is the immune system, the body's defense structure against disease-causing agents.

Certain stressors have been associated with temporarily lowered responsiveness of the im-

___
[1]A companion scale, the Uplifts Scale, consists of 135 events that can make a person feel good. Examples include "practicing your hobby," "buying clothes," and "being complimented."

mune system (Jemmott & Locke, 1984; Mc-Clelland, 1989), a condition known as *immuno-suppression,* which could make a person more susceptible to infectious diseases and other illnesses. For example, chronic stressors (e.g., taking care of a seriously ill relative) have been shown to lower immune system functioning, and even brief stressors like final-exam periods have been associated with a decline in the activity of immune system cells that fight viruses and tumors (Kiecolt-Glaser & Glaser, 1992). In one particularly interesting study of the relationship between stress and illness, researchers injected volunteer subjects with different cold viruses or a placebo and then measured the amount of stress experienced by the volunteers over a given time period (Cohen, Tyrell, & Smith, 1991). The results showed that the appearance of colds and infections was correlated with the amount of stress the subjects encountered.

Researchers have also begun to study whether psychological interventions aimed at countering stress can *enhance* the effectiveness of the body's immune system. Although initial results concerning relaxation training, hypnosis, and cognitive-behavior therapy are promising, the improvements tend to be small, and they have not yet been linked to reduced incidence or severity of illness (Kiecolt-Glaser & Glaser, 1992).

Other researchers question whether there is sufficient evidence to conclude that stress leads to illness. A correlation between stressful life events and symptoms can be explained in a number of ways. For example, many items on surveys of stressful life events involve illness; it is possible that the correlation between such surveys and measures of illness is because they simply contain identical items (Dohrenwend, Dohrenwend, Dodson, & Shrout, 1984). Another possibility is that people who are ill are more likely to remember negative life events from the past than are people who are well; if this is the case, the stress–illness correlation can be understood as an instance in which illness affects recall.

In addition, it is important to remember that most people who experience stress in its various forms do not become ill as a result. Although many methodological improvements have been made in the years since the first life events scales, most research indicates that the overall relationship between stress and illness onset is relatively small. This discovery has led to a search for variables that might help explain how people are protected from the assumed health-harming effects of stress. Among several *vulnerability* or *resistance* factors (Kessler et al., 1985), two variables, social support and coping strategies, have sparked the most interest.

Social Support

Social support has been defined in many ways (Schradle & Dougher, 1985). Cobb (1976) described it as experiences leading individuals to believe that they are cared for, loved, esteemed, and members of a network of communication and mutual obligation. Social support involves more than the mere presence of others. It provides relationships in which emotional support, feedback, cognitive guidance, tangible assistance, and shared values are exchanged between people.

Several studies have shown that the relationship between stress and illness is greater among individuals who perceive lower levels of social support in their lives (e.g., Mitchell, Billings, & Moos, 1982). Why is this the case? There are several possible answers, depending on how social support is measured (Cohen & Wills, 1985). The most popular explanation is that social support acts as a *buffer* against stress. The buffer model claims that social support enables people under high stress to neutralize the harmful effects of stress in any number of ways. By serving as an additional resource in a person's attempts at managing stressful problems, social support bolsters the efforts at coping (Thoits, 1986). Even more important than actual aid is the belief by recipients that others care for and value them. This *perception* of social support enhances self-esteem and may also increase feelings of self-efficacy about handling stress (Heller, Swindle, & Dusenbury, 1986). Another model, sometimes termed the *direct effect model,* holds that social support is helpful regardless of whether stressful events are experienced because there is a general benefit to being embedded in supportive relationships that manifests itself in better health. A third possibility is that high levels of social support, good health, and low levels of stress reflect the influence of some underlying characteristic like *social competence,* which has positive effects on many areas of functioning. Of course, some combination of all three models may operate as well. What does seem clear is that lack of social support, particularly emotional support, does put people at higher risk for both physical and psychological illnesses (Cohen & Wills, 1985; Kessler et al., 1985) and even mortality (House, Robbins, & Metzner, 1982).

Despite general advantages, attempts at social supportiveness do not always produce positive results. Social ties can create conflicts if recipients feel that helping efforts are so one-sided that they must be indebted to or dependent on others. If a recipient is not able to reciprocate helping efforts, she or he may feel disadvantaged in future interactions with the donor. In other instances, potential helpers may behave in misguided ways (giving too much advice or becoming upset when the advice is not followed) that lead the recipient to feel incompetent or rejected (Wortman & Lehman, 1985).

Coping Strategies

Coping refers to people's cognitive, emotional, and behavioral efforts at modifying, tolerating, or eliminating stressors that threaten them (Folkman & Lazarus, 1980; Pearlin & Schooler, 1978). People vary in their preferences for how to cope with stress. Some try to solve a problem directly; others attempt to change their way of thinking about a problem

to make it less stressful; still others concentrate on managing the emotional upsets that a stressor causes (Lazarus, 1993). The same person may employ different coping strategies to deal with different types of stress or may combine various coping approaches to reduce stress (see Box 12–2). Effective coping can lessen some effects of stress, but its success depends on several factors, including the type of stress to be reduced. For example, coping through denial (e.g., viewing a failed exam as being unimportant) appears to be an effective response to short-term stress but an ineffective strategy with chronic stress (Mullen & Suls, 1982).

A major question in this area is whether particular types of stress are better managed by problem-focused or emotion-focused coping efforts (Auerbach, 1989). For example, the multiple stresses of painful illnesses such as arthritis appear to be coped with better by people who actively seek information about the stressors so they can anticipate or control them (Revenson & Felton, 1989). On the other hand, when faced with a truly uncontrollable condition, emotion-focused coping, including ventilation of feelings but also occasional distraction from the trauma, might be an effective strategy (Meyerowitz, Heinrich, & Schag, 1983).

In line with these concepts, psychologists have developed interventions that bolster the social support and coping skills of stressed populations. Common examples include providing accurate information and emotional support before upcoming surgery (Johnson, 1984), cognitive restructuring in which clients learn to "inoculate" themselves against stress by developing new ways to think about it (Meichenbaum, 1975), and developing special social supports for people facing a crisis or frightening event (e.g., Cutrona, 1984).

Although there are many ways a psychologist can intervene to reduce stress, informational, behavioral, and cognitive-behavioral techniques appear especially well suited to building the social skills, behavioral compe-

Accurate measurement of the different ways people cope with stress is difficult because coping itself is a complex process consisting of several dimensions. Coping processes may change from one situation to another depending on how a person appraises stressful episodes; they may even change as a single stressful situation unfolds, leading to different appraisals of which coping options may be most effective. Two research groups at the University of California (Berkeley) and at the State University of New York (Stony Brook) have developed comprehensive instruments to measure the ways people cope with stress.

At Berkeley, Richard Lazarus and his colleague, Susan Folkman (Folkman & Lazarus, 1980), developed a Ways of Coping checklist that consists of 68 items that describe the methods that 100 middle-aged adults used to cope with stressful events in their daily lives. Folkman and Lazarus (1980) divided these items into two broad categories: *problem-focused* and *emotion-focused* coping. Examples of problem-focused strategies are "made a plan of action and followed it," and "got the person responsible to change his or her mind." Emotion-focused items involve steps like "look for the silver lining," "try to forget the whole thing," and "accept sympathy and understanding from someone."

The 100 respondents reported a total of 1332 stressful episodes. In 98% of these events, respondents used *both* problem-focused and emotion-focused coping. Furthermore, there was considerable variability in most persons' relative preference for one type of coping strategy versus the other. The typical person emphasized problem-solving approaches to some stresses but preferred emotional support approaches to other stresses. Problem-focused coping was favored for stress related to work,

but emotion-focused coping was used more often when the stress involved health. Men tended to use problem-focused coping more often than women in certain areas, but men and women did not differ in their use of emotion-focused coping.

At Stony Brook, Arthur Stone and John Neale initially tried to assess daily coping skills using an objective checklist like Folkman and Lazarus (1980), but gave up this method when they found that people were not consistent in their definitions and endorsements of different coping behaviors. Therefore, they developed an alternative instrument that asked subjects open-ended questions about how they handled problems (Stone & Neale, 1984). The format of the instrument was as follows: (a) Eight coping styles were listed and given a one-sentence summary (the eight categories were distraction, situation redefinition, direct action, catharsis, acceptance, seeking social support, relaxation, and religion); (b) subjects then indicated whether they had used each of the styles of coping to handle a problem on a given day; and (c) if they responded positively, subjects described in their own words the particular thoughts or actions they had used for each category of coping.

Despite differences in their methodologies, Folkman and Lazarus (1980) and Stone and Neale (1984) reached similar conclusions about coping. Men tended to use direct action a little more and distraction, catharsis and seeking social support a little less than women. The way a given problem was appraised or defined was significantly related to the ways people tried to cope with it. Finally, most people are flexible copers; although they may have one favorite coping style, they combine it with other strategies as their view of a problem requires.

BOX 12–2
Measuring Coping Skills

tencies, and cognitive strategies that can help mitigate stress. Psychologists can also learn much from the personal buffers and support systems that people fashion for themselves to cope with stress. Respect for the natural abilities of ordinary people to help one another (Lenrow & Cowden, 1980) is an important perspective for professionals to maintain.

Effects of Harmful Behavior on Health

The seven most important personal health problems facing Americans today are use of tobacco, faulty diet, excessive use of alcohol, accidents, suicidal behavior, violence, and unsafe sex practices. They are health problems because they involve behaviors that make people more likely to suffer various illnesses or death. For example, two of this country's leading killers, cardiovascular disease and cancer, have been strongly linked to smoking, overeating, lack of exercise, faulty diet, and alcoholism.

A behavior, personal characteristic, or environmental factor that increases a person's chances of developing an illness is called a *risk factor.* Each of the aforementioned health problems involves a human behavior, suggesting that psychologists could play a major role in promoting healthy behaviors and preventing disease or injury (VandenBos, DeLeon, & Belar, 1991).

In addition to behavioral risk factors, there are also biological (e.g., genetic defects), social (e.g., poverty), and environmental (unsafe cars or dangerous buildings) risk factors. Each of these factors suggests possible interventions by psychologists that might decrease or even prevent their effects (Lorion, 1991; Stokols, 1992).

Although not all researchers agree on the importance of behavioral risk factors in the etiology of specific illnesses (Angell, 1985), the current consensus is that many harmful behaviors do account for variations in rates of serious physical diseases (Krantz, Grunberg, & Baum, 1985). Conversely, certain behaviors or lifestyles promote better physical health. For example, Breslow (1979) reported that people who eat breakfast regularly, rarely snack between meals, exercise regularly, do not smoke, get 7 to 8 hours of sleep per day, and do not use alcohol excessively live on the average 11 years longer than people who practice none of these behaviors.

Treatments aimed at modifying behavioral risk factors can take many forms. Most interventions produce short-term improvements, but maintaining these changes for a long enough period to promote a healthier life is more difficult. For example, smoking is now considered to be the number one public health problem in America. Smoking cessation techniques produce short-term reductions in cigarette smoking, but more than 50% of smokers resume their habit (Lichtenstein & Glasgow, 1992). A similar picture exists for treatment of obesity (Brownell & Wadden, 1992). Although behavior modification appears to be the most effective psychological intervention for obesity, maintenance of weight loss and learning new eating behaviors are major difficulties for most people.

One psychological risk factor that has attracted a lot of attention in the past 10 years is the Type A behavior pattern (Friedman & Rosenman, 1974). Matthews (1982) listed the following characteristics of Type A behavior: (a) explosive, accelerated speech; (b) a heightened pace of living; (c) impatience with slowness; (d) trying to perform more than one activity at a time; (e) preoccupation with self; (f) dissatisfaction with life; (g) evaluation of one's accomplishments in terms of numbers; (h) competitiveness; and (i) free-floating hostility. In contrast to Type A persons, Type B persons are more relaxed and feel less time pressure. They appear less competitive, controlling, and hostile.

Friedman and Rosenman (1974) referred to Type A behavior as "hurry sickness" (examples: you become enraged at cars in front of you that go too slowly; you get angry and fidgety if you must wait in line), and believed that it was the most important behavioral risk factor in the development of coronary heart disease. However, current thinking among health psychologists is that Type A behavior is but one of several possibly interrelated risk factors that are difficult to disentangle from one another (e.g., the person who is always on the go is also less likely to maintain a balanced diet).

There are three basic procedures for measuring Type A behavior. *The Structured Interview* (Rosenman, 1978) consists of about 25 questions that tap how a person responds to frustrating situations and even presents some of the questions in a slow, halting manner designed to provoke Type A behavior. The *Jenkins Activity Survey* (Jenkins, Zyzanski, & Rosenman, 1971) contains approximately 50 questions that assess competitiveness, impatience, and job involvement (sample item: Do you ever have trouble finding time to get your hair cut or styled?) The *Framingham Type A Scale* (Haynes, Levine, Scotch, Feinleib, & Kannel, 1978) is a 10-item self-report measure that concentrates on competitiveness, time urgency, and sense of job pressure.

The different measures of Type A behavior do not agree well with one another in the classification of the Type A pattern (Matthews & Haynes, 1986), a serious complication for summarizing the research about this behavior. Although the Jenkins instrument is used frequently because of its convenience, the Structured Interview appears to be the superior measure because it is more strongly related to illness measures (Matthews, 1988).

Researchers do not agree on whether Type A behavior is a significant risk factor for coronary heart disease (Friedman & Booth-Kewley, 1988; Matthews, 1988). The different answers depend on whether cross-sectional versus prospective studies are emphasized and on whether initially healthy or high-risk subjects are included in the studies.

Not all components of Type A behavior are harmful. Some investigators suggest that it is the negative emotions associated with the Type A pattern that are the major carriers of risk. Hostility has often been singled out as the major culprit among the negative emotions, particularly for the person who broods rather than expresses hostility openly. Others are less certain that research has isolated hostility as the uniquely dangerous component in Type A behavior and suggest that all the elements (e.g., being overly invested in one self and living at a very fast pace) continue to be considered (Thoresen & Powell, 1992).

Recent evidence consistently suggests that reduction of Type A behavior improves the health and well-being of subjects. Several therapy techniques and treatment programs have been developed to reduce Type A behavior and, in turn, lower the risks for heart disease. Among the many techniques available, relaxation training, self-monitoring, and training in coping skills appear to have the largest effects on Type A behavior. Interventions that change Type A behavior also have beneficial effects on some physiological processes presumed to be at the root of disease. Reduced cholesterol, lowered systolic blood pressure, and slowed heart rate have all been discovered in association with reductions in Type A behavior.

Our Type A readers may have become anxious about their status, and are obsessing about whether they can change their behavior—by tonight, if possible. Box 12–3 contains several suggestions for reducing Type A behavior. Type A readers should read Box 12–3—slowly, please.

Health psychologists also have collaborated with physicians, health educators, and other professionals to develop large-scale programs that try to prevent illnesses by reducing behavioral risk factors in specified populations. Changes in diet, exercise, smoking and drinking habits, and Type A behavior are the most common examples, but other interventions, such as teaching children about healthy lifestyles, have been advocated (Matarazzo & Carmody, 1983). Box 12–4 summarizes large-scale illness-prevention projects.

Is it the case that "once a Type A always a Type A" or can a Type A person slow down, loosen up, and learn to relax? Can an A become more like a B? Friedman and Rosenman (1974) believed that Type A behavior can be changed if a person modifies his or her behavior at each of three levels: (a) philosophical guidelines, (b) reengineering the day, and (c) drills. A few examples of the changes Friedman and Rosenman (1974) recommended for each of those levels are presented below.

Philosophical Guidelines

1. Make an honest self-appraisal of your strengths and weaknesses so that you will be less dependent on the opinions of others and less driven to please them.
2. Develop broader interests in activities outside your career preoccupations—e.g., art, literature, making new friends.
3. Accept the fact that life consists of many unfinished processes, jobs, and events. Only some of these tasks will ever be finished no matter how compulsively you work at them.

Reengineering Your Day

1. Arrange your work environments so as to promote peace—e.g., schedule more time for appointments than you think they will require, keep a clean desk, don't be a slave to the telephone.
2. Talk less.
3. Reserve periods of time each week when you can be alone.

Drills

1. Go to a restaurant with a companion where you know you will have to wait in line to be served.
2. Whenever you go faster in your car to beat a red light at the intersection, punish yourself by circling the block and coming back to the same intersection.
3. Read books that demand patience and your full attention. For example, the prose of Proust and Faulkner moves at a pace that will force Type A persons to stop their tendency to skim read.

BOX 12-3
Can Type A Behavior Be Changed?

Psychological Interventions for Physical Diseases

Several psychological techniques, many of them drawn from behavior therapy, have been used to treat or prevent physical diseases. In some cases these methods constitute the primary treatment, but more often they are combined with medical procedures as part of an integrated treatment of illness. The success of these methods and the promise of new advances account in part for the rapid increase in the number of psychologists employed in hospitals and other health-care centers. In this section we highlight psychological treatments for cardiovascular diseases, gastrointestinal problems, pain, cancer, asthma, and acquired immune deficiency syndrome (AIDS). Extensive discussions of these methods can be found in Bellack, Hersen, and Kazdin (1990).

Cardiovascular Diseases

Coronary heart disease (CHD) and hypertension are two of the world's most lethal illnesses, claiming millions of lives each year.

Because illnesses like heart disease are so widespread and dangerous (cardiovascular diseases account for almost half the deaths in the United States); because population-wide prevention appears more cost effective than targeting just those people at high risk; and because large-scale programs might have positive side effects on other lifestyle changes, health psychologists have developed community-wide programs aimed at preventing heart disease through decreasing harmful habits such as smoking and promoting healthy habits such as regular exercise and good diet (Jeffery, 1988; Perry, Klepp, & Schultz, 1988).

Many different community-based prevention programs have been attempted. Some target a specific risk factor like obesity; others address several risk factors at the same time. The settings for implementing these programs also vary. Interventions in the workplace have become popular both because corporations believe they reduce the cost of health care and because occupational health promotion programs permit control and study of several motivational and environmental variables (Glasgow & Terborg, 1988). Mass media, correspondence, and agricultural extension programs have also been attempted.

A leading example of a community-based project aimed at preventing multiple risk factors associated with cardiovascular disease was the Stanford Heart Disease Prevention Program (SHDPP; Meyer, Nash, McAlister, Maccoby, & Farquhar, 1980).

Approximately 500 persons at high risk for heart disease were identified in three Northern California towns. In Community #1 (Watsonville), 56 subjects were assigned to a mass media campaign (TV and radio spots) that acquainted listeners with probable causes of heart disease and specific behaviors (smoking, diet, and exercise) that could reduce risk factors. One hundred and thirteen additional subjects in Watsonville received the same media packages plus "intensive instruction" involving face-to-face behaviorally oriented counseling about how to change diet, smoking habits, and exercise. In Community # 2 (Gilroy), 139 subjects received a comparable media intervention as the Watsonville participants. Community #3 (Tracy) subjects ($n = 136$) served as controls who received neither media nor intensive instructional intervention. Subjects were assessed at three annual follow-up surveys.

BOX 12–4
Illness Prevention in Communities

While surgery and medication are the most common treatments of these conditions, many patients have trouble tolerating these procedures. In addition, some persons may not currently have CHD or hypertension and are not receiving medical treatment, but because they are at risk for the diseases, they would benefit from preventive interventions. Several psychological treatments other than changing Type A behavior have been used to modify risk factors for cardiovascular diseases.

For example, because obesity is related to elevated blood pressure, maintaining a reasonable weight is an important goal in treatment of hypertension. Weight reduction can be achieved through a combination of behavior modification, low-calorie diets, relapse-prevention skills, and counseling about body-image distortions. As noted earlier, however, maintenance of weight loss remains an elusive goal in many cases (Brownell & Wadden, 1992). Lowered blood pressure can also result from biofeedback and relaxation methods aimed at reducing sympathetic nervous system activity (Agras,

All groups of treated subjects experienced reductions in the risk factors for cardiovascular disease plus an increase in their knowledge of behavioral factors that contribute to heart disease. On overall risk score reduction, greater and longer-lasting reductions occurred in the Watsonville group that received the mass media campaign combined with intensive instruction. For example, this group showed significantly greater reduction in smoking (a 50% cessation rate; a 51% reduction in cigarettes smoked per day) than any of the other groups. On other measures (e.g., increased physical exercise) there were no significant effects from intervention.

The Stanford investigators concluded that "intensive media plus face-to-face instruction had greater impact on cardiovascular disease risk and related knowledge and behavior than did the media only treatment or control." In addition, they found that the intensive instruction resulted in more durable changes in these factors over time.

The SHDPP has been subjected to several criticisms. A major difficulty was the high *attrition* or drop-out rate (around 25%), especially in the Watsonville intensive instruction group (e.g., when dropouts are considered in this group, its smoking cessation rate drops from 50 to 32%).

Other prominent examples of multiple-component prevention programs are the Multiple Risk Factor Intervention Trial (MRFIT, 1982) which attempted to lower blood pressure, smoking, and blood cholesterol in thousands of high-risk individuals; the North Karelia, Finland project (designed in the context of the international Know Your Body Program; Williams, Arnold, & Wynder, 1977); and the Minnesota Heart Health Program, a 5-year educational intervention targeting multiple heart disease risk factors (Blackburn et al., 1984). A special feature of these latter two programs is their attention to interventions for children and adolescents. Schools have been the primary setting for these interventions, which have concentrated on improving knowledge about health, changing peer norms about habits like cigarette smoking, and educating families about risk factors (Perry et al., 1988).

BOX 12–4
Continued

Taylor, Kraemer, Southam, & Schneider, 1987).

Because cardiovascular disease is less common among physically fit than among sedentary individuals, regular exercise has value in maintaining health. Unfortunately, most people do not adhere to a regular exercise program. Behavior modification techniques and social support programs have been shown to improve exercise adherence, though much work remains to be done on how best to promote enough regular exercise to have health benefits (Dubbert, 1992).

Gastrointestinal Problems

Included among these disorders are fecal incontinence, irritable bowel syndrome, inflammatory bowel disease, and repetitive vomiting among infants and retarded adults. Psychotherapy, stress management, and hypnosis have all proven to be effective in relieving symptoms of irritable bowel syndrome. Biofeedback and conditioning techniques which teach the patient to monitor and control internal sensations and reflexes are highly successful treatments for fecal incontinence and repetitive vomiting (Whitehead, 1992). Gastrointestinal problems are often symptoms of such chronic illnesses as cancer and diabetes; therefore, successful treatment methods are also useful in the management of these disorders.

Pain

Pain may be the single most common physical symptom experienced by medical patients (Turk & Rudy, 1990), so pain management is an important objective in many disorders. Psychologists have concentrated their pain research and treatment on three areas—chronic pain conditions, headaches, and rheumatoid arthritis. For headaches and chronic pain, biofeedback and relaxation training methods have a long record of success, and cognitive-behavioral techniques have also recently proved to be effective (Blanchard, 1992; Keefe, Dunsmore, & Burnett, 1992). Arthritic pain has generally been treated effectively via stress management and cognitive-behavioral therapy techniques (Young, 1992). These treatments also have some positive effects on the overall physical impairment associated with arthritis.

Cancer

Cancer strikes one of every three Americans. It remains one of this country's most lethal and frightening diseases. Psychological interventions have been applied to several aspects of the disease (Andersen, 1992), but two major goals are most prominent: helping patients overcome the negative side effects of chemotherapy, and encouraging coping skills that improve patients' quality of life and slow the progression of the disease.

Many drugs used to treat cancer cause severe nausea and vomiting. After several treatments, patients often become sick even before they are administered the drugs, an effect known as *anticipatory nausea*. This reaction in turn makes some patients reluctant to continue treatment. The common explanation for anticipatory nausea is that it is a conditioned response elicited by cues associated with the sights and smells of the hospital environment where the unconditioned stimulus (the chemotherapy) is delivered. Several behavior modification techniques, including systematic desensitization, biofeedback, and counterconditioning, have been used to reduce the severity of anticipatory nausea (Redd et al., 1987).

Cancer appears to progress more quickly in patients who feel hopeless and helpless about the illness (Taylor, 1983). Some researchers have described a passive, overly conforming, and repressed personality style as the *Type C* personality, which they suggest is associated with susceptibility to cancer and with poorer treatment outcomes. Although the evidence for Type C personality risk is not consistent, health psychologists often try to promote a higher quality of life for cancer patients by helping them (a) understand and confront the disease more actively, (b) cope more effectively with the stress of cancer, and (c) develop emotionally supportive relationships in which they can disclose their fears about the disease (Andersen, 1992).

Asthma

Asthma attacks appear to be related to periods of stress in some patients. In addition, because many patients are children, family dynamics are another important variable in the management of the disease. Relaxation-based treatments produce modest improvements in the anxiety problems related to asthma. Many family interventions are aimed at helping parents and children manage the child's illness better. They are taught to monitor the "triggers" of an attack as well as its early warning signs and symptoms. In addition, if the family can learn more effective coping behaviors (e.g., controlling harmful environmental agents, helping the child develop alternative breathing strategies, closely adhering to medical advice), the illness can be managed more safely. This goal is important because the number of deaths resulting from asthma is increasing in the United States (Lehrer, Sargunaraj, & Hochron, 1992).

AIDS

AIDS has become a world-wide disease epidemic. Between 1981 and 1992, more than 100,000 Americans died from AIDS, and by 1990 the incidence of HIV infection was as high as 25% of the population in some areas of Africa (Kelly & Murphy, 1992).

The main focus for psychologists working on the problems of AIDS is to reduce the risky behaviors known to contribute to HIV infection. These behaviors include unprotected sexual contact and sharing or reusing needles among intravenous drug users. Whether through individual contacts aimed at improving a high-risk person's knowledge about AIDS and promoting safer behavior on his or her part, or through mass communication efforts aimed at changing community attitudes, existing research suggests that moderate reductions in risk behavior and increased knowledge about AIDS can be achieved in targeted groups (gay men and intravenous drug users). However, relapse to risky behaviors is fairly common, and some subgroups of gays (e.g., racial minorities and adolescents) have not made large changes in their risk behavior.

A second target for health psychologists working on AIDS is to help patients with the disease cope with the adverse emotional and mental health consequences that often accompany it. A similar goal is to counsel family and friends of AIDS victims about the grief, fear, and stigmatization that they may feel in responding to a loved one with AIDS.

Improving Compliance With Treatment

Whether a given treatment for an illness is effective depends first on its being the correct treatment, and second on the patient's following through with the treatment. The extent to which patients adhere to the medical advice they have been given is called *compliance*.[2]

Estimates indicate that noncompliance occurs in up to 50% of patients prescribed certain medications and even more often for treatments that involve changes in lifestyle (Haynes, 1982). Physicians cite patients' noncompliance as a major source of dissatisfaction in their work, and noncompliance has been called "the best documented but least understood health-related behavior" (Becker & Maiman, 1975). Health psychologists are interested in the causes of noncompliance and in interventions that could improve compliance.

Causes of Noncompliance

The chief cause of noncompliance appears to be communication problems between physicians and patients. Patients frequently do not understand what physicians tell them about their illnesses or their treatments. As a result, they are confused about what they should do or they forget what they have been told. For example, Ley, Bradshaw, Eaves, and Walker (1973) found that only 5 minutes after seeing their physician, general-practice patients had forgotten 50% of what their doctor had told them.

The emotional aspects of patient–physician communications also are correlated with compliance. A common pattern of troubled communication involves patient antagonism toward the physician, accompanied by physician withdrawal from the patient. As an example, one study found a relationship between mothers' satisfaction with their interactions with pediatricians and their compliance with treatment (Francis, Korsch, & Morris, 1969). Dissatisfaction stemmed from the mothers not having ex-

---

[2]Health psychologists often prefer to use the term *adherence* rather than compliance because compliance suggests a passive process of obedience while adherence implies voluntary action by the individual (Rodin & Salovey, 1989).

pectations met, not feeling that the physician related warmly to them, and not receiving adequate explanations of illnesses.

A second source of noncompliance lies in the characteristics of treatment itself. Regimens that are more complex, that require greater changes in lifestyle, and that are of longer duration tend to impede compliance. Treatments that are painful or that produce negative side effects such as nausea or changes in appearance will lead to lower adherence.

Third, behavioral and environmental factors may reduce compliance. Researchers who emphasize these factors analyze compliance in operant terms; that is, compliance is a function of (a) environmental antecedents that prompt action by the patient and (b) consequences that follow that action. For example, Zifferblatt (1975) outlined a four-step functional analysis of noncompliance in which patients (a) keep a daily diary of antecedent cues, attending thoughts, and behavioral consequences of compliant behavior like taking medication; (b) arrange clear and compelling cues to trigger the prescribed behavior; (c) provide desirable reinforcers for the behavior; and (d) assess the success of the program through the continued use of the diary and redesign of the triggering cues and the consequences as necessary. Zifferblatt suggests the most effective cues and consequences for compliance possess (a) *salience* (cues or rewards that are meaningful for the patient); (b) *compatibility* (stimuli that are easily integrated into patients' daily routines); (c) *short latency* (brief delays between cues, prescribed responses, and consequences); and (d) *explicitness* (stimuli that are uniquely related to the prescribed response).

Most researchers have not attempted to formulate a theory that integrates what is known about noncompliance into a comprehensive explanation of its occurrence. One exception to this atheoretical approach is the Health Belief Model (HBM) originated by Rosenstock (1966) and focused by Becker and Maiman (1975) on the specific question of noncompliance. The HBM is a social-psychological theory that emphasizes the expectancies of certain outcomes an individual holds and the values these outcomes represent for the person. According to the HBM, individuals will comply with treatments depending on (a) how susceptible to a given illness individuals perceive themselves to be and how severe the consequences of the illness are thought to be; (b) how effective and feasible versus how costly and difficult the prescribed treatment is perceived to be; (c) the influence of internal cues (physical symptoms) plus external cues (media advertisements or advice from friends) in triggering health behaviors; and (d) demographic and personality variables as well as structural and social characteristics that modify the influences of the other variables. Subsequent versions of the HBM have incorporated general health motivations, faith in doctors, and characteristics of the doctor–patient relationship into the theoretical scheme, and Masur (1981) has integrated the HBM with traditional behavioral principles reminiscent of Zifferblatt's (1975) analysis.

Interventions to Improve Compliance

Attempts to improve compliance with treatment have developed on a piecemeal basis with little concern for theoretical justification (Haynes, 1982). Many commentators have attempted to impose some order on these different interventions by organizing them into three general approaches that Masur (1981) identified as education, modification of treatment plan, and behavioral techniques.

1. Education. One direct and effective intervention for improving compliance with short-term treatments is to give patients clear, explicit, written instructions that supplement oral instructions about how treatment is to proceed. This positive effect is less evident with long-term treatments, however. More extensive information about illnesses, the need for treatment, side effects of treatment, and the like do not improve compliance very much.

On the other hand, there may be benefits to educating physicians about the causes and management of noncompliance. In one study (Inui, Yourtee, & Williamson, 1976), physicians who had been educated about the HBM and ways to improve compliance had more compliant patients at a 6-month reassessment.

2. Modification of Treatment Plan. A second strategy for increasing compliance is to reorganize the treatment in ways that facilitate an individual's adherence to it. Examples include tailoring the taking of medications to existing daily habits (e.g., taking pills right after brushing teeth), giving the treatment in one or two injections rather than in several doses per day, packaging medicine in dosage strips or with pill calendars, and scheduling more frequent follow-up visits to supervise compliance. These procedures have shown promise (e.g., Boczkowski, Zeichner, & DeSanto, 1985), but many of them entail additional manufacturing costs and extra time from service providers, two characteristics likely to limit their application.

3. Behavior Modification. Arranging stimuli to prompt compliance and providing reinforcers for compliant behaviors have been used in innovative ways. Compliance can be prompted by *environmental cues* such as postcard reminders, telephone calls, or wristwatches set to emit a tone at the time a pill should be taken. *Self-monitoring* has improved compliance, particularly in the treatment of obesity and other conditions that have easily measured indices. Written *contingency contracts* between patient and physician can specify what compliance behaviors the patient must complete to earn a reward (e.g., future appointments scheduled at more convenient times). Such contracts encourage a more collaborative relationship between patient and physician and have demonstrated success in improving compliance (Swain & Steckel, 1981), although at least one study of hypertensives (Hoelscher, Lichstein, & Rosenthal, 1986)

found that a written contract condition produced less compliance in producing relaxation at home than a noncontract condition. *Token economies* have been employed to encourage compliance in a variety of patients. In a study by Magrab and Papadopoulou (1977), three children with renal failure were given points for maintaining their weight, potassium, and nitrogen levels at recommended levels. These points could then be exchanged for tangible rewards in the hospital. In comparison to their baseline levels, these children were able to make substantial weight gains, and two of them showed improvements in the other indices.

Many patients avoid essential medical procedures or treatments because they are painful or produce negative side effects. Behavior modification procedures have often been used to reduce these negative outcomes, thereby increasing patients' compliance with necessary interventions. Probably the best-known illustration of these methods is the previously described behavioral treatments to control anticipatory nausea suffered by cancer patients undergoing chemotherapy. Other examples include teaching children to use breathing exercises and distraction techniques to help them overcome the fear of receiving routine vaccination shots (Blount et al., 1992) and employing hypnosis to reduce the pain for burn patients who are undergoing debridement procedures (Patterson, Everett, Burns, & Marvin, 1992). Finally, behavioral treatments have been used for many years to treat dental phobias that may prevent people from maintaining regular dental care (Kleinknecht & Bernstein, 1978).

EXPERIMENTAL PSYCHOPATHOLOGY

A second area in clinical psychology where biological factors are receiving greater attention is *experimental psychopathology,* which is the study of the causes and characteristics of abnormal behaviors. Clinicians need to understand psychopathology because it has many implications for the way they diagnose and treat mental disorders. In addition, understanding the cause of a condition is usually a necessity for being able to prevent it. As a result of these implications, clinical psychologists have been interested in developing theories and conducting research that will promote their understanding of psychopathology.

Theories of abnormal behavior tend to fall into three categories: biological, psychological, and social-environmental. *Biological* theories stress genetic, biochemical, or structural problems as the underlying causes of disorders. *Psychological* theories emphasize problems in the psychological processes of thinking, emotion, perception, or motivation as causative agents. However, as Chapter 2 made clear, they differ widely on how these problematic processes themselves originate; some psychologists stress faulty learning experiences (behaviorists), some concentrate on early personality dynamics (psychoanalysts), and some look to current conditions that limit a person's ability to live an authentic, fully actualized life (phenomenologists). *Social-environmental* theories look for the causes of abnormal behavior in the conditions of society (poverty, discrimination, undereducation) or in environments that do not fit the needs of their inhabitants; they have been the basis for the interventions of community psychologists, as we described in Chapter 7.

Over the years the relationship between biological, psychological, and social-environmental theories has often been competitive. In one sense this competition is healthy because it stimulates new research that can improve all theories. In other cases, competition is less beneficial because it reflects political and financial motives. This problem arises when psychiatrists and psychologists bicker over competing biological and psychological theories of some disorder, believing that whoever is correct will be able to claim priority in treating the disorder. Disputes between advocates of different etiological explanations will al-

ways be with us, but in recent years the debate has shifted from framing the issue in terms of psychology versus biology to more balanced analyses of how biological, psychological, and social factors may all be implicated in causing disorders.

Most important for this chapter, psychologists have come to recognize that there are several patterns of causation that underlie serious psychological disorders. Psychologists' greater appreciation of biological etiology is due to several factors. First, improved research strategies have confirmed biological contributions that are hard to ignore. Second, psychologists have come to understand that the etiology of a disorder does not necessarily mean that only certain treatments can be applied to that disorder. For example, the fact that a person's fear of leaving home may have developed from faulty learning experiences does not restrict treatment to behavioral techniques, especially if there is a medication that might remedy the problem. Likewise, if a child's hyperactivity is traced to some neurological defect, this discovery does not eliminate the possibility that a behaviorally based program could help the child control his or her behavior. Third, psychologists are becoming more receptive to biological variables because they have come to realize that psychological processes can modify biological ones. As the field of health psychology has demonstrated, the relationship between biology and psychology is a reciprocal one, with cause and effect entwined in ways we are just beginning to understand.

In other words, recognizing the importance of biological variables in the causation of psychopathology does not need to lead to a form of reductionism in which psychological processes are nothing more than pale reflections of the real or more important biological influences. Understanding the biological components of a disorder is not the same as understanding the disorder itself. How the disorder expresses itself in behavior, how the person with the disorder perceives and feels about the symptoms, and how others react to signs of the disorder remain crucial to understanding the true nature of any psychological disturbance. Just as understanding how an automobile engine works doesn't mean a mechanic necessarily understands the overall experience of driving a car, understanding the underlying biology of an illness doesn't mean a researcher necessarily understands the day-to-day behavior of a person with schizophrenia, panic attacks, or depression.

Biological causes of disordered behavior take several forms. First, some conditions can be caused by biological abnormalities that exert a *direct influence* on behavior. Drug and alcohol intoxication, degenerative conditions like Alzheimer's disease, and most forms of profound mental retardation involve direct biological causation. A second pattern, suspected in many disorders, is that some aspects or subtypes of a problem have biological causes, while other aspects or subtypes are caused by psychological and/or social forces. This pattern, sometimes called *multiple pathways* etiology, is probably at work with subtypes of depression, some anxiety disorders, and perhaps even various personality disorders. The etiological pattern that has received the greatest attention involves biological, psychological, and social factors interacting with one another to cause a clinical disorder. This pattern, often termed the *diathesis-stress* model, involves three components:

1. A person has some defect which usually involves a biochemical or structural problem in the central or autonomic nervous system. This defect (or set of defects) is often inherited, but it can be acquired through trauma, infections, or other disease processes.

2. This defect or *diathesis* leaves the person vulnerable to developing a psychological disorder. Persons who carry the diathesis are said to be at risk, suggesting that they are predisposed to becoming disordered.

3. If at-risk persons are exposed to *pathogenic*

(disease-causing) stresses, their predispositions may worsen to the point that they become ill. On the other hand, if at-risk persons are exposed to mostly benign psychological, familial, and social influences, their predisposition may not express itself at a clinical level of disturbance.

Although the diathesis-stress model has been applied to several disorders, it has received its greatest support in the study of schizophrenia (Fowles, 1992).

The Etiology of Schizophrenia

About 3 million Americans (1% of the population) develop schizophrenia in their lifetimes. Schizophrenia is one of the most serious mental disorders, accounting for 100,000 hospitalized patients on any given day, or roughly 50% of all the persons in mental hospitals in the United States. It affects young adults, men usually before the age of 25 and women usually after the age of 25, and can last a lifetime. Although schizophrenia occurs in all social classes, it is particularly common among the urban poor.

Treatment of schizophrenia was very difficult until the mid-1950s, when the phenothiazines (major tranquilizers) were introduced. These drugs do not cure schizophrenia, but they are effective in controlling most of its more disturbing symptoms in the majority of patients. Nonetheless, the costs of schizophrenia remain enormous. It is estimated that schizophrenia costs society about $30 billion annually in treatment, disability payments, lost productivity and wages, legal expenses, and welfare support.

Schizophrenia is actually a group of disorders involving different combinations of symptoms. Schizophrenia is classified into five subtypes (disorganized type, catatonic type, paranoid type, undifferentiated type, and residual type). Each subtype presents a different clinical picture, but differentiating between them is not easy because schizophrenics show great variability in their symptoms.

Eight categories of symptoms are characteristic of schizophrenics. While at some point in their disorder all schizophrenics either have some type of thought disorder or hallucinations, they typically also show disturbances in several other symptom categories as well. The eight categories of symptoms are as follows:

1. *Content of thought*. The major symptom here is some delusion or false belief.

2. *Form of thought*. Formal thought disorder involves abnormalities in the way a person's thought processes are organized. "Loose associations," in which ideas shift from one unrelated topic to another, are a common example of this type of symptom.

3. *Perception*. Hallucinations or the reporting of experiences for which there appear to be no tangible stimuli are the major symptom in this category.

4. *Affect*. This category involves disturbed emotions. Most common are emotions that are blunted, flat, or inappropriate to the situation.

5. *Sense of self*. These symptoms refer to persons' confusion about their identities; they may feel unreal or controlled by forces outside their control.

6. *Volition*. These symptoms involve reduced motivation and interest in pursuing almost any sort of goal. They interfere severely with a person's ability to work.

7. *Relationship to the external world*. Schizophrenics often withdraw from the external world and become preoccupied with internal fantasies and odd ideas. These symptoms are sometimes called *autistic*.

8. *Psychomotor behavior*. Abnormalities of movement include rocking, pacing, stereotyped actions, and bizarre behavioral rituals. Some schizophrenics become almost totally immobile; others take on a very disheveled look or dress very strangely.

Because schizophrenia is such a serious disorder and because it affects so many people, research on its causes has been a priority among clinicians for several years. Progress in understanding the disorder has been slow, so there is still no definitive answer to the question, "What causes schizophrenia?" However, we have gained important knowledge about two organic factors in schizophrenia's development—genetics and biochemical abnormalities.

The Genetics of Schizophrenia

Family Studies

It has been known for some time that schizophrenia tends to run in families. This discovery was based on comparisons of the incidence of schizophrenia in the general population to the incidence of schizophrenia in families where one member has been diagnosed as schizophrenic. Rosenthal (1970) has reviewed the evidence on this question and reports the following figures: (a) The incidence of schizophrenia in the siblings of a schizophrenic ranges from 3.3 to 14.3%; (b) the incidence of schizophrenia in the parents of a schizophrenic ranges as high as 12%; and (c) the incidence of schizophrenia in children with two schizophrenic parents is about 35%. All these figures are much greater than the population base rate of 1%. These data suggest a genetic basis for schizophrenia, but they do not settle the issue because families share much more than their genetic inheritance. They also share a similar environment that could lead to schizophrenia. A better test of the genetic transmission of schizophrenia involves comparing incidence figures for different types of twins.

Twin Studies

The typical twin study of genetic etiology is based on the following logic: Holding other factors constant, people who are more similar in terms of their genetic makeup should be more similar in terms of genetically carried characteristics. Extending this logic to the inheritance of schizophrenia, a researcher should find that *monozygotic (MZ) twins,* who are genetically identical, will be more likely to be *concordant* (share the same diagnosis) for schizophrenia than *dizygotic (DZ) twins,* who are no more genetically similar than any siblings born at different times (such twins are sometimes called *fraternal*). The results have been consistent in study after study. Concordance rates for monozygotic twins are greater than that for dizygotic twins. If you have an identical twin who is schizophrenic, the risk of developing schizophrenia yourself is about 46%, while the risk is only about 14% if you have a fraternal twin who is schizophrenic (Gottesman & Shields, 1982).

While these figures lend support to the genetic hypothesis, they raise other questions. First, in no study has the concordance rate between MZ twins been 100%, indicating that nongenetic factors play some role in the etiology of schizophrenia. Second, as Rosenhan and Seligman (1989) observe, MZ twins share a unique environment involving slower maturation and language development and more frequent identity problems that could help cause their eventual schizophrenia. However, two lines of evidence suggest that nongenetic explanations of the high concordance rate among MZ twins are probably not correct. First, the rate of schizophrenia among all MZ twins is no greater than the overall population incidence. Second, the results of a third research strategy involving the study of adopted children provides even stronger evidence that there is a genetic component to schizophrenia.

Adoption Studies

The most convincing method for separating the effects of genetics from the confounding effects of similar environments is to compare the offspring of schizophrenic parents who are adopted at an early age to the offspring of nonschizophrenic parents who are adopted at equally early ages. Higher rates of schizophrenia in the first group relative to the general population and to the control group provide evidence for a genetic influence. Another research approach has been to locate a large number of adults who were adopted, identify those who have been diagnosed as schizophrenic, and then determine the incidence of schizophrenia among their biological and adoptive parents. Genetic factors would be implicated if the rate of schizophrenia is higher among the biological parents of the schizophrenics than it is in the general population or in the adoptive parents. Such studies are very time consuming, but when they have been accomplished (e.g., Heston, 1966; Kety, Rosenthal, Wender, & Schulsinger, 1968) they have always favored a strong role for genetic transmission of schizophrenia (Plomin, 1989).

Even though the role of genetics in the development of schizophrenia seems clear, questions remain as to how large a role it plays and just what abnormality is inherited. We have no final answers to either of these questions, but promising leads have turned up in the study of children considered at high risk for schizophrenia as a result of being born to mothers who were chronic schizophrenics (Mednick & Schulsinger, 1968). Several indirect clues about abnormalities in biochemical functions and brain structures have also been found.

The list of potential biological contributors to schizophrenia is a fairly long one (Berquier & Ashton, 1991). Among the suspected causes are atrophy or other structural abnormalities in certain areas of the brain, viral infections affecting the brain, and birth complications resulting in brain damage. The biological theory that has received the greatest attention is that schizophrenics suffer a disturbance in the level of one or more of the chemical neurotransmitters found in the brain. We review this theory next.

A Biochemical Theory of Schizophrenia— The Dopamine Hypothesis

A large number of studies have reported chemical and physical differences in the brains of schizophrenics. For example, in comparison to normal subjects, they show lower birth weights, more abnormal EEG readings, different blood-flow patterns, more difficulty in visually tracking a moving object, stronger galvanic skin responses, a larger number of unusual immune system antibodies, and a host of problems in some of their reflexes and motor responses (see Mirsky & Duncan, 1986, for a review). However, the discovery of these differences does not establish them as causes of schizophrenia. They may be caused by some other as-yet-undetected problem, or they may be by-products of schizophrenia itself. We know that most schizophrenics differ from nonschizophrenics in their exercise, nutrition, drug use, and general health; such factors are more likely to reflect lifestyle differences than fundamental causes of their disorder. Despite frequent disappointments in isolating a specific biochemical fault underlying schizophrenia, researchers have begun to concentrate on abnormal brain functioning involving one or more neurotransmitters in the brain.

One of the most popular neurotransmitter theories suggests that the symptoms of schizophrenia are caused by overactivity on the part of dopamine, one of about 20 chemicals in the brain responsible for carrying electrical impulses between neurons. Excessive activity in dopaminergic neural circuits is thought to push schizophrenics' brains into abnormally high levels of activation, particularly when they are stressed. The results are the florid symptoms that we associate with schizophrenia—jumbled thoughts, delusional beliefs, and hallucinations.

Evidence for the dopamine theory has been pieced together from three related discoveries that are summarized in Figure 12–1.

As line 1 of Figure 12–1 suggests, many symptoms of schizophrenia resemble the psychosis that can develop from an overdose of amphetamines (amphetamines will also worsen the symptoms of schizophrenia). There is good evidence that amphetamines induce psychotic symptoms by increasing available dopamine at the synapses. In addition, the pheno-

FIGURE 12–1   Patterns of evidence supporting the dopamine hypothesis of schizophrenia. (Reproduced from *Abnormal Psychology* by David L. Rosenhan and Martin E. P. Seligman, by permission of W. W. Norton & Company, Inc. Copyright © 1984 by W. W. Norton & Company, Inc.)

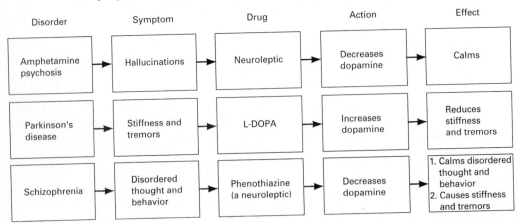

thiazines, which are effective in controlling the symptoms of schizophrenia, are also effective in calming patients suffering from amphetamine psychosis.

Line 2 of Figure 12–1 shows that Parkinson's disease, which is caused in part by lowered levels of dopamine in the area of the brain called the corpus striatum, can be successfully treated with L-dopa, a drug that increases available dopamine in the brain. The significance of this discovery is revealed by two findings that are depicted in the third line of Figure 12–1.

First, the phenothiazines, so successful in the treatment of schizophrenics' symptoms, exert a specific effect on brain chemistry: They decrease the amount of dopaminergic activity by blocking receptor sites of dopamine in the brain, but do not have as strong an effect on other neurotransmitters. Second, when schizophrenics are treated for long periods with large doses of phenothiazines they often develop symptoms almost identical to those found with Parkinson's disease!

These findings imply that the common mechanisms by which amphetamines stimulate psychotic behavior, L-dopa reduces Parkinsonian symptoms, and phenothiazines calm schizophrenic behavior is the dopamine system, which appears to be underactivated in Parkinson's disease and overactivated in schizophrenia. As you can see, the dopamine theory is based on a clever integration of what has been learned about the dopamine system and its responsiveness to various drugs. However, it remains only a theory about how schizophrenia might develop in some patients. In fact, some recent findings do not fit well with the theory. For example, despite the fact that phenothiazines rapidly block dopamine receptors, their therapeutic effect on schizophrenics is gradual, sometimes taking weeks before improvement is noted.

Another problem with the dopamine hypothesis is that the phenothiazines usually are beneficial for only the so-called *positive* symptoms that involve excesses of behavior such as

hallucinations and delusions. The *negative* symptoms of schizophrenia involving deficiencies of behavior like apathy and social withdrawal do not respond well to phenothiazine treatment. Therefore, the dopamine theory does not apply equally well to all forms of schizophrenia.

These are the sorts of puzzles that the dopamine hypothesis has yet to solve. Until it does and until there is direct evidence that excess dopamine activity precedes schizophrenia, this theory should not be accepted as an adequate causal explanation of schizophrenia.

Other Disorders

Schizophrenia has received the most attention as a mental disorder with possible biological causes. However, many other disorders have also been linked to possible biological and/or genetic etiologies. In fact, for most serious forms of psychopathology at least one prominent theory of biological causation has been proposed, and in some cases, these theories have received extensive support.

Biological differences have long been suspected as causes of various mood disorders (Goodwin & Jamison, 1990). Low levels of norepinephrine or serotonin have been associated with depression, and excesses of norepinephrine have been implicated in manic episodes. Another promising area of research involves the neuroendocrine system. Recent evidence suggests that the glands comprising this system may be overactive in depressed patients.

Some violent behavior has been reliably related to hormonal differences and to genetic differences (DiLalla & Gottesman, 1991). These discoveries have sparked controversy among the public and some scientists, who fear that a focus on biology may unfairly target minority groups and detract from efforts to improve the social and economic conditions long thought to increase violence.

Genetic and biological factors are also emphasized in current theories of suicidal behavior (Spoont, 1992), anxiety disorders (Gorman et al., 1988), alcoholism (Tarter, Alterman, & Edwards, 1985), and sexual aggression (Ellis, 1991).

A Final Word

In this chapter we have reviewed two areas in which clinical psychologists have become increasingly involved in studying relations between biological and psychological variables. The ultimate justification for this interest is that a complete understanding of human behavior requires it, and the scientific training of psychologists should leave them content with nothing less than an understanding of behavior that is as complete as possible. There are many practical advantages to clinicians becoming well informed about biological influences on behavior, but they are secondary to the most compelling reason—the advancement of scientific knowledge.

The interaction between clinical psychology and biological sciences is, of course, bidirectional. Biologically oriented scientists have an obligation to understand the influences psychological processes exert on physical phenomena. We are not implying, as is sometimes suggested, that all psychological variables must ultimately be reduced to a physical level before they can be understood. Biological and psychological variables are each legitimate targets of study in their own right. However, human behavior cannot be adequately explained without considering the complex interrelationships between both types of influences.

CHAPTER 13

Clinical Neuropsychology

Neuropsychology is the field of study that endeavors to define the relationship between brain processes and human behavior and psychological functioning. Neuropsychologists are interested in a wide range of functions, including cognitive abilities (language, mathematical, and visuospatial skills); motor abilities (gross and fine motor skills); emotional characteristics, such as the ability to express and understand feelings; personality traits (e.g., extraversion and hypnotic susceptibility); and mental disorders (e.g., depression and schizophrenia).

Historically, the main source of data in neuropsychology has been the study of behavior after brain damage. By observing the effects of specific kinds of brain damage on behavior, neuropsychologists were able to make inferences about the organization of the brain. More recently, the development of behavioral methods that allow neuropsychologists to study the organization of the brain in non-brain-damaged people has made it possible to confirm and expand our understanding of brain–behavior relationships. The power of the neuropsychological approach is revealed by the insights it has provided about brain damage and about psychological disorders such as learning disabilities, depression, schizophrenia, and psychopathy.

Knowledge that has been garnered from neuropsychological research is often applied by clinical neuropsychologists, who work with children and adults who have had trauma or injury to the brain, or who are experiencing problems in some area of functioning that may be related to a brain impairment. Often, the clinical neuropsychologist is called upon to assess how damage to the brain expresses itself in behavioral, cognitive, and emotional *deficits*. (A deficit is a deficiency in performance from the level shown by a normative or average group of people or from the level shown by an individual on an earlier occasion.) Clinical neuropsychologists typically seek to answer one or more of the following questions (Jones & Butters, 1983):

1. Does the client show deficits that suggest organic brain damage?

2. If there is impairment, how severe is it and what is its prognosis or likely course?

3. Can the impairment be localized to a certain area of the brain?

4. What is the probable cause of the impairment?

5. What are the consequences of the impairment for the client's daily, occupational, and interpersonal functioning?

6. What recommendations are there for the rehabilitation of the impairment?

In answering these questions, neuropsychologists must integrate data and knowledge from several sources. First, they must be proficient in the general assessment skills that we described in Chapters 3 through 6. Neuropsychological assessment should not be isolated from an assessment of the entire person, including social and family background, intellectual functioning, personality dynamics, and emotional reactions to possible brain dysfunction. Second, the neuropsychologist must be well versed in the neurosciences, including neuroanatomy (the study of the structures of the nervous system and the functions of these structures), neuropharmacology (the study of drugs that affect functioning of the nervous system), and neurophysiology (the study of the physiology of the nervous system, including the chemistry of nerve tissue and the relationship between the nervous system and endocrine functions). Third, neuropsychologists must be trained in human abilities (cognition, language, and perception) and developmental psychology (including behavioral genetics and life-span psychology). Fourth, the need to distinguish brain impairments from nonorganic psychopathology and the frequent requests to design rehabilitative programs require an in-depth understanding of clinical psychology. Finally, neuropsychologists must be thoroughly trained in the specialized assessment methods of neuropsychology.

The increasing demand for neuropsychologists has stimulated many clinical psychologists to list neuropsychology as one of their special-

ties. This rush to neuropsychology has led to serious questions about the education necessary to ensure competency in the field. An all too frequently traveled route has been to take one or two courses in neuropsychological assessment as part of a clinical psychology curriculum and then begin to "do neuropsychologicals." A worse practice is to acquire all of one's experience in neuropsychology through clinical workshops or a brief rotation on one's internship. The education of a competent clinical neuropsychologist is an ambitious process that requires multidisciplinary input, a large body of basic knowledge, research sophistication, supervised experience, and clinical acumen. Although various models are available for such preparation, all of them require extensive coordinated training for which there simply are no shortcuts (APA Division of Clinical Neuropsychology, 1989; Meier, 1981). Clinical neuropsychologists who work with children need even further specialized training, since many disorders have particular manifestations in children, and the problems that arise are unique (for example, family dynamics can play an important role in the management of children with seizure disorders). Pediatric neuropsychologists also need to be experienced in evaluating the educational programs and resources available to the client.

HISTORICAL DEVELOPMENT OF NEUROPSYCHOLOGY

Neuropsychology has only recently been defined as a field of study; the term appears to have been used first in the late 1940s. Behind it, however, lies a long history of thinking and speculation about the mind. As far back as 500 B.C., scholars debated about whether the mind was localized in the brain (the "brain hypothesis") or the heart (the "cardiac hypothesis") (Kolb & Whishaw, 1990), and many famous philosophers and physicians participated in the argument. Aristotle, in the fourth century B.C., decided that the mind must reside in the heart, because it was warm and active; the brain, which was cool and inert, was a "radiator" that cooled the blood. Others disagreed. For example, in the second century A.D., a famous Roman physician, Galen, had ample opportunity to study the effects of brain damage on behavior in his work with wounded gladiators. Based on his observations, Galen localized the mind in the brain.

Later, debate focused on exactly where in the brain the mind was localized; Galen believed that the mind resided in the fluid of the ventricles. In the 16th century, Anreas Vesalius put this theory to rest by dissecting brains and discovering that the ventricles are the same size in animals and people. Since people were considered to be far more rational than animals, the mind must therefore reside in their far larger brains. In the 17th century, Rene Descartes argued that the mind was located in a specific part of the brain, the pineal body.

Of greatest importance to neuropsychology were several lines of research in the 1800s that focused on possible relationships between selected behaviors and specific areas of the brain. At its extreme, this study of localization of function was popularized as phrenology by anatomists Franz Gall and his associate, Johann Spurzheim. As noted in Chapter 1, phrenology was a pseudoscience that claimed that individual differences in personality and intelligence could be assessed by measuring the bumps and indentations of the surface of the skull. These features supposedly corresponded to the part of the brain responsible for the characteristic in question. Phrenology was very popular with the public but was disdained by most scientists.

Discoveries made by Pierre Flourens earned greater scientific respectability. Flourens surgically destroyed parts of animals' brains and then observed the behavioral consequences of the loss. He concluded that although there was some localization of cortical function, the hemispheres of the cortex functioned more like an interrelated unit. This view was later supported by the work of Karl Lashley, who

emphasized the ability of one area of the cortex to substitute for the functions of a destroyed area, a capacity he described as *equipotentiality.*

Although the excesses of phrenology discredited early ideas about localization, careful work in behavioral neurology eventually provided convincing support for cortical localization of many cognitive functions. Paul Broca, a French physician, is often credited with the discovery that expressive speech was controlled by an area in the left cerebral cortex. However, there were already reports in the literature about speech deficits following left frontal damage. (One of these articles was published by the phrenologist Gall!) In 1825, Jean Baptiste Bouillaud presented a paper in which he argued that speech was localized in the frontal lobes. A few years later, Marc Dax is reported to have presented a similar paper (published by his son in 1865). Apparently, no one paid much attention until 1861, when Bouillaud's son-in-law, Ernest Auburtin, described yet another case demonstrating speech deficits associated with damage to the frontal lobes. Paul Broca was present at the meeting of the Anthropological Society of Paris, where Auburtin gave his paper. Shortly thereafter, Broca had the opportunity to confirm, by autopsy, that a patient with a profound speech deficit but otherwise normal intelligence had damage to the left frontal lobe. By 1863, Broca had collected a series of eight cases and had argued the case in such a way that localization of function was indisputable.

Another early clinical insight into localization of function was made by two Italian ophthalmologists: Antonio Quaglino, a professor at the University of Pavia, and Giambattista Borelli, a practicing ophthalmologist in Turin. In 1867, they published a paper describing the case of a man who lost the ability to recognize familiar faces after a cerebral hemorrhage that mainly damaged the right hemisphere of the brain. The loss of the capacity for facial recognition is known today as *prosopagnosia;* its precise cause is still a matter of great interest to researchers.

Development of Assessment Techniques

By the turn of the 20th century, Alfred Binet had begun to assess brain-damaged children in Paris. Although these tests are usually considered to be the beginning of intelligence testing, they also foreshadowed neuropsychological assessment. In addition, many of the disorders commonly assessed today with neuropsychological techniques had been identified by this time. *Aphasia* (disordered language abilities), *apraxias* (impaired abilities to carry out purposeful movements), *amnesias* (disorders of memory), and seizure disorders had all been classified, studied, and in some cases treated by the 1920s. In Russia, a Psychoneurological Institute was formed in 1907 to study the behavioral consequences of brain damage, and throughout the first decade of the 1900s, several investigators in the United States began to use psychological tests to study the effects of brain damage on behavior.

A crucial development in the history of neuropsychology was the work of Ward Halstead, who established a neuropsychology laboratory in 1935 at the University of Chicago. Halstead began his work by observing brain-damaged persons in natural settings. These observations led him to identify several characteristics of behavior, which he then tried to assess more thoroughly through existing psychological tests or through tests he developed himself. After testing a large number of patients who had been referred to him, Halstead compared the results of the brain-damaged referral cases to a group of control subjects and selected 10 measures for his assessment battery based on their ability to discriminate the patients from the controls (Reitan & Davison, 1974).

Halstead's first graduate student, Ralph M. Reitan, started his own neuropsychology laboratory in 1951 at the Indiana University Medical Center. Reitan eliminated two of Halstead's original tests and added several of his own, including a Wechsler intelligence scale and an MMPI. This revised battery became known as the Halstead-Reitan Battery, and it is still the most widely used neuropsychological battery in existence.

Basic research in neuropsychology and advances in assessment methods grew dramatically following World War II. Jones and Butters (1983) list five groups of scientists who made especially noteworthy contributions to the field in this period:

1. The Montreal Neurological Institute–McGill University Group, especially Brenda Milner and Doreen Kimura, who studied the effects of many types of specific or focal lesions on behavior. The Montreal investigators developed several neuropsychological assessment techniques, and their research (e.g., Branch, Milner, & Rasmussen, 1964; Kimura, 1967) led to the widespread acceptance of the view that each hemisphere of the brain has special importance for certain types of behavior.

2. Hans-Lukas Teuber who, with several colleagues at New York University College of Medicine and MIT, studied the behavioral effects of combat injuries to the brains (particularly the frontal lobes) of World War II veterans.

3. The Boston VA and Boston University School of Medicine group, including Edith Kaplan, Nelson Butters, and Harold Goodglass, who carefully classified different forms of aphasia and amnesia and who emphasized the need to study the process that contributes to objective performance deficits. In other words, patients may do poorly on the same neuropsychological tests for different reasons; the Boston group advocated assessment that measures not only the extent of deficits but also the qualitative problems that lead to the deficits. This approach has come to be known as the process approach.

4. Arthur L. Benton at the University of Iowa, who developed in 1945 the Benton Visual Retention Test, a test of visual memory still in use today. Benton also made numerous discoveries about the different behavioral effects of lesions in the right versus the left hemisphere and developed a number of other neuropsychological tests with admirable psychometric properties (see, e.g., Benton, Hamsher, Varney, & Spreen, 1983).

5. Alexander Luria, a Russian scientist, whose unique approach to neuropsychology became enormously influential in the West following the translation of his book, *Higher Functioning in Man,* in 1966 and the systematic description of his assessment methods by the Danish psychologist Anna-Lise Christensen in 1975. Luria's theory of functional systems in the brain is founded on important principles of brain functioning which we will examine in more detail later.

Split-Brain Patients

Another important event in the history of neuropsychology is the development of neurosurgical techniques that allowed for more precise localization of lesions in the brain. In this respect, the work of Roger Sperry and his colleagues at the California Institute of Technology deserves special mention (Sperry, 1961, 1982). These investigators studied the behavioral effects of cutting the corpus callosum, the band of fibers that connects the hemispheres of the brain and allows them to communicate with each other. This particular surgical procedure is occasionally used to prevent the spread of epileptic seizures from one side of the brain to the other in cases where pharmacological treatment is ineffective. When the corpus callosum is severed, there is no direct pathway between the hemispheres. Although vast sections of brain tissue devoted to complex information processing were presumably rendered incommunicado by this surgery, previous research in the forties had failed to note any significant differences between normal people and so-called split-brain patients. It was not until Roger Sperry (who won the Nobel Prize in 1981 for his work) and his associates used more sophisticated experimental procedures to test split-brain patients that it became possible to identify a disconnection syndrome.

Normative Studies

Research with split-brain patients stimulated an enormous number of studies investigating brain organization in non-brain-damaged people. These studies often used a tachistoscope, which is a stimulus presentation device that takes advantage of the fact that when the eyes are focused on a central point, stimuli in the left visual field are perceived first by the right hemisphere, whereas stimuli in the right visual field are perceived first by the left hemisphere. To get the information *directly* to both hemispheres, the person would have to move the eyes so as to place the information that was formerly in one visual field in the other. To forestall this possibility, the tachistoscope is designed to have split-second accuracy in the timing of the lights that illuminate the stimuli. Since it takes about 200 milliseconds to move the eyes, the stimuli are lit up for that amount of time or less. Researchers can thus be fairly certain that the only way the opposite hemisphere can obtain the information is to receive a second-hand copy via the corpus callosum.

Using tachistoscopic methods, experimenters were able to direct visual stimuli to one hemisphere or the other and measure a person's accuracy of performance or reaction time in response. Similarly, dichotic listening techniques, which direct auditory input simultaneously to both ears, rely on the tendency to ignore or suppress information in the ear opposite the hemisphere that is less adept at the task. Both approaches were based on the fact that pathways for sensory input are predominantly crossed in the nervous system.

By measuring the relative accuracy of responses for the two visual fields (for tachistoscopic presentation) or for the two ears (dichotic presentation), researchers from the 1960s on have been able to document and confirm unique hemispheric superiorities for a wide variety of cognitive and perceptual tasks (Kimura, 1961, 1966, 1967; Pirozollo & Rayner, 1977).

The Emergence of Clinical Neuropsychology

Our understanding of brain–behavior relationships has thus been enriched and expanded remarkably in the last few decades by research and scholarship that have provided converging evidence for many findings. At the same time, these findings have been increasingly applied in clinical settings in response to a variety of client needs. Clinical neuropsychology really emerged as a distinctive professional specialty in the 1970s. Two events marked this development: The founding of the *Journal of Clinical Neuropsychology* by Louis Costa and Byron Rourke, and the forming of the Division of Clinical Neuropsychology (Division 40) within the American Psychological Society. Division 40 now has about 1,800 members and is specifically concerned with neuropsychology as a field of professional practice. Part of Division 40's task has been to define the training and educational experiences that are necessary to become a competent clinical neuropsychologist, and to institute a procedure by which to obtain the credentials to demonstrate such competence. As a result, an American Board of Clinical Neuropsychology has been established, which is a component of the American Board of Professional Psychology. When an individual has undergone the proper training and has had sufficient experience in the practice of clinical neuropsychology (currently 5 years of postdoctoral practice), he or she can apply for the examination for the diplomate in clinical neuropsychology. The following statement defining a clinical neuropsychologist was adopted by the Executive Committee of Division 40 at the APA meeting on August 12, 1988:

A Clinical Neuropsychologist is a professional psychologist who applies principles of assessment and intervention based upon the scientific study of human behavior as it relates to normal and abnormal functioning of the central nervous system. The Clinical Neuropsychologist is a doctoral-level psychology provider of diagnostic and intervention services who has demonstrated competence in the application of such principles for human welfare following:

A. Successful completion of systematic didactic and experiential training in neuropsychology and neuroscience at a regionally accredited university;

B. Two or more years of appropriate supervised training applying neuropsychological services in a clinical setting;

C. Licensing and certification to provide psychological services to the public by the laws of the state or province in which he or she practices;

D. Review by one's peers as a test of these competencies.

Attainment of the ABCN/ABPP Diploma in Clinical Neuropsychology is the clearest evidence of competence as a Clinical Neuropsychologist, assuring that all of these criteria have been met.

This statement, along with a series of important documents relating to clinical neuropsychology, has recently appeared in a volume entitled *The TCN Guide to Professional Practice in Clinical Neuropsychology* (Adams & Rourke, 1992). This volume contains the Division 40 guidelines for doctoral training programs in neuropsychology and a listing of such programs on doctoral, postdoctoral, and internship levels. Undergraduates interested in pursuing the field of clinical neuropsychology can refer to a section describing the experiences that are useful to seek at the college level.

IMPORTANT PRINCIPLES OF NEUROPSYCHOLOGY

A thorough understanding of brain functioning is obviously beyond the scope of this chapter; it is even beyond the scope of any single book devoted to the topic. However, certain principles of brain–behavior relationships are so fundamental to neuropsychology that it is essential to review them before describing any assessment procedures.

Localization of Function

As we have already mentioned, the idea that certain parts of the brain control specific behaviors became the prevailing view of scientists in the 19th century, reaching an extreme with the phrenologists. *Localization theories* portray the brain in a compartmentalized fashion, with different parts responsible for different skills or senses. Localization of functioning continues to be an important idea among modern neuropsychologists, but they also recognize that the different areas of the brain are intricately interrelated and may even take over some of the functions formerly directed by an injured area.

Theorists who emphasize the interrelatedness of brain areas and who stress the holistic quality of brain functioning are sometimes known as *globalists* (Filskov, Grimm, & Lewis, 1981). John Hughlings Jackson, Karl Lashley, and Kurt Goldstein are three of the more influential globalists, but it was Alexander Luria who, more than any other scientist, proposed a theory of brain organization that emphasized its integration rather than its specificity.

Luria's theory was that the brain was ordered into three functional systems: (a) a system for regulating a person's overall tone or waking state, which involves the brain stem; (b) a system located in the back (posterior) portion of the cortex for obtaining, processing, and storing information received from the outside world; and (c) a system for planning, regulating, and verifying mental operations that is located mainly in the front (anterior) portion of the cortex. It is important to recognize that Luria, like all the other globalists, still believed the brain had some specialized division of labor.

Today, when neuropsychologists map the brain according to specific functions, they do so in a way that reflects both localization and global perspectives (Walsh, 1987). For example, Figure 13–1 depicts a side view of most of the human brain. The different areas identified in this figure are associated with particular functions; in general, the back of the brain is more sensory in function, while the front of the brain is more executive in function. Motor functions, including the movements involved in speech, are found in front of the central sulcus, and reception of sensory information involving touch, pressure, temperature, and body position is located behind the central sulcus.

The lobes of the brain also have particular functions associated with them. The *occipital lobes* are involved in processing visual information; signals from the retina are carried by the optic nerves to the thalamus and then to regions in the occipital lobes. Because of the way the nervous system is organized, visual information is represented *topographically* in the brain; in other words, neighboring parts of the brain respond to neighboring areas of the visual field. A similar arrangement for other sensory and motor information has given rise to the rather comical maps of the *homunculus* (see Figure 13–2), which display the relative size of cortical areas representing sensory information or motor output to and from different regions of the body.

After visual information is processed in the occipital lobes, it is relayed to association

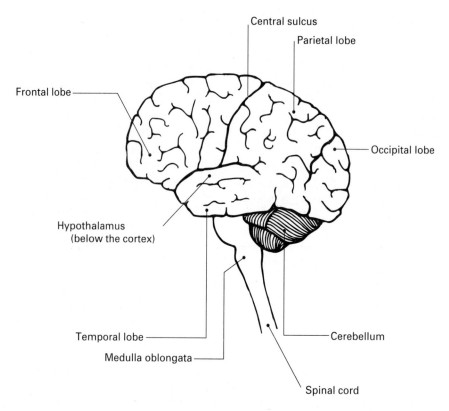

Central sulcus

Parietal lobe

Frontal lobe

Occipital lobe

Hypothalamus
(below the cortex)

Temporal lobe

Cerebellum

Medulla oblongata

Spinal cord

FIGURE 13-1 A lateral view of the human cortex and other brain structures.

areas in the *parietal lobes,* so called because these areas combine and integrate sensory information from a variety of sources. Because the parietal lobes are the meeting ground for visual, auditory, and sensory input, they are uniquely involved in creating a unified percept of an object. For example, when we pick up a rose, the pathways that convey its smell are separate from those that convey its visual image, and these are separate from the ones that convey the prick of its thorns. Yet we experience the rose as a single unified percept. Patients with damage to the parietal lobes often have difficulty recognizing objects, even highly familiar ones (see Box 13–1).

The parietal lobes are also involved in creating a spatial map of our environment and the objects in it, an organization that doesn't depend on the orientation or position of our bodies. Because of this specialty, the parietal lobes play a unique role in attention and awareness of spatial location. Patients with unilateral damage to the parietal lobes often display an intriguing deficit called *hemi-neglect,* in which they ignore the side of the body and the side of space opposite the lesioned hemisphere. Thus, if a patient has damage to the right parietal region, he or she might not eat the food on the left side of the plate, forget to comb the hair on the left side of the head, or fail to button the sleeve on the left arm. Such a patient might ignore words on the left side of the page, or fail to notice the doctor or family member who approaches from the left. Hemi-neglect can be so extreme that patients sometimes believe that parts of

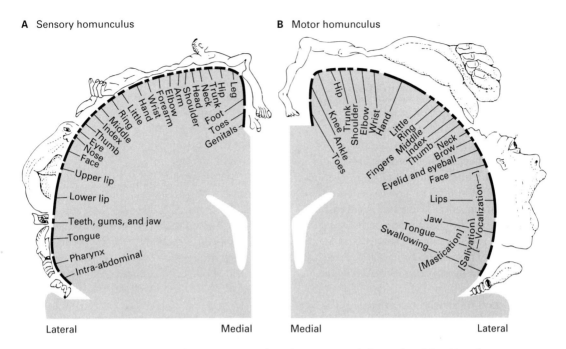

A Sensory homunculus   **B** Motor homunculus

Lateral   Medial   Medial   Lateral

FIGURE 13–2 These two maps show how sensory information (Map A) and motor (Map B) information are projected onto the human cortex. Note, for example, that those areas of the body that are more sensitive to sensory information (such as the tip of the tongue or the fingers) are represented by more cortical area than areas that are less sensitive (such as the back of the head or the upper leg). Source: Kandel, Schwartz, and Jessell (1991). Reprinted with the permission of Macmillan Publishing Company from *The Cerebral Cortex of Man* by Wilder Penfield and Theodore Rasmussen. Copyright 1950 Macmillan Publishing Company; copyright renewed © 1978 Theodore Rasmussen.

their bodies belong to other people. In another anecdote reported by Oliver Sacks in *A Leg to Stand On* (1990), a patient woke up in the middle of the night and tried to throw his leg out of bed, thinking that a stranger had gotten into bed with him. This syndrome is most common after damage to regions of the right parietal lobe, probably because of the unique specialization of the right hemisphere for processing spatial information, but it can occur after damage to the left parietal lobe as well.

Clinical neuropsychologists typically assess the presence of parietal lobe deficits by using tests such as the Benton Test of Facial Recog-

nition, tests of object recognition in which the patient is shown an object and asked to name it or point to it, and tests of visuospatial skills. Because the abilities to tell right from left and to comprehend abstract concepts are often disrupted by left parietal damage, these skills are carefully tested in cases where such damage is suspected. Hemi-neglect is often assessed by asking the patient to draw a clock or a flower. Problems are revealed when patients put all the numbers on the clock, or all the petals on the flower, only on one side. Other tests for neglect include letter cancellation tasks, where patients are asked to cross out all the letters or symbols on a page, and line bi-

The effects of brain damage can take an almost infinite number of forms. A common pattern with severe disorders is to find deficits in large areas of behavior like language, motor coordination, or memory. However, smaller deficits involving narrower functions are also encountered, and sometimes these deficits are of great interest because they permit neuroscientists to map brain–behavior relationships more specifically than they had been able to do previously.

In some instances these deficits are so unusual that they defy common sense. One such case is Doctor P., otherwise known as "the man who mistook his wife for a hat." This case history provides the title for Dr. Oliver Sacks's (1985) compassionate and insightful description of several extraordinary neurological patients whom he has encountered in his practice.

Dr. P. was a distinguished musician, a man of superior intelligence, refinement, and wit. In fact, his reputation as a man with an offbeat sense of humor may have hidden for a time the neurological significance of a strange set of symptoms that Dr. P.'s students and family began to observe—problems recognizing familiar people when he looked at them, but not when he heard them speak, and mistakenly seeing faces in place of such objects as fire hydrants, parking meters, and the knobs on furniture.

Dr. P. was referred to Dr. Sacks by an ophthalmologist who suspected brain damage while examining Dr. P.'s eyes. Upon examination, Dr. P. seemed a charming, healthy man, but Dr. Sacks was disquieted by what he called the "teasing strangeness" with which the patient looked at but seemed to not really see his face. Other oddities included his mistaking his foot for his shoe, and upon leaving the office his attempt to lift his wife's head off and put it on his head like a hat!

Intrigued by what he observed in the office, Dr. Sacks visited the patient's home. Here, he

BOX 13–1
A Case of Brain Damage:
The Man Who Mistook His Wife for a Hat

section tasks, where they are asked to bisect a line in the middle.

Once information is integrated in the parietal lobes, the *temporal lobes* come into play by categorizing, classifying, and storing the information in long-term memory. Although the temporal lobes are also involved in processing auditory information, the most dramatic effect of temporal lobe damage is the disruption of memory. Researchers at McGill University discovered, in the early 1950s, that patients with bilateral removal of the hippocampus, a part of the temporal lobe, have complete amnesia for everything that occurs after the surgery (Scoville & Milner, 1957). Such patients cannot remember where they live or how to find their way around, nor can they remember from one moment to the next a person they have just met. Every event is perceived as if it is happening for the very first time. Recent research has demonstrated that memory loss is most evident on a conscious level; although a patient may not experience any awareness of having seen a particular object in the past, there is sometimes unconscious recognition, as evidenced by changes in heart rate or skin conduction in response to a familiar stimulus (Jacoby & Kelley, 1987).

The temporal lobes are also important in linking affective or motivational significance to a particular stimulus. People with temporal lobe epilepsy often display a collection of emotional traits, which some researchers have termed the "temporal lobe personality" (Bear & Fedio, 1977). Included among these traits is a tendency to see mundane events as imbued observed that Dr. P.'s musical abilities were intact, as was his perception of abstract shapes, but his reactions to faces on the television or in family photographs were very bizarre. Dr. P. seemed incapable of visually perceiving real objects; instead, he saw only abstractions. His visual world was empty except for lifeless features which he could describe in almost geometric detail. An interesting confirmation of Dr. P.'s visual problems came in a series of paintings he had done over the years and had displayed throughout his house. Sacks (1985, p. 16) described them as follows:

All his earlier work was naturalistic and realistic, with vivid mood and atmosphere. . . . Then, years later, they became less vivid, less concrete, less realistic and naturalistic; but far more abstract, even geometrical and cubist. Finally, in the last paintings, the canvasses became intense—mere chaotic lines and blotches of paint.

Dr. P.'s disorder, of which he seemed to be almost happily unaware, was diagnosed as a *visual agnosia*; he was unable to derive a meaningful perception of objects by looking at them. Although he never ascertained the cause of the defect, Dr. Sacks speculated that it was a tumor or degenerative process in the part of the cortex that was responsible for object perception. Despite his difficulties, Dr. P. lived for several more years and played and taught music until the final days of his life.

Although Dr. P.'s case was unusually well documented, deficits in the ability to recognize familiar faces have often been reported in the literature. Indeed, whlie researching the problem, Dr. Sacks encountered reports of a farmer who suddenly could no longer distinguish the faces of his once-familiar cows and a museum worker who thought his own reflection was a three-dimensional picture of an ape.

BOX 13–1
Continued

with personal emotional significance, a characteristic that can lead to paranoia. Patients with temporal lobe epilepsy are also frequently described as "hypergraphic," which refers to their tendency to do a lot of writing, to be "hyperreligious," or to be "sticky" (a tendency to have difficulty disengaging from a conversation).

Clinical neuropsychologists typically test for problems associated with temporal lobe pathology with a variety of memory tests (e.g., Benton's Visual Retention Test, the Wechsler Memory Scale-Revised, or the California Verbal Learning Test). They also compare memory for verbal material, which would indicate left temporal disorder, with memory for visuospatial material, which would indicate right temporal disorder.

Current views of the *frontal lobes* view this region of the brain as primarily involved in the temporal organization of behavior (Kolb & Whishaw, 1990). Complex sequences of actions are planned and directed by the frontal lobes. As befits such a position of responsibility, the frontal lobes receive inputs from most other parts of the brain. This input is necessary because making appropriate decisions about responses and actions requires taking into account as much information as possible from the environment (including the position and current state of the body). This information must also be compared to previous information, and its motivational and affective significance needs to be assessed. Only then can appropriate motor responses be sequenced in time and space.

Frontal lobe damage can produce intriguing and highly disruptive effects on patients. For example, Eslinger and Damasio (1985) have reported a case of a patient whose performance on an entire battery of neuropsychological tests was completely unimpaired; yet the patient was unable to hold down a job, plan chores around the house, or even decide what to do next. Despite the patient's intact perceptual abilities and intellectual skills, he was unable to integrate all the information available to him and apply it to his daily activities in a constructive manner. Other frontal lobe impairments include changes in personality, failures to judge temporal order, and inability to use feedback from the environment to guide and modify behavior.

Typically, clinical neuropsychologists test for frontal lobe function by examining sequences of motor behavior, the person's ability to generate strategies, and his or her tendency to *perseverate* (an inability to inhibit behavior even when the behavior is inappropriate). Two tests commonly used to assess frontal lobe damage are the Wisconsin Card Sorting Test and the Categories Test from the Halstead-Reitan Battery. Both tests use feedback from the examiner to cue patients as to how to proceed, by informing them on each trial whether they were right or wrong. The feedback is designed to signal them to change their strategy for matching or categorizing information. Patients with frontal lobe lesions will often perseverate in the same strategy, regardless of whether it is successful.

Lateralization of Function

The cortex of the brain is divided into hemispheres. Each hemisphere is associated with different kinds of functions. Historically, this concept has been referred to as *cerebral dominance,* with the left hemisphere being viewed as the dominant hemisphere and the right as the nondominant or minor hemisphere. Current notions of cerebral dominance view each hemisphere as dominant for certain types of functions or processes.

Specialization of the Left Hemisphere

In most right-handers, the left hemisphere is specialized to handle speech and other aspects of linguistic processing, such as the ability to process phonological information. Thus, in right-handers, the right hemisphere has no direct access to speech mechanisms, nor can the right hemisphere process rhymes. Brain organization in left-handed people is more variable. Evidence that the left hemisphere is specialized for speech comes from a variety of sources. In addition to studies that have documented language deficits in brain-damaged patients (Rasmussen & Milner, 1975), a number of neurosurgical procedures have provided comprehensive evidence for the left hemisphere's special language abilities. Often, severe seizure disorders are caused by an area of damaged tissue in the brain; removal of this tissue can sometimes alleviate the occurrence of seizures. When neurosurgeons remove a section of the skull to prepare for surgery, they typically use electrodes to stimulate different regions of the brain, with the aim of avoiding damage to areas that are crucial for language. Thus, if they stimulate a particular area, and the patient cannot speak when instructed to, they conclude that the area is important for language. Investigations of this sort have shown that stimulation of the left hemisphere leads to disruptions in speech production and language processing. Furthermore, the disruption is consistent with the general area of function subserved by particular regions of the brain, as reviewed earlier. Thus, stimulation of the left temporal lobe disrupts verbal memory functions, whereas stimulation of the left frontal lobe disrupts speech production (since it involves complex motor sequences).

Another technique often used to investigate language lateralization was pioneered by Wada (Wada & Rasmussen, 1960) and involves injecting sodium amytal into the internal carotid artery. This procedure puts one hemisphere "to sleep" for a short period of time, during which the neuropsychologist or neurologist can test the patient. Milner (1974) and others have found that when the left hemisphere is put to sleep, nearly all right-handers lose the ability to speak.

Research with split-brain patients has also provided powerful evidence for left hemisphere lateralization of language. For example, a split-brain patient might sit before a screen that makes it impossible to see objects that are being placed in his or her hands. To identify the object, the patient must depend only on tactile information carried by the sensory nerves from the hand to the brain. Like most nerve pathways, these sensory nerves cross over before they *synapse* or connect with information processing areas in the cortex. As a result, information from the left hand is projected initially to the right side of the brain, and information from the right hand is projected to the left side of the brain. In a normal brain, the corpus callosum transfers the information from one hemisphere to the other in a split second—but when the corpus callosum is severed, the only way the opposite hemisphere can obtain the information is through direct visual input. By blocking such input, and asking a split-brain patient to describe the object in his or her hand, an experimenter can challenge the capabilities of the hemispheres.

Under these circumstances, Sperry and his associates (e.g., Sperry, 1974) found that split-brain patients had no difficulty naming objects that they were holding in the right hand (connecting with the left hemisphere). But when asked to name objects they were holding in the left hand (connecting with the right hemisphere), the patients were reduced to silence. When they were given the opportunity to point to a picture of the object, however, the left hand (which is controlled by the right hemisphere) was 100% accurate in identifying it. The obvious conclusion is that the right hemisphere is mute—it has no access to

speech mechanisms that are housed within the left hemisphere.

Specialization of the Right Hemisphere

Although the right hemisphere appears to lack speech functions, it is not stupid. Given a nonverbal means of communication, the right hemisphere is able to perform on a level equal to that of the left.

Indeed, one of the greatest contributions of research with split-brain patients was to demonstrate the right hemisphere's high-level information-processing capability. Although neuropsychological research with right-hemisphere-damaged patients had been documenting deficits in spatial information processing and facial recognition for decades, the prevailing attitude was that the right hemisphere is a poor cousin to the left, incapable of complex information processing. It was thought to be primarily devoted to lower level sensory perceptual analyses and to control of the inferior, nondominant left hand. Only a few researchers continue to endorse this view today.

We now know that the right hemisphere is crucial for analyzing a vast array of spatial and nonverbal information, including the highly complex signals involved in social communication. The right hemisphere is superior to the left hemisphere in its understanding of the relationships between objects in space and time. It seems to specialize in perceiving the *gestalt*, or whole. Thus, the left hemisphere would be more likely to focus on the trees, but miss the forest; whereas the right hemisphere sees the forest, but is likely to ignore the trees. These tendencies are revealed by drawings produced by right- versus left-brain-damaged patients. Patients with left brain damage are fairly good at drawing the parts of an object, but they are likely to misplace these parts relative to each other. Patients with right hemisphere damage are fairly good at drawing the overall shape, but their drawings lack the details.

Processing nonverbal information involves understanding the highly complex signals that are involved in social and emotional communication. Only part of the important information in a conversation is carried by the actual content of the utterances; a great deal of information is conveyed by *how* words are said rather than by *what* is said (Bates, 1976). Gestures, tone of voice, facial expressions, and body language can directly contradict verbal content. Sensitive decoding of this nonverbal information involves the ability to perceive nonverbal cues and then to integrate them into a coherent message. The right hemisphere is much better than the left at these tasks (Perecman, 1983).

Even the domain of language, long thought to be under the sole purview of the left hemisphere, depends, in part, on the right hemisphere. Recent research has shown that the right hemisphere plays an important role in understanding linguistic devices like metaphors. For example, right-brain-damaged patients interpret statements like "I cried my eyes out" as if they were literally true. Similarly, right-brain-damaged patients do not appreciate humor, and often lose the ability to "get a joke" (Gardner, Brownell, Wapner, & Michelow, 1983).

The difficulties of right-brain-damaged patients in judging situations appropriately, in relating to others, and in accurately perceiving social cues is compounded by another problem—they are often unaware of their deficits. The inability to comprehend the magnitude and severity of one's difficulties is called *anosognosia*. This problem poses a serious obstacle to rehabilitation programs because few remedial strategies will be effective if the patient does not perceive that he or she has a problem.

The Nature of Deficits

All neuropsychological approaches rely on the identification of cognitive, emotional, or behavioral deficits, followed by attempts to link these deficits to what is known about brain functioning. Therefore, it is important to understand what is meant by the concept of deficit. We have already defined *deficit* as a deficiency in a patient's performance from the level shown by a normative or average group of persons or from a level shown by the patient at an earlier time. Although normative comparisons are useful, the most important type of comparison is when a patient's current performance can be compared to prior performance.

The determination of a patient's performance level before any suspected brain damage is called a *premorbid* assessment of functioning. As the name implies, it supplies a benchmark standard against which current functioning can be compared. Repeated testing of the same patient can yield information about how rapidly a deficit is progressing or how general versus specific the deficit is. These data are useful for diagnosing brain disorders and for assessing their prognosis.

The measurement of deficits is not just a mathematical calculation. Under the best, but seldom possible, conditions, the clinician would be able to study earlier, standardized assessments of a patient's behavior and cognitive abilities. Because such assessments have usually not been performed, the clinical neuropsychologist must usually rely on the alternative strategy of estimating premorbid abilities from whatever clues can be assembled.

There are two methods for estimating premorbid functioning. An estimate can be derived from the correlations that are known to exist between cognitive abilities and such variables as age, ethnicity, sex, education level, and occupation. These correlations provide a basis for a formula that can be used to estimate premorbid levels of functioning (e.g., Barona & Chastain, 1986). The second approach is based on data showing that current reading ability is a good predictor of premorbid ability. The basis for this relationship is that reading is less affected by brain injury than most other cognitive tasks and can therefore be used to indicate how a subject might have performed in the past.

NEUROPSYCHOLOGICAL ASSESSMENT TECHNIQUES

Neuropsychologists usually follow one of two approaches to assess a patient suspected of suffering brain damage. The first approach is to administer a predetermined, standardized set of tests combined into a *battery*. Test batteries contain uniform assessment techniques for all patients. The second approach is the *individualized* method, in which a few tests are routinely given to all patients but the remaining tests are selected with the special needs of a particular patient in mind. The individualized approach tailors the choice of tests to specific diagnostic questions as well as to what is discovered about a patient from the initial core set of tests.

Both approaches have advantages. Batteries are comprehensive, useful for research because of their standardization and can be given by paraprofessionals since there is no need for expert judgments about what tests to use. Individualized approaches allow in-depth assessment of particular problems, permit the use of new tests as they are developed, and focus on specific deficits more thoroughly.

Each approach also has disadvantages. Batteries can be inefficient because they assess functions that are not disturbed in many patients; also, because of their fixed nature, batteries may become obsolete since it is difficult to incorporate new and perhaps better tests of abilities into them. Individualized approaches require their users to have more training and sophistication; and, because of the different combinations of tests they employ, research comparing different patients is more difficult.

In the following sections we briefly summarize some of the best-known examples of each approach to neuropsychological assessment.

Batteries

The most widely used battery is the Halstead-Reitan Neuropsychological Test Battery. As noted earlier, this battery was developed by Ward Halstead and later modified by his student Ralph Reitan. The Halstead-Reitan is suitable for persons aged 15 and older, but there are two other versions that can be used for children aged 9 to 14 and children between 5 and 8 years of age.

A complete Halstead-Reitan for adults consists of the following tests (Boll, 1981):

1. An MMPI (see Chapter 5 for a description).

2. A *Wechsler Adult Intelligence Scale-Revised* (WAIS-R) (see Chapter 5 for a description).

3. *The Categories Test,* which consists of 208 slides that require a subject to form correct categorizations of the visual stimuli in the slides. Initially the task is simple but later becomes difficult. The test measures mental efficiency and the ability to form abstract concepts.

4. *The Tactual Performance Test* consists of a board with spaces into which 10 blocks of various shapes can be fitted, somewhat like a big jigsaw puzzle. The subject is blindfolded and then asked to fit the blocks into the spaces as quickly as possible. The subject performs this task three times; first with the preferred hand, next with the nonpreferred hand, and finally with both hands. Following the last trial, the blindfold is removed, the board is moved from view, and the subject is asked to draw the board and blocks in their proper places from memory. This test measures abilities such as motor speed, tactile and kinesthetic perception, and incidental memory.

5. *The Rhythm Test* presents 30 pairs of rhythmic beats. The subject's task is to say whether the rhythms are the same or different. It is a measure of nonverbal auditory perception, attention, and concentration.

6. *The Speech-Sounds Perception Test* requires

Neuropsychological assessments have often been compared to and validated against methods used by neurologists. Neurodiagnostic procedures are based on directly observing damage to central nervous system tissue or monitoring some biophysical function of the brain that suggests impairment. The neuropsychologist examines how patterns of behavior are related to possible brain lesions, while the neurologist either observes lesions themselves or looks for chemical or physical evidence that a lesion is present.

Despite growing sophistication in recent years, neurological methods are not infallible. First, some neurological procedures are valid indicators for certain disorders but not for others. For example, the EEG is an excellent test for patients with seizure disorders, but it is not sensitive to Alzheimer's disease or brain infections. Second, some tests may show abnormalities in patients without any brain damage; the EEG is susceptible to this "false positive" mistake, particularly in children. A third difficulty with some neurological techniques is that they are risky for the patient. Arteriograms and repeated X-rays are two of the best-known examples.

The most common neurodiagnostic techniques are briefly described next.

1. *Neurological clinical exam.* The physician screens the patient's sensory abilities, eye movements, cognitive and perceptual abilities, language, motor and postural irregularities, and symptom history as a preliminary investigation of brain disturbance.

2. *Lumbar puncture.* Spinal fluid is extracted from the spinal cord by inserting a needle. Examination of the fluid's chemistry as well as its pressure upon extraction can help diagnose brain infections, hemorrhages, and some tumors. It is often not performed when any of several conditions are present (e.g., brain abscess), and it has some complications, the most common of which is headaches.

3. *Electroencephalogram (EEG).* The EEG monitors the electrical activity of the cerebral cortex. It is especially useful in the diagnosis of seizure disorders and some vascular diseases affecting large blood vessels in the brain. It is a safe procedure, but it yields a relatively high rate of false positives.

4. *Other electrical tests—electromyogram (EMG), evoked potentials, and nerve conduction velocities.* All three tests measure electrical activity of some sort—in muscles (EMG), in the brain when elicited by an external stimulus (evoked potentials), or in peripheral nerves (nerve conduction velocities). They are useful in the diagnosis of muscle disease, nerve disease caused by conditions such as diabetes, and certain sensory deficits.

BOX 13–2
Neurodiagnostic Procedures

that the subject match spoken nonsense words to words on written lists. Language processing, verbal auditory perception, attention, and concentration are measured by this task.

7. *The Finger Tapping Test* is a simple test of motor speed in which the subject taps a small lever with the index finger as fast as possible for 10 seconds. Several trials with both hands are used, allowing comparison of lateralized motor speed.

8. *The Trail Making Test* is a kind of "connect-the-dots" task involving a set of circles that

5. *X-rays.* There are many variations in X-ray pictures of brain structure. The technology of X-rays was revolutionized in the 1970s by the introduction of *computerized axial tomography* (CAT scans), which provides computer-enhanced three-dimensional pictures of successive slices of the brain. CAT scans are very valuable in the diagnosis of tumors, traumatic damage, degenerative diseases like Alzheimer's, and cerebrovascular disease.

6. *Positron Emission Tomography (PET scan).* PET scans show changes not just in the structure of the brain, but also in its metabolic function. It does this by tracking the rate at which a radioactive chemical injected into the brain is consumed by brain cells. Since diseased tissue uses the chemical at a different rate than normal tissue, the PET scan can reveal specific areas of abnormal brain physiology. In addition to neurological diagnoses, PET scans may help differentiate schizophrenics from bipolar patients.

7. *Arteriography.* Arteriograms involve injection of a dye into arteries, and then a series of X-rays reveals the condition of the arteries as the dye passes through them. It is used primarily to diagnose cerebrovascular disease, especially strokes and hemorrhages. Arteriograms can be very uncomfortable and sometimes dangerous procedures for some patients.

8. *Magnetic Resonance Imaging (MRI).* Another new technique that is still being refined, MRI works by tracking the activity of atoms in the body as they are "excited" by magnets in a chamber or coil placed around the patient. MRI is advantageous because it involves no X-ray exposure.

9. *Biopsies and exploratory surgery.* Both of these procedures involve direct examination of suspect tissue. Although they are risky, they can give a definite diagnosis of some neurological conditions.

10. *Single Photo Emission Computed Tomography (SPECT).* This procedure is similar to the PET scan, but because it uses a radioactive chemical that lasts longer than those used in the PET method, it permits imaging of cortical and subcortical brain sections from several different angles. It may also prove useful in the diagnosis of disorders like schizophrenia.

11. *Computerized Topographic Mapping of EEGs.* One problem with some EEG studies is that they produce too much data to be summarized effectively. Modern computer technology can be used to synthesize EEG data more efficiently. This technique relies on a computer to analyze EEG signals, code their different frequencies with different colors, and then print a multicolored map of the brain showing differences in EEG activity.

BOX 13–2
Continued

are numbered or lettered. The circles must be connected in a consecutive sequence requiring speed, visual scanning, and the ability to use and integrate different sets.

9. *The Strength of Grip Test* gives a right-side versus left-side comparison of strength. The subject simply squeezes a dynamometer twice with each hand.

10. *The Sensory-Perceptual Exam* assesses whether the subject can perceive tactile, auditory, and visual stimulation when presented on each side of the body (unilater-

ally) and on both sides simultaneously (bilaterally). Each of the three senses is assessed individually and with standard variations in the location of the stimulation used.

11. *Tactile Perception Tests* employ various methods to assess the subject's ability to identify objects when they are placed in the right and left hand, to perceive touch in different fingers of both hands, and to decipher numbers when they are traced on the fingertips while the subject's eyes are closed.

12. The *Aphasia Screening Test* is a short test that measures several aspects of language usage and recognition, as well as abilities to reproduce geometric forms and pantomime simple actions (see Reitan, 1984, for a thorough discussion of how he uses this test). Examples of 12 tasks from this test (there are a total of 32) are presented in Box 13–3.

Reitan recommended four procedures for evaluating performance on the Halstead-Reitan Battery. These procedures are generally followed by practitioners today, although there are variations in the extent each of them is emphasized. First, *level of performance* is assessed by comparing the patient's performance to that of normative groups; an impairment index is calculated based on the number of tests for which the patient's performance falls into a clinically deficient range. Second, *patterns of performance* are analyzed. Pattern analysis examines variations in performance on different components of a test; the most common example is the comparison of verbal to performance IQ scores. Third, because of the varying responsibilities of the brain's hemispheres, emphasis is placed on *comparing right-side to left-side performance* and drawing inferences from large differences. Fourth, the neuropsychologist looks for any *pathognomonic signs*. These signs involve specific deficits that are so strongly indicative of organic problems that their presence almost always indicates a disorder.

The Luria-Nebraska Neuropsychological Battery

In an attempt to administer and evaluate the neuropsychological approach pioneered by Luria in a standardized and reliable manner, Charles Golden and his colleagues at the University of Nebraska (Golden, 1981; Golden, Purisch, & Hammeke, 1985) compiled a battery based on Luria's methods but with explicit rules for quantitative scoring of the results. The latest version of this battery, known as the Luria-Nebraska Neuropsychological Battery, consists of 279 items and can be completed in about $2\frac{1}{2}$ hours, roughly half the time it takes to finish the Halstead-Reitan. The items in the test are those that best discriminated control subjects (psychiatric patients and normal subjects) from neurological patients in the original validation studies. The items are organized into 12 content scales: motor functions, rhythm and pitch, tactile and kinesthetic functions, visual functions, receptive language, expressive language, reading, arithmetic, writing, memory, intermediate memory, and intelligence. In addition, there is a pathognomonic scale composed of items that are rarely missed by normal subjects but rarely passed by brain-damaged ones, and a left hemisphere scale and a right hemisphere scale that measure motor and sensory functions of the right and left sides of the body, respectively. Scales for localization and lateralization have also been reported but are not as thoroughly validated as the initial scales (e.g., McKay & Golden, 1979).

Each item is given a score of 0 (normal performance), 1 (borderline performance), or 2 (defective performance). The items from each scale are summed, and the sums are converted to *T*-scores, allowing a profile to be drawn much like an MMPI profile.

In addition to profile analysis, the Luria-Nebraska can be interpreted qualitatively by analyzing patterns of item failures or the presence of pathognomonic signs. *T*-scores can also be adjusted for age and education, making the cutoff scores used to assess impairment specific to such characteristics.

Patient's Task	Examiner's Instructions to the Patient
Copy Square	First, draw this on your paper (examiner points to picture of a square). I want you to do it without lifting your pencil from the paper. Make it about this same size (points to square).
Name Square	What is that shape called?
Spell Square	Would you spell that word for me?
Copy Cross	Draw this on your paper (examiner points to picture of a cross). Go around the outside like this until you get back to where you started (examiner draws a finger line around the edge of the stimulus figure). Make it about this same size (points to cross).
Name Cross	What is that shape called?
Spell Cross	Would you spell that word for me?
Name Baby	What is this? (examiner points to picture of baby)
Repeat/Explain "He shouted the warning"	I am going to say something that I want you to say after me. So listen carefully: He shouted the warning. Now you say it. Would you explain what that means? Sometimes it is necessary to amplify by asking the kind of situation to which the sentence would refer. The patient's understanding is adequately demonstrated when he brings the concept of impending danger into his explanation.
Write "He shouted the warning"	Now I want you to write that sentence on the paper. Sometimes it is necessary to repeat the sentence so that the patient understands clearly what he is to write.
Name Key	What is this? (examiner points to picture of key)
Demonstrate Use of Key	If you had one of these in your hand, show me how you would use it (points to key).
Draw Key	Now I want you to draw a picture that looks just like this. Try to make your key look enough like this one so that I would know it was the same key from your drawing (points to key).

Source: Filskov and Boll, 1981. (© Copyright 1981. Used by permission of John Wiley & Sons.)

BOX 13–3

Examples of Items From the Aphasia Screening Test

Evaluation of Batteries

Both the Halstead-Reitan and the Luria-Nebraska batteries have shown impressive validities in discriminating brain-damaged patients from control subjects (Golden, Hammeke, & Purisch, 1978; Reitan, 1955; Vega & Parsons, 1967). The Halstead-Reitan has also demonstrated good validity in detecting the lateralization (Wheeler & Reitan, 1962) and localization (Reitan, 1964) of brain damage, but it does a relatively poor job of discriminating between brain damage and serious psychological disorders such as schizophrenia (Jones & Butters, 1983). Although strong claims are made for the Luria-Nebraska's ability to discriminate brain-damaged from schizophrenic patients, this battery has been severely criticized for flawed test construction, improper analysis of the data, inadequate standardization, and a distortion of Luria's original methods, which simply may not be translatable into items on a battery (Adams, 1980a,b; Golden, 1980; and Spiers, 1980, provide the flavor of this sometimes bitter controversy).

Individualized Approaches

One of the most thorough and best-described individualized approaches is that of Murial D. Lezak, a psychologist at the Oregon Health Sciences University and the Portland, Oregon, VA Hospital. Lezak's strategy, as described in her book, *Neuropsychological Assessment* (1983), is to perform several standard tests for all patients that assess "major functions in the auditory and visual receptive modalities and the spoken, written, graphic and constructional response modalities" (p. 107). This preliminary battery usually takes about 2 to 3 hours. Following the initial battery, Lezak proceeds with "hypothesis testing." During this part of the examination she shifts the focus of the assessment from one set of functions to another as the data indicate changes in what abilities may be most impaired.

The addition of specialized tests depends on continuing formulation and reformulation of hypotheses as new data answer some questions and raise others. Hypotheses involving differentiation of learning from retrieval, for instance, will dictate the use of techniques for assessing learning when retrieval is impaired. . . . every other function can be examined across modalities and in systematically varied formats. In each case, the examiner can best determine what particular combinations of modality, content, and format are needed to test the pertinent hypothesis. (Lezak, 1983, pp. 110–111)

The other well-known individualized approach to neuropsychological assessment was developed by the Boston group of Edith Kaplan, Harold Goodglass, and Nelson Butters. Their assessment begins with a core set of 11 tests that measure areas such as intelligence, memory, attention, construction, and sensory-perceptual abilities. Then, depending on the nature of the referral plus the results of the initial testing, additional tests are administered. Special attention is paid to language, memory, and other cortical functions. According to Jones and Butters (1983),

Attention to the strategies and processes involved in patients' failures and successes in test performance partially determines the selection of tests to be used in addition to those in the core group. Even more importantly, the emphasis on process and strategy contributes to a more than usually detailed analysis of patients' deficits, with the recognition that superficially similar deficits can reflect quite distinctive underlying processes. (p. 388)

Evaluation of Individualized Approaches

It is difficult to assess the validity of individualized approaches because they are tailored to each patient's needs and hence are not given to sufficient numbers of patients to permit large-scale comparisons. Furthermore, individualized approaches depend much more than batteries do on the skill of the examiner using them. It therefore becomes difficult to separate the validity of the tests from the clinical acumen of the examiner. Despite these limitations, individualized approaches offer a promising strategy when they are based on theoretical models that specify the impairments that one will encounter with various types of brain damage (Satz & Fletcher, 1981). In other words, individualized approaches usually reflect a theoretical justification for the use of particular tests while the typical neuropsychological battery does not; its construction depends only on the ability of its items to empirically differentiate brain-damaged subjects from others. This difference is another example of the distinction between empirical versus rational approaches to test construction that we outlined in Chapter 5.

NEUROPSYCHOLOGICAL APPROACHES TO PSYCHOPATHOLOGY

Recently, neuropsychological approaches have begun to shed light on a number of psychological disorders, including depression and schizophrenia. Neuropsychologists are also beginning to expand our understanding of several childhood problems, especially learning disabilities.

Depression

Neuropsychologists have been interested in depression ever since Gainotti (1972) documented in a systematic fashion that different kinds of brain damage produce different kinds of emotional reactions. Right-brain-damaged patients often show a rather cheerful, inappropriate, unconcerned reaction toward their impairment, change in status, and hospitalization. Gainotti termed this the "euphoric or indifference" reaction. (This reaction is often accompanied by anosognosia, which is an un-

awareness of deficit.) In contrast, left-brain-damaged patients often show what Gainotti called the "catastrophic" reaction, which is characterized by symptoms of depression such as tearfulness and despair.

More recently, a series of studies by Robinson and colleagues has confirmed that somewhere between one third and two thirds of patients become depressed after experiencing damage to the left side of the brain (Starkstein & Robinson, 1988). These researchers have also shown that the probability that a person will develop depression is highly correlated with the proximity of the lesion to the front part of the brain. The closer the lesion is to the frontal pole of the left hemisphere, the more severe the depression.

Other studies have suggested that these emotional responses are not simply a reaction to the experience of being impaired. When stroke patients were compared to orthopedic patients suffering a similar degree of disability, four times as many stroke patients were depressed (Folstein, Maiberger, & McHugh, 1977). Furthermore, the degree of depression doesn't correlate with the severity of the disability, suggesting that if there is a relationship, it is not a simple, linear one.

These findings have been corroborated by research measuring electrical activity over the left versus the right hemisphere. When depressed people are compared to nondepressed people, the left hemisphere in nondepressed people is not as active as the right. Similarly, when the same measurements are taken in nondepressed people in different moods, the left hemisphere is less active, compared to the right hemisphere, when people are sad. These differences in EEG activity are most evident over the frontal regions of the brain, confirming the importance of this area for these emotional effects.

It has also been shown, in tachistoscopic studies (Heller, 1990), that when visual stimuli are projected to both hemispheres, the left hemisphere typically rates pictures as more positive than the right hemisphere—even though each hemisphere has seen the exact same pictures. These results suggest that in the normal brain, frontal regions of the left hemisphere play some role in maintaining a positive perspective on things. When this area is underactive relative to the right hemisphere, because of a lesion or other unknown etiologies, negative mood states result.

Researchers have speculated that these effects on mood may be mediated by the neurotransmitter dopamine, which has been found to be unevenly distributed in the left hemisphere in both animals and people. Dopamine seems to play a special role in allowing people to find things rewarding or enjoyable; for example, the euphoric effects of amphetamine have been shown to be mediated by an increase in dopamine in the brain. It is possible, therefore, that interfering with the transmission of dopamine may affect the activity level of the left hemisphere as well as produce depression.

Other studies have found that depression is also associated with reduced functioning of the right hemisphere, but in this case, the posterior regions are most affected (Heller, 1990). People who are depressed show some of the same cognitive deficits displayed by patients with damage to parietal-temporal regions of the brain. They have difficulty with visuospatial information processing and show a number of attentional problems that are similar to right-brain-damaged patients. These effects may be caused by the interrelationship of the frontal and posterior regions of the brain. Since frontal regions often inhibit activation in posterior regions, relatively greater activation in the right frontal region compared to the left may be producing too much inhibition of the right posterior regions.

It is also possible that some of the characteristic cognitive and psychomotor symptoms of depression are due to these underlying neuropsychological patterns. For example, the frontal regions of the left hemisphere are involved in programming fine motor activities, and depressed patients display slowed responses and initiate fewer activities.

Neuropsychological findings have implications not only for our basic understanding of depression, but also for its diagnosis and treatment. It is important to consider the possibility that a brain-damaged patient is depressed, in addition to problems that the patient may have with impaired language comprehension or expression. Neuropsychologists typically ask family members whether a patient is sleeping normally, eating normally, or is recovering as expected. Often, when patients display disrupted sleep or appetite, or are not recovering as quickly as predicted, it is an indication of an underlying depression. Treatment with antidepressants can often alleviate these symptoms. It is also possible that depressed people can display neuropsychological deficits that might falsely imply brain impairment. With proper treatment of the depression, these deficits are typically reduced.

Schizophrenia

Neuropsychologists have also studied brain functioning in schizophrenia. Early studies, primarily using tachistoscopic methods, suggested the possibility that this disorder was characterized by an overactivation of the left hemisphere (Gur, 1978). Current studies present a more complicated picture, although the left hemisphere continues to be implicated. One of the most active areas of research involves the measurement of regional cerebral blood flow and glucose metabolism in schizophrenics compared to controls. These studies have suggested that the left prefrontal region of schizophrenics is abnormal because it is not activated during performance on tests like the Wisconsin Card Sort Test. In contrast, subcortical regions of the same hemisphere show a hyperactivation compared to controls (Rubin et al., 1991).

These results are compatible with several observations regarding the symptomatology of schizophrenia. First, many schizophrenics display what are termed *negative* symptoms.

These include flat affect, lack of initiative, lack of energy, absence of social engagement, and loss of spontaneity. These same symptoms are encountered in certain patients with prefrontal lesions. Second, the disruption in linear reasoning, logical thought, and language typically seen in schizophrenia is consistent with some kind of damage to the specialized regions of the left hemisphere.

We must be cautious in drawing conclusions, however. The prefrontal region is intricately connected to many other parts of the brain, and damage or dysfunction elsewhere could cause the prefrontal region to malfunction. Furthermore, the studies are usually based on small samples, since schizophrenia is relatively rare in the general population, the patients are difficult to test, and the technology is expensive and complicated. Nonetheless, many researchers believe that the results point to the possibility that schizophrenia is related to damage or dysfunction of the prefrontal regions of the left hemisphere (Rubin et al., 1991).

Learning Disabilities

Given neuropsychologists' interest in intellectual abilities and mental performance, it is not surprising that learning disabilities would be a popular area of research. Several studies have indicated that *dyslexia* (the inability to read) is related to dysfunction of the left hemisphere. Tachistoscopic studies and other behavioral measures have found that children with reading problems tend to show a reduced advantage for the left hemisphere relative to the right (Obrzut, 1988). These children tend to rely more on right than left hemisphere processes in learning to read. Dyslexia is correlated with other deficits in language skills; for example, children with reading difficulties often are slow to acquire spoken language.

Several studies have reported the results of brain autopsies in people who were known to have had dyslexia. These studies have found that the structure of the left hemisphere in dyslexics is different from that of most people. In other cases researchers have found evidence for misplaced brain cells, called *ectopias,* in the left hemisphere. These misplaced cells are likely to occur during the development of the brain, when cells are migrating to their proper places in the cortex. Such misplacements could cause developmental delays and deficits in the functioning of the left hemisphere.

Pediatric clinical neuropsychologists can often help document left hemisphere deficits in children with reading difficulties. Often, they also help design remedial programs for such children and consult with teachers and parents on how best to get academic information across.

Nonverbal Learning Disability

A different type of learning disability involves deficits in visuospatial and visuomotor skills, as well as other abilities that depend on the right hemisphere. This syndrome was first described by Myklebust (1975), but recent neuropsychological research has been at the forefront of delineating this disorder and communicating its significance to teachers and other professionals. Nonverbal learning disabilities have escaped the notice of professionals until recently, probably because these children often have high levels of verbal intelligence and are talkative. Consequently, they sound as though they should be more skillful than they actually are. Because their deficits are less obvious, they are more likely to be labeled as having an emotional or behavioral problem. Unfortunately, when a child has been viewed as bad, or uncooperative, or a problem long enough, he or she ends up being just that. Earlier diagnosis and treatment of children with nonverbal learning disabilities should help prevent some of these subsequent psychological problems.

In his recent book on nonverbal learning

disabilities, Rourke (1989) suggested that right hemisphere deficits early in childhood can dramatically interfere with normal development. Such deficits inhibit a child from exploring the environment, learning the consequences of actions, and gaining essential experience in coordinated visuomotor skills. Wendy Heller and her colleagues (Heller, Hopkins, & Cox, 1991) have studied infants with brain hemorrhages caused by immature development of the vascular system. They found that right-brain-damaged babies were less facially expressive and showed less reciprocity in interactions with their mothers than left-brain-damaged babies or non-brain-damaged controls. Since mother–infant interaction predicts quality of attachment at slightly older ages, and since quality of attachment predicts social adjustment in childhood, these results suggest that in addition to early motoric and cognitive handicaps, early abnormalities in social relationships place children with nonverbal learning disabilities at risk for emotional difficulties later in life.

Children with nonverbal learning disabilities often have difficulties keeping up with other children on nonverbal tasks. They are slow to learn skills like tying shoes, dressing, eating, and organizing time and space. They also have more difficulties in social development, probably because of the intense demands on nonverbal information processing during social situations. Under these circumstances, the need to integrate facial information, tone of voice, physical activity, and verbal content overwhelm them and they fail to follow even simple exchanges. Over time, the lack of experience and interaction with other children can cause them to feel isolated, lonely, and depressed. It has even been suggested that nonverbal learning disability may be a risk factor for the development of schizophrenia.

Pediatric clinical neuropsychologists typically administer a variety of tests to document a nonverbal learning disability. One of the first warning signals is the presence of a discrepancy between Verbal and Performance IQ on the Wechsler Intelligence Scale for Children. Often, Verbal IQ will be average or well above average, with Performance IQ significantly lower. If the pattern persists on other tests comparing verbal and visuospatial/visuomotor skills, a nonverbal learning disability is likely. Often, although not always, the pattern of poor performance on right hemisphere tasks is accompanied by left-sided signs on the Halstead-Reitan Battery, suggesting impaired right hemisphere performance.

As with verbal learning disabilities, pediatric clinical neuropsychologists work with teachers and parents to devise remedial programs. In the case of a child with a nonverbal learning disability, parents and teachers are encouraged to take advantage of the child's verbal skills to compensate for a lack of understanding in nonverbal domains. These children need individual attention from a learning disabilities specialist or tutor just as much as do children with verbal learning disabilities. Otherwise, their achievement is likely to fall far behind as the demands of school increase. Their difficulties in social skills can often be addressed by group therapy, social skills workshops, individual therapy, or facilitation of structured peer interactions such as scouting or participation in after-school programs.

FUTURE DIRECTIONS

One of the most obvious trends in neuropsychological research and practice is the increasing reliance on biological measures of brain functioning such as PET, MRI, and other indices of regional cerebral activation and organization. Continued development and refinement of these techniques are likely, making it likely that they will become more accessible to researchers and clinicians. In combination with other measures of neuropsychological, cognitive, attentional, and emotional functioning, brain activity measures will provide a new database for the field. Recently, Joseph Matarazzo (1992) predicted that these measures will eventually be used to index individual differences in brain structure and mental ability, "thus heralding the first clear break from test items and tests in the Binet tradition in a century" (p. 1012).

Matarazzo also argues that the future will bring refinement in the specificity of tests of ability as psychologists learn more about cognitive organization. At the same time, the links between specific kinds of abilities and the parts of the brain involved in those abilities will become clearer. Consequently, it will become easier to design tasks to measure even more precisely the functioning of particular brain regions, and to link these to individual differences in ability levels.

Increasing the sensitivity of the measures we have available, along with an improved ability to link these measures to specific brain regions, bodes well for our understanding of brain–behavior relationships in a variety of important groups. For example, as the elderly population increases, the incidence of Alzheimer's and other dementing illnesses will increase. Mapping the relationship between memory functions and brain regions promises to advance both basic knowledge about the problem as well as to improve clinical assessment and intervention. Similarly, our understanding of the neural architecture in schizophrenia will be advanced by the types of studies described in this chapter, where performance on neuropsychological tests is coupled with the measurement of brain activity.

CHAPTER 14

Professional Issues in Clinical Psychology

If Lightner Witmer were to return from the dead to review the field he founded, he would not recognize many modern clinicians as his colleagues. A few might match his original psychoeducational, child-oriented model. But many others would bewilder Witmer, because they practice something very different from the clinical psychology of the early 20th century.

Having read the previous 13 chapters, you should be able to sympathize with Witmer's confusion. Clinical psychology is an expanding profession that is becoming more and more difficult to summarize in a single volume. As we saw in Chapter 1, there is a long list of professional roles clinicians now fill. However, no list does full justice to the complexity of clinical psychology, because it does not indicate either the multiple functions required by each job or the new specialties that will emerge in the years to come. Struck by an almost geometric growth in the number of clinicians, a proliferation of alternative roles, and increasing specialization, commentators struggle for an apt description of clinical psychology's current status. A favorite summary is that clinical psychology is in a transitional state.

This claim is an understatement on at least two counts. First, it suggests that transition is a novel era in an otherwise tranquil history. This, of course, is not correct. Clinical psychology has been in constant transition. Witmer would not have had to wait until the 1990s to be surprised by changes in clinical psychology; he would have seen changes by the 1920s.

The words *transitional state* also underestimate the pace of change in clinical psychology. The rate of transition has been accelerating like an object falling through space. Each decade since World War II has seen more extensive changes in the field than any preceding period.

Consider these three examples: (a) In 1947 there were 787 members in APA's Division 12, the Division of Clinical Psychology. In 1964, there were 2,883 members (Shakow, 1968). In

1991 the membership of Division 12 stood at more than 6,000, approximately eight times its original size. (The next two largest divisions are also composed mainly of clinical psychologists—the Division of Psychotherapy and the Division of Psychologists in Independent Practice—each with more than 5,000 members.) (b) In the first 50 years of clinical psychology, there was only one conference on professional training, held in 1949 in Boulder, Colorado. Since that time there have been five national training conferences. In addition, several other conferences addressing specific issues in the training of clinical psychologists have been held; we discuss some of these conferences later in this chapter. (c) Early proposals for training in clinical psychology discouraged clinicians from entering private practice; only a handful of psychologists did so. Today, private practice is the number one type of employment for clinical psychologists, with more than one third of clinicians primarily employed in a private setting.

These changes, along with the community mental health movement, health insurance, behavioral medicine, and society's demand for mental health services, suggest that it would be more accurate to portray clinical psychology not so much in transition, as in an entirely new era.

The first era of clinical psychology extended from its birth in 1896 to World War II. This was the time when clinical psychology appeared as a subfield of scientific psychology and as a contributing member of the mental health team under the supervision of psychiatry. The approximately 50 years since the end of World War II have constituted clinical psychology's second era. During this period the field's identity became established and expanded vigorously. This modern era has seen the field largely transformed from an academic discipline into a service profession. It has seen clinical psychology liberate itself from the opposition of some members of nonclinical psychology and from the domination of psychiatry. It has been an era in which clinicians

struggled for autonomy, got it, and became determined to retain it.

The professionalization and current status of clinical psychology are the topics of this last chapter. It is a story that has many subplots because the professionalization of clinical psychology involves several overlapping developments that have reshaped clinical psychology's identity. We focus on five issues crucial to clinical psychology's struggle for professional recognition:

1. *Professional training.* What training does one need to become a clinical psychologist, and what are the options for obtaining this training?

2. *Professional regulation.* What are the mechanisms for insuring that a clinical psychologist possesses minimum skills and meets minimum requirements to function professionally?

3. *Professional ethics.* What principles guide clinicians in determining the ethical standards for their professional activities? How is unethical behavior handled?

4. *Professional independence.* What is the relationship between clinical psychology and other mental health professions?

5. *Perils of professionalization.* Has the professionalization of clinical psychology been an asset or a detriment? Has the public benefited? Has the quality of clinical psychology improved?

PROFESSIONAL TRAINING

Throughout the first 4 decades of the 20th century, advanced training for clinical psychologists made little progress. For clinicians of that period, experience was not only the best teacher, it was practically the only one. Psychologists were involved increasingly in clinical work during this time, but their training for these activities was unsystematic.

A few steps toward formalization of clinical training were taken by the APA during the 1930s and early 1940s, but they had little effect. In 1931 an APA Committee on Standards of Training for Clinical Psychologists was formed, and in 1935 this committee published several recommendations for clinical training. In 1936 the Psychology Department at Columbia University proposed a training curriculum for clinical psychologists that involved 2 years of graduate work and a 1-year internship (Shakow, 1948). In 1943 a Committee on Training in Clinical Psychology released a report entitled "Proposed Program of Professional Training in Clinical Psychology"; 2 years later a report on graduate internship training in psychology was published.

Very little was accomplished with respect to training clinical psychologists until the late 1940s, when the social needs brought about by World War II and the financial support provided by the Veterans Administration and the U.S. Public Health Service combined to offer psychology a unique opportunity for expansion, establishment, and esteem.

The most influential psychologist in the development of clinical training programs was David Shakow, for many years the chief psychologist at Worcester State Hospital in Massachusetts and later an important figure at the National Institute of Mental Health. As early as 1942, Shakow saw the need for a 4-year doctoral-level training program in clinical psychology that included an internship during the third year (Shakow, 1942).

Shakow attracted the attention of Carl Rogers, who was then president of the APA. Rogers asked Shakow to chair a Committee on Training in Clinical Psychology, whose task was to formulate a recommended clinical training program. The committee prepared a report entitled "Recommended Graduate Training in Clinical Psychology," which was accepted by the APA in September 1947 and published that same year in the *American Psychologist*. The Shakow report set the pattern for clinical training and remains, with surprisingly few exceptions, a standard against which modern clinical programs can be evaluated.

Three important recommendations of the Shakow report on clinical training were:

1. A clinical psychologist should be trained first and foremost as a psychologist.

2. Clinical training should be as rigorous as that for nonclinical areas of psychology.

3. Preparation of the clinical psychologist should be broad and directed toward assessment, research, and therapy.

In addition, several other principles for graduate clinical programs were advocated in the Shakow report:

4. The core content of clinical training programs should involve six areas: general psychology, psychodynamics of behavior, diagnostic methods, research methods, related disciplines, and therapy.

5. The program should offer basic courses in principles as opposed to a large number of courses on special techniques.

6. Training should integrate theory with practice. This emphasis on integrated training was a hallmark of Shakow's plan; mechanisms for integrating theory with practice are suggested in every one of his many articles on training.

7. Throughout the entire graduate program, beginning in the first year, the student should have contact with clinical material.

8. Opportunities should also be provided for contact with "normal" persons who never establish clinical contacts.

9. The training atmosphere should encourage maturity and the continued growth of desirable personality characteristics.

10. The program should promote a sense of responsibility for patients and clients.

11. Representatives of related disciplines should teach clinical trainees, and joint study with

students in these related disciplines should be arranged.

12. The program must emphasize the research implications of clinical phenomena.

13. Trainees "must acquire the ability to see beyond the responsibilities they owe the individual patient, to those they owe society" (Shakow, 1978, p. 151).

The Shakow report suggested a year-by-year curriculum to fulfill these criteria. This schedule was not offered as a blueprint for training but as an illustrative model of an adequate clinical program.

In this model, first-year clinical students would become acquainted with the foundations of general psychology. They would also be trained in observational techniques. The second year would be devoted primarily to the experimental, diagnostic, and therapeutic content of clinical psychology. In addition to didactic material, students would acquire direct, practical experience through practicum courses and clinical placements.

The third year would be the internship, a year of intensive and extensive experience with clinical phenomena at a hospital, clinic, or medical center. Shakow regarded the internship as an essential component that engendered the student's sense of professional identity and immersed her or him in practical clinical experience.

Several objectives were to be met during the fourth year. The dissertation would be completed; the student would take a seminar on professional problems and ethics as well as seminars involving related disciplines; and the student would undergo a period of self-evaluation. Self-evaluation usually meant being in individual psychotherapy, which would help the student uncover biases, attitudes, and personality problems that might interfere with later clinical work.

Many of today's clinical training programs are much like Shakow's prototype. However,

it usually takes 5 or 6, rather than 4, years to complete the entire training sequence (the internship is usually taken in the fourth or fifth year). The major reasons for the extra year are that most programs require a master's thesis (usually in the second year), some universities still retain requirements such as a foreign language, and many clinical programs have added required courses on professional ethics as well as such specialty areas as human diversity, substance abuse, sexual problems, and organic disorders.

While there are many variations in the curricula of APA-accredited programs, the sample schedule in Box 14–1 shows roughly what you might encounter in most PhD programs.

The greatest impact of the Shakow report was that it prescribed that special mix of scientific and professional preparation that has typified most clinical training programs ever since. This recipe for training (which we have already described as the scientist-professional model) was officially endorsed at clinical psychology's first major training conference held in Boulder, Colorado, 1949 (Raimy, 1950).

The Boulder Conference

The Boulder Conference on Training in Clinical Psychology was convened with the financial support of the Veterans Administration and the U.S. Public Health Service, which requested APA to (a) name those universities that offered satisfactory training programs and (b) develop acceptable programs in universities that did not have them.

The Boulder conferees accepted the recommendations of Shakow's committee for a scientist-professional model of training. Clinical psychologists were expected to be proficient in research and professional practice and to have earned a PhD in psychology from a university-based graduate program. A supervised, year-long internship would also be required. Shakow's plan became known as the *Boulder model.*

Fall Semester	*Spring Semester*

First Year

Psychological Statistics I	Psychological Statistics II
Introduction to Interviewing	Clinical Assessment II
Clinical Assessment I	Selected Proseminar (Social Psychology, Developmental Psychology, Psychology of Learning, Physiological Psychology)
Practicum in Assessment	
History and Systems of Psychology	
	Theories and Research in Personality

Second Year

Psychopathology	Psychotherapy Practicum
Selected Proseminar (choose one from list above)	Clinical Seminar (Group Therapy, Behavior Modification, Child and Family Therapy, Health Psychology, Community Psychology)
Systems of Psychotherapy	
MA research	MA research

Third Year

Psychotherapy Practicum	Advanced nonclinical seminar
Clinical Seminar (choose one from list above)	Clinical or nonclinical research seminar
Clinical Research Seminar (Research in Personlity, Psychopathology Research, Research in Psychotherapy)	Psychotherapy Practium
Advanced nonclinical seminar	

A written qualifying examination is to be taken during the third year of graduate work, but no later than the beginning of the fourth year. Only those students who have completed their MA thesis are permitted to register for the qualifying examination.

Fourth Year
Internship

Fifth Year

Clinical or nonclinical research seminar	Same as Fall Semester
Advanced nonclinical seminar	
Research on dissertation	

BOX 14–1
Sample Schedule of PhD Program in Clinical Psychology

The Boulder conferees further agreed that some mechanism was necessary for monitoring, evaluating, and officially accrediting clinical training programs and internship facilities. As a result, APA formed an Education and Training Board whose Committee on Accreditation was charged with these tasks. Currently, clinical training sites are visited by an APA accreditation team about every 5 years. The team consists of three psychologists (selected by the program from a list of potential visitors) who evaluate how well the program is meeting its own training goals and APA's training standards. The most recent version of APA's criteria for accreditation was published in 1986 in the form of an *Accreditation Handbook*. A new set of standards, developed by APA in 1989, are now being considered for adoption; they would apply to areas of specialization other than clinical, counseling and school, the currently accredited areas.

The results of accreditation site visits are published each year in the APA's official journal, *American Psychologist*. In 1992 there were about 160 clinical training programs fully approved by the APA (see Appendix) and more than 325 fully approved internships.[1] In addition, there are several doctoral training programs that function without APA approval, either because the program has not requested a site visit or because approval has not been granted after an accreditation visit.

The Conference at Stanford, Miami, and Chicago

Although the Boulder model remains dominant, some clinicians have expressed discontent with it since 1949. This discontent has grown in recent years, and there are now major alternatives to the Boulder model. We will describe these later; for now we need to examine the post-Boulder training conferences that set the stage for these alternatives.

---

[1]To acquaint prospective clinical students with the array of training possibilities, APA publishes a book annually called *Graduate Study in Psychology and Associated Fields,* which lists all graduate programs in psychology along with a brief description of requirements and training features. In addition, almost all clinical programs have a brochure that can be obtained on request. These brochures discuss the program's orientation, faculty interests, requirements, and means of financial support for students (see Appendix).

Stanford

The Stanford conference, held at Stanford University in 1955 (Strother, 1956), offered no new direction for clinical training. It did anticipate some of the effects that the community mental health movement would later have on clinical psychology, and it stressed the need to prepare clinicians for the new professional roles community mental health would offer.

Miami

The Miami Beach training conference was held in 1958 (Roe, Gustad, Moore, Ross, & Skodak, 1959). By then, clinical psychology had undergone enough changes to warrant reevaluation of the scientist-professional model. The conferees again concluded that the PhD program should be retained as the primary training vehicle, although departments were encouraged to develop programs that best suited their own resources and needs. The need for psychology to train its graduates in the techniques of empirical research was also emphasized.

Chicago

The 1965 Chicago Conference on the Professional Preparation of Clinical Psychologists was the first conference to seriously consider alternative models of clinical training. A theme of this conference was that, while the scientist-professional model should be continued, the value of a purely *professional* model of training should also be appreciated.

The interest in a professional model that stressed training for the delivery of clinical services stemmed from two sources. First, the need for psychological service providers was burgeoning, due in large part to the community mental health movement. Second, only a small percentage of psychologists, probably about 10%, publish research in psychology. Critics of the Boulder model argued that too much time was being spent training students for activities that, as professionals, they did not perform. At the same time, research-oriented departments of psychology were accepting increasing numbers of practice-oriented graduate students. The fit was often a bad one.

In place of the scientist-professional model, a professional program was proposed (Zimet & Throne, 1965):

The distinctive feature of this pattern of doctoral training would be the effort to prepare a broadly trained psychological clinician prepared to intervene in a wide variety of settings for the purpose of fostering change and forestalling psychological problems. His training would include psychological science but would stress those areas in which clinical methods find their support. It would also include relevant material from related disciplines such as medicine and sociology. He would be introduced to a variety of diagnostic, remedial, and preventive procedures. His training would include analysis of the manner in which clinical methods are developed with the intent to make him a sophisticated evaluator of new methods developed in the future. Because he would not carry out a doctoral dissertation or learn foreign languages, he would have more time available for professional training and experience. Should he wish to develop the competence of a specialist in specified diagnostic, remedial, or preventive procedures he will need additional training—either on the job or in formal postdoctoral training programs.

We would expect a clinical psychologist trained in this manner to devote full time to professional practice oriented toward treatment, prevention, or both. He would use diagnostic instruments, carry out psychotherapy, engage in milieu therapy, use behavior therapy, consult in community mental health projects, work with groups, organizations, and communities—as the occasion demanded. He would, as far as his limited scientific training would permit, keep abreast of new methods as they developed and critically appraise them prior to adoption. He would contribute to the development of methods of practice by exchanging his professional experience with that of his colleagues. (pp. 21–22)

In the end, the conferees refused to endorse the explicitly professional model, preferring instead a flexible scientist-professional plan that would not shortchange training in clinical activities. Training programs were urged to add faculty who were practicing clinicians and also to broaden their criteria for acceptable research activities.

Diversity in training was encouraged by calling for pilot programs that would experiment with innovative ways of implementing the professional model. Special interest focused on the first PsyD (Doctor of Psychology) program then under development at the University of Illinois at Urbana-Champaign. The appropriate levels (doctoral and subdoctoral) and locations (department of psychology, medical center, independent professional school) of clinical training were also debated at Chicago.

The importance of the Chicago conference was that professional training models and subdoctoral programs, while not officially endorsed, were gaining support among clinical psychology's leadership. Many of the ideas considered for the first time at Chicago were adopted by the participants at psychology's next training conference.

The Vail Conference

The National Conference on Levels and Patterns of Professional Training in Psychology was held in 1973 in Vail, Colorado. Sponsored by a grant from the National Institute of Mental Health (NIMH), the Vail conference included a wide range of psychological specialties, training orientations, graduate students, and minority-group psychologists. In only 5 days the conference passed 150 resolutions, which introduced sweeping changes in the training of psychologists. These recommendations were organized around the following themes (Korman, 1976):

1. Professional Training Models. The conference officially recognized professional training as an acceptable model for programs that defined their mission as the preparation of students for the delivery of clinical services. These "unambiguously professional" programs were to be given status equal to their more traditional scientist-professional counterparts. Professional programs could be housed in a number of settings, including academic psychology departments, medical schools, or specially established professional schools. When emphasis was on the delivery and evaluation of professional services, the PsyD would be the appropriate degree. When emphasis was on the development of new knowledge in psychology, the PhD would be preferred.

2. Levels of Training. The conferees believed that priority should be given to programs that provided multiple levels of training or demonstrated coordination with degree programs at varying levels. They advocated the idea of a *career lattice,* a structure that would allow upward professional mobility through continued, integrated training.

One of the most controversial of the Vail recommendations was that persons trained at the master's level should be considered professional psychologists. This sentiment reversed the opinion of previous conferences, which envisioned psychology as a doctoral-level profession. The Vail participants, on the other hand, felt that many services performed by doctoral psychologists could be performed with equal competence by personnel trained at the master's or submaster's level. The conference called for professional master's programs and full APA membership for the master's-level individual. Soon, universities in several states had developed MA training programs in clinical psychology. Today, master's-level clinicians continue to outnumber PhDs in some states, and there are about 200 programs

that offer an "MA-only" curriculum in psychology (Quereshi & Kuchan, 1988).

The MA proposal was short lived because the tide later turned against the MA as a recognized degree for the professional psychologist. In 1977 the APA voted that the title *psychologist* should be reserved for those who have completed a *doctoral* training program, a policy that remains in effect today.

The status of the MA clinician was also jeopardized by Vail advocates who, while willing to endorse MA-trained persons as professionals, were unwilling to recommend licensure for them. Another obstacle for the master's-level clinician has been a political one. Quite simply, the status of psychology as a profession vis-à-vis psychiatry is threatened by including the MA holder along with the PhD psychologist. Most observers agree that the professional autonomy of psychology is best preserved by defining it exclusively as a doctoral-level enterprise. Financial considerations have also exerted pressure against granting full standing to MA recipients. Psychologists' eligibility for reimbursement as health-care providers is strengthened by portraying clinical psychology as a doctoral-level profession (we return to this topic later).

3. Desirable Characteristics of Professional Training. The Vail conference considered many issues related to the social obligations of psychology, affirmative action, racism and sexism, and the need for continuing professional development. Although those issues are beyond the scope of this chapter, the attention paid to them at Vail proves that this conference, more than any of its predecessors, seriously challenged both the history and the future of professional psychology.

Salt Lake City

The sixth National Conference on graduate education in psychology was held in July, 1987 at the University of Utah in Salt Lake City. The conference was needed for several reasons, primarily the need to evaluate the several changes that had taken place in the training of professional psychologists during recent years, and the desire to reduce growing tensions between scientists and practitioners over numerous training and organizational issues. The conference produced 67 separate resolutions. The most important ones for our purposes are listed here (see also Bickman, 1987; and a special issue of the *American Psychologist,* December 1987):

1. For programs seeking accreditation, their trainees must be trained in a core of psychological knowledge that should include research design and methods; statistics; ethics; assessment; history and systems of psychology; biological, social, and cognitive-affective bases of behavior; and individual differences.

2. By 1995, in order to be accredited by APA, doctoral training programs must be academic units within a regionally accredited university *or* must be formally affiliated with a regionally accredited university. This resolution was aimed at gaining tighter control of professional schools of psychology that were not associated with a university. We discuss these free-standing schools later.

3. Education in psychology occurs along a continuum from precollege, undergraduate, graduate, to postdoctoral levels. Training at the lower levels should be broad, with greater depth and specialization introduced at the advanced levels.

After six national training conferences, several smaller conferences, countless hours of discussion, contention, and argument among clinicians, educators, and students, what is the state of training in clinical psychology? That question allows no easy answer, although we can give some general responses. First, the scientist-professional model has proven to be a tough competitor that is still the champ in terms of the number of programs professing it

as their training philosophy (O'Sullivan & Quevillon, 1992). This model now comes in an increasing number of different packages. Most programs have increased the time devoted to professional training in psychotherapy, at the expense of courses in psychodiagnostics or general psychology. Several programs follow a special theoretical model (e.g., behavioral or psychoanalytic), which offers a relatively narrow approach to the field. Other programs emphasize a specialty such as child-clinical or community psychology.

Despite the continuing popularity of the Boulder model, many programs that favor the model still struggle with the best way to train psychologists so that their practical skills are well integrated with scientific foundations and knowledge. This struggle stems from at least two sources: (a) the increasing tendency for accreditation standards to create more and more course requirements that may not promote integration of science and practice and (b) the difficulty clinical faculty members experience in modeling the scientist-professional role while meeting the many other demands on their time as university faculty.

These concerns led to a National Conference on Scientist-Practitioner Education and Training for the Professional Practice of Psychology in Gainesville, Florida in 1990. This conference reaffirmed the Boulder model as the best foundation for training clinicians and stressed the need for such training to involve more than just equal attention to practice and science (Belar & Perry, 1992). The basic principle for "scientist × practitioner" training, said the conferees, is that students must be trained to "embody a research orientation in their practice and a practice relevance in their research" (p. 72). This principle should be realized in all aspects of the curriculum, including coursework, research training, and practicum experiences, they said, and must be modeled as much as possible by clinical faculty.

As described earlier, other training programs with very different philosophies about how to train clinicians have been created in the past few decades. These programs envision the clinician as more of a health-care or human-service professional and therefore tend to deemphasize the integration of science and practice. Two training models of this type—the PsyD program and the professional school of psychology—are discussed next.

The Doctor of Psychology (PsyD) Degree

One of the earliest and most influential professional training programs was the PsyD program begun by the Department of Psychology at the University of Illinois (Urbana-Champaign) in 1968 (it was discontinued in 1980). PsyD programs give students desiring careers in clinical service training that concentrates on that goal. Emphasis is placed on the skills necessary for the delivery of psychological services. A master's thesis is not required, nor is a research-oriented dissertation, although a written, doctoral-level report of professional quality is usually required for the PsyD.

As of 1992, there were 15 fully accredited PsyD programs and five programs with provisional accreditation. Of course, the PsyD has been criticized by some clinicians. Goldenberg (1973) summarized early objections to the program:

(1) The Psy.D. program is likely to acquire second-class status in the eyes of faculty, students and the public; (2) the fact that support for the alternate doctorate comes from the unlikely quarter of academic psychology is suspect as being perhaps a device for shunting aside the bothersome problem of professional training in clinical psychology; (3) the profession of clinical psychology is in a state of flux, with new roles and practices emerging, making this a particularly inappropriate time to create a new profession with activities that are only dimly foreseeable at present and whose present clinical skills may soon be obsolete; (4) two parallel programs, producing two different degrees, will tend to separate clinical

practice from the rest of psychology even further, thus cutting the profession off from its scientific roots; (5) expert practitioners, necessary in a professional degree program, are likely to find it as difficult to be appointed and later promoted at the university as is the case now of competent clinical professors who do not publish research findings; and (6) future graduates of such programs are likely to be stigmatized because of their different degree and different training. (p. 85)

Peterson and Baron (1975) found that PsyD and PhD students at the University of Illinois performed equivalently on qualifying exams and course grades, and showed similar attrition rates. Shemberg and Leventhal (1981) found that internship supervisors did not differentiate the quality of work by PhD versus PsyD interns (see also Snepp & Peterson, 1988). Although very limited in scope, these data belie the gloomy predictions that were made about PsyD programs. However, serious reservations about the quality of training in some PsyD programs remain (Strickland, 1985), even among proponents of the degree (Peterson, 1985). Large numbers of students trained by part-time faculty in settings that do not encourage comprehensive education are characteristic of too many PsyD programs.

The Professional School

Professional schools of psychology have formed as free-standing clinical training units, independent of university departments of psychology. This arrangement is thought to free clinical psychology from the academic constraints of the university, to allow rewards for professional as well as scholarly achievements, and to provide students with faculty role models who are active, practicing clinicians.

Professional schools of psychology are sometimes associated with a university (e.g., at Rutgers or Yeshiva), but free-standing organizations are more common. The earliest example of a free-standing school was the California School of Professional Psychology, founded under the auspices of the California Psychological Association in 1969. The school has four campuses (Los Angeles, Berkeley, San Diego, and Fresno) and is generally regarded as the leading free-standing professional school in the country.

There are more than 50 professional schools operating in the United States, the majority of which are free standing. Some award the PsyD and some the PhD degree (Peterson, 1985). These schools are estimated to enroll about 40% of all students in doctoral training programs in psychology (Kohout, Wicherski, & Pion, 1991). This is because the average entering class of a professional school is about five times larger than the typical first-year class in a university psychology department. Further, professional schools admit a higher percentage of applicants than do programs in university psychology departments (Peterson, 1985).

The growth of the professional schools stems from several influences. First, well-intentioned, competent psychologists have honest differences about the best way to educate students (Bourg, Bent, McHolland, & Stricker, 1989). Were this not the case, debate about PhDs and PsyDs would have ended long ago. Second, the curricula of professional schools reflect the expressed interest of most graduate students, which is to be trained as providers of psychological services rather than as academicians and researchers. Third, economic factors and changing employment opportunities have encouraged more psychologists to start independent and group practices, work in healthcare facilities, and take other applied positions for which professional schools appear especially relevant. Fourth, many professional schools have admitted the large number of graduates from terminal MA programs who, not finding much success in being admitted to traditional programs, have flocked to the professional schools. Finally, professional schools provide a training atmosphere that many stu-

dents prefer to what they perceive in academic programs. The professional schools' emphasis on clinical practice and their provision of practitioner role models create a culture in tune with the applied interests of most of today's clinical students.

Professional schools have challenged the nature of clinical training. They have forced clinicians to consider seriously the type of knowledge upon which their services should be based and the standards against which they should evaluate their practices. Despite the apparent appeal of programs that emphasize the training of practitioners, we believe the single most important goal in training clinical psychologists is to teach them to choose and evaluate whatever services they offer in light of the empirical methods of science.

If clinical training moves too far from its foundation in psychological science and concentrates only on teaching therapy techniques, assessment methods, and other professional skills, the clinical psychologist of the 21st century is likely to be a narrowly specialized practitioner for whom research is of only passing interest. As a result, clinical psychology may become a better profession, but a poorer science.

Thorough discussions of the pros and cons of professional and Boulder model training can be found in Fox and Barclay (1989), Matarazzo (1987), Perry (1979), Peterson (1985), and Stricker (1992).

PROFESSIONAL REGULATION

One major responsibility of a human service profession is the establishment of standards of competence which members of the profession must meet before they are authorized to practice. The purpose of such regulation is to protect the public from unauthorized or incompetent practice of psychology by impostors, untrained persons, or psychologists who are unable to function at a minimum level of competence. Though some doubt the value of regulation (e.g., Gross, 1978; Hogan, 1983), psychology has developed an active system of professional regulation.

Certification and Licensure

The most important type of regulation lies in state laws that establish requirements for practice of psychology and/or restrict use of the term *psychologist* to persons with certain qualifications. This legislative regulation comes in two kinds of statutes: certification and licensure. The legal basis of these laws rests in the right of the state to pass legislation that protects its citizens. Caveat emptor ("let the buyer beware") is insufficient protection when buyers are not sufficiently informed about the services to know what to beware *of*.

Certification laws restrict use of the title *psychologist* or *certified psychologist* to people who have met requirements specified in the law. Certification only protects the *title* of psychologist; it does not regulate the practice of psychology.

Licensure, on the other hand, is a more restrictive type of statute. Licensure laws define the practice of psychology by specifying the services that the psychologist is authorized to offer the public. The requirements for licensure are usually more comprehensive than for certification. To distinguish between certification and licensure, remember the following rule of thumb: A certification law would not prevent a nonpsychologist from doing the same things as a certified psychologist; it would only prevent the person from being called a psychologist. A licensure law, on the other hand, would prevent a nonpsychologist from using the term *psychologist,* and it would also prohibit the person from offering services that the average citizen would believe to be among the professional functions of a psychologist.

Licensing laws are administered by state boards of psychology, which are charged by legislatures with regulating the practice of psy-

chology in the states. There are two major functions of state boards of psychology: (a) to determine the standards for admission to the profession and administer procedures for the selection and examination of candidates, and (b) to regulate professional practice and conduct disciplinary proceedings involving violators of professional standards.

Thus, a PhD in clinical psychology does not allow you to hang out a shingle and start to practice psychology. While the steps involved in becoming licensed differ somewhat from state to state, there is enough uniformity in the procedures of most states to offer a rough sketch of how the aspiring clinical psychologist would approach this task. Box 14–2 outlines the basic steps involved.

In 1945 Connecticut enacted the first psychology licensing law; Virginia, Kentucky, and Ohio followed suit within 5 years (Carlson, 1978). Today, all 50 states, the District of Columbia, and the Canadian provinces have certification or licensure laws. Several states combine their certification and licensure laws into one statute.

As more states passed licensing statutes, it became obvious there was a need for an organization to coordinate the activities of the state boards of psychology and to bring about uniformity in standards and procedures. To answer these needs, the American Association of State Psychology Boards (AASPB) was formed in 1961. In 1991 this organization was renamed the Association of State and Provincial Psychology Boards (ASPPB). ASPPB has also developed a Code of Conduct for psychologists consisting of enforceable rules of professional behavior intended to protect the public from unscrupulous, incompetent, and unethical licensed psychologists.

In addition, the ASPPB has developed a standardized, objective examination for use by state boards in examining candidates for licensure. First released in 1964 and revised frequently since then, this Examination for Professional Practice in Psychology is sometimes called the *multistate* or *national exam* be-

Imagine you have just received your PhD or PsyD from a clinical training program and are now interested in becoming a licensed clinical psychologist. What are the steps you would have to take? The following hurdles will be encountered in most states.

First, you must ask that the state board of psychology review your credentials to determine your eligibility for examination. Their decision is based on several criteria.

1. *Administrative requirements.* You must have reached a certain age, be a U.S. citizen, and have been a resident in the state for some minimum period. There is not too much to be done about these requirements; you either meet them or you do not. One bit of advice: Don't commit any felonies, engage in treason, or libel your governor. Those activities are judged to be indicative of poor moral character and may leave you plenty of time to fantasize about licensure while in prison.

2. *Education.* Most states require a doctoral degree in psychology from an accredited university (accreditation in this case refers not to APA approval but to accreditation of the university by a recognized accrediting agency). Official graduate and undergraduate transcripts are required.

3. *Experience.* This will usually amount to 1 to 2 years of supervised professional experience in a setting approved by the board. Some of the experience may have to be postdoctoral; letters of reference will be required from your supervisor(s).

If, after scrutinizing your credentials, the board finds you are eligible for examination, you will be invited for an exam. Here is what to expect.

1. *Examination fee.* There is a charge for the examination; it is usually between $100 and 200.

BOX 14–2
So You Want to Be a Licensed Psychologist?

cause all jurisdictions can use it as a part of their exam procedure. The ASPPB also helped develop a system of *reciprocity,* meaning that someone licensed in one state can sometimes transfer licensure to another jurisdiction.

Licensure of psychologists has been criticized on several grounds. A major objection has been that licensure does not assure competence of practitioners because the examination procedures do not adequately assess professional abilities. Some critics further contend that licensure may be detrimental to the public interest because it functions to curtail competition and increase the cost of psychologists' services. Legal challenges to licensure of psychologists involving alleged due process violations and antitrust considerations have been

attempted by disgruntled parties, but the success of these attacks has been limited.

In the 1970s, as part of a general sentiment favoring governmental deregulation of various activities, psychology licensure statutes were eliminated in some states (they have now been reenacted) through a process known as "sunset" legislation (laws requiring unnecessary regulations would be terminated or have "the sun set" on them). Today, licensure laws are applauded by a majority of clinicians and are upheld by courts if there is a plausible reason to believe they protect the public.

In 1975 the first edition of the *National Register of Health Service Providers in Psychology* was published. The *Register* is a listing of psychologists who possess the training and expe-

2. *The examination.* Many states will use the national exam. It contains about 200 objective items covering general psychology, methodology, applications of psychology, and professional conduct and ethics. Since many candidates will want to practice a specialty like clinical, school, or industrial psychology, boards also prepare essay examinations in these areas. You may also be required to take an oral examination by the board in which any material relevant to psychology may be covered.

3. *Reexamination.* If you should fail any part of the exam, you will probably be given another chance at that portion. Most boards feel that twice is enough, however; so if you fail the second time, it might be wise to reconsider the advantages of the family business.

In most states, you will be required to keep your license or certificate up to date by paying a periodic renewal fee. By the early 1990s, 27 states required *continuing professional education* (CPE) as a condition for maintaining licensure (VandeCreek, Knapp, & Brace, 1990). Continuing professional education is usually provided in special postdoctoral institutes, seminars, or workshops conducted by an expert in a particular area. The purpose of this activity is to keep the practicing psychologist abreast of current progress in important professional areas. In states requiring CPE, psychologists must document their participation in a certain number of CPE units of instruction. Although psychology has not yet developed its CPE plan to the level of professions like law or medicine, most psychologists agree that the future will see a strengthening of CPE requirements for their field.

BOX 14–2
Continued

---

rience to be considered a health service provider. The primary use of the *Register* is to identify psychologists who specialize in delivering health services and to help various organizations and insurance companies identify those psychologists who should be eligible for reimbursement for delivering mental health services. Over 14,000 psychologists are now listed in the *Register,* and hundreds of organizations, including many of the country's largest insurance companies, subscribe to the *Register.*

ABPP Certification

Another type of professional regulation is certification by the American Board of Professional Psychology (ABPP). ABPP was founded in 1947 as a national organization that would certify the professional competence of psychologists. Its certification is signified by the award of a diploma in one of several specialty areas including clinical, counseling, industrial/organizational, school, family, forensic, health, and neuropsychology. In 1992 the ABPP reorganized itself so that each of these specialty areas has its own board (all organized under the ABPP umbrella) that develops and administers its own exams and awards the diplomas.

An ABPP diploma is considered more prestigious than licensure, although it carries no legal authority. While licensure signifies a minimal level of competence, diplomate status is an endorsement of professional expertise, an indication that the person possesses a masterful knowledge of the specialty field.

Requirements for the ABPP diploma are more rigorous than for licensure. Three years of experience is a prerequisite to take the ABPP examination, which is conducted by a group of diplomates who observe the candidate dealing directly with clinical phenomena (e.g., testing or interacting with a client).

Other Forms of Legal Regulation

An interesting by-product of psychology's professionalization is greater legal scrutiny of the profession. Historically, courts have been disinclined to pass judgment on what constitutes acceptable psychological treatment. Recently, this reluctance has given way to a willingness to evaluate the legality of mental health care. Courts are no longer willing to permit what they see as violations of clients' rights, despite the hazards in the nonexpert evaluation of treatment methods.

A comprehensive review of the legal status of psychological treatments exceeds our purpose here, but we will highlight three frequently cited legal principles that have been used to challenge some forms of intervention. The first two (right to treatment and informed consent) are usually concerned with institutionalized persons such as mental patients or prison inmates. The third (privileged communication) is particularly relevant to outpatient psychotherapy clients.

Right to Treatment

The concept of the right to treatment for patients committed to psychiatric hospitals found legal support in the landmark *Rouse v. Cameron*[2] decision. In this case, the patient, who had been confined for 4 years without receiving treatment, petitioned the court to release him from the institution. In *Wyatt v. Stickney*,[3] a federal court held that involuntarily hospitalized persons had a constitutional right to individual treatment that would give them a realistic opportunity to be cured or improved.

The U.S. Supreme Court has also ruled that a state cannot confine without treatment nondangerous individuals who can survive by themselves or with the help of others outside the institution (*O'Connor v. Donaldson*[4]). Since *O'Connor,* mentally retarded patients also have had their treatment rights strengthened, although not guaranteed as an absolute right (*Youngberg v. Romero*[5]).

The *Wyatt* decision included a ban on involuntary labor by patients unless compensated by the minimum wage and a requirement that the physical and psychological resources to which patients are entitled as constitutional rights be specified. *Wyatt* directed that a patient is entitled to the "least restrictive conditions necessary to achieve the purposes of commitment." The "least restrictive conditions" doctrine was first applied in a case where a mental patient was being involuntarily committed to a hospital (*Lessard v. Schmidt*[6]). This doctrine holds that a state cannot stifle a person's civil liberties any more than is necessary for accomplishing legitimate treatment goals. Whenever less drastic means of effective treatment are available, they should be implemented rather than more drastic means. Like many well-intentioned reforms, the "least restrictive conditions" requirement poses problems for mental health professionals. An example is the young chronic mental patient whose frequent history of substance abuse and acting out make voluntary care in noninstitutional settings difficult.

The *Wyatt* case also had many implications for the legally acceptable reinforcers that can be used in institutional token economies. While based on principles of reward, rein-

---

[2]373 F. 2d 451 (D.C. Cir. 1966).

[3]344 F. Supp. 373 (1972).
[4]422 U.S. 563 (1975).
[5]457 U.S. 307 (1982).
[6]349 F. Supp. 1078 (E.D. Wis. 1972).

forcement programs require an initial state of deprivation to insure their motivational potency. *Wyatt* requires, however, the noncontingent availability of the following rights:

1. Payment of the minimum wage for institutional work;

2. A right to privacy, including a bed, closet, chair, and bedside table;

3. Meals meeting minimum daily dietary requirements;

4. The right to visitors, religious services, and clean personal clothing;

5. Recreational privileges (e.g., television in the day room); and

6. An open ward and ground privileges when clinically acceptable.

Many psychologists viewed *Wyatt* with concern. Berwick and Morris (1974, p. 436) commented: "The field of law is beginning to step in and demand that mental patients get fair treatment; however, they may inadvertently be undermining attempts to establish adequate treatments." No doubt *Wyatt* jeopardizes traditional token economies. At the same time, the decision is not incompatible with all possible behavior-modification programs.

Wexler (1973) recommended the contingent use of "idiosyncratic reinforcers," nonbasic items that certain patients particularly prefer (e.g., eating hard-boiled rather than soft-boiled eggs). Token economies utilizing idiosyncratic reinforcers are legally permissible because, by definition, idiosyncratic reinforcers are not the same as general rights. Another alternative (Wexler, 1974) is to use the *Wyatt* basics as reinforcers, but require informed consent of all participants in the program (see next section). One problem with this solution is that courts have held that informed consent to "drastic therapies" can be revoked at any time. This requirement would permit residents to convert contingent privileges into noncontingent rights whenever they wished, thereby depriving the program of its motivational impact.

Informed Consent

The claim that institutionalized persons have a right to treatment is complicated by the suggestion that they also may have a right to refuse at least some treatments. An individual's control over her or his treatment often takes the form of giving or withholding informed consent. Full informed consent involves several elements, including full specification of the nature of treatment; a description of its purpose, risks, and likely outcomes; notification that consent may be terminated at any time without prejudice to the individual; and demonstration of a capacity to consent. Written informed consent is usually required for treatments of an experimental, intrusive, or aversive nature.

From a practical perspective, the right to refuse treatment usually involves a patient's right to refuse psychotropic medication, since it is the major treatment for most seriously disturbed patients whether they are in hospitals or not.

When a mental patient refuses medication that a physician believes is beneficial, a fundamental question of personal autonomy is raised. Should society "help" patients against their will? Should they be forced to take medication? Concerns about the side effects of psychoactive drugs, about patients' right to privacy, and about patients' control of their own bodies led federal district courts in Massachusetts (*Rogers v. Okin*[7]) and New Jersey (*Rennie v. Klein*[8]) to hold that mentally ill patients did have the right to refuse medications, even if the medications were likely to be beneficial. However, this right to refuse was held not to

---

[7]478 F. Supp. 1342, 1369 (Mass. 1979).
[8]462 F. Supp. 1131 (D.N.J. 1978).

be absolute. A patient's desire not to be medicated could be overridden in three general situations: (a) if the patient was behaving dangerously toward self or others, (b) if the patient was so ill as to not be able to make a competent decision about treatment, and (c) if there was an emergency that a physician concluded made forced medication necessary. In the 1990 case of *Washington v. Harper*,[9] the U.S. Supreme Court held that a mentally ill prisoner could not be medicated against his will *unless* it was determined by the application of professional standards that the medication was necessary for safety reasons.

The Supreme Court has refused to hold that mentally ill patients have a Constitutional right to refuse treatment. It has used a doctrine of deferring to the professional judgment of physicians who are treating the patient. In *Youngberg v. Romeo,* the Supreme Court held that honoring the rights of patients cannot be used to restrict unnecessarily the professional judgment of treating physicians. Some states still allow patients a right to refuse treatment, but the availability of numerous ways to override a patient's refusal converts this right into more of a right to object to treatment and have the medical necessity of the treatment reviewed (Brooks, 1986). In reality, few patients refuse medication over a long period of time (Appelbaum & Hoge, 1986), and those who persistently do so typically have their refusal ultimately overridden (Godard, Bloom, Williams, & Faulkner, 1986).

Privileged Communication

Numerous states have laws that establish a psychotherapist–client *privilege*. Privilege is a legal right imposed to protect the client from public disclosure of confidences by the therapist without the client's permission. Privilege is

similar but not identical to confidentiality. The main difference is that confidentiality is an ethical obligation of a profession, not a legal requirement. Passage of therapist–client privilege statutes is due mainly to the recognition that confidentiality of treatment is essential to the success of psychotherapy.

Just as the law of some states recognizes this type of privilege, it recognizes several exceptions to it. The most common are (a) where a therapist determines that a client needs commitment to a hospital, (b) where a client has undergone a court-ordered examination and been informed that his or her communications would not be privileged, (c) where a patient introduces his or her mental condition as an element of a defense against a criminal conviction, and (d) where a therapist believes the client may be abusing other persons.

Another area in which a breach of confidentiality may be legally mandated is where a client communicates to a therapist the intention to commit harmful acts. This exception presents a dilemma for the psychotherapist who, by the open and trusting character of the therapeutic relationship, encourages verbal expressions of violent impulses from clients. The courts have held that privilege does not apply where its use would conceal information necessary for public safety or the administration of justice.

This brings us to a practical question: Should a therapist who has heard a client threaten to harm another person be required to protect the intended victim? This question was raised in the now-famous case of *Tarasoff v. Regents of University of California*,[10] and the answer—at least in some states—is yes. In the *Tarasoff* case, a couple sued the University of California, psychotherapists employed by the university, and the campus police to recover damages for the murder of their daughter (a

---

[9]494 U.S. 210 (1990).

[10]529 P. 2d 553 (Col. 1974) *Vac. reheard in bank and affirmed* 131 Cal. Rptr. 14, 551 P. 2d 334 (1976).

UC coed) by a client of one of the psychotherapists. A lower court sustained the defendants' answers to the suit, but the Supreme Court of California reversed that decision and found for the plaintiffs.

Here are the facts of the case. The client, Prosenjit Poddar, told his psychotherapist, Dr. Lawrence Moore, he intended to kill a young woman, Tatiana Tarasoff. The therapist informed his superior, Dr. Harvey Powelson, of this threat, and the campus police were called and requested in writing to confine the client. They did so, but shortly thereafter they released him, concluding that he was rational and believing his promise that he would stay away from the Tarasoffs' home. He didn't. After terminating his relationship with his therapist, Poddar killed Tatiana. He was later convicted of murder. No one had warned the woman or her parents of the threat. In fact, Powelson had asked the police to return Moore's letter and further ordered that all copies of the letter and Moore's therapy notes be destroyed and that Poddar not be confined.

In reaching its decision, the court weighed the importance of confidential therapy relationships against society's interest in protecting itself from dangerous persons. The balance was struck in favor of society's protection. The therapist's situation was like that of a physician who would be held liable for the failure to warn persons threatened with a contagious disease: "The protective privilege ends where the public peril begins."

Tarasoff's conclusion that therapists have a duty to protect specific victims from clients that the therapist believes or should believe to be dangerous has been implemented in other states. However, it is not legally binding in all states, a fact that many psychologists misunderstand. About 15 states have now passed laws that specify the conditions where a therapist is liable for failing to take precautions to protect third parties from the dangerous acts of the therapist's clients. At the same time, some other states have extended "*Tarasoff* liability" to persons other than those specifically threatened; in *Peterson v. State,*[11] the Supreme Court of Washington held that therapists are responsible "to protect anyone who might foreseeably be endangered" by their clients.[12] One thing is clear: Therapists are responsible for knowing what their state requires regarding protection of third parties.

PROFESSIONAL ETHICS

A code of professional ethics is a set of principles that encourages or forbids certain professional conduct. Ethics are normative statements that justify certain goals and patterns of behavior. All professions have ethical principles about the proper way for professionals to behave toward the public and toward each other. As psychology moved into its professional era, it needed to articulate the ethical principles that should guide its members.

Psychology's first code of ethics was published in 1953 (APA, 1953). A unique feature of this code was the manner by which it was developed. True to their empirical foundations, psychologists submitted to an APA committee a large number of "critical incidents" involving some ethical dilemma that had occurred in a professional context. By analyzing this real-life material, the committee distilled a comprehensive ethical code, which was summarized in a set of general principles 6 years later (APA, 1959). After this version had been in use for 3 years, it was amended and formally adopted (APA, 1963). The ethical principles underwent several revisions through the 1960s, 1970s, and 1980s.

The current version of the ethical principles, entitled *Ethical Principles of Psychologists and Code of Conduct,* became official on December 1, 1992 after 6 six years of debate and

---

[11]100 Wn. 2d 421, 671 P. 2d 320 (1983).
[12]A related issue concerns therapists' possible obligation to protect third parties from the behavior of their clients who have AIDS (Totten, Lamb, & Reeder, 1990).

revision. This document consists of a Preamble, six General Principles, and a large number of specific Ethical Standards. The Preamble and General Principles (presented in Box 14–3) are not enforceable rules. They state the aspirations of psychologists to attain the highest ideals of psychology, and they can serve as guides to psychologists who are evaluating what would be ethically desirable behavior in certain situations.

The Ethical Standards *do* establish enforceable rules of conduct for psychologists. They apply to members of APA and may be used by other organizations (state boards of psychology, courts) to judge the behavior of a psychologist, whether a member or not. These standards are organized under the following headings:

1. *General Standards.* Rules prohibiting discrimination, sexual and other types of harassment, and misuse of work products are included here, as are rules about maintaining competence, recognizing the limits of one's competence, proper recordkeeping, fees, and financial relationships.

2. *Evaluation, Assessment, or Intervention.* Rules pertaining to the use and interpretation of tests are listed here.

3. *Advertising and Other Public Statements.* Standards that control the way psychologists publicize their services and their professional credentials are presented under this category.

4. *Therapy.* Rules about the structuring, conduct, and termination of therapy are identified here. Specific standards prohibit psychologists from

---

BOX 14–3
Preamble and General Principles in the APA Ethical Principles
of Psychologists and Code of Conduct

Preamble

Psychologists work to develop a valid and reliable body of scientific knowledge based on research. They may apply that knowledge to human behavior in a variety of contexts. In doing so, they perform many roles, such as researcher, educator, diagnostician, therapist, supervisor, consultant, administrator, social interventionist, and expert witness. Their goal is to broaden knowledge of behavior and, where appropriate, to apply it pragmatically to improve the condition of both the individual and society. Psychologists respect the central importance of freedom of inquiry and expression in research, teaching, and publication. They also strive to help the public in developing informed judgments and choices concerning human behavior. This Ethics Code provides a common set of values upon which psychologists build their professional and scientific work.

This Code is intended to provide both the general principles and the decision rules to cover most situations encountered by psychologists. It has as its primary goal the welfare and protection of the individuals and groups with whom psychologists work. It is the individual responsibility of each psychologist to aspire to the highest possible standards of conduct. Psychologists respect and protect human and civil rights, and do not knowingly participate in or condone their discriminatory practices.

The development of a dynamic set of ethical standards for a psychologist's work-related conduct requires a personal commitment to a lifelong effort to act ethically; to encourage ethical behavior by students, supervisees, employees, and colleagues, as appropriate; and to consult with others, as needed, concerning ethical problems. Each psychologist supplements, but does not violate, the Ethics Code's values and rules on the basis of guidance drawn from personal values, culture, and experience.

having sexual intimacies with current clients and accepting persons as clients if they have had previous sexual intimacies with them. Furthermore, psychologists should not have sexual intimacies with former therapy clients for at least 2 years after the termination of therapy, and even then only if the psychologist can demonstrate that no exploitation of the client has occurred.

5. *Privacy and Confidentiality.* These rules cover the obligation that psychologists have to protect the confidentiality and privacy of their clients.

6. *Teaching, Training, Supervision, Research and Publication.* This section contains several ethical standards that control psychologists' conduct as they teach and supervise students and perform psychological research.

7. *Forensic Activities.* When performing forensic evaluations or other services, psychologists must comply with special rules about such services.

8. *Resolving Ethical Issues.* This last section contains standards about how psychologists are to resolve ethical questions or complaints.

In 1967 the APA published its first *Casebook on Ethical Standards of Psychologists,* which contained a restatement of the 1963 ethical principles as well as actual cases drawn from discussions of the APA's Committee on Scientific and Professional Ethics and Conduct between 1959 and 1962. The *Casebook* is intended as a guide for how ethical principles are applied to real cases. It is the source most

---

BOX 14-3
Continued

General Principles

Principle A: Competence

Psychologists strive to maintain high standards of competence in their work. They recognize the boundaries of their particular competencies and the limitations of their expertise. They provide only those services and use only those techniques for which they are qualified by education, training, or experience. Psychologists are cognizant of the fact that the competencies required in serving, teaching, and/or studying groups of people vary with the distinctive characteristics of those groups. In those areas in which recognized professional standards do not yet exist, psychologists exercise careful judgment and take appropriate precautions to protect the welfare of those with whom they work. They maintain knowledge of relevant scientific and professional information related to the services they render, and they recognize the need for

ongoing education. Psychologists make appropriate use of scientific, professional, technical, and administrative resources.

Principle B: Integrity

Psychologists seek to promote integrity in the science, teaching, and practice of psychology. In these activities psychologists are honest, fair, and respectful of others. In describing or reporting their qualifications, services, products, fees, research, or teaching, they do not make statements that are false, misleading, or deceptive. Psychologists strive to be aware of their own belief systems, values, needs, and limitations and the effect of these on their work. To the extent feasible, they attempt to clarify for relevant parties the roles they are performing and to function appropriately in accordance with those roles. Psychologists avoid improper and potentially harmful dual relationships.

psychologists study in order to educate themselves about the profession's ethical standards. A more recent edition of the *Casebook* was published in 1987. Periodically, summaries of actual ethical cases and their resolutions are published in the *American Psychologist,* and several books on psychology ethics are now available (Keith-Spiegel & Koocher, 1985; Pope & Bouhoutsos, 1986).

Most clinicians believe in and are guided by the APA *Ethical Principles*. As exemplified by the case presented in Box 14–4, they take great pains to deal with complex and ethically ambiguous situations in accordance with the highest standards of professional conduct. On those rare occasions when, as a fallible human being, a psychologist behaves in a questionable manner, she or he is subject to censure by local,

state, and national organizations whose task it is to deal with violations of ethical practice.

Once a complaint of unethical behavior has been brought against an APA member and the appropriate committee has decided that the conduct in question was in fact unethical, the question of punishment must be decided. The most severe APA sanction is to dismiss the offender from the association and to inform the membership of this action. This penalty is embarrassing for most transgressors, humiliating for a few, but seldom devastating for any. Unethical conduct can also cause a psychologist to be threatened with the loss of his or her license by the board of psychology in the state where the psychologist practices.

The largest number of ethical violations involve (a) sexual intimacy between a therapist

---

BOX 14–3
Continued

Principle C: Professional and Scientific Responsibility

Psychologists uphold professional standards of conduct, clarify their professional roles and obligations, accept appropriate responsibility for their behavior, and adapt their methods to the needs of different populations. Psychologists consult with, refer to, or cooperate with other professionals and institutions to the extent needed to serve the best interests of their patients, clients, or other recipients of their services. Psychologists' moral standards and conduct are personal matters to the same degree as is true for any other person, except as psychologists' conduct may compromise their professional responsibilities or reduce the public's trust in psychology and psychologists. Psychologists are concerned about the ethical compliance of their colleagues' scientific and professional conduct. When appropriate, they consult with colleagues in order to prevent or avoid unethical conduct.

Principle D: Respect for People's Rights and Dignity

Psychologists accord appropriate respect to the fundamental rights, dignity, and worth of all people. They respect the rights of individuals to privacy, confidentiality, self-determination, and autonomy, mindful that legal and other obligations may lead to inconsistency and conflict with the exercise of these rights. Psychologists are aware of cultural, individual, and role differences, including those due to age, gender, race, ethnicity, national origin, religion, sexual orientation, disability, language, and socioeconomic status. Psychologists try to eliminate the effect on their work of biases based on those factors, and they do not knowingly participate in or condone unfair discriminatory practices.

and a client, (b) violations of state or federal laws (e.g., fraudulent billing practices), and (c) breaches of confidentiality. In addition to clear-cut violations, a large number of questionable behaviors often occur that raise possible ethical problems. Pope and Vetter (1992) mailed a survey to 1,319 members of APA, asking them to describe any ethical dilemmas they or a colleague had recently encountered. A total of 679 psychologists returned the questionnaire and indicated the following three areas to be the most ethically troubling for them:

1. *Confidentiality.* Eighteen percent of the troubling incidents involved problems of confidentiality. Reporting of suspected child abuse and warning victims about the potential vio-

lence of a client were common examples. A typical response was the following:

> One girl underwent an abortion without the knowledge of her foster parents. . . . I fully evaluated her view of the adults' inability to be supportive and agreed but worried about our relationship being damaged if I was discovered to know about the pregnancy and her action. (Pope & Vetter, 1992, p. 599)

2. *Dual or conflictual relationships with clients.* Seventeen percent of the incidents involved difficulties maintaining the proper boundaries around professional relationships. Here is an example:

> I was conducting therapy with a child and soon became aware that there was a mutual attraction between myself and the child's

BOX 14–3
Continued

Principle E: Concern for Others' Welfare

Psychologists seek to contribute to the welfare of those with whom they interact professionally. In their professional actions, psychologists weigh the welfare and rights of their patients or clients, students, supervisees, human research participants, and other affected persons, and the welfare of animal subjects of research. When conflicts occur among psychologists' obligations or concerns, they attempt to resolve these conflicts and to perform their roles in a responsible fashion that avoids or minimizes harm. Psychologists are sensitive to real and ascribed differences in power between themselves and others, and they do not exploit or mislead other people during or after professional relationships.

Principle F: Social Responsibility

Psychologists are aware of their professional and scientific responsibilities to the community and the society in which they work and live. They apply and make public their knowledge of psychology in order to contribute to human welfare. Psychologists are concerned about and work to mitigate the causes of human suffering. When undertaking research, they strive to advance human welfare and the science of psychology. Psychologists try to avoid misuse of their work. Psychologists comply with the law and encourage the development of law and social policy that serve the interests of their patients and clients and the public. They are encouraged to contribute a portion of their professional time for little or no personal advantage.

The following case history is drawn from the original APA *Casebook* on ethical standards (1967, pp. 29–30). It deals with the difficult issue of a clinician protecting the welfare of a client while remaining sensitive to the social interests inherent in criminal conduct. It raises a somewhat different problem than the one involved in the *Tarasoff* case because in this case the violent act has already been committed.

Case 6A

A fully trained clinical psychologist in private practice was referred a patient for treatment because of a "near nervous breakdown." The background of the patient revealed many stressful and traumatic circumstances. After a few visits the patient admitted to having committed murder, something that weighed heavily on his conscience. The psychologist wrote to the committee for advice, pointing out that no ethical principle fitted the case exactly, the closest being one dealing with situations in which knowledge and intent are revealed but in which an act has not yet been committed. The psychologist wrote further as follows:

I find myself in a very uncomfortable position of not knowing whether accepting him in a treatment basis would be in effect condoning his act. It is possible to understand the internal pressures and the dynamics which led him to behave as he did. Nor am I sure when he says that he thinks he ought to make public what he has done and bear punishment for it that it is my responsibility to encourage this action. Theoretically I know that I should help him to clarify his own thinking to the point where he can take the course of action which he deems most suitable. However, as he himself states, not only is he involved, but the public knowledge of his act would have to be borne by his wife and daughters. From a psychotherapeutic point of view there is no doubt that this man is in intense psychic pain and regardless of what course he decides to follow I suppose that I could justify seeing him in a professional role in an attempt to make him more comfortable. Yet I do not find it possible to completely encapsulate his act. There is no indication that he is suspected of the act or that he would ever do it again.

I am afraid that my own ethical values and social conscience are being intruded, and in a sense I suppose I am asking whether, in this case, they should not be. I do hope that I have outlined the situation clearly enough that your committee can help me to ascertain my ethical responsibilities as a psychologist.

Opinion

The committee felt the client should be accepted in therapy without condoning his act, but that the decision in such a case rested with the psychologist involved. In reaching such a decision, it is necessary to take into account responsibilities to both the profession and the community, in addition to recognizing the legal considerations as well. Since the laws in the different states vary with respect to privileged communication, the committee also recommended that the psychologist confronted with such a question consult an attorney about his legal obligations under the particular circumstances.

BOX 14–4
An Example of an Ethical Dilemma

mother. The strategies I had used and my rapport with the child had been positive. Nonetheless, I felt it necessary to refer to avoid a dual relationship (at the cost of the gains that had been made). (Pope & Vetter, 1992, p. 400)

3. *Trouble collecting payments for services and conflicts with insurance carriers.* Fourteen percent of the incidents focused on difficulties collecting fees or providing adequate treatment under insurance policy limitations. The following example illustrates this type of problem:

A 7 year old boy was severely sexually abused and severely depressed. I evaluated the case and recommended 6 months treatment. My recommendation was evaluated by a managed health care agency and approved for 10 sessions by a nonprofessional in spite of the fact that there is no known treatment program that can be performed in 10 sessions on a 7 year old that has demonstrated efficacy. (Pope & Vetter, 1992, p. 401)

Other Ethical Standards

Because of increasing public concern, new governmental research regulations, and outrage about the alleged mistreatment of animals in some laboratories, APA has found it necessary to supplement its ethical standards with a detailed set of guidelines covering research with animals. A copy of these *Guidelines for Ethical Conduct in the Care and Use of Animals* is available from APA's Office of Scientific Affairs.

Clinical psychologists are responsible for being knowledgeable about other standards that govern their delivery of psychological services. The major sources for these various standards are *Ethical Principles in the Conduct of Research with Human Participants* (APA, 1982), *General Guidelines for Providers of Psychological Services* (APA, 1987), *Specialty Guidelines for the Delivery of Services by Clinical Psychologists* (APA, 1981), *Standards*

for Educational and Psychological Testing (APA, 1985), and the *Publication Manual of the American Psychological Association* (APA, 1983).

PROFESSIONAL INDEPENDENCE

The clinical psychologist must consult and collaborate with people from other professions in many aspects of clinical practice. Clinical psychologists often work closely with educators, attorneys, ministers, social workers, nurses, physicians, and other psychologists.

For the most part, psychology's interprofessional relationships are healthy, profitable, and characterized by good will. The most obvious sign of this harmony is the frequency of referrals made across groups. A teacher with a child whose classroom misbehavior is related to a serious emotional problem is likely to suggest that the family consult a psychologist. Psychologists, on the other hand, may encounter clients who are in legal trouble; rather than offer legal advice, they urge such clients to hire an attorney.

Psychologists have had considerable friction with physicians, particularly psychiatrists. In fact, clinical psychology's most persistent problem in its efforts at professionalization has been its wary, often stormy relationships with the medical profession. Garfield (1965) observes that as early as 1917, psychiatrists were critical of psychologists, particularly "those who have termed themselves 'clinical psychologists'" and work in "so-called 'psychological clinics'" and provide "so-called expert testimony."

There have been several battles between clinical psychology and psychiatry. The first involved the independent practice of psychotherapy by psychologists. More recently, the squabble has concentrated on psychologists' eligibility for reimbursement under an increasing array of public, private, and prepaid health insurance covering treatment for mental disorders. Although the two controversies are related, we look at them individually in order to understand the development of each.

Independent Practice of Psychotherapy

As long as psychologists confined themselves to research, consultation, and testing, physicians did not interfere with them. Psychologists, by the same token, found no problem with the fact that physicians were the authority on physical disorders or organic treatments such as medication, electroconvulsive therapy, and surgery. Disagreement, when it came, centered on psychotherapy, which both professions (along with several others) offered to the public. When psychologists began to engage in the independent practice of psychotherapy, psychiatrists objected and insisted that a psychotherapist must be either a physician or under the supervision of a physician.

The rationale for the psychiatrists' position is that physicians are the experts on the functioning of the *whole person* and that with many types of abnormal behaviors it is essential that the therapist differentiate mental and physical aspects of the disorder and treat both aspects thoroughly. For their part, psychologists contend that the vast majority of mental disorders involve psychological and social processes rather than physical ones, and that they are better trained about these processes than physicians are. In addition, when physical etiology and/or medical treatments are indicated, psychologists are aware of their ethical obligations to refer such clients to physicians. Finally, psychologists point out that many of the most influential therapists over the years have been nonphysicians (Anna Freud, Carl Rogers, Erich Fromm, Erik Erickson).

Psychologists themselves were at one time opposed to practicing psychotherapy independently. In 1949 the APA discouraged the practice of psychotherapy by psychologists who were not working in collaboration with psychiatrists (Goldenberg, 1973).

Psychologists reconsidered their position on the independent practice of psychotherapy (APA, 1958), but psychiatrists did not. In fact, the American Medical Association (1954) adopted an official policy that psychotherapy was a medical procedure to be performed only by medically trained personnel. The strategy of the AMA in this battle was to oppose certification and licensure of psychologists. This strategy was unsuccessful, a fact for which most clinical psychologists are grateful. Psychologists now provide more office-based mental health care than do psychiatrists (McGuire, 1989).

Relations between psychologists and psychiatrists improved throughout the 1970s and early 1980s. Psychiatrists came to accept psychologists as professionals and were less likely to treat them with the condescension of earlier days. In turn, psychologists shed some of their defensive armor and were less prone to feel that they constantly must guard against psychiatrists. Both fields have been enhanced by the growing number of well-qualified persons who have entered the two professions.

In the 1990s relationships between psychologists and psychiatrists have again become strained. This time the tensions are primarily economic, although they also involve questions about whether psychologists should be excluded from offering certain professional services (e.g., prescribing medication, admitting patients to hospitals) that historically have been reserved for physicians. These issues are made more urgent by the changes that are anticipated in the way health care will be funded in the United States in the next century.

The Economics of Mental Health Care

Having won the battles over licensure and recognition of psychology as an independent profession in the 1970s and 1980s, clinicians turned to struggles involving the economic aspects of mental health care. The focus of these struggles was whether psychologists should be eligible for reimbursement for their services by insurance companies. Physicians opposed psychologists' inclusion because they said it would be too costly to third-party payers and consumers. Physicians argued that if psychologists were to be included, their services should be reimbursed *only* when they were treating clients referred and supervised by physicians. As a result, many major health insurance companies (such as Blue Cross/Blue Shield), run by and for physicians, excluded psychologists from third-party payments except when billing under a physician's supervision.

Psychologists found this intolerable for a profession that aspired to full autonomy. As a result, in the late 1960s and early 1970s psychologists began to lobby state legislatures to pass what is known as *freedom-of-choice* laws. A freedom-of-choice law mandates that services rendered by qualified mental health professionals licensed to practice in a given state shall be reimbursed by insurance plans covering such services regardless of whether the provider is a physician.

Physicians fought hard against such legislation, using the term *medical psychotherapy* to refer to the services they believed should be reimbursable. This term was seen by psychology as a political maneuver intended to guarantee that physicians would be the only professionals identified as appropriate providers of psychotherapy.

Psychologists argued that there is nothing "medical" about psychotherapy. In addition, psychologists presented data to counter the claims that including them as providers or even including coverage of mental disorders treated by any provider would be too costly for third-party payers. For example, one study showed that a *single session of psychotherapy* reduced subsequent use of medical resources by 60% among the recipients, and there was about a 75% reduction in medical utilizations by patients receiving two to eight sessions of psychotherapy (Cummings, 1977; see also Olbrisch, 1977). Far from being economically

disadvantageous, reimbursing psychotherapy can be cost effective because it saves money that would otherwise be spent for more expensive medical services. This reduction, known as "medical offset," has been replicated in larger, more recent studies (e.g., Holder & Blose, 1987).

Over the years psychologists have succeeded in having freedom-of-choice laws enacted in most states. By 1983 40 states covering 90% of the country's population had passed legislation that provided free choice of licensed psychologists as reimbursable providers of mental health services (Lambert, 1985). In addition, other legislation at the federal level promoted recognition of psychologists as independent clinicians. The Rehabilitation Act of 1973 (PL 93–112) provided parity for psychologists with physicians in both assessment and treatment services. Services provided by clinical psychologists are reimbursable under both the Federal Employee Health Benefits Act (PL 93–363) and the Federal Work Injuries Compensation Program (PL 94–212). Licensed psychologists are also recognized as *independent* providers by CHAMPUS (The Civilian Health and Medical Program of the Uniformed Services), a federal program covering several million beneficiaries in all 50 states and the District of Columbia.

For 25 years, psychologists have fought for legislative changes that would make it possible for them to be directly reimbursed for their services under Medicaid (a shared federal/state program for the medically needy) and Medicare (a federal program for elderly and disabled clients). Physicians have successfully lobbied against such amendments, arguing that including psychologists would be too costly and that psychologists are not qualified to diagnose and treat many mental disorders without the supervision of a physician.

However, the tide has turned at last, at least with respect to Medicare, the federal program that provides health-care funds for 30 million aged and 3 million disabled recipients. Late in 1989, an amendment allowing psychologists to be included and reimbursed as direct providers was signed into law by President George Bush.

Psychologists have been less successful obtaining coverage for their services under Medicaid (DeLeon, Wedding, Wakefield, & Vanden-Bos, 1992). This program, established by Congress in the 1960s to help the states supply health care to the poor and needy, grew dramatically in the last decade; federal expenditures for Medicaid increased from $14 billion to $41 billion. The individual states are free to determine their own criteria for recipient eligibility and to control which services will be covered at what cost. As a result, states that have been concerned about excessive use of mental health services have limited the kinds of treatment they will reimburse; as of 1989 only half the states reimbursed psychologists for their services under Medicaid (DeLeon et al., 1992).

Even though a state or the federal government passes a freedom-of-choice law, some insurance companies will ignore it unless forced to comply. Resnick (1985) describes the $3\frac{1}{2}$ years of litigation needed to require Blue Cross/Blue Shield of Virginia to comply with that state's freedom-of-choice law. A related area of litigation lies in suits challenging the practice of denying staff privileges to non-physicians. California, North Carolina, Washington, DC, Georgia, and several other states have passed laws allowing hospital privileges for psychologists, although physician-based attacks on California's law required psychologists to go to court to protect the original law.

The skyrocketing costs of health care (accounting for more than 13% of the gross national product; Frank, 1993) are causing insurance companies to invent new reimbursement plans and various self-insurance packages to curtail costs and extent of health-care coverage. Many of the newer forms of health insurance, especially the self-insurance packages offered by large corporations, either exclude mental health benefits or put a cap on how much reimbursement is allowed for such services. Psychologists now find themselves facing a situation where the victories they won in the freedom-of-choice legislation may be made obsolete by new insurance plans. Economics determine to a large degree the nature, quality, and extent of health care, a lesson that psychologists have been slow to learn. In the near future, clinical psychology will face at least three important changes in health-care economics that it must be prepared for if it is to remain viable in the health-care marketplace (Zimet, 1989).

1. Debate over how our nation's health-care system should be reformed is sure to continue, and well it should, because the makeover of our current system into one that provides basic health-care for all Americans will have a tremendous impact on mental health services in this country. Although the conservative politics of federal administrations throughout the 1980s discouraged federal revamping of health-care services and financing, most politicians and policy makers have, as we entered the 1990s, begun to agree that providing health care to all Americans will require increased governmental control over the costs and coverage of health services. The two questions about health-care reform of most interest to clinical psychologists are what mental health services will be covered in the basic package of guaranteed care and whether psychologists delivering these services will be reimbursed as independent professionals.

Approximately 35 million Americans have no medical insurance. Not only is this situation morally unacceptable, it is economically foolish. National health-care reform will occur; it is only a question of what form it will take. Will we have universal coverage under a single carrier or will we have separate plans provided by private businesses and regulated by the government? Under any system, containing costs and increasing access will be primary goals, and psychologists will need to become increasingly able to integrate mental health services into general health-care approaches (DeSantis & Walker, 1991) similar to those we describe next.

2. The newest form of health insurance plans is what has been termed "managed care," including HMOs (Health Maintenance Organizations), PPOs (Preferred Provider Organizations), and IPAs (Independent Practice Associations). Despite various differences, these plans provide health care to subscribers for a fixed, prepaid price in contrast to the traditional free-choice plans. Thus, these plans offer an incentive for keeping subscribers healthy as opposed to increasing their utilization of services (Tulkin & Frank, 1985).

Managed health care represents a significant change in the financing of health care. As large private corporations move into the health-care market, the promise of federal health controls competes with the prospects of profit-driven, privately owned and operated health-care plans (Bickman & Dokecki, 1989; Simons, 1989).

How will a shift toward managed care affect the practice of clinical psychology? A number of alternatives are possible. Clinicians may increasingly decide to join HMOs or PPOs and abandon their private or group practices. Or they may try to create their own health-care organizations or plans and aggressively market their services to businesses and industries. The larger question concerns the effects of managed care on the quality of services offered. Will quality suffer under profit-driven managed care plans, or will mental health services become more cost effective and responsive to consumer needs? These questions are being heatedly debated by clinicians (Cummings, 1988; Shadish, 1989; Shulman, 1988).

Organized psychology, as represented by APA, has responded to the questions about managed care[13] by developing an aggressive

marketing strategy aimed at the following goals:

1. Educating consumers and employers about several perceived dangers and shortcomings of most managed care systems. These dangers include an emphasis on cost containment rather than improving service quality, frequent evaluations of services by nonprofessional reviewers, inappropriate limits on the number of allowable in-patient treatment days or out-patient therapy sessions, and intrusions by nonprofessional reviewers into the confidentiality of treatment.

2. Educating consumers and employers about the value of psychology in any comprehensive health-care system. This effort involves extensive advertising and public relations activities focusing on psychology's effectiveness in treating the problems of children, the elderly, the seriously mentally ill, and substance abusers.

3. Helping psychologists diversify their services so they can expand their practice. These specialty training programs are aimed at areas such as health psychology, sports psychology, drug and alcohol abuse, and severe mental disorders.

This campaign has been welcomed by many practitioners as politically necessary if clinical psychology is to ensure its economic viability and professional identity. However, aggressive marketing runs the risk of making claims for psychology that go beyond available scientific data (Sechrest, 1992). The skeptical attitude that underlies the scientist's insistence on empirical proof is difficult to maintain in the face of pressures to promise effective interventions for every type of social problem and mental disorder. In the long run, the profession of clinical psychology will prosper most if it makes claims that are clearly tied to a scientific base (Garfield, 1992; Sechrest, 1992).

3. In an effort to control the price of medical services, in 1983 the United States Con-

[13]For a more complete discussion of the range of opinions that clinical psychologists hold about managed mental health care, see a special section on managed care in the February 1991 issue of the journal *Professional Psychology*. See also the March 1993 issue of the *American Psychologist*.

gress implemented a new system for reimbursing hospitals at a predetermined rate for their treatment of Medicare patients. Under this system, payment is determined on the basis of the diagnosis a patient receives rather than on the basis of the actual cost of treatment (as was the case prior to 1983). Patients are classified into *diagnosis-related groups* (known as DRGs), and payment is based on the average cost of treating patients with that diagnosis. Thus, if a hospital treats a patient for less money than the DRG payment provides, it makes a profit; if it spends more than the allocated amount, it loses money.

Currently, several types of settings in which psychologists are employed are exempted from the DRG system because the disorders treated in these settings make them inappropriate for DRG classification. Psychiatric hospitals and specialty settings that treat alcoholics, drug abusers, or children are exempt, for example. However, there are new proposals for expanding the DRG system to these settings. Should such an expansion occur, psychologists will encounter powerful restraints on the treatments they deliver to patients in these settings. The DRG system may also influence the diagnosis of patients because it provides an incentive to give patients diagnoses that are associated with larger reimbursements. It is important that the possible effects of expanding the DRG system be studied and understood before being implemented; psychologists might want to take the initiative and be involved in empirical studies of this proposal (Essock & Goldman, 1989; Kiesler & Morton, 1989).

The legal struggles and political combat over issues of professional independence have negative effects that clinical psychology must consider. First, litigation is very expensive. Legal costs are usually encumbered by state psychological associations, APA, or other organizations of psychologists. As a result, funds may not be available for other activities (e.g., sponsorship of research or prevention programs) that might be of greater interest to academic or nonclinical psychologists, who are justifiably concerned that clinicians will bankrupt psychological associations by constantly expanding their resources in court cases.[14] Clinicians need to take seriously the questions raised by nonpractitioners about the best use of organized psychology's limited resources.

Another risk of litigation is that, as previously described in relation to psychology's high-profile marketing strategy, psychologists may be tempted to exaggerate their accomplishments and claims for success, particularly in psychotherapy. The profession will not be served well by promising more than it can deliver, especially when consumers must bear whatever additional costs expanding healthcare coverage might bring. Finally, there are disadvantages in maintaining an adversarial stance toward psychiatry. As Resnick (1985, p. 983) put it, "today's adversaries are tomorrow's allies." Psychology and psychiatry have mutual interests in several areas that will be jeopardized by continued interprofessional sparring. For example, some forms of managed care might omit mental health services, an exclusion that both psychology and psychiatry should oppose. Members of both professions may find that the most serious threats to mental health care do not come from each other, but from outside forces that require a cooperative and unified response.

PERILS OF PROFESSIONALISM

Have the first 50 years of clinical psychology's professional era made it a better profession, or have they simply made it more of a guild that employs meaningless membership criteria? Has clinical psychology become a better profession by endorsing standards of training, competence, and service, or is it merely a more closed profession? We consider such questions in these final pages.

The ultimate justification for the profession-

---

[14]Clinicians also have mounted successful litigation to allow them to be admitted to psychoanalytic training institutes, formerly open only to physicians.

alization of any discipline is that the public will benefit from the standards that govern the profession. Of course these restrictions also benefit members of the profession because they control the profession's size and reduce competition. There is little objection to this latter function when it is a by-product of protecting the public from unqualified practitioners. The problem arises when the priorities of a profession are reversed, so that the promotion of its members takes precedence over its obligations to the public.

As early as 1951, Fillmore Sanford, then executive secretary of the APA, warned about the perils of professionalization. In an effort to call psychology's attention to its obligations as a profession, Sanford proposed 16 principles that should be considered "the criteria of a good profession" (Sanford, 1951, p. 667). He hoped that these criteria would guide the development of psychology as a socially useful and responsive profession. Sanford's criteria of a good profession are summarized in Box 14–5.

Sanford's statement remains timely. Al-

BOX 14–5

Fillmore Sanford's Criteria for a Good Profession

1. A good profession is motivated by a sense of social responsibility.

2. A good profession is sufficiently perceptive of its place in society to guide its practices and policies so they conform to the best and changing interests of that society.

3. A good profession is continually on guard lest it represent itself as able to render services that are beyond its demonstrable competence.

4. A good profession continually seeks to find its unique pattern of competence and concentrates its efforts on the rendering of the unique service based on its pattern of competencies.

5. A good profession devotes relatively little of its energy to "guild" functions, to the building of its own in-group strength, and relatively much of its energy to the serving of its social function.

6. A good profession engages in rational and non-invidious relations with other professions having related competencies and common purposes.

7. A good profession devotes a proportion of its energies to the discovery of new knowledge.

8. A good profession develops channels of communication between the discoverers of knowledge and the appliers of knowledge.

9. A good profession does not relegate its discoverers of knowledge to positions of second-rate status.

10. A good profession is free of nonfunctional entrance requirements.

11. A good profession provides preparatory training which is validly related to the ultimate function of the members of the profession.

12. A good profession is one in which the material benefits accruing to its members are proportional to social contributions.

13. A good profession is one whose members are socially and financially accessible to the public.

14. A good profession has a code of ethics designed primarily to protect the client and only secondarily to protect the members of the profession.

15. A good profession facilitates the continuing education and training of all its members.

16. A good profession is continually concerned with the validity of its techniques and procedures.

though it was written as an idealistic vision of what psychology should strive for, it can be used today as a yardstick for measuring what psychology has become. The first two criteria deal with the need for psychologists to adjust to social needs and changes. At several points we have emphasized that clinical psychology has responded to the social and political events surrounding it. The growth of the profession itself was a reaction to social upheaval and virtually unprecedented human needs. In a similar fashion, the evolution of such disparate psychological activities as assessment, psychotherapy, community psychology, and behavior modification had roots in the fact that psychology has always been well tuned to the current *zeitgeist*.

Several criteria (3, 4, 13, and 14) are concerned with professional ethics. Psychologists are justifiably proud of their code of ethics because it remains the only set of professional standards developed with explicitly empirical procedures. This pride has not fostered complacency, however, and the code continues to be revised and updated.

Three criteria (10, 11, and 15) involve professional training. Clinical psychology is committed to training programs that are appropriate for the roles clinicians are asked to fill. Value is still placed on the Boulder model of training, but it is valued in the context of experimentation with other systems of training intended to prepare psychologists who will deliver clinical services. The one area that has lagged behind is continuing professional education (CPE). Progress is being made on this front, however, and we believe that within the next few years a majority of states will be mandating CPE as a condition for the licensing of psychologists.

The sixth of Sanford's criteria is related to interprofessional relationships. This issue, especially as it relates to psychiatrists and clinical psychologists, will continue to be the focus of much attention. An adequate response to our sometimes troubled relations with psychiatry requires a balancing act. On the one hand, clinicians must search for new opportunities to collaborate and cooperate with *all* professions. At the same time, psychology must also be a free profession, unwilling to enter into any Faustian pact where the goodwill of the medical profession is purchased with acquiescence to its domination of psychology.

The greatest number of Sanford's criteria discuss the priorities of the profession, the essential contributions it should make to the public. Sanford, like many psychologists before and after him, affirmed research and advancement of new knowledge as psychology's primary activity. The creation of basic knowledge is the one function that separates the professional from the technician, who applies methods based on existing knowledge. This judgment is especially accurate for a new profession like clinical psychology, where "the fewer its techniques of demonstrable utility, the more of its resources it should devote to research" (Sanford, 1951, p. 669).

THE FUTURE OF CLINICAL PSYCHOLOGY

When authors reach the end of their books, they often feel it necessary to become prophets who cast a wise eye toward the future and predict the development of their fields. Although we cannot completely resist this temptation, we hope to avoid the excesses and unrealistic optimism that often bedevils the inveterate forecaster. Our outlook for the future of clinical psychology emphasizes the following expectations:

1. The number of clinicians will continue to increase, although at a slower pace than in recent years. Clinical psychology has had a growth spurt over the past few decades. Whether one considers the number of training programs established, the number of PhDs graduated, or the number of psychologists licensed to practice, the field has expanded enormously. Some analysts suggest that the number of clinical psychologists (one for every 100,000 persons) already exceeds the national need for them and predict economic hard times for clinicians about to start their careers (Robiner, 1991). Other scholars disagree with these conclusions. Some argue that such dire predictions neglect the need for researchers and prevention-oriented psychologists as opposed to practitioners offering traditional clinical services (Pion, 1991; Schneider, 1991). Others respond that the knowledge base about professional supply and consumer demand is currently inadequate for answering questions about how many clinical psychologists are needed (VandenBos, DeLeon, & Belar, 1991).

Although we believe the *rate* of increase in the production of clinical psychologists will slow somewhat in the next decade, the number of clinicians available is not as important an issue as two others—for what roles will clinicians be trained and how good will the quality of this training be?

Several areas will continue as "growth stocks" for clinicians. First, as described in Chapter 12, health psychology and behavioral medicine should remain important specialty areas because of the contributions psychologists can make to treatment and the promotion of physical health. Although these activities pose exciting opportunities for psychologists, we must be realistic in our appraisals and in our claims of success so as not to promise more than our knowledge allows us to deliver.

A second burgeoning specialty area is forensic psychology. Psychologists are being consulted on a range of topics of relevance to the legal system (Pope, Butcher, & Seelen, 1993). Box 14–6 summarizes 16 areas of expert testimony frequently offered by psychologists. For each category of testimony, the ultimate question that the expert is usually asked is identified. The list of topics in Box 14–6 is not exhaustive. Demand for psychologists' expertise in litigation is growing dramatically. While this demand is gratifying and potentially lucrative, psychologists must be careful not to

testify on matters that exceed their competence and not to exaggerate the scientific support for the conclusions they report. (For criticism of psychologists' expert testimony, see McCloskey & Egeth, 1983; Morse, 1978; Ziskin, 1981; and the June 1986 issue of *Law & Human Behavior,* which discusses ethical problems in expert testimony.)

A third specialty area in which clinical psychologists will face an increasing demand for services relates to children. Assessment and treatment of childhood disorders have advanced remarkably in the past decade, as has research on basic child development and the etiology of child psychopathology. As we discussed in Chapter 11, this greater attention to children has generated much knowledge on the unique qualities and problems of children and has led to an emphasis on early interventions with children in order to prevent emotional and academic problems (Zigler, Taussig, & Black, 1992). Another direction that has gained popularity in recent years is the prevention of drug and alcohol abuse among children and adolescents.

2. Clinical psychology will take on more of a consumer orientation. This trend is apparent in the large number of self-help groups that have been formed (Jacobs & Goodman, 1989), the emphasis on professional accountability to clients, and the expectation that psychologists must develop their own standards as health-service providers. The result of these movements is that clinicians will need to evaluate the effectiveness of their interventions as well as the financial costs of producing certain outcomes (Banta & Saxe, 1983; Newman & Howard, 1986). The psychologist as researcher will always have a place in the future.

3. The question of how to train clinical psychologists will continue to be controversial in the next decade. Currently, there is enthusiasm for preparing clinicians to work with specialty problems and/or groups such as the chronically mentally ill, children and youth,

1. Insanity defense	What is the relationship between the defendant's mental condition at the time of the alleged offense and the defendant's responsibility for the crime with which the defendant is charged?
2. Competence to stand trial	Does the defendant have an adequate understanding of the legal proceedings?
3. Sentencing	What are the prospects for the defendant's rehabilitation? What deterrent effects do certain sentences have?
4. Eyewitness identification	What are the factors that affect the accuracy of eyewitness identification? How is witness confidence related to witness accuracy?
5. Trial procedure	What effects are associated with variations in pretrial and/or trial procedures?
6. Civil commitment	Does a mentally ill person present an immediate danger or threat of danger to self or others which requires treatment no less restrictive than hospitalization?
7. Psychological damages in civil cases	What psychological consequences has an individual suffered as a result of tortious conduct? How treatable are these consequences? To what extent are the psychological problems attributable to a preexisting condition?
8. Psychological autopsies	In equivocal cases, do the personality and circumstances under which a person died indicate a likely mode of death?
9. Negligence and product liability	How do environmental factors and human perceptual abilities affect an individual's use of a product or ability to take certain precautions in its use?

BOX 14–6

Topics of Expert Testimony by Psychologists

rural populations, substance abusers, and older patients. NIMH has concentrated training grant money on these priorities (sometimes designated as "underserved groups"), and they will probably remain a focus for some clinical programs in the future.

Along with more specialty training, there is bound to be continuing pressures and proposals for revamping the way clinical psychologists are trained. We anticipate a widening split between Boulder model programs that stress training in research methods and the scientific traditions of psychology and professionally oriented programs that concentrate on training practitioner skills. This gap may be accompanied by the development of alternative or competing systems of accreditation—one for scientist-practitioner programs and one for professional practitioner programs.

Some psychologists are urging that clinical internships become 2 years in length, rather than the traditional 1-year rotation (Belar et al., 1989). Others are calling for a formal system of postdoctoral education that would emphasize training in specialty skills (Graham & Fox, 1991).

10. Trademark litigation	Is a certain product name or trademark confusingly similar to a competitor's? Are advertising claims likely to mislead consumers?
11. Class action suits	What psychological evidence is there that effective treatment is being denied or that certain testing procedures are discriminatory against minorities in the schools or in the workplace?
12. Guardianship and conservatorship	Does an individual possess the necessary mental ability to make decisions concerning living conditions, financial matters, health, etc.?
13. Child custody	What psychological factors will affect the best interests of the child whose custody is in dispute? What consequences are these factors likely to have on the family?
14. Adoption and termination of parental rights	What psychological factors affect the best interests of a child whose parents' disabilities may render them unfit to raise and care for the child?
15. Professional malpractice	Did defendant's professional conduct fail to meet the standard of care owed to plaintiff?
16. Social issues in litigation	What are the effects of pornography, violence, spouse abuse, etc. on the behavior of a defendant who claims that his or her misconduct was caused by one of these influences?

Source: Based on Nietzel and Dillehay, 1986.

BOX 14–6
Continued

4. The growing emphasis on evaluation may be accompanied by abandonment of a "brand name" approach to psychotherapy. As research indicates the effectiveness of behavior-change techniques, regardless of their theoretical origins, clinicians will find little advantage in identifying themselves as behaviorists, gestaltists, or analysts.

5. Psychologists will continue to push for the freedom of their profession. Organized psychology will intensify its political efforts for inclusion in all types of health-care plans. Individual psychologists will strive to keep abreast of the most modern clinical techniques so that they can continue to offer top-quality services.

The most controversial of these attempts is the move by some psychologists to be allowed to prescribe psychoactive medication as part of their treatment of clients. To explore the possibility that psychologists might prescribe psychotropic medications, the Department of Defense began a demonstration project at the Uniformed Services Hospital of the Health Sciences and Walter Reed Army Medical Center to train and supervise a few clinical psychologists in psychopharmacology and the prescribing of these medications (DeLeon, Fox, & Graham, 1991). The profession is divided over this idea; advocates within the leadership of APA see it as a necessary and socially responsible step (DeLeon et al., 1991), but opponents (May & Belsky, 1992) question the value of its long-term impact either for clinical psychology or the public it serves. The pros and cons of prescription privileges for psychologists are listed in Box 14–7.

Of course, none of these forecasts tells us what clinical psychology should strive for and what it should avoid. For this wisdom we will rely on the ideas of a clinical psychologist who has given the question a career's worth of serious attention:

Clinical psychology, after a long period spent as part of an academic discipline, is in the early stages of becoming a profession. It is going through the natural disturbances and difficulties which attend a growth process of this kind. However, if it selects its students carefully, for personality as well as intellect; if it trains thoroughly, in spirit as well as letter; if it trains broadly, recognizing that "specialists" . . . are not clinical psychologists; if it remains flexible about its training and encour-

---

BOX 14–7
Should Psychologists Be Trained
to Prescribe Psychoactive Medication?

Clinical psychologists themselves have not reached a consensus on the question of whether they should have prescription privileges. Although many psychologists remain ambivalent (Jarrett & Fairbank, 1987), recent surveys suggest a shift toward a more favorable opinion (Frederick/Schneiders, 1990). The major arguments for and against psychologists' gaining prescribing privileges are summarized below.

Arguments For	*Arguments Against*
1. Helps provide a fuller range of mental health services to underserved groups (e.g., elderly, chronically mentally ill, rural populations).	1. Produces an increase in malpractice insurance rates.
2. Compensates for the shortage of physicians in many areas.	2. Increases the length and expense involved in training clinical psychologists.
3. Allows psychologists to use a technique that is necessary for effective treatment of some clinical problems.	3. Increases the medicalization of social problems that are primarily economic, social, and/or psychological in nature.
4. Is a logical extension of psychologists' increasing interest in the reciprocal influence of psychological and physiological factors.	4. Erodes psychologists' traditional expertise in the area of assessment and research.
5. Ensures the economic survivability and professional autonomy of psychology.	5. Pulls psychology away from its distinctive emphasis as the science of human behavior.

ages experimentation; if it does not become overwhelmed by immediate needs at the cost of important, remoter goals; if it maintains its contact with its scientific background, remaining aware of the importance of theory as well as practice; if it remains modest in the face of the complexity of its problems, rather than becoming pretentious—in other words, if it finds good people and gives them good training—these disturbances and difficulties need not be of serious concern. Its future, both for itself as a profession and for society in the contribution it can make, is then assured. Fortunately, there are many reasons for believing that these are the prevailing aspirations in clinical psychology. (p. 246)

These lofty aspirations were written by David Shakow in 1948. We believe Shakow's goals can be reached by clinical psychology *only if* in the future it firmly establishes itself, in Schneider's (1991) eloquent phrase, as "a profession based on science that is informed by practice." We hope this book plays a role in moving some of you to join in the creation of that future.

APPENDIX

Getting into Graduate School in Clinical Psychology

Students ask a number of questions when they are thinking of applying to graduate school in clinical psychology. The purpose of this Appendix is to answer some of these questions. The first step in applying to graduate school is to ask yourself these questions: (a) Do I want to go to graduate school at this time? (b) Are my credentials strong enough for admission to graduate school? (c) In what type of program am I interested? and (d) Given my credentials, to what type of program can I realistically aspire? We first discuss the issues you should consider as you answer these four questions.

Do I Want to Go to Graduate School at This Point in Time?

A PhD program in clinical psychology requires major time, financial, and emotional

commitments on the part of a student. At least 5 years are needed to complete the program, during which time you will be living on subsistence wages, at best. In addition, you will be asked to work harder in school than you have in the past. For example, typical requirements may involve a full course load of academic work, a 20-hour-per-week placement at a clinical agency, as well as independent research toward completion of your thesis or dissertation.

It is not only the time and effort that make graduate school so demanding. The academic expectations and requirements are aimed at a higher level than those with which most students are familiar. Much more independent thinking is expected of graduate students than undergraduates. Finally, the method of instruction shifts dramatically. The classes are predominantly seminars, with discussion and student-directed presentations rather than faculty lectures. Journal articles, rather than textbooks, are the primary reading material.

How can you determine whether you are ready for graduate school? The answer may

---

The Appendix was written by John P. Fiore, MEd, Associate Head for Undergraduate Affairs, Department of Psychology, University of Illinois, Urbana-Champaign.

depend on how you feel about going to graduate school. It is appropriate to be apprehensive—some anxiety can serve as an effective motivator for increased effort. However, if you are ambivalent about graduate school, you might consider taking some time off before pursuing further education. Graduate school is a demanding and stressful experience, and ambivalence on your part will interfere with successful completion of the program. Your application to graduate school will not be jeopardized if you decide to take some time off after completing your undergraduate studies to explore other options. You may realize that graduate school is not for you. Alternatively, many graduate students report that they become more motivated after having taken time off from study. Either way, you are better off for exploring this issue.

Are My Credentials Strong Enough for Graduate School in Clinical Psychology?

It is difficult to evaluate your own credentials objectively. However, we can outline the criteria graduate programs employ, so you can determine your strengths and weaknesses. A recent survey of Directors of Clinical Training programs indicated there are four main criteria employed when evaluating applicants: (a) Graduate Record Exam (GRE) scores; (b) Grade Point Average (GPA); (c) letters of recommendation; (d) research experience and publications/presentations. We list the criteria in the order in which they were ranked. Although programs may weigh these criteria differently, these are the data used in determining whom to accept into a program. Notice that clinical experience was not listed by the program directors. Such experience is more beneficial to the students in determining whether clinical work is the field they wish to pursue. It is not deemed especially important in the application process. We will discuss the criteria that are employed in evaluating applicants.

1. GRE Scores. Students do not like to hear this, but performance on the GREs is an impor-

tant predictor of success in graduate school, and thus one of the most important selection criteria. A recent study found that GRE scores, but not college GPAs, significantly predicted performance in a graduate program in clinical psychology (Dollinger, 1989). GRE scores represent the only data for which comparisons can be made across all applicants. All students take the exact same test, so performance is not influenced by differences in collegiate standards, as are letters of recommendation and college grades. A total score of 1,200 for a student in Alaska means the same as a 1,200 in Florida. Also, the GREs offer a summary of a student's potential for performance in graduate school. However, keep in mind that traditional test indicators, such as GRE scores, are deemphasized when programs are considering applications from nontraditional or minority students.

2. GPA. If GRE scores are good measures of potential for performance in graduate school, GPA is the best indicator of the effort a student is willing to exert. Some undergraduate institutions are more demanding than others, and directors of admission take this into account. However, when examining a student's transcript, three questions are addressed: (a) Does this student apply herself equally to all courses, or only to those in which she is interested? (b) Does this student have the necessary breadth of training in psychology? (c) Does this student do as well in the research methodology courses (e.g., statistics, experimental design) as he does in the clinical courses?

3. Letters of Recommendation. There are several features admission directors will look for when examining letters of recommendation. These include students' potential for graduate school, their willingness to work hard, their interpersonal skills, and their potential for successfully handling clinical work. For these reasons, it is crucial that you develop means of interacting with the faculty outside the classroom. The best way to do this is to get involved in faculty research programs.

4. Research Experience. There are many reasons why students need to gain research experience prior to applying to graduate school in clinical psychology. First, the PhD in clinical psychology is both a research and a clinical degree. Therefore, directors of admission want to ensure that applicants understand what is involved in research, and that they enjoy participating in such activities, before they enter graduate school. Second, as we noted earlier, working with faculty on their research is an excellent way to obtain letters of recommendation that define more precisely a student's potential for graduate school. Third, working on research projects helps students determine which areas they would like to pursue in graduate school, and therefore, which schools to apply to. Finally, research experience gives the applicant useful information to discuss during the graduate school interview.

In What Type of Program Am I Interested?

Many students seem to think that if they want to do clinical work, they must enter a graduate program in clinical psychology. In fact, there are many different types of programs that offer training leading to careers in the mental health profession. Schools of social work, as well as counseling and school psychology programs, all offer extensive training and experience in clinical work. Graduates of these programs enter many of the same positions as do clinical psychologists. Before you invest all of your effort in applying to graduate school in clinical psychology, you should explore the clinical opportunities offered by these other training programs.

Given My Credentials, to What Type of Program Can I Realistically Aspire?

One of the most difficult things students need to do, when applying to graduate school, is realistically evaluate their credentials. Unfortunately, the credentials of many applicants are not strong enough to gain entry into PhD programs in clinical psychology. Unless these students have pursued other options, they are setting themselves up for disappointment. Fortunately, there are other options these students can explore: (a) MA programs in clinical psychology usually have lower criteria for admission than PhD programs. Students can enter these programs to earn a terminal degree or to provide a stepping stone to a PhD program. (b) Other programs that offer clinical training (e.g., counseling or school psychology) often are less competitive than PhD programs in clinical psychology. As we discussed earlier, students in these programs receive as much applied training and experience as students in clinical psychology programs. (c) Other programs in psychology (e.g., developmental, social) are less competitive than clinical programs. Students who are committed to the field of psychology, and want to remain in a research environment, may find a nonclinical PhD program in psychology more rewarding than a clinical program in another field.

PhD programs in clinical psychology are not for everyone; they are highly competitive, they place great demands on their students, and they emphasize research training as much as clinical experience. We have offered some guidelines to help you better assess your credentials and aspirations, to determine whether you should apply to programs in clinical psychology. If the answer is yes, we now offer guidelines on the application process.

GENERAL ISSUES

I Have Decided to Apply to Graduate School in Clinical Psychology. What Should I Do First?

In choosing graduate programs, you will want to make sure they provide the training and professional environment that will meet your needs. Therefore, you should clarify your personal goals, objectives, and plans. Are you most interested in research, balanced training in clinical practice and research, or primarily in clinical practice? Are you interested in doctoral-level or master's-level programs? Do you have an interest in a specific client population? Do you have preferences related to types and/or locations of future employment? These are a few of the questions you should be asking yourself before the application process begins. You will not have definitive answers for all possible questions, but you will have some, and these will probably indicate what is most important to you in choosing a graduate program.

Should I Apply to a Master's Degree Program and Complete It Before I Apply to a Doctoral Program?

There are different routes one can take to earn the doctorate in clinical psychology. A number of graduate programs provide master's degree training only. Many graduates from these programs terminate their formal education at the MA; others apply to doctoral programs.

Some graduate schools have separate training programs at the master's and doctoral levels and accept students for each. The master's program in these schools sometimes serves as a "feeder" to the doctoral program. However, each program is separate, so that the student who does not enter the doctoral program will have completed training similar to that offered at "master's only" schools.

Other programs are designed to prepare doctoral-level clinicians only. They may award the master's degree after a minimum number of credits and a master's thesis have been completed, but it is important to recognize that these departments accept applicants for the doctoral degree only.

If I Earn a Master's Degree, Are My Chances for Then Being Admitted to a Doctoral Program Better or Worse?

Generally, the possession of a master's degree has little impact on a student's application. Graduate schools are interested in the best candidates they can find. If your credentials are excellent, your chances for being admitted to a doctoral program are good. Some students who feel they need to improve their credentials may find master's degree work helpful in achieving that goal, but doctoral admission committees consider all academic work when making their decision. A mediocre undergraduate academic record is not disregarded because it has been supplemented with a master's degree and good graduate school grades, but these graduate credentials can improve a student's chances for being considered seriously.

If I Choose to Terminate My Training After Earning a Master's Degree, Will My Opportunities for Doing Clinical Work Be Limited?

Though there are many good clinicians whose highest academic degree is the master's, the doctorate is the standard of the profession. The following resolution was adopted by the American Psychological Association (APA) Council of Representatives.

The title "Professional Psychologist" has been used so widely and by persons with such a wide variety of training and experience that it does not provide the information the public deserves.

As a consequence, the APA takes the position and makes it a part of its policy that the use of the titles "Professional Psychologist," "School Psychologist," and "Industrial Psychologist" is reserved for those who have completed a doctoral training program in psychology in a university, college, or professional school of psychology that is APA or regionally accredited. In order to meet this standard, a transition period will be acknowledged for the use of the title "School Psychologist," so that ways may be sought to increase opportunities for doctoral training and to improve the level of the educational codes pertaining to the title.

The APA further takes the position and makes part of its policy that only those who have completed a doctoral training program in professional psychology in a university, college, or professional school of psychology that is APA or regionally accredited are qualified to independently provide unsupervised direct delivery of professional services including preventive, assessment, and therapeutic services. The exclusions mentioned above pertaining to school psychologists do not apply to the independent, unsupervised, direct delivery of professional services discussed in this paragraph.

Licensed or certified master's-level psychologists, having met earlier standards of the profession (i.e., were accorded grandmother/grandfather recognition) are to be regarded as comparably qualified through education, experience, examination, and the test of time, as are present and future doctoral psychologists, and shall be entitled under APA guidelines to include as part of their title the word "psychologist." (APA, 1992, p. vii)

Another fact that needs to be considered is that all states employ some form of licensing or certification for psychologists (see Chapter 14). Though requirements vary from state to state, an earned doctorate is a prerequisite in most of them. Before you decide to prepare for clinical work by earning a master's degree, be certain your career expectations can be met with this degree.

Are All Doctoral Programs in Clinical Psychology Research Oriented?

All university-based PhD programs in clinical psychology provide training in research as well as in clinical functions, but there are differences in emphasis from one institution to another. It is worth your effort to learn of each program's emphasis when you are securing other information about the program. Programs that are strictly research oriented make this fact clear in their information and refrain from using "clinical psychology" as a title (ex-

perimental psychopathology is a common substitute). Some graduate programs offer a Doctor of Psychology (PsyD) degree in addition to, or instead of, a traditional PhD. This degree puts the emphasis on clinical training while reducing the emphasis on research. These programs still require their students to acquire knowledge of research tools, but do not require students to do basic research. In other words, students still develop their knowledge of statistics and research methods but are not required to do a thesis or dissertation.

How Do I Identify Good Graduate Programs?

It is difficult to label graduate programs as good and bad. The question to be answered is whether a specific program fits a particular student's needs. A research versus clinical emphasis has already been discussed and can be ascertained for a specific program by corresponding with current graduate students and faculty at the particular school. If you can identify graduates of particular programs, ask them for their evaluation. Other things to consider include the size of the department and the program, the student/faculty ratio, opportunities for a variety of practicum experiences, the size and location of the campus and the community, the type and extent of department resources, and the particular philosophical school of thought that may be dominant in the program. Any of the foregoing important to *you* should be considered when you attempt to identify good programs.

One final caution concerns generalizing the quality of the department to the program. There are some psychology departments considered to be the best by many psychologists. Since your interest is in clinical psychology, do not assume that the clinical program is one of the best because the department is considered one of the best. Identify what is the best for *you* and judge each program against *your* criteria.

What Does American Psychological Association (APA) Accreditation of a Clinical Psychology Graduate Program Mean?

APA accreditation means the program has met a minimum standard of quality. The APA publication *Graduate Study in Psychology and Associated Fields* explains that APA accreditation should be interpreted to mean:

1. The program is recognized and publicly labeled as a doctoral program in clinical, counseling, or school psychology (or combination thereof). It is located in and supported by an institution of higher education, which itself is accredited by one of six regional accrediting bodies also recognized by COPA.

2. The program voluntarily applied for accreditation and, in so doing, engaged in extensive self-study of its program objectives, educational and training practices, its resource support base, and its faculty, students, and graduates. The program also participated in a peer review of its operations by a site-visit team of distinguished professional colleagues.

3. The program was thoroughly evaluated by the APA Committee on Accreditation (comprised of professional and public members) and judged to be in sufficient compliance with the APA Criteria for Accreditation to warrant accreditation status. Those criteria against which a program is evaluated include institutional support; sensitivity to cultural and individual differences; training models and curricula; faculty; students; facilities; and practicum and internship training.

Accreditation, in summary, applies to educational institutions and programs, not to individuals. It does not guarantee jobs or licensure for individuals, though being a graduate of an accredited program may facilitate such achievement. It does speak to the manner and quality by which an educational institution or program conducts its business. It speaks to a sense of public trust, as well as professional quality. (APA, 1992, p. ix)

Students should be aware that there may be excellent departments that have not applied for accreditation or that have not had a doctoral program in clinical psychology long enough to be eligible for approval. Table A–1 lists the clinical training programs that were APA accredited through 1992.

APPLICATION PROCEDURES

How Do I Get Initial Information About Graduate Schools?

There are several sources of information; you should use *all* of them. Some of the best informants are psychology faculty, especially those who are clinical psychologists. Preparing for courses, doing research, and keeping current for clinical practice require review of new ideas and research as well as participation at professional meetings and workshops. This exposure to the field helps faculty know about various schools, training and research staff, the nature and philosophies of different programs, recent changes in certain departments, and other pertinent information. Though it is not reasonable to expect the faculty to know about all or even most doctoral programs, they will be able to provide you with good information about many of them.

Professional journals and related publications are information sources that are often overlooked. An excellent way to find programs that meet your needs is to use these sources to identify faculty who are studying topics that interest you. A thorough search of the literature will highlight programs that have several faculty with whom you might like to study. Find out where they are teaching by consulting the APA and APS (American Psychological Society) membership directories (most psychology departments have recent editions).

Some colleges or undergraduate departments have a special advising staff for their students. The advisors or counselors may or may not be faculty, but if part of their job is to

In addition to over 150 fully approved programs, several clinical programs have received provisional approval. This is a category for relatively new programs whose development shows promise or for programs that are innovative and consequently do not fit the usual accreditation criteria. For the institutions listed, the training programs are housed in the department of psychology unless otherwise indicated; the majority of training programs still follow Shakow's recommendation that clinical students be trained in an environment that stresses general psychological knowledge. Programs awarding the PsyD degree rather than the PhD are noted.

Adelphi University, Institute of Advanced
  Psychological Studies
University of Alabama
University of Alabama at Birmingham
American University
University of Arizona
University of Arkansas
Arizona State University
Auburn University
Baylor University (PsyD)
Biola University, Rosemead School of
  Psychology (PhD, PsyD)
Boston University
Bowling Green State University
Brigham Young University
University of British Columbia
University of California (Berkeley)

University of California (Los Angeles)
California School of Professional Psy-
  chology (Berkeley)
California School of Professional Psy-
  chology (Fresno)
California School of Professional Psy-
  chology (Los Angeles) (PhD and PsyD)
Case Western Reserve University
Catholic University of America
University of Cincinnati
City College, CUNY
Clark University
University of Colorado
Columbia University, Teachers College
  Department of Clinical Psychology
Concordia University
University of Connecticut

TABLE A–1
APA-Accredited Programs in Clinical Psychology, 1992

help with graduate school applications, you can benefit from their experience with former students. Even if this source of information does not exist at your school, all department offices receive pamphlets, notices, and general information brochures from many graduate psychology programs in the United States and Canada. Use this information; it may answer some of your questions and inform you of new programs.

There are numerous books that list graduate schools and programs. The best of these for psychology is published by the American Psychological Association. It is called *Graduate Study in Psychology*. This book is revised semi-annually and has over 500 pages of information, including application addresses, types of programs and degrees offered by each institution, size of faculty, financial aid information, tuition, degree requirements, admission requirements, average grades and entrance test scores for students admitted the previous year, comments

University of Delaware

University of Denver

University of Denver, School of Professional Psychology (PsyD)

DePaul University

University of Detroit-Mercy

Duke University

Emory University

Farleigh Dickinson (Teaneck-Hackensack Campus)

University of Florida Department of Clinical Psychology

Florida Institute of Technology (PsyD)

Florida State University

Fordham University

Fuller Theological Seminary Graduate School of Psychology (PhD, PsyD)

George Mason University

George Washington University

University of Georgia

Georgia State University

Hahnemann University

University of Hawaii

University of Health Sciences Chicago Medical School

University of Houston

Howard University

University of Illinois (Chicago)

University of Illinois (Urbana-Champaign)

Illinois Institute of Technology

Illinois School of Professional Psychology (PsyD)

Indiana University at Bloomington

Indiana University of Pennsylvania (PsyD)

Indiana State University (PsyD)

University of Iowa

University of Kansas

Kent State University

University of Kentucky

Long Island University

Louisiana State University

University of Louisville

Loyola University of Chicago

University of Maine at Orono

University of Manitoba

University of Maryland

University of Maryland-Baltimore County

University of Massachusetts

Massachusetts School of Professional Psychology (PsyD)

McGill University

Memphis State University

Miami University (Ohio)

University of Miami (Florida)

TABLE A–1

Continued

about the program, and other valuable information. You may purchase a copy of this publication from the American Psychological Association, 1200 Seventeenth Street N.W., Washington, DC 20036. The cost of *Graduate Study in Psychology* in 1992 was $19.50. There is a discount if you are an APA student affiliate.

Finally, your library should have catalogs from most universities. Once you have identified clinical programs that interest you, look at the graduate catalog for the university to get some idea of general university structure and requirements. If course descriptions are listed, you may be able to identify a particular program's emphasis.

How Many Potential Programs in Clinical Psychology Should Be on My Initial List?

Your *initial* list should include as many programs as possible. The APA's *Graduate*

University of Michigan
Michigan State University
University of Minnesota
University of Mississippi
University of Missouri (Columbia)
Univerity of Missouri (St. Louis)
University of Montana
University of Nebraska (Lincoln)
University of Nevada (Reno)
University of New Mexico
New York University
University of North Carolina (Chapel Hill)
University of North Carolina (Greensboro)
University of North Dakota
University of North Texas
Northern Illinois University
Northwestern University
Northwestern University Medical School
  Department of Psychiatry and Behav-
  ioral Sciences
Nova University School of Psychology
Nova University School of Psychology
  (PsyD)
Ohio University
Ohio State University
Oklahoma State University
University of Oregon
University of Ottawa (School of Psychology)

University of Pennsylvania
Pennsylvania State University
Pepperdine University School of Educa-
  tion and Psychology (PsyD)
University of Pittsburgh
Purdue University Department of Psycho-
  logical Services
University of Rhode Island
University of Rochester
Rutgers—The State University of New Jer-
  sey
Rutgers—The State University of New Jer-
  sey, Department of Clinical Psychol-
  ogy (PsyD)
St. John's University
St. Louis University
San Diego State University/University of
  California-San Diego
University of Saskatchewan
Simon Fraser University
University of South Carolina
University of South Dakota
University of South Florida
University of Southern California
Southern Illinois University
University of Southern Mississippi
State University of New York
  at Albany

TABLE A–1
Continued

Study in Psychology lists almost every clinical psychology program in the United States and Canada. As you use the various sources of information mentioned above and decide about location and degree preferences, you will begin to eliminate programs from your initial list. Once you have eliminated as many programs as possible by using the information you have compiled, you should write to each remaining program to request descriptions. This will allow you to continue to reduce the list on the basis of new information.

When Should I Write to Graduate Programs for Information?

You should request information in August and September, approximately a year before the projected admission date (e.g., September 1994 for Fall 1995 admission). Requesting ma-

State University of New York at Birmingham

State University of New York at Buffalo

State University of New York at Stony Brook

Syracuse University

Temple University

University of Tennessee

Texas A&M University

University of Texas at Austin

University of Texas Southwestern Medical Center at Dallas

Texas Tech University

University of Toledo

University of Utah

Vanderbilt University

Vanderbilt University (George Peabody College for Teachers)

University of Vermont

University of Virginia

University of Virginia (Department of Human Services)

Virginia Commonwealth University

Virginia Consortium for Professional Psychology (PsyD)

Virginia Polytechnic Institute and State University

University of Washington

Washington State University

Washington University in St. Louis

University of Waterloo

Wayne State University

West Virginia University

University of Western Ontario

Widener University, Institute for Graduate Clinical Psychology (PsyD)

University of Windsor

University of Wisconsin (Madison)

University of Wisconsin (Milwaukee)

Wright State University School of Professional Psychology (PsyD)

University of Wyoming

Yale University

Yeshiva University (PsyD)

Yeshiva University, Ferkauf Graduate School of Psychology

Hofstra University*

Utah State University*

---

*Fully accredited programs offering training in more than one specialty, one of which is clinical.

TABLE A–1
Continued

terial earlier than this sometimes gets you old information or places you on a waiting list until material is available. If you make a request too late, the material may not arrive in time for you to make effective use of it. Remember, you may have questions that arise from your reading the material and you may wish to correspond with some departments before a final decision is made about whether to apply to them. This all requires time—give yourself plenty!

When Writing for Application Information, What Should I Ask for and What Format Should I Use?

At minimum, you should ask for information about the clinical psychology program, appropriate department and graduate school application forms, a graduate school program and course catalog, financial aid information, financial aid application forms, and a list of faculty and their research interests.

Your request for information need not be elaborate. A postcard or form letter addressed to the department's graduate admission committee can be used, but be sure it includes a request for all the information you will need.

When Should I Apply?

Department application deadlines vary, but most are from January 15 to February 15. A few come as early as December, while others (mostly for master's degree programs) run as late as August. A rule of thumb is to use January 15 as an application deadline except for schools having earlier dates. Some schools that use later deadlines are often selecting students as applications are being processed. Therefore, it is to your advantage to submit your application early to these schools.

Submitting *very* early applications (September or October) is usually of no particular value since departments are not "tooled up" for the admission process. Also, required test scores (to be discussed later) are usually not available this early in the school year.

How Many Programs Should I Apply To?

It is difficult to identify a specific number of applications appropriate for all students. I am reminded of two cases: One student applied to six schools and was admitted to all of them, while another applied to 27 and was admitted to one. Since competition is keen, the general rule is apply to as many programs as you can reasonably afford. The larger the number of applications, the better your chances of being accepted.

Once you have decided on a final list of schools, ask yourself what you will do if you are not accepted by any of them. Perhaps at this point you may want to add one or two "safety valve" programs to fall back on. However, do not apply to programs that are really not acceptable to you. Such applications waste admission committee time, your time (and

money), and may prevent a serious applicant from being admitted.

How Much Does Applying Cost?

Total testing costs can run over $100. Application fees usually vary from nothing to $65. Transcript costs (usually $2 to $5 each), additional test report fees, postage, and phone calls add up quickly. A total cost of $60 per application is about average.

QUALIFICATIONS AND CREDENTIALS

What Kinds of Courses and Experiences Will Help My Application?

Your undergraduate department will have designed a graduate preparatory major to meet your course needs. This will probably include a core program of introductory psychology, statistics, and experimental psychology (including a laboratory). These are the minimum requirements for most graduate programs, regardless of specialization area. In addition to these core courses and some breadth in psychology, PhD programs often look for course work in mathematics, laboratory work in other sciences, and computer science courses. Remember, graduate programs are looking for the best students they can find, so a strong academic preparation is essential.

In addition to standard course work, independent research such as a bachelor's thesis and/or experience as an assistant to faculty who are involved in research is very helpful. This not only provides you with desired experience, but also allows faculty supervisors to observe your potential for scholarly endeavors and to include their evaluations and impressions in letters of recommendation.

Psychology departments will not expect you to enter their programs as a trained clinician, but they may look for evidence of experience in "helping relationships." Practica and relevant volunteer work will assist in establishing that your career decision is based in part on some first-hand knowledge of the field. Remember, impressions of what it is like to work in a field and actual working experiences are often very different. It is important that you know what you are getting into when you choose clinical psychology as a career.

What Grade Average Is Necessary to Be Accepted?

Grade average requirements will vary across programs, degrees, and institutions. Some admissions committees will be concerned with a 4-year average, while others will consider the last 2 years only. For clinical psychology doctoral programs, a 3.5 grade average (on a 4-point system) is generally considered *minimum*. At highly competitive schools a 3.7 grade average may be more common, but other criteria are also taken into consideration. It is not unusual for a department to select a student with a 3.5 grade average over a student with a 4.0 grade average when other admissions data (test scores, research experience, course selection, and the like) are more in line with the program's goals, requirements, and orientation.

Admission to master's degree programs is less competitive than for doctoral programs. Many master's programs have a minimum grade average requirement of B– (approximately 2.75), though the typical student admitted to such programs is likely to have a solid B (3.25) grade average.

What Testing Is Involved in Applying to Graduate School?

Most graduate schools use standardized tests to assist them in evaluating applicants. The most common are the Graduate Record Examination (GRE) and the Miller Analogies Test (MAT).

The GRE General Test is described in the *GRE Information Bulletin* as follows:

The GRE General Test measures certain developed verbal, quantitative, and analytical abilities that are important for academic achievement. In doing so, the test necessarily reflects the opportunities and efforts that have contributed to the development of those abilities.

The General Test is only one of several means of evaluating likely success in graduate school. It is not intended to measure inherent intellectual capacity or intelligence. Neither is it intended to measure creativity, motivation, perseverance, or social worth. The test does, however, make it possible to compare students with different backgrounds. A GRE score of 500, for example, has the same meaning whether earned by a student at a small, private liberal arts college or by a student at a large public university.

Because several different forms (or editions) of the test are in active use, all students do not receive exactly the same test edition. However, all editions measure the same skills and meet the same specifications for content and difficulty. The scores from different editions are made comparable to one another by a statistical procedure known as equating. This process makes it possible to assure that all reported scores of a given value denote the same level of developed ability regardless of which edition of the test is taken.

Since students have wide-ranging backgrounds, interests, and skills, the *verbal sections* of the General Test use questions from diverse areas of experience. The areas tested range from the activities of daily life to broad categories of academic interest such as the sciences, social studies, and the humanities. Knowledge of high school level arithmetic, plane geometry, and algebra provides adequate preparation for the *quantitative sections* of the test. Questions in the *analytical sections* measure analytical skills developed in virtually all fields of study. No formal training in logic or methods of analysis is needed to do well in these sections. (ETS, 1992, p. 19)

The GRE Subject Test in Psychology is described in the 1992–1993 information booklet as follows:

The test has about 220 questions drawn from courses most commonly offered at the undergraduate level, in three categories:

1. Experimental or natural science oriented (about 43% of the questions), including learning, language, memory, thinking, perception, ethology, comparative, sensation, and physiological psychology.

2. Social or social science oriented (about 43% of the questions), including clinical and abnormal, developmental, personality, and social psychology.

3. General (about 14% of the questions), including the history of psychology, applied psychology, measurement, research designs, and statistics. (ETS, 1992, p. 21)

The General Test is given in the morning on each international testing date, while the Subject Test is given in the afternoon. Each test requires about 3 hours.

Another option for taking the GRE General Test is computer-based testing. In October 1992, over 100 test centers throughout the United States were available to give the GRE General Test, by appointment, using PC-type computers. An advantage of using this form of testing is that your results are made known to you immediately after you have finished the examination, and paper score reports are mailed to you and your designated institution recipients within 15 days after the test. This option is available for the General Test only. The cost for computer-based testing in 1992 was $90.

The GRE information bulletins include all application material for the scheduled test dates and for the computer-based testing. They are available at most colleges and universities, or you may receive a copy by writing to

Graduate Record Examinations
Educational Testing Service

P.O. Box 6000
Princeton, NJ 08541–6000

The basic fees for 1992–1993 were $45 for the General Test, $45 for the Subject Test, and $90 for computer-based testing (General Test only).

The Miller Analogies Test (MAT) consists of 100 difficult verbal analogy items. Although the MAT is not as widely used as the GRE, a substantial number of programs require MAT scores. As with the GRE, testing is often available on college and university campuses. Further information about the MAT and testing locations can be obtained by writing to

Psychological Corporation
304 East 45th Street
New York, NY 10017

Should I Take Both the GRE General Test and the GRE Subject Test?

Since the General Test is almost always required, there is no choice but to take it. As for the Subject Test, your decision will be determined in part by your choice of schools. If you have decided on the graduate programs to which you will apply, the application information from these schools will indicate whether the Subject Test is required. If you have not decided on a specific list of schools, you had better take both the General Test and the Subject Test. If you wish to send only General Test results or only Subject Test results to a particular school, Educational Testing Service will honor your request.

When Should I Take the Graduate Record Exam?

Most students choose to take the exam on the October test date in the fall of their senior year. The results of this test are usually in the mail to the student and to all schools designated by the student by the end of November. There are six test dates scheduled each year. Educational Testing Service reports that it takes approximately 6 weeks to score tests and have the results in the mail. Therefore, the latest you can take the exam is on a scheduled date that is at least 6 weeks before the application deadline for a given institution. If February 1 is the deadline date, only October and December tests in the school year will meet the deadline.

When selecting test dates, keep in mind that you are likely to be taking both the General Test and the Subject Test. Three hours of testing in the morning and three more hours in the afternoon can be tiring, so many students take the General Test on one test date and the Subject Test on another.

Another consideration in selecting test dates is whether or not you wish to use the results in making decisions about where to apply. If you choose test dates that are sufficiently early, you will be able to look over your scores, consult advisors, and review resource material. For example, the APA's *Graduate Study in Psychology* lists average GRE scores for students admitted to specific schools. Students who apply to graduate programs without knowing their GRE scores are taking a chance. Scores at the 90th percentile permit application to a different set of schools than do scores at the 40th percentile. Being fully informed when you apply will save time and money as well as increase your chances of being admitted to a clinical psychology program.

One test-scheduling strategy that has worked well for some students is to take the General Test in June, at the end of the junior year. The summer is then spent reviewing for the Subject Test in Psychology, which is taken in October of the senior year. This allows time for retaking tests, if necessary, and using the results for choosing schools.

Can I Study for the Tests?

There are several how-to-prepare books on the market. Generally, they provide a mathematics and vocabulary review, give tips on test taking, and provide sample GRE test items. The GRE *Information Bulletin* provides a sample GRE General Test, and Educational Testing Services sells practice material including GRE General Tests and Subject Tests actually administered in previous years. These sources can be helpful in familiarizing yourself with the types and forms of questions you are likely to encounter and can give you practice at pacing yourself during an examination.

You can review for the quantitative portion of the General Test, especially if you have been away from mathematics for a while. Brushing up on basic algebra and geometry will help you during the exam by reducing the time needed to recall how to solve particular problems. Students report that the quantitative portion of the test is not difficult but that it is fast paced. Know your basic math "cold" so you can work quickly and accurately.

Sources frequently used by students in preparing for the GRE General Test include test preparation courses, videotaped preparation courses, and annually revised test preparation books. Courses and tapes can get quite expensive, so most students use the test preparation books. Some of the more frequently used how-to-prepare books are published by Barron's Educational Series, Arco Publishing Company, and Monarch Press. These are readily available at most bookstores.

As for the Subject Test in Psychology, remember that it covers all areas of psychology. Names, theories, and definitions are likely to be a part of the test, as are basic concepts. No one is expected to know about every area, so if you have not been exposed to certain aspects of psychology, you will no doubt have trouble with some questions. You can prepare for the Subject Test in Psychology by thoroughly reviewing a comprehensive textbook in introductory psychology. In addition, books that present the history of psychology and/or systems and theories in psychology are available and provide information that is particularly useful in preparing for the Psychology Subject Test.

Will I Need Letters of Recommendation for Graduate School Application? If so, How Many and From Whom?

Three letters of recommendation are usually required by the overwhelming majority of graduate programs in clinical psychology. At least two letters should be academic (i.e., from psychology faculty who are thoroughly familiar with your academic ability). If faculty from other disciplines can provide a better picture of your academic achievement and potential for graduate study, use them. The quality of the recommendation could be more important than whether or not the writer is a psychologist.

Letters from practicum or (relevant) job supervisors can also be helpful, since they help establish your success at working within the mental health field. Letters from people such as senators, governors, and other political figures do not help your application. Generally, these say nothing more than "I've been asked to write . . . " and "please give this student full consideration." Such letters are likely to leave the impression that the student feels incapable of making it on his or her own. Unless the writer is in a position to judge the candidate's potential as a graduate student or a clinician, such prestige letters should not be submitted.

What Should I Know About Asking for Letters of Recommendation?

First, ask permission before you use someone's name as a reference. Many faculty will want to talk with you about your academic and career objectives before agreeing to write a letter. Some will ask you to provide additional written information about yourself and may want to discuss this information with you. Be prepared to do this.

It is appropriate for you to provide faculty with information about yourself. Faculty with many students can easily forget individual students' work, when they took courses, and other details. Also, it is not unusual for faculty to know little about a student other than what has been observed in the classroom setting. General knowledge of the student's activities, accomplishments, and jobs can supplement classroom contacts in a way that enhances a reference letter.

Here is a list of information items you should provide faculty who are writing letters of reference for you:

1. Your full name.

2. Major, minor, curriculum, and specialization.

3. A computation of grade average in your major, in all college work, and in work since the end of the sophomore year.

4. A transcript of your college courses and grades.

5. A list of the psychology laboratory courses you have had.

6. A description of other research experiences, including comments on the full extent of your participation (include a copy of any major research papers).

7. A list of honor societies, clubs, and organizations to which you belong, along with comments on your participation (be sure to include positions of responsibility you held).

8. A brief discussion of jobs you have held and volunteer work you have done. Some students carry heavy work loads while being enrolled as full-time students in order to pay for their education. This type of information should be included.

9. An outline of your personal and professional plans and goals.

10. Any other information which it might be appropriate for this person to know as she or he writes a letter of recommendation.

Be sure to ask for letters and provide appropriate recommendation materials early. Faculty often write letters for several students; give them plenty of time to prepare yours. To reduce the possibility of error and to speed the process:

1. Include a stamped, addressed envelope for each program for which a recommendation is being sent.

2. When forms are included, *your name* and other information which is not part of the formal recommendation should be *typed* in the appropriate space. *Do not hand blank forms to the recommender.*

3. Include a list of all the schools to which a recommendation is to be sent. Indicate which have forms to be completed and those that did not provide forms. This can later be used by the writer as a checklist against which actual references can be compared.

Will I Be Able to See My Recommendation?

Letters of reference are not confidential unless you waive your right to see them. You are encouraged to consider doing so since some readers feel that the recommendation is more likely to be a candid assessment of the student if the writer knows the student will not see the letter. If you are concerned about what the letter might include, ask the writer if he or she can write a letter *supporting* your application.

Are Personal Interviews Required?

When interviews are part of the admissions procedure, they are likely to come only after the admission committee has considerably narrowed the number of applicants. Interviews are usually held on the school's campus, but when a visit requires long-distance travel, a representative of the school may interview applicants at a location closer to their residences. Telephone interviews are sometimes used, but they are the exception rather than the rule. On the other hand, a student who has already been interviewed in person should be prepared for a follow-up telephone call. When final decisions are being made, the committee may want to ask some candidates a few more questions.

One bit of strategy used by one successful applicant might be considered. He kept information about the programs to which he had applied (e.g., who was on the faculty, particular emphases and strengths), along with notes about his interests and goals near his telephone. He felt that if he received a call, this preparation would reduce his anxiety about the conversation and help him organize his responses so that the emphasis would be appropriate for each institution. This also assured that he would include all the points he wanted to make so that he could avoid blaming himself later for not remembering to mention something important. He did receive a call and the strategy worked.

Interviews are not always part of the applicant review process. Once you have received a formal letter of acceptance, it is appropriate to visit the school and talk with department representatives and graduate students about their program. It is *not* appropriate to show up unannounced and expect department representatives to be available. Make an appointment ahead of time by calling the director of clinical training and asking to meet with members of the clinical psychology program and with graduate students. Be prepared to outline briefly the nature of your questions and have a number of alternate dates in mind before you call.

Often, students want to schedule interview appointments before they apply or before they are admitted to a program. Some departments, usually those offering a master's degree, welcome such requests. However, most departments have so many potential applicants that it is impossible for them to accommodate such requests. Usually, the department's printed material is sufficiently detailed so that a decision on whether or not to apply can be made by interested individuals. Once admitted, students can use interviews to compare programs and make the accept or reject decision.

If the written material is not sufficiently informative for you to get a clear and accurate picture of the program, seek additional information by writing or calling the department. However, be sure you have read what was sent to you before contacting the department, and that your questions do not cover what is presented in the printed material.

Are My College Transcripts Required?

Most programs will ask for a transcript of your college work from each institution at which you have studied. Transfer work summarized on the transcript from the last school you attended is not usually accepted—separate transcripts are required. You should call the schools you have attended to find out about transcript charges. Once that has been determined, send a letter to the director of student records at each school, enclosing a list of institutions to which a copy of your transcript is to be sent. Include a check to cover the cost.

FINANCIAL AID

What Kind of Financial Aid Is Available for Graduate Study?

Financial aid comes in three forms: loans, grants, and work programs. The major sources of all financial aid are the universities themselves. This aid is, of course, limited to their own students. Other sources include guaranteed loan programs (many of which are government sponsored) and national awards, which are competitive and have specific criteria for application. These are awarded directly to the student for use at the school of her or his choice. One example of this type of aid is the Danforth graduate fellowship, which provides support for 4 years. It is awarded to seniors who intend to obtain the highest degree in their fields and who have a serious interest in college teaching. Students applying to clinical programs with the intention of teaching in colleges or universities are eligible.

Since the availability of awards and loans changes regularly, you are encouraged to check for current information with the financial aid officer at your college or at the institution to which you are applying.

Since financial support is usually received through the program to which you are admitted, the aid information you will receive with your application material is very important—read it carefully!

Loan programs exist on most campuses as a way of assisting students to invest in their own future. They usually carry a low interest rate with payments beginning after the students leave graduate school.

Fellowships and scholarships are given on many campuses as outright grants to support and encourage very bright students with excellent potential. These are few in number and highly competitive in nature.

Assistantships come in two forms: research assistantships and teaching assistantships. Both are *jobs* in the university that require graduate students to assist faculty in research projects or in teaching responsibilities (e.g., as discussion leaders, laboratory instructors, or paper graders). Assistantships usually require 10 to 20 hours of work each week.

Some programs have received grants from the federal government to provide *traineeships* in clinical psychology. As a result, there may be training grant funds available for a limited number of students at some institutions. Like fellowships, these are usually outright gifts, but do require that you carry a full academic load. They, too, are few in number, and competition for them is keen.

Not all types of aid are offered at all schools. Be sure you understand what is available at each school and at each level of graduate standing by carefully reading the financial aid information you receive.

Are There Assistantships Available From Departments Other Than the One to Which I Have Applied?

Assistantships of various types may be available on a campus. If you are accepted to a program with little or no financial aid, it is well worth your time to check on the availability of assistantships in other departments. For example, administrators of residence halls may hire graduate students to serve as hall counselors. Departments with large enrollments in undergraduate courses may have more teaching assistantships than graduate students in their programs and thus import assistants from related areas. Identify your skills and experiences and seek out jobs that fit them.

Do All Financial Aid Packages Involve About the Same Amount of Money?

Financial aid will vary from campus to campus and between departments on the same campus. For example, one school may give more money, but recipients are required to pay their own tuition. Others will give a smaller sum of money, but also pay tuition and fees. Some residence hall assistantships provide room and board only; others provide room, board, tuition, and fees. If the amount of financial aid is an important factor in your selection of a graduate program, be sure you know both the amount you will receive and the costs you will incur before you make a final decision to accept or reject an offer of admission.

Are Separate References Required When Applying for Financial Aid?

Sometimes, separate application deadlines and reference letters are involved for financial aid consideration. Usually the letters of reference, when required, are copies of those used by departments in the admission process. The reference letters are usually used to assess the

student's academic potential, not financial need. Read your application material carefully to determine just what is required in order to apply for financial aid, and remember that *deadlines for financial aid applications are sometimes earlier than deadlines for applying to clinical psychology graduate programs.*

OTHER IMPORTANT QUESTIONS

Are There Any Last-Minute Things I Need to Do When Applying?

Once your applications are sent out, you are encouraged to check with each department to which you have applied for the purpose of assuring that your application is complete. Each year, some applications are not considered because the students were unaware that they were incomplete. Some departments notify students when letters of reference or GRE scores are missing, but many do not. To eliminate this potential problem, ask each department to verify that your application is complete. Be sure to enclose a stamped, self-addressed envelope for their response. The brief note and checklist shown in Figure A–1 provide examples of what might be sent.

When I Am Admitted to a Program, How Long Will I Have to Make a Decision About Whether to Accept?

Most offers are made with a specific deadline for accepting or rejecting them. For doctoral programs, this is usually April 15. This date was adopted by the APA Council of Graduate Schools to protect students from being pressured to make decisions before having full information about their alternatives. The council's statement reads as follows:

Acceptance of an offer of financial aid (such as graduate scholarship, fellowship, traineeship, or assistantship) for the next academic

Graduate Admissions Committee
Department of Psychology
University of Illinois
Champaign, Illinois 61820

To Whom It May Concern:

    I have applied to your graduate program in clinical psychology. Since I am very interested in being accepted to your program, I would like to verify that my application file is complete. I have enclosed a checklist and a self-addressed, stamped envelope to assist you in providing me with that information. Thank you for your cooperation.

Sincerly,

Mary Smith

Date: _____   (PLEASE CHECK APPROPRIATE LINES)

<u>Received</u>

Application for Admission	_____
Application for Financial Aid	_____
GRE General Test Scores	_____
GRE Subject Test Scores	_____
Miller Analogies Test Score	_____
Recommendation letters from:	
Professor Abigail Jones	_____
Professor Herbert Long	_____
Mr. Ben Wright	_____
Transcripts from:	
City Junior College	_____
University of Colorado	_____

Are there other required materials which have not been received?

_____
_____
_____

    (PLEASE RETURN IN ENCLOSED STAMPED AND ADDRESSED ENVELOPE.)

FIGURE A–1   An example of a brief note and checklist to send to the admissions committee when applying to a graduate program in clinical psychology.

year by an actual or prospective graduate student completes an agreement which both student and graduate school expect to honor. In those instances in which the student accepts the offer before April 15 and subsequently desires to withdraw, the student may submit in writing a resignation of the appointment at any time through April 15. However, an acceptance given or left in force after April 15 commits the student not to accept another offer without first obtaining a written release from the institution to which a commitment has been made. Similarly, an offer by an institution after April 15 is conditional on presentation by the student of the written release from any previously accepted offer. It is further agreed by the institutions and organizations subscribing to the above Resolution that a copy of this Resolution should accompany every scholarship, fellowship, traineeship, and assistantship offer. (APA, 1992, p. viii)

However, this resolution has been modified by the Counsel of Graduate Departments of Psychology to read:

An acceptance given or left in force after April 15 commits the student not to solicit or accept another offer. Offers made after April 15 must include the proviso that the offer is void if acceptance of a previous offer from a department accepting this resolution is in force on that date. These rules are binding on all persons acting on the behalf of the offering institution. (APA, 1992, p. viii)

In 1988, the following motion was passed:

That the currently prevailing procedures dealing with the offering and acceptance of financial aid are intended to cover graduate admissions as well as offers of financial aid. To protect candidates against the need to make premature decisions, graduate programs should allow applicants until April 15 to make final decisions. (APA, 1992, p. viii)

If financial aid as described in this statement is not involved, the student is not under the same obligation. In such cases, however, courtesy dictates that you inform the department of your decision as soon as possible. This will be appreciated by the department and may provide space for another student. If you do not receive an acceptance letter in April, you may receive one later because space does become available as students decline offers.

Will I Be Successful in Gaining Admission?

Obviously, this is not a question that can be answered. We hope the information and suggestions that have been presented are helpful to you. A careful examination of your own credentials and the advice and counsel of those who have experience with students applying to graduate school in clinical psychology will help you apply to appropriate programs. It is also a good idea to explore related human-service areas. Many students have found it valuable to explore counseling psychology and clinical social work programs as alternatives to programs in clinical psychology. We wish you success!

References

AMERICAN PSYCHOLOGICAL ASSOCIATION. (1992). *Graduate study in psychology*. Washington, DC: Author.

EDUCATIONAL TESTING SERVICE. (1992). *GRE 1992–93 Registration and Information Bulletin, 1992*. Princeton, NJ: Author.

References

ABIKOFF, H. (1985). Efficacy of cognitive training interventions in hyperactive children: A critical review. *Clinical Psychology Review, 5,* 479–512.

ABIKOFF, H., & GITTELMAN, R. (1985). Hyperactive children maintained on stimulants: Is cognitive training a useful adjunct? *Archives of General Psychiatry, 42,* 953–961.

ABIKOFF, H., GITTELMAN-KLEIN, R., & KLEIN, D. (1977). Validation of a classroom observation code for hyperactive children. *Journal of Consulting and Clinical Psychology, 45,* 772–783.

ABLES, B. S., & BRANDSMA, J. M. (1977). *Therapy for couples.* San Francisco: Jossey-Bass.

ABOOD, L. G. (1960). A chemical approach to the problem of mental illness. In D. D. Jackson (Ed.), *The etiology of schizophrenia* (pp. 91–119). New York: Basic Books.

ABRAMOWITZ, S. I., ABRAMOWITZ, C. V., JACKSON, C., & GOMES, B. (1973). The politics of clinical judgment: What nonliberal examiners infer about women who do not stifle themselves. *Journal of Consulting and Clinical Psychology, 41,* 385–391.

ABRAMSON, L. Y., SELIGMAN, M. E. P., & TEASDALE, J. D. (1978). Learned helplessness in humans: Critique and reformulation. *Journal of Abnormal Psychology, 87,* 49–74.

ACHENBACH, T. M. (1978). The Child Behavior Profile: I. Boys aged 6–11. *Journal of Consulting and Clinical Psychology, 46,* 478–488.

ACHENBACH, T. M. (1982). *Developmental psychopathology* (2nd ed.). New York: John Wiley.

ACHENBACH, T. M. (1985). *Assessment and taxonomy of child and adolescent psychopathology.* Newbury Park, CA: Sage.

ACHENBACH, T. M. (1988). Integrating assessment and taxonomy. In M. Rutter, A. H. Tuma, & I. S. Lann (Eds.), *Assessment and diagnosis in child psychopathology* (pp. 300–343). New York: Guilford Press.

ACHENBACH, T. M., & EDELBROCK, C. S. (1978). The classification of child psychopathology: A review and analysis of empirical efforts. *Psychological Bulletin, 85,* 1275–1301.

ACHENBACH, T. M., & EDELBROCK, C. S. (1979). The child behavior profile: II. Boys aged 12–16 and girls aged 6–11. *Journal of Consulting and Clinical Psychology, 47,* 223–233.

ACHENBACH, T. M., & EDELBROCK, C. S. (1981). Behavioral problems and competencies reported by parents of normal and disturbed children aged four to sixteen. *Monographs of the Society for Research in Child Development, 46,* Serial No. 188.

ACKERMAN, N. W. (1958). *The psychodynamics of family life.* New York: Basic Books.

ACKERMAN, R., & DERUBEIS, R. J. (1991). Is depressive

realism real? *Clinical Psychology Review, 11,* 565–584.

ADAMS, H. E., DOSTER, J. A., & CALHOUN, K. S. (1977). A psychologically based system of response classification. In A. R. Ciminero, K. S. Calhoun, and H. E. Adams (Eds.), *Handbook of behavioral assessment* (pp. 47–78). New York: John Wiley.

ADAMS, K. M. (1980a). An end of innocence for behavioral neurology? Adams replies. *Journal of Consulting and Clinical Psychology, 48,* 522–524.

ADAMS, K. M. (1980b). In search of Luria's battery: A false start. *Journal of Consulting and Clinical Psychology, 48,* 511–516.

ADAMS, K. M., & ROURKE, B. P. (1992). *The TCH guide to professional practice in clinical neuropsychology.* The Netherlands: Swets & Zeitlinger.

ADLER, A. (1933). *Social interest: A challenge to mankind.* Vienna, Leipzig: Rolf Passer.

ADLER, A. (1963). *The practice and theory of individual psychology.* Paterson, NJ: Littlefield.

ADLER, A. (1964). *Problems of neurosis.* New York: Harper & Row.

AGRAS, W. S., KAZDIN, A. E., & WILSON, G. T. (1979). *Behavior therapy: Towards an applied clinical science.* San Francisco: W. H. Freeman.

AGRAS, W. S., TAYLOR, C. B., KRAEMER, H. C., SOUTHAM, M. A., & SCHNEIDER, J. A. (1987). Relaxation training for essential hypertension at the worksite: II. The poorly controlled hypertensive. *Psychosomatic Medicine, 49,* 264–273.

ALBEE, G. W. (1959). *Mental health manpower trends.* New York: Basic Books.

ALBERTI, R. E., & EMMONS, M. L. (1974). *Your perfect right: A guide to assertive behavior.* San Luis Obispo, CA: Impact.

ALEXANDER, F. M. (1937). *The medical value of psychoanalysis.* New York: W. W. Norton.

ALEXANDER, F. M. (1956). *Psychoanalysis and psychotherapy.* New York: W. W. Norton.

ALEXANDER, F. M. (1963). *Fundamentals of psychoanalysis.* New York: W. W. Norton.

ALEXANDER, F. M., & FRENCH, T. M. (1946). *Psychoanalytic therapy.* New York: Ronald Press.

ALEXANDER, J. F., & PARSONS, B. V. (1973). Short-term behavioral intervention with delinquent families: Impact on family process and recidivism. *Journal of Abnormal Psychology, 81,* 219–225.

ALEXANDER, J. F., & PARSONS, B. V. (1982). *Functional family therapy.* Monterey, CA: Brooks/Cole.

ALLEN, G. J. (1971). The effectiveness of study counseling and desensitization in alleviating test anxiety in college students. *Journal of Abnormal Psychology, 77,* 282–289.

ALLPORT, F. H. (1924). *Social psychology.* Cambridge, MA: Riverside Press.

ALLPORT, G. W., VERNON, C. E., & LINDZEY, G. (1970). *Study of values* (rev. manual). Boston: Houghton-Mifflin.

AMERICAN MEDICAL ASSOCIATION. (1954). Report of committee on mental health. *Journal of the American Medical Association, 156,* 72.

AMERICAN PSYCHIATRIC ASSOCIATION. (1952). *Diagnostic and statistical manual of mental disorders* Washington, DC: Author.

AMERICAN PSYCHIATRIC ASSOCIATION. (1968). *Diagnostic and statistical manual of mental disorders* (2nd ed.). Washington, DC: Author.

AMERICAN PSYCHIATRIC ASSOCIATION. (1980). *Diagnostic and statistical manual of mental disorders* (3rd ed.). Washington, DC: Author.

AMERICAN PSYCHIATRIC ASSOCIATION. (1987). *Diagnostic and statistical manual of mental disorders* (3rd ed.-Revised). Washington, DC: Author.

AMERICAN PSYCHOLOGICAL ASSOCIATION. (1947). Recommended graduate training programs in clinical psychology. *American Psychologist, 2,* 539–558.

AMERICAN PSYCHOLOGICAL ASSOCIATION. (1953). *Ethical standards of psychologists.* Washington, DC: Author.

AMERICAN PSYCHOLOGICAL ASSOCIATION. (1958). Committee on Relations with Psychiatry, Annual Report. *American Psychologist, 13,* 761–763.

AMERICAN PSYCHOLOGICAL ASSOCIATION. (1959). Ethical standards of psychologists. *American Psychologist, 14,* 279–282.

AMERICAN PSYCHOLOGICAL ASSOCIATION. (1963). Ethical standards of psychologists. *American Psychologist, 18,* 56–60.

AMERICAN PSYCHOLOGICAL ASSOCIATION. (1967). *Casebook on ethical standards of psychologists.* Washington, DC: Author.

AMERICAN PSYCHOLOGICAL ASSOCIATION. (1981). *Specialty guidelines for the delivery of services by clinical psychologists.* Washington, DC: Author.

AMERICAN PSYCHOLOGICAL ASSOCIATION. (1982). *Ethical principles in the conduct of research with human subjects.* Washington, DC: Author.

AMERICAN PSYCHOLOGICAL ASSOCIATION. (1983). *Publication manual of the American Psychological Association* (3rd ed.). Washington, DC: Author.

AMERICAN PSYCHOLOGICAL ASSOCIATION. (1985). *Standards for educational and psychological tests.* Washington, DC: Author.

AMERICAN PSYCHOLOGICAL ASSOCIATION. (1986). *Guidelines for computer-based tests and interpretations.* Washington, DC: Author.

AMERICAN PSYCHOLOGICAL ASSOCIATION. (1987). General guidelines for providers of psychological services. *American Psychologist, 42,* 712–723.

AMERICAN PSYCHOLOGICAL ASSOCIATION. (1990). Ethical principles of psychologists (amended June 2, 1989). *American Psychologist, 45,* 390–395.

AMERICAN PSYCHOLOGICAL ASSOCIATION. (1992). Ethical principles of psychologists and code of conduct. *American Psychologist, 47,* 1597–1611.

AMERICAN PSYCHOLOGICAL ASSOCIATION DIVISION OF NEUROPSYCHOLOGY. (1989). Definition of a neuropsychologist. *The Clinical Neuropsychologist, 3,* 22.

AMUNDSON, M. E., HART, C. A., & HOLMES, T. H. (1986). *Manual for the schedule of recent experience.* Seattle: University of Washington Press.

ANASTASI, A. (1988). *Psychological testing* (6th ed.). New York: Macmillan.

ANCHIN, J. C., & KIESLER, D. J. (Eds.). (1982). *Handbook of interpersonal psychotherapy.* New York: Pergamon Press.

ANDERSEN, B. L. (1992). Psychological interventions for cancer patients to enhance the quality of life. *Journal of Consulting & Clinical Psychology, 60,* 552–568.

ANDREWS, G., & HARVEY, R. (1981). Does psychotherapy benefit neurotic patients? A re-analysis of the Smith, Glass, and Miller data. *Archives of General Psychiatry, 38,* 1203–1208.

ANDREWS, J. D. W. (1989). Integrating visions of reality: Interpersonal diagnosis and the existential vision. *American Psychologist, 44,* 803–817.

ANGELL, M. (1985). Disease as a reflection of the psyche. *New England Journal of Medicine, 312,* 1570–1572.

APPELBAUM, P. S., & HOGE, S. K. (1986). The right to refuse treatment: What the research reveals. *Behavioral Sciences and the Law, 4,* 279–292.

ARCHER, R. (1987). *Using the MMPI with adolescents.* Hillsdale, NJ: Lawrence Erlbaum Associates.

ARKES, H. A. (1981). Impediments to accurate clinical judgment and possible ways to minimize their impact. *Journal of Consulting and Clinical Psychology, 49,* 323–330.

ARKOWITZ, H., & MESSER, S. B. (Eds.). (1984). *Psychoanalytic therapy and behavior therapy: Is integration possible?* New York: Plenum Press.

ARRINGTON, R. E. (1932). *Interrelations in the behavior of young children.* New York: Columbia University Press.

ASH, P. (1949). The reliability of psychiatric diagnosis. *Journal of Abnormal and Social Psychology, 44,* 272–276.

ASHER, S. R., & WHEELER, V. A. (1985). Children's loneliness: A comparison of rejected and neglected peer status. *Journal of Consulting and Clinical Psychology, 53,* 500–505.

ATKINSON, J. W. (1981). Studying personality in the context of an advanced motivational psychology. *American Psychologist, 36,* 117–128.

AULD, F., JR., & MURRAY, E. J. (1955). Content-analysis studies of psychotherapy. *Psychological Bulletin, 52,* 377–395.

AUERBACH, A. H., & JOHNSON, M. (1977). Research on the therapist's level of experience. In A. S. Gurman & A. M. Razin (Eds.), *Effective psychotherapy: A handbook of research* (pp. 84–102). New York: Pergamon Press.

AUERBACH, S. M. (1989). Stress management and coping research in the health care setting: An overview and methodological commentary. *Journal of Consulting and Clinical Psychology, 57,* 388–395.

AUERBACH, S. M., & KILMANN, P. R. (1977). Crisis intervention: A review of outcome research. *Psychological Bulletin, 84,* 1189–1217.

AXLINE, V. M. (1976). Play therapy procedures and results. In C. Schaefer (Ed.), *The therapeutic use of child's play.* New York: Jason Aronson.

AYLLON, T., & AZRIN, N. H. (1965). The measurement and reinforcement of behavior of psychotics. *Journal of the Experimental Analysis of Behavior, 8,* 357–383.

AZAR, S. T., & WOLFE, D. A. (1989). Child abuse and neglect. In E. J. Mash & R. A. Barkley (Eds.), *Treatment of childhood disorders,* pp. 451–489. New York: Guilford Press.

AZRIN, N. H., & PETERSON, A. L. (1989). Reduction of an eye tic by controlled blinking. *Behavior Therapy, 20,* 467–473.

BACKER, T. E., & RICHARDSON, D. (1989). Building bridges: Psychologists and families of the mentally ill. *American Psychologist, 44,* 546–550.

BAEKELAND, F., & LUNDWALL, L. (1975). Dropping out of treatment: A critical review. *Psychological Bulletin, 82,* 738–783.

BAER, D. M. (1973). The control of development process: Why not? In J. R. Nesselroade & H. W. Reese (Eds.), *Life-span developmental psychology.* New York: Academic Press.

BAER, R., & NIETZEL, M. T. (1990). *Treatment of impulsivity in children: A meta-analytic review of the outcome literature.* Unpublished manuscript. University of Kentucky, Lexington.

BALAY, J., & SHEVRIN, H. (1988). The subliminal psychodynamic activation method: A critical review. *American Psychologist, 43,* 161–174.

BALES, R. F. (1950). *Interaction process analysis.* Cambridge, MA: Addison-Wesley.

BANDURA, A. (1969). *Principles of behavior modification.* New York: Holt, Rinehart & Winston.

BANDURA, A. (1977). Self-efficacy: Toward a unifying theory of behavioral change. *Psychological Review, 84,* 191–215.

BANDURA, A. (1978). The self system in reciprocal determinism. *American Psychologist, 33,* 344–358.

BANDURA, A. (1982). Self-efficacy mechanism in human agency. *American Psychologist, 33,* 122–147.

BANDURA, A. (1986). *Social foundations of thought and action: A social cognitive theory.* Englewood Cliffs, NJ: Prentice Hall.

BANDURA, A., BLANCHARD, E. B., & RITTER, B. (1969). The relative efficacy of desensitization and modeling approaches for inducing behavioral, affective, and attitudinal changes. *Journal of Personality and Social Psychology, 13,* 173–199.

BANDURA, A., ROSS, D., & ROSS, S. A. (1963). Imitation of film-mediated aggressive models. *Journal of Abnormal and Social Psychology, 66,* 3–11.

BANTA, H. D., & SAXE, L. (1983). Reimbursement for psychotherapy: Linking efficacy research and public policymaking. *American Psychologist, 38,* 918–923.

BARKER, R. G., DEMBO, T., & LEWIN, K. (1941). Frustration and regression: An experiment with young children. *University of Iowa Student Child Welfare, 18,* No. 1.

BARKER, R. G., SCHOGGEN, M. F., & BARKER, L. S. (1955). Hemerography of Mary Ennis. In A. Burton & R. E. Harris (Eds.), *Clinical studies of personality* (pp. 768–808). New York: Harper & Row.

BARKER, R. G., & WRIGHT, H. F. (1951). *One boy's day.* New York: Harper.

BARKER, R. G., & WRIGHT, H. F. (1955). *Midwest and its children: The psychological ecology of an American town.* New York: Row, Peterson.

BARKLEY, R. A., & CUNNINGHAM, C. E. (1979). The effects of Ritalin on the mother-child interaction of hyperactive children. *Archives of General Psychiatry, 36,* 201–208.

BARLOW, D. H. (1980). Behavior therapy: The next decade. *Behavior Therapy, 11,* 315–328.

BARLOW, D. H. (1981). *Behavioral assessment of adult disorders.* New York: Guilford Press.

BARLOW, D. H., & HERSEN, M. (1984). *Single- case experimental designs: Strategies for studying behavior* (2nd ed.). New York: Pergamon Press.

BARLOW, D. H., O'BRIEN, G. T., & LAST, C. G. (1984). Couples treatment of agoraphobia. *Behavior Therapy, 15,* 41–58.

BARLOW, D. H., & WADDELL, M. T. (1985). Agoraphobia. In D. H. Barlow (Ed.), *Clinical handbook of psychological disorders* (pp. 1–68). New York: Guilford Press.

BARLOW, D. H., & WOLFE, B. (1981). Behavioral approaches to anxiety disorders: A report on the NIMH-SUNY, Albany, research conference. *Journal of Consulting and Clinical Psychology, 49,* 448–454.

BARONA, A., & CHASTAIN, R. L. (1986). An improved estimate of premorbid IQ for blacks and whites on the WAIS-R. *International Journal of Clinical Neuropsychology, 8,* 169–173.

BARROM, C. P., SHADISH, W. R., JR., & MONTGOMERY, L. M. (1988). Ph.D.s, Psy.D.s, and real-world constraints on scholarly activity: Another look at the Boulder model. *Professional Psychology: Research and Practice, 19,* 93–101.

BARTHELL, C. N., & HOLMES, D. S. (1968). High school yearbooks: A nonreactive measure of social isolation in graduates who later became schizophrenic. *Journal of Abnormal Psychology, 73,* 313–316.

BARTLETT, C. J., & GREEN, C. G. (1966). Clinical prediction: Does one sometimes know too much? *Journal of Counseling Psychology, 13,* 267–270.

BARTON, A. (1974). *Three worlds of therapy: An existential-phenomenological study of the therapies of Freud, Jung, and Rogers.* Palo Alto, CA: National Press Books.

BATES, E. (1976). *Language and context: The acquisition of pragmatics.* New York: Academic Press.

BATESON, C., JACKSON, D. D., HALEY, J., & WEAKLAND, J. H. (1956). Toward a theory of schizophrenia. *Behavioral Science, 1,* 251–264.

BAUCOM, D. H., EPSTEIN, N., SAYERS, S., & SHER, T. G. (1989). The role of cognitions in marital relationships: Definitional, methodological, and conceptual issues. *Journal of Consulting and Clinical Psychology, 57,* 31–38.

BAUM, C. G., FOREHAND, R., & ZEIGOB, L. E. (1979). A review of observer reactivity in adult-child interactions. *Journal of Behavioral Assessment, 1,* 167–178.

BAYLEY, N. (1965). Comparisons of mental and motor test scores for ages 1–15 months by sex, birth order, race, geographic location, and education of parents. *Child Development, 36,* 379–411.

BEAR, D. M., & FEDIO, P. (1977). Quantitative analysis of interictal behavior in temporal lobe epilepsy. *Archives of Neurology, 34,* 454–467.

BECK, A. T. (1976). *Cognitive therapy and the emotional disorders.* New York: International Universities Press.

BECK, A. T., WARD, C. H., MENDELSON, M., MOCK, J., & ERBAUGH, J. (1961). An inventory for measuring depression. *Archives of General Psychiatry, 4,* 561–571.

BECKER, M. H., & MAIMAN, L. A. (1975). Sociobehavioral determinants of compliance with health and medical care recommendations. *Medical Care, 13,* 10–24.

BEIDEL, D. C., & TURNER, S. M. (1986). A critique of the theoretical base of cognitive-behavioral theories and therapy. *Clinical Psychology Review, 6,* 177–197.

BELAR, C. D., BIELIAUSKAS, L. A., LARSEN, K. G., MENSH, I. N., POEY, K., & ROELKE, H. J. (1989). The National Conference on internship training in psychology. *American Psychologist, 44,* 60–65.

BELAR, C. D., & PERRY, N. W. (1992). National conference on scientist-practitioner education and training for the professional practice of psychology. *American Psychologist, 47,* 71–75.

BELL, R. Q., & HARPER, L. V. (1977). *Child effects on adults.* Lincoln and London: University of Nebraska Press.

BELLACK, A. S. (1983). Recurrent problems in the behavioral assessment of social skill. *Behaviour Research and Therapy, 21,* 29–42.

BELLACK, A. S., & HERSEN, M. (Eds.). (1988). *Behavioral assessment: A practical handbook* (3rd ed.). New York: Pergamon Press.

BELLACK, A. S., HERSEN, M., & HIMMELHOCH, J. M. (1983). A comparison of social skills training, pharmacotherapy and psychotherapy for depression. *Behaviour Research and Therapy, 21,* 101–107.

BELLACK, A. S., HERSEN, M., & KAZDIN, A. E. (Eds.). (1990). *International handbook of behavior modification and therapy* (2nd ed.). New York: Plenum Press.

BELLAK, L. (1954). *The Thematic Apperception Test and the Children's Apperception Test in clinical use.* New York: Grune & Stratton.

BELLAK, L. (1986). *The Thematic Apperception Test, the Children's Apperception Test, and the Senior Apperception Technique in Clinical Use* (4th ed.). New York: Grune & Stratton.

BELLAK, L. (1992). *The TAT, CAT, and SAT in clinical use* (5th ed.). Odessa, FL: Psychological Assessment Resources.

BEMPORAD, J. R., & SCHWAB, M. E. (1986). The DSM-III and clinical child psychiatry. In T. Millon & G. L. Klerman (Eds.), *Contemporary directions in psychopathology: Toward the DSM-IV* (pp. 135–150). New York: Guilford Press.

BENDER, L. A. (1938). A visual motor Gestalt test and its clinical use. *American Orthopsychiatric Association Research Monograph, No. 3.*

BENJAMIN, L. S. (1980). *INTREX users' manual.* Madison, WI: INTREX Interpersonal Institute.

BENNETT, C. C. (1965). Community psychology: Impressions of the Boston conference on the education of psychologists for community mental health. *American Psychologist, 20,* 832–835.

BENNEY, M., RIESMAN, D., & STAR, S. A. (1956). Age and sex in the interview. *American Journal of Sociology, 62,* 143–152.

BEN-PORATH, Y. S., & BUTCHER, J. N. (1991). The historical development of personality assessment. In C. E. Walker (Ed.), *Clinical psychology: Historical and research foundations* (pp. 121–158). New York: Plenum Press.

BEN-PORATH, Y. S., & WALLER, N. G. (1992). "Normal" personality inventories in clinical assessment: General requirements and potential for using the NEO Personality Inventory. *Psychological Assessment, 4,* 14–19.

BENTON, A. L. (1974). *Revised visual retention test: Clinical and experimental applications* (4th ed.). New York: Psychological Corporation.

BENTON, A. L., HAMSHER, K., VARNEY, N. R., & SPREEN, O. (1983). *Contributions to neuropsychological assessment: A clinical manual.* New York: Oxford University Press.

BERG, I. A. (1955). Response bias and personality: The deviation hypothesis. *Journal of Psychology, 40,* 61–71.

BERGIN, A. E. (1971). The evaluation of therapeutic outcomes. In A. E. Bergin & S. L. Garfield (Eds.), *Handbook of psychotherapy and behavior change: An empirical analysis* (pp. 217–270). New York: John Wiley.

BERGIN, A. E., & LAMBERT, M. J. (1978). The evaluation of therapeutic outcomes. In S. L. Garfield & A. E. Bergin (Eds.), *Handbook of psychotherapy and behavior change: An empirical analysis* (2nd ed., pp. 139–190). New York: John Wiley.

BERMAN, J. S., & NORTON, N. C. (1985). Does professional training make a therapist more effective? *Psychological Bulletin, 98,* 401–406.

BERNARDONI, L. C. (1964). A culture fair intelligence test for the ugh, no, and oo-la-la cultures. *Personnel and Guidance Journal, 42,* 554–557.

BERNE, E. (1964). *Games people play.* New York: Grove Press.

BERNSTEIN, D. A. (1973). Behavioral fear assessment: Anxiety or artifact? In H. Adams & P. Unikel (Eds.), *Issues and trends in behavior therapy* (pp. 225–267). Springfield, IL: Charles C. Thomas.

BERNSTEIN, D. A., & BORKOVEC, T. D. (1973). *Progressive relaxation training.* Champaign, IL: Research Press.

BERNSTEIN, D. A., & CARLSON, C. R. (1993). Progressive relaxation: Abbreviated methods. In P. M. Lehrer & R. Woolfolk (Eds.), *Principles and practices of stress management* (2nd ed., pp. 53–87). New York: Guilford Press.

BERNSTEIN, D. A., & NIETZEL, M. T. (1977). Demand characteristics in behavior modification: A natural history of a "nuisance." In M. Hersen, R. M. Eisler, & P. M. Miller (Eds.), *Progress in behavior modification* (Vol. 4, pp. 119–162). New York: Academic Press.

BERNSTEIN, D. A., & PAUL, G. L. (1971). Some comments on therapy analogue research with small animal "phobias." *Journal of Behavior Therapy and Experimental Psychiatry, 2,* 225–237.

BERNSTEIN, L., BERNSTEIN, R. S., & DANA, R. H. (1974). *Interviewing: A guide for health professionals* (2nd ed.). New York: Appleton-Century-Crofts.

BERQUIER, A., & ASHTON, R. (1991). A selective review of possible neurological etiologies of schizophrenia. *Clinical Psychology Review, 11,* 645–661.

BERRY, D., BAER, R., & HARRIS, M. (1991). Detection of malingering on the MMPI: A meta-analysis. *Clinical Psychology Review, 11,* 585–598.

BERRY, D. T., WETTER, M. W., BAER, R. A., WIDIGER, T. A., SUMPTER, J. C., REYNOLDS, S. K., & HALLEM, R. A. (1991). Detection of random responding on the MMPI-2: Utility of F, Back F, and VRIN scales. *Psychological Assessment: A Journal of Consulting and Clinical Psychology, 3,* 418–423.

BERSOFF, D. N. (1981). Testing and the law. *American Psychologist, 36,* 1047–1056.

BERSOFF, D. N. (1988). Should subjective employment devices be scrutinized? It's elementary, my dear Ms. Watson. *American Psychologist, 43,* 1016–1018.

BERWICK, P., & MORRIS, L. A. (1974). Token economies: Are they doomed? *Professional Psychology, 5,* 434–439.

BERZINS, J. I. (1977). Therapist-patient matching. In A. S. Gurman & A. M. Razin (Eds.), *Effective psychotherapy: A handbook of research* (pp. 222–251). New York: Pergamon Press.

BETTLEHEIM, B. (1967). *The empty fortress.* New York: Free Press.

BEUTLER, L. E., CRAGO, M., & ARIZMENDI, T. G. (1986). Research on therapist variables in psychotherapy. In S. L. Garfield & A. E. Bergin (Eds.), *Handbook of psychotherapy and behavior change* (3rd ed., pp. 257–310). New York: John Wiley.

BICKMAN, L. (1987). Graduate education in psychology. *American Psychologist, 42,* 1041–1047.

BICKMAN, L., & DOKECKI, P. R. (1989). Public and private responsibility for mental health services. *American Psychologist, 44,* 1133–1137.

BIERI, J., ATKINS, A. L., BRIAR, S., LEAMAN, R. L., MILLER, H., & TRIPOLDI, T. (1966). *Clinical and social judgment: The discrimination of behavioral information.* New York: John Wiley.

BIERMAN, K. L., MILLER, C. L., & STABB, S. D. (1987). Improving the social behavior and peer acceptance of rejected boys: Effects of social skill training with instructions and prohibitions. *Journal of Consulting and Clinical Psychology, 55,* 194–200.

BIJOU, S. W., PETERSON, R. F., & AULT, M. H. (1968). A method to integrate descriptive and experimental field studies at the level of data and empirical concepts. *Journal of Applied Behavior Analysis, 1,* 175–191.

BINGHAM, W. V. D., MOORE, B. V., & GUSTAD, J. W. (1959). *How to interview.* New York: Harper & Row.

BLACKBURN, H., LUEPKER, R. V., KLINE, F. G., BRACHT, N., CARLAW, R., JACOBS, D., MITTELMARK, M., STAUFFER, L., & TAYLOR, H. L. (1984). The Minnesota Heart Health Program: A research and demonstration project in cardiovascular disease prevention. In J. D. Matarazzo et al. (Eds.), *Behavioral health: A handbook of health enhancement and disease prevention* (pp. 1171–1178). New York: John Wiley.

BLAKE, B. G. (1965). The application of behaviour therapy to the treatment of alcoholism. *Behaviour Research and Therapy, 3,* 75–85.

BLANCHARD, E. B. (1992). Psychological treatment of benign headache disorders. *Journal of Consulting and Clinical Psychology, 60,* 537–551.

BLANCK, G. (1976). Psychoanalytic technique. In B. B. Wolman (Ed.), *The therapist's handbook: Treatment methods of mental disorders* (pp. 61–86). New York: Van Nostrand Reinhold.

BLATT, S. J., & LERNER, H. (1983). Psychodynamic perspectives on personality theory. In M. Hersen, A. E. Kazdin, & A. S. Bellack (Eds.), *The clinical psychology handbook* (pp. 87–106). New York: Pergamon Press.

BLAU, T. H. (1988). *Psychotherapy tradecraft: The technique and style of doing therapy.* New York: Brunner/Mazel.

BLECHMAN, E. A., & BROWNELL, K. D. (Eds.). (1986). *Behavioral medicine for women.* New York: Pergamon Press.

BLEULER, M. (1978). *The schizophrenic disorders; Long-term patient and family studies* (S. M. Clemens, Trans.). New Haven, CT: Yale University Press.

BLOCK, J. H., BLOCK, J., & GJERDE, P. F. (1986). The personality of children prior to divorce: A prospective study. *Child Development, 57,* 827–840.

BLOOM, B. L., HODGES, W. F., & CALDWELL, R. A. (1982). A preventive program for the newly separated: Initial evaluation. *American Journal of Community Psychology, 10,* 251–264.

BLOUNT, R. L., BACHANAS, P. J., POWERS, S. W., COTTER, M. C., FRANKLIN, A., CHAPLIN, W., MAYFIELD, J., HENDERSON, M., & BLOUNT, S. D. (1992). Training children to cope and parents to coach them during routine immunizations: Effects on child, parent, and staff behavior. *Behavior Therapy, 23,* 689–705.

BOCZKOWSKI, J. A., ZEICHNER, A., & DESANTO, N. (1985). Neuroleptic compliance among chronic schizophrenic outpatients: An intervention outcome report. *Journal of Consulting and Clinical Psychology, 53,* 666–671.

BOICE, R., & MYERS, P. E. (1987). Which setting is healthier and happier, academe or private practice? *Professional Psychology: Research and Practice, 18,* 526–529.

BOLGAR, H. (1965). The case study method. In B. B. Wolman (Ed.), *Handbook of clinical psychology* (pp. 28–39). New York: McGraw-Hill.

BOLL, T. J. (1981). The Halstead-Reitan Neuropsychology Battery. In S. B. Filskov & T. J. Boll (Eds.), *Handbook of clinical neuropsychology* (pp. 577–607). New York: John Wiley.

BONGAR, B. (1988). Clinicians, microcomputers, and confidentiality. *Professional Psychology: Research and Practice, 19,* 286–289.

BONGAR, B. (1991). *The suicidal patient: Clinical and legal standards of care.* Washington, DC: American Psychological Association.

BONIME, W. (1962). *The clinical use of dreams.* New York: Basic Books.

BORDIN, E. S. (1955). Ambiguity as a therapeutic variable. *Journal of Consulting Psychology, 19,* 9–15.

BORGATTA, E. F. (1955). Analysis of social interaction: Actual, role playing, and projective. *Journal of Abnormal and Social Psychology, 51,* 394–405.

BORING, E. G. (1950). *A history of experimental psychology* (2nd ed.). New York: Appleton-Century-Crofts.

BORKOVEC, T. D., & O'BRIEN, G. T. (1976). Methodological and target behavior issues in analogue therapy outcome research. In M. Hersen, R. M. Eisler, & P. M. Miller (Eds.), *Progress in behavior modification* (pp. 133–172). New York: Academic Press.

BOROFSKY, G. L. (1974). Issues in the diagnosis and classification of personality functioning. In A. I. Rabin (Ed.), *Clinical psychology: Issues of the seven-*ties (pp. 24–48). East Lansing: Michigan State University Press.

BOUDIN, H. (1972). Contingency contracting as a therapeutic tool in the deceleration of amphetamine use. *Behavior Therapy, 3,* 604–608.

BOURG, E. F., BENT, R. J., MCHOLLAND, J., & STRICKER, G. (1989). Standards and evaluation in the education and training of professional psychologists: The National Council of Schools and Professional Psychology Mission Bay Conference. *American Psychologist, 44,* 66–72.

BOURNE, L. E., & EKSTRAND, B. R. (1976). *Psychology: Its principles and meanings* (2nd ed.). New York: Holt, Rinehart & Winston.

BRAGINSKY, B. M., BRAGINSKY, D. D., & RING, K. (1969). *Methods of madness: The mental hospital as a last resort.* New York: Holt, Rinehart & Winston.

BRAGINSKY, B. M., GROSSE, M., & RING, K. (1966). Controlling outcomes through impression management: An experimental study of the manipulative tactics of mental patients. *Journal of Consulting Psychology, 30,* 295–300.

BRANCH, C., MILNER, B., & RASMUSSEN, T. (1964). Intracarotid sodium Amytal for the lateralization of cerebral speech dominance. *Journal of Neurosurgery, 21,* 399–405.

BRASWELL, L, & KENDALL, P. C. (1988). Cognitive behavioral methods with children. In K. S. Dobson (Ed.), *Handbook of cognitive-behavioral therapies* (pp. 167–213). New York: Guilford Press.

BREMS, C., THEVENIN, D. M., & ROUTH, D. K. (1991). The history of clinical psychology. In C. E. Walker (Ed.), *Clinical psychology: Historical and research foundations* (pp. 3–36). New York: Plenum Press.

BRENNER, C. (1974). *An elementary textbook of psychoanalysis.* New York: Anchor Books.

BRESLOW, L. (1979). A positive strategy for the nation's health. *Journal of the American Medical Association, 242,* 2093–2094.

BRILL, A. A. (1938). *The basic writings of Sigmund Freud.* New York: Random House.

BRODY, G. H., & FOREHAND, R. (1986). Maternal perceptions of child maladjustment as a function of the combined influence of child behavior and maternal depression. *Journal of Consulting and Clinical Psychology, 54,* 237–240.

BROOKS, A. (1986). Law and antipsychotic medications. *Behavioral Sciences and the Law, 4,* 247–264.

BROTEMARKLE, B. A. (1947). Fifty years of clinical psychology: Clinical psychology 1896–1946. *Journal of Consulting Psychology, 11,* 1–4.

BROVERMAN, I. K., BROVERMAN, D. M., CLARKSON, F. E., ROSENKRANTZ, P. S., & VOGEL, S. R. (1970). Sex role stereotypes and clinical judgments of mental health. *Journal of Consulting and Clinical Psychology, 34,* 1–7.

BROWN, E. (1972). Assessment from a humanistic perspective. *Psychotherapy: Theory, Research, and Practice, 9,* 103–106.

BROWN, G. W., BONE, M., DALISON, B., & WING, J. K. (1966). *Schizophrenia and social care.* London: Oxford University Press.

BROWN, G. W., & HARRIS, T. (1978). *The social origins of depression.* New York: Free Press.

BROWN, , R., & HERRNSTEIN, R. J. (1975). *Psychology.* Boston: Little, Brown.

BROWNELL, K. D. (1981). Assessment of eating disorders. In D. H. Barlow (Ed.), *Behavioral assessment of adult disorders* (pp. 329–404). New York: Guilford Press.

BROWNELL, K. D., & FOREYT, J. P. (1985). Obesity. In D. H. Barlow (Ed.), *Clinical handbook of psychological disorders* (pp. 299–343). New York: Guilford Press.

BROWNELL, K. D., & WADDEN, T. A. (1992). Etiology and treatment of obesity: Understanding a serious, prevalent, and refractory disorder. *Journal of Consulting and Clinical Psychology, 60,* 505–517.

BRUININK, S. A., & SCHROEDER, H. E. (1979). Verbal therapeutic behavior of expert psychoanalytically oriented, Gestalt, & behavior therapists. *Journal of Consulting and Clinical Psychology, 47,* 567–574.

BRUNSWICK, E. (1947). *Systematic and representative design of psychological experiments with results in physical and social perception.* Berkeley: University of California Press.

BRYNTWICK, S., & SOLYOM, L. (1973). A brief treatment of elevator phobia. *Journal of Behavior Therapy and Experimental Psychiatry, 4,* 355–356.

BUCK, J. N. (1948). The H-T-P technique: A qualitative and quantitative scoring manual. *Journal of Clinical Psychology, 4,* 319–396.

BUGENTAL, J. F. T. (1978). *Psychotherapy and process: The fundamentals of an existential-humanistic approach.* Reading, MA: Addison-Wesley.

BUGENTAL, J. F. T., & ZELEN, S. (1950). Investigations into the "self-concept." I. The W-A-Y technique. *Journal of Personality, 18,* 483–498.

BURBACK, D. J., & PETERSON, L. (1986). Children's concepts of physical illness: A review and critique of the cognitive-developmental literature. *Health Psychology, 5,* 307–325.

BURCHARD, J. D. (1967). Systematic socialization: A programmed environment for the habilitation of antisocial retardates. *Psychological Record, 17,* 461–476.

BURCHARD, J. D., & BURCHARD, S. N. (Eds.). (1987). *Prevention of delinquent behavior.* Newbury Park, CA: Sage.

BURISCH, M. (1984). Approaches to personality inventory construction: A comparison of merits. *American Psychologist, 39,* 214–227.

BURKE, M. J., & NORMAND, J. (1987). Computerized psychological testing: Overview and critique. *Professional Psychology: Research and Practice, 18,* 42–51.

BURNAM, M. A., STEIN, J. A., GOLDING, J. M., SIEGEL, J. M., SORENSON, S. B., FORSYTHE, A. B., & TELLES, C. A. (1988). Sexual assault and mental disorders in a community population. *Journal of Consulting and Clinical Psychology, 56,* 843–850.

BUROS, O. K. (Ed.). (1938). *The 1940 mental measurements yearbook.* Highland Park, NJ: Gryphon Press.

BUSS, D. M., & CRAIK, K. H. (1983). The act frequency approach to personality. *Psychological Review, 90,* 105–126.

BUSS, D. M., & CRAIK, K. H. (1986). Acts, dispositions, and clinical assessment: The psychopathology of everyday conduct. *Clinical Psychology Review, 6,* 387–406.

BUTCHER, J. N. (Ed.). (1987). *Computerized psychological assessment: A practitioner's guide.* New York: Basic Books.

BUTCHER, J. N., DAHLSTROM, W. G., GRAHAM, J. R., TELLEGEN, A., & KAEMMER, B. (1989). *Manual for administration and scoring of the MMPI-2.* Minneapolis: University of Minnesota Press.

BUTCHER, J. N., & KELLER, L. S. (1984). Objective personality assessment. In G. Goldstein & M. Hersen (Eds.), *Handbook of psychological assessment* (pp. 307–331). New York: Pergamon Press.

BUTCHER, J. N., & KOSS, M. P. (1978). Research on brief and crisis-oriented psychotherapies. In S. L. Garfield & A. E. Bergin (Eds.), *Handbook of psychotherapy and behavior change: An empirical analysis* (2nd ed., pp. 725–767). New York: John Wiley.

BUTCHER, J. N., & WILLIAMS, C. L. (1992). *Essentials of MMPI-2 and MMPI-A interpretation.* Minneapolis: University of Minnesota Press.

BUTLER, G., FENNELL, M., ROBSON, P., & GELDER, M. (1991). Comparison of behavior therapy and cognitive behavior therapy in the treatment of generalized anxiety disorder. *Journal of Consulting and Clinical Psychology, 59,* 167–175.

CAIRNS, R. B., & GREEN, J. A. (1979). How to assess personality and social patterns: Observations or ratings? In B. Cairns (Ed.), *The analysis of social interactions: Methods, issues, and illustrations* (pp. 209–226). Hillsdale, NJ: Lawrence Erlbaum Associates.

CAMPBELL, D. T., & FISKE, D. W. (1959). Convergent and discriminant validation by the multitrait-multimethod matrix. *Psychological Bulletin, 56,* 81–105.

CAMPBELL, M., GREEN, W. H., & DEUTSCH, S. I. (1985). *Child and adolescent psychopharmacology* (Vol. 2). Beverly Hills, CA: Sage.

CAMPBELL, S. B. (1989). Developmental perspectives in child psychopathology. In M. Hersen & T. Ollendick (Eds.), *Handbook of child psychopathology* (2nd ed., pp. 5–28). New York: Plenum Press.

CANTWELL, D. P. (1980). The diagnostic process and diagnostic classification in childhood psychiatry—DSM-III. *Journal of the American Academy of Child Psychiatry, 19,* 345–355.

CANTWELL, D. P. (1983). Depression in childhood: Clinical picture and diagnosis criteria. In D. P. Cantwell & G. A. Carlson (Eds.), *Affective disorders in childhood and adolescence* (pp. 3–18). New York: Spectrum.

CAPLAN, G. (1961). *An approach to community mental health.* New York: Grune & Stratton.

CAPLAN, G. (1964). *Principles of preventive psychiatry.* New York: Basic Books.

CARLSON, H. S. (1978). The AASPB Story: The beginnings and first 16 years of the American Association of State Psychology Boards, 1961–1977. *American Psychologist, 33,* 486–495.

CARSON, R. C. (1969). *Interaction concepts of personality.* Chicago: Aldine.

CARSON, R. C. (1983). The social-interactional viewpoint. In M. Hersen, A. E. Kazdin, & A. S. Bellack (Eds.), *The clinical psychology handbook* (pp. 143–154). New York: Pergamon Press.

CARSON, R. C. (1991). Dilemmas in the pathway of the DSM-IV. *Journal of Abnormal Psychology, 100,* 302–307.

CARTWRIGHT, R. A. (1966). A comparison of the response to psychoanalytic and client-centered therapy. In L. A. Gottschalk & A. H. Auerbach (Eds.), *Methods of research in psychotherapy* (pp. 517–529). New York: Appleton-Century-Crofts.

CASEY, R. J., & BERMAN, J. S. (1985). The outcome of psychotherapy with children. *Psychological Bulletin, 98,* 388–400.

CASSISSI, J. E., & McGLYNN, F. D. (1988). Effects of EMG-activated alarms on nocturnal bruxism. *Behavior Therapy, 19,* 133–142.

CATTELL, R. B., EBER, H. W., & TATUSOKA, M. M. (1970). *Handbook for the Sixteen Personality Factor Questionnaire.* Champaign, IL: Institute for Personality and Ability Testing.

CAUTELA, J., & KEARNEY, A. J. (1986). *The covert conditioning handbook.* New York: Springer.

CAUTELA, J. R. (1966). Treatment of compulsive behavior by covert sensitization. *Psychological Record, 86,* 33–41.

CAUTELA, J. R., & KASTENBAUM, R. A. (1967). A reinforcement survey schedule for use in therapy, training, and research. *Psychological Reports, 20,* 1115–1130.

CECI, S. J., & BRUCK, M. (1993). Suggestibility of the child witness: A historical review and synthesis. *Psychological Bulletin, 113,* 403–439.

CECI, S., TOGLIA, M., & ROSS, D. (1987). *Children's eyewitness memory.* New York: Springer-Verlag.

CHANDLER, M. (1973). Egocentrism and antisocial behavior: The assessment and training of social perspective-taking skills. *Developmental Psychology, 9,* 326–332.

CHAPMAN, L. J., & CHAPMAN, J. P. (1967). The genesis of popular but erroneous psychodiagnostic observations. *Journal of Abnormal Psychology, 72,* 193–204.

CHARLTON-SEIFERT, J., STRATTON, B. D., & WILLIAMS, M. G. (1980). Sweet and slow: Diet can affect learning. *Academic Therapy, 16,* 211–217.

CHESLER, P. (1972). *Women and madness.* New York: Doubleday.

CHESS, S., & THOMAS, A. (1986). *Temperament in clinical practice.* New York: Guilford Press.

CHRISTENSEN, A., MARGOLIN, G., & SULLAWAY, M. (1992). Interparental agreement on child behavior problems. *Psychological Assessment, 4,* 419–425.

CHRISTIANSEN, B. C., SMITH, G. T., ROEHLING, P. V., & GOLDMAN, M. S. (1989). Using alcohol expectancies to predict adolescent drinking behavior after one year. *Journal of Consulting and Clinical Psychology, 57,* 93–99.

CIMINERO, A. R., CALHOUN, K. S., & ADAMS, H. E. (1986). *Handbook of behavioral assessment* (2nd ed.). New York: John Wiley.

CLARK, R. W. (1980). *Freud: The man and the cause.* New York: Random House.

CLINE, V. B., & RICHARDS, J. M., JR. (1961). The generality of accuracy of interpersonal perception. *Journal of Abnormal and Social Psychology, 62,* 446–449.

COBB, S. (1976). Social support as a moderator of life stress. *Psychosomatic Medicine, 38,* 300–314.

COHEN, H. L. (1968). Educational therapy: The design of learning environments. *Research in Psychotherapy, 3,* 21–58.

COHEN, L. H., SARGENT, M. M., & SECHREST, L. B. (1986). Use of psychotherapy research by professional psychologists. *American Psychologist, 41,* 198–206.

COHEN, R. J., SWERDLIK, M. E., & SMITH, D. K. (1992). *Psychological testing and measurement.* Mountain View, CA: Mayfield.

COHEN, S., MERMELSTEIN, R., KAMARCK, T., & HOBERMAN, H. (1985). Measuring the functional components of social support. In I. G. Sarason & B. R. Sarason (Eds.), *Social support: Theory, research, and application* (pp. 73–94). The Hague: Nijhoff.

COHEN, S., TYRRELL, D. A., & SMITH, A. P. (1991). Psychological stress in humans and susceptibility to the common cold. *New England Journal of Medicine, 325,* 606–612.

COHEN, S., & WILLS, T. A. (1985). Stress, social support, and the buffering hypothesis. *Psychological Bulletin, 98,* 310–357.

COLLINS, R. L., PARKS, G. A., & MARLATT, G. A. (1985). Social determinants of alcohol consumption: The effects of social interactions and model status on the self-administration of alcohol. *Journal of Consulting and Clinical Psychology, 53,* 189–200.

COLMEN, J. G., KAPLAN, S. J., & BOULGER, J. R. (1964, August). *Selection and selecting research in the Peace Corps.* (Peace Corps Research Note No. 7).

CONE, J. D. (1988). Psychometric considerations and the multiple models of behavioral assessment. In A. S. Bellack & M. Hersen (Eds.), *Behavioral assessment: A practical handbook* (3rd ed., pp. 42–66). New York: Pergamon Press.

CONE, J. D., & FOSTER, S. L. (1982). Direct observation in clinical psychology. In P. C. Kendall & J. N. Butcher (Eds.), *Handbook of research methods in clinical psychology* (pp. 311–354). New York: John Wiley.

CONE, J. D., & HAWKINS, R. P. (Eds.). (1977). *Behavioral assessment: New directions in clinical psychology.* New York: Brunner/Mazel.

CONNERS, C. K. (1973). Rating scales for use in drug studies with children. *Psychopharmacology Bulletin* (Special issue, Pharmacotherapy of Children), 24–84.

CONOLEY, C. W., CONOLEY, J. C., McCONNELL, J. A., & KIMZEY, C. E. (1983). The effect of the ABCs of rational emotive therapy and the empty-chair technique of Gestalt therapy on anger reduction. *Psychotherapy: Theory, Research, and Practice, 20,* 112–117.

CONOLEY, J. C., & KRAMER, J. J. (Eds.). (1989). *The tenth mental measurements yearbook.* Lincoln: The Buros Institute of Mental Measurements of the University of Nebraska.

CONWAY, J. B. (1988). Differences among clinical psychologists: Scientists, practitioners, and scientist-practitioners. *Professional Psychology: Research and Practice, 19,* 642–655.

COOK, T. D., & CAMPBELL, D. T. (1979). *Quasi-experimentation: Design and analysis issues for field settings.* Chicago: Rand-McNally.

COOPER, N. A., & CLUM, G. A. (1989). Imaginal flooding as a supplementary treatment for PTSD in combat veterans: A controlled study. *Behavior Therapy, 20,* 381–392.

CORMIER, W. H., & CORMIER, L. S. (1979). *Interviewing strategies for helpers: A guide to assessment, treatment, and evaluation.* Monterey, CA: Brooks/Cole.

COSTA, P. T., & McCRAE, R. R. (1992a). *Manual for the Revised NEO Personality Inventory (NEO-PIR) and the NEO Five-Factor Inventory (BEO-FFI).* Odessa, FL: Psychological Assessment Resources.

COSTA, P. T., & McCRAE, R. R. (1992b). Normal personality inventories in clinical assessment: General requirements and potential for using the NEO Personality Inventory. *Psychological Assessment, 4,* 5–13.

COSTELLO, A. J., EDELBROCK, C., KALAS, R., KESSLER, M. D., & KLARIC, S. (1982). *The NIMH Diagnostic Interview Schedule for Children (DISC).* Pittsburgh: Author.

COVNER, B. J. (1942). Studies in phonographic recordings. I. The use of phonographic recordings in counseling practice and research. *Journal of Consulting Psychology, 6,* 105–113.

COVNER, B. J. (1944). Studies in phonographic recordings of verbal material. III. The completeness and accuracy of counseling interview reports. *Journal of General Psychology, 30,* 181–203.

COWEN, E., PEDERSON, A., BABIGIAN, H., IZZO, L., & TROST, M. (1973). Long-term follow-up of early detected vulnerable children. *Journal of Consulting and Clinical Psychology, 41,* 438–446.

COWEN, E. L. (1973). Social and community intervention. *Annual Review of Psychology, 24,* 423–472.

COWEN, E. L. (1977). Psychologists in primary prevention: Blowing the cover story. An editorial. *American Journal of Community Psychology, 5,* 481–490.

COWEN, E. L. (1980). The wooing of primary prevention. *American Journal of Community Psychology, 8,* 258–284.

COWEN, E. L. (1982). Help is where you find it: Four informal helping groups. *American Psychologist, 37,* 385–395.

COWEN, E. L. (1983). Primary prevention in mental health: Past, present and future. In R. D. Felner, L. A. Jason, J. N. Moritsugu, & S. S. Farber (Eds.), *Preventive psychology: Theory, research and practice* (pp. 11–30). New York: Pergamon Press.

COWEN, E. L., GESTEN, E. L., & WILSON, A. B. (1979). The primary mental health project (PMHP): Evaluation of current program effectiveness. *American Journal of Community Psychology, 7,* 293–303.

COWEN, E. L., & WORK, W. C. (1988). Resiliant children, psychological wellness, and primary prevention.

American Journal of Community Psychology, 16, 591–607.

COYNE, J. C. (1976). Toward an interactional description of depression. *Psychiatry, 39,* 28–39.

CRAIG, J. R. (1988). Diagnostic interviewing with drug abusers. *Professional Psychology: Research and Practice, 19,* 14–20.

CRITELLI, J. W., & NEUMANN, K. F. (1984). The placebo: Conceptual analysis of a construct in transition. *American Psychologist, 39,* 32–39.

CRITS-CHRISTOPH, P., COOPER, P., & LUBORSKY, L. (1988). The accuracy of therapists' interpretations and the outcome of dynamic psychotherapy. *Journal of Consulting and Clinical Psychology, 56,* 490–495.

CRONBACH, L. J. (1946). Response sets and test validity. *Educational and Psychological Measurement, 6,* 475–494.

CRONBACH, L. J. (1960). *Essentials of psychological testing* (2nd ed.). New York: Harper & Row.

CRONBACH, L. J. (1970). *Essentials of psychological testing* (3rd ed.). New York: Harper & Row.

CRONBACH, L. J. (1975). Five decades of public controversy over mental testing. *American Psychologist, 30,* 1–14.

CRONBACH, L. J., & GLESER, G. C. (1965). *Psychological tests and personnel decisions* (2nd ed.). Urbana: University of Illinois Press.

CRONBACH, L. J., & GLESER, G. C., NANDA, H., & RAJARATNAM, N. (1972). *The dependability of behavioral measurements*. New York: John Wiley.

CRONBACH, L. J., & MEEHL, P. E. (1955). Construct validity in psychology tests. *Psychological Bulletin, 52,* 281–302.

CROSS, D. G., SHEEHAN, P. W., & KHAN, J. A. (1980). Alternative advice and counsel in psychotherapy. *Journal of Consulting and Clinical Psychology, 48,* 615–625.

CROW, W. J., & HAMMOND, K. R. (1957). The generality of accuracy and response sets in interpersonal perception. *Journal of Abnormal and Social Psychology, 54,* 384–390.

CRUMBAUGH, J. C. (1968). Cross-validation of the Purpose in Life test based on Frankl's concepts. *Journal of Individual Psychology, 24,* 74–81.

CUMMINGS, J. A. (1986). Projective drawings. In H. M. Knoff (Ed.), *The assessment of child and adolescent personality* (pp. 199–244). New York: Guilford Press.

CUMMINGS, N. A. (1977). The anatomy of psychotherapy under national health insurance. *American Psychologist, 32,* 711–718.

CUMMINGS, N. A. (1986). The dismantling of our health system: Strategies for the survival of psychological practice. *American Psychologist, 41,* 426–431.

CUMMINGS, N. A. (1988). Emergence of the mental health complex: Adaptive and maladaptive responses. *Professional Psychology: Research and Practice, 19,* 308–315.

CUNNINGHAM, C. E., SIEGEL, L. S., & OFFORD, D. R. (1985). A developmental dose-response analysis of the effects of methylphenidate on the peer interactions of Attention Deficit Disordered boys. *Journal of Child Psychology and Psychiatry, 26,* 955–971.

CUTRONA, C. E. (1984). Social support and stress in the transition to parenthood. *Journal of Abnormal Psychology, 93,* 378–390.

DAHLSTROM, W. G., LACHAR, D., & DAHLSTROM, L. E. (1986). *MMPI patterns of American minorities*. Minneapolis: University of Minnesota Press.

DAHLSTROM, W. G., & WELSH, G. S. (1960). *An MMPI handbook: A guide to use in clinical practice and research*. Minneapolis: University of Minnesota Press.

DAHLSTROM, W. G., WELSH, G. S., & DAHLSTROM, L. E. (1972). *An MMPI handbook: Vol. 1. Clinical interpretation* (rev. ed.). Minneapolis: University of Minnesota Press.

DAHLSTROM, W. C., WELSH, G. S., & DAHLSTROM, L. E. (1975). *An MMPI handbook: Vol. 2. Research applications*. Minneapolis: University of Minnesota Press.

DAILEY, C. A. (1952). The effects of premature conclusions upon the acquisition of understanding a person. *Journal of Psychology, 33,* 133–152.

DAILEY, C. A. (1953). The practical utility of the clinical report. *Journal of Consulting Psychology, 17,* 297–302.

DANA, R. H. (1959). The perceptual organization TAT score, number, order, and frequency. *Journal of Projective Techniques, 23,* 307–310.

DANA, R. H., & LEECH, S. (1974). Existential assessment. *Journal of Personality Assessment, 38,* 428–435.

DANGEL, R. F., & POLSTER, R. A. (Eds.). (1984). *Parent training*. New York: Guilford Press.

DAVIDSON, W. S. (1974). Studies of aversive conditioning for alcoholics: A critical review of theory and research methodology. *Psychological Bulletin, 81,* 571–581.

DAVIDSON, W. S., REDNER, R., BLAKELY, C., MITCHELL, C. M., & EMSHOFF, J. G. (1987). Diversion of juvenile offenders: An experimental comparison. *Journal of Consulting and Clinical Psychology, 55,* 68–75.

DAVISON, G. C., & NEALE, J. M. (1990). *Abnormal psychology* (5th ed.). New York: John Wiley.

DAWE, H. C. (1934). An analysis of two-hundred quarrels of pre-school children. *Child Development, 5,* 139–157.

Dawes, R. M. (1986). Representative thinking in clinical judgment. *Clinical Psychology Review, 6,* 425–442.

Dawes, R. M. (1992). *Psychology and psychotherapy: The myth of professional expertise.* New York: Free Press.

Dawes, R. M., Faust, D., & Meehl, P. E. (1989). Clinical versus actuarial judgment. *Science, 243,* 1668–1674.

Delameter, A. M. (1986). Psychological aspects of diabetes mellitus in children. In B. B. Lahey & A. E. Kazdin (Eds.), *Advances in clinical child psychology* (Vol. 9, pp. 333–375). New York: Plenum Press.

DeLeon, P. H., Fox, R. E., & Graham, S. R. (1991). Prescription privileges: Psychology's next frontier. *American Psychologist, 46,* 384–393.

DeLeon, P. H., Wedding, D., Wakefield, M. K., & VandenBos, G. R. (1992). Medicaid policy: Psychology's overlooked agenda. *Professional Psychology: Research and Practice, 23,* 96–107.

Dembo, R., Weyant, J. M., & Warner, J. L. (1982). The impact of intake experiences on clients dropping out of treatment at a community mental health center. *Journal of Psychiatric Treatment and Evaluation, 4,* 345–353.

Dennis, W. (1948). *Readings in the history of psychology.* New York: Appleton-Century-Crofts.

DeSantis, B. W., & Walker, C. E. (1991). Contemporary clinical psychology. In C. E. Walker (Ed.), *Clinical psychology: Historical and research foundations* (pp. 513–535). New York: Plenum Press.

Deutsch, F., & Murphy, W. F. (1955). *The clinical interview.* New York: International Universities Press.

Diener, C. I., & Dweck, C. S. (1978). An analysis of learned helplessness: Continuous changes in performance, strategy, and achievement cognitions following failure. *Journal of Personality and Social Psychology, 36,* 451–462.

DiGiusepee, R. A., & Miller, N. J. (1977). A review of outcome studies on rational-emotive therapy. In A. Ellis & R. Grieger (Eds.), *Handbook of rational emotive therapy* (pp. 72–95). New York: Springer.

DiLalla, L. F., & Gottesman, I. I. (1991). Biological and genetic contributions to violence—Widom's untold tale. *Psychological Bulletin, 109,* 125–129.

Dillehay, R. C. (1973). On the irrelevance of the classical negative evidence concerning the effect of attitudes on behavior. *American Psychologist, 28,* 887–891.

DiNardo, P. A. (1975). Social class and diagnostic suggestion as variables in clinical judgment. *Journal of Consulting and Clinical Psychology, 43,* 363–368.

DiNardo, P. A., O'Brien, G. T., Barlow, D. H., Waddell,

M. T., & Blanchard, E. B. (1983). Reliability of DSM-III anxiety disorder categories using a new structural interview. *Archives of General Psychiatry, 40,* 1070–1075.

Dobson, K. S. (1989). A meta-analysis of the efficacy of cognitive therapy for depression. *Journal of Consulting and Clinical Psychology, 57,* 414–419.

Dodge, K. A. (1986). A social information processing model of social competence in children. In M. Perlmutter (Ed.), *Minnesota Symposia on Child Psychology* (Vol. 18, pp. 77–125). Hillsdale, NJ: Lawrence Erlbaum Associates.

Dodge, K. A., McClaskey, C. L., & Feldman, E. (1985). Situational approach to the assessment of social competence in children. *Journal of Consulting and Clinical Psychology, 53,* 344–353.

Dohrenwend, B. S. (1978). Social stress and community psychology. *American Journal of Community Psychology, 6,* 1–14.

Dohrenwend, B. S., & Dohrenwend, B. P. (Eds.). (1981). *Stressful life events and their contexts.* New Brunswick, NJ: Rutgers University Press.

Dohrenwend, B. S., Dohrenwend, B. P., Dodson, M., & Shrout, P. E. (1984). Symptoms, hassles, social supports, and life events: Problem of confounding measures. *Journal of Abnormal Psychology, 93,* 222–230.

Dohrenwend, B. S., Krasnoff, L., Askenasy, A. R., & Dohrenwend, B. P. (1978). Exemplification of a method for scaling life events: The PERI life events scale. *Journal of Health and Social Behavior, 19,* 205–229.

Doleys, D. M. (1983). Enuresis and encopresis. In T. Ollendick & M. Hersen (Eds.), *Handbook of child psychopathology* (pp. 201–226). New York: Plenum Press.

Dollard, J., & Miller, N. E. (1950). *Personality and psychotherapy: An analysis in terms of learning, thinking and culture.* New York: McGraw-Hill.

Dollinger, S. J. (1989). Predictive validity of the Graduate Record Examination in a clinical psychology program. *Professional Psychology: Research and Practice, 20,* 56–58.

Douglas, V. I. (1972). Stop, look and listen: The problem of sustained attention and impulse control in hyperactive and normal children. *Canadian Journal of Behavioral Science, 4,* 259–282.

Dreikurs, R. (1954). The psychological interview in medicine. *American Journal of Individual Psychology, 10,* 99–122.

Dryden, W., & Trower, P. (1989). *Cognitive psychotherapy.* New York: Springer.

Dubbert, P. M. (1992). Exercise in behavioral medicine.

Journal of Consulting and Clinical Psychology, 60, 613–618.

DuBois, P. H. (1970). *A history of psychological testing.* Boston: Allyn & Bacon.

Dulany, D. E. (1968). Awareness, rules, and propositional control: A confrontation with S-R behavior theory. In T. R. Dixon & D. L. Horton (Eds.), *Verbal behavior and general behavior theory* (pp. 340–387). Englewood Cliffs, NJ: Prentice-Hall.

Dunham, H. W. (1965). Community psychiatry: The newest therapeutic bandwagon. *Archives of General Psychiatry, 12,* 303–313.

Dunlap, G., Koegel, R. L., & O'Neill, R. (1985). Pervasive developmental disorders. In P. H. Bornstein & A. E. Kazdin (Eds.), *Handbook of clinical behavior therapy with children* (pp. 499–540). Homewood, IL: Dorsey Press.

Durlak, J. (1979). Comparative effectiveness of paraprofessional and professional helpers. *Psychological Bulletin, 86,* 80–92.

Dush, D. M., Hirt, M. L., & Schroeder, H. (1983). Self-statement modification with adults: A meta-analysis. *Psychological Bulletin, 94,* 408–422.

Dush, D. M., Hirt, M. L., & Schroeder, H. E. (1989). Self-statement modification in the treatment of child behavior disorders: A meta-analysis. *Psychological Bulletin, 106,* 97–106.

Eagle, M. (1984). *Recent developments in psychoanalysis: A critical evaluation.* New York: McGraw-Hill.

Edelbrock, C., Costello, A. J., Dulcan, M. K., Kalas, R., & Conover, N. C. (1985). Age differences in the reliability of the psychiatric interview of the child. *Child Development, 56,* 265–275.

Edelstein, B. A., & Eisler, R. M. (1976). Effects of modeling and modeling with instructions and feedback on the behavioral components of social skills. *Behavior Therapy, 7,* 382–389.

Edelstein, B. A., & Michelson, L. (Eds.). (1986). *Handbook of prevention.* New York & London: Plenum Press.

Edwards, A. L. (1957). *The social desirability variable in personality assessment and research.* New York: Dryden.

Edwards, A. L. (1959). *Edwards Personal Preference Schedule.* New York: Psychological Corporation.

Einhorn, H. J., & Hogarth, R. M. (1978). Confidence in judgment: Persistence of the illusion of validity. *Psychological Review, 85,* 395–416.

Elias, M. J., Dalton, J. H., & Godin, S. (1987). A survey of graduate education in community psychology. *The Community Psychologist, 20,* 10–34.

Elkind, D. (1981). *The hurried child.* Reading, MA: Addison-Wesley.

Elkins, R. (1975). Aversion therapy for alcoholism: Chemical, electrical, or verbal imagery. *The International Journal of the Addictions, 10,* 157–209."

Ellenberger, H. F. (1972). The story of "Anna O.": A critical review with new data. *Journal of the History of the Behavioural Sciences, 8,* 267–279.

Ellis, A. (1962). *Reason and emotion in psychotherapy.* New York: Lyle Stuart.

Ellis, A. (1973). Rational-emotive therapy. In R. Corsini (Ed.), *Current psychotherapies* (pp. 167–206). Itasca, IL: F. E. Peacock.

Ellis, A., & Bernard, M. E. (Eds.). (1985). *Clinical applications of rational-emotive therapy.* New York: Plenum Press.

Ellis, A., & Dryden, W. (1987). *The practice of rational-emotive therapy.* New York: Springer.

Ellis, A., & Grieger, R. (Eds.). (1977). *Handbook of rational-emotive therapy.* New York: Springer.

Ellis, L. (1991). A synthesized (biosocial) theory of rape. *Journal of Consulting and Clinical Psychology, 59,* 631–642.

Emery, R. E. (1982). Interparental conflict and the children of discord and divorce. *Psychological Bulletin, 92,* 310–330.

Emmelkamp, P. M. G., & Felten, M. (1985). The process of exposure *in vivo:* Cognitive and physiological changes during treatment of acrophobia. *Behaviour Research and Therapy, 23,* 219–224.

Emmelkamp, P. M. G., Van Der Hout, A., & DeVries, K. (1983). Assertive training for agoraphobics. *Behaviour Research and Therapy, 21,* 63–68.

Endicott, J., & Spitzer, R. L. (1978). A diagnostic interview: The schedule for affective disorders and schizophrenia. *Archives of General Psychiatry, 35,* 837–844.

Englemann, S. (1974). The effectiveness of direct verbal instruction on IQ performance and achievement in reading and arithmetic. In R. Ulrich, T. Stachnik, & J. Mabry (Eds.), *Control of human behavior* (Vol. 3, pp. 69–84). Glenview, IL: Scott, Foresman.

Epstein, N., & Baucom, D. H. (1989). Cognitive-behavioral marital therapy. In A. Freeman, K. M. Simon, L. E. Beutler, & H. Arkowitz (Eds.), *Comprehensive handbook of cognitive therapy* (pp. 491–513). New York: Plenum Press.

Erdberg, P. (1990). Rorschach assessment. In G. Goldstein & M. Hersen (Eds.), *Handbook of psychological assessment* (pp. 387–399). New York: Pergamon Press.

Erdman, H. P., Klein, M. H., & Greist, J. H. (1985). Direct patient computer interviewing. *Journal of Consulting and Clinical Psychology, 53,* 760–773.

Erikson, E. H. (1946). Ego development and historical

change. *The psychoanalytic study of the child* (Vol. 2, pp. 359–396). New York: International Universities Press.

ERIKSON, E. H. (1959). Identity and the life cycle. *Psychological Issues,* Monograph 1. New York: International Universities Press.

ERIKSON, E. H. (1963). *Childhood and society* (rev. ed.). New York: W. W. Norton.

ERON, L. D. (1950). A normative study of the thematic apperception test. *Psychological Monographs, 64* (9).

ESLINGER, P. J., & DAMASIO, A. R. (1985). Severe disturbance of higher cognition after bilateral frontal lobe ablation: Patient EVR. *Neurology, 35,* 1731–1741.

ESSOCK, S. M., & GOLDMAN, H. H. (1989). Prospective payment in retrospect. *American Psychologist, 44,* 1237–1239.

EXNER, J. E. (1976). Projective techniques. In I. B. Weiner (Ed.), *Clinical methods in psychology* (pp. 61–121). New York: John Wiley.

EXNER, J. E. (1978). *The Rorschach: A comprehensive system, Vol. 2: Current research and advanced interpretation.* New York: John Wiley.

EXNER, J. E. (1986). *The Rorschach: A comprehensive system, Vol. 1: Basic foundations* (2nd ed.). New York: John Wiley.

EYSENCK, H. J. (1952). The effects of psychotherapy: An evaluation. *Journal of Consulting Psychology, 16,* 319–324.

EYSENCK, H. J. (1959). Learning theory and behaviour therapy. *Journal of Mental Science, 105,* 61–75.

EYSENCK, H. J. (1966). *The effects of psychotherapy.* New York: International Science Press.

EYSENCK, H. J. (1978). An exercise in mega-silliness. *American Psychologist, 33,* 517.

EYSENCK, H. J. (1982). Neobehavioristic (S-R) theory. In G. T. Wilson & C. M. Franks (Eds.), *Contemporary behavior therapy: Conceptual and empirical foundations* (pp. 205–276). New York: Guilford Press.

EYSENCK, H. J. (1985). *The decline and fall of the Freudian empire.* London: Allen Lane.

EYSENCK, H. J., & EYSENCK, S. B. G. (1975). *Manual for Eysenck Personality Questionnaire.* San Diego, CA: Educational and Individual Testing Service.

EYSENCK, H. J., WAKEFIELD, J. A., & FRIEDMAN, A. F. (1983). Diagnosis and clinical assessment: The DSM-III. *Annual Review of Psychology, 34,* 167–193.

FAIRBAIRN, W. R. D. (1952). *Psychoanalytic studies of the personality.* London: Tavistock Publications/Routledge & Kegan Paul.

FAIRWEATHER, G. W. (1980). *New directions for mental health services: The Fairweather lodge: A twenty-five year retrospective.* San Francisco: Jossey-Bass.

FAIRWEATHER, G. W., SANDERS, D. H., & TORNATZKY, L. G. (1974). *Creating change in mental health organizations.* New York: Pergamon Press.

FANCHER, R. E. (1973). *Psychoanalytic psychology: The development of Freud's thought.* New York: W. W. Norton.

FARKAS, G. M. (1980). An ontological analysis of behavior therapy. *American Psychologist, 35,* 364–374.

FARRELL, A. D., CAMPLAIR, P. S., & McCULLOUGH, L. (1987). Identification of target complaints by computer interview: Evaluation of the computerized assessment system for psychotherapy evaluation and research. *Journal of Consulting and Clinical Psychology, 55,* 691–700.

FAUST, D., & ZISKIN, J. (1988). The expert witness in psychology and psychiatry. *Science, 242,* 31–35.

FEINGOLD, A. (1989). Assessment of journals in social science psychology. *American Psychologist, 44,* 961–964.

FEINGOLD, B. F. (1975). *Why your child is hyperactive.* New York: Random House.

FELDMAN, S. S. (1959). *Mannerisms of speech and gestures in everyday life.* New York: International Universities Press.

FELNER, R. D. (1985). Prevention. *The Community Psychologist, 19,* 31–34.

FELNER, R. D., JASON, L. A., MORITSUGU, J. N., & FARBER, S. S. (Eds.). (1983). *Preventive psychology: Theory, research and practice.* New York: Pergamon Press.

FIEDLER, F. E. (1950). A comparison of therapeutic relationships in psychoanalytic, nondirective, and Adlerian therapy. *Journal of Consulting Psychology, 14,* 436–445.

FILSKOV, S. B., & BOLL, T. J. (Eds.). (1981). *Handbook of clinical neuropsychology.* New York: John Wiley.

FILSKOV, S. B., GRIMM, B. H., & LEWIS, J. A. (1981). Brain-behavior relationships. In S. B. Filskov & T. J. Boll (Eds.), *Handbook of clinical neuropsychology* (pp. 39–73). New York: John Wiley.

FINE, R. (1971). *The healing of the mind: The technique of psychoanalytic psychotherapy.* New York: David McKay.

FISCHER, C. T. (1985). *Individualizing psychological assessment.* Monterey, CA: Brooks/Cole.

FISCHER, C. T. (1989). A life-centered approach to psychodiagnostics: Attending to lifeworld, ambiguity, and possibility. *Person-Centered Review, 4,* 163–170.

FISCHER, C. T., & FISCHER, W. F. (1983). Phenomenological-existential psychotherapy. In M. Hersen, A. E. Kazdin, & A. S. Bellack (Eds.), *The clinical psychology handbook* (pp. 489–505). New York: Pergamon Press.

FISHER, S., & FISHER, R. (1950). Test of certain assumptions regarding figure drawing analysis. *Journal of Abnormal and Social Psychology, 45,* 727–732.

FISHER, S., & GREENBERG, R. P. (1977). *The scientific credibility of Freud's theories and therapy.* New York: Basic Books.

FISK, J. D., BRAHA, R. E. D., WALKER, A., & GRAY, J. (1991). The Halifax Mental Status Scale: Development of a new test of mental status for use with elderly clients. *Psychological Assessment: A Journal of Consulting and Clinical Psychology, 3,* 162–167.

FLYNN, J. R. (1984). The mean IQ of Americans: Massive gains 1932 to 1978. *Psychological Bulletin, 95,* 29–51.

FOA, E. B., ROTHBAUM, B. O., & KOZAK, M. J. (1989). Behavioral treatments for anxiety and depression. In P. C. Kendall & D. Watson (Eds.), *Anxiety and depression: Distinctive and overlapping features* (pp. 413–454). San Diego: Academic Press.

FOA, E. G., STEKETEE, G. S., & ROTHBAUM, B. (1989). Behavioral/cognitive conceptualizations of post-traumatic stress disorder. *Behavior Therapy, 20,* 155–176.

FOLKMAN, S., & LAZARUS, R. S. (1980). An analysis of coping in a middle-aged community sample. *Journal of Health and Social Behavior, 21,* 219–239.

FOLLETTE, W. C., & HOUTS, A. C. (1992). Philosophical and theoretical problems for behavior therapy. *Behavior Therapy, 23,* 251–262.

FOLSTEIN, M. F., MAIBERGER, P., & McHUGH, P. R. (1977). Mood disorders as a specific complication of stroke. *Journal of Neurology, Neurosurgery & Psychiatry, 40,* 1018–1020.

FORD, D. H., & URBAN, H. B. (1963). *Systems of psychotherapy: A comparative study.* New York: John Wiley.

FOREHAND, R., LAUTENSCHLAGER, G. J., FAUST, J., & GRAZIANO, W. G. (1986). Parent perceptions and parent-child interactions in clinic-referred children: A preliminary investigation of the effects of maternal depressive moods. *Behaviour Research and Therapy, 24,* 73–76.

FOREHAND, R., & McMAHON, R. J. (1981). *Helping the noncompliant child: A clinician's guide to parent training.* New York: Guilford Press.

FOSTER, S. L., BELL-DOLAN, D. J., & BURGE, D. A. (1988). Behavioral observation. In A. S. Bellack & M. Hersen (Eds.), *Behavioral assessment: A practical handbook* (3rd ed., pp. 119–160). New York: Pergamon Press.

FOSTER, S. L., & ROBIN, A. L. (1988). Family conflict and communication in adolescence. In E. J. Mash & L. G. Terdal (Eds.), *Behavioral assessment of child-*hood disorders (2nd ed., pp. 717–775). New York: Guilford Press.

FOWLER, R. D. (1985). Landmarks in computer-assisted psychological assessment. *Journal of Consulting and Clinical Psychology, 53,* 748–759.

FOWLES, D. C. (1992). Schizophrenia: Diathesis-stress revisited. *Annual Review of Psychology, 43,* 303–336.

FOX, L. H., & ZIRKIN, B. (1984). Achievement tests. In G. Goldstein & M. Hersen (Eds.), *Handbook of psychological assessment* (pp. 119–131). New York: Pergamon Press.

FOX, R. E., & BARCLAY, A. (1989). Let a thousand flowers bloom: Or, weed the garden. *American Psychologist, 44,* 55–59.

FOY, D. W., NUNN, L. B., & RYCHTARIK, R. G. (1984). Broad-spectrum behavioral treatment for chronic alcoholics: Effects of training controlled drinking skills. *Journal of Consulting and Clinical Psychology, 52,* 218–230.

FRANCES, A. J., FIRST, M. B., WIDIGER, T. A., MIELE, G. M., TILLY, S. M., DAVIS, W. W., & PINCUS, H. A. (1991). An A to Z guide to DSM-IV conundrums. *Journal of Consulting and Clinical Psychology, 100,* 407–412.

FRANCES, A. J., WIDIGER, T. A., & PINCUS, H. A. (1989). The development of DSM-IV: Work in progress. *Archives of General Psychiatry, 46,* 373–375.

FRANCIS, V., KORSCH, B. M., & MORRIS, M. J. (1969). Gaps in doctor-patient communications. *New England Journal of Medicine, 280,* 535–540.

FRANK, J. D. (1957). Some determinants, manifestations, and effects of cohesiveness in therapy groups. *International Journal of Group Psychotherapy, 7,* 53–63.

FRANK, J. D. (1973). *Persuasion and healing* (rev. ed.). Baltimore, MD: Johns Hopkins University Press.

FRANK, L. K. (1939). Projective methods for the study of personality. *Journal of Psychology, 8,* 343–389.

FRANK, R. G. (1993). Health-care reform: An introduction. *American Psychologist, 48,* 258–260.

FRANKL, V. (1963). *Man's search for meaning.* New York: Washington Square Press.

FRANKL, V. (1965). *The doctor and the soul.* New York: Knopf.

FRANKL, V. (1967). *Psychotherapy and existentialism: Selected papers on logotherapy.* New York: Washington Square Press.

FRANKS, C. M. (1964). *Conditioning techniques in clinical practice and research.* New York: Springer.

FRANKS, C. M. (1976). Forward. In E. J. Mash & L. G. Terdal (Eds.), *Behavior therapy assessment* (pp. xi–xiii). New York: Springer.

FREDERICK/SCHNEIDERS, INC. (1990). *Survey of American Psychological Association members*. Washington, DC: Author.

FREEMAN, A., SIMON, K. M., BEUTLER, L. E., & ARKOWITZ, H. (1989). *Comprehensive handbook of cognitive therapy*. New York: Plenum Press.

FREMER, J., DIAMOND, E. E., & CAMARA, W. J. (1989). Developing a code of fair testing practices in education. *American Psychologist, 44,* 1062–1067.

FREUD, A. (1946). *The ego and mechanisms of defense*. New York: International Universities Press.

FREUD, A., & BURLINGHAM, D. T. (1943). *War and children*. London: Medical War Books.

FREUD, S. (1900). *The interpretation of dreams*. (Avon Edition, 1965). New York: Avon Books.

FREUD, S. (1901). *The psychopathology of everyday life*. New York: Macmillan.

FREUD, S. (1904). *On psychotherapy*. Lecture delivered before the College of Physicians in Vienna. Reprinted in S. Freud, *Therapy and technique*. New York: Collier Books, 1963.

FREUD, S. (1905). Jokes and their relation to the unconscious. In the *Standard edition of the complete psychological works of Sigmund Freud* (Vol. 8). London: Hogarth Press, 1953–1964.

FREUD, S. (1912). Recommendations for physicians on the psychoanalytic method of treatment. *Zentralblatt,* DS. II. Reprinted in S. Freud, *Therapy and technique*. New York: Collier Books, 1963.

FREUD, S. (1915). Further recommendations in the technique of psychoanalysis. *Zeitschrift,* BD. III. Reprinted in S. Freud, *Therapy and technique*. New York: Collier Books, 1963.

FREUD, S. (1938). *The basic writings of Sigmund Freud*. New York: Modern Library.

FREUD, S. (1949). *An outline of psychoanalysis*. (J. Strachey, trans.). New York: W. W. Norton.

FREUD, S. (1953–1964). *The standard edition of the complete psychological works of Sigmund Freud* (24 vols.). London: Hogarth Press.

FRIEDMAN, H. S., & BOOTH-KEWLEY, S. (1988). Validity of the Type A construct: A reprise. *Psychological Bulletin, 104,* 381–384.

FRIEDMAN, M., & ROSENMAN, R. H. (1974). *Type A behavior and your heart*. New York: Knopf.

FURMAN, W. (1980). Promoting appropriate social behavior: A developmental perspective. In B. Lahey & A. Kazdin (Eds.), *Advances in clinical child psychology* (Vol. 3, pp. 1–41). New York: Plenum Press.

FURSTENBERG, F. F., BROOKS-GUNN, J., & CHASE-LANSDALE, L. (1989). Teenaged pregnancy and childbearing. *American Psychologist, 44,* 313–320.

GAFFNEY, L. R., & McFALL, R. M. (1981). A comparison of social skills in delinquent and nondelinquent girls using a behavioral role-playing inventory. *Journal of Consulting and Clinical Psychology, 49,* 959–967.

GAINOTTI, G. (1972). Emotional behavior and hemispheric side of lesion. *Cortex, 8,* 41–55.

GALTON, F. (1983). *Inquiries into human faculty and its development*. London: Macmillan.

GANZER, V. J., & SARASON, I. G. (1964). Interrelationships among hostility, experimental conditions, and verbal behavior. *Journal of Abnormal and Social Psychology, 68,* 79–84.

GARB, H. N. (1984). The incremental validity of information used in personality assessment. *Clinical Psychology Review, 4,* 641–656.

GARB, H. N. (1989). Clinical judgment, clinical training, and professional experience. *Psychological Bulletin, 105,* 387–396.

GARB, H. N. (1992). The trained psychologist as expert witness. *Clinical Psychology Review, 12,* 451–468.

GARBER, J. (1984). Classification of childhood psychopathology: A developmental perspective. *Child Development, 55,* 30–48.

GARCIA, J., McGOWAN, B., & GREEN, K. (1972). Biological constraints on conditioning. In A. H. Block & W. F. Prokasky (Eds.), *Classical conditioning* (pp. 3–27). New York: Appleton-Century-Crofts.

GARDNER, H., BROWNELL, H. H., WAPNER, W., & MICHELOW, D. (1983). Missing the point: The role of the right hemisphere in the processing of complex linguistic materials. In E. Perecman (Ed.), *Cognitive processing in the right hemisphere* (pp. 169–191). New York: Academic Press.

GARDNER, R. A. (1971). *Therapeutic communication with children: The mutual story-telling technique*. New York: Jason Aronson.

GARFIELD, S. L. (1965). Historical introduction. In B. B. Wolman (Ed.), *Handbook of clinical psychology* (pp. 125–140). New York: McGraw-Hill.

GARFIELD, S. L. (1974). *Clinical psychology: The study of personality and behavior*. Chicago: Aldine.

GARFIELD, S. L. (1986). Research on client variables in psychotherapy. In S. L. Garfield & A. E. Bergin (Eds.), *Handbook of psychotherapy and behavior change* (3rd ed., pp. 213–256). New York: John Wiley.

GARFIELD, S. L. (1992). Comments on "Retrospect: Psychology as a profession." *Journal of Consulting and Clinical Psychology, 60,* 9–15.

GARFIELD, S. L., & KURTZ, R. (1976). Clinical psychologists in the 1970s. *American Psychologist, 31,* 1–9.

GARMEZY, N. (1978). Never mind the psychologists: Is it good for the children? *Clinical Psychologist, 31,* 1–6.

GARMEZY, N. (1983). Stressors of childhood. In N. Garmezy and M. Rutter (Eds.), *Stress, coping, & development in children* (pp. 43–84). New York: McGraw-Hill.

GARMEZY, N. (1985). Stress resilient children: The search for protective factors. In J. E. Stevenson (Ed.), *Recent research in developmental psychopathology. Journal of Child Psychology and Psychiatry, Book Supplement No. 4* (pp. 213–233). Oxford: Pergamon Press.

GARNER, A. M., & SMITH, G. M. (1976). An experimental videotape technique for evaluating trainee approaches to clinical judging. *Journal of Consulting and Clinical Psychology, 44,* 945–950.

GARNER, H. H. (1970). *Psychotherapy.* St. Louis: Warren H. Green.

GAY, P. (1988). *Freud: A life for our time.* New York: W. W. Norton.

GEER, J. H. (1965). The development of a scale to measure fear. *Behaviour Research and Therapy, 3,* 45–53.

GELFAND, D. M., JENSON, W. R., & DREW, C. J. (1982). *Understanding child behavior disorders* (2nd ed.). New York: Holt, Rinehart & Winston.

GELFAND, D. M., & PETERSON, L. (1985). *Child development and psychopathology.* Beverly Hills, CA: Sage.

GERGEN, K. J. (1985). The social constructionist movement in modern psychology. *American Psychologist, 40,* 266–275.

GETKA, E. J., & GLASS, C. R. (1992). Behavioral and cognitive-behavioral approaches to the reduction of dental anxiety. *Behavior Therapy, 23,* 433–448.

GILBERSTADT, H., & DUKER, J. (1965). *A handbook for clinical and actuarial MMPI interpretation.* Philadelphia: Saunders.

GILL, M. M., & HOFFMAN, I. Z. (1982). A method of studying the analysis of aspects of the patient's experience of the relationship in psychoanalysis and psychotherapy. *Journal of the American Psychoanalytic Association, 30,* 137–167.

GITTELMAN, R. (1980). The role of tests for differential diagnosis in child psychiatry. *Journal of the American Academy of Child Psychiatry, 19,* 413–438.

GLASGOW, R. E., & TERBORG, J. R. (1988). Occupational health promotion programs to reduce cardiovascular risk. *Journal of Consulting and Clinical Psychology, 56,* 365–373.

GLASS, G. V., & KLIEGL, R. M. (1983). An apology for research integration in the study of psychotherapy. *Journal of Consulting and Clinical Psychology, 51,* 28–41.

GLENWICK, D., & JASON, L. A. (Eds.). (1980). *Behavioral community psychology.* New York: Praeger.

GODARD, S. L., BLOOM, J. D., WILLIAMS, M. H., & FAULKNER, L. R. (1986). The right to refuse treatment in Oregon: A two-year statewide experience. *Behavioral Sciences and the Law, 4,* 293–304.

GOFFMAN, E. (1959). *The presentation of self in everyday life.* Garden City, NY: Doubleday.

GOFFMAN, E. (1961). *Asylums.* Garden City, NY: Doubleday.

GOLDBERG, L. R. (1959). The effectiveness of clinicians' judgments: The diagnosis of organic brain damage from the Bender-Gestalt test. *Journal of Consulting Psychology, 23,* 25–33.

GOLDBERG, L. R. (1968). Simple models or simple processes? Some research on clinical judgments. *American Psychologist, 23,* 483–496.

GOLDEN, C. J. (1980). In reply to Adams' "In search of Luria's battery: A false start." *Journal of Consulting and Clinical Psychology, 48,* 517–521.

GOLDEN, C. J. (1981). A standardized version of Luria's neuropsychological tests: A quantitative and qualitative approach to neuropsychological evaluation. In S. B. Filskov & T. J. Boll (Eds.), *Handbook of clinical neuropsychology* (pp. 608–642). New York: John Wiley.

GOLDEN, C. J., HAMMEKE, T., & PURISCH, A. (1978). Diagnostic validity of the Luria-Nebraska Neuropsychological battery. *Journal of Consulting and Clinical Psychology, 46,* 1258–1265.

GOLDEN, C. J., PURISCH, A. D., & HAMMEKE, T. A. (1985). *Luria-Nebraska Neuropsychological Battery: Forms I and II Manual.* Los Angeles: Western Psychological Services.

GOLDEN, C. J., SAWICKI, R. B., & FRANZEN, M. D. (1990). Test construction. In G. Goldstein & M. Hersen (Eds.), *Handbook of psychological assessment* (2nd ed., pp. 21–40). New York: Pergamon Press.

GOLDEN, M. (1964). Some effects of combining psychological tests on clinical inferences. *Journal of Consulting Psychology, 28,* 440–446.

GOLDENBERG, H. (1973). *Contemporary clinical psychology.* Monterey, CA: Brooks/Cole.

GOLDFRIED, M. R. (1980). Toward the delineation of therapeutic change principles. *American Psychologist, 35,* 991–999.

GOLDFRIED, M. R., & DAVISON, G. C. (1976). *Clinical behavior therapy.* New York: Holt, Rinehart & Winston.

GOLDFRIED, M. R., & D'ZURILLA, T. J. (1969). A behavior-analytic model for assessing competence. In C. D. Spielberger (Ed.), *Current topics in clinical and community psychology* (Vol. 1, pp. 151–196). New York: Academic Press.

GOLDFRIED, M. R., & SPRAFKIN, J. N. (1974). *Behavioral personality assessment.* Morristown, NJ: General Learning Press.

GOLDFRIED, M. R., STRICKER, G., & WEINER, I. B. (1971). *Rorschach handbook of clinical and research applications.* Englewood Cliffs, NJ: Prentice-Hall.

GOLDING, S. L., ROESCH, R., & SCHREIBER, J. (1984). Assessment and conceptualization of competency to stand trial: Preliminary data on the Interdisciplinary Fitness Interview. *Law and Human Behavior, 8,* 321–334.

GOLDING, S. L., & RORER, L. G. (1972). Illusory correlation and subjective judgment. *Journal of Abnormal Psychology, 80,* 249–260.

GOLDSCHMID, M. L., STEIN, D. D., WEISSMAN, H. N., & SORRELS, J. A. (1969). A survey of the training and practices of clinical psychologists. *The Clinical Psychologist, 22,* 89–94, 107.

GOLDSMITH, J. B., & McFALL, R. M. (1975). Development and evaluation of an interpersonal skill-training program for psychiatric inpatients. *Journal of Abnormal Psychology, 84,* 51–58.

GOLDSTEIN, A. J. (1973). Behavior therapy. In R. Corsini (Ed.), *Current psychotherapies* (pp. 207–249). Itaska, IL: F. E. Peacock.

GOLDSTEIN, A. P. (1971). *Psychotherapeutic attraction.* New York: Pergamon Press.

GOLDSTEIN, A. P. (1976). Relationship-enhancement methods. In F. H. Kanfer & A. P. Goldstein (Eds.), *Helping people change* (pp. 15–49). New York: Pergamon Press.

GOLDSTEIN, G., & HERSEN, M. (Eds.). (1990). *Handbook of psychological assessment.* New York: Pergamon Press.

GOODENOUGH, F. L. (1931). Children's drawings. In C. Murchison (Ed.), *A handbook of child psychology* (pp. 480–514). Worcester, MA: University Press.

GOODENOUGH, F. L. (1949). *Mental testing.* New York: Rinehart.

GOODWIN, F. K., & JAMISON, K. R. (1990). *Manic-depressive illness.* New York: Oxford University Press.

GORMAN, J. M., FYER, M. R., GOETZ, R., ASKANAZI, J., LEIBOWITZ, M. R., FYER, A. J., KINNEY, J., & KLEIN, D. F. (1988). Ventilation physiology of patients with panic disorder. *Archives of General Psychiatry, 45,* 53–60.

GOTTESMAN, I. I., & SHIELDS, J. (1982). *Schizophrenia: The epigenetic puzzle.* Cambridge: Cambridge University Press.

GOTTMAN, J. M. (1979). *Marital interaction: Experimental investigations.* New York: Academic Press.

GOTTMAN, J. M., & KROKOFF, L. J. (1989). Marital interaction and satisfaction: A longitudinal view. *Journal of Consulting and Clinical Psychology, 57,* 47–52.

GOTTMAN, J. M., & MARKMAN, H. J. (1978). Experimental designs in psychotherapy research. In S. Garfield & A. Bergin (Eds.), *Handbook of psychotherapy and behavior change* (2nd ed., pp. 12–62). New York: John Wiley.

GOTTMAN, J. M., MARKMAN, H. J., & NOTARIUS, C. (1977). The topography of marital conflict: A sequential analysis of verbal and nonverbal behavior. *Journal of Marriage and the Family, 39,* 461–477.

GOUGH, H. (1987). *California Psychological Inventory: Administrator's guide.* Palo Alto, CA: Consulting Psychologists Press.

GRAHAM, F. K., & KENDALL, B. S. (1960). Memory-for-designs test: Revised general manual. *Perceptual and Motor Skills, 11,* 147–188.

GRAHAM, J. R. (1990). *MMPI-2: Assessing personality and psychopathology.* New York: Oxford University Press.

GRAHAM, S. R., & FOX, R. E. (1991). Postdoctoral education for professional practice. *American Psychologist, 46,* 1033–1035.

GRANTHAM, R. J. (1973). Effects of counselor sex, race, and language style on black students in initial interviews. *Journal of Counseling Psychology, 20,* 553–559.

GREENBERG, L. (1986). Change process research. *Journal of Consulting and Clinical Psychology, 54,* 4–9.

GREENBERG, L. S., & SAFRAN, J. D. (1989). Emotion in psychotherapy. *American Psychologist, 44,* 19–29.

GREENBLATT, M. (1959). Discussion of papers by Saslow, Matarazzo, & Lacey. In E. A. Rubinstein & M. B. Parloff (Eds.), *Research in psychotherapy* (Vol. 1. pp. 209–220). Washington, DC: American Psychological Association.

GREENSPOON, J. (1962). Verbal conditioning and clinical psychology. In A. J. Bachrach (Ed.), *Experimental foundations of clinical psychology* (pp. 510–553). New York: Basic Books.

GREENWOOD, C. R., WALKER, H. M., TODD, N. M., & HOPS, H. (1979). Selecting a cost-effective screening measure for the assessment of preschool social withdrawal. *Journal of Applied Behavior Analysis, 12,* 639–652.

GRENCAVAGE, L. M., & NORCROSS, J. C. (1992). Where are the commonalities among the therapeutic common factors? *Professional Psychology: Research and Practice, 21,* 372–378.

GRIEST, D. L., FOREHAND, R., ROGERS, T., BREINER, J., FUREY, W., & WILLIAMS, C. A. (1982). Effect of parent enhancement therapy on the treatment outcome and generalization of a parent training program. *Behaviour Research and Therapy, 20,* 429–436.

GRIEST, D. L., WELLS, K. C., & FOREHAND, R. (1979). An examination of predictors of maternal perceptions of maladjustment in clinic-referred children. *Journal of Abnormal Psychology, 88,* 277–281.

GROSS, A. M., & DRABMAN, R. S. (1990). *Handbook of clinical behavioral pediatrics.* New York: Plenum Press.

GROSS, M. L. (1962). *The brain watchers.* New York: Random House.

GROSS, S. J. (1978). The myth of professional licensing. *American Psychologist, 33,* 1009–1016.

GROSSBERG, J. M., & GRANT, B. F. (1978). Clinical psychophysics: Applications of ratio scaling and signal detection methods to research on pain, fear, drugs, and medical decision making. *Psychological Bulletin, 85,* 1154–1176.

GROTH-MARNAT, G. (1984). *Handbook of psychological assessment.* New York: Van Nostrand Reinhold.

GROTJAHN, M. (1957). *Beyond laughter: Humor and the subconscious.* New York: McGraw-Hill.

GROVE, H. (1987). The reliability of psychiatric diagnosis. In C. G. Last & M. Hersen (Eds.), *Issues in diagnostic research* (pp. 99–117). New York: Plenum Press.

GRYCH, J. H., & FINCHAM, F. D. (1992). Interventions for children of divorce: Toward greater integration of research and action. *Psychological Bulletin, 111,* 434–454.

GUERNEY, B. G. (Ed.). (1969). *Psychotherapeutic agents: New roles of nonprofessionals, parents, and teachers.* New York: Holt, Rinehart & Winston.

GUNTRIP, H. (1973). *Psychoanalytic theory, therapy, and the self.* New York: Basic Books.

GUR, R. E. (1978). Left hemisphere dysfunction and left hemisphere overactivation in schizophrenia. *Journal of Abnormal Psychology, 87,* 225–238.

GURIN, G., VEROFF, J., & FELD, S. (1960). *Americans view their mental health.* New York: Basic Books.

GURMAN, A. S. (1985). *Casebook of marital therapy.* New York: Guilford Press.

GURMAN, A. S., & KNISKERN, D. P. (Eds.). (1981). *Handbook of family therapy.* New York: Brunner/Mazel.

GURMAN, A. S., KNISKERN, D. P., & PINSOF, W. M. (1986). Research on marital and family therapies. In S. L. Garfield & A. E. Bergin (Eds.), *Handbook of psychotherapy and behavior change* (3rd ed., pp. 565–624). New York: John Wiley.

GURMAN, A. S., & RAZIN, A. M. (1977). *Effective psychotherapy: A handbook of research.* New York: Pergamon Press.

GUTHRIE, E. R. (1935). *The psychology of learning.* New York: Harper & Row.

HAAGA, D. A. (1986). A review of the common principles approach to integration of psychotherapies. *Cognitive Therapy and Research, 10,* 527–538.

HAAGA, D. A., & DAVISON, G. C. (1989). Outcome studies of rational-emotive therapy. In M. E. Bernard & R. Digiuseppe (Eds.), *Inside rational-emotive therapy* (pp. 155–197). New York: Academic Press.

HAAGA, D. A. F., & DAVISON, G. C. (1991). Cognitive change methods. In F. H. Kanfer & A. P. Goldstein (Eds.), *Helping people change* (4th ed., pp. 248–305). New York: Pergamon Press.

HAAGA, D. A. F., DYCK, M. J., & ERNST, D. (1991). Empirical status of cognitive theory of depression. *Psychological Bulletin, 110,* 215–236.

HAHLWEG, K., REVENSTORF, D., & SCHINDLER, L. (1984). Effects of behavioral marital therapy on couples' communication and problem-solving skills. *Journal of Consulting and Clinical Psychology, 52,* 553–566.

HALL, C. S., LINDZEY, G., LOEHLIN, J. C., MANOSEVITZ, M. (1985). *Introduction to theories of personality.* New York: John Wiley.

HALL, G. C. N. (1990). Prediction of sexual aggression. *Clinical Psychology Review, 10,* 229–245.

HALLECK, S. L. (1969). Community psychiatry: Some troubling questions. In L. M. Roberts, S. L. Halleck, & M. B. Loeb (Eds.), *Community psychiatry* (pp. 58–71). Garden City, NY: Doubleday, Anchor Books.

HAMMER, E. F. (1968). Projective drawings. In A. I. Rabin (Ed.), *Projective techniques in personality assessment* (pp. 366–393). New York: Springer.

HAMMOND, K. R., & ALLEN, J. M. (1953). *Writing clinical reports.* Englewood Cliffs, NJ: Prentice-Hall.

HANDELSMAN, M. M., & GALVIN, M. D. (1988). Facilitating informed consent for outpatient psychotherapy: A suggested written format. *Professional Psychology: Research and Therapy, 19,* 223–225.

HANDLER, L. (1974). Psychotherapy, assessment, and clinical research: Parallels and similarities. In A. I. Rabin (Ed.), *Clinical psychology: Issues of the seventies* (pp. 49–62). East Lansing: Michigan State University Press.

HANSEN, D. J., ST. LAWRENCE, J. S., & CHRISTOFF, K. A. (1985). Effects of interpersonal problem-solving training with chronic aftercare patients on problem-solving component skills and effectiveness of solutions. *Journal of Consulting and Clinical Psychology, 53,* 167–174.

HANSEN, D. J., ST. LAWRENCE, J. S., & CHRISTOFF, K. A. (1989). Group conversational-skills training with inpatient children and adolescents. *Behavior Modification, 3,* 4–31.

HANSEN, J. C. (1984). Interest inventories. In G. Goldstein & M. Hersen (Eds.), *Handbook of psychological assessment* (pp. 157–177). New York: Pergamon Press.

HANSEN, J. C., & CAMPBELL, D. P. (1985). *Manual for the SVIB-SCII* (4th ed.). Palo Alto, CA: Consulting Psychologists Press.

HARBECK, C., PETERSON, L., & STARR, L. (1992). Previously abused child victims' response to a sexual abuse prevention program: A matter of measures. *Behavior Therapy, 23,* 375–388.

HARLEY, J. P., RAY, R. S., TOMASI, L., EICHMAN, P. L., MATTHEWS, C. G., CHUN, R., CLEELAND, C. S., & TRAISMAN, E. (1978). Hyperkinesis and food additives: Testing the Feingold hypothesis. *Pediatrics, 61,* 818–828.

HARPER, R. A. (1959). *Psychoanalysis and psychotherapy: Thirty-six systems.* Englewood Cliffs, NJ: Prentice-Hall.

HARRIS, F. C., & LAHEY, B. B. (1982a). Recording system bias in direct observational methodology: A review and critical analysis of factors causing inaccurate coding behavior. *Clinical Psychology Review, 2,* 539–556.

HARRIS, F. C., & LAHEY, B. B. (1982b). Subject reactivity in direct observational assessment: A review and critical analysis. *Clinical Psychology Review, 2,* 523–538.

HARRIS, J. G. (1980). Nomovalidation and idiovalidation: A quest for the true personality profile. *American Psychologist, 35,* 729–744.

HARRIS, M. J., MILICH, R., JOHNSTON, E. M., & HOOVER, D. W. (1990). Effects of expectancies on children's social interactions. *Journal of Experimental Social Psychology, 26,* 1–12.

HARRIS, V. W., & SHERMAN, J. A. (1973). Effects of peer tutoring and consequences on the math performance of elementary classroom students. *Journal of Applied Behavior Analysis, 6,* 587–598.

HARRIS, W. G. (1987). Computer-based test interpretations: Some developments and application issues. *Applied Psychology: An International Review, 36,* 237–247.

HARRISON, R. (1965). Thematic apperceptive methods. In B. B. Wolman (Ed.), *Handbook of clinical psychology* (pp. 562–620). New York: McGraw-Hill.

HARROWER, M. R. (1945). *Psychodiagnostic inkblots.* New York: Grune & Stratton.

HARROWER, M. R. (1961). *The practice of clinical psychology.* Springfield, IL: Charles C. Thomas.

HARROWER, M. R. (1965). Clinical psychologists at work.

In B. B. Wolman (Ed.), *Handbook of clinical psychology* (pp. 1443–1458). New York: McGraw-Hill.

HARROWER, M. R., & STEINER, M. (1945). *Large scale Rorschach techniques.* Springfield, IL: Charles C. Thomas.

HART, S. N., & BRASSARD, M. R. (1987). A major threat to children's mental health: Psychological maltreatment. *American Psychologist, 42,* 160–165.

HARTMANN, H. (1939). Psychoanalysis and the concept of health. *International Journal of Psychoanalysis, 20,* 308–321.

HARTMANN, H. (1958). *Ego psychology and the problem of adaptation.* New York: International Universities Press.

HARTSHORNE, H., & MAY, M. A. (1928). *Studies in deceit.* New York: Macmillan.

HARTUP, W. W. (1983). Peer relations. In E. M. Hetherington (Ed.), *Handbook of child psychology* (Vol. 4): *Socialization, personality, and social development* (pp. 103–198). New York: John Wiley.

HATHAWAY, S. R. (1958). A study of human behavior: The clinical psychologist. *American Psychologist, 13,* 255–265.

HATHAWAY, S. R., & McKINLEY, J. C. (1967). *The Minnesota Multiphasic Personality Inventory Manual.* New York: Psychological Corporation.

HAUGAARD, J. J., & REPPUCCI, N. D. (1988). *The sexual abuse of children.* San Francisco: Jossey-Bass.

HAYES, S. C. (1983). The role of the individual case in the production and consumption of clinical knowledge. In M. Hersen, A. E. Kazdin, & A. S. Bellack (Eds.), *The clinical psychology handbook* (pp. 181–195). New York: Pergamon Press.

HAYNES, R. B. (1982). Improving patient compliance: An empirical view. In R. B. Stuart (Ed.), *Adherence, compliance, and generalization in behavioral medicine* (pp. 56–78). New York: Brunner/Mazel.

HAYNES, S. G., LEVINE, S., SCOTCH, N., FEINLEIB, M., & KANNEL, W. B. (1978). The relationship of psychosocial factors to coronary heart disease in the Framingham study: I. Methods and risk factors. *American Journal of Epidemiology, 107,* 362–383.

HAYNES, S. N. (1978). *Principles of behavioral assessment.* New York: Gardner Press.

HAYNES, S. N. (1984). Behavioral assessment of adults. In G. Goldstein & M. Hersen (Eds.), *Handbook of psychological assessment* (pp. 369–401). New York: Pergamon Press.

HAYNES, S. N. (1990). Behavioral assessment of adults. In G. Goldstein & M. Hersen (Eds.), *Handbook of psychological assessment* (2nd ed., pp. 423–463). New York: Pergamon Press.

HAYVREN, M., & HYMEL, S. (1984). Ethical issues in sociometric testing: Impact of sociometric measures on interaction behavior. *Developmental Psychology, 20,* 844–849.

Hedges, L. V., & Olkin, L. (1982). Analyses, reanalyses, and meta-analysis. *Contemporary Education Review, 1,* 157–165.

Heidegger, M. (1968). *Being and time* (J. Macquarrie & E. Robinson, Trans.). New York: Harper & Row. (Original work published 1927)

Heinrich, R. L., & Schag, C. C. (1985). Stress and activity management: Group treatment for cancer patients and spouses. *Journal of Consulting and Clinical Psychology, 53,* 439–446.

Heitler, J. B. (1976). Preparatory techniques in initiating expressive psychotherapy with lower-class, unsophisticated patients. *Psychological Bulletin, 83,* 339–352.

Helfer, R. E., & Kempe, C. H. (Eds.). (1968). *The battered child.* Chicago: University of Chicago Press.

Heller, K. (1971). Laboratory interview research as an alogue to treatment. In A. E. Bergin & S. L. Garfield (Eds.), *Handbook of psychotherapy and behavior change* (pp. 126–153). New York: John Wiley.

Heller, K. (1972). Interview structure and interviewer style in initial interviews. In A. W. Siegman & B. Pope (Eds.), *Studies in dyadic communication* (pp. 9–28). New York: Pergamon Press.

Heller, K., Davis, J. D., & Myers, R. A. (1966). The effects of interviewer style in a standardized interview. *Journal of Consulting Psychology, 30,* 501–508.

Heller, K., Holtzman, W., & Messick, S. (Eds.). (1982). *Placing children in special education: A strategy for equity.* Washington, DC: National Academy Press.

Heller, K., Price, R. H., Reinharz, S., Riger, S., & Wandersman, A. (1984). *Psychology and community change* (2nd ed.). Homewood, IL: Dorsey.

Heller, K., Swindle, R. W., Jr., & Dusenbury, L. (1986). Component social support processes: Comments and integration. *Journal of Consulting and Clinical Psychology, 54,* 466–470.

Heller, W. (1990). The neuropsychology of emotion: Developmental patterns and implications for psychopathology. In N. L. Stein, B. L. Leventhal, & T. Trabasso (Eds.), *Psychological and biological approaches to emotion* (pp. 167–211). Hillsdale, NJ: Lawrence Erlbaum Associates.

Heller, W., Hopkins, J., & Cox, S. (1991). Effects of lateralized brain damage on infant socioemotional development. *Journal of Clinical and Experimental Neuropsychology, 13,* 64.

Helmes, E., & Reddon, J. R. (1993). A perspective on developments in assessing psychopathology: A crit-

ical review of the MMPI and MMPI-2. *Psychological Bulletin, 113,* 453–471.

Helzer, J. E. (1983). Standardized interviews in psychiatry. *Psychiatry Developments, 2,* 161–178.

Henry, W. E. (1956). *The analysis of fantasy: The thematic apperception technique in the study of personality.* New York: John Wiley.

Herink, R. (Ed.). (1980). *The psychotherapy handbook: The A to Z guide to more than 250 different therapies in use today.* New York: New American Library.

Hermalin, J. E., & Morell, J. A. (Eds.). (1987). *Prevention planning in mental health.* Newbury Park, CA: Sage.

Hersen, M. (1981). Complex problems require complex solutions. *Behavior Therapy, 12,* 15–29.

Hersen, M., & Turner, S. M. (Eds.). (1985). *Diagnostic interviewing.* New York: Plenum Press.

Heston, L. L. (1966). Psychiatric disorders in foster home reared children of schizophrenic mothers. *British Journal of Psychiatry, 112,* 819–825.

Hetherington, E. M. (1989). Coping with family transitions: Winners, losers, and survivors. *Child Development, 60,* 1–14.

Hetherington, E. M., & Arasteh, J. D. (Eds.). (1988). *Impact of divorce, single parenting, and stepparenting on children.* Hillsdale, NJ: Lawrence Erlbaum Associates.

Hetherington, E. M., Stanley-Hagan, M., & Anderson, E. R. (1989). Marital transitions: A child's perspective. *American Psychologist, 44,* 303–312.

Hewitt, L. E., & Jenkins, R. L. (1946). *Fundamental patterns of maladjustment: The dynamics of their origin.* Springfield: State of Illinois.

Himelein, M. (1988). *Adjustment to victimization by burglary: Cognitive coping and perceptions of support.* Unpublished doctoral dissertation. University of Kentucky, Lexington.

Hodgson, R. J., & Rachman, S. (1977). Obsessional-compulsive complaints. *Behaviour Research and Therapy, 15,* 389–395.

Hoelscher, T. J., Lichstein, K. L., & Rosenthal, T. L. (1986). Home relaxation practice in hypertension treatment: Objective assessment and compliance induction. *Journal of Consulting and Clinical Psychology, 54,* 217–221.

Hoffman, B. (1962). *The tyranny of testing.* New York: Crowell-Collier.

Hoffman, P. J. (1960).The paramorphic representation of clinical judgment. *Psychological Bulletin, 57,* 116–131.

Hoffman, R. S. (1973). The varieties of psychotherapeutic experience. *Journal of Irreproducible Results, 19,* 76–77.

HOGAN, D. B. (1983). The effectiveness of licensing: History, evidence, and recommendations. *Law and Human Behavior, 7,* 117–138.

HOGAN, R., & NICHOLSON, R. A. (1988). The meaning of personality test scores. *American Psychologist, 43,* 621–626.

HOLDER, H. D., & BLOSE, J. D. (1987). Changes in health care costs and utilization associated with mental health treatment. *Hospital and Community Psychiatry, 38,* 1070–1075.

HOLLAND, J. L. (1985). *Self-Directed Search: Professional manual—1985 edition.* Odessa, FL: Psychological Assessment Resources.

HOLLAND, J. L. (1986). New directions for interest testing. In B. S. Plake & J. C. Witt (Eds.), *The future of testing* (pp. 245–267). Hillsdale, NJ: Lawrence Erlbaum Associates.

HOLMES, M. R., HANSEN, D. J., & ST. LAWRENCE, J. S. (1984). Conversational skills training with aftercare patients in the community: Social validation and generalization. *Behavior Therapy, 15,* 84–100.

HOLMES, T. H., & MASUDA, M. (1974). Life change and illness susceptibility. In B. S. Dohrenwend & B. P. Dohrenwend (Eds.), *Stressful life events: Their nature and effects* (pp. 45–72). New York: John Wiley.

HOLROYD, K. A., NASH, J. M., PINGEL, J. D., CORDINGLEY, G. E., & JEROME, A. (1991). A comparison of pharmacological (Amitriptyline HCL) and non-pharmacological (cognitive-behavioral) therapies for chronic tension headaches. *Journal of Consulting and Clinical Psychology, 59,* 387–393.

HOLT, R. R. (1958). Formal aspects of the TAT: A neglected resource. *Journal of Projective Techniques, 22,* 163–172.

HOLT, R. R. (1970). Yet another look at clinical and statistical prediction: Or is clinical psychology worthwhile? *American Psychologist, 25,* 337–349.

HOLT, R. R. (1978). *Methods in clinical psychology: Projective assessment* (Vol. 1). New York: Plenum Press.

HOLT, R. R., & LUBORSKY, L. (1958). *Personality patterns of psychiatrists: A study of methods for selecting residents* (Vol. 1). New York: Basic Books.

HOLTZMAN, W. H., THORPE, J. W., SWARTZ, J. D., & HERRON, E. W. (1961). *Inkblot perception and personality: Holtzman Inkblot Technique.* Austin: University of Texas Press.

HOLTZWORTH-MONROE, A. (1992). Social skill deficits in maritally violent men: Interpreting the data using a social information processing model. *Clinical Psychology Review, 12,* 605–618.

HOROWITZ, L. M., & VITKUS, J. (1986). The interpersonal basis of psychiatric symptoms. *Clinical Psychology Review, 6,* 443–469.

HOSHMAND, L. T., & POLKINGHORNE, D. E. (1992). Redefining the science-practice relationship and professional training. *American Psychologist, 47,* 55–66.

HOUSE, J. S., LANDIS, K. R., & UMBERSON, D. (1988). Social relationships and health. *Science, 241,* 540–545.

HOUSE, J. S., ROBBINS, C., & METZNER, H. L. (1982). The association of social relationships and activities with mortality: Prospective evidence from the Tecumseh Community Health Study. *American Journal of Epidemiology, 116,* 123–140.

HOWARD, A., PION, G. M., GOTTFREDSON, G. D., FLATTAU, P. E., OSKAMP, S., PFAFFLIN, S. M., BRAY, D. W. (1986). The changing face of American psychology: A report from the Committee on Employment and Human Resources. *American Psychologist, 41,* 1311–1327.

HUBER, C. H., & BARUTH, L. G. (1989). *Rational-emotive family therapy.* New York: Springer.

HUBERT, N., WACHS, T. D., PETERS-MARTIN, P., & GANDOUR, M. (1982). The study of early temperament: Measurement and conceptual issues. *Child Development, 53,* 571–600.

HULL, C. L. (1943). *Principles of behavior.* New York: Appleton.

HUMPHREY, L. L., APPLE, R. F., & KIRSCHENBAUM, D. S. (1986). Differentiating bulimic-anorexic from normal families using interpersonal and behavioral observational systems. *Journal of Consulting and Clinical Psychology, 54,* 190–195.

HUNT, W. A., & JONES, N. F. (1962). The experimental investigation of clinical judgment. In A. J. Bachrach (Ed.), *Experimental foundations of clinical psychology* (pp. 26–51). New York: Basic Books.

HUSSERL, E. (1969). *Ideas: General introduction to pure phenomenology.* New York: Humanities Press. (Original work published 1913)

HUTT, C., & HUTT, S. J. (1968). Stereotypy, arousal and autism. *Human Development, 11,* 277–286.

HYND, G. W., SNOW, J., & BECKER, M. G. (1986). Neuropsychological assessment in clinical child psychology. In B. B. Lahey & A. E. Kazdin (Eds.), *Advances in clinical child psychology* (Vol. 9, pp. 35–86). New York: Plenum Press.

INGRAM, R. E. (Ed.). (1986). *Information processing approaches to clinical psychology.* Orlando, FL: Academic Press.

INSTITUTE OF PERSONALITY ASSESSMENT AND RESEARCH. (1970). *Annual report: 1969–1970.* Berkeley: University of California.

INUI, T., YOURTEE, E., & WILLIAMSON, J. (1976). Improved

outcomes in hypertension after physician tutorials. *Annals of Internal Medicine, 84,* 646–651.

Iscoe, I., & Harris, L. C. (1984). Social and community interventions. *Annual Review of Psychology, 35,* 333–360.

Jackson, D. N. (1975). The relative validity of scales prepared by naive item writers and those based on empirical methods of personality scale construction. *Educational and Psychological Measurement, 35,* 361–370.

Jackson, D. N. (1984). *Personality Research Form manual.* Port Huron, MI: Research Psychologists Press.

Jackson, D. N. (1989). *Basic Personality Inventory manual.* Port Huron, MI: Sigma Assessment Systems.

Jackson, D. N., & Messick, S. (1958). Content and style in personality assessment. *Psychological Bulletin, 55,* 243–252.

Jackson, D. N., & Messick, S. (1961). Acquiescence and desirability as response determinants on the MMPI. *Educational and Psychological Measurement, 21,* 771–790.

Jacob, T., & Tennenbaum, D. L. (1988). Family assessment methods. In M. Rutter, A. H. Tuma, & I. S. Lann (Eds.), *Assessment and diagnosis in child psychopathology* (pp. 196–231). New York: Guilford Press.

Jacobs, M. K., & Goodman, G. (1989). Psychology and self-help groups: Predictions on a partnership. *American Psychologist, 44,* 536–545.

Jacobson, N. S., & Gurman, A. S. (Eds.). (1986). *Clinical handbook of marital therapy.* New York: Guilford Press.

Jacobson, N. S., & Truax, P. (1991). Clinical significance: A statistical approach to defining meaningful change in psychotherapy research. *Journal of Consulting and Clinical Psychology, 59,* 12–19.

Jacoby, L. L., & Kelley, C. M. (1987). Unconscious influences of memory for a prior event. *Personality and Social Psychology Bulletin, 13,* 314–336.

Jansson, L., & Ost, L. G. (1982). Behavioral treatments for agoraphobia: An evaluative review. *Clinical Psychology Review, 2,* 311–336.

Jarrett, R. B., & Fairbank, J. A. (1987). Psychologists' views: APA's advocacy of and resource expenditure on social and professional issues. *Professional Psychology, 18,* 643–646.

Jeffery, R. W. (1988). Dietary risk factors and their modification in cardiovascular disease. *Journal of Consulting and Clinical Psychology, 56,* 350–357.

Jemmott, J. B., & Locke, S. E. (1984). Psychosocial factors, immunologic mediation, and human suscepti-bility to infectious diseases: How much do we know? *Psychological Bulletin, 95,* 52–77.

Jemmott, J. B., & Magloire, K. (1988). Academic stress, social support, and secretory immunoglobulin A. *Journal of Personality and Social Psychology, 55,* 803–810.

Jenkins, C. D., Zyzanski, S. J., & Rosenman, R. H. (1971). Progress toward validation of a computer-scored test for the Type A coronary-prone behavior pattern. *Psychosomatic Medicine, 33,* 193–202.

Jensen, J. P., Bergin, A. E., & Greaves, D. W. (1990). The meaning of eclecticism: New survey and analysis of components. *Professional Psychology: Research and Practice, 21,* 124–130.

Johansson, C. B. (1982). *Manual for Career Assessment Inventory* (2nd ed.). Minneapolis: National Computer Systems.

Johnson, J. E. (1984). Psychological interventions and coping with surgery. In A. Baum, S. E. Taylor, & J. E. Singer (Eds.), *Handbook of psychology and health: Vol. 4. Social psychological aspects of health* (pp. 167–187). Hillsdale, NJ: Lawrence Erlbaum Associates.

Johnson, J. H., Rasbury, W. G., & Siegel, L. J. (1986). *Approaches to child treatment: Introduction to theory, research, and practice.* New York: Pergamon Press.

Johnson, M. L. (1953). Seeing's believing. *New Biology, 15,* 60–80.

Johnson, S. M., & Bolstad, O. D. (1973). Methodological issues in naturalistic observation: Some problems and solutions for field research. In L. A. Hamerlynck, L. C. Handy, & E. J. Mash (Eds.), *Behavior change: Methodology, concepts and practice* (pp. 7–67). Champaign, IL: Research Press.

Johnson, S. M., & Lobitz, G. K. (1974). Parental manipulation of child behavior in home observations. *Journal of Applied Behavior Analysis, 7,* 23–32.

Jones, B. P., & Butters, N. (1983). Neuropsychological assessment. In M. Hersen, A. E. Kazdin, & A. S. Bellack (Eds.), *The clinical psychology handbook* (pp. 377–396). New York: Pergamon Press.

Jones, E. (1953, 1955, 1957). *The life and work of Sigmund Freud* (Vols. 1–3). New York: Basic Books.

Jones, E. E., Cumming, J. D., & Horowitz, M. J. (1988). Another look at the nonspecific hypothesis of therapeutic effectiveness. *Journal of Consulting and Clinical Psychology, 56,* 48–55.

Jones, H. E. (1943). *Development in adolescence.* New York: Appleton-Century.

Jones, M. C. (1924a). The elimination of children's fears. *Journal of Experimental Psychology, 7,* 382–390.

JONES, M. C. (1924b). A laboratory study of fear: The case of Peter. *Pedagogical Seminary and Journal of Genetic Psychology, 31,* 308–315.

JONES, R. R., REID, J. B., & PATTERSON, G. R. (1975). Naturalistic observation in clinical assessment. In P. McReynolds (Ed.), *Advances in psychological assessment* (Vol. 3, pp. 42–95). San Francisco: Jossey-Bass.

JOURILES, E. N., & FARRIS, A. M. (1992). Effects of marital conflict on subsequent parent–child interactions. *Behavior Therapy, 23,* 355–374.

JOURILES, E. N., & O'LEARY, K. D. (1985). Interspousal reliability of reports of marital violence. *Journal of Consulting and Clinical Psychology, 53,* 419–421.

JULIEN, R. M. (1988). *Drugs and the body.* New York: Freeman.

KAGAN, J. (1989). Temperamental contributions to social behavior. *American Psychologist, 44,* 668–674.

KAGAN, N. (1974). Influencing human interaction—Eleven years with IPR. In B. A. Jacobs, R. K. Buschman, R. F. Dency, D. T. Schaeffer, & J. Stieber (Eds.), *Counselor training* (pp. 329–346). Arlington, VA: National Drug Abuse Training Center.

KAHN, E. (1985). Heinz Kohut and Carl Rogers: A timely comparison. *American Psychologist, 40,* 893–904.

KAHN, T. C. (1955). Personality projection on culturally structured symbols. *Journal of Projective Techniques, 19,* 431–442.

KAHNEMAN, D., & TVERSKY, A. (1979). Intuitive prediction: Biases and corrective procedures. *TIMS Studies in the Management Sciences, 12,* 313–327.

KANDEL, E. P., SCHWARTZ, J. H., & JESSELL, T. M. (1991). *Principles of neural science.* Norwalk, CT: Appleton & Lange.

KANFER, F. H. (1968). Verbal conditioning: A review of its current status. In T. R. Dixon & D. L. Horton (Eds.), *Verbal behavior and general behavior theory* (pp. 245–290). Englewood Cliffs, NJ: Prentice-Hall.

KANFER, F. H., & GAELICK, L. (1986). Self-management methods. In F. H. Kanfer & A. P. Goldstein (Eds.), *Helping people change: A textbook of methods* (3rd ed., pp. 283–345). New York: Pergamon Press.

KANFER, F. H., & McBREARTY, J. F. (1962). Minimal social reinforcement and interview content. *Journal of Clinical Psychology, 18,* 210–215.

KANFER, F. H., & SASLOW, G. (1969). Behavioral diagnosis. In C. M. Franks (Ed.), *Behavior therapy: Appraisal and status* (pp. 210–215). New York: McGraw-Hill.

KANNER, A. D., COYNE, J. C., SCHAEFER, C., & LAZARUS, R. S. (1981). Comparison of two modes of stress measurement: Daily hassles and uplifts versus major life events. *Journal of Behavioral Medicine, 14,* 1–39.

KANNER, L. (1943). Autistic disturbances of affective contact. *Nervous Child, 2,* 217–250.

KAPLAN, A. (1964). *The conduct of inquiry.* San Francisco: Chander.

KAPLAN, M. (1983). A woman's view of DSM-III. *American Psychologist, 38,* 786–792.

KAPLAN, R. M. (1990). Behavior as the central outcome in health care. *American Psychologist, 45,* 1211–1220.

KASLOW, N. J., & REHM, L. P. (1985). Conceptualization, assessment, and treatment of depression in children. In P. H. Bornstein & A. E. Kazdin (Eds.), *Handbook of clinical behavior therapy with children* (pp. 599–657). Homewood, IL: Dorsey Press.

KASLOW, N. J., REHM, L. P., & SIEGEL, A. W. (1984). Social and cognitive correlates of depression in children: A developmental perspective. *Journal of Abnormal Child Psychology, 12,* 605–620.

KAUFMAN, A. S. (1990). *Assessing adolescent and adult intelligence.* Boston: Allyn & Bacon.

KAUFMAN, A. S., & HARRISON, P. L. (1991). Individual intellectual assessment. In C. E. Walker (Ed.), *Clinical psychology: Historical and research foundations* (pp. 91–120). New York: Plenum Press.

KAUFMAN, A. S., & KAUFMAN, N. L. (1983). *KABC: Kaufman Assessment Battery for Children.* Circle Pines, MN: American Guidance Service.

KAUFMAN, A. S., & KAUFMAN, N. L. (1985). *Kaufman Test of Educational Achievement.* Circle Pines, MN: American Guidance Service.

KAUFMAN, J., & ZIGLER, E. (1987). Do abused children become abusive parents? *American Journal of Orthopsychiatry, 57,* 186–192.

KAZDIN, A. E. (1972). Response cost: The removal of conditioned reinforcers for therapeutic change. *Behavior Therapy, 3,* 533–546.

KAZDIN, A. E. (1973). Covert modeling and reduction of avoidance behavior. *Journal of Abnormal Psychology, 81,* 87–95.

KAZDIN, A. E. (1974). Self-monitoring and behavior change. In M. J. Mahoney & C. E. Thoresen (Eds.), *Self-control: Power to the person* (pp. 218–246). Monterey, CA: Brooks/Cole.

KAZDIN, A. E. (1978). *History of behavior modification: Experimental foundations of contemporary research.* Baltimore, MD: University Park Press.

KAZDIN, A. E. (1982a). *Single-case research designs: Methods for clinical and applied settings.* New York: Oxford University Press.

KAZDIN, A. E. (1982b). Single-case experimental designs. In P. C. Kendall & J. N. Butcher (Eds.), *Handbook of research methods in clinical psychology* (pp. 461–490). New York: John Wiley.

KAZDIN, A. E. (1984). *Behavior modification in applied settings* (3rd ed.). Homewood, IL: Dorsey Press.

KAZDIN, A. E. (1985). *Treatment of antisocial behavior in children and adolescents.* Homewood, IL: Dorsey Press.

KAZDIN, A. E. (1989). Developmental psychopathology: Current research, issues, and directions. *American Psychologist, 44,* 180–187.

KAZDIN, A. E. (1993). Evaluation in clinical practice: Clinically sensitive and systematic methods of treatment delivery. *Behavior Therapy, 24,* 11–45.

KAZDIN, A. E., BASS, D., SIEGEL, T., & THOMAS, C. (1989). Cognitive-behavioral therapy and relationship therapy in the treatment of children referred for antisocial behavior. *Journal of Consulting and Clinical Psychology, 57,* 522–535.

KAZDIN, A. E., ESVELDT-DAWSON, K., FRENCH, N. H., & UNIS, A. S. (1987). Problem-solving skills training and relationship therapy in the treatment of antisocial child behavior. *Journal of Consulting and Clinical Psychology, 55,* 76–85.

KAZDIN, A. E., ESVELDT-DAWSON, K., & MATSON, J. L. (1983). The effects of instructional set on social skills performance among psychiatric inpatient children. *Behavior Therapy, 14,* 413–423.

KAZDIN, A. E., ESVELDT-DAWSON, K., SHERICK, R. B., & COLBUS, D. (1985). Assessment of overt behavior and childhood depression among psychiatrically disturbed children. *Journal of Consulting and Clinical Psychology, 53,* 201–210.

KAZDIN, A. E., & KOPEL, S. A. (1975). On resolving ambiguities of the multiple baseline design: Problems and recommendations. *Behavior Therapy, 6,* 601–608.

KAZDIN, A. E., MATSON, J. L., & ESVELDT-DAWSON, K. (1984). The relationship of role-play assessment of children's social skills to multiple measures of social competence. *Behaviour Research and Therapy, 22,* 129–140.

KAZDIN, A. E., & WILCOXON, L. A. (1976). Systematic desensitization and nonspecific treatment effects: A methodological evaluation. *Psychological Bulletin, 83,* 729–758.

KAZDIN, A. E., & WILSON, G. T. (1978). *Evaluation of behavior therapy: Issues, evidence and research strategies.* Cambridge, MA: Ballinger.

KEEFE, F. J., DUNSMORE, J., & BURNETT, R. (1992). Behavioral and cognitive-behavioral approaches to chronic pain: Recent advances and future directions. *Journal of Consulting and Clinical Psychology, 60,* 528–536.

KEITH-SPIEGEL, P. C., & KOOCHER, G. (1985). *Ethics in psychology: Professional standards and cases.* New York: Random House.

KELLY, E. L. (1961). Clinical psychology—1960: A report of survey findings. *Newsletter, Division of Clinical Psychology of APA, 14,* 1–11.

KELLY, E. L., & FISKE, D. W. (1951). *The prediction of performance in clinical psychology.* Ann Arbor: University of Michigan Press.

KELLY, G. A. (1955). *The psychology of personal constructs.* New York: W. W. Norton.

KELLY, G. A. (1958). The theory and technique of assessment. *Annual review of psychology* (Vol. 9, pp. 323–352). Palo Alto, CA: Annual Review.

KELLY, J. A. (1982). *Social skills training: A practical guide for interventions.* New York: Springer.

KELLY, J. A., & MURPHY, D. A. (1992). Psychological interventions with AIDS and HIV: Prevention and treatment. *Journal of Consulting and Clinical Psychology, 60,* 576–585.

KEMPLER, W. (1973). Gestalt therapy. In R. Corsini (Ed.), *Current psychotherapies* (pp. 251–286). Itasca, IL: F. E. Peacock.

KENDALL, P. C. (1984). Behavioral assessment and methodology. In G. T. Wilson, C. M. Franks, K. D. Brownell, & P. C. Kendall (Eds.), *Annual Review of Behavior Therapy* (Vol. 9, pp. 123–163). New York: Guilford Press.

KENDALL, P. C., & BRASWELL, L. (1985). *Cognitive behavioral modification with impulsive children.* New York: Guilford Press.

KENDALL, P. C., & INGRAM, R. E. (1989). Cognitive-behavioral perspectives: Theory and research on depression and anxiety. In P. C. Kendall & D. Watson (Eds.), *Anxiety and depression: Distinctive and overlapping features* (pp. 27–53). San Diego, CA: Academic Press.

KENDALL, P. C., & ZUPAN, B. A. (1981). Individual versus group application of cognitive-behavioral self-control procedures with children. *Behavior Therapy, 12,* 344–359.

KENT, R. N., & FOSTER, S. L. (1977). Direct observational procedures: Methodological issues in naturalistic settings. In A. R. Ciminero, K. S. Calhoun, & H. E. Adams (Eds.), *Handbook of behavioral assessment* (pp. 279–328). New York: John Wiley.

KERN, J. M. (1982). The comparative external and concurrent validity of three role-plays for assessing heterosocial performance. *Behavior Therapy, 13,* 666–680.

KERN, J. M. (1991). An evaluation of a novel role-play methodology: The standardized idiographic approach. *Behavior Therapy, 22,* 13–30.

KERN, J. M., CAVELL, T. A., & BECK, B. (1985). Predicting

differential reactions to males' versus females' assertions, empathic-assertions, and non-assertions. *Behavior Therapy, 16,* 63–75.

KERNBERG, O. (1976). *Object relations, theory and clinical psychoanalysis.* New York: Jason Aronson.

KESSLER, R. C., PRICE, R. H., & WORTMAN, C. B. (1985). Social factors in psychopathology: Stress, social support, and coping processes. *Annual Review of Psychology, 36,* 531–572.

KETY, S. S., ROSENTHAL, D., WENDER, P. H., & SCHULSINGER, F. (1968). The types and prevalence of mental illness in the biological and adoptive families of adopted schizophrenics. In D. Rosenthal & S. S. Kety (Eds.), *The transmission of schizophrenia* (pp. 345–362). Oxford: Pergamon Press.

KIECOLT-GLASER, J. K., & GLASER, R. (1992). Psychoneuroimmunology: Can psychological interventions modulate immunity? *Journal of Consulting and Clinical Psychology, 60,* 569–575.

KIESLER, C. A., & MORTON, T. (1989). Keeping an open mind: A rejoinder. *American Psychologist, 44,* 1239–1241.

KIESLER, D. J. (1983). The 1982 Interpersonal Circle: A taxonomy for complementarity in human transactions. *Psychological Review, 90,* 185–214.

KIESLER, D. J. (1986a). The 1982 interpersonal circle: An analysis of DSM-III personality disorders. In T. Millon & G. L. Klerman (Eds.), *Contemporary directions in psychopathology: Towards the DSM-IV* (pp. 571–597). New York: Guilford Press.

KIESLER, D. J. (1986b). Interpersonal methods of diagnosis and treatment. In J. O. Cavenar, Jr. (Ed.), *Psychiatry* (Vol. 1, pp. 1–23). Philadelphia: Lippincott.

KIESLER, D. J. (1987a). *Check List of Psychotherapy Transactions-Revised (CLOPT-R) and Check List of Interpersonal Transactions-Revised (CLOIT).* Richmond: Virginia Commonwealth University.

KIESLER, D. J. (1987b). *Research manual for the Impact Message Inventory.* Palo Alto, CA: Consulting Psychologists Press.

KIESLER, D. J. (1988). *Therapeutic metacommunication: Therapist impact disclosure as feedback in psychotherapy.* Palo Alto, CA: Consulting Psychologists Press.

KIESLER, D. J. (1991). Interpersonal methods of assessment and diagnosis. In C. R. Snyder & D. R. Forsyth (Eds.), *Handbook of social and clinical psychology: The health perspective* (pp. 438–468). Elmsford, NY: Pergamon Press.

KIESLER, D. J., ANCHIN, J. C., PERKINS, M. J., CHIRICO, B. M., KYLE, E. M., & FEDERMAN, E. J. (1985). *The Impact Message Inventory: Form II.* Palo Alto, CA: Consulting Psychologists Press.

KILBURG, R. R. (1984). Psychologists in management: The unseen career path in psychology. *Professional Psychology: Research and Practice, 15,* 613–625.

KIMURA, D. (1961). Cerebral dominance and the perception of verbal stimuli. *Canadian Journal of Psychology, 15,* 166–171.

KIMURA, D. (1966). Dual functional asymmetry of the brain in visual perception. *Neuropsychologia, 4,* 275–285.

KIMURA, D. (1967). Functional asymmetry of the brain in dichotic listening. *Cortex, 3,* 163–178.

KIRCHNER, E. P., & DRAGUNS, J. G. (1979). Assertion and aggression in adult offenders. *Behavior Therapy, 10,* 452–471.

KLEIN, D. F., ZITRIN, C. M., WOERNER, M. G., & ROSS, D. C. (1983). Treatment of phobias: Behavior therapy and supportive psychotherapy: Are there any special ingredients? *Archives of General Psychiatry, 40,* 139–145.

KLEIN, M. (1960). *The psychoanalysis of children.* New York: Grove Press.

KLEIN, M. (1975). *The writings of Melanie Klein* (Vol. III). London: Hogarth Press.

KLEIN, R. H. (1983). Group treatment approaches. In M. Hersen, A. E. Kazdin, & A. S. Bellack (Eds.), *The clinical psychology handbook* (pp. 593–610). New York: Pergamon Press.

KLEINKNECHT, R. A., & BERNSTEIN, D. A. (1978). Assessment of dental fear. *Behavior Therapy, 9,* 626–634.

KLEINMUNTZ, B. (1963). MMPI decision rules for the identification of college maladjustment: A digital computer approach. *Psychological Monographs, 77* (14, Whole No. 477).

KLEINMUNTZ, B. (1969). Personality test interpretation by computer and clinician. In J. N. Butcher (Ed.), *MMPI: Research developments and clinical applications* (pp. 97–104). New York: John Wiley.

KLEINMUNTZ, B. (1982). *Personality and psychological assessment.* New York: St. Martin's Press.

KLEINMUNTZ, B. (1984). The scientific study of clinical judgment in psychology and medicine. *Clinical Psychology Review, 4,* 111–126.

KLOPFER, B., & KELLEY, D. M. (1937). The techniques of the Rorschach performance. *Rorschach Research Exchange, 2,* 1–14.

KLOPFER, B., & KELLEY, D. M. (1942). *The Rorschach technique.* New York: Harcourt, Brace & World.

KLOPFER, W. G. (1960). *The psychological report.* New York: Grune & Stratton.

KLOPFER, W. G. (1983). Writing psychological reports. In C. E. Walker (Ed.), *The handbook of clinical psychology* (Vol. 1, pp. 501–527). Homewood, IL: Dow Jones-Irwin.

Koffka, K. (1935). *Principles of Gestalt psychology.* New York: Harcourt, Brace.

Kohler, W. (1925). *The mentality of apes.* New York: Harcourt, Brace.

Kohout, J., & Wicherski, M. (1991). *1989 doctorate employment survey.* Washington, DC: American Psychological Association.

Kohout, J., Wicherski, M., & Pion, G. (1991). *1988–89 characteristics of graduate departments of psychology.* Washington, DC: American Psychological Association.

Kohut, H. (1971). *The analysis of self.* New York: International Universities Press.

Kohut, H. (1977). *The restoration of the self.* New York: International Universities Press.

Kohut, H. (1983). Selected problems of self-psychological theory. In J. D. Lichtenberg & S. Kaplan (Eds.), *Reflections on self psychology* (pp. 387–416). Hillsdale, NJ: Lawrence Erlbaum Associates.

Kolb, B., & Whishaw, I. Q. (1990). *Fundamentals of neuropsychology* (3rd ed.). New York: Freeman.

Kolotkin, R. H. (1980). Situation specificity in the assessment of assertion: Considerations for the measurement of training and transfer. *Behavior Therapy, 11,* 651–661.

Koppitz, E. M. (1968). *Psychological evaluation of children's human figure drawings.* New York: Grune & Stratton.

Korchin, S. J. (1976). *Modern clinical psychology: Principles of intervention in the clinic and community.* New York: Basic Books.

Koriat, A., Lichtenstein, S., & Fischhoff, B. (1980). Reasons for confidence. *Journal of Experimental Psychology: Human Learning and Memory, 6,* 107–118.

Korman, M. (1974). National conference on levels and patterns of professional training in psychology: The major themes. *American Psychologist, 29,* 441–449.

Korman, M. (Ed.). (1976). *Levels and patterns of professional training in psychology.* Washington, DC: American Psychological Association.

Korsch, B. M., & Negrete, V. F. (1972). Doctor-patient communication. *Scientific American, 227,* 66–74.

Kostlan, A. (1954). A method for the empirical study of psychodiagnosis. *Journal of Consulting Psychology, 18,* 83–88.

Kovacs, M., Rush, A. J., Beck, A. T., & Hollon, S. D. (1981). Depressed outpatients treated with cognitive therapy or pharmacotherapy: A one-year follow-up. *Archives of General Psychiatry, 38,* 33–39.

Kraemer, H. C. (1981). Coping strategies in psychiatric clinical research. *Journal of Consulting and Clinical Psychology, 49,* 309–319.

Kraemer, H. C., & Thiemann, S. (1989). A strategy to use soft data effectively in randomized controlled clinical trials. *Journal of Consulting and Clinical Psychology, 57,* 148–154.

Krantz, D. S., Grunberg, N. E., & Baum, A. (1985). Health psychology. *Annual Review of Psychology, 36,* 349–383.

Krasner, L. (1965). Verbal conditioning and psychotherapy. In L. Krasner & L. P. Ullmann (Eds.), *Research in behavior modification: New developments and implications* (pp. 211–228). New York: Holt, Rinehart & Winston.

Krasner, L., & Ullmann, L. P. (Eds.). (1965). *Research in behavior modification: New developments and implications.* New York: Holt, Rinehart & Winston.

Krasner, L., & Ullmann, L. P. (1973). *Behavior influence and personality.* New York: Holt, Rinehart & Winston.

Kratochwill, T. R., Mott, S. E., & Dodson, C. L. (1984). Case study and single-case research in clinical and applied psychology. In A. S. Bellack & M. Hersen (Eds.), *Research methods in clinical psychology* (pp. 55–99). New York: Pergamon Press.

Krehbiel, G., & Milich, R. (1986). Issues in the assessment and treatment of socially rejected children. In R. J. Prinz (Ed.), *Advances in behavioral assessment of children and families* (Vol. 2, pp. 249–270). Greenwich, CT: JAI Press.

Kroger, R. O., & Turnbull, W. (1975). Invalidity of validity scales: The case of the MMPI. *Journal of Consulting and Clinical Psychology, 43,* 48–55.

Kutash, S. B. (1976). Modified psychoanalytic therapies. In B. B. Wolman (Ed.), *The therapist's handbook* (pp. 87–116). New York: Van Nostrand Reinhold.

L'Abate, L. (1969). Introduction. In L. L'Abate (Ed.), *Models of clinical psychology.* Research paper number 22. Atlanta: Georgia State College.

La Greca, A. M. (1990). Issues and perspectives on the child assessment process. In A. M. La Greca (Ed.), *Through the eyes of the child* (pp. 3–17). Boston, MA: Allyn & Bacon.

La Greca, A. M., Dandes, S. K., Wick, P., Shaw, K., & Stone, W. L. (1988). Development of the Social Anxiety Scale for Children: Reliability and concurrent validity. *Journal of Clinical Child Psychology, 17,* 84–91.

Laing, R. D. (1967). *The politics of experience.* New York: Pantheon.

Lamb, H. R., & Zusman, J. (1981). Primary prevention in perspective. *American Journal of Psychiatry, 9,* 1–26.

Lambert, D. (1985). *Political and economic determi-*

nants of mental health regulations. Unpublished doctoral dissertation, Brandeis University.

LAMBERT, M. J., SHAPIRO, D. A., & BERGIN, A. E. (1986). The effectiveness of psychotherapy. In S. L. Garfield & A. E. Bergin (Eds.), *Handbook of psychotherapy and behavior change* (3rd ed., pp. 157–211). New York: John Wiley.

LAMBERT, N. M. (1981). Psychological evidence in Larry P. v. Wilson Riles: An evaluation by a witness for the defense. *American Psychologist, 36,* 937–952.

LAMBERT, N. M., COX, H. W., & HARTSOUGH, C. S. (1970). The observability of intellectual functioning of first graders. *Psychology in the Schools,* 74–85.

LAMIELL, J. T., & TRIERWEILER, S. J. (1986). Personality measurement and intuitive personality judgments from an idiothetic point of view. *Clinical Psychology Review, 6,* 471–491.

LANDAU, S., & MILICH, R. (1990). Assessment of children's social status and peer relations. In A. M. La Greca (Ed.), *Through the eyes of the child* (pp. 259–291). Boston: Allyn & Bacon.

LANDMAN, J. T., & DAWES, R. (1982). Experimental outcome: Smith and Glass' conclusions stand up under scrutiny. *American Psychologist, 37,* 504–516.

LANG, A. R., PELHAM, W. E., JOHNSTON, C., & GELERNTER, S. (1989). Levels of adult alcohol consumption induced by interactions with child confederates exhibiting normal versus externalizing behaviors. *Journal of Abnormal Psychology, 98,* 294–299.

LANG, P. J., & LAZOVIK, A. D. (1963). Experimental desensitization of a phobia. *Journal of Abnormal and Social Psychology, 66,* 519–525.

LANGER, E. J., & ABELSON, R. (1974). A patient by any name: Clinician group differences in labeling bias. *Journal of Consulting and Clinical Psychology, 42,* 4–9.

LANYON, B. P., & LANYON, R. I. (1980). *Incomplete sentences task: Manual.* Chicago: Stoelting.

LANYON, R. I. (1984). Personality assessment. *Annual Review of Psychology, 35,* 667–701.

LANYON, R. I., & GOODSTEIN, L. D. (1982). *Personality assessment* (2nd ed.). New York: John Wiley.

LAPOUSE, R., & MONK, M. A. (1958). An epidemiologic study of behavior characteristics in children. *American Journal of Public Health, 48,* 1134–1140.

LAST, C. G., & FRANCIS, G. (1988). School phobia. In B. B. Lahey & A. E. Kazdin (Eds.), *Advances in clinical child psychology* (Vol. 11, pp. 193–222). New York: Plenum Press.

LAST, C. G., & HERSEN, M. (Eds.). (1987). *Issues of diagnostic research.* New York: Plenum Press.

LAURENT, J., SWERDLIK, M., & RYBURN, M. (1992). Review of validity research on the Stanford-Binet Intelli-

gence Scale: Fourth Edition. *Psychological Assessment, 4,* 102–112.

LAWLIS, G. F. (1971). Response styles of a patient population on the Fear Survey Schedule. *Behaviour Research and Therapy, 9,* 95–102.

LAZARUS, A. A. (1976). *Multimodal behavior therapy.* New York: Springer.

LAZARUS, A. A. (1977). Has behavior therapy outlived its usefulness? *American Psychologist, 32,* 550–554.

LAZARUS, A. A. (1981). *The practice of multimodal therapy.* New York: McGraw-Hill.

LAZARUS, A. A. (1985). *Casebook of multimodal therapy.* New York: Guilford Press.

LAZARUS, R. S. (1993). From psychological stress to the emotions: A history of changing outlooks. *Annual Review of Psychology, 44,* 1–21.

LEAHEY, T. H. (1987). *A history of psychology* (2nd ed.). Englewood Cliffs, NJ: Prentice Hall.

LEAHEY, T. H., & HARRIS, R. J. (1989). *Human learning* (2nd ed.). Englewood Cliffs, NJ: Prentice Hall.

LEARY, T. (1957). *Interpersonal diagnosis of personality. A functional theory and methodology for personality evaluation.* New York: Ronald Press.

LEARY, T., & GILL, M. (1959). The dimensions and a measure of the process of psychotherapy: A system for the analysis of the content of clinical evaluations and patient-therapist verbalizations. In E. A. Rubinstein & M. B. Parloff (Eds.), *Research in psychotherapy* (Vol. 1, pp. 62–95). Washington, DC: American Psychological Association.

LEDERER, W. J., & JACKSON, D. D. (1968). *The mirages of marriage.* New York: W. W. Norton.

LEDVINKA, J. (1971). Race of interviewer and the language elaboration of black interviewees. *Journal of Social Issues, 27,* 185–197.

LEDWIDGE, B. (1978). Cognitive behavior modification: A step in the wrong direction? *Psychological Bulletin, 85,* 353–375.

LEE, S. D., & TEMERLIN, M. K. (1970). Social class, diagnosis, and prognosis for psychotherapy. *Psychotherapy: Theory, Research, and Practice, 7,* 181–185.

LEFKOWITZ, M. M., & BURTON, N. (1978). Childhood depression: A critique of the concept. *Psychological Bulletin, 85,* 716–726.

LEHRER, P. M., SARGUNARAJ, D., & HOCHRON, S. (1992). Psychological approaches to the treatment of asthma. *Journal of Consulting and Clinical Psychology, 60,* 639–643.

LEHRER, P. M., & WOOLFOLK, R. L. (1982). Self-report assessment of anxiety: Somatic, cognitive, and behavioral modalities. *Behavioral Assessment, 4,* 167–177.

LEITENBERG, H., AGRAS, W. S., BARLOW, D. H., & OLIVEAU, D. C. (1969). Contribution of selective positive reinforcement and therapeutic instructions to systematic desensitization therapy. *Journal of Abnormal Psychology, 74,* 113–118.

LEITENBERG, H., & ROSEN, J. C. (1988). Cognitive-behavioral treatment of bulimia nervosa. In M. Hersen, R. M. Eisler, & P. M. Miller (Eds.), *Progress in behavior modification* (Vol. 23, pp. 11–35). Newbury Park, CA: Sage.

LENNARD, H. L., & BERNSTEIN, A. (1960). *The anatomy of psychotherapy: Systems of communication and expectation.* New York: Columbia University Press.

LENROW, P., & COWDEN, P. (1980). Human services, professionals, and the paradox of institutional reform. *American Journal of Community Psychology, 8,* 463–484.

LESHER, E. L., & WHELIHAN, M. (1986). Reliability of mental status instruments administered to nursing home residents. *Journal of Consulting and Clinical Psychology, 54,* 726–727.

LEVENBERG, S. B. (1975). Professional training, psychodiagnostic skill, and kinetic family drawings. *Journal of Personality Assessment, 39,* 389–393.

LEVENSON, R. W., & GOTTMAN, J. M. (1983). Marital interaction: Physiological linkage and affective exchange. *Journal of Personality and Social Psychology, 45,* 587–597.

LEVINE, F. J. (1985). Self-psychology and the new narcissism in psychoanalysis. *Clinical Psychology Review, 5,* 215–230.

LEVY, J., TREVARTHEN, C., & SPERRY, R. W. (1972). Perception of bilateral chimeric figures following hemispheric deconnection. *Brain, 95,* 61–78.

LEVY, L. H. (1963). *Psychological interpretation.* New York: Holt, Rinehart & Winston.

LEVY, L. H. (1984). The metamorphosis of clinical psychology: Toward a new charter as human services psychology. *American Psychologist, 39,* 486–494.

LEWINSOHN, P. M., & SHAFFER, M. (1971). Use of home observations as an integral part of the treatment of depression: Preliminary report and case studies. *Journal of Consulting and Clinical Psychology, 37,* 87–94.

LEY, P., BRADSHAW, P. W., EAVES, D. E., & WALKER, C. M. (1973). A method for increasing patient recall of information presented to them. *Psychological Medicine, 3,* 217–220.

LEZAK, M. D. (1983). *Neuropsychological assessment* (2nd ed.). New York: Oxford University Press.

LIBET, J. M., & LEWINSOHN, P. M. (1973). Concept of social skill with special reference to the behavior of depressed persons. *Journal of Consulting and Clinical Psychology, 40,* 304–312.

LICHT, B. G., & KISTNER, J. A. (1986). Motivational problems of learning-disabled children: Individual differences and their implications for treatment. In J. K. Torgesen & B. Y. L. Wong (Eds.), *Psychological and educational perspectives on learning disabilities* (pp. 225–255). New York: Academic Press.

LICHTENSTEIN, E., & GLASGOW, R. E. (1992). Smoking cessation: What have we learned over the past decade? *Journal of Consulting and Clinical Psychology, 60,* 518–527.

LIDZ, R. W., & LIDZ, T. (1949). The family environment of schizophrenic patients. *American Journal of Psychiatry, 106,* 332–345.

LIEBERT, R. M., & SPIEGLER, M. D. (1990). *Personality: Strategies and issues* (6th ed.). Homewood, IL: Dorsey Press.

LINDEMANN, E. (1944). Symptomology and management of acute grief. *American Journal of Psychology, 101,* 141–148.

LINDEMANN, J. E., & MATARAZZO, J. D. (1990). Assessment of adult intelligence. In G. Goldstein & M. Hersen (Eds.), *Handbook of psychological assessment* (2nd ed., pp. 79–101). New York: Pergamon Press.

LINDESMITH, A. R., & STRAUSS, A. (1950). A critique of culture-personality writings. *American Sociological Review, 15,* 587–600.

LINDNER, R. (1954). *The fifty minute hour.* New York: Rinehart.

LINDSLEY, O. R., SKINNER, B. F., & SOLOMON, H. C. (1953). *Studies in behavior therapy. Status report 1.* Waltham, MA: Metropolitan State Hospital.

LINDZEY, G. (1952). The thematic apperception test: Interpretive assumptions and related empirical evidence. *Psychological Bulletin, 49,* 1–25.

LINDZEY, G. (1961). *Projective techniques and cross-cultural research.* New York: Appleton-Century-Crofts.

LINDZEY, G., BRADFORD, J., TEJESSY, C., & DAVIDS, A. (1959). Thematic apperception test: An interpretive lexicon. *Journal of Clinical Psychology Monograph Supplement,* No. 12.

LINEHAN, M. M. (1984). *Dialectical behavior therapy for treatment of parasuicidal women: Treatment manual.* Seattle: University of Washington, Psychology Department.

LINEHAN, M. M. (1987). Dialectical behavior therapy for borderline personality disorder: Theory and method. *Bulletin of the Menninger Clinic, 51,* 261–276.

LINEHAN, M. M., & NIELSEN, S. L. (1983). Social desirability: Its relevance to the measurement of hopelessness and suicidal behavior. *Journal of Consulting and Clinical Psychology, 51,* 141–143.

LIPINSKI, D. P., BLACK, J. L., NELSON, R. O., & CIMINERO, A. R. (1975). The influence of motivational variables on the reactivity and reliability of self-recording. *Journal of Consulting and Clinical Psychology, 43,* 637–646.

LIPTON, D. N., McDONEL, B. C., & McFALL, R. M. (1987). Heterosexual perception in rapists. *Journal of Consulting and Clinical Psychology, 55,* 17–21.

LITTLE, K. B., & SHNEIDMAN, E. S. (1959). Congruences among interpretations of psychological test and anamnestic data. *Psychological Monographs, 73* (Whole No. 476).

LITTLE, L. M., & CURRAN, J. P. (1978). Covert sensitization: A clinical procedure in need of some explanation. *Psychological Bulletin, 85,* 513–531.

LITTLE, L. M., & KELLEY, M. L. (1989). The efficacy of response cost procedures for reducing children's noncompliance to parental instructions. *Behavior Therapy, 20,* 525–534.

LOCHMAN, J. E. (1992). Cognitive-behavioral intervention with aggressive boys: Three-year follow-up and preventive effects. *Journal of Consulting and Clinical Psychology, 60,* 426–432.

LORION, R. P. (1991). Prevention and public health: Psychology's response to the nation's health care crisis. *American Psychologist, 46,* 516–519.

LORR, M. (1986). Classifying psychotics: Dimensional and categorical approaches. In T. Millon & G. L. Klerman (Eds.), *Contemporary directions in psychopathology: Toward the DSM IV* (pp. 331–345). New York: Guilford Press.

LORR, M., McNAIR, D. M., & KLETT, C. J. (1966). *Inpatient Multidimensional Psychiatric Scale.* Palo Alto, CA: Consulting Psychologists Press.

LORR, M., & YOUNISS, R. P. (1986). *Interpersonal Style Inventory (ISI): Manual.* Los Angeles: Western Psychological Services.

LOUTTIT, C. M., & BROWN, C. G. (1947). Psychometric instruments in psychological clinics. *Journal of Consulting Psychology, 11,* 49–54.

LUBIN, B., LARSEN, R. M., & MATARAZZO, J. D. (1984). Patterns of psychological test usage in the United States: 1935–1982. *American Psychologist, 39,* 451–454.

LUBIN, B., LARSEN, R. M., MATARAZZO, J. D., & SEEVER, M. (1985). Psychological test usage patterns in five professional settings. *American Psychologist, 40,* 857–861.

LUBIN, B., WALLIS, R. R., & PAINE, C. (1971). Patterns of psychological test usage in the United States: 1935–1969. *Professional Psychology, 2,* 70–74.

LUBORSKY, L. (1984). *Principles of psychoanalytic psychotherapy: A manual for supportive-expressive treatment.* New York: Basic Books.

LUBORSKY, L., CRITS-CHRISTOPH, P., & MELLON, J. (1986). Advent of objective measures of the transference concept. *Journal of Consulting and Clinical Psychology, 54,* 39–47.

LUBORSKY, L., SINGER, B., & LUBORSKY, L. (1975). Comparative studies of psychotherapies: Is it true that "Everyone has won and all must have prizes"? *Archives of General Psychiatry, 32,* 995–1008.

LUBORSKY, L., & SPENCE, D. P. (1978). Quantitative research on psychoanalytic therapy. In S. L. Garfield & A. E. Bergin (Eds.), *Handbook of psychotherapy and behavior change* (2nd ed., pp. 331–368). New York: John Wiley.

LYMAN, R. D. (1984). The effect of private and public goal setting on classroom on-task behavior of emotionally disturbed children. *Behavior Therapy, 15,* 395–402.

LYONS, H. A. (1971). Psychiatric sequelae of the Belfast riots. *British Journal of Psychiatry, 118,* 265–273.

LYONS, L. C., & WOODS, P. J. (1991). The efficacy of rational-emotive therapy: A quantitative review of the outcome research. *Clinical Psychology Review, 11,* 357–370.

MACHOVER, K. (1949). *Personality projection in the drawing of the human figure.* Springfield, IL: Charles C. Thomas.

MacKINNON, R. A. (1980). Psychiatric interview. In H. I. Kaplan, A. M. Freedman, & B. J. Sadock (Eds.), *Comprehensive textbook of psychiatry, Vol. III.* Baltimore, MD: Williams & Wilkins.

MacPHILLAMY, D. J., & LEWINSOHN, P. M. (1976). *Manual for the Pleasant Events Schedule.* Eugene, OR: Authors.

MAGARET, A. (1952). Clinical methods: Psychodiagnostics. *Annual Review of Psychology, 3,* 283–320.

MAGRAB, P., & PAPADOPOULOU, Z. L. (1977). The effect of a token economy on dietary compliance for children on hemodialysis. *Journal of Applied Behavioral Analysis, 10,* 573–578.

MAHL, G. F. (1959). Exploring emotional states by content analysis. In I. Pool (Ed.), *Trends in content analysis* (pp. 89–130). Urbana: University of Illinois Press.

MAHLER, M. S., PINE, F., & BERGMAN, A. (1975). *The psychological birth of the human infant.* New York: Basic Books.

MAHONEY, M. J. (1991). *Human change processes.* New York: Basic Books.

MAHONEY, M. J., & FREEMAN, A. (Eds.). (1985). *Cognition and psychotherapy.* New York: Plenum Press.

Mahrer, A. R. (Ed.). (1970). *New approaches to personality classification.* New York: Columbia University Press.

Mahrer, A. R. (1988). Discovery-oriented psychotherapy research: Rationale, aims, and methods. *American Psychologist, 43,* 694–702.

Mahrer, A. R., & Nadler, W. P. (1986). Good moments in psychotherapy: A preliminary review, a list, and some promising research avenues. *Journal of Consulting and Clinical Psychology, 54,* 10–15.

Maisto, S. A., & Maisto, C. A. (1983). Institutional measures of treatment outcome. In M. J. Lambert, E. R. Christensen, & S. S. DeJulio (Eds.), *The assessment of psychotherapy outcome* (pp. 603–625). New York: John Wiley.

Malmo, R. B., Shagass, C., & Davis, F. H. (1950). Symptom specificity and bodily reactions during psychiatric interviews. *Psychosomatic Medicine, 12,* 362–376.

Maloney, M. P., & Ward, M. P. (1976). *Psychological assessment: A conceptual approach.* New York: Oxford University Press.

Mann, P. A. (1978). *Community psychology: Concepts and applications.* New York: Free Press.

Margolin, G., Michelli, J., & Jacobson, N. (1988). Assessment of marital dysfunction. In A. S. Bellack & M. Hersen (Eds.), *Behavioral assessment: A practical handbook* (3rd ed., pp. 441–489). New York: Pergamon Press.

Marks, I. (1975). Behavioral treatments of phobic and obsessive compulsive disorders: A critical appraisal. In M. Hersen, R. M. Eisler, & P. M. Miller (Eds.), *Progress in behavior modification* (Vol. 1, pp. 187–207). New York: Academic Press.

Martin, G., & Pear, J. (1983). *Behavioral modification: What it is and how to do it.* Englewood Cliffs, NJ: Prentice-Hall.

Martin, R. P. (1988). *Assessment of personality and behavior problems: Infancy through adolescence.* New York: Guilford Press.

Marx, J. A., Gyorky, Z. K., Royalty, G. M., & Stern, T. E. (1992). Use of self-help books in psychotherapy. *Professional Psychology: Research and Practice, 23,* 300–305.

Marx, M. B., Garrity, T. F., & Bowers, F. R. (1975). The influence of recent life experience on the life of college freshmen. *Journal of Psychosomatic Research, 19,* 87–98.

Mash, E. J. (1985). Some comments on target selection in behavior therapy. *Behavioral Assessment, 7,* 63–78.

Mash, E. J., & Barkley, A. (1986). Assessment of family interaction with the Response-Class Matrix. In R. J. Prinz (Ed.), *Advances in behavioral assessment of children and families* (Vol. 2, pp. 29–67). Greenwich, CT: JAI Press.

Mash, E. J., & McElwee, J. D. (1974). Situational effects on observer accuracy: Behavior predictability, prior experience, and complexity of coding categories. *Child Development, 45,* 367–377.

Mash, E. J., & Terdal, L. G. (Eds.). (1988). *Behavioral assessment of childhood disorders* (2nd ed.). New York: Guilford Press.

Masling, J. (1966). Role-related behavior of the subject and psychologist and its effect upon psychological data. In D. Levine (Ed.), *Nebraska symposium on motivation* (pp. 67–103). Lincoln: University of Nebraska Press.

Masling, J. (Ed.). (1982). *Empirical studies of psychoanalytical theories* (Vol. 1). Hillsdale, NJ: Lawrence Erlbaum Associates.

Maslow, A. H. (1954). *Motivation and personality.* New York: Harper.

Maslow, A. H. (1962). *Toward a psychology of being.* Princeton, NJ: D. Van Nostrand.

Maslow, A. H. (1968). *Toward a psychology of being* (2nd ed.). New York: Van Nostrand Reinhold.

Maslow, A. H. (1971). *The farther reaches of human nature.* New York: Viking Press.

Masserman, J. H. (1943). *Behavior and neurosis: An experimental psycho-analytic approach to psychobiologic principles.* Chicago: University of Chicago Press.

Masson, J. M. (1983). *The assault on the truth: Freud's suppression of the seduction theory.* New York: Farrar, Straus & Giroux.

Masterpasqua, F. (1989). A competence paradigm for psychological practice. *American Psychologist, 44,* 1366–1371.

Masters, J. C., Burish, T. G., Hollon, S. D., & Rimm, D. C. (1987). *Behavior therapy: Techniques and empirical findings* (3rd ed.). San Diego, CA: Harcourt, Brace, Jovanovich.

Masur, F. T. (1981). Adherence to health care regimens. In C. K. Prokop & L. A. Bradley (Eds.), *Medical psychology: Contributions to behavioral medicine* (pp. 442–470). New York: Academic Press.

Matarazzo, J. D. (1965). The interview. In B. B. Wolman (Ed.), *Handbook of clinical psychology* (pp. 403–450). New York: McGraw-Hill.

Matarazzo, J. D. (1983a). Computerized psychological testing. *Science, 221,* 323.

Matarazzo, J. D. (1983b). The reliability of psychiatric and psychological diagnosis. *Clinical Psychology Review, 3,* 103–145.

Matarazzo, J. D. (1986). Computerized clinical psychological test interpretations: Unvalidated plus all mean and no sigma. *American Psychologist, 41,* 14–24.

MATARAZZO, J. D. (1987). There is only one psychology, no specialties, but many applications. *American Psychologist, 42,* 893–903.

MATARAZZO, J. D. (1992). Psychological testing and assessment in the 21st century. *American Psychologist, 47,* 1007–1018.

MATARAZZO, J. D., & CARMODY, T. P. (1983). Health psychology. In M. Hersen, A. J. Kazdin, & A. S. Bellack (Eds.), *The clinical-psychology handbook* (pp. 657–682). New York: Pergamon Press.

MATARAZZO, J. D., WEITMAN, M., SASLOW, G., & WIENS, A. N. (1963). Interviewer influence on durations of interviewee speech. *Journal of Verbal Learning and Verbal Behavior, 1,* 451–458.

MATTHEWS, K. A. (1982). Psychological perspectives on the Type A behavior pattern. *Psychological Bulletin, 91,* 293–323.

MATTHEWS, K. A. (1988). Coronary heart disease and Type A behaviors: Update on and alternative to the Booth-Kewley and Friedman (1987) quantitative review. *Psychological Bulletin, 104,* 373–380.

MATTHEWS, K. A., & HAYNES, S. G. (1986). Type A behavior pattern and coronary risk: Update and critical evaluation. *American Journal of Epidemiology, 123,* 923–960.

MAVISSAKALIAN, M., & MICHELSON, L. (1986). Agoraphobia: Relative and combined effectiveness of therapist-assisted *in vivo* exposure and imipramine. *Journal of Clinical Psychiatry, 56,* 117–122.

MAY, R. (1969). *Love and will.* New York: W. W. Norton.

MAY, R., ANGEL, E., & ELLENBERGER, H. F. (Eds.). (1958). *Existence: A new dimension in psychiatry and psychology.* New York: Basic Books.

MAY, W. T., & BELSKY, J. (1992). Response to "Prescription privileges: Psychology's next frontier?" or the siren call: Should psychologists medicate? *American Psychologist, 47,* 427.

MCARTHUR, D. S., & ROBERTS, G. E. (1982). *Roberts Apperception Test for Children: Manual.* Los Angeles: Western Psychological Services.

MCCLELLAND, D. C. (1989). Motivational factors in health and disease. *American Psychologist, 44,* 675–683.

MCCLELLAND, D. C., ATKINSON, J. W., CLARK, R. A., & LOWELL, E. L. (1953). *The achievement motive.* New York: Appleton-Century-Crofts.

MCCLOSKEY, M., & EGETH, H. E. (1983). Eyewitness identification: What can a psychologist tell a jury. *American Psychologist, 38,* 550–563.

MCCOY, S. A. (1976). Clinical judgments of normal childhood behavior. *Journal of Consulting and Clinical Psychology, 44,* 710–714.

MCCRAE, R. R., & COSTA, P. T. (1983). Social desirability scales: More substance than style. *Journal of Consulting and Clinical Psychology, 51,* 882–888.

MCFALL , R. M. (1991). Manifesto for a science of clinical psychology. *The Clinical Psychologist, 44,* 75–88.

MCFALL, R. M., & LILLESAND, D. B. (1971). Behavior rehearsal with modeling and coaching in assertion training. *Journal of Abnormal Psychology, 77,* 313–323.

MCGLYNN, F. D., MEALIEA, W. L., & LANDAU, D. L. (1981). The current status of systematic desensitization. *Clinical Psychology Review, 1,* 149–180.

MCGUIRE, T. G. (1989). Outpatient benefits for mental health services in medicare: Alignment with the private sector. *American Psychologist, 44,* 818–824.

MCINTYRE, T. J., BORNSTEIN, P. H., ISAACS, C. D., WOODY, D. J., BORNSTEIN, M. T., CLUCAS, T. J., & LONG, G. (1983). Naturalistic observation of conduct-disordered children: An archival analysis. *Behavior Therapy, 14,* 375–385.

MCKAY, S., & GOLDEN, C. J. (1979). Empirical derivation of neuropsychological scales for the lateralization of brain damage using the Luria-Nebraska Neuropsychological Battery. *Clinical Neuropsychology, 1,* 1–5.

MCLEMORE, C. W., & BENJAMIN, L. S. (1979). Whatever happened to interpersonal diagnosis: A psychosocial alternative to DSM-III. *American Psychologist, 34,* 17–34.

MCREYNOLDS, P. (1975). Historical antecedents of personality assessment. In P. McReynolds (Ed.), *Advances in psychological assessment* (Vol. 3, pp. 477–532). San Francisco: Jossey-Bass.

MCREYNOLDS, P. (1987). Lightner Witmer: Little-known founder of clinical psychology. *American Psychologist, 42,* 849–858.

MCREYNOLDS, P. (1989). Diagnosis and clinical assessment: Current status and major issues. In M. R. Rosenzweig & L. W. Porter (Eds.), *Annual Review of Psychology* (pp. 83–108). Palo Alto, CA: Annual Reviews.

MEAD, M. (1928). *Coming of age in Samoa.* New York: Morrow.

MEAD, M. (1939). *From the South Seas.* New York: Morrow.

MEADOR, B. D., & ROGERS, C. R. (1973). Client-centered therapy. In R. Corsini (Ed.), *Current psychotherapies* (pp. 119–165). Itasca, IL: F. E. Peacock.

MEDNICK, S. A., & SCHULSINGER, F. (1968). Some premorbid characteristics related to breakdown in children with schizophrenic mothers. In D. Rosenthal

& S. S. Kety (Eds.), *The transmission of schizophrenia* (pp. 267–291). Oxford: Pergamon Press.

MEEHL, P. E. (1954). *Clinical versus statistical prediction*. Minneapolis: University of Minnesota Press.

MEEHL, P. E. (1956). Wanted—A good cookbook. *American Psychologist, 11,* 263–272.

MEEHL, P. E. (1957). When shall we use our heads instead of the formula? *Journal of Consulting Psychology, 4,* 268–273.

MEEHL, P. E. (1960). The cognitive activity of the clinician. *American Psychologist, 15,* 19–27.

MEEHL, P. E. (1965). Seer over sign: The first good example. *Journal of Experimental Research in Personality, 1,* 27–32.

MEEHL, P. E., & ROSEN, A. (1955). Antecedent probability and the efficiency of psychometric signs, patterns, and cutting scores. *Psychological Bulletin, 52,* 194–216.

MEICHENBAUM, D. H. (1971). Examination of model characteristics in reducing avoidance behavior. *Journal of Personality and Social Psychology, 17,* 298–307.

MEICHENBAUM, D. H. (1975). A self-instructional approach to stress management: A proposal for stress inoculation training. In C. Spielberger & I. Sarason (Eds.), *Stress and anxiety* (Vol. 2). New York: John Wiley.

MEICHENBAUM, D. H. (1977). *Cognitive-behavior modification*. New York: Plenum Press.

MEICHENBAUM, D. H., & GOODMAN, J. (1971). Training impulsive children to talk to themselves: A means of developing self-control. *Journal of Abnormal Psychology, 77,* 115–126.

MEIER, M. J. (1981). Education for competency assurance in human neuropsychology: Antecedents, models, and directions. In S. B. Filskov & T. J. Boll (Eds.), *Handbook of clinical neuropsychology* (pp. 754–781). New York: John Wiley.

MEIER, S. T., & WICK, M. T. (1991). Computer-based unobtrusive measurement: Potential supplements to reactive self-reports. *Professional Psychology: Research and Practice, 22,* 410–412.

MELTON, A. W. (Ed.). (1947). *Apparatus tests*. Washington, DC: Government Printing Office.

MELTZOFF, J., & KORNREICH, M. (1970). *Research in psychotherapy*. New York: Atherton Press.

MENNINGER, K. (1958). *The theory of psychoanalytic technique*. New York: Basic Books.

MERCATORIS, M., & CRAIGHEAD, W. E. (1974). The effects of non-participant observation on teacher and pupil classroom behavior. *Journal of Educational Psychology, 66,* 512–519.

MERLEAU-PONTY, M. (1962). *Phenomenology of perception* (C. Smith, Trans.). New York: Humanities Press. (Original work published 1945)

MERMELSTEIN, R., LICHTENSTEIN, E., & MCINTYRE, K. (1983). Partner support and relapse in smoking-cessation programs. *Journal of Consulting and Clinical Psychology, 51,* 331–337.

MESSER, S. B., & WINOKUR, M. (1980). Some limits to the integration of psychoanalytic and behavior therapy. *American Psychologist, 35,* 818–827.

MESSER, S. B., & WINOKUR, M. (1986). Eclecticism and the shifting visions of reality in three systems of psychotherapy. *International Journal of Eclectic Psychotherapy, 5,* 115–124.

MEYER, A. J., NASH, J. D., MCALISTER, A. L., MACCOBY, N., & FARQUHAR, J. W. (1980). Skills training in a cardiovascular education campaign. *Journal of Consulting and Clinical Psychology, 48,* 129–142.

MEYEROWITZ, B. E., HEINRICH, R. L., & SCHAG, C. C. (1983). A competency-based approach to coping with cancer. In T. G. Burish & L. A. Bradley (Eds.), *Coping with chronic disease* (pp. 137–158). New York: Academic Press.

MEYERS, J. (1975). Consultee centered consultation with a teacher as a technique in behavior management. *American Journal of Community Psychology, 3,* 111–122.

MEZZICH, A. C., MEZZICH, J. E., & COFFMAN, G. A. (1985). Reliability of DSM-III vs. DSM-II in child psychopathology. *Journal of the American Academy of Child Psychiatry, 24,* 281–285.

MILICH, R., & FITZGERALD, G. (1985). Validation of inattention/overactivity and aggression ratings with classroom observations. *Journal of Consulting and Clinical Psychology, 53,* 139–140.

MILICH, R., & KRAMER, J. (1984). Reflections on impulsivity: An empirical investigation of impulsivity as a construct. In K. D. Gadow (Ed.), *Advances in learning and behavioral disabilities: A research annual* (Vol. 3, pp. 57–94). Greenwich, CT: JAI Press.

MILICH, R., LONEY, J., & LANDAU, S. (1982). Independent dimensions of hyperactivity and aggression: Validation with playroom observation data. *Journal of Abnormal Psychology, 91,* 183–198.

MILICH, R., WIDIGER, T. A., & LANDAU, S. (1987). Differential diagnosis of attention deficit and conduct disorders using conditional probabilities. *Journal of Consulting and Clinical Psychology, 55,* 762–767.

MILICH, R., WOLRAICH, M., & LINDGREN, S. (1986). Sugar and hyperactivity: A critical review of empirical findings. *Clinical Psychology Review, 6,* 493–513.

MILLER, L. K., & MILLER, O. (1970). Reinforcing self-help

group activities of welfare recipients. *Journal of Applied Behavior Analysis, 3,* 57–64.

MILLER, N. E. (1951). Learnable drives and rewards. In S. S. Stevens (Ed.), *Handbook of experimental psychology* (pp. 435–472). New York: John Wiley.

MILLER, N. E. (1969). Learning of visceral and glandular responses. *Science, 163,* 434–445.

MILLER, N. E. (1983). Behavioral medicine: Symbiosis between laboratory and clinic. *Annual Review of Psychology, 34,* 1–31.

MILLER, N. E., & DOLLARD, J. (1941). *Social learning and imitation.* New Haven, CT: Yale University Press.

MILLER, R. C., & BERMAN, J. S. (1983). The efficacy of cognitive behavior therapies: A quantitative review of the research evidence. *Psychological Bulletin, 94,* 39–53.

MILLER, W. R., & DiPILATO, M. (1983). Treatment of nightmares via relaxation and desensitization: A controlled evaluation. *Journal of Consulting and Clinical Psychology, 51,* 870–877.

MILLON, T. (1981). *Disorders of personality: DSM-III, Axis II.* New York: John Wiley.

MILLON, T. (1987a). *Millon Clinical Multiaxial Inventory-II.* Minneapolis: National Computers System.

MILLON, T. (1987b). On the nature of taxonomy in psychopathology. In C. G. Last & M. Hersen (Eds.), *Issues in diagnostic research* (pp. 3–85). New York: Plenum Press.

MILLON, T. (1991). Classification in psychopathology: Rationale, alternatives, and standards. *Journal of Abnormal Psychology, 100,* 245–261.

MILLON, T., GREEN, C. J., & MEAGHER, R. B., JR. (1982). *Millon Adolescent Personality Inventory manual.* Minneapolis: National Computer Systems.

MILLON, T., & KLERMAN, G. L. (Eds.). (1986). *Contemporary directions in psychopathology: Toward the DSM-IV.* New York: Guilford Press.

MILNER, B. (1974). Hemispheric specialization: Scope and limits. In F. O. Schmitt & F. G. Worden (Eds.), *The neurosciences: Third study program* (pp. 75–89). Cambridge, MA: MIT Press.

MINUCHIN, S. (1974). *Families and family therapy.* Cambridge, MA: Harvard University Press.

MIRSKY, A. F., & DUNCAN, C. C. (1986). Etiology and expression of schizophrenia: Neurobiological and psychosocial factors. *Annual Review of Psychology, 37,* 291–319.

MISCHEL, W. (1968). *Personality and assessment.* New York: John Wiley.

MISCHEL, W. (1971). *Introduction to personality.* New York: Holt, Rinehart & Winston.

MISCHEL, W. (1984). Convergences and challenges in the search for consistency. *American Psychologist, 39,* 351–364.

MISCHEL, W. (1986). *Introduction to personality* (4th ed.). New York: Holt, Rinehart & Winston.

MISHLER, E. G., & WAXLER, N. E. (1968). *Interaction in families: An experimental study of family process in schizophrenia.* New York: John Wiley.

MITCHELL, J. V. (Ed.). (1985). *The ninth mental measurements yearbook.* Lincoln: Buros Institute of Mental Measurements, University of Nebraska.

MITCHELL, R. E., BILLINGS, A. G., & MOOS, R. H. (1982). Social support and well-being: Implications for prevention programs. *Journal of Primary Prevention, 3,* 77–98.

MITCHELL, S. K. (1979). Interobserver agreement, reliability, and generalizability of data collected in observational studies. *Psychological Bulletin, 86,* 376–390.

MONAHAN, J. (1984). The prediction of violent behavior: Toward a second generation of theory and practice. *American Journal of Psychology, 141,* 10.

MONAHAN, J. (1988). Risk assessment of violence among the mentally disordered: Generating useful knowledge. *International Journal of Law and Psychiatry, 11,* 249.

MONCHER, F. J., & PRINZ, R. J. (1991). Treatment fidelity in outcome studies. *Clinical Psychology Review, 11,* 247–266.

MOOS, R. H., & SHAEFER, J. A. (Eds.). (1989). *Coping with physical illness. 2: New perspectives.* New York: Plenum Press.

MORELAND, K. L. (1987). Computer-based test interpretations: Advice to the consumer. *Applied Psychology: An International Review, 36,* 385–399.

MORENO, J. L. (1946). *Psychodrama.* New York: Beacon House.

MOREY, L. (1991). *Personality assessment inventory manual.* Odessa, FL: Psychological Assessment Resources.

MORGAN, C., & MURRAY, H. A. (1935). A method for investigating phantasies: The thematic apperception test. *Archives of Neurology and Psychiatry, 34,* 289–306.

MORGANSTERN, K. P., & TEVLIN, H. E. (1981). Behavioral interviewing. In M. Hersen & A. S. Bellack (Eds.), *Behavioral assessment: A practical handbook* (2nd ed., pp. 71–100). New York: Pergamon Press.

MORGANSTERN, K. P. (1988). Behavioral interviewing. In A. S. Bellack & M. Hersen (Eds.), *Behavioral assessment: A practical handbook* (3rd ed., pp. 86–108). New York: Pergamon Press.

MORRIS, E. K., & BRAUKMANN, C. J. (Eds.). (1987). *Behavioral approaches to crime and delinquency: A handbook of application, research, and concepts.* New York: Plenum Press.

MORRIS, R. J., & KRATOCHWILL, T. R. (1983). *Treating children's fears and phobias: A behavioral approach.* New York: Pergamon Press.

MORRISON, R. L. (1988). Structured interviews and rating scales. In A. S. Bellack & M. Hersen (Eds.), *Behavioral assessment: A practical handbook* (3rd ed., pp. 252–277). New York: Pergamon Press.

MORSE, S. J. (1978). Law and mental health professionals: The limits of expertise. *Professional Psychology, 9,* 389–399.

MOSAK, H. H., & DREIKURS, R. (1973). Adlerian psychotherapy. In R. Corsini (Ed.), *Current psychotherapies* (pp. 35–83). Itasca, IL: F. E. Peacock.

MOSAK, H. H., & GUSHURST, R. S. (1972). Some therapeutic uses of psychological testing. *American Journal of Psychotherapy, 26,* 539–546.

MOWRER, O. H. (1939). A stimulus-response analysis of anxiety and its role as a reinforcing agent. *Psychological Review, 46,* 553–565.

MOWRER, O. H. (1960). *Learning theory and behavior.* New York: John Wiley.

MRFIT (MULTIPLE RISK FACTORS INTERVENTION TRIAL RESEARCH GROUP). (1982). Multiple risk factor intervention trial: Risk factor changes and mortality results. *Journal of the American Medical Association, 248,* 1465–1477.

MULLEN, B., & SULS, J. (1982). The effectiveness of attention and rejection as coping styles. *Journal of Psychosomatic Research, 26,* 43–49.

MUNROE, R. (1955). *Schools of psychoanalytic thought.* New York: Dryden Press.

MURAN, J. C. (1991). A reformulation of the ABC model of cognitive psychotherapies: Implications for assessment and treatment. *Clinical Psychology Review, 11,* 399–418.

MURRAY, H. A. (1938). *Explorations in personality.* Fair Lawn, NJ: Oxford University Press.

MURRAY, H. A. (1943). *Thematic Apperception Test.* Cambridge, MA: Harvard University Press.

MURSTEIN, B. I. (1972). Normative written TAT responses for a college sample. *Journal of Personality Assessment, 36,* 109–147.

MUSSEN, P. H., & SCODEL, A. (1955). The effects of sexual stimulation under varying conditions on TAT sexual responsiveness. *Journal of Consulting Psychology, 19,* 90.

MYKLEBUST, H. R. (1975). Nonverbal learning disabilities: Assessment and intervention. In H. R. Myklebust (Ed.), *Progress in learning disabilities* (Vol. 3, pp. 85–121). New York: Grune & Stratton.

NATHAN, P. E. (1987). DSM-III-R and the behavior therapist. *Behavior Therapy, 10,* 203–205.

NATIONAL CENTER FOR EDUCATION STATISTICS (1991). *Digest of educational statistics: 1990.* Washington, DC: U.S. Department of Education.

NEALE, J. M., & OLTMANNS, T. F. (1980). *Schizophrenia.* New York: John Wiley.

NELSON, R. O. (1977). Assessment and therapeutic functions of self-monitoring. In M. Hersen, R. M. Eisler, & P. M. Miller (Eds.), *Progress in behavior modification* (pp. 264–308). New York: Academic Press.

NELSON, R. O., & HAYES, S. C. (Eds.). (1986). *Conceptual foundations of behavioral assessment.* New York: Guilford Press.

NELSON, R. O., HAYES, S. C., FELTON, J. L., & JARRETT, R. B. (1985). A comparison of data produced by different behavioral assessment techniques with implications for models of social-skills adequacy. *Behaviour Research and Therapy, 23,* 1–12.

NEWMAN, F. L., & HOWARD, K. I. (1986). Therapeutic effort, treatment outcome, and national health policy. *American Psychologist, 41,* 181–187.

NEWMARK, C. S. (1985). *Major psychological assessment instruments.* Rockleigh, NJ: Allyn & Bacon.

NICHOLSON, R. A., & BERMAN, J. S. (1983). Is follow-up necessary in evaluating psychotherapy? *Psychological Bulletin, 93,* 261–278.

NIETZEL, M. T., & BERNSTEIN, D. A. (1976). The effects of instructionally mediated demand upon the behavioral assessment of assertiveness. *Journal of Consulting and Clinical Psychology, 44,* 500.

NIETZEL, M. T., BERNSTEIN, D. A., & RUSSELL, R. L. (1988). Assessment of anxiety and fear. In A. S. Bellack & M. Hersen (Eds.), *Behavioral assessment: A practical handbook* (3rd ed., pp. 280–312). New York: Pergamon Press.

NIETZEL, M. T., & DILLEHAY, R. C. (1986). *Psychological consultation in the courtroom.* New York: Pergamon Press.

NIETZEL, M. T., & FISHER, S. G. (1981). Effectiveness of professional and paraprofessional helpers: A reply to Durlak. *Psychological Bulletin, 89,* 555–565.

NIETZEL, M. T., GUTHRIE, P. R., & SUSMAN, D. T. (1991). Utilization of community and social support services. In F. H. Kanfer & A. P. Goldstein (Eds.), *Helping people change* (4th ed., pp. 396–421). New York: Pergamon Press.

NIETZEL, M. T., & HARRIS, M. J. (1990). Relationship of dependency and achievement/autonomy to depression. *Clinical Psychology Review, 10,* 279–298.

NIETZEL, M. T., RUSSELL, R. L., HEMMINGS, K. A., & GRETTER, M. L. (1987). The clinical significance of psychotherapy for unipolar depression: A meta-analytic approach to social comparison. *Journal of Consulting and Clinical Psychology, 55,* 156–161.

NIETZEL, M. T., & TRULL, T. J. (1988). Meta-analytic approaches to social comparisons: A method for measuring clinical significance. *Behavioral Assessment, 10,* 159–169.

NIETZEL, M. T., WINETT, R. A., MacDONALD, M. L., & DAVIDSON, W. S. (1977). *Behavioral approaches to community psychology.* New York: Pergamon Press.

NISBETT, R. E., & ROSS, L. (1980). *Human inference: Strategies and shortcomings of social judgment.* Englewood Cliffs, NJ: Prentice-Hall.

NISBETT, R. E., & WILSON, T. D. (1977). Telling more than we can know: Verbal reports on mental processes. *Psychological Review, 84,* 231–259.

NORCROSS, J. C., NASH, J. M., & PROCHASKA, J. O. (1985). Psychologists in part-time independent practice: Description and comparison. *Professional Psychology: Research and Practice, 16,* 565–575.

NORCROSS, J. C., & PROCHASKA, J. O. (1983). Psychotherapists in independent practice: Some findings and issues. *Professional Psychology: Research and Practice, 14,* 869–881.

NORCROSS, J. C., PROCHASKA, J. O., & GALLAGHER, K. M. (1989a). Clinical psychologists in the 1980s: I. Demographics, affiliations, and satisfactions. *The Clinical Psychologist, 42,* 29–39.

NORCROSS, J. C., PROCHASKA, J. O., & GALLAGHER, K. M. (1989b). Clinical psychologists in the 1980s: II. Theory, research, and practice. *The Clinical Psychologist, 42,* 45–53.

NOVACO, R. W., & MONAHAN, J. (1980). Research in community psychology: An analysis of works published in the first six years of the *American Journal of Community Psychology. American Journal of Community Psychology, 8,* 131–145.

NYE, R. D. (1975). *Three views of man: Perspectives from Sigmund Freud, B. F. Skinner, and Carl Rogers.* Monterey, CA: Brooks/Cole.

OBRZUT, J. E. (1988). Deficient lateralization in learning-disabled children: Developmental lag or abnormal cerebral organization? In D. L. Molfese & S. J. Segalowitz (Eds.), *Brain lateralization in children: Developmental implications.* New York: Guilford Press.

OFFICE OF STRATEGIC SERVICES ASSESSMENT STAFF (1948). *Assessment of men.* New York: Rinehart.

OLBRISCH, M. E. (1977). Psychotherapeutic interventions in physical health: Effectiveness and economic efficiency. *American Psychologist, 32,* 761–777.

O'LEARY, K. D., & BECKER, W. C. (1967). Behavior modification of an adjustment class: A token reinforcement program. *Exceptional Children, 33,* 637–642.

O'LEARY, K. D., & KENT, R. (1973). Behavior modification for social action: Research tactics and problems. In L. A. Hamerlynck, L. C. Handy, & E. J. Mash (Eds.), *Behavior change: Methodology, concepts, and practice* (pp. 69–96). Champaign, IL: Research Press.

O'LEARY, K. D., & O'LEARY, S. G. (Eds.). (1972). *Classroom management.* New York: Pergamon Press.

O'LEARY, K. D., & WILSON, G. T. (1987). *Behavior therapy: Applications and outcome* (2nd ed.). Englewood Cliffs, NJ: Prentice-Hall.

OLIN, J. T., & ZELINSKI, E. M. (1991). The 12-month reliability of the Mini-Mental State Examination. *Psychological Assessment: A Journal of Consulting and Clinical Psychology, 3,* 427–432.

OLIVE, H. (1972). Psychoanalysts' opinions of psychologists' reports: 1952 and 1970. *Journal of Clinical Psychology, 28,* 50–54.

OLLENDICK, T. H. (1983). Reliability and validity of the Revised-Fear Survey Schedule for Children (FSSC-R). *Behaviour Research and Therapy, 21,* 685–692.

OLLENDICK, T. H., & GREENE, R. (1990). Behavioral assessment of children. In G. Goldstein & M. Hersen (Eds.), *Handbook of psychological assessment* (2nd ed., pp. 403–422). New York: Pergamon Press.

OLLENDICK, T. H., & HERSEN, M. (1984). *Child behavioral assessment: Principles and procedures.* New York: Pergamon Press.

OMER, H., & DAR, R. (1992). Changing trends in three decades of psychotherapy research: The flight from theory into pragmatics. *Journal of Consulting and Clinical Psychology, 60,* 88–93.

O'NEILL, P., & TRICKETT, E. J. (1982). *Community consultation.* San Francisco: Jossey-Bass.

ORLINSKY, D. E. (1989). Researchers' image of psychotherapy: Their origins and influence on research. *Clinical Psychology Review, 9,* 413–442.

ORLINSKY, D. E., & HOWARD, K. I. (1986). Process and outcome in psychotherapy. In S. L. Garfield & A. E. Bergin (Eds.), *Handbook of psychotherapy and behavior change* (3rd ed., pp. 311–381). New York: John Wiley.

ORNE, M. T. (1962). On the social psychology of the psychological experiment: With particular reference to demand characteristics and their implications. *American Psychologist, 17,* 776–783.

ORNE, M. T., & SCHEIBE, K. E. (1964). The contribution of nondeprivation factors in the production of sensory deprivation effects: The psychology of the panic button. *Journal of Abnormal and Social Psychology, 68,* 3–12.

ORNE, M. T., & WENDER, P. (1968). Anticipatory socialization for psychotherapy. Method and rationale. *American Journal of Psychiatry, 124,* 88–98.

OSKAMP, S. (1965). Overconfidence in case-study judgments. *Journal of Consulting Psychology, 29,* 261–265.

OSSIP-KLEIN, D. J., MARTIN, J. E., LOMAX, B. D., PRUE, D. M., & DAVIS, C. J. (1983). Assessment of smoking topography generalization across laboratory, clinical, and naturalistic settings. *Addictive Behaviors, 8,* 11–17.

OST, L. G., JERREMALM, A., & JOHANSSON, J. (1981). Individual response patterns and the effects of different models in the treatment of social phobia. *Behaviour Research and Therapy, 19,* 1–16.

O'SULLIVAN, J. J., & QUEVILLON, R. P. (1992). 40 years later: Is the Boulder model still alive? *American Psychologist, 47,* 67–70.

PARKER, K. C. H. (1983). A meta-analysis of the reliability and validity of the Rorschach. *Journal of Personality Assessment, 47,* 227–231.

PARKER, K. C. H., HANSON, R. K., & HUNSLEY, J. (1988). MMPI, Rorschach, and WAIS: A meta-analytic comparison of reliability, stability, and validity. *Psychological Bulletin, 103,* 367–373.

PATTERSON, C. H. (1973). *Theories of counseling and psychotherapy* (2nd ed.). New York: Harper & Row.

PATTERSON, D. R., EVERETT, J. J., BURNS, G. L., & MARVIN, J. A. (1992). Hypnosis for the treatment of burn pain. *Journal of Consulting and Clinical Psychology, 60,* 713–717.

PATTERSON, G. R. (1974). Interventions for boys with conduct problems: Multiple settings, treatments, and criteria. *Journal of Consulting and Clinical Psychology, 42,* 471–481.

PATTERSON, G. R. (1975). *Families.* Champaign, IL: Research Press.

PATTERSON, G. R. (1976). The aggressive child: Victim and architect of a coercive system. In L. A. Hamerlynck, L. C. Handy, & E. J. Mash (Eds.), *Behavior modification and families: Theory and research* (Vol. 1, pp. 267–316). New York: Brunner/Mazel.

PATTERSON, G. R. (1982). *Coercive family process.* Eugene, OR: Castalia.

PATTERSON, G. R., RAY, R. S., SHAW, D. A., & COBB, J. A. (1969). *Manual for coding of family interactions* (Document NO. 01234). Available from ASIS/NAPS, c/o Microfiche Publications, 305 East 46th St., New York, NY 10017.

PAUL, G. L. (1966). *Insight versus desensitization in psychotherapy: An experiment in anxiety reduction.* Stanford, CA: Stanford University Press.

PAUL, G. L. (1969a). Behavior modification research: Design and tactics. In C. M. Franks (Ed.), *Behavior therapy: Appraisal and status* (pp. 29–62). New York: McGraw-Hill.

PAUL, G. L. (1969b). Outcome of systematic desensitization II. In C. M. Franks (Ed.), *Behavior therapy: Appraisal and status* (pp. 63–159). New York: McGraw-Hill.

PAUL, G. L., & LENTZ, R. J. (1977). *Psychosocial treatment of chronic mental patients: Milieu versus social-learning programs.* Cambridge, MA: Harvard University Press.

PAVLOV, I. P. (1927). *Conditioned reflexes.* New York: Oxford University Press.

PAYNE, A. F. (1928). *Sentence completions.* New York: New York Guidance Clinic.

PEARLIN, L. I., & SCHOOLER, C. (1978). The structure of coping. *Journal of Health and Social Behavior, 22,* 337–356.

PECK, C. P., & ASH, E. (1964). Training in the Veterans Administration. In L. Blank & H. P. David (Eds.), *Sourcebook for training in clinical psychology* (pp. 61–81). New York: Springer.

PEDRO-CARROLL, J. L., & COWEN, E. L. (1985). The children of divorce intervention program: An investigation of the efficacy of a school-based prevention program. *Journal of Consulting and Clinical Psychology, 53,* 603–611.

PEELE, S. (1981). Reductionism in the psychology of the eighties: Can biochemistry eliminate addiction, mental illness, and pain? *American Psychologist, 36,* 807–818.

PELHAM, W. E., & BENDER, M. E. (1982). Peer relationships in hyperactive children: Description and treatment. In K. D. Gadow & I. Bialer (Eds.), *Advances in learning and behavioral disabilities* (Vol. 1). Greenwich, CT: JAI Press.

PELHAM, W. E., MCBURNETT, K., HARPER, G. W., MILICH, R., MURPHY, D. A., CLINTON, J., & THIELE, C. (1990). Methylphenidate and baseball playing in ADHD children: Who's on first. *Journal of Consulting and Clinical Psychology, 58,* 130–133.

PELHAM, W. E., MURPHY, D. A., VANNATTA, K., MILICH, R., LICHT, B. G., GNAGY, E. M., GREENSLADE, K. E., GRENIER, A. R., & VODDE-HAMILTON, M. (1992). Methylphenidate and attributions in boys with attention-deficit hyperactivity disorder. *Journal of Consulting and Clinical Psychology, 60,* 282–292.

PELHAM, W. E., & MURPHY, H. A. (1986). Attention deficit and conduct disorders. In M. Hersen (Ed.), *Pharmacological and behavioral treatments: An integrative approach* (pp. 108–148). New York: John Wiley.

PENNEBAKER, J., & BEALL, S. (1986). Confronting a traumatic event: Toward an understanding of inhibition and disease. *Journal of Abnormal Psychology, 95,* 274–281.

PENNEBAKER, J., KIECOLT-GLASER, J. K., & GLASER, R. (1988). Disclosure of traumas and immune function: Health implications for psychotherapy. *Journal of Consulting and Clinical Psychology, 56,* 239–245.

PERECMAN, E. (1983). *Cognitive processing in the right hemisphere.* New York: Academic Press.

PERLS, F. S. (1947). *Ego, hunger and aggression: A revision of Freud's theory and method.* New York: Random House.

PERLS, F. S. (1965). Gestalt therapy. Film no. 2. In Everett Shostrom (Ed.), *Three approaches to psychotherapy.* (Three 16 mm color motion pictures). Santa Ana, CA: Psychological Films.

PERLS, F. S. (1969). *Gestalt therapy verbatim.* Lafayette, CA: Real People Press.

PERLS, F. S. (1970). Four lectures. In J. Fagan & I. L. Shepherd (Eds.), *Gestalt therapy now* (pp. 14–38). Palo Alto, CA: Science and Behavior Books.

PERLS, F. S., HEFFERLINE, R. F., & GOODMAN, P. (1951). *Gestalt therapy.* New York: Julian Press.

PERRY, C. L., KLEPP, K., & SHULTZ, J. M. (1988). Primary prevention of cardiovascular disease: Communitywide strategies for youth. *Journal of Consulting and Clinical Psychology, 56,* 358–364.

PERRY, N. W. (1979). Why clinical psychology does not need alternative training models. *American Psychologist, 34,* 603–611.

PERSONS, J. B. (1991). Psychotherapy outcome studies do not accurately represent current models of psychotherapy: A proposed remedy. *American Psychologist, 46,* 99–106.

PERVIN, L. A. (1984). *Personality: Theory and research* (4th ed.). New York: John Wiley.

PETERSON, C., & VILLANOVA, P. (1988). An Expanded Attributional Style Questionnaire. *Journal of Abnormal Psychology, 97,* 87–89.

PETERSON, D. R. (1968). *The clinical study of social behavior.* New York: Appleton-Century-Crofts.

PETERSON, D. R. (1983). The case for the Psy.D. In S. Walfish & G. Sumprer (Eds.), *Clinical, counseling, and community psychology.* New York: Irvington.

PETERSON, D. R. (1985). Twenty years of practitioner training in psychology. *American Psychologist, 40,* 441–451.

PETERSON, D. R., & BARON, A. (1975). Status of the University of Illinois doctor of psychology program, 1974. *Professional Psychology, 6,* 88–95.

PETERSON, L. (1989). Latchkey children's preparation for self-care: Overestimated, underestimated, and unsafe. *Journal of Clinical Child Psychology, 18,* 36–43.

PETERSON, L., & ROBERTS, M. C. (1991). Treatment of children's problems. In C. E. Walker (Ed.), *Clinical psychology: Historical and research foundations* (pp. 313–342). New York: Plenum Press.

PHARES, A. J. (1988). *Introduction to personality* (2nd ed.). Glenview, IL: Scott, Foresman.

PIAGET, J. (1947). *The psychology of intelligence.* London: Kegan Paul.

PIAGET, J. (1962). *Play, dreams, and imitation in childhood.* New York: W. W. Norton.

PIKOFF, H. (1984). A critical review of autogenic training in America. *Clinical Psychology Review, 4,* 619–640.

PILKONIS, P. A., HEAPE, C. L., RUDDY, J., & SERRAO, P. (1991). Validity in the diagnosis of personality disorders: The use of the LEAD standard. *Psychological Assessment: A Journal of Consulting and Clinical Psychology, 3,* 46–54.

PION, G. M. (1991). A national human resources agenda for psychology: The need for a broader perspective. *Professional Psychology: Research and Practice, 22,* 449–455.

PIOTROWSKI, Z. (1972). Psychological testing of intelligence and personality. In A. M. Freedman & H. I. Kaplan (Eds.), *Diagnosing mental illness: Evaluation in psychiatry and psychology* (pp. 41–85). New York: Atheneum.

PIPER, W. E., DEBBANE, E. G., BIENVENU, J. P., & GARANT, J. (1984). A comparative study of four forms of psychotherapy. *Journal of Consulting and Clinical Psychology, 52,* 268–279.

PIROZZOLO, F. J., & RAYNER, K. (1977). Hemispheric specialization in reading and word recognition. *Brain and Language, 4,* 248–261.

PITTENGER, R. E., HOCKETT, C. F., & DANEHY, J. J. (1960). *The first five minutes: A sample of microscopic interview analyses.* Ithaca, NY: Paul Martineau.

PLOMIN, R. (1989). Environment and genes: Determinants of behavior. *American Psychologist, 44,* 105–111.

PLOUS, S., & ZIMBARDO, P. G. (1986). Attributional biases among clinicians: A comparison of psychoanalysts and behavior therapists. *Journal of Consulting and Clinical Psychology, 54,* 568–570.

POLSTER, E., & POLSTER, M. (1973). *Gestalt therapy integrated: Contours of theory and practice.* New York: Brunner/Mazel.

POLSTER, R. A., & DANGEL, R. G. (1984). Behavioral parent training: Where it came from and where it's at. In R. F. Dangel & R. A. Polster (Eds.), *Parent training* (pp. 1–14). New York: Guilford Press.

POLYSON, J., NORRIS, D., & OTT, E. (1985). The recent decline in TAT research. *Professional Psychology: Research and Practice, 16,* 26–28.

POMERANZ, D. M., & GOLDFRIED, M. R. (1970). An intake

report outline for behavior modification. *Psychological Reports, 26,* 447–450.

POPE, K. S., & BOUTHOUSOS, J. C. (1986). *Sexual intimacy between therapists and patients.* New York: Praeger.

POPE, K. S., BUTCHER, J. N., & SEELEN, J. (1993). *MMPI MMPI-2 MMPI-A in court: A practical guide for expert witnesses and attorneys.* Washington, DC: American Psychological Association.

POPE, K. S., & VETTER, V. A. (1992). Ethical dilemmas encountered by members of the American Psychological Association: A national survey. *American Psychologist, 47,* 397–411.

PORTER, E. H., JR. (1943). The development and evaluation of a measure of counseling interview procedures. *Educational and Psychological Measurement, 3,* 105–126.

POWELL, T. J. (1987). *Self-help organizations and professional practice.* Silver Springs, MD: National Association of Social Workers.

PROCHASKA, J. O., & DICLEMENTE, C. C. (1984). *The transtheoretical approach: Crossing traditional boundaries of therapy.* Homewood, IL: Dow Jones-Irwin.

PURDY, J. E., REINEHR, R. C., & SWARTZ, J. D. (1989). Graduate admissions criteria of leading psychology departments. *American Psychologist, 44,* 960–961.

PUTTALAZ, M., & GOTTMAN, J. (1983). Social relationship problems in children. In B. B. Lahey & A. E. Kazdin (Eds.), *Advances in clinical child psychology* (Vol. 6, pp. 1–39). New York: Plenum Press.

QUAY, H. (1986). A critical analysis of DSM-III as a taxonomy of psychopathology in childhood and adolescence. In T. Millon & G. L. Klerman (Eds.), *Contemporary directions in psychopathology: Toward the DSM-IV* (pp. 151–165). New York: Guilford Press.

QUERESHI, M Y., & KUCHAN, A. M. (1988). The master's degree in clinical psychology: Longitudinal program evaluation. *Professional Psychology: Research and Practice, 19,* 594–599.

QUINSEY, V. L., CHAPLIN, T. C., & UPFOLD, D. (1984). Sexual arousal to nonsexual violence and sadomasochistic themes among rapists and non-sex offenders. *Journal of Consulting and Clinical Psychology, 52,* 651–657.

RACHMAN, S. J., & WILSON, G. T. (1980). *The effects of psychological therapy.* Oxford: Pergamon Press.

RAHE, R. H. (1975). Epidemiological studies of life change and illness. *International Journal of Psychiatry in Medicine, 6,* 133–146.

RAIMY, V. C. (1950). *Training in clinical psychology.* New York: Prentice-Hall.

RAPAPORT, D. (1951). *Organization and pathology of thought.* New York: Columbia University Press.

RAPAPORT, D., GILL, M. M., & SCHAFER, R. (1945). *Diagnostic psychological testing* (Vol. 1). Chicago: Yearbook.

RAPAPORT, D., GILL, M. M., & SCHAFER, R. (1946). *Diagnostic psychological testing* (Vol. 2). Chicago: Yearbook.

RAPP, D. W. (1965). *Detection of observer bias in the written record.* Unpublished manuscript, University of Georgia.

RAPPAPORT, J. (1977). *Community psychology: Values, research and action.* New York: Holt, Rinehart & Winston.

RAPPAPORT, J. (1981). In praise of paradox: A social policy of empowerment over prevention. *American Journal of Community Psychology, 9,* 1–25.

RAPPAPORT, J., & CHINSKY, J. M. (1974). Models for delivery of services from a historical and conceptual perspective. *Professional Psychology, 5,* 42–50.

RAQUEPAW, J. M., & MILLER, R. S. (1989). Psychotherapist burnout: A componential analysis. *Professional Psychology: Research and Practice, 20,* 33–36.

RASMUSSEN, T., & MILNER, B. (1975). Clinical and surgical studies of the cerebral speech areas in man. In K. J. Zulch, O. Creutzfeldt, & G. C. Galbraith (Eds.), *Cerebral localization.* Berlin & New York: Springer-Verlag.

RAUSCH, H. L., & BORDIN, E. S. (1957). Warmth in personality development and in psychotherapy. *Psychiatry, 20,* 351–363.

RAYMOND, M. J. (1956). Case of fetishism treated by aversion therapy. *British Medical Journal, 2,* 854–857.

REDD, W. H., JACOBSEN, P. B., DIE-TRILL, M., DERMATIS, H., McEVOY, M., & HOLLAND, J. C. (1987). Cognitive/attentional distraction in the control of conditioned nausea in pediatric cancer patients receiving chemotherapy. *Journal of Consulting and Clinical Psychology, 55,* 391–395.

REED, S. D., KATKIN, E. S., & GOLDBAND, S. (1986). Biofeedback and behavioral medicine. In F. H. Kanfer & A. P. Goldstein (Eds.), *Helping people change: A textbook of methods* (3rd ed., pp. 381–436). New York: Pergamon Press.

REHM, L. P., KORNBLITH, S. J., O'HARA, M. W., LAMPARSKI, D. J., ROMANO, J. M., & VOLKIN, J. I. (1981). An evaluation of major components in a self-control therapy program for depression. *Behavior Modification, 5,* 459–489.

REHM, L. P., & MARSTON, A. R. (1968). Reduction of social anxiety through modification of self-reinforcement: An instigation therapy technique. *Journal of Consulting and Clinical Psychology, 32,* 565–574.

REID, J. B. (Ed.). (1978). *A social learning approach to*

family intervention: Observation in home settings (Vol. 2). Eugene, OR: Castalia Publishing.

REID, J. B. (1985). Behavioral approaches to intervention and assessment with child-abusive families. In P. H. Bornstein & A. E. Kazdin (Eds.), *Handbook of clinical behavior therapy with children* (pp. 772–802). Homewood, IL: Dorsey Press.

REID, J. B., & PATTERSON, G. R. (1976). The modification of aggression and stealing behavior of boys in the home setting. In A. Bandura & E. Ribes (Eds.), *Behavior modification: Experimental analysis of aggression and delinquency* (pp. 123–146). Hillsdale, NJ: Lawrence Erlbaum Associates.

REIK, T. (1948). *Listening with the third ear.* New York: Farrar, Straus & Giroux.

REISMAN, J. M. (1976). *A history of clinical psychology.* New York: Irvington.

REITAN, R. M. (1955). An investigation of the validity of Halstead's measure of biological intelligence. *Archives of Neurology and Psychiatry, 73,* 28–35.

REITAN, R. M. (1964). Psychological deficits resulting from cerebral lesions in man. In J. M. Warren & K. Akert (Eds.), *The frontal grandular cortex and behavior.* New York: McGraw-Hill.

REITAN, R. M. (1984). *Aphasia and sensory-perceptual deficits in adults.* Tucson, AZ: Reitan Neuropsychology Laboratories.

REITAN, R. M., & DAVISON, L. A. (Eds.). (1974). *Clinical neuropsychology: Current status and applications.* Washington, DC: V. H. Winston.

RENSHAW, P. D., & ASHER, S. R. (1983). Children's goals and strategies for social interaction. *Merrill-Palmer Quarterly, 29,* 353–375.

RESCHLY, D. J. (1984). Aptitude tests. In G. Goldstein & M. Hersen (Eds.), *Handbook of psychological assessment* (pp. 132–156). New York: Pergamon Press.

RESCHLY, D. J. (1990). Aptitude tests in educational classification and placement. In G. Goldstein & M. Hersen (Eds.), *Handbook of psychological assessment* (pp. 148–172). New York: Pergamon Press.

RESNICK, J. H. (1991). Finally, a definition of clinical psychology: A message from the President, Division 12. *The Clinical Psychologist, 44,* 3–11.

RESNICK, R. J. (1985). The case against the Blues: The Virginia challenge. *American Psychologist, 40,* 975–983.

REVENSON, T. A., & FELTON, B. J. (1989). Disability and coping as predictors of psychological adjustment to rheumatoid arthritis. *Journal of Consulting and Clinical Psychology, 57,* 344–348.

REYNOLDS, C. R. (1982). The problem of bias in psychological assessment. In C. R. Reynolds & T. B. Gutkin (Eds.), *The handbook of school psychology.* New York: John Wiley.

REYNOLDS, W. M. (1979). Psychological tests: Clinical usage versus psychometric quality. *Professional Psychology, 10,* 324–329.

REYNOLDS, W. M. (in press). *Suicidal Ideation Questionnaire: Professional manual.* Odessa, FL: Psychological Assessment Resources.

RHOLES, W. S., BLACKWELL, J., JORDAN, C., & WALTERS, C. (1980). A developmental study of learned helplessness. *Developmental Psychology, 16,* 616–624.

RICE, L., & GREENBERG, L. (1984). *Patterns of change: Intensive analysis of psychotherapy process.* New York: Guilford Press.

RICE, S. A. (1929). Contagious bias in the interview: A methodological note. *American Journal of Sociology, 35,* 420–423.

RICHTERS, J. E. (1992). Depressed mothers as informants about their children: A critical review of the evidence for distortion. *Psychological Bulletin, 112,* 485–499.

RICKEL, A. U., & ALLEN, L. (1987). *Preventing maladjustment from infancy through adolescence.* Newbury Park, CA: Sage.

RIEU, E. V. (Trans.). (1950). *Homer: The Iliad.* Hammondsworth, Middlesex: Penguin.

ROAZEN, P. (1975). *Freud and his followers.* New York: Knopf.

ROBBINS, L. C. (1963). The accuracy of parental recall of child development and of child rearing practices. *Journal of Abnormal and Social Psychology, 66,* 261–270.

ROBINER, W. N. (1991). How many psychologists are needed? A call for a national psychology human resource agenda. *Professional Psychology: Research and Practice, 22,* 427–440.

ROBINS, L. N., HELZER, J. E., CROUGHAN, J. L., WILLIAMS, J. B. W., & RATCLIFF, R. L. (1981). *The NIMH Diagnostic Interview Schedule: Version III.* Washington, DC: Public Health Service. (HSS) ADM-T-42–3 (5/81, 8/81).

ROCK, D. L., BRANSFORD, J. D., MAISTO, S. A., & MOREY, L. (1987). The study of clinical judgment: An ecological approach. *Clinical Psychology Review, 7,* 645–661.

RODIN, J., & SALOVEY, P. (1989). Health psychology. *Annual Review of Psychology, 40,* 533–580.

RODRIGUEZ, R., NIETZEL, M. T., & BERZINS, J. I. (1980). Sex role orientation and assertiveness among female college students. *Behavior Therapy, 11,* 353–366.

ROE, A., GUSTAD, J. W., MOORE, B. V., ROSS, S., & SKODAK, M. (Eds.). (1959). *Graduate education in psychol-*

ogy. Washington, DC: American Psychological Association.

ROGERS, C. R. (1939). *The clinical treatment of the problem child.* Boston: Houghton Mifflin.

ROGERS, C. R. (1942). *Counseling and psychotherapy.* Boston: Houghton Mifflin.

ROGERS, C. R. (1951). *Client-centered therapy.* Boston: Houghton Mifflin.

ROGERS, C. R. (1954). *Psychotherapy and personality change.* Chicago: University of Chicago Press.

ROGERS, C. R. (1959). A theory of therapy, personality, and interpersonal relationships as developed in the client-centered framework. In S. Koch (Ed.), *Psychology: A study of a science: Vol. III. Formulations of the person and the social context* (pp. 184–256). New York: McGraw-Hill.

ROGERS, C. R. (1961). *On becoming a person.* Boston: Houghton Mifflin.

ROGERS, C. R. (1965). Client-centered therapy, Film no. 1. In Everett Shostrom (Ed.), *Three approaches to psychotherapy* (three 16 mm color motion pictures). Santa Ana, CA: Psychological Films.

ROGERS, C. R. (Ed.). (1967). *The therapeutic relationship and its impact: A study of psychotherapy with schizophrenics.* With E. T. Gendlin, D. J. Kiesler, & C. Louax. Madison: University of Wisconsin Press.

ROGERS, C. R. (1969). *Freedom to learn.* Columbus, OH: Merrill.

ROGERS, C. R. (1970). *Carl Rogers on encounter groups.* New York: Harper & Row.

ROGERS, C. R. (1972). *On becoming partners: Marriage and its alternatives.* New York: Delacorte.

ROGERS, C. R. (1974). Remarks on the future of client-centered therapy. In D. A. Wexler & L. N. Rice (Eds.), *Innovations in client-centered therapy* (pp. 7–13). New York: John Wiley.

ROGERS, C. R. (1980). *A way of being.* Boston: Houghton Mifflin.

ROGERS, R., GILLIS, J. R., DICKENS, S. E., & BAGBY, R. M. (1991). Standardized assessment of malingering: Validation of the Structured Interview of Reported Symptoms. *Psychological Assessment: A Journal of Consulting and Clinical Psychology, 3,* 89–96.

ROGERS, R., WASYLIW, O. E., & CAVANAUGH, J. L. (1984). Evaluating insanity: A study of construct validity. *Law and Human Behavior, 8,* 293–304.

ROMANCZYK, R. G., KENT, R. N., DIAMENT, C., & O'LEARY, K. D. (1973). Measuring the reliability of observational data: A reactive process. *Journal of Applied Behavior Analysis, 6,* 175–184.

RORER, L. G., & WIDIGER, T. A. (1983). Personality structure and assessment. *Annual Review of Psychology, 34,* 431–463.

ROSE, S. D., & LECROY, C. W. (1991). Group methods. In F. H. Kanfer & A. P. Goldstein (Eds.), *Helping people change* (4th ed., pp. 422–453). New York: Pergamon Press.

ROSEN, R. C., & KOPEL, S. A. (1977). Penile plethysmography and biofeedback in the treatment of a transvestite-exhibitionist. *Journal of Consulting and Clinical Psychology, 45,* 908–916.

ROSENBLATT, D. (1975). *Opening doors: What happens in Gestalt therapy.* New York: Harper & Row.

ROSENHAN, D. L. (1973). On being sane in insane places. *Science, 179,* 250–258.

ROSENHAN, D. L., & SELIGMAN, M. E. (1989). *Abnormal psychology* (2nd ed.). New York: W. W. Norton.

ROSENMAN, R. H. (1978). The interview method of assessment of the coronary-prone behavior pattern. In T. M. Dembroski, S. M. Weiss, J. L. Shields, S. G. Haynes, & M. Feinleib (Eds.), *Coronary-prone behavior* (pp. 55–69). New York: Springer-Verlag.

ROSENSTOCK, I. M. (1966). Why people use health services. *Milbank Memorial Fund Quarterly, 44,* 94–127.

ROSENTHAL, D. (1970). *Genetic theory and abnormal behavior.* New York: McGraw-Hill.

ROSENTHAL, H. R. (1959). The final dream: A criterion for the termination of therapy. In A. Adler & D. Deutsch (Eds.), *Essays in individual psychology* (pp. 400–409). New York: Grove Press.

ROSENTHAL, R. (1966). *Experimenter effects in behavioral research.* New York: Appleton-Century-Crofts.

ROSENTHAL, R. (1983). Assessing the statistical and social importance of the effects of psychotherapy. *Journal of Consulting and Clinical Psychology, 51,* 4–13.

ROSENTHAL, R., & RUBIN, D. B. (1978). Interpersonal expectancy effects: The first 345 studies. *Behavioral and Brain Sciences, 3,* 377–386.

ROSENTHAL, T. L. (1982). Social learning theory. In G. T. Wilson & C. M. Franks (Eds.), *Contemporary behavior therapy: Conceptual and empirical foundations.* (pp. 339–363). New York: Guilford Press.

ROSENTHAL, T. L., & STEFFEK, B. D. (1991). Modeling methods. In F. H. Kanfer & A. P. Goldstein (Eds.), *Helping people change* (4th ed., pp. 70–121). New York: Pergamon Press.

ROSENZWEIG, S. (1949). Apperceptive norms for the Thematic Apperception Test. I. The problem of norms in projective methods. *Journal of Personality, 17,* 475–482.

ROSENZWEIG, S., & FLEMING, E. E. (1949). Apperceptive norms for the Thematic Apperception Test. II. An empirical investigation. *Journal of Personality, 17,* 483–503.

ROSS, A. O. (1985). To form a more perfect union: It is

time to stop standing still. *Behavior Therapy, 16,* 195–204.

ROSS, D. M., & ROSS, S. A. (1982). *Hyperactivity: Current issues, research, and theory* (2nd ed.). New York: John Wiley.

ROTTER, J. B. (1954). *Social learning and clinical psychology.* Englewood Cliffs, NJ: Prentice-Hall.

ROTTER, J. B., & RAFFERTY, J. E. (1950). *The Rotter Incomplete Sentences Test.* New York: Psychological Corporation.

ROURKE, B. P. (1989). *Nonverbal learning disabilities: The syndrome and the model.* New York: Guilford Press.

ROUTH, D. K., & KING, K. M. (1972). Social class bias in clinical judgment. *Journal of Consulting and Clinical Psychology, 38,* 202–207.

RUBIN, R., HOLM, S., FRIBERG, L., VIDEBECH, P., ANDERSEN, H. S., BENDSEN, B. B., STROMSO, N., LARSEN, J. K., LASSEN, N. A., & HEMMINGSEN, R. (1991). Altered modulation of prefrontal and subcortical brain activity in newly diagnosed schizophrenia and schizophreniform disorder: A regional cerebral blood flow study. *Archives of General Psychiatry, 48,* 987–995.

RUBLE, D. N., & RHOLES, W. S. (1981). The development of children's perceptions and attributions about their social world. In J. H. Harvey, W. Ickes, & R. F. Kidd (Eds.), *New directions in attribution research* (Vol. 3, pp. 1–36). Hillsdale, NJ: Lawrence Erlbaum Associates.

RUDE, S., & REHM, L. P. (1991). Response to treatments for depression: The role of initial status on targeted cognitive and behavioral skills. *Clinical Psychology Review, 11,* 493–514.

RUGH, J. D., GABLE, R. S., & LEMKE, R. R. (1986). Instrumentation for behavioral assessment. In A. R. Ciminero, C. S. Calhoun, & H. E. Adams (Eds.), *Handbook of behavioral assessment* (2nd ed., pp. 79–108). New York: John Wiley.

RUSH, A. J., BECK, A. T., KOVACS, M., & HOLLON, S. D. (1977). Comparative efficacy of cognitive therapy and pharmacotherapy in the treatment of depressed outpatients. *Cognitive Therapy and Research, 1,* 17–38.

RUTTER, M. (1981). Stress, coping, and development: Some issues and some questions. In N. Garmezy & M. Rutter (Eds.), *Stress, coping & development* (pp. 1–41). New York: McGraw-Hill.

RUTTER, M., MAUGHAM, B., MORTIMORE, P., OUSTON, J., & SMITH, A. (1979). *Fifteen thousand hours: Secondary schools and their effects on children.* London: Open Books; Cambridge, MA: Harvard University Press.

RUTTER, M., & SHAFFER, D. (1980). DSM-III. A step forward or a step backward in terms of the classification of child psychiatric disorders. *Journal of the American Academy of Child Psychiatry, 19,* 371–394.

RYCHLAK, J. F. (1970). *Introduction to personality and psychotherapy: A theory-construction approach.* Boston: Houghton Mifflin.

SACKS, O. (1985). *The man who mistook his wife for a hat.* New York: Summit Books.

SACKS, O. (1990). *A leg to stand on.* New York: Summit Books.

SAFRAN, J. D. (1990a). Towards a refinement of cognitive therapy in light of interpersonal theory: I. Theory. *Clinical Psychology Review, 10,* 107–122.

SAFRAN, J. D. (1990b). Towards a refinement of cognitive therapy in light of interpersonal theory: II. Practice. *Clinical Psychology Review, 10,* 123–150.

SAFRAN, J. D., & SEGAL, Z. V. (1990). *Interpersonal process in cognitive therapy.* New York: Basic Books.

SALOVEY, P., & SINGER, J. A. (1991). Cognitive behavior modification. In F. H. Kanfer & A. P. Goldstein (Eds.), *Helping people change* (4th ed., pp. 361–395). New York: Pergamon Press.

SALTER, A. (1949). *Conditioned reflex therapy: The direct approach to the reconstruction of personality.* New York: Creative Age Press.

SALZINGER, K. (1959). Experimental manipulation of verbal behavior: A review. *Journal of Genetic Psychology, 61,* 65–95.

SAMUDA, R. J. (1975). *Psychological testing of American minorities: Issues and consequences.* New York: Dodd, Mead.

SANDLER, J., & STEELE, H. V. (1991). Aversion methods. In F. H. Kanfer & A. P. Goldstein (Eds.), *Helping people change* (4th ed., pp. 202–247). New York: Pergamon Press.

SANFORD, F. H. (1951). Annual report of the executive secretary. *American Psychologist, 6,* 664–670.

SANTOSTEFANO, S. (1962). Performance testing of personality. *Merrill-Palmer Quarterly, 8,* 83–97.

SARASON, I. G., JOHNSON, J. H., & SIEGEL, J. M. (1978). Assessing the impact of life changes: Development of the life experiences survey. *Journal of Consulting and Clinical Psychology, 46,* 932–946.

SARASON, S. B. (1974). *The psychological sense of community: Prospects for community psychology.* San Francisco: Jossey-Bass.

SARBIN, T. R., TAFT, R., & BAILEY, D. E. (1960). *Clinical inference and cognitive theory.* New York: Holt, Rinehart & Winston.

SASLOW, G., & MATARAZZO, J. D. (1959). A technique for studying changes in interview behavior. In E. A. Rubinstein & M. B. Parloff (Eds.), *Research in psycho-*

therapy (Vol. 1, pp. 125–159). Washington, DC: American Psychological Association.

SATIR, V. (1967). *Conjoint family therapy* (rev. ed.). Palo Alto, CA: Science and Behavior Books.

SATTERFIELD, J. H., HOPPE, C. M., & SCHELL, A. M. (1982). A prospective study of delinquency in 110 adolescent boys with attention deficit disorder and 88 normal adolescent boys. *American Journal of Psychiatry, 139,* 795–798.

SATTLER, J. M. (1988). *Assessment of children's intelligence and special abilities* (3rd ed.). Boston: Allyn & Bacon.

SATZ, P., & FLETCHER, J. M. (1981). Emergent trends in neuropsychology: An overview. *Journal of Consulting and Clinical Psychology, 49,* 851–865.

SAWYER, J. (1966). Measurement and prediction, clinical and statistical. *Psychological Bulletin, 66,* 178–200.

SAYLOR, C. F., FINCH, A. J., BASKIN, C. H., FUREY, W., & KELLY, M. M. (1984). Construct validity for measures of childhood depression: Application of multitrait-multimethod methodology. *Journal of Consulting and Clinical Psychology, 52,* 977–985.

SAYWITZ, K. (1990). The child as witness: Experimental and clinical considerations. In A. La Greca (Ed.), *Through the eyes of the child: Obtaining self-reports from children and adolescents* (pp. 329–367). Boston: Allyn & Bacon.

SCHAAR, K. (1978). Vermont: Getting through the adult years. *APA Monitor, 9,* 7.

SCHAEFER, H. H., & MARTIN, P. L. (1975). *Behavior therapy* (2nd ed.). New York: McGraw-Hill.

SCHAEFER, R. (1967). *Projective testing and psychoanalysis.* New York: International Universities Press.

SCHEFF, T. J. (1966). *Being mentally ill.* Chicago: Aldine.

SCHMIDT, H. O., & FONDA, C. P. (1956). The reliability of psychiatric diagnosis: A new look. *Journal of Abnormal and Social Psychology, 52,* 262–267.

SCHNEIDER, S. F. (1991). No fluoride in our future. *Professional Psychology: Research and Practice, 22,* 456–460.

SCHRADLE, S. B., & DOUGHER, M. J. (1985). Social support as a mediator of stress: Theoretical and empirical issues. *Clinical Psychology Review, 5,* 641–662.

SCHUCKMAN, H. (1987). Ph.D. recipients in psychology and biology: Do those with dissertation advisors of the same sex publish scholarly papers more frequently? *American Psychologist, 42,* 987–992.

SCHWITZGEBEL, R. K., & KOLB, D. A. (1974). *Changing human behavior.* New York: McGraw-Hill.

SCOVILLE, W. B., & MILNER, B. (1957). Loss of recent memory after bilateral hippocampal lesions. *The Journal of Neurology, Neurosurgery, & Psychiatry, 20,* 11–21.

SECHREST, L. (1992). The past future of clinical psychology: A reflection on Woodworth (1937). *Journal of Consulting and Clinical Psychology, 60,* 18–23.

SECHREST, L. B. (1963). Incremental validity: A recommendation. *Educational and Psychological Measurement, 23,* 153–158.

SEEMAN, J. A. (1949). A study of the process of nondirective therapy. *Journal of Consulting Psychology, 13,* 157–168.

SEIDMAN, E. (Ed.). (1983). *Handbook of social intervention.* Beverly Hills, CA: Sage.

SELIGMAN, M. E. P., ABRAMSON, L. Y., SEMMEL, A., & VON BAEYER, C. (1979). Depressive attributional style. *Journal of Abnormal Psychology, 88,* 242–247.

SELIGMAN, M. E. P., PETERSON, C., KASLOW, N. J., TANENBAUM, R. L., ALLOY, L. B., & ABRAMSON, L. Y. (1984). Explanatory style and depressive symptoms among school children. *Journal of Abnormal Psychology, 93,* 235–238.

SELYE, H. (1956). *The stress of life.* New York: McGraw-Hill.

SHADEL, C. A. (1944). Aversion treatment of alcohol addiction. *Quarterly Journal of Studies of Alcohol, 5,* 216–228.

SHADISH, W. R., JR. (1989). Private-sector care for chronically mentally ill individuals: The more things change, the more they stay the same. *American Psychologist, 44,* 1142–1147.

SHAFFER, G. W., & LAZARUS, R. S. (1952). *Fundamental concepts in clinical psychology.* New York: McGraw-Hill.

SHAKOW, D. (1942). The training of the clinical psychologist. *Journal of Consulting Psychology, 6,* 277–288.

SHAKOW, D. (1948). Clinical psychology: An evaluation. In L. G. Lowrey & V. Sloane (Eds.), *Orthopsychiatry, 1923–1948: Retrospect and prospect* (pp. 231–247). New York: American Orthopsychiatric Association.

SHAKOW, D. (1965). Seventeen years later: Clinical psychology in the light of the 1947 CTCP report. *American Psychologist, 20,* 353–362.

SHAKOW, D. (1968). Clinical psychology. In D. L. Sills (Ed.), *International encyclopedia of the social sciences* (pp. 513–518). London: Collier Macmillan.

SHAKOW, D. (1978). Clinical psychology seen some 50 years later. *American Psychologist, 33,* 148–158.

SHANNON, D., & WEAVER, W. (1949). *The mathematical theory of communication.* Urbana: University of Illinois Press.

SHAPIRO, A. K. (1971). Placebo effects in medicine, psychotherapy, and psychoanalysis. In A. E. Bergin & S. L. Garfield (Eds.), *Handbook of psychotherapy and behavior change: An empirical analysis* (pp. 439–473). New York: John Wiley.

SHAPIRO, D. A., & SHAPIRO, D. (1982). Meta-analysis of comparative therapy outcome research: A critical appraisal. *Behavioral Psychotherapy, 10,* 4–25.

SHEA, S. (1988). *Interviewing: The art of understanding.* Philadelphia: W. B. Saunders.

SHEMBERG, K. M., & LEVENTHAL, D. B. (1978). A survey of activities of academic clinicians. *Professional Psychology, 9,* 580–586.

SHEMBERG, K. M., & LEVENTHAL, D. B. (1981). Attitudes of internship directors toward preinternship training and clinical training models. *Professional Psychology, 12,* 639–646.

SHEPARD, L. A. (1982). Definitions of bias. In R. A. Berk (Ed.), *Handbook of methods for detecting item bias* (pp. 9–30). Baltimore, MD: Johns Hopkins University Press.

SHEPHERD, M., OPPENHEIM, B., & MITCHELL, S. (1971). *Childhood behavior and mental health.* London: University of London Press.

SHERMAN, M., TRIEF, P., & SPRAFKIN, R. (1975). Impression management in the psychiatric interview: Quality, style, and individual differences. *Journal of Consulting and Clinical Psychology, 43,* 867–871.

SHNEIDMAN, E. S. (1965). Projective techniques. In B. B. Wolman (Ed.), *Handbook of clinical psychology* (pp. 498–521). New York: McGraw-Hill.

SHOHAM-SALOMON, V. (1985). Are schizophrenics' behaviors schizophrenic? What medically versus psychosocially oriented therapists attribute to schizophrenic persons. *Journal of Abnormal Psychology, 94,* 443–453.

SHOSTROM, E. L. (1968). *Personal orientation inventory: An inventory for the measurement of self-actualization.* San Diego, CA: Educational and Industrial Testing Service.

SHULMAN, M. E. (1988). Cost containment in clinical psychology: Critique of Biodyne and the HMOs. *Professional Psychology: Research and Practice, 19,* 298–307.

SHWEDER, R. A. (1982). Fact and artifact in trait perception: The systematic distortion hypothesis. *Progress in Experimental Personality Research, 11,* 65–100.

SIASSI, I. (1984). Psychiatric interviews and mental status examinations. In G. Goldstein & M. Hersen (Eds.), *Handbook of psychological assessment* (pp. 259–275). New York: Pergamon Press.

SIEGMAN, A. W. (1972). Do interviewer mm-hmm's reinforce interviewee verbal productivity? *Proceedings of the 80th Annual Convention of the American Psychological Association, 7,* 323–324.

SIEGMAN, A. W. (1974). The gain-loss principle and interpersonal attraction in the interview. *Proceedings of the Division of Personality and Social Psychology,* pp. 83–85.

SIEGMAN, A. W. (1976). Do noncontingent interviewer mm-hmm's facilitate interviewee productivity? *Journal of Consulting and Clinical Psychology, 44,* 171–182.

SILVERMAN, L. H., & WEINBERGER, J. (1985). Mommy and I are one: Implications for psychotherapy. *American Psychologist, 40,* 1296–1308.

SIMONS, L. S. (1989). Privatization and the mental health system: A private sector view. *American Psychologist, 44,* 1138–1141.

SINES, L. K. (1959). The relative contribution of four kinds of data to accuracy in personality assessment. *Journal of Consulting Psychology, 23,* 483–492.

SKINNER, B. F. (1948). *Verbal behavior.* Cambridge, MA: Harvard University Press.

SKINNER, B. F. (1953). *Science and human behavior.* New York: Macmillan.

SKINNER, B. F. (1957). *Verbal behavior.* New York: Appleton-Century-Crofts.

SKINNER, B. F. (1971). *Beyond freedom and dignity.* New York: Knopf.

SLEATOR, E. K., & ULLMANN, R. K. (1981). Can the physician diagnose hyperactivity in the office? *Pediatrics, 67,* 13–17.

SLIPP, S. (Ed.). (1981). *Curative factors in psychodynamic therapy.* New York: McGraw-Hill.

SLOANE, R. B., STAPLES, F. R., CRISTOL, A. H., YORKSTON, N. J., & WHIPPLE, K. (1975). *Psychotherapy versus behavior therapy.* Cambridge, MA: Harvard University Press.

SMITH, D. (1982). Trends in counseling and psychotherapy. *American Psychologist, 37,* 802–809.

SMITH, M. L., GLASS, G. V., & MILLER, T. I. (1980). *The benefits of psychotherapy.* Baltimore, MD: Johns Hopkins University Press.

SNEPP, F. P., & PETERSON, D. R. (1988). Evaluative comparison of Psy.D. and Ph.D. students by clinical internship supervisors. *Professional Psychology: Research and Practice, 19,* 180–183.

SNOWDEN, L. (Ed.). (1982). *Reaching the underserved: Mental health needs of neglected populations.* Beverly Hills, CA: Sage.

SNYDER, D. K. (1981). *Marital Satisfaction Inventory: Manual.* Los Angeles: Western Psychological Services.

SNYDER, D. K., LACHAR, D., & WILLS, R. M. (1988). Computer-based interpretation of the Marital Satisfaction Inventory: Use in treatment planning. *Journal of Marital and Family Therapy, 14,* 397–409.

SNYDER, D. K., WIDIGER, T. A., & HOOVER, D. H. (1990). Methodological considerations in validating computer-based test interpretations: Controlling for response bias. *Journal of Consulting and Clinical Psychology, 2,* 470–477.

SNYDER, D. K., & WILLS, R. M. (1989). Behavioral versus insight-oriented marital therapy: Effects on individual and interspousal functioning. *Journal of Consulting and Clinical Psychology, 57,* 39–46.

SNYDER, W. V. (1945). An investigation of the nature of nondirective psychotherapy. *Journal of General Psychology, 33,* 193–232.

SNYDER, W. V. (Ed.). (1953). *Group report of a program of research in psychotherapy.* State College: Department of Psychology, Pennsylvania State University.

SNYDER, W. V. (1954). Client-centered therapy. In L. A. Pennington & I. A. Berg (Eds.), *An introduction to clinical psychology* (pp. 529–556). New York: Ronald Press.

SOBELL, L. C., & SOBELL, M. B. (1975). Outpatient alcoholics give valid self-reports. *Journal of Nervous and Mental Disease, 161,* 32–42.

SOLDZ, S., BUDMAN, S., DEMBY, A., & JERRY, J. (1993). Representation of personality disorders in circumplex and five-factor space: Explorations with a clinical sample. *Psychological Assessment, 5,* 41–52.

SOLLOD, R. N. (1978). Carl Rogers and the origins of client-centered therapy. *Professional Psychology, 9,* 93–104.

SOLOMON, R. L., KAMIN, L. J., & WYNNE, L. C. (1953). Traumatic avoidance learning: The outcomes of several extinction procedures with dogs. *Journal of Abnormal and Social Psychology, 49,* 291–302.

SOSKIN, W. F. (1954). Bias in postdiction from projective tests. *Journal of Abnormal and Social Psychology, 49,* 69–74.

SPANOS, N. P. (1978). Witchcraft in histories of psychiatry: A critical analysis and an alternative conceptualization. *Psychological Bulletin, 85,* 417–439.

SPEER, P., DEY, A., GRIGGS, P., GIBSON, C., LUBIN, B., & HUGHEY, J. (1992). In search of community: An analysis of community psychology research from 1984–1988. *American Journal of Community Psychology, 20,* 195–210.

SPENCE, K. W. (1956). *Behavior theory and conditioning.* New Haven, CT: Yale University Press.

SPERRY, R. W. (1961). Cerebral organization and behavior. *Science, 133,* 1749–1757.

SPERRY, R. W. (1974). Lateral specialization in the surgically separated hemispheres. In F. O. Schmitt & F. G. Worden (Eds.), *The neurosciences: Third study program* (pp. 5–20). Cambridge, MA: MIT Press.

SPERRY, R. W. (1982). Some effects of disconnecting the cerebral hemispheres. *Science, 217,* 1223–1226.

SPIEGEL, T. A., WADDEN, T. A., & FOSTER, G. D. (1991). Objective measurement of eating rate during behavioral treatment of obesity. *Behavior Therapy, 22,* 61–68.

SPIELBERGER, C. D., GORSUCH, R. L., LUSHENE, R., VAGG, P. R., & JACOBS, G. A. (1983). *Manual for the State-Trait Anxiety Inventory.* Palo Alto, CA: Consulting Psychologists Press.

SPIERS, P. A. (1980). Have they come to praise Luria or to bury him? The Lurio-Nebraska controversy. *Journal of Consulting and Clinical Psychology, 49,* 331–341.

SPIKER, D. G., & EHLER, J. G. (1984). Structured psychiatric interviews for adults. In G. Goldstein & M. Hersen (Eds.), *Handbook of psychological assessment* (pp. 291–304). New York: Pergamon Press.

SPITZER, R. L. (1991). An outsider-insider's views about revising DSMs. *Journal of Abnormal Psychology, 100,* 294–296.

SPITZER, R. L., FLEISS, J. L., BURDOCK, E. I., & HARDESTY, A. S. (1964). The mental status schedule: Rationale, reliability, and validity. *Comprehensive Psychiatry, 5,* 384–394.

SPITZER, R. L., WILLIAMS, J. B., GIBBON, M., & FIRST, M. B. (1988). *Instruction manual for the Structured Clinical Interview for DSM-III-R (SCID, 6/1/88 revision).* Biometrics Research Department, New York State Psychiatric Institute, 722 W. 168th St., New York, NY 10032.

SPIVAK, G., & SHURE, M. B. (1974). *Social adjustment of young children: A cognitive approach to solving real-life problems.* San Francisco: Jossey-Bass.

SPOONT, M. R. (1992). Modulatory role of serotonin in neural information processing: Implications for human psychopathology. *Psychological Bulletin, 112,* 330–350.

SROUFE, L. A., & RUTTER, M. (1984). The domain of developmental psychopathology. *Child Development, 55,* 17–29.

STAMPFL, T. G., & LEVIS, D. J. (1973). *Implosive therapy: Theory and technique.* Morristown, NJ: General Learning Press.

STANGL, D., PFOHL, B., ZIMMERMAN, M., BOWERS, W., & CORENTHAL, C. (1985). A structured interview for the DSM-III personality disorders. *Archives of General Psychiatry, 42,* 591–597.

STAPP, J., & FULCHER, R. (1983). The employment of APA members. *American Psychologist, 38,* 1298–1320.

STAPP, J., FULCHER, R., & WICHERSKI, M. (1984). The employment of 1981 and 1982 doctorate recipients in psychology. *American Psychologist, 39,* 1408–1423.

STAPP, J., TUCKER, A. M., & VANDENBOS, G. R. (1985). Census of psychological personnel: 1983. *American Psychologist, 40,* 1317–1351.

STARKSTEIN, S. E., & ROBINSON, R. G. (1988). Lateralized emotional response following stroke. In M. Kinsbourne (Ed.), *Cerebral hemisphere function in depression.* Washington, DC: American Psychiatric Press.

STEIN, D. M., & LAMBERT, M. J. (1984). On the relationship between therapist experience and psychotherapy outcome. *Clinical Psychology Review, 4,* 127–142.

STEIN, D. M., & POLYSON, J. (1984). The Primary Mental Health Project reconsidered. *Journal of Consulting and Clinical Psychology, 52,* 940–945.

STEKETEE, G., & CHAMBLESS, D. L. (1992). Methodological issues in prediction of treatment outcome. *Clinical Psychology Review, 12,* 387–400.

STEKETEE, G., & FOA, E. B. (1985). Obsessive-compulsive disorders. In D. H. Barlow (Ed.), *Clinical handbook of psychological disorders* (pp. 69–104). New York: Guilford Press.

STERNBERG, R. J., & DETTERMAN, D. K. (Eds.). (1986). *What is intelligence? Contemporary viewpoints on its nature and definition.* Norwood, NJ: Ablex.

STEVENS, M. R., & REILLY, R. R. (1980). MMPI short forms: A literature review. *Journal of Personality Assessment, 44,* 368–376.

STEWART, D. J., & PATTERSON, M. L. (1973). Eliciting effects of verbal and nonverbal cues on projective test responses. *Journal of Consulting and Clinical Psychology, 41,* 74–77.

STILES, W. A., SHAPIRO, D. A., & ELLIOT, R. (1986). "Are all psychotherapies equivalent?" *American Psychologist, 41,* 165–180.

STOKES, T. F., & BAER, D. M. (1977). An implicit technology of generalization. *Journal of Applied Behavior Analysis, 10,* 349–367.

STOKOLS, D. (1992). Establishing and maintaining healthy environments: Toward a social ecology of health promotion. *American Psychologist, 47,* 6–22.

STONE, A. A., & NEALE, J. M. (1984). New measures of daily coping: Developments and preliminary results. *Journal of Personality and Social Psychology, 46,* 892–906.

STRAYHORN, J. M. (1988). *The competent child.* New York: Guilford Press.

STRICKER, G. (1992). The relationship of research to clinical practice. *American Psychologist, 47,* 543–549.

STRICKLAND, B. R. (1985). Over the Boulder(s) and through the Vail. *The Clinical Psychologist,* 52–56.

STROTHER, C. R. (1956). *Psychology and mental health.* Washington, DC: American Psychological Association.

STRUPP, H. H. (1960). *Psychotherapists in action: Explorations of the therapist's contribution to the treatment process.* New York: Grune & Stratton.

STRUPP, H. H. (1972). Freudian analysis today. *Psychology Today, 6* (2), 33–40.

STRUPP, H. H. (1989). Psychotherapy: Can the practitioner learn from the researcher? *American Psychologist, 44,* 717–724.

STRUPP, H. H., & BLINDER, J. L. (1984). *Psychotherapy in a new key: A guide to time-limited dynamic psychotherapy.* New York: Basic Books.

STRUPP, H. H., & BLOXOM, A. L. (1973). Preparing lower-class patients for group psychotherapy: Development and evaluation of a role-induction film. *Journal of Consulting and Clinical Psychology, 41,* 373–384.

STRUPP, H. H., & HADLEY, S. W. (1977). A tripartite model of mental health and therapeutic outcomes. *American Psychologist, 32,* 187–196.

STRUPP, H. H., & HADLEY, S. W. (1979). Specific vs. nonspecific factors in psychotherapy. *Archives of General Psychiatry, 36,* 1125–1137.

STUART, R. B. (1971). Behavioral contracting within the families of delinquents. *Journal of Behavior Therapy and Experimental Psychiatry, 2,* 1–11.

STUMPHAUZER, J. S. (1986). *Helping delinquents change: A treatment manual of social learning approaches.* New York: Haworth Press.

SULLIVAN, H. S. (1953). *The interpersonal theory of psychiatry.* New York: W. W. Norton.

SULLIVAN, H. S. (1954). *The psychiatric interview.* New York: W. W. Norton.

SULLIVAN, M. A., & O'LEARY, S. G. (1990). Maintenance following reward and cost token programs. *Behavior Therapy, 21,* 139–151.

SULZER, E. (1965). Behavior modifications in adult psychiatric patients. In L. P. Ullmann & L. Krasner (Eds.), *Case studies in behavior modification* (pp. 196–200). New York: Holt, Rinehart & Winston.

SUMMIT, R. (1983). The child sexual abuse accommodation syndrome. *Child Abuse and Neglect, 7,* 177–193.

SUNDBERG, N. D. (1961). The practice of psychological testing in clinical services in the United States. *American Psychologist, 16,* 79–83.

SUNDBERG, N. D. (1977). *Assessment of persons.* Englewood Cliffs, NJ: Prentice-Hall.

SUNDBERG, N. D., TAPLIN, J. R., & TYLER, L. E. (1983). *Introduction to clinical psychology: Perspectives, issues, and contributions to human service.* Englewood Cliffs, NJ: Prentice-Hall.

SUNDBERG, N. D., & TYLER, L. E. (1962). *Clinical psychology: An introduction to research and practice.* New York: Appleton-Century-Crofts.

SUNDBERG, N. D., TYLER, L. E., & TAPLIN, J. R. (1973). *Clinical psychology: Expanding horizons* (2nd ed.). Englewood Cliffs, NJ: Prentice-Hall.

SVARTBERG, M., & STILES, T. C. (1991). Comparative effects of short-term psychotherapy: A meta-analysis. *Journal of Consulting and Clinical Psychology, 59,* 704–714.

SWAIN, M. A., & STECKEL, S. B. (1981). Influencing adherence among hypertensives. *Research Nursing and Health, 4,* 213–218.

SWEENEY, J. A., CLARKIN, J. F., & FITZGIBBON, M. L. (1987). Current practice of psychological assessment. *Professional Psychology: Research and Practice, 18,* 377–380.

SWEET, A. A. (1984). The therapeutic relationship in behavior therapy. *Clinical Psychology Review, 4,* 253–272.

SZASZ, T. S. (1960). The myth of mental illness. *American Psychologist, 15,* 113–118.

SZONDI, L., MOSER, U., & WEBB, M. W. (1959). *The Szondi test in diagnosis, prognosis and treatment.* Philadelphia: Lippincott.

TAFT, J. (1951). *The dynamics of therapy in a controlled relationship.* New York: Harper.

TAFT, R. (1955). The ability to judge people. *Psychological Bulletin, 52,* 1–23.

TALLENT, N. (1976). Psychological report writing. Englewood Cliffs, NJ: Prentice-Hall.

TALLENT, N. (1992). *The practice of psychological assessment.* Englewood Cliffs, NJ: Prentice-Hall.

TALLENT, N., & REISS, W. J. (1959). Multidisciplinary views on the preparation of written psychological reports. *Journal of Clinical Psychology, 15,* 444–446.

TAPLIN, P. S., & REID, J. B. (1973). Effects of instructional set and experimenter influence on observer reliability. *Child Development, 44,* 547–554.

TARDE, G. (1903). *The laws of imitation.* New York: Holt.

TARTER, R. E., ALTERMAN, A. I., & EDWARDS, K. L. (1985). Vulnerability to alcoholism in men: A behavior-genetic perspective. *Journal of Studies on Alcoholism, 46,* 329–356.

TASK FORCE ON PEDIATRIC AIDS, AMERICAN PSYCHOLOGY ASSOCIATION. (1989). Pediatric AIDS and human immunodeficiency virus infection. *American Psychologist, 44,* 258–264.

TAYLOR, H. G. (1988). Learning disabilities. In E. J. Mash & L. G. Terdal (Eds.), *Behavioral assessment of childhood disorders* (2nd ed., pp. 402–450). New York: Guilford Press.

TAYLOR, S. E. (1983). Adjustment to threatening events: A theory of cognitive adaptation. *American Psychologist, 38,* 1161–1173.

TAYLOR, S. E., & BROWN, J. D. (1988). Illusion and well-being: A social psychological perspective on mental health. *Psychological Bulletin, 103,* 193–210.

TELLEGEN, A. (1982). *Brief manual for the Multidimensional Personality Questionnaire.* Unpublished manuscript, University of Minnesota.

TELLEGEN, A., & BEN-PORATH, Y. S. (1992). The new uniform T scores for the MMPI-2: Rationale, derivation, and appraisal. *Psychological Assessment, 4,* 145–155.

TEMERLIN, M. K. (1968). Suggestion effects in psychiatric diagnosis. *Journal of Nervous and Mental Disease, 147,* 349–353.

TENDLER, A. D. (1930). A preliminary report on a test for emotional insight. *Journal of Applied Psychology, 14,* 123–136.

TEPLIN, L. A., & SCHWARTZ, J. (1989). Screening for severe mental disorder in jails: The development of the Referral Decision Scale. *Law and Human Behavior, 13,* 1–18.

THOITS, P. A. (1982). Conceptual, methodological, and theoretical problems in studying social support as a buffer against life stress. *Journal of Health and Social Behavior, 23,* 145–159.

THOITS, P. A. (1986). Social support as coping assistance. *Journal of Consulting and Clinical Psychology, 54,* 416–423.

THOMAS, A., & CHESS, S. (1977). *Temperament and development.* New York: Brunner/Mazel.

THOMAS, A., CHESS, S., & BIRCH, H. G. (1968). *Temperament and behavior disorders in children.* New York: New York University Press.

THOMAS, D. S. (1929). *Some new techniques for studying social behavior.* New York: Columbia University.

THOMAS, E. J. (1973). Bias of therapist influence in behavioral assessment. *Journal of Behavior Therapy and Experimental Psychiatry, 4,* 107–111.

THORESEN, C. E., & POWELL, L. H. (1992). Type A behavior pattern: New perspectives on theory, assessment, and intervention. *Journal of Consulting and Clinical Psychology, 60,* 595–604.

THORNDIKE, E. L. (1911). *Animal intelligence.* New York: Macmillan.

THORNDIKE, R. L., HAGEN, E. P., & SATTLER, J. M. (1986). *What is intelligence? Contemporary viewpoints on its nature and definition.* Chicago: Riverside.

THORNE, F. C. (1948). Theoretical foundations of directive psychotherapy. *Current Trends in Clinical Research, 49,* 867–928.

THORNE, F. C. (1967). *Integrative psychology.* Brandon, VT: Clinical Psychology Publishing Co.

THORNE, F. C. (1972). Clinical judgment. In R. H. Woody & J. D. Woody (Eds.), *Clinical assessment in counseling and psychotherapy* (pp. 30–85). Englewood Cliffs, NJ: Prentice-Hall.

THORNE, F. C. (1973). Eclectic psychotherapy. In R. Corsini (Ed.), *Current psychotherapies* (pp. 445–486). Itasca, IL: F. E. Peacock.

THORNTON, E. M. (1983). *Freud and cocaine: The Freudian fallacy.* London: Blond & Briggs.

TISDELLE, D. A., & ST. LAWRENCE, J. S. (1988). Adolescent interpersonal problem-solving skill training: Social validation and generalization. *Behavior Therapy, 19,* 171–182.

TOLAN, P., KEYS, C., CHERTOK, F., & JASON, L. (Eds.). (1991). *Researching community psychology: Issues of theory and methods.* Washington, DC: American Psychological Association.

TOLMAN, E. C. (1932). *Purposive behavior in animals and men.* New York: Naiburg.

TOTTEN, G., LAMB, D. H., & REEDER, G. D. (1990). *Tarasoff* and confidentiality in AIDS-related psychotherapy. *Professional Psychology: Research and Practice, 21,* 155–160.

TRYON, W. W. (1976). A system of behavioral diagnosis. *Professional Psychology, 7,* 495–506.

TULKIN, S. R., & FRANK, G. W. (1985). The changing role of psychologists in health maintenance organizations. *American Psychologist, 40,* 1125–1130.

TURK, D. C., & RUDY, T. E. (1990). Pain. In A. S. Bellack, M. Hersen, & A. E. Kazdin (Eds.), *International handbook of behavior modification and therapy* (2nd ed., pp. 399–413). New York: Plenum Press.

TURNER, R. M. (1989). Case study evaluations of a bio-cognitive-behavioral approach for the treatment of borderline personality disorder. *Behavior Therapy, 20,* 477–489.

TURNER, S. M., BEIDEL, D. C., DANCU, C. V., & STANLEY, M. A. (1989). An empirically derived inventory to measure social fears and anxiety: The Social Phobia and Anxiety Inventory. *Psychological Assessment: Journal of Consulting and Clinical Psychology, 1,* 35–40.

TURNER, S. M., BEIDEL, D. C., & LONG, P. J. (1992). Reduction of fear in social phobics: An examination of extinction patterns. *Behavior Therapy, 23,* 389–404.

TVERSKY, A., & KAHNEMAN, D. (1974). Judgment under uncertainty: Heuristics and biases. *Science, 185,* 1124–1131.

TVERSKY, A., & KAHNEMAN, D. (1983). Extensional versus intuitive reasoning: The conjunction fallacy in probability judgment. *Psychological Review, 90,* 293–315.

TWENTYMAN, C. T., ROHRBECK, C. H., & AMISH, P. (1984). A cognitive-behavioral model of child abuse. In Sanders (Ed.), *Violent individuals and families: A practitioner's handbook* (pp. 86–111). Springfield, IL: Charles C. Thomas.

ULLMANN, L. P., & HUNRICHS, W. A. (1958). The role of anxiety in psychodiagnosis: Replication and extension. *Journal of Clinical Psychology, 14,* 276–279.

ULLMANN, L. P., & KRASNER, L. (Eds.). (1965). *Case studies in behavior modification.* New York: Holt, Rinehart & Winston.

ULLMANN, L. P., & KRASNER, L. (1975). *A psychological approach to abnormal behavior.* Englewood Cliffs, NJ: Prentice-Hall.

VAILLANT, G. E. (1984). The disadvantages of DSM-II outweigh its advantages. *American Journal of Psychiatry, 141,* 542–545.

VANDECREEK, L., KNAPP, S., & BRACE, K. (1990). Mandatory continuing education for licensed psychologists: Its rationale and current implementation. *Professional Psychology: Research and Practice, 21,* 135–140.

VANDENBOS, G. R., DELEON, P. H., & BELAR, C. D. (1991). How many psychological practitioners are needed? It's too early to know. *Professional Psychology: Research and Practice, 22,* 441–448.

VANDENBOS, G. R., & STAPP, J. (1983). Service providers in psychology: Results of the 1982 APA human resources survey. *American Psychologist, 38,* 1330–1352.

VANDIVER, T., & SHER, K. J. (1991). Temporal stability of the Diagnostic Interview Schedule. *Psychological Assessment: A Journal of Consulting and Clinical Psychology, 3,* 277–281.

VANE, J. R. (1981). The Thematic Apperception Test: A review. *Clinical Psychology Review, 1,* 319–336.

VANE, J. R., & MOTTA, R. W. (1990). Group intelligence tests. In G. Goldstein & M. Hersen (Eds.), *Handbook of psychological assessment* (pp. 102–119). New York: Pergamon Press.

VAUGHN, C. L., & REYNOLDS, W. A. (1951). Reliability of personal interview data. *Journal of Applied Psychology, 35,* 61–63.

VEGA, A., & PARSONS, O. A. (1967). Cross-validation of the Halstead-Reitan tests for brain damage. *Journal of Consulting Psychology, 31,* 619–625.

VON BERTALANFFY, L. (1968). *General systems theory.* New York: Braziller.

WACHTEL, P. (1977). *Psychoanalysis and behavior therapy.* New York: Basic Books.

WADA, J., & RASMUSSEN, T. (1960). Intracarotid injection of sodium amytal for the lateralization of cerebral speech dominance. *Journal of Neurosurgery, 17,* 266–282.

WADE, T. C., & BAKER, T. B. (1977). Opinions and use of psychological tests: A survey of clinical psychologists. *American Psychologist, 32,* 874–882.

WALKER, C. E., HEDBERG, A., CLEMENT, P. W., & WRIGHT, L. (1981). *Clinical procedures for behavior therapy.* Englewood Cliffs, NJ: Prentice-Hall.

WALKER, R. S., & WALSH, J. A. (1969). As others see us? The Medieval Multi-Purpose Inquiry. *Perceptual and Motor Skills, 28,* 414.

WALLEN, R. W. (1956). *Clinical psychology: The study of persons.* New York: McGraw-Hill.

WALLERSTEIN, J., CORBIN, S. B., & LEWIS, J. M. (1988). Children of divorce: A ten-year study. In E. M. Hetherington & J. Arasteh (Eds.), *Impact of divorce, single-parenting and stepparenting on children* (pp. 198–214). Hillsdale, NJ: Lawrence Erlbaum Associates.

WALLERSTEIN, R. S. (1986). *Forty-two lives in treatment: A study of psychoanalysis and psychotherapy.* New York: Guilford Press.

WALLERSTEIN, R. S. (1989). The Psychotherapy Research Project of the Menninger Foundation: An overview. *Journal of Consulting and Clinical Psychology, 57,* 195–205.

WALLERSTEIN, R. S., & SAMPSON, H. (1971). Issues in research in the psychoanalytic process. *International Journal of Psychoanalysis, 52,* 11–50.

WALSH, K. (1987). *Neuropsychology: A clinical approach* (2nd ed.). Edinburgh: Churchill Livingstone.

WATERHOUSE, G. J., & STRUPP, H. H. (1984). The patient-therapist relationship: Research from the psychodynamic perspective. *Clinical Psychology Review, 4,* 77–92.

WATKINS, C. E. (1985). Counseling psychology, clinical psychology, and human services psychology: Where the twain shall meet. *American Psychologist, 40,* 1054–1056.

WATKINS, C. E., TIPTON, R. M., MANUS, M., & HOUTON-SHOUP, J. (1991). Contemporary clinical psychology: Reflections about role relevance and role engagement. *The Clinical Psychologist, 44,* 45–52.

WATLEY, D. J. (1968). Feedback training and improvement of clinical forecasting. *Journal of Counseling Psychology, 15,* 167–171.

WATSON, D., & FRIEND, R. (1969). Measurement of social-evaluative anxiety. *Journal of Consulting and Clinical Psychology, 33,* 448–457.

WATSON, J. B. (1913). Psychology as the behaviorist views it. *Psychological Review, 20,* 158–177.

WATSON, J. B. (1924). *Behaviorism.* New York: W.W. Norton.

WATSON, J. B. (1930). *Behaviorism* (rev. ed.). New York: W. W. Norton.

WATSON, J. B., & RAYNER, R. (1920). Conditioned emotional reactions. *Journal of Experimental Psychology, 3,* 1–14.

WATSON, R. I. (1951). *The clinical method in psychology.* New York: Harper.

WATSON, R. I. (1953). A brief history of clinical psychology. *Psychological Bulletin, 50,* 321–346.

WEBB, E., CAMPBELL, D. T., SCHWARTZ, R. D., & SECHREST, L. B. (1966). *Unobtrusive measures: Nonreactive research in the social sciences.* Chicago: Rand-McNally.

WEBSTER-STRATTON, C. (1988). Mothers' and fathers' perceptions of child deviance: Roles of parent and child behaviors and parent adjustment. *Journal of Consulting and Clinical Psychology, 56,* 909–915.

WECHSLER, D. (1967). *Manual for the WPPSI.* New York: Psychological Corporation.

WECHSLER, D. (1981). *Wechsler Adult Intelligence Scale-Revised.* New York: Psychological Corporation.

WECHSLER, D. (1991). *WISC-III: Manual.* San Antonio, TX: Psychological Corporation.

WEICK, K. E. (1968). Systematic observational methods. In G. Lindzey & E. Aronson (Eds.), *Handbook of social psychology* (Vol. 2, 2nd ed., pp. 357–451). Reading, MA: Addison-Wesley.

WEINBERG, R. A. (1989). Intelligence and IQ: Landmark issues and great debates. *American Psychologist, 44,* 105–111.

WEISS, G., & HECHTMAN, L. T. (1986). *Hyperactive children grow up.* New York: Guilford Press.

WEISS, J. H. (1963). The effect of professional training and amount and accuracy of information on behavioral prediction. *Journal of Consulting Psychology, 27,* 257–262.

WEISSBERG, R. P., COWEN, E. L., LOTYCZEWSKI, B. S., & GESTEN, E. L. (1983). The Primary Mental Health Project: Seven consecutive years of outcome research. *Journal of Consulting and Clinical Psychology, 51,* 100–107.

WEISZ, J. R., WEISS, B., ALICKE, M. D., & KLOTZ, M. L. (1987). Effectiveness of psychotherapy with children and adolescents: A meta-analysis for clinicians. *Journal of Consulting and Clinical Psychology, 55,* 542–549.

WENAR, C., & COULTER, J. B. (1962). A reliability study of developmental histories. *Child Development, 33,* 453–462.

WERNICK, R. (1956). *They've got your number.* New York: W. W. Norton.

WERRY, J. S., & QUAY, H. C. (1971). The prevalence of behavior symptoms of younger elementary school children. *American Journal of Orthopsychiatry, 41,* 136–143.

WERTHEIMER, M. (1923). Studies in the theory of Gestalt psychology. *Psychological Forschung, 4,* 300–350.

WESTEN, D. (1991). Social cognition and object relations. *Psychological Bulletin, 109,* 429–455.

WEXLER, D. B. (1973). Token and taboo: Behavior modification, token economies and the law. *California Law Review, 61,* 81–109.

WEXLER, D. B. (1974). Of rights and reinforcers. *San Diego Law Review, 11,* 957–971.

WHALEN, C. K., HENKER, B., & DOTEMOTO, S. (1980). Methylphenidate and hyperactivity: Effects on teacher behaviors. *Science, 208,* 1280–1282.

WHEELER, D. R. (1938). Imaginal productivity tests: Beta inkblot test. In H. A. Murray (Ed.), *Explorations in personality* (pp. 111–150). New York: Oxford University Press.

WHEELER, L., & REITAN, R. M. (1962). The presence and laterality of brain damage predicted from responses to a short aphasia screening test. *Perceptual and Motor Skills, 15,* 783–799.

WHITE, R. F., & WATT, N. F. (1973). *The abnormal personality* (4th ed.). New York: Ronald Press.

WHITEHEAD, W. E. (1992). Behavioral medicine approaches to gastrointestinal disorders. *Journal of Consulting and Clinical Psychology, 60,* 605–612.

WHITT, J. K., DYKSTRA, W., & TAYLOR, C. A. (1979). Chidren's conceptions of illness and cognitive development: Implications for pediatric practitioners. *Clinical Pediatrics, 18,* 327–335.

WICKER, A. W. (1969). Attitudes versus actions: The relationship of verbal and overt behavioral responses to attitude objects. *Journal of Social Issues, 25,* 41–78.

WICKS-NELSON, R., & ISRAEL, A. C. (1991). *Behavior disorders of childhood* (2nd ed.). Englewood Cliffs, NJ: Prentice Hall.

WIDIGER, T. A. (1985). Review of Millon Clinical Multiaxial Inventory. In J. V. Mitchell (Ed.), *The ninth mental measurements yearbook* (pp. 986–988). Lincoln: Buros Institute of Mental Measurements, University of Nebraska.

WIDIGER, T. A., & FRANCES, A. (1985). The DSM-III personality disorders: Perspectives from psychology. *Archives of General Psychiatry, 42,* 615–623.

WIDIGER, T. A., FRANCES, A. J., PINCUS, H. A., DAVIS, W. W., & FIRST, M. B. (1991). Toward an empirical classification for the DSM-IV. *Journal of Abnormal Psychology, 100,* 280–288.

WIDIGER, T. A., & RORER, L. G. (1984). The responsible psychotherapist. *American Psychologist, 39,* 503–515.

WIDIGER, T. A., TRULL, T. J., HURT, S. W., CLARKIN, J., & FRANCES, A. (1987). A multidimensional scaling of the DSM-III personality disorders. *Archives of General Psychiatry, 44,* 557–563.

WIENS, A. N., & MATARAZZO, J. D. (1983). Diagnostic interviewing. In M. Hersen, A. E. Kazdin, & A. S. Bellack (Eds.), *The clinical psychology handbook* (pp. 309–328). New York: Pergamon Press.

WIGDOR, A. K., & GARNER, W. R. (Eds.). (1982). *Ability testing: Uses, consequences, and controversies.* Washington, DC: National Academy Press.

WIGGINS, J. S. (1973). *Personality and prediction: Principles of personality assessment.* Reading, MA: Addison-Wesley.

WIGGINS, J. S. (1981). Clinical and statistical prediction: Where are we and where do we go from here? *Clinical Psychology Review, 1,* 3–18.

WIGGINS, J. S. (1982). Circumplex models of interpersonal behavior in clinical psychology. In P. C. Kendall & J. N. Butcher (Eds.), *Handbook of research methods in clinical psychology* (pp. 183–221). New York: John Wiley.

WIGGINS, J. S., & BROUGHTON, R. (1985). The interpersonal circle: A structural model for the integration of personality research. In R. Hogan & W. C. Jones (Eds.), *Perspective in personality: Theory, measurement, and interpersonal dynamics* (Vol. 1, pp. 1–48). Greenwich, CT: JAI Press.

WIGGINS, J. S., & PINCUS, A. L. (1989). Conceptions of personality disorders and dimensions of personality. *Psychological Assessment: A Journal of Consulting and Clinical Psychology, 1,* 305–316.

WILKINS, W. (1971). Desensitization: Social and cognitive factors underlying the effectiveness of Wolpe's procedure. *Psychological Bulletin, 76,* 311–317.

WILKINS, W. (1979). Expectancies in therapy research: Discriminating among heterogeneous nonspecifics. *Journal of Consulting and Clinical Psychology, 47,* 837–845.

WILKINS, W. (1984). Psychotherapy: The powerful placebo. *Journal of Consulting and Clinical Psychology, 52,* 570–573.

WILLIAMS, C. L., ARNOLD, C. B., & WYNDER, E. L. (1977). Primary prevention of chronic disease beginning in childhood: The Know Your Body Program: Design of study. *Preventive Medicine, 6,* 344–357.

WILLIAMS, C. L., & POLING, J. (1989). An epidemiological perspective on the anxiety and depressive disorders. In P. C. Kendall & D. Watson (Eds.), *Anxiety and depression: Distinctive and overlapping fea-*

tures (pp. 317–339). San Diego, CA: Academic Press.

WILLIAMS, R. L. (1972). *The Black Intelligence Test of Cultural Homogeneity (BITCH)—A culture-specific test.* Paper presented at the American Psychological Association meeting, Honolulu.

WILLIAMS, S. L., & ZANE, G. (1989). Guided mastery and stimulus exposure treatments for severe performance anxiety in agoraphobics. *Behaviour Research and Therapy, 27,* 237–246.

WILLIAMS, T. R. (1967). *Field methods in the study of culture.* New York: Holt, Rinehart & Winston.

WILLIAMSON, D. A., DAVIS, C. J., & PRATHER, R. C. (1988). Assessment of health-related disorders. In A. S. Bellack & M. Hersen (Eds.), *Behavioral assessment: A practical handbook* (3rd ed., pp. 396–440). New York: Pergamon Press.

WILLIS, J., & GILES, D. (1978). Behaviorism in the twentieth century: What we have here is a failure to communicate. *Behavior Therapy, 9,* 15–27.

WILSON, G. T. (1978). On the much discussed term "behavior therapy." *Behavior Therapy, 9,* 89–98.

WILSON, G. T. (1982). Psychotherapy process and procedure: The behavioral mandate. *Behavior Therapy, 13,* 291–312.

WILSON, G. T. (1985). Limitations of meta-analysis in the evaluation of the effects of psychological therapy. *Clinical Psychology Review, 5,* 35–47.

WILSON, G. T., & RACHMAN, S. J. (1983). Meta-analysis and the evaluation of psychotherapy outcome: Limitations and liabilities. *Journal of Consulting and Clinical Psychology, 51,* 54–64.

WILSON, M. L., & RAPPAPORT, J. (1974). Personal self-disclosure: Expectancy and situational effects. *Journal of Consulting and Clinical Psychology, 42,* 901–908.

WINNICOTT, D. W. (1965). *The maturational processes and the facilitating environment.* New York: International Universities Press.

WIRT, R. D., LACHAR, D., KLINEDINST, J. K., & SEAT, P. D. (1984). *Multidimensional description of child personality: A manual for the Personality Inventory of Children.* Los Angeles: Western Psychological Services.

WOLBERG, L. R. (1967). *The technique of psychotherapy* (2nd ed). New York: Grune & Stratton.

WOLFE, D. A. (1987). *Child abuse: Implications for child development and psychopathology.* Newbury Park, CA: Sage.

WOLPE, J. (1958). *Psychotherapy by reciprocal inhibition.* Stanford, CA: Stanford University Press.

WOLPE, J. (1982). *The practice of behavior therapy* (3rd ed.). New York: Pergamon Press.

WOLPE, J. (1984). Behavior therapy according to Lazarus. *American Psychologist, 39,* 1326–1327.

WOLPE, J., & LANG, P. J. (1969). *Fear Survey Schedule.* San Diego, CA: Educational and Industrial Testing Service.

WOLPE, J., & LAZARUS, A. A. (1966). *Behavior therapy techniques: A guide to the treatment of neuroses.* New York: Pergamon Press.

WONG, B. Y. L. (1986). Problems and issues in the definition of learning disabilities. In J. K. Torgesen & B. Y. L. Wong (Eds.), *Psychological and educational perspectives on learning disabilities* (pp. 3–26). New York: Academic Press.

WOOD, L. F., & JACOBSON, N. S. (1985). Marital distress. In D. Barlow (Ed.), *Clinical handbook of psychological disorders* (pp. 344–416). New York: Guilford Press.

WOODCOCK, R., & JOHNSON, M. (1977). *Woodcock-Johnson Psycho-educational Battery.* Allen, TX: DLM/Teaching Resources.

WOODCOCK, R. W., & JOHNSON, M. B. (1989). *Woodcock-Johnson Psycho-educational Battery-Revised.* Allen, TX: DLM/Teaching Resources.

WOODS, P. A., HIGSON, P. J., & TANNAHILL, M. M. (1984). Token-economy programmes with chronic psychotic patients: The importance of direct measurement and objective evaluation for long-term maintenance. *Behaviour Research and Therapy, 22,* 41–51.

WOODWORTH, R. S. (1920). *Personal data sheet.* Chicago: Stoelting.

WORTMAN, C. B., & LEHMAN, D. R. (1985). Reactions to victims of life crises: Support attempts that fail. In I. G. Sarason & B. R. Sarason (Eds.), *Social support: Theory, research, and applications* (pp. 463–489). Dordrecht, The Netherlands: Martinus Nijhoff.

WRIGHTSMAN, L., NIETZEL, M., & FORTUNE, W. (1994). *Psychology and the legal system* (3rd ed.). Monterey, CA: Brooks/Cole.

WYATT, F. (1968). What is clinical psychology? In A. Z. Guiora & M. A. Brandwin (Eds.), *Perspectives in clinical psychology* (pp. 222–238). Princeton, NJ: D. Van Nostrand.

YALOM, I. D. (1985). *The theory and practice of group psychotherapy* (3rd ed.). New York: Basic Books.

YOUNG, L. D. (1992). Psychological factors in rheumatoid arthritis. *Journal of Consulting and Clinical Psychology, 60,* 619–627.

ZAJONC, R. B. (1980). Feeling and thinking: Preferences need no inferences. *American Psychologist, 35,* 151–175.

ZAX, M., & SPECTER, G. A. (1974). *An introduction to community psychology.* New York: John Wiley.

ZEGIOB, L. E., ARNOLD, S., & FOREHAND, R. (1975). An examination of observer effects in parent-child interactions. *Child Development, 46,* 509–512.

ZETTLE, R. D., & HAYES, S. C. (1980). Conceptual and empirical status of rational-emotive therapy. In M. Hersen, R. M. Eisler, & P. M. Miller (Eds.), *Progress in behavior modification* (Vol. 9, pp. 125–162). Orlando, FL: Academic Press.

ZIFFERBLATT, S. M. (1975). Increasing compliance through the applied analysis of behavior. *Preventive Medicine, 4,* 173–182.

ZIGLER, E., TAUSSIG, C., & BLACK, K. (1992). Early childhood intervention: A promising preventative for juvenile delinquency. *American Psychologist, 47,* 997–1006.

ZILBOORG, G., & HENRY, G. W. (1941). *A history of medical psychology.* New York: W. W. Norton.

ZIMET, C. N. (1989). The mental health revolution: Will psychology survive? *American Psychologist, 44,* 703–708.

ZIMET, C. N., & THRONE, F. M. (1965). *Preconference materials.* Conference on the Professional Preparation of Clinical Psychologists. Washington, DC: American Psychological Association.

ZIMMERMAN, M (1983). Methodological issues in the assessment of life events: A review of issues and research. *Clinical Psychology Review, 3,* 339–370.

ZISKIN, J. (1981). *Coping with psychiatric and psychological testimony* (3rd ed.). Venice, CA: Law and Psychology Press.

ZOOK A., II, & WALTON, J. M. (1989). Theoretical orientations and work settings of clinical and counseling psychologists: A current perspective. *Professional Psychology: Research and Practice, 20,* 23–31.

ZUBIN, J. (1969). The role of models in clinical psychology. In L. L'Abate (Ed.), *Models of clinical psychology* (pp. 5–12). Atlanta: Georgia State College.

ZUBIN, J., ERON, L. D., & SCHUMER, F. (1965). *An experimental approach to projective techniques.* New York: John Wiley.

ZUCKERMAN, M., & LUBIN, B. (1965). *Manual for the multiple affect adjective checklist.* San Diego, CA: Educational and Industrial Testing Service.

ZWANG, G. (1985). *La statue de Freud.* Paris: Robert Lafont.

ZYTOWSKI, D. G. (1985). *Kuder Occupational Interest Survey manual supplement.* Chicago: Science Research Associates.

Index

SUBJECTS

DATE DUE	
JUL 2 8 1997	
APR 1 5 1998	
MAY 7 1998	
FEB 1 3 1999	
APR 2 3 1999	
APR 1 1 2006	